BEHAVIOR DISORDERS OF CHILDHOOD

RITA WICKS-NELSON

Process-Strategies Institute
Charleston, West Virginia

ALLEN C. ISRAEL
State University of New York
at Albany

PRENTICE-HALL, INC., ENGLEWOOD CLIFFS, NEW JERSEY 07632

Library of Congress Cataloging in Publication Data

WICKS-NELSON, RITA
    Behavior disorders of childhood.

    Bibliography.
    Includes index.
    1. Child psychopathology.   I. Israel, Allen C.
II. Title.   [DNLM: 1. Child behavior disorders—Psy-
chology. 2. Child development.   3. Mental disorders—In
infancy and childhood.   WS 350.6 W637b]
RJ499.W45   1984   618.92'89   83-13719
ISBN 0-13-071753-3

Editorial/production supervision: Jeanne Hoeting
Cover design: Ben Santora
Manufacturing buyer: Ron Chapman

Printed in the United States of America

10   9   8   7   6   5   4   3   2   1

ISBN 0-13-071753-3

PRENTICE-HALL INTERNATIONAL, INC., *London*
PRENTICE-HALL OF AUSTRALIA PTY. LIMITED, *Sydney*
EDITORA PRENTICE-HALL DO BRASIL, LTDA., *Rio de Janeiro*
PRENTICE-HALL CANADA INC., *Toronto*
PRENTICE-HALL OF INDIA PRIVATE LIMITED, *New Delhi*
PRENTICE-HALL OF JAPAN, INC., *Tokyo*
PRENTICE-HALL OF SOUTHEAST ASIA PTE. LTD., *Singapore*
WHITEHALL BOOKS LIMITED, *Wellington, New Zealand*

To my Mother, my Father,
and Len
RW–N

To my Parents,
and Alice
ACI

CONTENTS

Preface   xvii

 1 A DEFINITIONAL AND HISTORICAL INTRODUCTION 1

DEFINING DISORDERED BEHAVIOR   2

   Sociocultural Norms   2
   Developmental Norms   5
   Other Criteria   5

HOW COMMON ARE CHILDHOOD DISORDERS?   6

   Sex Differences   7
   The Stability of Problems   7

CHILDHOOD DISORDERS: A BRIEF HISTORY   8

   BOX 1.1   EARLY VIEWS OF CHILDREN AND THEIR DISORDERS   9
   The Influence of Sigmund Freud   8
   Behaviorism and Social Learning Theory   10
   The Mental Hygiene and Child Guidance Movements   10
   The Scientific Study of the Child   12

WORKING WITH THE CHILD CLIENT   13

   BOX 1.2   TREATMENT ETHICS AND GENDER DISORDERS   15

SUMMARY   16

v

2 THE DEVELOPMENTAL CONTEXT   18

WHAT IS DEVELOPMENT?   19

Nature and Nurture   19
   BOX 2.1   HEREDITY AND ENVIRONMENT: THE EXAMPLE OF PKU   21

A SCHEMA OF NORMAL DEVELOPMENT   20

The Genetic Context   20
The Child as a Physical Being   21
The Child as an Intellectual Being   25
   Piaget's cognitive theory 26   Language and communication 26

The Child as a Social Being   28
The Social Context   29
   Socioeconomic status 29   The family 31   The influence of peers 34   School 35

SOME IMPORTANT DEVELOPMENT ISSUES   36

Levels of Development   36
Individual Differences   37
   BOX 2.2   THE "DIFFICULT" CHILD NEED NOT BECOME THE DIFFICULT ADULT   38

Early Experience and Critical Events   39
Risk and Invulnerability to Psychopathology   40

SUMMARY   41

3 PERSPECTIVES ON CHILDHOOD BEHAVIOR DISORDERS   43

WHAT ARE PERSPECTIVES?   44

THE BIOLOGICAL / PHYSIOLOGICAL PERSPECTIVE   45

Genetic Influences   46

   Inheritance through a single-gene, recessive mechanism   46
   Inheritance through a single-gene, dominant mechanism   46
   Inheritance of sex-linked characteristics   46
   Characteristics influenced by many genes   47
   Noninheritable genetic effects: chromosome aberrations   48
   BOX 3.1   INVESTIGATING HEREDITARY EFFECTS ON HUMANS   49

Biochemical Influences   50
Structural and Physiological Damage   52
   Prenatal influences 52   Later influences 53

THE PSYCHODYNAMIC PERSPECTIVE   54

    The Structures of the Mind   54
    Psychosexual Stages   55
        Oral stage 55   Anal stage 55   Phallic stage 56   Lagency and genital stages 56

    Anxiety and the Defense Mechanisms   57
    Criticisms and Modifications of Psychoanalytic Theory   57

THE BEHAVIORAL/SOCIAL LEARNING PERSPECTIVE   59

    Classical Conditioning   59
    Instrumental (operant) Conditioning   60
    Observational Learning   62

SOME OTHER PERSPECTIVES   63

    The Cognitive-Behavioral Approach   63
    The Psychoeducational Approach   64
        BOX 3.2   PROJECT RE—ED: A PSYCHOEDUCATIONAL AND ECOLOGICAL APPROACH   65
    The Family Systems Approach   67

SUMMARY   68

4 RESEARCH: ITS ROLE AND METHODS   69

THE NATURE OF SCIENCE   70

    Observation and Measurement   71
    Reliability   71
    Validity   71

BASIC METHODS OF RESEARCH   72

    Simple Descriptive Methods   72
        The clinical case study 72   Systematic direct observation 74

    Correlational Research   75
        The problem of directionality and of other variables   77

    Experimental Research   78
        Single-subject experiments   81

    Mixed Designs   82

LONGITUDINAL AND CROSS—SECTIONAL STRATEGIES   83
ETHICAL ISSUES IN RESEARCH WITH CHILDREN   85
SUMMARY   88

5 **CLASSIFICATION AND ASSESSMENT** **90**

CLASSIFICATION AND DIAGNOSIS 91

Clinically Derived Classification Systems 91
DSM 91
GAP and ICD-9 93
Empirical Approaches to Classification 94
The Similarity of Derived Syndromes 95
Syndromes according to age and sex 96   Reliability and validity 97

The Dangers of Labeling 98

ASSESSMENT 99

Assessment of Physical Functioning 99
Neurophysiological assessment 100   Neuropsychological assessment 100

Personality-Behavior Assessment 103
The interview 103   Psychological tests 103   Observational assessment 104
Problem checklists and dimensional rating scales 107

Intellectual-Educational Assessment 108
Intelligence tests 108   Developmental scales 109
Ability and achievement tests 109

DOING A COMPREHENSIVE ASSESSMENT 109
SUMMARY 109

6 **DISORDERS OF EATING, ELIMINATION, AND SLEEP** **111**

DISORDERS OF EATING 112

Rumination 112
Etiology and treatment 112

Pica 13
Etiology and treatment 114

Obesity 115
Eating patterns and activity levels of obese children 116   The etiology of obesity 118
Behavioral treatment 119

Anorexia Nervosa 120
Predisposing variables 122   Biological model 122   Psychodynamic model 123
The behavioral model 124   Family systems approach 125

DISORDERS OF ELIMINATION   126

Enuresis   126
The cause of enuresis 127   Treatment approaches 129

Encopresis   132
The causes of encopresis 132   Treatment approaches 133

SLEEP DISORDERS   133

Sleepwalking   134
Nightmares and Night Terrors   134
Causes and Treatment of Sleep Disorders   134

SUMMARY   136

7   INTERNALIZING DISORDERS   138

FEARS AND PHOBIAS   139

Clinical Description and Classification   140
Developmental Characteristics of Children's Fears   140
The general incidence of fears 140   Sex differences 140   Age trends 142

Etiological Paradigms   142
The psychoanalytic view 143   Behavioral paradigms 143
A biological perspective 145

Treatment of Childhood Phobias   146
The use of therapeutic models 146   Cognitive treatments 147

School Phobia   148
Prevalence 148   Theoretical viewpoints 149   Treatment 150

OTHER ANXIETY DISORDERS   150

The Overanxious Child   150
Clinical description 150   Prevalence and predisposing factors 151

Obsessive-Compulsive Disorder   151
Description and prevalence 151   Treatment   152

THE SOCIALLY WITHDRAWN CHILD   153

Peer Relations and Development   153
Peer Relations and Adjustment   153

Behaviors Related to Peer Status and Social Competence   155
   Responding positively to peers   155
   Perspective taking and accurate communication   156
   Initiating interactions   156

Treatment of the Withdrawn Child   156

CHILDHOOD DEPRESSION   158

Prevalence   158
   BOX 7.1   CHILD AND ADOLESCENT SUICIDE   159
Classification of Childhood Depression   160
Is Childhood Depression a Distinct Disorder?   160
   A development perspective   161

Theories of Depression   162
   Separation-loss   162   Other psychological theories   163   Biological theories   163

Assessment and Treatment   163

SUMMARY   164

**8   CHILDHOOD PSYCHOSES:
PERVASIVE DEVELOPMENTAL DISORDERS**   **166**

THE PROBLEM OF DEFINITION   167
EARLY ONSET: INFANTILE AUTISM   168

What Is the Basic Defect?   171
   Perceptual disturbances   171   Selective attention and learning   172
   Communication   172

Etiology   173
   Psychogenic determinants   173   Biological factors   175   Summary   176

LATER ONSET PSYCHOSES   176

Clinical Features   177
   Bender's descriptions   177   Char and Lubetsky's descriptions   178
   Eggers's descriptions   179

Etiology   180
   Psychogenic variables   180   Organic factors   182   Genetic influence   182
   Summary   182

WHAT HAPPENS TO PSYCHOTIC CHILDREN? 183
HELPING THE PSYCHOTIC CHILD 184
PHYSICAL METHODS OF TREATMENT 186
TRADITIONAL THERAPIES 187
BEHAVIOR MODIFICATION 187
    Language Training 188
    Self-injurious Behavior 189
    Training Parents as Therapists 191
    Efficacy 192

SUMMARY 192

9 MENTAL RETARDATION 195

HOW IS MENTAL RETARDATION DEFINED? 196
THE NATURE AND MEASUREMENT OF INTELLIGENCE 197

    Conceptualizing Intelligence 197
    Tests of Intelligence: The Binet and Wechsler Scales 197
        The Binet scales 197   *Wechsler scales 198*

    Infant Tests of Intelligence 199
    Interpretation of IQ 199
        What does IQ measure? 199   *Is IQ constant? 200*
        Are intelligence tests biased? 201

ADAPTIVE BEHAVIOR 201
    Vineland Social Maturity Scale 202
    AAMD's Adaptive Behavior Scale 203

LEVELS OF RETARDATION 203
EPIDEMIOLOGY 205
ETIOLOGY 206

    Chromosome Aberrations 207
        Down's syndrome 207   *Sex chromosome aberrations 209*
        BOX 9.1 THE "FRAGILE X" CHROMOSOME AND MENTAL RETARDATION 210
    Mendelian Inheritance 209
    Prenatal, Perinatal, and Postnatal Variables 210
    Family and Sociocultural Factors 210
        BOX 9.2 NATURE VERSUS NURTURE: CONTINUING DEBATE ABOUT INTELLIGENCE 213

COGNITION AND LEARNING   214

Piagetian Theory   214
Developmental versus difference controversy   215

Learning and Information Processing   215
Attention in discrimination learning   215
Mediation in paired-associate learning 216   Problem solving 216
Memory 217

PERSONALITY AND MOTIVATIONAL VARIABLES   219

Effects of Social Deprivation   219
Effectiveness of Reinforcers   219
Expectations for Failure and Success   220

FAMILY ADJUSTMENT   221
ISSUES IN TREATMENT AND EDUCATION   222

The Right to Education and the Least Restrictive Environment   223
Least restrictive environments   224

Deinstitutionalization   224
Behavior Modification   225

SUMMARY   227

10   HYPERACTIVITY AND LEARNING DISABILITIES   **229**

MINIMAL BRAIN DYSFUNCTION   230
HYPERACTIVITY   232

What Is Hyperactivity?   232
Secondary manifestations 233   Is hyperactivity a syndrome? 235

Etiology   235
Genetics 235   Perinatal factors 236   Dysfunctioning nervous system 236
Diet 236   Ecological variables: Lead and lighting 237
Psychosocial factors   238

Identifying the Hyperactive Child   239
Treatment   240
Pharmacologic   240
Behavioral intervention 243   Medication versus behavior modification 245
     BOX 10.1   ATTITUDES THAT AFFECT PHARMACOLOGICAL TREATMENT
           OF CHILDREN   244

The Changing Face of Hyperactivity   245

LEARNING DISABILITIES 245

    Definition and Clinical Description 246
    What Causes Learning Disabilities? 248
    Specific Learning Disabilities 249
        Language 249 Articulation 249 Reading 250 Arithmetic 252

    Treatment and Assessment 252
        Perceptual-motor approaches 252 Behavioral Approaches 254

SUMMARY 255

11   CONDUCT DISORDERS

256

WHAT ARE CONDUCT DISORDERS? 257

    The DSM-III Definition 257
    Empirically Derived Syndromes 258
    Prevalence 258
    The Stability of Conduct Disorders 259

CAUSES AND CORRELATES OF CONDUCT DISORDERS 260

    Family Influences 260
        Marital discord 260 Parent-child interactions 260
        BOX 11.1   THE BROKEN FAMILY AND BEHAVIOR DISORDERS 261

    Moral Development 260
    Underarousal and Conduct Disorders 263
    Biological Influences on Conduct Disorders 264

CONDUCT DISORDERED BEHAVIORS 265

    Aggression 265
        Freud's theory 265 The frustration-aggression hypothesis 266
        Aggression as a learned behavior 266 The Work of Patterson
        and his colleagues 269
        BOX 11.2   DOES WATCHING TELEVISED AGGRESSION CAUSE AGGRESSIVE
            BEHAVIOR? 267

    Oppositional-Noncompliant Behavior 272
    Juvenile Delinquency 274
        The problem of definition 275 Subtypes of delinquency 275
        Treatment of delinquency 277
        BOX 11.3   THE USE OF DRUGS AND ALCOHOL 276

SUMMARY 280

12 PSYCHOLOGICAL FACTORS AFFECTING PHYSICAL CONDITIONS   282

ASTHMA   283

    BOX 12.1   LIFE STRESS AND ILLNESS   284
Prevalence and Prognosis   285
Causes   285
Psychological Aspects of Asthma   287
    Psychological causes 287   Psychological irritants 289
    Psychological intervention in childhood asthma   291

ULCERATIVE COLITIS   292

Description and Incidence   292
Etiology   293
Treatment   293

PSYCHOLOGICAL CONSEQUENCES OF CHRONIC ILLNESS   294

A Description of Juvenile Diabetes Mellitus   294
Management of the Diabetic Condition   295
Reactions to the Illness   297
    BOX 12.2   SURVIVING PEDIATRIC CANCER   298

PSYCHOLOGICAL MODIFICATION OF PHYSICAL FUNCTIONS   300
FACILITATING MEDICAL TREATMENT   303

Fear Reduction in Dental Treatment   303
Compliance with Medical Regimens   303
Hospitalization   304

THE DYING CHILD   307
SUMMARY   309

13 EVOLVING CONCERNS FOR THE CHILD   310

PREVENTION OF BEHAVIOR DISORDERS   311

Rochester Primary Mental Health Project (PMHP)   312
Head Start and Early Intervention   313
    Education 313   Health 314   Parent Involvement 314   Social Services 314
    Evaluation 314

Child Abuse and Its Prevention   315
    BOX 13.1   CHILD ABUSE: THE DEATHS OF MARIA AND RUBIN   317
    The voluntary intervention and treatment program (VITP)   *318*

Crisis Intervention: Sudden Infant Death Syndrome   319
Prevention of Schizophrenia   320
Issues in Prevention   322

THE CHILD AS A COMPETENT HUMAN   323

Building Competencies in Children   324

THE RIGHTS OF CHILDREN   327

The Problem of Child Placement   327
What Children Think about Their Rights   329
Progress in Children's Rights   329

THE CHALLENGE OF THE FUTURE: WHO IS FOR CHIDREN?   331
SUMMARY   333

GLOSSARY   335
REFERENCES   345
NAME INDEX   380
SUBJECT INDEX   388

PREFACE

We are witnessing a time of escalating study and activism regarding youth. The desire to optimize the quality of life for various peoples, including the young, and practical concern about childhood dysfunction have led to heightened interest in childhood behavior disorders. The entire range of problems in development, from specific minor habit disorders to severe and pervasive dysfunction, is being explored. Moreover, the search to understand and ameliorate behavioral disturbance is beginning to benefit from knowledge that has accumulated in this century—and from advances in the ways in which knowledge is gained.

Our goal in writing this text is to present a relatively comprehensive introduction to childhood psychopathology. Thus, we have included issues central to the field, theoretical and methodological underpinnings, descriptions and discussion of many disorders, clinical and research data, and various treatment efforts. Space mandates some selectivity in approach and topic. Still, we hope that our readers will come away with clear, systematic, and broad understanding if what is known and yet to be discovered.

Three overriding themes are paramount in our view of childhood disorders. First is the belief that problem behaviors ultimately will be most clearly perceived within a *developmental context*. Although present knowledge limits this approach, facts about typical developmental sequences and processes will increasingly aid in the elucidation of disturbed behavior. This text reflects our interest in relating ''normal'' and ''abnormal'' growth.

Also obvious is a *strong interactionist* approach to the causes of dysfunction. With few if any exceptions, behavior can be explained only by multiple influences and their continuous interaction. A vast array of variables—biological structure and function, inheritance, cognition, socioemotional status, family, social class, culture—can usually be expected to come into play.

The third theme that runs through the text is our bias toward *empirical approaches* to the study of psychopathology. It is fascinating to delve into myths and possibilities—and we do this for the sake of history and interest. But the complexity of human behavior calls for systematic conceptualization, data collection, and hypothesis testing. Thus the methods and results of research are discussed in virtually every chapter. This should not be taken as a rejection of the clinical case study, for clinical examples and insight can provide rich ground for hypotheses. Nevertheless, only scientific study can take us beyond clinical observations and guesses—to firm evidence about our subject matter. For this reason *Behavior Disorders of Childhood* tends to emphasize theoretical frameworks that rely heavily on the scientific method.

Although the book is not formally broken into sections, it will be apparent to the reader that the first five chapters present the broad underpinnings of the field: historical context, normal development, theoretical perspectives, research, and classification/ diagnosis. All of these chapters draw heavily on psychology but they also reflect the multidisciplinary character of the field. We assume that many of our readers have some background in psychology or related areas but we have made an effort to serve those who come with relatively limited experience.

Chapters 6–12 cover specific behavior disorders: sleep and eating dysfunctions, phobias, autism, mental retardation, hyperactivity, to name a few. Since much is yet to be learned, we have focused on the dominant descriptions, causal hypotheses, and treatments for each disorder. Chapter 13, the closing chapter, speaks to growing concerns about children, including the enormous need for prevention and interest in children's competency and rights.

Problems of the young are intricately tied to broad cultural and social issues—and we have addressed many of these. Discussions of suicide, child abuse, the influence of television, educational mainstreaming, a child's reactions to cancer, and the like are woven into the text, sometimes emphasized by boxed material. Much of this material has an applied aspect, as do descriptions of treatment programs.

We extend our sincere thanks to several individuals who lent a hand to this project. John Isley and Jeanne Hoeting of Prentice-Hall have been of invaluable assistance. Appreciation goes to those who reviewed the manuscript. Victor Young, Director of the Library at West Virginia Institute of Technology, was most helpful in locating materials. Mary Rumbach drafted sections for a few chapters and made other contributions as well. For their various efforts, we acknowledge Olga Bleser, Cynthia Guile, Jennifer Lokant, Linda Simon, Marjory Simmons, Lauren Solotar, Laurie Stolmaker, Sharon Tackett, Jodi Weinstein, Anne Wichman, and William Worthington. Finally, a special thanks to Sara for her understanding, patience, and cooperation.

As colleagues we have shared equally in the delights and frustrations of this work: order of authorship was thus decided by a flip of the coin.

Rita Wicks-Nelson   Allen C. Israel

ACKNOWLEDGMENTS

Our grateful appreciation goes to those who reviewed our manuscript during its preparation;

Sharon S. Brehm, *University of Kansas*
Laurie Chassin, *University of Missouri at Columbia*
Thomas Fagan, *Memphis State University*
Bruce D. Grossman, *Hofstra University*
Raymond C. Hawkins, *The University of Texas at Austin*
Thomas H. Ollendick, *Virginia Polytechnic Institute and State University*
Karen A. Paulsen, *The University of Arizona*
L. Alan Sroufe, *University of Minnesota*
Susan Waldman, *San Francisco State University*
Elaine Walker, *Cornell University*
Richard Young, *Indiana University*

1

A DEFINITIONAL AND HISTORICAL INTRODUCTION

DEFINING DISORDERED BEHAVIOR

Sociocultural Norms
Developmental Norms
Other Criteria

HOW COMMON ARE CHILDHOOD DISORDERS?

Sex Differences
The Stability of Problems

CHILDHOOD DISORDERS: A BRIEF HISTORY

The Influence of Sigmund Freud
Behaviorism and Social Learning
  Theory
The Mental Hygiene and Child
  Guidance Movements
The Scientific Study of the Child

WORKING WITH THE CHILD CLIENT

SUMMARY

This book is written for all those concerned with behavioral or psychological problems displayed by the young. Disordered behavior attracts attention because it is often atypical, strange, or annoying. We may react to it with sadness, anger, embarrassment, repulsion, fear, or confusion. We may also be motivated to change it because it does not fit easily into the fabric of social life. But the drive to understand and ameliorate childhood problems also has its basis in the discrepancy between behavioral disturbance and each child's ideal potential.

Central to our concern and fascination with disordered behavior are the questions of its origins and maintenance. Why is a child excessively shy, aggressive, or fearful? Why do some youngsters have difficulty in developing the usual patterns of eating, sleeping, and acting "appropriately" female or male? What processes underlie intellectual deficits and severe disturbances such as lack of language, social isolation, and even self-mutilation? When we ask these questions, we raise the fundamental issues of how people develop and how normal developmental processes go awry.

Considerable progress is now being made in describing the sequences of typical development and in understanding the basic processes involved. This knowledge serves as a guide to identifying, describing, and ameliorating behaviors that fall short of normative standards. Conversely, investigations of disordered behavior increase our understanding of normal development. Interest in problem behavior and development therefore go hand in hand.

DEFINING DISORDERED BEHAVIOR

There is no concise and simple way to define disordered functioning. Frequently problem behavior is viewed as "abnormal." Inspecting the roots of this term, we find that *ab* means "away," "from," and "off," while *normal* refers to the average, standard, and regular (*Webster's new collegiate dictionary*, 1973). Thus, *abnormal* simply means something that deviates from the average, although common usage also assumes that the direction of deviation is negative or pathological. Psychological or behavioral disorders are therefore often labeled psychopathological.

It is obvious that judgment is involved in determining abnormality: We must be able to define the standard and decide whether the instance is qualitatively or quantitatively different from the standard. Dramatic differences cause no difficulty of definition. Most of us would agree that individuals who cannot learn to speak or to feed and dress themselves are abnormal. Less dramatic instances are harder to judge. Children may function in ways that appear only slightly deviant and quite prevalent—and thus not abnormal in the strict sense—but that are nevertheless considered problematic. In these instances parents, teachers, other adults, and occasionally children themselves may rely on numerous criteria to make the judgment that "something is wrong."

Sociocultural Norms

The role of *sociocultural norms*, perhaps the broadest criterion for judging behavior as disordered, was tellingly described many years ago by the anthropologist Ruth Benedict. After studying widely diverse cultures, Benedict (1934b) proposed that each society selects certain behaviors that are of value to it and socializes its members to act accordingly. Individuals who do not display these behaviors, by dint of temperamental predisposition or learning experiences, are considered deviant by the society. Deviance is always relative to cultural norms. Benedict noted, for example, that in one Melanesian culture the degree of suspiciousness typically exhibited would be considered pathological in our society. The Melanesians were so preoccupied with being harmed by others that women would not leave their cooking pots for fear of the food being poisoned (Benedict, 1934a). Moreover, the Melanesians who displayed the helpfulness, kindness, and cheerfulness that is considered positive in our

Ken Karp

The behavior that is expected of or appropriate for a child may vary among cultures.

United Nations/Photo by Bruno J. Zehnder

society were considered abnormal in their own culture. Thus, in Benedict's words:

Normality, in short, within a very wide range, is culturally defined. It is primarily a term for the socially elaborated segment of behavior in any culture; and abnormality, a term for the segment that that particular civilization does not use. The very eyes with which we see the problem are conditioned by the long traditional habits of our own society. (1934a, p. 75)

Cultural norms are applied to children as well as to adults. Youngsters in the United States are expected to be assertive and aggres-sive, as compared to children in some other parts of the world. We would be relatively more likely, then, to express concern about the quiet, passive child. Similarly, in technologically advanced societies, in which certain intellectual skills are highly valued, concern would be voiced about the child who does not measure up to standards of intellectual development.

In a society as complex as that of the United States, *subcultural norms* are also found. Consider, for example, the findings of a study that compared two groups of New York City families (Thomas, Chess, Sillen, and Mendez, 1974). Puerto Rican working-class families comprised one group, while predominantly Jewish middle- and upper-middle-class families comprised the other. Both groups had high family stability, and no differences were reported in prenatal and birth complications for the children. The groups differed markedly, though, in the number and kinds of problems they presented in their offspring. By the time the youngsters reached age 9, only 10 percent of the working-class children—as opposed to 31 percent of the middle-class children—had been diagnosed as having behavior disorders. Working-class parents appeared to place fewer demands on their children to dress and feed themselves and to follow through on verbal directions. They were relatively less oriented to childhood problems, less psychologically oriented, and less optimistic about obtaining help.

Ken Karp

Expectations for behavior vary across situations as well. What is appropriate in the city may be inappropriate in the country.

Ken Karp

They were also more likely to believe that young children would outgrow their disturbances. Thus, the working-class parents reported fewer problems, and the kinds of disorders they reported were relatively severe.

It is important to note that cultural norms are prescribed for specific situations. Energetic running may be quite acceptable on the playground but would create havoc in the classroom or in a dentist's office. Similarly, singing aloud may be tolerated at home, but rarely is it allowed in the library. Children are expected to act in certain ways in certain situations—in short, to meet *situational norms*.

Another way in which sociocultural norms are specified is in terms of gender. Of all the classifications individuals receive, perhaps none is as ladened with differential expectations as is sex. In most societies males are expected to be aggressive, objective, dominant, active, and adventurous; females are considered dependent, emotional, subjective, submissive, and sensitive (D'Andrade, 1966; Tresemer and Pleck, 1974). These *sex stereotypes* strongly guide our judgments about normality. We are probably less inclined to worry about the hypersensitive, shy girl and the excessively dominant boy than about their opposite-sex counterparts.

Finally, it must be noted that sociocultural norms of psychopathology may *change over time*, due to broad societal transitions or to changes in the popularity of particular views of abnormality. For example, the psychopathological category of "masturbatory insanity" was applied to children in the 1800s but no longer exists (Rie, 1971). Similarly, nail biting, considered relatively harmless today, was once regarded as a "stigma of degeneration" and "an exquisite psychopathic symptom" (Kanner, 1960, cited by Anthony, 1970, p. 668).

Developmental Norms

Because children change rapidly and dramatically, their functioning cannot be adequately assessed without consideration of developmental norms. The typical rate and sequence of the growth of skills, knowledge, and social behavior can be charted, and these developmental standards can be extremely helpful in evaluating the possibility that "something is wrong." Adults would be mistaken to worry about the 1-year-old boy who is not yet walking, because many children of this age do not walk. However, if the same child is unable to sit alone, concern would be appropriate, because virtually all babies can sit well before the end of the first year of life. Norms for social behavior are not as well established as those for motor and intellectual development, but children are expected to act generally like their peers.

Developmental norms can be used inappropriately. Adults tend to believe that every child should meet at least the average standards. But when an average is calculated, individuals fall on both sides of it, and a range of values must be taken into account. Table 1-1 exemplifies this point by showing the range of ages at which certain percentages of children successfully perform three different behaviors. Here we see, for example, that although in this sample of babies 50 percent were able to sit alone steadily at 6.6 months, 9.0 months was the time required before 95 percent of them could do so.

Other Criteria

Several other factors may be considered in evaluating a child's behavior. Behavior that is adequately performed at the usual age level may be viewed as disturbed in degree if it occurs too frequently or infrequently, is too intense or insufficiently intense, or endures over too long or

Table 1-1 Months at Which Children Perform Certain Behaviors

	5%	50%	95%
Sits alone steadily	5.0	6.6	9.0
Repeats performance laughed at	8.0	10.8	17.0
Sentence of two words	16.0	20.6	30.0

(Adapted and reproduced by permission from the Bayley Scales of Infant Development Manual. Copyright © 1969 by the Psychological Corporation. All rights reserved.)

too short a period of time. It is not unusual for a child to display fear, for example, but fear may be judged problematic if it occurs in an excessive number of situations, is extremely intense, and does not abate over time. Concern might also be expressed for the child whose reactions appear to have changed, such as when a friendly and outgoing girl turns reclusive and morose. Adults seem to worry, too, when a child is troubled simultaneously by several things.

Finally, the subjective feelings of others are also a factor. The labeling of a problem is likely to occur when the child disturbs others, as when a sibling continuously complains of being physically attacked or when a teacher is uncomfortable with a withdrawn student. Childhood disorders are typically identified by adults, so adult attitudes, sensitivity, tolerance, and ability to cope are bound to influence how children are perceived and handled. Shepherd, Oppenheim, and Mitchell (1966) addressed this issue when they contrasted parents of youngsters seen in a clinic with parents of children with comparable problems who were not brought to the clinic. After the clinic and nonclinic children were matched according to problems, the parents were interviewed. Among other findings the investigators discovered that clinic mothers felt helpless and unable to cope with their children's behavior. Nonclinic mothers, in contrast, viewed their offsprings' behavior as temporary difficulties. Thus, the individual mother's reaction to her child's behavior appeared to be a factor in whether the child was considered disturbed.

In summary, then, we can see that identifying psychological or behavioral disorders is a complex matter, depending upon an array of very different considerations. This has direct implications for determining the prevalence and incidence of childhood problems.

HOW COMMON ARE CHILDHOOD DISORDERS?

An often-asked question about childhood disorders is: How common are they? *Prevalence* can be ascertained by counting the number of children with a disorder at any one time. It is usually expressed as the number of such children in the population, or as a percentage (for example, there are 2,000 children suffering from a disorder, or 10 out of every 1,000, or 1 percent of all children). *Incidence* can be determined by counting the number of new cases within a specific time period. There is good reason for wanting to determine prevalence and incidence. Aside from satisfying sheer intellectual curiosity, these data signal the need for prevention, treatment, rehabilitation, and research. However, they must be considered with caution.

If one wanted to determine the presence of childhood disorders in a population, it would seem reasonable to survey the settings directly involved with children's mental health; namely clinics, hospitals, residential homes, private professional offices, and the like. Indeed, such a tactic is often followed. However, the youngsters actually brought to these settings may not provide an accurate or reliable index of disordered behavior. We have already seen that the criteria for judging the presence of a disorder are complex. In addition, cases frequently go unreported out of shame, fear of stigma, and neglect. On the other side of the coin, high interest in an anomaly can result in its being reported more frequently or even being overreported. For example, publicity in the media about a particular behavior disorder may result in adults "seeing" the problem in a child who they had previously considered normal. Another serious matter is that diagnostic categories are not used in a consistent manner: One clinician may label a child as hyperactive, while another may diagnose the same child as learning disabled. Such unreliability obviously casts doubt on information gathered about the occurrence of specific disorders.

A second way in which the presence of disordered behaviors might be evaluated is by examining all children in a geographic area or a representative sample of the area. Such epidemiologic studies have several weaknesses, among which are poor sampling and reliance on adult reports rather than on clinical observation (e. g., Gould, Wunsch-Hitzig, and Dohrenwend, 1981). Nevertheless, the results of several investigations of this kind conducted in the United States and in Europe are striking in that they reveal a high prevalence in the general population of behaviors often considered signs of disturbance.

In a carefully designed investigation Lapouse and Monk (1958) contacted almost 500 mothers of a representative sample of all 6 to 12-year-olds in Buffalo, New York. The mothers were requested to evaluate their children's behavior in detail. They reported that 49 percent of the offspring were overactive, 48 percent lost their tempers twice weekly, 43 percent had seven or more fears and worries, 28 percent experienced nightmares, 27 percent bit their nails, 17 percent wet the bed, and 10 percent sucked their thumbs. Many of these figures are similar to the results obtained from other epidemiologic investigations (Anthony, 1970). Again they indicate the complexities involved in labeling a problem: The children surveyed were not of a clinic population but displayed behaviors often regarded as signs of psychopathology.

Sex Differences

One of the most pervasive findings regarding prevalence is that a large variety of behavior disorders are more commonly found in boys than in girls. These include severe mental dysfunction, hyperactivity, bed-wetting, antisocial behavior, and learning difficulties (Anthony, 1970; Eme, 1979). When girls show greater prevalence, the problems involve shyness, fear, anxiety, bodily complaints, and the like (Achenbach, 1974; Quay, 1972; Schultz, Salvia, and Feinn, 1974). This difference can be attributed to several factors. In general, males appear more biologically vulnerable than females: They have a higher death rate from the moment of conception and seem more affected by major diseases, malnutrition, and poverty (Birns, 1976; Eme, 1979; Knobloch and Pasamanick, 1974). However, differential socialization may also account for sex differences. For example, aggressive acting-out behavior is undoubtedly more readily encouraged in males than in females. There is also evidence, though, that the greater prevalence of problems in males can be attributed to relatively more reporting of male deviance. Mothers expect that boys' difficulties are longer lasting than those of girls (Shepherd, Oppenheim, and Mitchell, 1966), and parents and teachers are less tolerant of male hyperactivity, lack of persistence, distractibility, and disruption (Battle and Lacey, 1972; Chess and Thomas, 1972; Eme, 1979; Serbin and O'Leary, 1975). At the same time, it is possible that adult tolerance is lower for boys because males have been more difficult to handle from the beginning of life. In effect, then, biological endowment may interact with socialization and social expectation to create a vicious cycle for the male child.

The Stability of Problems

From some of the prevalence studies it can be concluded that childhood disorders, at least the less serious ones, wax and wane and sometimes disappear spontaneously. Thus, they may represent transient developmental crises. Such a conclusion is strengthened by the findings that many childhood problems appear to remit without specific treatment (Levitt, 1957, 1963; Shepherd, Oppenheim, and Mitchell, 1966). If early behavior problems disappear, are markedly reduced by adulthood, or have no relationship to later disturbance, they would be of less concern than if they were highly predictive of later problems.

What is the association between early behavioral disorders and later problems? Many severely disordered children clearly do not escape dysfunction in later life (Lotter, 1974b, 1978). There is also evidence that childhood antisocial behavior is associated with adult disability (Robins, 1966, 1974) and that hyperactive children tend to display academic deficiencies and inadequate social relationships at least into adolescence (Barkley, 1978; Hoy, Weiss, Minde, and Cohen, 1978; Milich and Loney, 1979). However, early behaviors such as nailbiting, nervousness, masturbation, fears, shyness, inhibition, and irritability do not seem to predict most adult disorders (Kanner, 1960;

Kohlberg, LaCrosse, and Ricks, 1972; Robins, 1966).

Thus, on the basis of present data, it is difficult to draw a simple picture of spontaneous remission and the relationship between early and late disorders. Perhaps this is not surprising—development is often notoriously difficult to predict. It is hazardous to predict what will happen to any one child, since individual attributes interact with particular environmental variables to produce an array of outcomes. Also, tracing stability or change is no easy matter. At different developmental levels behaviors that appear quite different may actually fall into the same class. For example, the 5-year-old child may demonstrate aggression by slapping a playmate, while the adolescent is more likely to use subtle sarcasm. Slapping and verbal abuse seem quite different; in fact, they may represent the same class of behavior, the form of which was transformed over time by socialization and intellectual growth. On the other hand, actions that seem to fall into different classes may actually serve the same functions. For example, consider the reactions to feelings of fear. A young child may act quite timid in a fearful situation but later, due to social experience, may try to overcome fear by behaving overly courageous or assertive. While timidity and courageousness are dissimilar in topography, they are functionally similar in this case. Would it be correct, then, to conclude that the child's problem in coping with fear disappeared, or has it merely taken another, equally maladaptive, form?

From even these few illustrations we can see the complexities associated with the stability or instability of behavior. It clearly would be a mistake to conclude that attempts at treatment are useless because childhood disorders disappear anyway. Moreover, from a humanitarian perspective it is valuable to relieve dysfunction and suffering even when they are temporary. Care should be taken not to overemphasize behavior problems, but treatment is desirable if children experience immediate discomfort or if there is reason to suspect that their potential development is being hindered. While this posi-

tion may seem obvious, it is a relatively new one in the history of humankind.

CHILDHOOD DISORDERS: A BRIEF HISTORY

Human beings are probably the only species that minutely analyzes its own behavior. Conjectures have been offered about the etiology of psychopathology, and serious attempts have been made to classify and treat deranged individuals. Until the late nineteenth century these efforts focused primarily on adults (see Box 1-1). Several subsequent developments dramatically altered this state of affairs.

The Influence of Sigmund Freud

Prior to the twentieth century most theories of disordered behavior emphasized organic etiologies. The work of Sigmund Freud radically changed this situation. When Freud was a young neurologist, he began collaborating with others, especially Joseph Breuer, who had growing convictions that certain disorders were caused by psychological events. In particular, Breuer and Freud were interested in the fact that childhood experiences appeared related to later hysterical symptoms, such as paralysis, blindness, and deafness, for which no known physical etiology was evident. These symptoms seemed to be alleviated when the patient was able to talk emotionally about earlier experiences. Such observations of adults set Freud on a lifelong course: He attempted to construct a grand theory of development and a treatment method for disordered behavior.

While Freudian theory will be discussed in greater detail in later chapters of this book, we should note here the pervasive influence Freud had on the field of childhood psychopathology. Although Freud virtually never treated children, he was nevertheless convinced that childhood conflicts among the id, ego, and superego were the key to understanding subsequent behavior. Moreover, Freudian theory specified universal developmental stages through which

---

Box 1-1   Early Views of Children and Their Disorders

It is interesting to speculate how medieval and early modern attitudes and views about children might have caused lack of concern and knowledge of childhood behavior disorders. Although the historical bits and pieces are not yet woven into a completed tapestry, a few dominant themes have emerged.

One theme concerns an indifference to children that seems quite remarkable today. The child was widely viewed as unimportant and unworthy of much consideration (Ariès, 1962). Abandonment of children—many were given away, sold as slaves, and left at monasteries and orphanages—was common practice from the fourth to thirteenth centuries (de Mause, 1974). One apparent reason for children having such low value was the high risk of early death. It is estimated that until 1750 the odds were only 1 to 3 that a child would survive to age 5 (Rie, 1971). Thus, as Ariès (1962) noted, people could not allow themselves to become attached to a child regarded as a probable loss. This climate hardly lent itself to taking children seriously, much less to the study of children.

A related phenomenon was that childhood was not viewed as a stage of life separate from adulthood (Ariès, 1962). As soon as children could live without adult help, they were considered miniature adults. They mingled freely with adults, participated in adult activities, and dressed like adults. This lasted into the seventeenth and eighteenth centuries. Gradually the young came to be regarded in the family circle as agreeable, amusing, and charming toys; outside of the family they were viewed by churchmen and moralists as fragile creatures who needed to be reformed and safeguarded (Ariès, 1962). This was the beginning of the awareness in modern times of the unique nature of children. Without recognition of childhood as a unique developmental stage, there could be no substantial progress in studying children and in identifying childhood disorders.

Although passing references to children's dysfunctions were made in earlier times, the first recordings of specific problems were made at the beginning of the nineteenth century (Rie, 1971). By the end of the century a few prominent persons had attempted to classify childhood disorders and had proposed causes for them. Psychoses, aggression, hyperactivity, and "masturbatory insanity" had all been noted, but mental retardation received most attention. Heredity and biological determinants were greatly emphasized; psychological causes, when suggested, were believed to act directly on the nervous system by, for example, irritating the brain or exhausting the nerves. Efforts to understand disturbed behavior coincided with increased interest in the education of the young and in observing and charting the course of development of individual children. Indeed, the so-called "baby biographies" of men such as Charles Darwin and the Swiss educator Johann Pestolozzi were forerunners of modern scientific observation of children (Rie, 1971).

---

children pass, described the stages in depth, and drew relationships between the stages and later behavior. In *Three Essays on the Theory of Sexuality*, published in 1905, Freud introduced his radical ideas about childhood and the early determinants of psychological disorders (Rie, 1971). These views, although controversial from the start (particularly with regard to children's sexuality), provided a systematic framework for conceptualizing both childhood and adult be-

havior. By the 1930s Freud's ideas had been widely interpreted by Melanie Klein, Freud's daughter Anna, Erik Erikson, Heinz Hartmann, and numerous others. These investigations helped to establish psychiatry as a major discipline in the study and treatment of childhood disorders, as indicated by the publication in 1935 of a text by Leo Kanner that is considered the first child psychiatry text in the United States (Rie, 1971).

Behaviorism and Social Learning Theory

At the approximate time that Freud was stirring up the academic world with his innovative ideas, a system of behavioral psychology was being introduced in the United States that would eventually rival Freud's ideas (Sears, 1975). Behaviorism was launched by John B. Watson's essay *Psychology as a Behaviorist Views It* (1913). Unlike Freud, Watson placed little value on describing stages of development or on past psychic conflicts. Instead, drawing on Pavlov and other learning theorists, he emphasized the centrality of learning processes in shaping behavior, claiming that most behaviors can be learned, given the appropriate environmental circumstances. Watson stated enthusiastically:

Give me a dozen healthy infants, well-formed, and my own specified world to bring them up in and I'll guarantee to take any one at random and train him to become any type of specialist I might select—doctor, lawyer, merchant, chief and yes, even beggar-man and thief, regardless of his talents, penchants, tendencies, abilities, vocations, and race of his ancestors. (Watson, 1924, reprinted 1963, p. 104)

E. L. Thorndike also made an early, crucial contribution to the development of behaviorism by formulating what he called the *Law of Effect*. Simply put, the Law of Effect states that behavior is shaped by its consequences. If the consequence is satisfying, the behavior will be strengthened in the future; if the consequence is discomforting, the behavior will be weakened (Thorndike, 1905). Thorndike considered the Law of Effect a fundamental principle of learning and teaching, and later researchers were to substantiate his claim. Notable among them is B. F. Skinner, who has written widely on the application of behavioral consequences to the shaping of behavior (Skinner, 1948, 1953, 1968).

Behaviorism thrived in the United States during the first half of this century, led by theorists such as Hull, Spence, Skinner, and Tolman. Its impact on the area of childhood psychopathology came only gradually, however, as Mowrer, Bijou, Baer, and Bandura, among others, began to apply learning principles directly to children's behavior. Although their work focused on different aspects of the learning process, all emphasized the importance of the social context. Thus, their approach is often described as the social learning perspective. When applied explicitly to the assessment and treatment of disordered behavior, it is called behavior modification or behavior therapy. This perspective and its progress are further discussed in Chapter 3.

The Mental Hygiene and Child Guidance Movements

Even though adult psychopathology had received considerable attention by the early twentieth century, there remained much to be learned, and treatment was characterized by custodial hospital care. The mental hygiene movement in the United States was an effort to increase understanding, improve treatment, and prevent dysfunctioning from occurring in the first place.

In 1908 Clifford Beers wrote an autobiographical account, *A Mind That Found Itself*, telling of his experiences as a mental patient. He described the insensitive and ineffective treatment to which he had been exposed, and proposed extensive reform. Beers was successful in obtaining the interest and support of renowned professionals, such as the psychiatrist Adolf Meyer. Recognizing psychological as well as biological determinants of mental dysfunction, Meyer believed that disordered behavior stemmed from a failure to adapt, and he recommended a "commonsense" approach both to studying the patient's environment and to counseling. He set the course for a new professional role—that of psychiatric social worker—and suggested the name for the movement that Beers was struggling to create (Achenbach, 1974). Beers's efforts led to the establishment of the National Committee for Mental Hygiene, which was to study mental dysfunction, initiate treatment programs, and focus on pre-

Wide World Photos

Both Sigmund Freud (center) and his daughter Anna Freud (foreground) were influential in the development of the psychodynamic conceptualization of childhood disorders.

John B. Watson was a highly influential figure in the application of the behavioral perspective.

The Bettmann Archive

vention. The importance attributed to the effects of childhood on later mental health resulted in the child guidance movement (Rie, 1971).

In 1896 Lightner Witmer had already set up a clinic at the University of Pennsylvania, primarily to assess the intellectual functioning of children who were having school difficulties. This clinic is considered the first child psychology clinic in the United States, and it is some-

times cited as the original source of clinical child psychology (Ross, 1972). Witmer coined the term *psychological clinic*; founded and for many years edited a journal, *Psychological Clinic*; and began a hospital school for long-term observation of children (Rie, 1971). He emphasized a psychoeducational approach and also drew attention to the relationship of psychology to sociology. According to Witmer, the school room, the juvenile court, and the streets all served as a laboratory for psychology (1907, cited by Rossi, 1962).

Such an interdisciplinary approach, albeit a somewhat different one, was taken by psychiatrist William Healy and psychologist Grace Fernald in Chicago in 1909, when they founded the Juvenile Psychopathic Institute, the model for the child guidance movement. The focus of the Institute was delinquent children. It was not the problem, however, but the approach, that became the mark of child guidance. Healy was convinced that antisocial behavior could be treated by psychological means, by helping youngsters adjust to the circumstances in which they lived (Santostefano, 1978). This required understanding the entire personality and the multiple causes of behavior. Freudian theory provided the central conceptualizations for dealing with children's intrapsychic conflicts, but attempts were made to gather information about familial and other significant relationships (Santostefano, 1978; Strean, 1970). The psychiatrist, psychologist, and social worker formed a collaborative team toward this end, meeting to share case histories.

Healy and his wife, psychologist Augusta Bronner, continued to use this approach when they opened the Judge Baker Guidance Center in Boston. The National Committee for Mental Hygiene subsequently established several urban and rural child clinics, adopting Healy's approach. Increasingly the types of cases treated there included personality and emotional problems, in addition to delinquency. These clinics flourished during the 1920s and 1930s (Santostefano, 1978). In 1924 the child guidance movement was formally represented by the formation of the American Orthopsychiatric Association, with Healy as its first president and Bronner as its second. To this day the Association includes a variety of professionals concerned about children.

The Scientific Study of the Child

It was also during the early twentieth century that the scientific study of children became systematic and widespread. A central figure in the new area of inquiry was G. Stanley Hall, who received the first Ph.D. in psychology awarded by an American university.

Like many others of this period, Hall knew little about children's development, and so he set about collecting questionnaire data concerning their fears, dreams, preferences, play, and the like (Grinder, 1967; Sears, 1975). Although Hall's method was later found wanting (for example, the samples were unknown and the procedures were not standardized), his enthusiasm and deep involvement resulted in his being considered the founder of child psychology in the United States. He authored numerous books and articles on children and adolescents and trained students who would later become leaders in the study of children. In 1909, as president of Clark University, Hall invited Sigmund Freud to Clark to lecture on psychoanalysis. He also played a central role in establishing the American Psychological Association and was its first president.

At about the same time, an important event was occurring in Europe: Alfred Binet and Theophil Simon were commissioned by public school officials in Paris to design a test to identify children who were likely to need special education (Tuddenham, 1963). In order to do so, Binet and Simon presented children of various ages with different kinds of tasks and problems, thereby establishing age-norms by which school-children's intellectual development could be evaluated. The 1905 Binet-Simon test became the basis for the development of intelligence tests. It also encouraged professionals to search for ways to measure other psychological attributes.

Another figure who stands out in the study of children is Arnold Gesell. A student of Hall's at Clark University, Gesell observed and charted children's motor and social behavior at the Clinic of Child Development at Yale University. Gesell relied heavily on photography as a method of study, using hundreds of thousands of feet of film to examine the actions of infants and children (Knobloch and Pasamanick, 1974). The organizing concept of Gesell's work was *maturation,* the intrinsic unfolding of development relatively independent of environmental influences. In his voluminous writings Gesell attempted to chart the typical maturational sequences of development, and deviations from them. His early practical interest in education expanded into efforts concerning adoption, guidance, and developmental assessment. Some of Gesell's followers are actively involved in studying and diagnosing developmental deviations, using as a guide the behavioral manifestations of the maturing nervous system.

Beginning around 1920 child study profited from several longitudinal research projects that evaluated children as they developed over several years. Some of the major studies, which focused on both physical and psychological growth, had their headquarters at Fels Research Institute (Antioch, Ohio), the University of California's Institute of Child Welfare at Berkeley, and the Merrill-Palmer Institute (Chicago). In addition, Columbia University's Teachers College, the Iowa Child Welfare Research Station, John Hopkins University, Harvard University, and the universities of Michigan, Colorado, Minnesota, Ohio, and Washington all produced substantial child research by the 1930s. The result was a body of knowledge about the sequences and processes of normal development that eventually could be applied to the study of childhood disorders.

WORKING WITH THE CHILD CLIENT

As we have already seen, professional care of children with behavioral problems involves various disciplines. Most notable are psychology, psychiatry, social work, and special education.

Psychologists interested in childhood disorders usually have specialized in clinical psychology, sometimes in developmental, school, and educational psychology. Most often they hold the doctoral degree (Ph.D. or Psy. D.), which demands four or five years of graduate study. As

Table 1-2   Some Historical Landmarks

1896	The first child clinic in the U.S. was established at the University of Pennsylvania by Lightner Witmer.
1905	Alfred Binet and Theophil Simon developed the first intelligence tests to identify feeble-minded children.
1905	Sigmund Freud's *Three Essays on the Theory of Sexuality* described a startlingly different view of childhood development.
1908	In *A Mind That Found Itself,* Clifford Beers recounted his mental breakdown and advocated an enlightened view of mental disorders, initiating the mental hygiene and child guidance movements.
1909	G. Stanley Hall invited Sigmund Freud to Clark University to lecture on psychoanalysis.
1909	William Healy and Grace Fernald established the Juvenile Psychopathic Institute in Chicago, which would become the model for the child guidance clinics.
1911	The Yale Clinic of Child Development was established for child development research under the guidance of Arnold Gesell.
1913	John B. Watson introduced behaviorism in his essay *Psychology as a Behaviorist Views It.*
1917	William Healy and Augusta Bronner established the Judge Baker Guidance Center in Boston.
1922	The National Committee on Mental Hygiene and the Commonwealth Fund initiated a demonstration program of child guidance clinics.
1924	The American Orthopsychiatric Association was established.
1928–1929	Longitudinal studies of child development began at Berkeley and Fels Research Institute, respectively.
1935	Leo Kanner authored *Child Psychiatry,* the first child psychiatry text published in the U.S.

a discipline, psychology has sturdy roots in the laboratory and in academe and is interested in both normal and abnormal behavior. Training in clinical psychology thus includes psychological research as well as direct contact with troubled people. Many psychologists have a strong background in assessing behavior by means of psychological tests. *Psychiatrists*, on the other hand, hold the M.D. degree; they are medical doctors who have specialized in the care of the mentally disturbed. Psychiatrists make a unique contribution to childhood psychopathology by conducting medical evaluations and prescribing medication when appropriate. *Social workers* generally hold the master's degree in social work. Like psychologists and psychiatrists, they may counsel and do therapy, but historically their special focus has been working with the family and with other social systems in which children are enmeshed. *Special education teachers*, who usually have obtained the master's degree in special education, emphasize the importance of providing troubled children with optimal educational experiences. They are able to plan and implement such programs, thereby contributing strongly to the amelioration of many childhood disorders.

Troubled children also come to the attention of other professionals, such as nurses, general physicians, teachers in regular classrooms, and professionals in the legal system. Thus, interdisciplinary consultation is a common occurrence and is regarded as ideal in most cases. The interdisciplinary approach requires a good deal of coordination. Who functions as the coordinator may depend on the type of disorder, the developmental level of the child, the first point of professional contact, and the treatment setting.

These factors also partly determine the mode of treatment; that is, the selection of individual therapy, family therapy, medical procedures, special education, and the like. In many instances several modes of treatment may be used simultaneously or consecutively. Moreover, although an association exists between disciplines and modes of treatment (for example, psychiatry and medical procedures; special education

and educational programs), there is considerable overlap in the kinds of services rendered by the various disciplines.

Regardless of the approach, evaluating and treating the young are difficult endeavors, insofar as children are often incapable of identifying their problems and seeking treatment. This means that children usually enter the therapeutic situation at the suggestion or coercion of adults. Professionals must therefore be sensitive to the child's perspective and work to create and maintain the child's motivation.

Dealing with childhood disorders also frequently demands working closely with parents, who vary greatly in their capacity to participate. Although it is safe to assume that most parents desire to help their offspring, parental needs can interfere with assessment of their child. For example, consider the hypothetical case of authoritarian parents who require excessive obedience from their son and actually seek therapy to change the child's behavior in ways that may be detrimental to him. Similarly, due to personality or situational circumstances, parents vary in their capacity to understand, support, and conduct recommended therapeutic procedures. The competent and sensitive professional is aware of these factors and works toward optimizing the quality of parental involvement—compensating for its lack whenever necessary.

When working with child clients, professionals always face the question of the degree to which the child is "disturbed" or "disturbing" (Algozzine, 1977). In the hypothetical case of the overly authoritarian parents, the child may be disturbing to the parents but may not be disturbed, by most standards. Similarly, it may be necessary to view a disorder as located neither within the child nor the parents but within the larger social system. In many classrooms, for example, children are expected to sit still and attend diligently. And yet, in one teacher survey of third- and fourth-grade students, about 40 percent of the boys were rated restless, disruptive, and inattentive (Schultz, Salvia, and Feinn, 1974). Such a high prevalence of deviation suggests that the situation itself, unreasonable situational norms, or an inadequate assessment procedure may account for the "children's problems." In working with the young, one of the most difficult tasks is to balance these considerations in the best interests of the child as an individual in the family and in society (see Box 1–2).

Finally, the overall approach to working with children is strongly influenced by the conceptual or theoretical perspective held by the professional. In this chapter most of the widely held perspectives have been mentioned, at least in passing. The following two chapters will describe these views more fully and draw out their

---

Box 1–2 Treatment Ethics and Gender Disorder

A clear demonstration of the complexities that can arise in the treatment of childhood disorders involves gender disturbance. The gender-disturbed child exhibits cross-sex mannerisms, prefers the activities of the other sex, and perhaps even expresses the desire to be of the other sex. No known biological dysfunction exists. The condition has been treated with behavioral techniques to reduce the "inappropriate" behaviors and strengthen those considered more normal for the biological sex of the child. These efforts have raised serious ethical questions.

A case that precipitated much discussion concerned a 5-year-old boy, Kraig, whose parents had sought professional help for their offspring. Rekers and Lovaas, the clinician/researchers who provided the treatment, offered this description of the boy:

He had a history of cross-dressing since he was 2 yrs. old; at that time, he also began to play with cosmetic items. . . . Kraig continually displayed pronounced feminine mannerisms, gestures, and gait, as well as exaggerated feminine inflection and feminine content of speech. . . . At the same time, he seemed void of masculine behaviors, being both unable and unwilling to play the "rough and tumble" games of boys his age in his immediate neighborhood. . . . He preferred to play with girls, and one neighborhood girl in particular; even when playing house with the girls, he invariably insisted on playing the part of the "mother" and assigned the part of the "father" to one of the girls. For a child his age, Kraig had an overly dependent relationship with his mother; he demanded her attention almost continuously. He appeared to be very skillful at manipulating her to satisfy his feminine interests (e.g., he would offer to "help mommy" by carrying her purse

when she had other packages to carry). He seemed almost compulsive or "rigid" in the extent to which he insisted on being a girl and in his refusal of all contact with masculine-like activities. (1974, p. 174)

With parental cooperation Rekers and Lovaas constructed an intervention that centered on the social reinforcement of masculine mannerisms, activities, and interests. They reported a successful outcome. In their presentation of the case, Rekers and Lovaas justified their treatment goal by noting that (1) the boy was handicapped socially, being the victim of ridicule and rejection, (2) Kraig was at high risk for developing hard-to-treat adult gender disorders such as homosexuality, transvestism (cross-sex dressing), and transsexualism (the desire to be of the opposite sex that sometimes leads to voluntary medical sex change), and (3) Kraig's parents, his legitimate advocates, had requested consultation and aid.

Nevertheless, not all professionals agreed with this ethical stance. At the heart of the criticism, in one way or another, are value-laden issues. One team of writers suggested that diversity of behavior must be recognized as valuable (Nordyke, Baer, Etzel, and LeBlanc, 1977). Wolfe (1979) noted that stereotypes associated with sex are of questionable value—that what behaviorally constitutes a male or female is an open question. Thus, the use of sex stereotypes as a guide for change, which is how Rekers and Lovaas proceeded, may be inappropriate. For example, playing with dolls could be quite beneficial for boys in preparation for fatherhood, while reduction of "feminine" interests could diminish the likelihood of later artistic accomplishments. Moreover, Wolfe argued that the a priori labeling of behaviors according to gender may occur because cross-sex behaviors are more disturbing than disturbed. Ollendick and Cerny (1981), while fundamentally sympathetic to the Rekers and Lovaas position, would have liked to have seen Kraig involved in the treatment decision to the extent that one so young can be involved. These writers state, however, that in the final analysis they value the goal of Rekers and Lovaas to expand the child's options by helping him become less femininely sex-stereotyped and more flexible in his behavioral repertoire.

While ethical dilemmas about treatment of behavioral or psychological problems are common, they are of special concern when children are involved (for example, Rosen, Rekers, and Bentler, 1978). Value judgments are a part of ethical considerations, and children—by dint of developmental level and legal status—are limited in speaking for themselves. Similar concerns apply also to children's participation in research, a topic to which we return in later discussion.

implications for explanations and treatment of childhood disorders.

SUMMARY

Although most behavioral disturbance elicits interest and motivation to bring about change, the drive to understand and treat childhood problems is heightened by the desire to optimize development of the young. Central to questions about psychopathology are basic issues about development and about how typical development goes awry. The study of childhood disorders and development thus go hand in hand.

The identification of behavioral disturbance rests on several criteria, including sociocultural and developmental norms. Behavior that appears atypical in frequency, intensity, and duration, or that changes abruptly, is likely to be pinpointed as problematic. Since children's disorders are commonly identified by parents and teachers, the attitudes, sensitivities, and tolerances of adults are crucial variables in determining whether a child is or is not labeled a problem.

Assessing the occurrence of childhood disorders (that is, prevalence and incidence) relies on surveying the settings directly involved in mental health as well as observing the general population of children (epidemiologic studies). Because both methods are imperfect, caution is appropriate in interpreting the data. Neverthe-

less, some of the findings are pervasive. Behaviors that are often viewed as signs of disturbance are actually quite prevalent in the general population of children. Also widely reported is the higher prevalence of disorder in boys as compared to girls, although girls show greater frequency of shyness, fear, anxiety, and bodily complaints. Sex differences can be attributed to biological and environmental factors and their interaction. Prevalence studies also suggest that many childhood problems may be nothing more than transient developmental crises that may remit spontaneously. However, remission is not a certainty, and some early behavior problems are associated with later difficulties. Tracing the stability or instability of disorders is difficult because relatively little is known about developmental transformations of behavior and the various changing functions of behavior. Treatment thus appears warranted on the basis of the immediate discomfort of the child and the danger to potential development.

Current interest in and intervention on behalf of the young is a recent trend that required the growth of certain beliefs and attitudes about children. Only in this century have children's problems become a focus of concern. Several historical influences are notable: the work of Freud, the rise of the behavioral/social learning approach, the mental hygiene and child guidance movement, and the dramatic increase in scientific study of the child. These events have shaped the belief that childhood disorders are worthy of investigation. They have also provided several conceptual frameworks and considerable knowledge of children's development.

Professional care of children is interdisciplinary, most commonly involving psychologists, psychiatrists, social workers, and educational specialists, as well as general medical practitioners, teachers, and professionals in the legal system. As a result, various modes of treatment and evaluation are offered.

The care of the child, as compared to that of the adult, brings with it some special considerations. Since children typically enter the therapeutic setting due to the decision of adults, particular effort is required to understand the child's perspective. In most instances, however, parents play an important part in the child's treatment, and so their needs, motivations, and capacities cannot be ignored. Working with the child client also raises several ethical dilemmas. The extent to which the child is "disturbed"—rather than "disturbing"—is of utmost concern. Behavior disorders are best viewed within the context of the family and larger social systems. Value judgments are almost always involved in treatment. The need for value-ladened decisions is made especially complex by children's developmental level and legal status, both of which may limit their ability to represent themselves. Ethical issues in intervention are not easy to resolve.

2

THE DEVELOPMENTAL CONTEXT

WHAT IS DEVELOPMENT?

Nature and Nurture

A SCHEMA OF NORMAL DEVELOPMENT

The Genetic Context
The Child as a Physical Being
The Child as an Intellectual Being
The Child as a Social Being
The Social Context

SOME IMPORTANT DEVELOPMENTAL ISSUES

Levels of Development
Individual Differences
Early Experience and Critical Events
Risk and Invulnerability

SUMMARY

The developmental orientation to childhood problems takes as its guiding principle the proposition that behavioral disturbance can best be understood in terms of the child as a developing entity. This view has made several specific contributions to understanding behavior disorders.

Perhaps the most obvious of these contributions is that descriptions of the usual course of growth provide a standard by which abnormality can be judged and conceptualized. Theories of development offer hypotheses, too, as to how growth and change occur and thus how they might go awry. Since no one theory can account for the numerous changes that take place throughout the early years of life, diverse explanations must be considered. The study of developmental phenomena also suggests several issues that may be critical for the task of understanding, preventing, and ameliorating childhood disturbance. In this chapter we will survey normal development, with a particular eye toward how developmental issues can be applied to the study of abnormality. For those readers who already possess considerable knowledge about development, the overview will serve as a reminder of the developmental context of childhood behavior disorders. For other readers the overview will additionally provide some important conceptualizations and factual information about children's growth.

WHAT IS DEVELOPMENT?

If we were to ask strangers passing on the street to define the term *development*, many would surely offer "growth" and "change" as synonyms. These are reasonably good substitute terms. Development does indeed include growth; that is, an increase in the size or the number of elements with age (Thompson and Grusec, 1970). For example, children become physically taller and progressively display a larger number of social responses. But development also implies direction—a change to-

ward complexity and organization. Within a relatively short period of time, the fertilized egg typically becomes the infant who crawls, smiles, and says "da-da," and then the preschooler who jumps, speaks in complex sentences, and acts in socially "grown-up" ways. Development thus proceeds in an orderly fashion, with early structures and competencies laying the groundwork for later, qualitatively more advanced ones.

Although the orderliness of development is widely agreed upon, the specific course of change is debated. For our purposes it is necessary only to recognize that some theorists view development as discrete steps or stages that occur in the same order in all children. Other investigators suggest that children progress in steps so gradual that development may be considered continuous, or without discrete stages. Both stage and continuity theorists have contributed much to our knowledge about growth. In particular, the former have offered comprehensive schemes of development, while the latter have emphasized the study of learning phenomena and of environmental impact.

Nature and Nurture

Perhaps the most fundamental question about development concerns its determinants. Development is attributable to both biological and environmental factors—although the contributions of each has been one of the most hotly debated issues in psychology. Known variously as the nature-nurture, heredity-environmental, and maturational-learning controversy, the specific question has evolved from Which one? to How much? to How? (Anastasi, 1958).

Investigators initially questioned whether it was heredity or the environment that was responsible for individual development (Which one?). The extreme heredity view was exemplified by the Swiss-born philosopher Jean Jacques Rousseau, who argued that the inborn nature of the child is primarily responsible for the results of development. The British philosopher John Locke dramatically expressed the extreme environmentalist position by likening the child's mind at birth to a *tabula rasa,* a blank slate upon which experience is yet to be sketched (Thomas, 1979). Since neither of these extremes appeared reasonable, investigators shifted their focus to study the degree to which nature and nurture separately contribute to developmental outcomes (How much?). This question receives considerable attention today. For example, some researchers claim that genes account for a certain percentage of the variation in intelligence and that environmental experiences account for the remaining amount. The How much? question is limited, though, because it emphasizes to the idea that genetic and environmental influences are independent of each other. In fact, since both influences are always 100 percent present, and since they work together to shape development, the most appropriate question concerns the way in which they produce development (How?).

Today most investigators hold either an interactional or transactional model of development. With regard to the nature-nurture issue, the former emphasizes that behavior results from the interaction of biological dispositions and environmental factors. The transactional model goes beyond this to suggest that biological and environmental factors continuously influence each other so that each modifies the other. In a strict sense these models are not identical (e.g., Sameroff and Chandler, 1975), and the transactional model requires that continuous interplay between the organism and the environment be followed. Conceptually, such a task is possible, but it is extremely difficult to accomplish. In practice, even at the conceptual level, the models often are not distinguished. What they hold in common, however, is extremely important—a commitment to the view that development depends on the interplay of nature and nurture. Box 2–1 provides a striking example of how genetic and environmental factors can interact to produce behavior that falls into the "normal" or "abnormal" range. Later points of discussion also bear directly on this issue.

A SCHEMA OF NORMAL DEVELOPMENT*

When the topic of normal development is discussed, a wide array of processes are referred to. Volumes of texts are required to cover all that is known or under investigation. The purpose of the present discussion is thus a modest one: to survey some aspects of development as a broad framework for subsequent consideration of the behavior problems of childhood.

The Genetic Context

That human beings are fundamentally biological organisms is a truism. All body cells have a nucleus that contains chromosomes, segments of which are referred to as *genes*. Chromosomes are composed of deoxyribonucleic acid (DNA), which directs development and cell activity and bears the information of inheritance. Except for the gametes (the reproductive cells, the ova and sperm), human cells contain twenty-three pairs of chromosomes, each member of which influences the same attributes of the individual. One of the pairs, the sex chromosomes, differs overtly in females and males, with females having two X chromosomes and males having one X and one Y chromosome. The Y chromosome is smaller and lighter, having fewer genes than the X chromosome.

The gametes, in contrast to other cells, undergo a specialized cell division—*meiosis*—during maturation, which results in their carrying only twenty-three single chromosomes, one from each of the original pairs. Thus, at conception the ovum of the mother and sperm of the father each contribute half of the normal complement of chromosomes to the offspring. The processes of meiosis and conception assure billions of possible chromosome combinations for any one individual. Other genetic mechanisms result in even greater variability. For example, in *crossing over*, pieces of chromosomes break off and reattach on different chromo-

---

*Much of the material in this section is drawn from Liebert and Wicks-Nelson, 1981.

Box 2–1 Heredity and Environment: The Example of PKU

Phenylketonuria (PKU) is a heredity condition that was discovered by Fölling in 1934. It occurs only when both parents pass on a particular defective (recessive) gene. The frequency of PKU varies from 1 in 10,000 persons to 1 in 20,000 persons in parts of the United States and Europe (Cytryn and Lourie, 1980). The disease is reported primarily among those of northern European origin.

In PKU the amino acid phenylalanine is not metabolized normally because a liver enzyme is absent or inactive. Elevated levels of phenylalanine are found in the blood, cerebrospinal fluid, and urine. Phenylpyruvic acid is also abnormally secreted in the urine. The neurotransmitters serotonin, epinephrine, and norepinephrine are at low blood levels. The exact way in which the brain is affected is unknown, but intelligence can range from normal to severely retarded. The PKU child may be undersized, with a small head, coarse features, and a light complexion. Many are blue-eyed and blond due to a lack of melanin. By and large, PKU children are difficult to manage: They may be unpredictable and hyperactive, and display bizarre movements. Communication is impaired, coordination is poor, and perceptual difficulties are common.

Of enormous importance was the discovery that PKU can be markedly alleviated by early diagnosis and dietary control. Children are easily screened for high phenylalanine blood levels or phenylpyruvic acid in the urine. Once PKU is identified, the intake of phenylalanine can be reduced by restriction of foods such as eggs, cheese, milk, and fish. It turns out that normal or near-normal intelligence may be attained if dietary treatment is begun during the first few months of life. The later diet control is initiated, the less effective it is. In untreated older children and adolescents, diet restriction does not remediate retardation but may decrease irritability, social unresponsiveness, and short attention span.

Here then is a telling example of how heredity interacts with the environment. When PKU children receive a normal diet, some levels of intellectual retardation is likely. But this level may be substantially influenced depending on how early a restricted diet is initiated.

somes, which are then passed on to offspring. Chromosomes may also change by *mutation*, spontaneous alterations in the DNA molecule. Environmental interaction with the chromosomal complement contributes further to produce an almost infinite variety of individuals.

Although it is said that genes influence or control physical attributes and behavior, genes operate only indirectly by controlling the biochemical substances that are involved in the many related functions of the body. The relationship of the genes to the characteristics of the organism is made still more complicated by the interacting influence of the environment. Any one set of genes (genotype) may lead to a range of observable attributes (phenotypes), and any one phenotype may be associated with different genotypes. Moreover, it can never be assumed that characteristics for which genetic influence

has been established cannot be altered to some degree by the environment. Many traits can be altered substantially; for example, height is determined genetically but is affected by diet or disease. Thus, the contribution of the genes to the development of behavior, including behavioral problems in childhood, is likely to be quite complex.

The Child as a Physical Being

It is only in this century that we have come to understand the processes of early physical growth. The previously popular doctrine of *preformation* held that adults were actually preformed in either the ova or the sperm and that development was simply an enlargement of already-existing parts (Grinder, 1967). It was believed that each gamete contained a tiny human being whose reproductive cells held another tiny human being, and so on. This view gradually gave way in light of evidence that the union of the ovum and the sperm forms the *zygote*, which differentiates the body parts during prenatal development.

Conception takes place in the Fallopian tube, and within a few days the zygote travels down the tube and attaches itself to the wall of the uterus. The growing organism floats freely in the amniotic fluid in the amniotic sac except for its attachment by the umbilical cord to the placenta of the mother (Figure 2-1). The very early stages of development are referred to as the *pe-riod of the ovum*. During the subsequent *period of the embryo* (from the second to eighth week after conception), the inner cell layers—the ectoderm, mesoderm, and endoderm—grow rapidly and give rise to the organs. The upper part of the embryo develops more rapidly than the lower, so that it is disproportionately large. The *period of the fetus* (from the eighth week to birth) is characterized by further growth of existing structures, changes in body proportion, and the first appearance of hair, nails, and external sex organs. The bones ossify, and the brain becomes convoluted. The rate of growth reaches a peak early and then declines, and the upper

Figure 2-1   Schema of the developing child showing indirect contact with the mother's circulatory system.

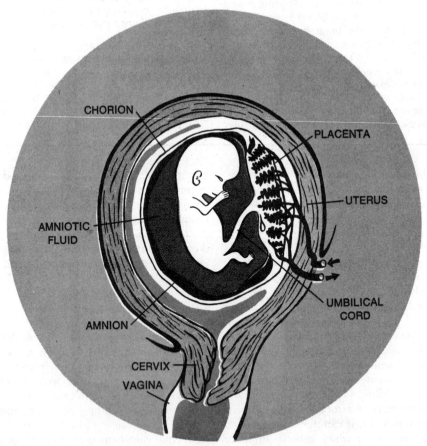

body is no longer quite as predominant. Spontaneous movement begins at about sixteen weeks. Many reflexes, which are automatic responses to specific stimuli, appear: for example, sucking, swallowing, and coughing. During the last trimester it is as if the fetus were preparing for birth: Vital functions become increasingly refined and weight gain is noticeable as fatty tissue increases. If all goes uneventfully, birth occurs about thirty-eight weeks after conception. These weeks of prenatal life are crucial; the body plan that is so rapidly laid down can be dramatically affected by genetic and environmental variables.

From the first moments of life, physical growth occurs in a quite predictable manner, following certain general principles. Growth takes place in a *cephalocaudal* direction—that is, from the head to the tail regions. Thus, the head region undergoes prenatal development earlier than the remainder of the body; at birth it still comprises one-fourth of the length of the body, but by age 25, it comprises only one-eighth (Jackson, 1929). Growth also occurs in a *proximodistal* direction, from the center axis to the extremities or more distal areas. This is illustrated in prenatal development by the growth of the chest and trunk prior to the limbs, fingers, and toes. Throughout life, however, different body parts exhibit diverse developmental patterns. For example, the skeleton, muscles,

and internal organs grow rapidly during infancy and early childhood, slow down during middle childhood, and accelerate in adolescence. In contrast, the reproductive system develops only slowly until adolescence, when it undergoes rapid growth, while the neural system is almost completely developed by 6 years of age (Tanner, 1970).

Like physical growth, motor development is quite predictable. The infant's behavior is replete with reflexes, such as those described in Table 2-1. Some reflexes (for example, blinking, sneezing, and rooting) are directly related to vital functions and to the orientation of the body in space (for example, walking reflex). Others, the so-called primitive reflexes (for example, Moro, Babinski, and grasp), seem of little importance, although it is postulated that they once were adaptive mechanisms in the evolution of the human species. Many reflexes persevere into adulthood, but several of the postural and primitive reflexes disappear during the first year of life or perhaps develop into more mature voluntary action (Capute, Accardo, Vining, Rubenstein, and Harryman, 1978; Kessen, Haith, and Salapatek, 1970). The absence of reflexes at birth, and the undue persistence of some that typically disappear, are signs of improper development of the nervous system. Thus, they may give early warning of later developmental problems.

Table 2-1   A Few of the Many Neonatal Reflexes

Babinski	Stroking the sole of the foot results in the spreading out of the toes and the upward extension of the big toe.
Galant	Stroking the neonate's back along the spine results in the trunk arching toward that side.
Moro	Withdrawal of physical support (dropping, allowing the head to drop, change in position) or a sharp noise results in the arms extending outward and returning to midline.
Palmar grasp	Touching the palm causes the fingers to grasp the object.
Rooting	Stroking the cheek or corner of the mouth causes the head to turn toward the object and precipitates movements that look as if the infant is searching for something to suck.
Sucking	Placing an object in the mouth results in sucking.
Walking	Holding the infant upright and allowing the feet to touch a surface results in stepping movements.

Voluntary movement appears to follow the rules of cephalocaudal and proximodistal growth. Moreover, mass motor control involving large areas of the body is achieved earlier than control of small muscle groups. Thus, when children begin to use crayons, they tend to use the entire arm, and only gradually do they master the fine hand control required to stay within the lines and to shade areas of the picture. Such differentiation is the foundation of complex motor skills, which necessitate the child integrating several specific skills. Before infants can sit without support, for example, they must acquire control of the legs, trunk, arms, neck and head—and then integrate this control into a cohesive motor act. Table 2-2 shows the average age for a few of the motor milestones.

The determinants of motor development are not well understood. It is sometimes assumed that the lower brain governs early reflexive movement and that the cortex takes over regulation as motor action becomes voluntary. Both learning and biological maturation appear to play a role. The importance of maturation is illustrated by Dennis and Dennis's (1940) well known study of Hopi Indian children. Hopi babies were traditionally secured to cradle boards in a manner that prevented them from rolling over, raising their bodies, or moving their arms and legs. But the investigators also had the opportunity to observe Hopi infants who were not so restricted, their parents having been influenced by European ways. Dennis and Dennis found no difference in the age at which the children walked: Both groups did so at about 15 months. It is highly likely that human children

Table 2-2   Some Early Gross Motor Milestones

Rolls over	2–4 months
Sits without support	5–7
Stands holding on to furniture	8–9
Creeps on hands and knees	9–10
Stands without support	10–13
Walks alone	11–14
Walks upstairs alone, two feet per step	21–25

would learn to walk even if the environment failed to encourage it. Nevertheless, practice clearly has a role in motor development, particularly in the performance of complex action. Most people are certainly capable of simple gymnastic feats but cannot perform on the uneven bars. The acquisition of a particular complex movement depends upon physical maturation, practice with feedback, and the child's ability to understand and process the feedback (Newell and Kennedy, 1978). When these processes go awry, the child may be considerably disadvantaged in manipulating and learning about the environment. In addition to adverse effects on intellectual growth, poor motor development can also influence the child's self-concept.

Other aspects of physical growth may affect children's psychological development. For example, several investigators have delved into the effects of early and late maturation (Carron and Bailey, 1974; Eichorn, 1963; Faust, 1960; Mussen and Jones, 1957; Weatherley, 1964). Boys appear to benefit from early growth: They excel athletically, possess superior physical strength, are rated as attractive, and as adults are poised, responsible, and achieving in a conventional way. Those who mature late are likely to be considered childish, talkative, and restless, although as adults they are relatively more active, exploring, insightful, independent, and perceptive. For girls the picture is less clear. Early maturers may be disadvantaged initially by their large size and by having relationships with males for which they are socially and emotionally unprepared—but these disadvantages appear to vanish quickly and perhaps reverse themselves. With regard to intellectual ability, the overall evidence points to an advantage for early maturers of both sexes, but social class and type of task play a role (Westin-Lindgren, 1982). For example, early-maturing boys of lower socioeconomic status (SES), but not of higher SES, seem disadvantaged on verbal tasks.

Another area of investigation has focused on the influence of physical attractiveness—showing its many advantages. Physically attractive people are more popular and are viewed as hav-

Practice plays an important role in the development of complex motor skills. A child's motor development is likely to have significant impact on other areas of functioning and to influence the child's self-concept.

ing more desirable personalities and behavior (Berscheid and Walster, 1974; Dion, 1972; Dion, Berscheid, and Walster, 1972). In contrast, the physically handicapped are often responded to by avoidance, overindulgence, and a mixture of sympathy and contempt (Diller, 1972). Individuals may be overly polite or avoid the handicapped altogether because they are unsure of how they should act. In turn, the handicapped may be further disadvantaged in social development due to distorted feedback about their own interpersonal behavior.

The Child as an Intellectual Being

The newborn is typically a six- to eight-pound organism that may seem quite unaware of its surroundings. Nevertheless, early life is

more dynamic than it appears. In order to respond, even reflexively, the infant must sense the environment. Because infants are limited in their capacity to respond motorically and cannot relate their experiences, it has been difficult to judge their sensory capacity. However, new techniques have provided better understanding of the world of the infant. One method, for example, allows us to track exactly what the infant is looking at and how long visual fixation lasts; another measures changes in heart rate and minute muscle activity in response to different odorants (Fantz, 1961; Lipsitt, Engen, and Kaye, 1963). Such techniques confirm that infants come into the world with considerable capacity to sense their surroundings. Seeing, hearing, smelling, tasting, and feeling—all of which develop rapidly during the first years of life—are the sensory basis for experiencing the environment. When these are disturbed, children's ability to function is variously intruded upon. However, in the normal course of events, knowledge of the world is acquired rapidly through learning and cognitive processes.

Despite the familiarity of the term *learning*, it is not easy to define. Hilgard and Bower describe it as:

. . . the process by which an activity originates or is changed through reacting to an encountered situation, providing that . . . the change in activity cannot be explained on the basis of native response tendencies, maturation, or temporary states of the organism (e.g., fatigue, drugs, etc.). (1966, p. 2)

Three basic learning processes have been widely recognized and studied: classical conditioning, instrumental learning, and observational learning. (They are more fully discussed in the next chapter). To some extent these processes operate from very early life, but they enter into increasingly complex environmental interactions as the so-called higher mental processes develop. Memory, attention, mediation, imagery, and concept formation all enable children to gather and make sense of the multitudinous information available in the environment. Although we do not attempt here to provide an extensive discussion of these higher mental functions, it should be noted that they are at the heart of thinking, reasoning, and cognition.

Piaget's cognitive theory. Cognition refers to *knowing* or *coming to know*. No name is as closely associated with children's cognition as that of Jean Piaget. Continuously interested in biology and in epistemology (the philosophical study of ways of knowing), Piaget scrutinized the young in hopes of explaining epistemological processes (Flavell, 1963). He began by detailing cognitive growth in his own children and eventually constructed a theory of cognitive development that stands as one of the greatest accomplishments of psychology in this century.

Piaget viewed the child as a biological organism that adapts to its environment by actively organizing and interpreting experiences through the higher mental functions. Such adaptation occurs by assimilation and accommodation. *Assimilation* is the process of taking in an experience in terms of already existing mental schemas or constructions of the world. *Accommodation* is the process of modifying the internal schemas based on new experiences. Through these reciprocal functions the child develops increasingly sophisticated schemas, or models, of the world. Both maturation and experience are considered necessary for such cognitive development, which is postulated to occur in four distinct periods, roughly correlated with chronological age. Consistent with stage theory, the following is assumed: (1) The periods occur in an invariant order; (2) no period can be skipped; (3) each period is more complex than the preceding one and represents a transformation of what previously existed; and (4) each period is based on the preceding one and prepares for the succeeding one (Breger, 1974, after Loevinger, 1966).

During the *sensorimotor period* (0 to 2 years), the infant begins to construct reality with the sensory and reflexive motor abilities with which it is born. The child knows the environment only through sensorimotor interactions. These capacities become progressively more refined, coordinated, and integrated and come more under the control of planned action. Thus, the child moves from automatic, gross responses to refined reactions that serve some goal-directed purpose. As striking as these changes are, the most remarkable achievement of this early period is the child's growing ability to construct and manipulate mental representations of the world, at first in the form of images. During the *pre-operational* period (2 to 7 years) there occurs a shift in emphasis from sensorimotor functioning to internal manipulation of symbols, and children are able to deal with a variety of problems. Language development is especially important at this time. At first children are hindered by egocentrism, the inability to take another's perspective, but this gradually gives way to broader possible interpretations. Still, cognition is limited in many ways: by the inability to simultaneously view different aspects of a problem, to understand the idea of reversibility, and to perceive transformations. These abilities are largely attained during the third period, *concrete operations* (7 to 11 years), during which children come to better understand relationships among environmental events. It is in the final period of *formal operations* (11 years and after) that true logical thinking appears. At this time people are able to mentally free themselves even more than before from the concrete—they can make hypotheses, draw and hold complex comparisons in their minds, and deduce and induce principles. Piaget (1972) recognized, however, that perhaps not all individuals reach formal operations in all areas of thinking, due to individual differences in aptitude, interests, and opportunity.

In offering a stage theory of cognition, Piaget argued that at any one stage the child's intelligence is qualitatively different than it is at any other stage. This has implications for how children might perceive the world at any particular time, what they are prepared to learn, and how developmental problems might be interpreted.

Language and communication. The growth of language, viewed by many as the most dramatic development of the early years, is closely linked to learning and cognition. Among the skills that are required are the ability to receive and interpret stimulation, produce highly specific sounds, attribute meaning to particular utterances, string sounds into words and words into grammatically correct sentences, and grasp the social context in which a message is being received or sent.

Table 2-3 presents some of the widely recognized early steps in language acquisition, categorized into receptive (taking in) and expressive communication. With regard to expressive skills, the infant's early vocalizations change rapidly from cries and coos to social babbling, in which an array of sounds are made.

These increase to such an extent that it has been suggested that the 1-year-old can produce all the sounds of the various different human languages (Jespersen, 1922). Interestingly, as the native tongue is adopted, certain sounds are eliminated. Of the remainder, some (for example, *f, s, ch*) are more difficult to produce than others (for example, *p, t*); so children are prone to say *pish* instead of *fish* and *tarter* instead of *father*. By 1 year of age they have usually said their first words, used *mama* and *dada* accurately, spontaneously imitated adult sounds, and given signs of recognizing simple statements, instructions, and gestures. First words commonly refer to animals, food, and toys and

Table 2-3 Acquisition of Language and Communication

	Receptive	Expressive
Birth to 3 months	Reacts to sudden noise Is quieted by voice	Cries Some sounds
3 to 6 months	Turns when a voice is heard Locates the source of sounds Recognizes own name and words such as *bye-bye, no,* and *daddy*	Babbles and laughs Initiates vocal play Vocalizes to self and toys and experiments with own voice
6 to 9 months	Stops activity to *no-no* Raises arms to *come up* Sustains interest in pictures when a person names them	Develops sounds of the culture's language Combines vowel sounds Develops rhythm
9 to 12 months	Obeys simple instructions Understands simple statements Understands gestures	Says first words Uses *mama* and *dada* correctly Spontaneously imitates adult sounds Uses gestures Plays peek-a-boo
12 to 18 months	Carries out two consecutive commands Understands new words Listens to nursery rhymes	Uses ten words Requests by naming objects Repeats words of adult conversation Connects sounds so that they seem to flow like a sentence
18 to 24 months	Recognizes many sounds Understands action words like *show me*	Uses short sentences Uses pronouns Echoes last words of a rhyme
24 to 36 months	Understands taking turns Follows commands using *in, on, under* Follows three verbal commands given in one utterance	Mother understands 90 percent of communication attempts Uses noun-verb combinations Relates experiences Names siblings on request

Adapted from Bryant, 1977.

thus seem to be drawn from the child's immediate experience (Nelson, 1973, 1974). In virtually all societies the first sentence consists of a single word that is used to assert, command, or question. So, for example, the word *boy* may assert "He is a boy." Soon, two-word utterances emerge, and then still longer word strings that more or less follow the rules for acceptable sentence structure. The complexity of this task can be grasped by considering the nuances of word and sentence meanings and the many ways in which an event or idea can be verbally described. By age 5, however, the major period of language growth is over (Nelson, 1981), although basic language and communication skills continue to be perfected for several years.

The processes that underlie the development of language are still hotly debated in spite of the fascination they have long held for philosophers and scientists. Theoretical perspectives range from an extreme focus on biological determinants to an extreme emphasis on environmental factors (Lenneberg, 1967; McNeill, 1970). This dichotomy is not fruitful. The human biological system is obviously constructed in such a way that language can be comprehended and expressed, but the development of communication skills relies heavily on cognitive development and social transmission.

The development of language is clearly an index of, and has implication for, the growth of cognitive capabilities. However, language is both affected by and affects the child's social development. Social stimulation facilitates early language acquisition, and the child's babbling and talking attracts the attention of caretakers. Thus, language development is also related to the development of social competencies and difficulties.

The Child as a Social Being

Social development addresses children's interactions with others and their adoption of social roles. It thus includes the growth of altruism, honesty, aggression, dependency, cooperation, self-control, and achievement motivation, as well as learning to be a student, sibling, friend, daughter or son, or girl or boy. It is these realms of behavior that are usually referred to as "personality," although on careful analysis it is clear that physical attributes and intellectual functioning are also a part of personality.

Developmental theorists have had much to say about the growth of the child as a social being. At one time it was quite common to hold inheritance responsible for a child's bad temper or timidity. Few researchers today would argue that the personality of the individual is determined by genetic endowment. Nevertheless, there is some evidence that certain behavioral tendencies are genetically influenced. Research suggests, for example, that genes have a role in determining introversion-extroversion (Freedman and Keller, 1963; Scarr, 1969). This dimension of behavior refers to an opposing orientation to the social environment: The introvert tends to be shy, socially anxious, and socially withdrawn; the extrovert is outgoing, friendly, and at ease with people. Heredity also has been implicated in investigations of a person's overall activity level and emotionality (e.g., Buss, Plomin, and Willerman, 1973; Scarr, 1966; Willerman, 1973). These findings do not mean, of course, that introversion-extroversion, activity level, and emotionality are inextricably set. Instead, they suggest that each of us is born with a disposition toward certain reactions that enter immediately into our relationships with our surroundings.

Regardless of individual predispositions, it is likely that each infant will become attached to an adult. Attachment refers to a socioemotional bond that is formed between the baby and another individual, initially the caretaker and usually the mother. Observed in virtually all infants in all cultures, it seems that only quite atypical circumstances prevent infants and adults from bonding (Ainsworth, 1977). Perhaps for this reason theorists from different persuasions have come to suggest that this relationship is a foundation for later social adjustment.

Attachment displays itself by the infant orienting toward the adult—watching, crying, smiling, staying in proximity—and in the adult responding to the infant. The growth of attachment involves the infant discriminating the adult, setting up specific expectations of the adult, and then developing trust and confidence (e.g., Yarrow, 1972; Yarrow and Pedersen, 1972). It appears that the quality of this developmental progression depends strongly on the specific interaction between the child and the adult. Parental sensitivity to the child, emotional intensity, and tender loving care (Ainsworth and Bell, 1974; Hunt, 1979) are critical, but the infant, too, plays a role in determining attachment. The child who meets parental expectations, is easy to feed and otherwise care for, and smiles and vocalizes to the adult is likely to foster attachment in the adult. Clearly, the process is reciprocal.

Because the mother is often the primary caretaker, research and theoretical conceptualizations about attachment have focused on the mother-child relationship. However, with the recent new interest in the father's role in child development, researchers have revealed that infants almost invariably soon become attached to both parents (Kotelchuck, 1976; Lamb, 1976; Schaffer and Emerson, 1964). Moreover, attachment to grandparents, siblings, and even to other children has been observed to occur by 18 months of age. Thus, the social world of the child rapidly takes on ever-broadening relationships and experiences.

Although most theorists recognize early attachment as a root of social development, they diverge markedly in overall explanation of how children come to be socialized human beings. Freud's intrapsychic conceptualizations stand in sharp contrast to the environmentalism of the social learning approach. Of more recent interest is the contribution of cognitive theory to explanations of social development. Central to this approach is the assumption that children's cognitive level—their world schemes and intellective processes—interacts with experience to bring about social growth. Since the psychodynamic, social learning, and cognitive approaches are detailed in later chapters, we turn now to the broad social contexts within which development occurs.

The Social Context

The social context of development includes social class, family, peers, and the school. It is within these settings that social as well as physical and intellectual attributes are shaped.

Socioeconomic status. Socioeconomic status, or social class, is determined by the in-

United Nations/Photo by John Isaac

The child's expanding world of social relationships soon extends to the father, grandparents, siblings, and other family members.

come, educational achievement, and occupational level of the family, all of which are correlated with each other. Virtually all societies are stratified according to SES, and socioeconomic class is marked by differences in almost all facets of life—environmental conditions, child-care interactions, values, attitudes, and expectations. Furthermore, SES variables begin to affect children even prior to their entrance into the world.

The pervasive influence of socioeconomic variables can be seen in all classes, but they are particularly notable in the lower classes. The 1960s saw a resurgence of concern for the children of the poor. Indeed, these youngsters are at high risk for a broad range of difficulties. From the moment of conception they are more likely to die and to suffer from disease and disability. Figure 2-2 depicts the relationship between number of infant deaths and SES, with education of the father as the SES indicator. For all ages examined, death increases as SES decreases. In general, this pattern has been found to hold for other SES indicators and for the black population (U.S. Bureau of the Census, 1979; Vital and Health Statistics, 1972). Moreover, birth weight, one of the most important predictors of infant death, deformity, and later developmental problems, is inversely related to socioeconomic status. This unfortunate association has its basis largely in poor maternal health and medical care. In too many cases poor children also continue to suffer from inadequate diet, health care, and other adverse environmental circumstances. In turn, the poor do less well in school and, upon reaching adulthood, acquire less desirable jobs and have higher rates of unemployment. This tragic pattern is a vicious cycle (Figure 2-3) that tends to repeat itself over generations (Birch and Gussow, 1970).

The poor child is at risk in many other ways as well. Poverty works against family stability,

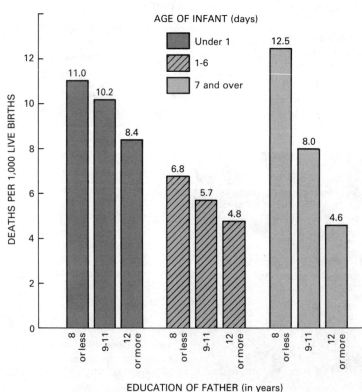

Figure 2–2 Estimated number of infant deaths per 1,000 white legitimate live births according to education of the father and age of infant at death. *Source: Infant mortality rates: Socioeconomic factors.* Vital and Health Statistics, 1972.

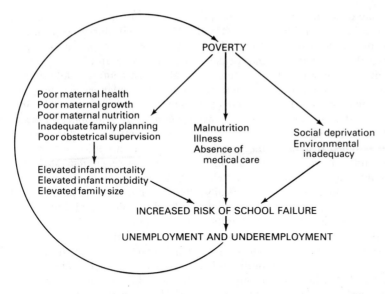

Figure 2–3 The poor suffer a vicious cycle of inadequate health care, illness, environmental inadequacy, school failure, and unemployment that for at least some begins even before birth. *Adapted from Birch and Gussow, 1970, by permission.*

as do many other factors: Those of lower status marry at younger ages; they marry more often as the result of pregnancy; and more offspring are born to such families at a faster rate. Family disorganization and crises increase the likelihood of children being neglected, although poverty itself does not necessarily lead to child neglect (Giovannoni and Billingsley, 1971). One of the most obvious SES differences with regard to parent-child interaction itself involves the extent to which parents allow their offspring self-direction and freedom. Lower class parents are, in general, more restrictive. Mothers, for example, more often punish failures of self-control (such as toilet accidents), are more concerned with outward appearances, and anticipate less independence from their children (Bronfenbrenner, 1958). It has been postulated that such a restrictive mode teaches the child to be impulsive rather than reflective, to deal with immediate happenings rather than plan for the future, and to be compliant rather than consider alternatives (Hess and Shipman, 1968). These behaviors, in turn, may prevent the child from succeeding in systems dominated by the less-restrictive, middle-class mode of social interaction.

The family. In most, if not all, societies, the family is viewed as a critical determinant of development. Family influence begins immediately, appears especially strong and pervasive, and may endure over one's lifetime. Both theoretical and empirical analyses of the family have focused primarily on the parent-child relationship, assigning priority to parental effects on the child. Greater recognition has more recently been given to the child's impact on other family members and on the entire family as an interacting unit.

Historically the most influential views of the family have been offered by psychoanalytic, social learning, and role theories (Lynn, 1974). Psychoanalytic theory traditionally views development as the result of the child moving through psychosexual conflicts that are largely played out between the child and the parents. Although the mother is viewed as central during the first few years, the father soon becomes the source of motivation, especially for boys, to incorporate societal rules, prohibitions, and values. Social learning theorists rely heavily on learning principles to conceptualize family influence, and with few exceptions they, too, emphasize parental dominance. Parents are seen as shaping their offspring's behavior by dispensing reinforcement and punishment and by serving as models for behavior. Because the mother is often in closer contact than the father with the child, her influence may be viewed as stronger, but the conditions and content of learning are considered the crucial variables. Role theory focuses on the claim that all societies differentiate social roles, including sex roles. In general, females are assigned responsibility for expressive behavior and males for instrumental behavior. Mothers are thus expected to maintain smooth family relationships, provide emotional support, and love unconditionally. Fathers are expected to be the disciplinarians, to stress competence and achievement, and to prepare the child for independence.

PARENT-CHILD INTERACTIONS. Although theoretical perspectives of the family have long offered hypotheses and "food for thought," recent heightened interest in the infant and in family dynamics has led to a burgeoning of research and analyses of specific parent-child interactions as well as their influences on behavior.

Mothers' early reactions to their infants may be determined partly by their attitudes about pregnancy and mothering, whether or not the pregnancy was planned, and the type of hospital care after delivery (Hunt, 1979; Kennell, Trause, and Klaus, 1980; Moss, 1967). There is some evidence that opportunity for physical contact soon after delivery facilitates early mother-child attachment, but the strength of this variable over time has not been substantiated (Grossmann, Thane, and Grossmann, 1981). As we have seen, socioemotional attachment between the infant and mother develops gradually during the first year of life, and attachment to the father, once considered irrelevant at best, appears to occur simultaneously or relatively early.

Direct observations of mother-child and father-child interactions indicate some noteworthy differences, at least when the mother is the primary caretaker (Hodapp and Mueller, 1982). Mothers hold their infants for caretaking, display more nurturance, and vocalize more (Lamb, 1978; Weinraub and Frankel, 1977). Their play is conventional (for example, pat-a-cake and peek-a-boo) and focuses on intellectual stimulation. In contrast, fathers pick up their babies more for play, which tends to be active, physical, and idiosyncratic. Infants seem to prefer fathers as playmates. Unsurprisingly, a few investigations of interaction of the infant with both parents have shown that the presence of a third person changes social exchange (Belsky, 1981; Clarke-Stewart, 1978). Specifically, there is a reduction in parent-child interaction. As Belsky (1981) has pointed out, the family system is comprised of parent-infant and marital relations that influence each other. Moreover, it has become clear that the child is not merely a passive end product of the care it receives; it influences its own treatment (Bell, 1968; Belsky, 1981). Low birth-weight babies are treated less favorably than average-weight babies; girls are more often cuddled, held, and restrained; and fathers soon interact more with sons than with daughters (Frodi et al., 1978; Goldberg, 1978; Lamb, 1978). The implications of all these findings have yet to be determined.

Studies of how parents handle their older children suggest the importance of two dimensions of parental behavior: acceptance-rejection and permissiveness-restrictiveness (Becker, 1964; Martin, 1975; Sears, Maccoby, and Levin, 1957). *Acceptance-rejection* refers to the amount of respect and love parents give to their children. Accepting parents show affection, approval, warmth, and understanding; discipline tends to include praise and encouragement and little physical punishment. Rejecting parents are disapproving, punitive, and cold; they seem not to enjoy their offspring nor to show sensitivity to their children's needs. *Permissiveness-restrictiveness* refers to the amount of autonomy and freedom parents allow their children. Permissive parents permit freedom in decision making and in carrying out decisions. They tend to set few rules and do not consistently enforce them. Restrictive parents, on the other hand, maintain a good measure of control.

Based on observations of mothers' interactions with their children from 1 month to 3 years of age, Schaefer (1959) suggested that permissive and restrictive parents can be either accepting or rejecting. Becker (1964) found that children's behavior may be related to the styles of their parents' behavior, as shown in Table 2-4. Other investigators have shown that restrictiveness, permissiveness, hostility, rejection, power-assertive discipline (such as physical punishment), and inconsistency all can be related to children's antisocial behavior, lack of control, and lack of prosocial behavior. In contrast, parental warmth, acceptance, stimulation, responsiveness, nonrestrictiveness, and the use of verbal reasoning in discipline are associated with children's socioemotional security, intellectual competence, and prosocial behavior (Belsky, 1981; Hetherington and Martin, 1979). These results must be viewed cautiously, however. They are based largely on interview data; moreover, we cannot conclude from the existence of these associations that parental styles *cause* certain childhood behaviors. For any one family many other variables operate that moderate the relationship between parental style and children's behavior. Nevertheless, the fact that permissiveness-restrictiveness and acceptance-rejection are so often found as dimensions of parental handling argues for continued examination of their influence.

FAMILY STRUCTURE AND ROLES. Another aspect of the family that might be expected to influence child development is family structure. It is relatively well established, for example, that firstborn children are more successful than later-born children in a variety of ways: They speak at an earlier age, tend to perform better on intelligence tests, and are more likely to attend college. They also tend to be achievement oriented and conformist and to adopt the standards of their parents. There is some evidence that the older children in a family perform better on intelligence tests than do the younger children (Belmont and Marolla, 1973). The sex of siblings also has been found to be related to behavior. For example, boys of preschool age exhibit more feminine behavior when they have older sisters and more masculine behavior when they have older brothers. Girls with older brothers rather than older sisters tend to be "tomboys"; further, they are ambitious and aggressive and perform better on intelligence tests (Brim, 1958; Sutton-Smith and Rosenberg, 1970).

Of increasing interest is the question of how children are influenced by maternal employment outside the home. About 50 percent of all women are now in the work force, and over one-half of working mothers have school-age children (*Handbook on women workers,* 1975). Research suggests that employed mothers provide a model that leads to less traditional sex-role stereotyping by their children, higher approval of maternal employment, and higher evaluation of female competence (Hoffman, 1974). Working mothers also seem to give their offspring more household tasks and to train them for independence. Nevertheless, concern has been expressed about inadequate supervision and about the quality of nonmaternal child care (e.g., Etaugh, 1980).

When we think of family structure, we are inclined to consider the nuclear family of two parents and children. However, about 16 percent of all families are headed by a single parent

Table 2-4   Relationship of Parental Styles and Children's Behaviors

	Permissiveness	Restrictiveness
Acceptance	Independent Outgoing; friendly Creative Low hostility Active	Dependent Polite Obedient Compliant
Rejection	Noncompliance Delinquency Hostility Criminality	Socially withdrawn Quarrelsome Self-hostility Inhibition

From Becker, 1964.

(Sussman, 1978), and about one in six children under the age of 18 is living in a single-parent family (Bronfenbrenner, 1978). In most cases the female is the single parent, whether due to death or to some kind of marital separation. How are children affected by the absence of their fathers? Research suggests that it can negatively influence intellectual performance, social adjustment, and sex-role identity of sons, and daughters' social behavior (Biller, 1974; Hetherington, 1972; Lynn, 1974; Shinn, 1978; Young and Parish, 1977). However, the age of the child, length of absence, cause of absence, and subsequent family adjustment all play a role in affecting the child. (See Box 11.1 for discussion of the effects of divorce.) Loss of a father is also linked to his previous contributions and to the quality of the marriage. Two parents are better than one only when the marriage and the parent-child relationships meet certain standards (Lynn, 1974).

The influence of peers.   As children grow older, peers come to play an important part in their lives. From ages 2 to 5, children engage more frequently in parallel, associative, and cooperative activities and less frequently in solitary play and onlooker behavior (Hartup, 1970). A shift from a family focus to a peer focus has been documented as the young move from the fourth to the tenth grades: They increasingly identify with peers, prefer to associate more with peers, and consider peer values and norms more like their own (Bowerman and Kinch, 1969). In the United States it is likely that peer influence is stronger today than in past times. Children enter into organized peer groups at younger ages than previously (approximately two-thirds of all 3- and 4-year-olds now attend preschool), and the number of years in which children stay in school has increased markedly during this century (Asher, 1978). Moreover, technical progress has removed adults from the home and decreased children's contact with the adult world of work (Bronfenbrenner, 1972).

Whether the young relate to each other through informal or formal groups (for exam-

Learning to interact appropriately and effectively with peers is one of the many socialization tasks addressed in the school setting.

ple, classroom, Girl Scouts, Little League), peers serve many different kinds of functions:

1. They provide each other with a sense of emotional security and support.
2. They provide each other with information about normative standards in many situations and serve as a standard against which accomplishments and failures can be judged. In serving as models and reinforcers of each other's behaviors, peers may strengthen actions that are consonant or disconsonant with adult values.
3. They teach each other many types of skills, usually informally, but at times in structured, formal contexts.
4. In play, discussion, and practice they provide the opportunity for rehearsal and for explanation of alternative roles and behaviors.
5. They may lessen the adult burden of socialization and, in some cases, protect each other from the coercion of adults.

Peer acceptance and popularity is a topic that has been widely researched; children have been asked to nominate friends or working partners or to otherwise indicate with which children they prefer to associate (Hartup, 1970). High preference and status accorded to peers in this manner are relatively stable over time and are associated with friendliness, sociability, compliance, cooperation, good adjustment, and intelligence. As we shall see later, the significance of peer relationships is highlighted by the provocative finding that poor relationships are linked to several unfortunate developmental outcomes (Asher, 1978). Although this does not mean that poor peer relationships necessarily cause later difficulties, it seems reasonable that children who have trouble getting along well with peers and who are given low preference and status would be disadvantaged.

School. The school, especially in highly technical societies, is the workplace of the child. Its clearly denoted purpose is to teach the child academic and intellectual skills and knowledge accumulated by the society. The degree to which this goal is accomplished can affect individuals throughout their lives—in terms of their work and leisure activities and in terms of how they evaluate themselves. But formal education also has been charged, albeit sometimes only covertly, with the broader tasks of socialization (Busch-Rossnagel and Vance, 1982). Schools in the United States are expected to transmit moral, social, and political values consonant with a democratic form of government. The messages given to the child about these values certainly act powerfully on development. However, the influence of the school cannot be completely understood without an awareness that whatever its stated purposes, the school operates as a social system in and of itself. The structure of the classroom, pedagogical techniques, methods of discipline, and the setting of standards and expectations all play a role in shaping children.

One ongoing issue in education that has come to the fore again in recent years concerns the structure and discipline of the classroom in relation to learning and social behavior. Educators such as Silberman (1970) and Weber (1971) have argued strenuously that the classroom milieu is often so restrictive and confining that it precludes learning, thinking, and curiosity. They advocate a more open, free, or informal atmosphere in which children can explore, discover, and enjoy learning. Taking up this argument in part, Winett and Winkler (1972) challenged their behavior-modification colleagues for overemphasizing behaviors such as attending to the teacher, raising hands, and working at one's seat. In the opinion of these writers, the classroom that follows these rules teaches the child to "be still, be quiet, be docile." O'Leary (1972), who has used behavior modification extensively in educational settings, countered that although Winett and Winkler's suggestion is well taken, they failed in several ways to accurately describe the success of behavior modification. Most important for our purposes are two related points made by O'Leary. First, he noted that children with special needs often have been helped by behavioral techniques. Second, he questioned whether the informal classroom is salutary for unmotivated, withdrawn, hyperactive, and otherwise disadvantaged youngsters. Indeed, there is evidence that structure seems to help these children in the classroom (e.g., Kazdin and Bootzin, 1972; Weikart, 1972). What seems noteworthy, however, is that structure can be implemented in various ways and that informal classrooms do not necessarily indicate loose, chaotic environments.

Another widely discussed issue in education today is its influence on children's self-expectations and self-esteem. It has been shown, for example, that youngsters who expect to achieve in school tend to do so, and that those who have low grades hold low self-images and occupational expectancy (Crandall, 1967; Rosenberg, 1965). Moreover, it is likely that teacher expectation affects children's performance or judgment of their performance (Brophy and Good, 1970; Rist, 1970). Rist's study of black children in an all-black elementary school describes the way in which teachers may set up expectations of children about whom they know little. Prior to the children's entrance into kindergarten, the teachers had information regarding medical histories, place of residence, number of siblings and parents in the home, welfare status of the family, previous school experiences, and problems reported by the mothers. By the eighth day the teachers had placed the youngsters at three tables based on assessment of ability to learn. At Table 1 were "fast learners." In contrast to the other children, they were dressed neatly and cleanly, were quite verbal, used standard English rather than black dialect, and came from smaller, more educated, and wealthier families. Rist found that table placement became the foundation for social interaction. The fast learners received much teacher attention, while the other children eventually withdrew and became verbally and physically hostile. In following these children into the first and second grades, Rist noted that they tended to be organized in the same way. Of course, by this time the teachers had more information—namely, how the children had behaved in previous grades. One cannot help but wonder how these children would have fared had they not been judged so early in their academic careers. In this study judgment apparently was based on social-class variables, and, indeed, the school has been criticized for its middle-class orientation. But it seems reasonable to assume that race, sex, physical attributes, behavioral tendencies, and personal preference all might contribute to teacher expectancy and treatment of students. This, in turn, undoubtedly affects children's experiences in their workplace. Thus, the classroom, like all social settings, influences children in many different ways, some much more subtle than others.

SOME IMPORTANT DEVELOPMENTAL ISSUES

So far in this chapter we have offered some descriptions and theoretical propositions about normal growth and its implication for both competencies and difficulties in children. Inherent in much of what has already been said

are several overlapping issues that offer guidelines for the way in which childhood disorders might be viewed.

Levels of Development

Developmental change is so much a part of childhood that it is virtually impossible to speak of a child's problems without making inquiries about his or her level of growth. Chronological age may be a rough indicator of developmental level; ideally, actual performance or attributes are evaluated to determine functional level. In some instances precise determination is possible, as when we measure height, check motor and language milestones, and give Piagetian tasks or an intelligence test. Specific evaluations of this sort allow comparison of children with their age-mates and can thus inform us of developmental lag or precocity.

Even when imprecise, knowledge of a child's developmental level can be helpful in interpreting the significance of problems. For example, we can expect that certain kinds of disorders will display themselves with greater frequency at particular times in development. The crisis of parental separation when a child enters school might indeed be difficult, as is the struggle to forge an identity at adolescence; however, they can be expected in a proportion of young people. Likewise, certain fears can be anticipated to decrease during childhood, while drug use and abuse can be expected to increase during puberty (Achenbach and Edelbrock, 1981). Such developmental patterns were indicated by the Berkeley Child Guidance Study, which followed the growth of normal children from 21 months into adolescence (MacFarland, Allen, and Honzik, 1954). As shown in Table 2-5, some problems simply declined with age, some increased, some declined and then increased, some increased and then declined, and some showed no change at all. Knowledge that such temporal patterns might exist provides a framework for evaluating and interpreting the seriousness of a child's difficulties.

Finally, knowledge of a child's developmental competencies and failures also provides

Table 2-5 Five Developmental Patterns of Behavior Problems and Examples of Each

Type of Pattern	Example
Symptoms declining with age	Enuresis and encopresis (bladder and bowel incontinence), speech problems, fears, thumb sucking, overeating, temper tantrums, destructiveness
Symptoms increasing with age	Nail biting
Symptoms declining and then increasing with age	Restless sleep, disturbing dreams, timidity, irritability, attention seeking, dependency, jealousy, food finickiness (boys), somberness
Symptoms increasing and then declining with age	Poor appetite, lying
Symptoms unrelated to age	Oversensitivity

From MacFarland, Allen, and Honzik, 1954.

clues for amelioration. For example, suppose an intellectually retarded boy has difficulty getting along amicably with his peers. Whether appropriate treatment would consist solely of punishment/rewards or also include verbal rules and explanations might indeed depend on the intellectual level of the child.

Individual Differences

Although it is helpful to place children at a developmental level, it is equally important to recognize the enormous variability in human beings. Examples of individual differences abound in the child development literature (Birns, 1965; Schaffer and Emerson, 1964; Tanner, 1963).

One of the most extensive studies of individual differences in behavior is the New York Longitudinal Study conducted by Thomas, Chess, and Birch, and their colleagues (Thomas, Chess, and Birch, 1970; Chess and Thomas, 1977). Shortly after birth a group of children were rated for several years on measures of "temperament" such as motor activity, responses to new stimuli, and intensity of reactions to stimulation. Ratings were based on parental interviews that were structured so as to encourage specific descriptions. Home observations also were conducted by observers who had no information about any child's behavioral tendencies. The researchers discov-

ered that distinct individual differences appeared to exist very early in life. Moreover, many of the children were classifiable into one of three disposition groups. The "easy" child was characterized by regularity, a positive approach to new stimuli, easy adaptability to change, positive mood, and mild to moderate intensity of reactions. The "difficult" child exhibited irregularity of biological functions, negative withdrawal from new stimuli, frequent negative mood, and high-intensity reactions. In between these two types was the "slow-to-warm-up" child, who only slowly adapted to new stimuli but who, compared to the "difficult" child, displayed less irregularity of function, less negative mood, and mild initial negative reactions.

The fact of individual differences poses two main considerations for the study of childhood problems. First, it cautions us that individual variability must always be taken into account when we evaluate development of any kind of behavior. But second, it cannot be concluded that what the child brings to the situation produces a certain developmental outcome. Rather, organismic variables—regardless of their origins—transact with other factors in the environment in which the child is operating. In interpreting their findings, for example, Chess and Thomas (1977) suggest that early temperamental differences occur in the presence of parents who themselves differ in style and reactions and thus handle their children in different ways. Differential handling, in turn, influences early individual differences in children, producing nuances in temperament and behavior. These new behavioral patterns interact, in turn, with recurrent and new features of the environment, and so on. Chess and Thomas have provided several case studies to demonstrate that developmental outcome depends upon a multitude of factors. Box 2-2 contains their description of Carl, who was classified as a "difficult" child early in life. Although many "difficult" children do display problem behaviors over time, Carl fared quite well, due at least in part to a positive parent-child interaction that began early in Carl's development.

Box 2-2   The "Difficult" Child Need Not Become the Difficult Adult

Carl requested a discussion with one of us (S.C.) after his first term in college because of feelings of depression and inability to cope with the academic and social situation at college. He had made virtually no friends and found studying difficult, experiences he could not recall ever having had before. He had done well academically in high school, had many friends, found school enjoyable, and had a wide range of interests, including the piano. In the interview he was alert, articulate, and in very good contact. He did not appear depressed, but rather bewildered at what was happening, exclaiming, "This just isn't me!"

The . . . data showed that in earlier life Carl had been one of our most extreme "difficult child" temperamental types, with intense, negative reactions to new situations and slow adaptability only after many exposures. This was true whether it was the first bath or first solid foods in infancy, the beginning of nursery school and elementary school, first birthday parties, or the first shopping trip. Each experience evoked stormy responses, with loud crying and struggling to get away. However, his parents learned to anticipate Carl's reactions, knew that if they were patient, presented only one or a few new situations at a time, and gave Carl the opportunity for repeated exposure to the new, he would finally adapt positively. Furthermore, once he adapted, his intensity of responses gave him a zestful enthusiastic involvement, just as it gave his initial negative reactions a loud and stormy character. His parents recognized that the difficulties in raising Carl were due to his temperament and not to their being "bad parents." The father even looked on his son's shrieking and turmoil as a sign of "lustiness." As a result of this positive parent-child interaction Carl never became a behavior problem even though the "difficult child" as a group is significantly at higher risk for disturbed development.

In his later childhood and high-school years Carl met very few new situations and developed an appropriately positive and self-confident self-image. However, the entry to college away from home suddenly confronted him simultaneously with a number of new situations—strange surroundings, an entirely new peer group, new types of faculty approaches and learning demands, and a complex relationship with a girl student with whom he was living. This resulted in a recrudescence of his "difficult child" pattern of response to the new and brought him for help.

Only one discussion was necessary with Carl, consisting primarily in clarifying for him his temperamental pattern and the techniques he could use for adapting to the new. Actually, Carl had already begun to take these steps on his own—cutting down the number of new subjects, insisting with himself that he study each subject daily for specific times, attenuating his involvement with the girl, and making a point of attending peer social group activities, no matter how uncomfortable he felt. By the end of the academic year his difficulties had disappeared and his subsequent functioning has been on the previous positive level. He was told that similar negative reactions to the new might occure in the future. His response was, "That's all right. I know how to handle them now." (Chess and Thomas, 1977, pp. 220-221)

Early Experience and Critical Events

Since the child's transaction with the world is set on its course early in life, particular importance may be attributed to early events. In fact, theorists of different persuasions and interests note that early experience is crucial for later development. Some go as far to suggest that it is critical. The *critical period hypothesis* refers to the idea that at certain times in life organisms are maximally sensitive to certain events, so the occurrence and quality of these events are extremely, sometimes irrevocably, influential. This hypothesis has largely been applied to the early period of life. It derives in part from demonstrations of the critical importance of the timing of events for biological development. For example, the first three months of pregnancy is a time of maximal sensitivity to exposure to the rubella (German measles) virus. Such exposure results in a much higher rate of prenatal death and defect than exposure later in pregnancy (Chess, 1974; Rugh and Shettles, 1971).

Research with animals provides examples of the influence of early experience on social development. Konrad Lorenz's demonstration of the following response in geese is particularly noteworthy (Lorenz, 1965, 1967). Lorenz showed that these animals have a strong tendency to follow the first object that crosses their visual field during a specific short period early in life. By placing himself in the visual pathway of goslings during this critical period, Lorenz demonstrated that the geese became attached even to him, following him through a field or when he swam in a lake. Under ordinary circumstances such attachment would occur with the mother, setting up social interaction that would ensure protection and guidance. If the phenomenon—labeled imprinting by Lorenz—does not take place during the critical time period, it is less likely to occur at all, seriously affecting the development of the goslings.

Other animal research provides evidence that a variety of early experiences, such as handling, shock, and temperature alterations, have an impact on emotionality, exploration, and re-

sponse to stress (Thompson and Grusec, 1970). Rearing rats in sensory-enriched environments has been shown to increase learning and perhaps even to influence the weight and chemistry of the brain (Forgus, 1954; Hebb, 1949; Rosenzweig, Bennett, and Diamond, 1972). Harlow and Harlow's (1970) work with rhesus monkeys reared in social isolation for three to twelve months showed that the young animals were terror stricken when isolation was removed. The monkeys isolated for only three months soon recovered, but the others continued to be fearful and never progressed beyond minimal social interaction.

Turning to humans, we have already seen that early attachment is viewed as important for normal development. Freud regarded the infant's love for its mother as the prototype of all later love relationships, and early parent-child interaction as crucial for personality development (Freud, 1949; Thompson and Grusec, 1970). Following Freud, Bowlby (1969) and Goldfarb (1943) argued that early defective mothering of orphans resulted in socially, intellectually, and physically impaired individuals. Social learning theorists have suggested that early learning is of special importance because it escapes interference by previous learning and becomes the foundation for all later learning (Lamb, 1978).

The varied experimental work and theoretical proposals concerning the impact of early experience leave little doubt of its importance. Nevertheless, it is unlikely that *strict* critical periods are at all common in the human species. Humans appear remarkably malleable (Hunt, 1979). Most developmental outcomes are *multiply determined* and *overdetermined*—that is, they rely on many factors, all of which may not be necessary. This implies that a "critical" experience need not have a profound effect on the child (Lamb, 1978) and that the presence of other, even later, experiences can moderate outcome. Moreover, the exact nature of any early experience requires specification for a reasonable account of its influence. Lack of "good mothering," for example, may refer to lack of warmth and affection, sensory stimulation, verbalization, or all of these deprivations. We would hardly expect each of these to affect the child in an identical way.

Risk and Invulnerability

As is quite obvious by now, the prediction of individual growth is very "iffy" (Chess and Thomas, 1977). Two concepts that are helpful in any attempt to conceptualize the development of psychopathology are the concepts of risk and invulnerability.

Risk may be viewed as having two foci (Garmezy, 1975). One is predispositions of the individual to respond maladaptively to life's experiences. Such organismic tendencies may arise through heredity or experience, or through their interaction. The other focus is life experience itself that in some way brings stress to the child. The study of these domains may permit the early identification of children who have a higher-than-usual chance of developing problems and may allow early intervention to minimize or prevent the difficulties from occurring at all.

What puts a child at high risk for behavioral disturbance in general, or for a particular disturbance? If etiology were completely understood, this question would be relatively simple to answer. Unfortunately, this is rarely the case. Thus, we must look to models of development and psychopathology to provide hypotheses about risk factors. We may also draw on astute observations and research with children who do and do not develop problems. Table 2-6 lists some of the factors that are most likely to prove fruitful in conceptualizing risk. To some extent all these factors have been studied and implicated in childhood psychopathology, as will be apparent in subsequent chapters.

On the other side of the coin, the child is increasingly being recognized as a competent and adaptive individual. Interestingly, this is a relatively new theme. For example, in 1948 Anderson drew attention to what he considered a misrepresentation of children (Cohen, 1976). He noted that the child too often was viewed as passive and as so delicate that exceptional

Table 2-6   Some Factors That May Increase Risk of Behavior Disorders

Hereditary influence
Prenatal influence
Birth defects, complications, prematurity
Detrimental early social experiences
Disease and damage, especially to the nervous system
Poverty
Child abuse, neglect
Family stress and negative interactions
Poor peer relations

amounts of protection, love, affection, and security were required for healthy growth. Anderson argued that the child should be seen as an active, resilient individual who selects environmental input to a large degree. Fifteen years later Kessen (1963) put forth a similar thesis, backed by research findings, that even in infancy children act on the world with individual competence and play a reciprocal role in relationships with caretakers. Meanwhile, Murphy and Moriarty (1976) had begun to analyze the competence and coping capacity observed in a longitudinal study of children growing up in Kansas in the 1950s and 1960s. On the basis of this and other work, developmentalists have increasingly begun to conceptualize the criteria for adaptability and competence. Garmezy (1975) and his research team, for example, selected the following as central indicators of competence:

1. Effectiveness in work, play, and love.
2. Expectancies that "good outcomes" will result from effort and initiative.
3. Self-esteem and the belief that one can control events rather than being a passive victim.
4. Self-discipline as shown by an ability to delay gratification and to be future-oriented.
5. Control and regulation of impulsive behavior.

6. The ability to think abstractly and flexibly in new situations.

Perhaps even more interesting is the question of *how* children grow up healthy, sometimes in the face of considerable biological and environmental vulnerabilities. Unfortunately, beyond the widely held belief that basic biological, socioemotional, and educational needs must be met for psychological well-being, remarkably little is known about the resiliency and adaptability of individuals as they confront developmental tasks within their specific environments. In reviewing his own and others' research on attachment, Sroufe (1979) reported that the child who is securely attached to its caretaker early in life shows peer competence at 3 ½ years and resiliency at 5 years (for example, self-reliance, curiosity, resourcefulness, moderate control). However, substantially more research is needed on the fascinating topic of adaptability. What is already clear, is that the development of adaptability, like other behavioral tendencies, cannot be viewed without taking into account the child's transaction with the environment. The stressful situations encountered by the child, and the way in which important individuals respond to the child's endeavors, certainly help shape competence and adaptability.

If any one outstanding impression can be drawn from looking at the child as a developing entity, it is a picture of enormous complexity and variability. Indeed, the dynamic of development is what makes the topic so fascinating, if at times also exasperating. Understanding developmental processes is essential to understanding childhood disorders because problem behaviors have the same fundamental determinants as "normal" behaviors. Furthermore, *normal* and *abnormal* can be defined only in terms of each other. Many of the descriptions and issues discussed in this chapter will reappear throughout the book. In Chapter 3 we shall explore perspectives on childhood problems—an area that is intricately entwined with developmental theory.

SUMMARY

The developmental orientation to childhood problems makes several contributions to the area of psychopathology. Descriptions of normal development provide a framework for judging all behavior, while theoretical hypotheses can help explain how normal processes go awry. Certain developmental issues can alert us to the most appropriate ways in which to view and interpret childhood problems.

Development is defined in terms of change or growth—both quantitative and qualitative—that occurs over time as the result of the interaction or transaction between biological and environmental variables. The old argument concerning the impact of nature and nurture has evolved from the question of Which one? to How much? to How?

Development is set on its course by the gene complement, which influences attributes and behavior by control of the biochemical functioning of the body. Enormous variability in individuals is assured by the processes of meiosis and conception and by genetic events such as crossing over and mutation. Gene-environment interaction adds to this variability.

The developing child can be viewed as a physical, intellectual, and social entity, although these aspects are obviously tied to each other. Considerable knowledge has accumulated about the typical sequence of growth. For example, it is known that physical growth occurs in a quite orderly direction and fashion. When the child comes into the world, he or she has substantial capacity to sense and react to stimulation and to learn. Many of these processes are being explored. Piaget's investigation of cognitive growth is an outstanding example of developmental stage theory and empirical exploration. Children show early differences in social behavior, some of which may be predisposed genetically. Social attachment begins early and is considered an important basis for later development.

The social context of development includes the influence of socioeconomic class, family, school, and peers. Numerous examples exist of variations among socioeconomic classes. Concern about the effects of low SES has established that children of low social class are at high risk for later disorders, due to inadequate prenatal care, health care, and diet, and other environmental circumstances. Of all the socializing agents, the family is perhaps seen as the most crucial. Much is being discerned about family interactions and structure, but the impact of these variables is not firmly determined. Increasing recognition is now given to the influence of peers, who play a progressively important role as the child develops. Poor peer relationships are associated with poor developmental outcome. The well-known influence of the school includes not only what children learn but also how their behavior and self-expectations are shaped.

Several developmental issues are especially important to understanding and interpreting childhood behavioral problems. Assessment of developmental level aids in evaluating children and constructing an appropriate treatment plan. Demonstrations of individual differences remind us both of the need to evaluate each child as an individual and of the necessity to examine organismic-environmental interactions. Extensive research with animals and humans has established the importance of early experience. Given the flexibility of human beings, strict critical periods are unlikely; rather, most developmental outcomes are multiply determined and overdetermined. The prediction of individual development would be less "iffy" if more were known about risk and invulnerability to behavior disorders. Several variables have been implicated as putting the child at high risk. However, little is understood about invulnerability and about how children often develop in a healthy way despite substantial risk.

3

PERSPECTIVES ON CHILDHOOD BEHAVIOR DISORDERS

WHAT ARE PERSPECTIVES?

THE BIOLOGICAL/PHYSIOLOGICAL PERSPECTIVE

Genetic Influences
Biochemical Influences
Structural and Physiological Damage

THE PSYCHODYNAMIC PERSPECTIVE

The Structures of the Mind
Psychosexual Stages
Anxiety and the Defense Mechanisms
Criticisms and Modifications
 of Psychoanalytic Theory

THE BEHAVIORAL/SOCIAL LEARNING PERSPECTIVE

Classical Conditioning
Instrumental (Operant) Conditioning
Observational Learning

SOME OTHER PERSPECTIVES

The Cognitive-Behavioral Approach
The Psychoeducational Approach
The Family Systems Approach

SUMMARY

Baddeley (Hunter and Macalpine, 1963), writing in 1622, described a boy who was thought by many to be possessed of the devil "by reason of many strange fits, and much distemper," which came upon him at the reading of a particular biblical verse. It was decided that the verse should be read to the boy in Greek, which he did not understand and, if he reacted violently again, it would have been demonstrated that he was possessed of the devil who, as everyone knew, was well versed in all languages. The boy responded but not at the proper time, and it was therefore determined that he was a "fraud" (having even put ink in his urine to make it black). The boy "brast into plentiful teares, confessing all, to his owne shame" when he was confronted, and that presumably settled that. There was no want of ingenuity, either on the part of the boy or his diagnosticians but it is obvious that the disturbed behavior—while described in sufficient detail—could be understood only in terms of possession or volition. No one, apparently, inquired into the boy's reasons for perpetrating so hazardous a hoax! (Rie, 1971, p. 8)

Possession by demons is no longer popular as an explanation of behavioral disorders in children. However, the above case study reminds us that the perspective we employ to understand abnormal behavior affects the questions we ask and the treatments we offer.

In Chapter 2 we looked at the child as a developing organism to help us understand the genesis of both normal and abnormal behavior. We now turn to perspectives, or paradigms, that have traditionally been brought to bear on behavioral disorders. The biological/physiological, the psychodynamic, and the behavioral/social learning perspectives are the three major viewpoints that have been used to understand aberrant behavior. This chapter also mentions some additional viewpoints that have been applied to childhood disorders. Before turning to particular approaches,

however, let us look at the meaning of the terms *perspective* and *paradigm*.

WHAT ARE PERSPECTIVES?

Much of what we have learned about children's behavioral problems has come from the attempt to apply the methods of science to the study of this phenomenon. However, the writings of Thomas Kuhn (1962) and others have made us increasingly aware that while the scientific method seeks objectivity, science itself is not a completely objective endeavor. Scientists must employ certain conceptions in order to make sense of and deal with the world. The human mind is unable to experience an infinite series of stimuli, while attending to each new stimulus and seeing it as unique. In order to simplify the world, concepts—or assumptions about the nature of events—are constructed. These assumptions lead us to "see" only certain phenomena and to react to new events from our existing perspective. Kuhn refers to the set of general assumptions that are shared by a group of investigators as a paradigm. Here we employ the terms *perspective* and *paradigm* interchangeably. The terms *model* and *theory* frequently are used in the same way as *perspective* and *paradigm,* but they suggest a greater precision and organization of principles than often seems warranted. Historically a variety of paradigms has been employed to explain abnormal behavior. The paradigm that is dominant at any time is likely to be consistent with the prevailing *zeitgeist*, the general viewpoint of a given society at a particular time.

What are the implications of adopting a particular perspective or paradigm? Perspectives help make sense out of a puzzling and complex universe, but at the same time as they aid us, they limit us as well. Perspectives guide us in "selecting" the issues chosen for investigation. An investigator cannot (or does not) think of asking all possible questions. Once a question is selected for investigation, however, a decision must be made—what will be observed in order to answer this question? We do not choose to observe all things, just some things. How we observe is also influenced by a chosen perspective. Particular methods and instruments help in detecting certain phenomena but result in our missing others. The observation of certain phenomena may, in fact, be impossible with particular instruments.

Finally, the adoption of a paradigm affects the interpretations we make of our "facts." The history of astronomy offers a classic example of how paradigms give meaning to "facts" (Davison and Neale, 1982). Ptolemy's view that the earth was at the center of the universe, with the other planets and stars revolving around it, was the dominant paradigm from the second through sixteenth centuries A.D. This basic assumption, along with other concepts that elaborated the perspective, was indeed able to handle the appreciable amount of astronomical data that was available. The explanations of the Ptolemaic paradigm could predict fairly well things such as the positions of the planets and the occurrence of eclipses. Minor problems and discrepancies did not cause astronomers to abandon this widely held belief system but rather to look for ways to elaborate and expand it. Fourteen centuries later, in 1543, Copernicus proposed a different paradigm, with the sun as the center of the universe. The information available to him was about the same as had been available 1,400 years earlier: The paradigm shift occurred for subjective reasons rather than because earlier perspectives failed to handle the data. Copernicus felt that the Ptolemaic view had become overly complex and loose in order to avoid being disproved. Religious-cosmological beliefs also led Copernicus to think that the planetary orbits should be circular—the most perfect form in nature—rather than moving in the complex motions described in the Ptolemaic system. Although this new viewpoint initially did no better at predicting planetary phenomena than the old one, a paradigm shift had occurred due to the subjective views of an observer.

Throughout the book we emphasize an empirical approach to understanding behavior disorders of childhood. The scientific approach, as we have seen, is not entirely objective. Psychologists, like all scientists, like all humans, are aided and limited by their assumptions and conceptions. Let us now look at some of the perspectives offered for understanding children's problems.

THE BIOLOGICAL/PHYSIOLOGICAL PERSPECTIVE

In its most general form the biological perspective holds that biology plays a central role in the development of behavioral disorders in children. The conjecture that psychopathology is due to a defective or malfunctioning biological system can be traced in the Western world to Greek culture. Hippocrates (460–370 B.C.), who is considered the father of medicine, was an advocate of *somatogenesis* (*soma* refers to body, *genesis* means origin). He postulated that proper mental functioning relied on a healthy brain and thus that deviant thinking or behavior was the result of brain pathology. The physiological paradigm initially took the form of a "strong" biological position—biology directly causes abnormal behavior. The original psychiatric classification system developed by Kraeplin in the late 1800s, and the forerunner of current systems, was clearly based on this assumption. Early discoveries of biological causes for particular behavioral problems (for example, the revelation that a spirochete caused syphillis and the mental deterioration of its late stages) led to the hope that similar causes would be found for all abnormal behavior. With limited exception, this has not proven to be the case. Currently the most popular conceptualization of the role of biology is the notion of *diathesis-stress*—that a biological predisposition toward a disorder (a diathesis) interacts with environmental or life events (stress) to produce a particular behavioral problem. The influence of biological factors on a child's behavior can occur through a variety of mechanisms. Here we will examine three: genetic influences, biochemical malfunctioning, and structural damage or malfunction caused by disease or trauma.

Genetic Influences

Beginning with the work of Gregor Mendel, several mechanisms of hereditary influence have been recognized. Our discussion briefly describes some of the mechanisms most widely studied.

Inheritance through a single-gene, recessive mechanism. Among Mendel's first publications was a report on the inheritance of certain characteristics that are genetically controlled by one gene pair. In cross-fertilizing pea plants Mendel observed, for example, that violet-flower plants sometimes produced offspring that were either violet or white. To explain the occurrence of the white-flowered plants, Mendel hypothesized that each parent plant carried two hereditary factors (later called genes) influencing color but passed on only one in the gamete. He also proposed that one form of the factor was *dominant*, in that its transmission by either parent led to the display of that form of the characteristic. The other form, the *recessive*, displayed itself only when it was transmitted by both parents. Thus, white-flowered plants could spring from violet-flowered plants, provided that each parent carried and passed on the recessive gene. Mendel's hypothesis has stood the test of time, and today we know that many human attributes (for example, blue eyes, straight hair, sickle-cell anemia, albinism) are influenced by one gene pair and are carried recessively. The inheritance of Tay-Sachs disease provides an example of this pattern.

A degenerative disease of the nervous system, Tay-Sachs is evident very early in life, causing progressive deterioration of mental abilities, motor capacities, and vision. Many Tay-Sachs youngsters exhibit seizures and convulsions and never develop the ability to sit and stand (Jabbour, Duenas, Gilmartin, and Gottlieb, 1976). The absence of an enzyme required for fat metabolism is associated with the condition. No treatment exists, and death typically ensues by the age of 1 to 3 years. An estimated 60 to 90 percent of all cases of Tay-Sachs is found among children of Ashkenazic Jewish extraction. One out of every thirty people in this population carries the disease heterozygously; that is, carries one recessive gene for the condition and one dominant gene for the normal condition. When both parents are heterozygous, the chance is 1 in 4 that their offspring will inherit the gene for Tay-Sachs from both parents, thereby displaying the disease. Figure 3-1 depicts this pattern of inheritance.

Inheritance through a single-gene, dominant mechanism. An attribute can be transmitted by a dominant gene; whenever the gene is inherited from either parent, the condition will theoretically display itself. A well-known pattern occurs when such a gene is carried heterozygously by one parent and not at all by the other. In this case there is a 50 percent chance of offspring exhibiting the condition. Examples of human attributes carried by a single dominant gene are curly hair, free ear lobes, extra fingers and toes, and Huntington's chorea (Figure 3-2). The latter is a disease that causes death but does not show up until adulthood, when limb spasms, mental deterioration, and psychotic behavior become evident. The onset of this disease and the devastating deterioration that follows are described in the biography of the well-known folk singer Woody Guthrie, who died of Huntington's chorea (Yurchenco, 1970).

Inheritance of sex-linked characteristics. Another widely recognized pattern of inheritance is sex linkage. Certain attributes are said to be sex linked because they are influenced by genes on the sex chromosomes. Of special interest is the situation in which the relevant gene is recessive and carried on the X chromosome, such as red-green color blindness, hemophilia, and Lesch-Nyhan Syndrome.

Lesch-Nyhan Syndrome is a rare, untreatable X-linked disorder that results in unusual motor development, mental retardation, and extreme self-mutilation in children. Children

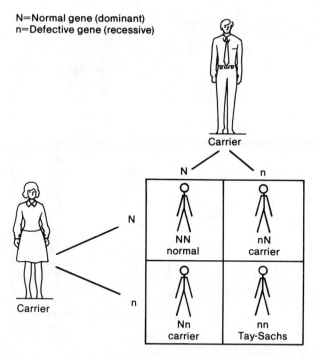

N=Normal gene (dominant)
n=Defective gene (recessive)

Figure 3-1 Inheritance of Tay-Sachs disease when both parents carry the defective gene. Because Tay-Sachs is transmitted by a single recessive gene, it is displayed only when the gene is inherited from both parents, in about 25% of all offspring.

suffering from the disorder compulsively and repetitively bite their lips, tongue, and fingers. The disorder is found only in males. Since the condition is so severe, causing death before adulthood, Lesch-Nyhan males do not have offspring. The Lesch-Nyhan child has a normal father and a mother who carries the disorder, having one normal X chromosome and one affected X chromosome. Sons receive their only X chromosome from their mothers. Those who receive the recessive defective gene will develop the disorder, since the Y chromosome transmitted from the father carries no gene at all to offset the defective gene. Daughters receive one X chromosome from each parent. If a girl received the defective recessive gene from her mother, it would be offset by the dominant normal gene from her father; she would have no affliction herself but could carry Lesch-Nyan to her son. This pattern, which always affects the male more adversely than the female, is now widely recognized in human inheritance.

Characteristics influenced by many genes. So far our discussion has focused on characteristics that are influenced by one gene pair. These characteristics tend to fall into all-or-none categories: Pea plant flowers are violet or white, and individuals have or do not have Huntington's chorea. Many attributes, however, are influenced by several genes, and they are displayed along a continuum. Individuals are not only extremely tall or short, for example; they fall into a range between these extremes. So too do individuals vary continuously with regard to intellectual and personality characteristics that may be genetically influenced. In studying such polygenetic inheritance it is im-

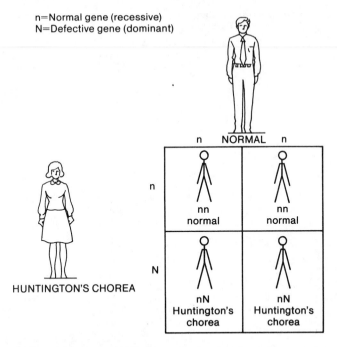

Figure 3–2 Inheritance of Huntington's chorea when one parent carries the dominant gene heterozygously (and thus has the disease) and the other does not carry it at all. On the average, 50% of all offspring will display the disease.

possible to trace gene patterns in the same manner as when one or only a few gene pairs are involved. Complex statistical methods must be used. Furthermore, it is frequently the case that a number of different, complex patterns of genetic influence seem to explain the available data equally well. Also, it is usually difficult to eliminate competing environmental models. As we examine a variety of childhood behavioral problems, we will see that inherited genetic mechanisms are posited for many of these disorders. If inheritance does indeed play a role in these problems, it is likely that the mechanism in most cases involves a complex polygenetic influence. Box 3-1 illustrates some of the research methods that are currently employed to study the genetic contribution to behavioral disorders.

Noninheritable genetic effects: chromosome aberrations. Chromosomes that are aberrant in either number or structure are known to cause death or a variety of deficiencies. As many as 22 to 50 percent of early spontaneous abortions are attributed to chromosome aberrations, and 1 in every 200 live births involves some kind of gross chromosome abnormality (Reed, 1975). Abnormality in the number of chromosomes is thought to occur during maturation of the ova and sperm (meiosis) or in early cell division in the fertilized ova (mitosis). The chromosome pair fails to separate, resulting in either an extra chromosome or the loss of a chromosome in cells. Abnormality in structure occurs when a piece of a chromosome breaks off, often attaching itself to another chromosome. These ''accidents'' are often not

Box 3-1 Investigating Hereditary Effects on Humans

The idea that physical and behavioral characteristics can be passed from parent to child through some biological mechanism is a very old one. Only in this century, however, have we begun to understand hereditary processes and to construct ways of investigating their influence. The search is difficult, requiring that genetic and environmental influences be separated. But how can this be accomplished when these effects are so intertwined? In fact, the goal can only be approximated.

Putting aside all ethical and practical concerns, the task could be approached by selectively mating humans of a known attribute and observing their offspring. Or we could take genetically identical individuals (identical twins) and expose them to differentially controlled environments. If the individuals came to differ, environmental influence would be implicated. If they did not, it could be inferred that genetic influence was quite strong or that the environmental differences had little to do with the attribute being examined. All these considerations are quite irrelevant, nevertheless, since ethical and practical concerns cannot be put aside. For human subjects, at least, direct manipulation of any sort is out of the question.

Direct manipulation is employed in animal research, however. In one now-classic study, for example, rats which rapidly learned to find their way through a maze were mated with each other, as were those which performed extremely poorly in the maze (Thompson, 1954). After several generations of such selective breeding, two strains of rats had been developed, a "maze bright" and a "maze dull" strain. Since all the animals had been reared in the identical environment, it was concluded that the ability to perform on the maze task is influenced by heredity. Various other investigations involving control of breeding and environmental factors have demonstrated that heredity plays a role in determining aggressiveness, emotionality, activity level, alcohol preference, susceptibility to seizures, and the like in animals (DeFries and Plomin, 1978; McClearn, 1970). These findings support the general concept of

hereditary influence but cannot give firm evidence about human inheritance. For that we must turn to family, twin, and adoption studies.

One way to study the family is by pedigree analysis. This entails identifying family members who display the attribute of interest and then determining whether the presence of the characteristic in family members follows one of the known inheritance patterns. Pedigree analysis is obviously limited to attributes that are carried by relatively simple hereditary mechanisms. For other attributes—in particular, those carried by many genes—*consanguinity study* is employed. This is based on the assumption that the occurrence of an attribute should increase as the degree of relationship increases (due to an increase in the number of shared genes). In consanguinity studies several index cases of the attributes are identified, and their various family members are examined. If inheritance is a factor, it would be expected, for example, that parents and siblings of the index cases would show the attribute with greater frequency than cousins of the index cases, who in turn would display the attribute more than the general population. When such a pattern is revealed, it is consistent with a hereditary explanation. Nevertheless, such data are not conclusive when applied to behavior because social transmission could account for the findings. Close relatives, when compared to those less close, would be expected to be more alike due to shared environments as well as shared genes.

The study of twins provides an opportunity to overcome some of these difficulties. Twin study involves the comparison of monozygotic (identical) twins and dizygotic (fraternal) twins. In the former each twin carries the same genes, while in dizygotic twins one child genetically resembles the co-twin only to the extent that regular siblings resemble each other. The hypothesis of genetic transmission predicts that monozygotic twins are more alike (concordant) than are dizygotic twins. Twin study is a powerful tool in genetic research. However, it has some disadvantages. One is that the identification of twins as identical and fraternal has not always been reliable. It is also argued that monozygotic twins may be more alike because they are treated more alike than are dizygotic pairs. So far there is inadequate substantiation for this position.

The influence of genes and of the environment can also be examined by adoption studies (or foster family studies). Although various comparisons can be made, they all focus on the fact that when immediate adoption occurs, later resemblances between a child and the adoptive parents are due to social transmissions, while resemblances to biological parents are due to genetic factors. If greater similarity among biologically related pairs is revealed, genetic transmission is evidenced. However, to the degree that the child is like the adoptive family, social transmission is implicated.

As is obvious from this discussion, hereditary influence is examined by quite indirect methods. This is especially true in investigations of behavioral characteristics, which usually involve complicated polygene inheritance.

inherited, so that they influence only the specific developing embryo.

Perhaps the most widely recognized disorder attributed to a chromosome aberration is Down's syndrome (see Chapter 9). Characterized by mental deficiency, it is usually caused by an extra #21 chromosome. A group of abnormalities that results from sex chromosome aberrations has also been discovered. These sex chromosome disorders are often characterized by below-average intelligence, atypical sexual development, and other difficulties.

Biochemical Influences

Much of both early and current thinking about the role of biological influences on disordered behavior implicates imbalances in body chemistry. Hippocrates speculated that adequate mental functioning relied on a proper balance of the four bodily humors: blood, phlegm, yellow bile, and black bile. Thus, for example, excessive black bile was thought to produce melancholia, or what we would today label depression. Biochemical theories of depression as well as other disorders have gained prominence more recently as well. For example, there is a long history of speculation regarding a biochemical basis for schizophrenia. As early as 1883, Kraeplin postulated that schizophrenia was due to a chemical imbalance. Since that time numerous biochemical agents have been thought to cause schizophrenia. Most recent biochemical theories have stressed the role of neurotransmitters. These are substances that are released by one neuron and relay the neural impulse across the synapse to the special receptor of the next neuron. The neurotransmitter that is currently receiving the greatest attention is dopamine. It is postulated that schizophrenia is caused by an excess production of dopamine. Support for this theory comes from two indirect sources. Phenothiazines, drugs that are currently employed to alleviate the symptoms of schizophrenia, are thought to interfere with dopamine activity. It is therefore reasoned that since phenothiazines help schizophrenics, an excess of dopamine probably caused the schizophrenia originally. Caution must be exercised in employing such reasoning. A treatment that is successful may *suggest* a cause for the disorder, but it cannot *prove* that the disorder was originally produced in this manner. The second indirect source of support for the dopamine hypothesis comes from observations that high doses of amphetamines can produce behavior that resembles some of the symptoms of schizophrenia. These drugs are known to act through their impact on dopamine production.

At present there has been a great deal of research on the dopamine hypothesis, but none of it is conclusive. The research, like other biochemical research, faces a number of appreciable difficulties. Most schizophrenic individuals are given some form of medication—usually some tranquilizing agent. These drugs have effects on the biochemistry of the body that last a considerable time, even after they have been

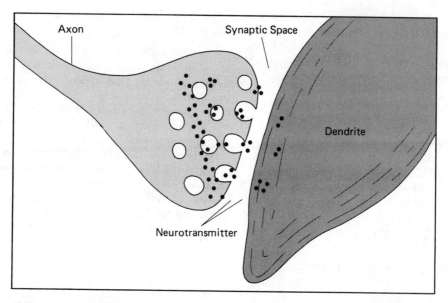

Figure 3-3 Neurotransmitters are substances that are released by one neuron and relay the neural impulse across the synapse to the special receptor of the next neuron.

discontinued. Also, severely disturbed individuals are often different from control subjects in a number of other ways that have an impact on the body's biochemistry. Unusual or inadequate diet, inactivity, and particular stressors are not easily controlled and thus may account for biochemical differences between schizophrenics and control subjects. It is also difficult to determine whether a biochemical imbalance was the cause of or was caused by a disorder. While biochemical theories may contribute to our understanding of certain behavior disorders, caution regarding any particular hypothesis is warranted. In addition, it seems likely that any complete explanation will have to incorporate environmental factors as well.

Most research on biochemical factors has emphasized genetic influences. The chemistry of the body, however, can be affected in a number of other ways: infection, diet, stress, ingestion of foreign substances, and drug and alcohol abuse. It has been postulated that these influences contribute to several disorders. For example, a biochemical theory of hyperactivity was offered by Feingold (1975). Through his work on allergies Feingold suggested that hyperactivity might be caused by a sensitivity to certain food additives. Still other examples are the possible contribution of lead poisoning to hyperactivity and of prenatal viral infections to the development of childhood psychosis. Like many genetic-biochemical explanations, these mechanisms, too, are largely speculative.

While specific mechanisms for specific disorders are often questioned, there is fairly broad agreement and speculation that biochemistry in some form contributes to disturbed behavior. For example, it is speculated that individual differences in physiological reactivity may be related to the development of anxiety problems or depression in children. Similarly, it has been suggested that differences in biochemistry contribute to the severe loss of appetite characteristic of anorexia nervosa. Early individual differences in temperament, and their consequences for child-parent interaction (described earlier, p. 37), are yet another example of the possible role that biochemical factors may play in the development of behavioral disorders.

Structural and Physiological Damage

We have seen how genetic and biochemical influences are thought to contribute to behavioral disorders. Actual damage to the structural or physiological integrity of the biological system may also produce a variety of intellectual and behavioral difficulties. These known or presumed influences may occur during pregnancy (prenatal influences), at about the time

of birth (perinatal effects), or during later development.

Prenatal influences. At the present time we are witnessing much interest in *teratogens*, conditions or agents that appear related to fetal death, disease, and defect. The possible effects of a number of teratogens are presented in Table 3-1. However, a word of caution is appropriate about these presumed effects. Ethical considerations do not permit research that would provide clear conclusions, such as studies in which pregnant women would be exposed to various conditions of diet, drug ingestion, disease, and the like. We must therefore rely on animal studies, the results of which may not

Table 3-1 Some Possible Prenatal Effects

Diseases and Conditions	
Diabetes mellitus	Fetal death; stillbirth; respiratory difficulties; metabolic disturbances
Herpes Simplex 2	Death; encephalitis; local and generalized infection
Influenza A	Malformations
Maternal diet deficiencies	Prematurity; low birth weight; stillbirth; growth retardation; and poor mental functioning—also, indirect effects by raising mother's susceptibility to disease and pregnancy complications
Rh incompatibility	Early death; mental retardation
Rubella	Death; prematurity; deafness; blindness; heart, liver, pancreas defects; mental retardation
Syphilis	Death; blindness; deafness; mental retardation
Drugs and Chemicals	
Alcohol	Growth retardation; microcephaly; disfigurations; cardiac anomalies; behavioral and cognitive deficits
Aspirin (in excess)	Bleeding in the newborn; possible circulatory anomalies
Barbiturates	Depressed breathing; drowsiness during the first week of life
Heroin, morphine	Convulsions; tremors; newborn death; newborn withdrawal symptoms
Hormones given prenatally for medical reasons (e.g., DES, progestin)	Cancer; abnormal external sex organs
Lead	Anemia; hemorrhage; miscarriage
Radiation	Abnormalities of structure and function: leukemia, cataracts, stunted growth, microcephally (abnormally small head), miscarriage, stillbirth
Thalidomide	Malformations, especially of the limbs
Tobacco	Low birth weight; prematurity; high heart rate; convulsions

This table and related materials are adapted from Liebert and Wicks-Nelson, 1981.

hold for humans, and on investigations of humans under natural (uncontrolled) conditions.

Although exposure to teratogens cannot be completely controlled, pregnant women can exert special care not to expose themselves to disease, and they can obtain treatment if they do contract disease. For example, the ravages of rubella can be dramatically reduced by the administration of a vaccine at least two months before pregnancy (Rugh and Shettles, 1971). Drug and chemical ingestion can be voluntarily controlled but often is not. In one study Dalby (1978) found that 42 to 73 percent of all pregnant women smoked tobacco and that approximately eleven drugs were ingested during pregnancy. These included aspirin, antacids, antibiotics, barbiturates, and antihistamines. Pleasure, and relief of discomfort, were the common reasons for drug ingestion.

In addition to the teratogens and their possible effects, as outlined in Table 3-1, several other variables, such as age of the mother and maternal stress, have been associated with infant death and developmental difficulties. Also, while the discussion of prenatal influences has focused on maternal matters, there is some evidence that birth defects may be unusually high for the children of males who are exposed to certain agents before their offspring are conceived (Kolata, 1978). An interesting study of humans involved men who, as operating room personnel, had been exposed to anesthetic gases. Wives of these men, as compared to those of men not so exposed, had a higher prevalence of miscarriages, and their infants were more likely to have birth defects.*

Later influences. It is important to note that brain damage may also occur after birth due to accident, illness, malnutrition, or accidental poisoning. Both the site and the severity of the brain damage determine the nature of the difficulties the child experiences. A precise description of the relationship between damage and dysfunction cannot always be made, how-

*Many chromosome anomalies and developmental defects can now be detected prenatally by examining fluid drawn from the amniotic sac surrounding the fetus. This procedure is *amniocentesis.*

Courtesy of March of Dimes Birth Defects Foundation

The girl pictured above is one of two daughters born to a, since deceased, alcoholic mother. On the basis of history, mental deficiency, and physical findings, both were diagnosed as having fetal alcohol syndrome. Several key features of the syndrome are visible in this girl, including: narrow eye openings, underdeveloped-thin upper lip, flattening or absence of the usual indentation under the nose, and possible drooping of the upper eyelids.

ever. Thus, the link between brain damage and psychopathology is unclear and in many ways controversial (Werry, 1979b). Perhaps most controversial is the concept of minimal brain damage or dysfunction. Problems such as hyperactivity and learning disabilities are often presumed to be caused by minimal degrees of brain damage that are undetectable with current clinical methods. This concept and its relationship to behavioral and learning problems will be explored further in Chapter 10.

One of the major concerns of those who work with children is whether problems arising from brain damage can be remediated. The optimistic view suggests that the immature central nervous system is highly "plastic." It can recuperate following damage, or lost functions can be taken over by other brain tissue. While this position encourages continued work to develop lost or unachieved functioning, it may have some negative consequences as well. Frustration for the child, parent, and teacher may result where complete plasticity is assumed but is not realized. The assumption that the young brain is highly plastic may also lead to imprecise forms of intervention. On the other hand, identification of loss and acceptance of non-plasticity can lead to advances in our understanding and to improved remediation (St. James-Roberts, 1979).

THE PSYCHODYNAMIC PERSPECTIVE

Probably the best known perspective on childhood disorders is the psychoanalytic theory of Sigmund Freud. Although it was the first modern systematic attempt to understand mental disorders in psychological terms, Freud's theory drew heavily on biology. Freud was a physician who had trained to be a neurologist. His thinking about how the psychic system operated was formulated to parallel the workings of biological systems and to reflect the then-current developments in the natural sciences.

Freud's ideas went through a number of transitions during his lifetime. The evolution of his conceptualizations has come to be known as classical psychoanalytic theory. Only a brief description of this complex and highly systematized theory will be given here. More elaborate and detailed summaries have been provided by a number of writers (e.g., Kessler, 1966; Wolman, 1972).

Freud's theory of the human mind has at its core biologically given instincts. According to Freud, two instincts are present in all individuals. *Eros* is the impulse to seek pleasure and gratification; the energy associated with this sexual instinct is referred to as *libido*. *Thanatos* is the destructive, aggressive instinct, which

aims to destroy life. These instincts serve as the energy sources of all psychological activity.

Freud's theory has a number of other important characteristics as well. The theory is *deterministic*—there is a specific cause for all behavior, even the most trivial. The principles that describe how behavior is determined are universal, applying to both "normal" and "abnormal" behavior. Emphasis is also given to intrapsychic factors rather than environmental or social influences in explaining behavior. Equally important is the idea that mental processes are *unconscious*; that is, determined by forces that are inaccessible to rational awareness. The analogy of an iceberg, nine-tenths of which is below the surface, illustrates the importance placed on unconscious influences. The theory thus emphasizes instinctual-irrational forces, not rational problem solving.

Although Freud based his theory on clinical observations of adults, he came to view personality as being essentially set during the first five to six years of life. Since the child is viewed as moving through a series of distinct stages of growth, Freud's theory is *developmental*, with a distinct emphasis on early childhood. Psychological difficulties in children as well as in adults are seen as the result of problems experienced during these first few years of life.

To move through early development and beyond, the individual is provided with a fixed amount of psychic energy. The theory describes a dynamic process of transfer of this energy among various aspects of the personality. To explain this ongoing transfer psychoanalytic theory employs a *structural* and *conflict* model as a metaphor for this process. What we seek to do in this brief discussion is to provide an overview of the framework Freud used in talking about the structural-conflict model, stages of development, and the development of psychopathology. We turn first to a description of the structural system.

The Structures of the Mind

Freud described three parts of the mental apparatus: the *id*, the *ego*, and the *superego*. Each of these "structures" is intended to describe part of a system of psychic functioning. The id, present at birth, is the earliest structure and is the source of all psychic energy. Operating entirely at an unconscious level, the id seeks immediate and unconditional gratification of all instinctual urges (the *pleasure principle*). If this cannot be done directly, the id employs *primary process* thinking—obtaining what is desired through fantasy.

The other psychic structures, the ego and superego, both evolve from the id and must obtain their energy from it. The ego is primarily conscious, and its principle task is to mediate between instinctual urges and the outside world. The mature ego employs its cognitive and decision-making functions to test reality. The superego develops when the immature ego cannot handle all conflicts. In order to deal with some of these, the ego incorporates or *introjects* the parents' standards, and this is the beginning of a separate superego. The superego sets ideal standards for behavior and is the conscience, or self-critical part, of the individual. In trying to satisfy the id's instinctual urges, the ego must consider not only reality but also the ideals of the superego. The *psychodynamics* of the Freudian perspective arise out of the attempts of these three systems to achieve their frequently conflicting goals.

Psychosexual Stages

The psychoanalytic perspective relies on a stage theory of development. As the child develops, the focus of psychic energy passes from one bodily zone to the next. The process leads the individual through stages of psychosexual development in a fixed order. Each stage derives its name from the bodily zone that is the primary source of gratification during that period (for example, oral, anal, phallic). Each of these stages also involves a developmental crisis, and the child is hindered in development by not more-or-less resolving the conflicts at any one stage. Failure to reach resolution results in the individual becoming psychologically fixated at the stage. Two situations are at the root of *fixation*. The child may not be able to meet the demands of the environment while also satis-

fying its own needs—and may thus be psychologically frustrated. Alternatively, needs may be met so well that the child is unwilling to leave the stage; and behaviors associated with the stage continue inappropriately. Thus, either frustration or the results of overindulgence can fixate the child at a particular stage, adversely affecting development at all subsequent stages.

Oral stage. From birth through approximately the first year of life, the mouth is the center of pleasure. For example, the infant experiences pleasurable sensations associated with sucking. During this stage the child is highly dependent upon the mother. The themes of this stage are thus not only oral pleasure but also dependency and taking in. Freud and Abraham have suggested that the oral stage can be divided into the oral-passive and oral-aggressive phases (Abraham, 1911). The *oral-passive* stage is associated with the pleasures of sucking and gratification. The *oral-aggressive phase*, which usually coincides with teething, results from the infant realizing that the mother's breast is not always available. When gratification is not available, the child seeks satisfaction by acts of aggression, such as biting. These two styles of oral activity can serve as the prototype for later behavior. The gullible person, who swallows everything, may have a significant amount of libido fixated at the incorporative or oral-passive stage. Alternatively, the oral instinct may be displaced (diverted to another object), and the person may gain pleasure from the acquisition of possessions or information. Displacements of oral aggression (biting) may produce argumentativeness or sarcasm. The child who has a great deal of psychic energy fixated at the oral stage may also continue an interpersonal or problem-solving style characteristic of this stage. For example, dependency may be central to this child's behavior. The final and crucial conflict that ends this period of oral and dependency themes is weaning. If weaning is difficult, a significant proportion of libido may be fixated at this stage.

Anal stage. During the second and third years of life the locus of satisfaction shifts to the anal zone. The retention and expulsion of feces

are the major sources of stimulation and pleasure during this period, and toilet training is
the major task for resolving the conflicts of the
anal stage. Abraham (1911) suggests that the
period can be divided into *anal-expulsive* and *anal-
retentive* phases. The period has several themes;
primary among them are holding and giving.
Later behavior and attitudes regarding possessions and giving (for example, the bowel movement as a gift of love to the mother) are thus
developed during this stage. Presumed sexual
roles of masculine-active-expulsion and femi-
nine-passive-reception begin to be distinguished during this stage as well (Wolman,
1972). According to psychoanalytic theory, if
parental demands are met with relative ease, the
basis for self-control is established. If there is
difficulty, children may retaliate by, for instance, deliberately defecating when and where
they please (Liebert and Wicks-Nelson, 1981).
Such aggressiveness and hostility, may be carried into adulthood, where they take the form
of excessive stubbornness and willfulness. On
the other hand, the child may react by retaining
the feces, setting the stage for later stinginess
and stubbornness.

Phallic stage.   During the phallic stage the
genitals become the focus of pleasure, as indicated in the young child's masturbation, curiosity, and inspection of the sexual organs. The
chief conflict of this period is the desire to possess the opposite-sex parent and the fear of retaliation from the same-sex parent. For the boy
this conflict is called the *Oedipus complex*. It derives its name from the legend of the King of
Thebes who killed his father and married his
mother. Since Oedipus did not know that these
people were his father and mother, this action
is symbolic of an inevitable fate. Similarly,
Freud viewed a boy's desire to possess his
mother and to eliminate his father-competitor
as an inevitable part of the developmental process. The boy's fear that the father will retaliate
by cutting off his penis is known as *castration
anxiety*. To resolve this conflict the boy abandons his direct desire to possess the mother and
identifies with the father. This process, in which

the boy introjects the attitudes and values of the
father, is the basis for the formation of the superego as well as masculine identity.

The parallel process for the girl is known as
the *Electra complex*. The young girl's observation
of the large male organ results in *penis envy* and
leads her to blame her mother for her deficiency. Resentment and anger toward the
mother result in the girl fearing loss of the
mother's love. According to psychoanalytic theory, normal resolution of the Electra complex
involves giving up the wish for a penis and
identifying with the mother, thus accepting the
feminine-respective-passive role, and desiring
to have a baby, which becomes a penis substitute (Wolman, 1972).

The resolution of the Oedipal and Electra
complexes is central to both sex-role and moral
development. Difficulties in either of these areas
are traced back to patterns developed during
this period. For example, castration fears may
be so strong that the boy not only abandons his
incestuous desire for the mother but also gives
up masturbation and the active male role. This
passive attitude, similar to the mother's, may
also conceal an increased fear and hatred of the
father and develop into a defiance of all men in
authority positions. Another example of a problematic Oedipal resolution is the so-called negative Oedipal complex. A strong and aggressive
mother and a weak father may produce a boy
who represses his desires for his mother, identifies with her, and forms a passive affection for
the father. Such a pattern, it is hypothesized,
may lead to homosexuality.

Latency and genital stages.   Following the
resolution of the conflicts of the phallic stage,
the child enters the latency stage. As the name
suggests, this is a period of relative stability.
The sexual and aggressive impulses of the child
are subdued. With puberty, however, these impulses are revived, and the adolescent enters the
genital stage, during which pleasure presumably comes from heterosexual activities. This
stage continues for the remainder of the individual's life. These final two stages are less important to the understanding of behavioral

disorders, since Freud suggested that the basic personality structure is laid down by the end of the phallic stage.

According to classical Freudian theory, children's psychological disorders develop from one of two general sources. The child may be experiencing difficulty in resolving the psychosexual conflict of a particular stage or may be fixated at an earlier stage of development. In either case anxiety is seen as central to symptom formation.

Anxiety and the Defense Mechanisms

Anxiety is the danger signal to the ego that some unacceptable impulse is seeking to gain consciousness. When this signal reaches consciousness, the ego creates defenses to deal with the anxiety. *Repression* and *denial* are two of these defenses. Both seek to make something unconscious by "forgetting" it or denying its existence. *Projection* and *displacement* are defenses which "recognize" the impulse but alter its source. In projection the child may say, for example, "I don't hate her, she hates me." An instance of displacement is when the child's anger at the father is directed instead at the teacher. *Reaction formation* is a defense in which the child develops a behavior that is the opposite of the original impulse. For example, when the child undergoing toilet training cannot express pleasure in being dirty, fastidiousness is displayed as a defensive substitute. Symptoms arising from these and other defense mechanisms are a compromise between impulses seeking expression and the demands of the ego. Thus, symptoms are disguised expressions of unacceptable impulses. Their true "meaning" remains unconscious and is hidden from the person's awareness. One of Freud's most frequently cited cases illustrates the latent meaning of a child's symptoms.

The case of a five-year-old boy, Hans, who was afraid of horses, has served as a model for the psychoanalytic interpretation of childhood phobias (Freud, 1909, 1953). Freud actually saw Hans only once, and the case is based upon treatment by the boy's father under Freud's direction. Hans was very affectionate toward his mother and enjoyed spending time "cuddling" with her. When Hans was almost 5, he returned from his daily walk with his nursemaid frightened, crying, and wanting to cuddle with his mother. The next day, when the mother took him for the walk herself, Hans expressed a fear of being bitten by a horse and that evening insisted upon cuddling with his mother. He cried about having to go out the next day and expressed considerable fear concerning the horse. These symptoms, which continued to get worse, were interpreted by Freud as reflecting the child's sexual impulses toward his mother and his fear of castration by the father. The ego began its defenses against these unacceptable impulses by repressing Hans's wish to attack his rival for his mother's affection, the father. This was an attempt to make the unacceptable impulse unconscious. The next step was projection: Hans believed that his father wished to attack him, rather than that he wished to attack his father. The final step was displacement. The horse was viewed as dangerous, not the father. According to Freud, the choice of the horse as a symbol of the father was due to numerous associations of horses with Hans's father, danger, and penises. For example, the black muzzle and blinders on the horse were viewed as symbolic of the father's mustache and eyeglasses. The fear Hans displaced onto the horse permitted the child's ambivalent feelings toward the father to be resolved. He could now love his father. In addition, thinking of horses as the source of anxiety allowed Hans to avoid anxiety by simply avoiding horses (Kessler, 1966).

Criticisms and Modifications of Psychoanalytic Theory

It would be remiss not to point out that many of Freud's hypotheses have been severely criticized, particularly in the last few decades. For example, psychoanalytic formulations rest primarily on the impressions and recollections of clinical cases. They also involve large inferential leaps from what is observed to what is interpreted as existing. In addition, the mechanisms Freud postulated are intrapsychic and often unconscious and are therefore difficult, if not impossible, to investigate. Thus, much of the criticism of psychoanalytic theory has rested on its untestability. A number of specific assumptions, such as the universality of the psychosexual stages, have also been questioned. It is doubtful, for example, that the Oedipal conflict exists in cultures in which uncles play a dominant role in family life (Malinowski, 1927). Moreover, social learning theorists in particular have rejected psychodynamic formulations, arguing that social behavior and patterns of interaction are rooted in basic learning processes. Even some theorists who retain much of psychoanalytic theory object to Freud's emphasis on erotic gratification and on the early years as the basis of development. Still others insist that personality and social behavior arise from a broader social context and that ego functions are far more central than id drives.

Ego psychology, the elaboration of Freud's conceptions of the ego and its function, is probably the major revision of his theory. Anna Freud, Heinz Hartmann, and Erik Erikson have contributed to this perspective, giving considerable emphasis to children and adolescents in their writings. In the 1920s Anna Freud was one of the first to begin psychoanalytic work with children on a formal basis. Through this work she suggested that the ego, rather than unconscious id impulses, should be the focus of interest. This did not mean abandoning the analytic goal of identifying and interpreting unconscious mental activity. Rather, the analyst's task was expanded to include bringing into consciousness the unconscious defense activities undertaken by the ego. Both Anna Freud and Melanie Klein emphasized the importance and meaning of play. The recognition that children express through play what adults can communicate verbally led to the development of play therapy. Toys and play are used by the therapist to encourage the child to express the fantasies and conflicts that then become the material of therapy.

Anna Freud's interest in ego development led her to emphasize development as a continuous process and thus place less emphasis on psychosexual stages. The concept of *developmental lines* emerged from her view of continuities. The sequence from the complete dependence of the newborn to the young adult's self-reliance is the most basic developmental line and the prototype of all others. So, for example, the child's reactions to separations will change as development occurs. The reaction at any one point in time will depend on the degree of progress along this line of dependence through self-reliance.

Erik Erikson, in addition to stressing the

Table 3-2 Comparison of Erikson's Psychosocial and Freud's Psychosexual Stages of Development

Approximate Chronological Age	Freudian Stages	Erikson's Conflicts or Crises
Infancy	Oral	Basic trust vs. mistrust
1 1/2–3 years	Anal	Autonomy vs. shame, doubt
3–6 years	Phallic	Initiative vs. guilt
6–12 years	Latency	Industry vs. inferiority
Adolescence	Genital	Identity vs. role confusion
Young adulthood		Intimacy vs. isolation
Adulthood		Generativity vs. stagnation
Maturity		Ego integrity vs. despair

problem-solving functions of the ego, has extended Freudian stages into the entire lifespan and incorporated various relationships beyond the parent-child relationship. Erikson's emphasis on the interaction of the individual and society is reflected in the concept of *modalities* of *social interaction*—the kinds of social relations that children learn at different stages as they relate to others. In Table 3–2 the social crisis faced during each developmental period is described, and for earlier periods the comparable Freudian stage is indicated. According to Erikson, the manner in which the child resolves the crisis of a particular developmental period serves as a prototype for social modalities—ways of dealing with others. In addition, the child who fails to achieve an adequate resolution of the central crisis of a particular psychosocial stage will fail to develop the attribute which is the goal of that stage. Role confusion, for example, may be reflected in the adolescent who fails to achieve a basic identity.

Freud's theory of psychosexual development has had tremendous historical impact on the field of child psychopathology. Despite its many critics, it is still a perspective employed by many current workers. The conceptual and methodological critiques of psychoanalytic theory have, however, led some to make significant modifications and others to abandon the theory entirely.

THE BEHAVIORAL/SOCIAL LEARNING PERSPECTIVE

The central concept of the behavioral/social learning perspective is that childhood disorders are learned in the same way that other behaviors are learned. As indicated in Chapter 1, the publication of John B. Watson's essay *Psychology as a Behaviorist Views It* (1913) set into motion a perspective that would serve as the major rival to the psychoanalytic position. While this perspective was also deterministic, it differed from the psychoanalytic paradigm in a number of key ways. Unlike Freud, Watson emphasized observable events rather than unconscious in-

trapsychic conflicts. Developed in the psychological laboratory rather than in a clinical setting, the behavioral perspective heavily emphasized objective empirical verification. Learning and the influence of the environment were seen as the appropriate focus of study. Furthermore, development was viewed as a continuous process rather than as a fixed sequence of stages. The process of learning continues throughout the life span, and therefore it was not assumed that "personality" was set by a certain age. Finally, unlike classical psychoanalytic theory, the behavioral perspective did not develop as a single comprehensive theory aimed at explaining all behavior. Rather, a number of theories, often employing similar language but each describing a different aspect of the learning process, were suggested.

Classical Conditioning

The demonstration by Pavlov that a dog could be taught to salivate in response to a previously neutral stimulus served to focus attention on the process of classical conditioning. Pavlov's basic demonstration was relatively simple. Meat powder (the unconditioned stimulus) initially produced salivation by the dog. A tone (the conditioned stimulus) was then repeatedly sounded, followed by presentation of the meat powder. Soon the tone itself produced salivation prior to the appearance of the meat powder. This salivation in response to the tone was termed a conditioned response. Once the conditioned response was learned, the sounding of a similar, but not identical, tone caused the dog to salivate. *Generalization* from the original conditioned stimulus had occurred. The dog, in contrast, could also be taught to salivate to a particular tone and not to others. This was the process of *discrimination* training.

Two early studies based on this model stand out because of the great impact they had on the application of classical conditioning to human problems. Watson and Rayner's (1920) now-famous case of Little Albert was an early illustration of the conditioning of fear. Albert, an 11-month-old child, initially showed no fear reactions to a variety of objects, including a white rat. He did, however, exhibit fear when a loud sound was produced by the striking of a steel bar. Watson and Rayner attempted to condition fear of the white rat by producing the loud clanging sound each time Albert reached for the animal. After several of these pairings, Albert reacted with crying and avoidance when the rat was presented without the noise (see Figure 3-4). Thus, it appeared that fear could be learned through classical conditioning. Needless to say, there are significant ethical difficulties with conducting studies such as Watson and Rayner's, and therefore behavioral researchers have tended to focus their attention on applying classical conditioning principles to the treatment of disorders.

The second landmark study was Mary Cover Jones's (1924) demonstration that the principles of classical conditioning could be applied to the removal of fearful responses. Peter, a boy of 2 years and 10 months, exhibited a fear of furry objects. Jones first attempted to treat Peter by placing him with children who liked the rabbit and petted it. The treatment appeared to be working but was interrupted when Peter became ill for nearly two months. Just prior to his return to treatment, he was also frightened by a large dog. With Peter's fear back at its original level, Jones decided to treat Peter with a counterconditioning procedure. This involved

allowing Peter to eat some of his favorite foods while the animal was moved progressively closer, thus pairing the feared stimulus with pleasantness. The procedure was apparently successful in reducing the boy's fears, and he was ultimately able to hold the animal by himself.

This case demonstration lacks sufficient control, and we cannot draw conclusions regarding the effectiveness of the procedures derived from classical conditioning. Of additional concern is Jones's inclusion of nonfearful children in treatment sessions. Did the presence of the children, like the food, make the situation pleasant, or did they also serve as models for nonfearful behavior? Despite these limitations, Jones's contribution was important. This demonstration helped to stimulate the development of numerous treatments based on the principles of classical conditioning.

Instrumental (Operant) Conditioning

The approach to learning set forth in Thorndike's *Law of Effect* and in the work of B. F. Skinner and his followers is probably the behavioral perspective most extensively applied to children's disorders. Instrumental conditioning places emphasis on the consequences of behavior. Behavior is acquired or reduced, is emitted in some circumstances but not in others,

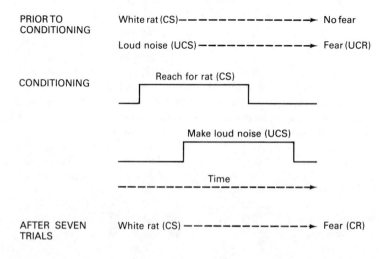

Figure 3–4 Watson and Rayner's case of Little Albert. The repeated pairing of an unconditioned stimulus (noise) that produced fear with a previously neutral stimulus (rat) resulted in the rat itself producing a conditioned response of fear.

through processes of consequation such as reinforcement, extinction, and punishment (see Table 3-3). As is the case for classical conditioning, the majority of efforts derived from the instrumental or operant conditioning paradigm have focused on the treatment rather than the etiology of disordered behavior.

Williams's (1959) report on altering a 21-month-old child's tantrums is an early example of the use of these principles for the treatment of childhood disorders. Following a long illness the child had developed severe tantrums. It was assumed that the parents had been reinforcing this behavior by attending to it. For example, the child's screaming as the parents left his bedroom was reinforced by their remaining in the room. After determining that there were no medical problems, a program of removing the reinforcement for the tantrum behavior (extinction) was begun. After leisurely putting the child to bed, the parents left and did not reenter the room. Although the child cried for forty-five minutes the first night, by the tenth occasion he no longer fussed when left alone. No negative side effects occurred, and the child was reported to be well-adjusted at 3 years of age.

The principles of instrumental conditioning have increasingly been applied to a broad range of difficult and complex problems, and the treatment procedures themselves have become more varied and complex. For example, Lovaas and his colleagues have employed instrumental learning principles to treat self-destructive, self-help, and speech behaviors of autistic children (Lovaas and Newsom, 1976). Token economy programs, which involve a set of rules for how tokens can be earned and exchanged for backup reinforcers such as prizes and privileges, have been applied to problem behaviors in the classroom (O'Leary and

Table 3-3   Some Frequently Employed Instrumental Conditioning Terms

Term	Definition	Example
Positive Reinforcement	A stimulus is presented following a response (*contingent* upon the response), increasing the frequency of that response.	Praise for good behavior increases the likelihood of good behavior.
Negative Reinforcement	A stimulus is withdrawn contingent upon a response, and its removal increases the frequency of that response.	Removal of mother's demands following a child's tantrum increases the likelihood of tantrums.
Extinction	A weakening of a learned response is produced when the reinforcement that followed it no longer occurs.	Parents ignore bad behavior, and it decreases.
Punishment	A response is followed by either an unpleasant stimulus or the removal of a pleasant stimulus, thereby decreasing the frequency of the response.	A parent scolds a child for hitting, and the child stops hitting; food is removed from the table after a child spits, and the spitting stops.
Generalization	A response is made to a new stimulus that is different from, but similar to, the stimulus present during learning.	A child is fearful of all men with mustaches like that of a stern uncle.
Discrimination	The process by which a stimulus comes to signal that a certain response is likely to be followed by a particular consequence.	An adult's smile indicates that a child's request is likely to be granted.
Shaping	A desired behavior that is not in the child's repertoire is taught by rewarding responses that are increasingly similar to (*successive approximations* of) the desired response.	A mute child is taught to talk by initially reinforcing any sound, then something that sounds a little like the word, and so on.

O'Leary, 1977) and to the behavior of predelinquent boys in a group home (cf. Phillips, Phillips, Fixsen, and Wolf, 1971). The specific applications of these procedures will be discussed throughout the succeeding chapters of this book. They all share the assumption that problem behavior can be changed through a learning process and that the focus on treatment should be on the consequences of behavior.

Observational Learning

The investigator most widely associated with *observational learning*, or *modeling*, is Albert Bandura, who, along with his associates, has conducted a large number of studies that bear upon the genesis and treatment of childhood disorders. It has been demonstrated that children can acquire a variety of behaviors—aggression, cooperation, delay of gratification, sharing,—by watching others perform them. These studies suggest how observational learning can lead to both the acquisition and removal of problem behaviors.

Studies by Bandura and his colleagues on children's imitation of aggressive behavior illustrate how a deviant behavior may be acquired through the observation of a model. In one well-known experiment, Bandura (1965) showed nursery school children a five-minute film in which an adult exhibited a number of unusual, aggressive behaviors toward a Bobo doll. The behaviors were also accompanied by distinctive verbalizations. One group of children saw a final scene in which the model was rewarded for aggression; another group saw a final scene in which the model was punished; and the remaining group did not see any final scene. Later, each child entered a playroom and was left alone to play freely. The child could thus engage in imitative aggressive behavior with the Bobo doll or in nonimitative behavior with the doll or other toys. As you might expect, the children who had seen the model punished exhibited far fewer imitative aggressive responses in the playroom. The experimenter then reentered the room and told the children that for each act of imitative aggression that he or she could reproduce, a treat would be given. This incentive eliminated the effects of vicarious punishment, as all three groups showed the same high level of imitative aggression. The study demonstrated that acquisition of the aggressive behavior had occurred and, moreover, that its performance depended on certain environmental "payoffs."

Bandura and others have also demonstrated

Observation of another child "getting his way" because of aggressive behavior can result in a child, even the "victim", being more aggressive in the future.

the usefulness of imitative learning in the treatment of children's problems. Bandura, Grusec, and Menlove (1967), for example, demonstrated that children's fear of dogs could be overcome by having them observe another child fearlessly approach the dog in a graded sequence. In this study the restraints on the dog were gradually lessened, and the model's closeness and duration of contact with the dog gradually increased.

While the phenomenon of learning by imitation seems straightforward and simple, the process of observational learning is actually quite complex. Attention has been given to the impact of numerous variables on the imitative process. For example, multiple models, conflicting models, and attributes of the models themselves are among the variables that have been demonstrated to affect whether imitation will occur. In addition to direct imitation of modeled behavior, observation can lead to inhibition or disinhibition of behavior. For example, a child who observes another child being scolded for running about may become quieter in other ways (inhibition). Observing a great deal of shooting and fighting on television, in contrast, may lead a child to exhibit other forms of aggression, such as verbal abuse and physical roughness, with peers (disinhibition). In neither case is the exact behavior of the model imitated; rather, a class of behaviors becomes less or more likely to occur due to observation of a model.

The complex processes that are required for observational learning to occur have also been described (Bandura, 1977b). Imitation relies on the child attending to the salient features of the model's behavior. The child must also organize and encode this information and remember it. The acquired behavior must then be performed when it is anticipated that it will meet with the desired consequences. The process of learning by observation is viewed by Bandura and others as more than a simple mimicking of behavior. The social learning perspective that has developed from this and other research has placed increasing emphasis on cognitive processes such as attention, memory, and problem solving.

SOME OTHER PERSPECTIVES

Other perspectives on childhood behavioral disorders have expanded on existing paradigms or have added some distinct and different viewpoints to the field. These perspectives are described briefly here, and further detail is provided in later chapters, where their application to specific childhood disorders is illustrated.

The Cognitive-Behavioral Perspective

Recent trends in American psychology have resulted in increased emphasis on cognitive processes. Research and theory in the areas of learning, personality, and developmental psychology, for example, reflect an increased awareness of processes such as thinking, imagery, expectancy, information processing, and attention (cf. Bolles, 1972; Epstein, 1979; Flavell, 1977; Greeno, 1980; Horowitz, 1979; Lieberman, 1979; Mischel, 1979; Neisser, 1967). This was not always the case. Watson, Skinner, and other early advocates of the behavioral perspective, in reaction to then-existing viewpoints, deliberately and specifically ignored the role of mediating events such as thoughts and images. It was argued that since these events could not be subjected to direct observation, they could not be studied. Influenced by the recent cognitive trend, some behaviorally oriented clinicians began to suggest that increased attention be paid to the role of cognitive processes (cf. Bandura, 1977b; Mahoney, 1977; Meichenbaum, 1977). It was suggested that behaviors are learned and maintained by interacting systems of external events and cognitions, and that cognitive factors influence whether environmental events are attended to, how events are perceived, and whether these events affect future behavior. What distinguished this new approach was the requirement that within the behavioral perspective, mediational processes must ultimately be measurable. They must also be subject to empirical evaluation.

The cognitive-behavioral perspective that has resulted has produced an interest in phenomena such as self-efficacy beliefs—an expectation that one can produce positive outcomes. It is hypothesized that behavior change occurs through changes in self-efficacy beliefs. Several different treatments (for example, modeling, reinforcement, verbal persuasion) may all help change a child's behavior, because they each can boost the child's perceived self-efficacy (Bandura, 1977a). The cognitive-behavioral perspective is also likely to attend to phenomena such as the child's self-statements and problem-solving strategies. These are aspects of the learning process that did not receive attention from earlier behaviorists.

In recent years a number of investigators have incorporated thinking, imagining, self-statements, self-control, and problem solving into the development of treatments for childhood behavior disorders (cf. Kendall and Hollon, 1979; Meichenbaum, 1979). Meichenbaum and Goodman's (1971) multifaceted training program to teach hyperactive children to "think before they act" is the prototype of much of this work. In this program children experienced the following sequential steps: (1) While the child watched, an adult model self-instructed aloud while performing the desired task; (2) the child performed the task as the adult instructed aloud; (3) the child self-instructed aloud while performing the task; (4) the child whispered the instructions while doing the

task; and (5) the child used private speech to guide performance. The number of self-statements employed by the child was then enlarged over several training sessions. When compared to control children who had been exposed to the same task material but given no self-instructional training, treated children did seem to learn to think before they acted. This was true immediately following treatment and at a one-month follow-up. These procedures have influenced the development of treatments for a variety of disorders.

The Psychoeducational Perspective

What we refer to here as the psychoeducational perspective is a view that arises out of an approach to working with children rather than a conceptual paradigm. Children's problems are viewed within an educational context, and commitment to reeducation is what characterizes the variety of approaches that fall within this rubric. Box 3–2 describes a program, Project Re-ED, that illustrates the appreciable potential of this perspective.

The term *special education* has also been used to describe the efforts of educators to deal with the problems of atypical children. That the vast majority of children receive extended formal education as a right rather than as a privilege is a given in today's society. This has not al-

Working with children in an educational context and a commitment to education as a means of intervention characterize the psychoeducational approach.

Box 3-2   Project Re-ED: A Psychoeducational and Ecological Approach

Project Re-ED ("a project for the reeducation of emotionally disturbed children") is an outstanding example of the use of the psychoeducational perspective that also takes into account the larger social context. Begun in the early 1960s at George Peabody College for Teachers, Project Re-ED has been detailed by Nicholas Hobbs in *The Troubled and Troubling Child* (1982). Twenty-three residential programs are currently operating, scattered across nine states, all having evolved from a national demonstration project funded largely by the National Institute of Mental Health and Tennessee and North Carolina. The programs vary somewhat, but they share a common philosophy. The children range in age from 1 to 18 years; many display seriously disturbed behaviors, as captured in the following description (Hobbs, 1982):

Cissy, a tall, slender, *eleven-year-old* girl, was brought into a hospital emergency room in a state of hysteria, alternately screaming and crying, her eyes bulging , her extremities shaking, her body covered with perspiration. . . .

During the first eleven years of her life, home for Cissy was a variety of houses in slum neighborhoods, peopled by a variety of relatives, four younger siblings, her mother's assorted men friends, and a drunken, paranoid stepfather . . . . A severe beating with a belt followed Cissy's slightest deviation from what her mother considered proper behavior. . . .

In school, soft spoken and affable, Cissy was generally accepted by her fifth-grade peers, but she had no sustained relationships with them. On the playground, she stayed on the fringe of a group, preferring to ingratiate herself with the teacher in charge. Academically, Cissy never functioned at a satisfactory level. She was retained in second grade, and psychological testing was recommended. Poor reading skills interfered with comprehension in all content subjects. She complained frequently that words disappeared from the page she was reading. (p. 160)

From the beginning the planners of Project Re-ED turned away from the traditional psychotherapy model, deciding it was too expensive and was impossible because of a limited supply of therapists. Instead, they employed various other "talented workers" (usually trained at the master's level) to carry out educational, psychological, and ecological strategies. At the heart of the project is the teacher-counselor and the liaison teacher-counselor. The individuals filling these roles are selected on the basis of their decency, training, ability to give and receive affection, hopefulness, confidence, joy, and commitment to the idea that disturbed children can be helped by reeducation with academic and social behavior. The counselors work and live with the children, defining each child's problem, choosing the means to bring about change, specifying the goals, carrying out the plan, and evaluating outcomes. The liaison teacher-counselor works with parents, schools, and the community to which the child will return.

The aim of the project is reeducation in the broadest sense. A small group of children is assigned to three teacher-counselors. Mornings are usually reserved for formal academic training. Always committed to academic competence, Project Re-ED has become even more convinced of the value of competence to a child's personal growth and social effectiveness. Rejected is the long-held assumption that emotionally disturbed children must be treated for their illness before they are able to learn. Perhaps the reverse is true—or more likely, learning and adjustment problems interact and must be continually addressed. In Hobbs's words, "The mastery of basic learning skills is a prerequisite to overcoming emotional problems." (p. 290) But the children are also taught the things that others take for granted: to catch a ball, go camping, improve one's appearance, write a note to a friend, avoid an argument, and the like. Principles of learning (for example, reinforcement or extinction) guide educational efforts. The days at the residential school are crammed with learning experiences embedded in the safety of structure, trusting relationships, and a belief in the possibility of competence.

At all times Project Re-ED children are viewed as part of a large interacting social system that includes the family, neighborhood, school, and legal and other systems. The liaison teacher-counselor keeps in touch with parents and the school, monitors home visits, plans for the return of the child to the community, and consults about ongoing or potential conflicts. It is no coincidence that the title of Hobbs's book carries the word "troubling," for there is keen awareness that children's problems are intricately tied to their environments and to how they are perceived by the major figures in their lives.

Project Re-ED has been able to conduct some evaluations of its effectiveness. During the development of one of the early programs, data were collected on 120 children previous to enrollment, at discharge, and at six and again at eighteen months after they returned home. All were in regular classrooms at the last follow-up. Project Re-ED children had made substantial gains as compared to a group of "normal" youngsters and a group of children judged to have comparable problems who received help from school psychologists and others. The Project children held more positive self-concepts, had better control of their behavior, had gained academically, and were rated by teachers and parents as having improved. It is thus not surprising that Project Re-ED has endured and expanded.

---

ways been the case, nor has education always been assigned an important role in dealing with children's problems.

Lilly (1979a) has provided an overview of the history of special education from the early nineteenth century to the present. The initial view of the special education approach, particularly for the mentally retarded, was optimistic. Residential treatment centers were developed so as to prepare handicapped individuals to return to the community. Residential schools evolved, however, into permanent residences for more severely handicapped children. Moreover, little attention was given to persons whose problems were milder. Compulsory education laws then forced the educational systems to provide services for the less severely handicapped.

Another development—the construction of general tests of intelligence—had a long-lasting and far-reaching impact on special education. These tests defined a new group of mildly handicapping conditions. The presence of "mildly mentally retarded" children and, later, children with "mild emotional disturbance" in the school systems led to the development of special classes as a means of working with these children. With expansion of services, legislation for mandatory special education, and the development of university-based research and training programs, special educational services

experienced rapid growth beginning in the 1950s.

The application of the psychoeducational perspective and special education interventions to particular problems will be described in later chapters of this book. However, it is appropriate to recognize here two matters that have been of particular concern (Lilly, 1979a). One is that special educators have been prominent among those who have questioned the necessity of employing traditional categories or special labels with children. They have often led the fight against the use of categorization and for recognition of the role of social and environmental factors in the etiology of childhood problems. (The controversy concerning the use of labels and categories is discussed more fully in Chapter 5.)

The second issue concerns the decision as to whether children should be placed in special classes. Although special classes were originally developed to help children who were not succeeding in regular classrooms, a number of educators began to question their efficacy. In a classic article entitled "Special education for the mildly-retarded—is much of it justifiable?" Dunn (1968) concluded that there was no evidence to justify the existence of special classes. However, the question of whether children with problems should be placed in special classrooms or "mainstreamed" into the regular school system remains a complex and controversial one, the impact of which has become far-reaching (Hallahan and Kauffman, 1978; Lilly, 1979a). Drawing attention to this concern is one of the current contributions of the psychoeducational approach.

The Family Systems Perspective

Virtually all approaches to behavior disorders that include social environmental influences acknowledge the family as having a major impact. A variety of viewpoints might describe how a family factor (for example, interparental conflict) contributes to a problem in the child (acting out or aggressive behavior). These family issues might be addressed in therapy sessions with the child, or the parents might be seen by a separate therapist. Alternatively, family members might be asked to participate in therapy sessions so as to assist in the child's change. Family therapy sessions have increasingly been employed by a variety of clinicians. The focus in the majority of these approaches, however, has remained on the designated child. The family's role is to assist the child in achieving change.

Family systems theorists, however, view family influences in a somewhat different way. Although no one theory guides this work, a central thesis is that families are more complicated than the sum of their parts (Bowen, 1980). The family is viewed as a complex social system that has designated the child as the "identified patient." The child's symptoms play a role in maintaining this system. Therapy, from such a perspective, must address family themes and methods of communication rather than individual child behaviors and parental reactions. Therefore, there are two key concepts involved in this viewpoint: a nonlinear, systems theory of family influences and a focus on the family rather than the individual as the problem unit.

Most explanations of family influences are linear; that is, A is seen as causing B. For example, it might be reasoned that family stress operating on a child with a certain psychological and biological make-up may cause a particular psychosomatic disease. The systems

Figure 3–5 The model of psychosomatic disease described by Minuchin illustrates a family systems perspective on psychological dysfunction. *From Minuchin, Rosman, and Baker, 1978. Reprinted by permission of the publishers.*

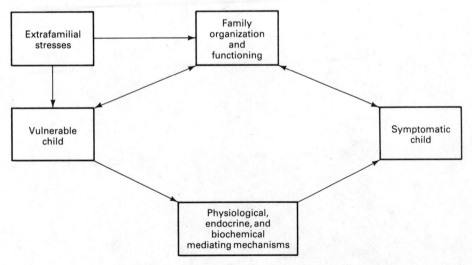

perspective, in contrast, suggests a circular relationship of parts, with complex and interrelated feedback mechanisms. Figure 3-5 illustrates how Minuchin, a family systems therapist, views the problem of psychosomatic disease differently from the linear model described above. The central argument of the systems perspective is that the behavior of any child cannot be attributed to biology or merely to a *reaction* to some outside agent. Rather, the view is offered that the child is engaged in an ongoing *interaction* in the family system. It is the system's interactions that are problematic and that maintain the child's "symptomatic" behavior.

The family systems perspective is not one but rather several different approaches offered by Bowen, Haley, Weakland, Watzlawick, Selvini Palazzoli, Minuchin, and others. Clinicians from other perspectives have become increasingly aware of the need to address the complex interaction of children's problems and family variables (Griest and Wells, 1983). All agree that it is unlikely that the child will be able to change unless the family changes. Furthermore, family systems themselves exist in and are affected by larger systems (Wahler and Graves, 1983). The family system thus may be influenced by relationships with extended family or public agencies. A systems perspective suggests a sensitivity to multiple levels of influence.

SUMMARY

In this chapter we have attempted to introduce the major perspectives that have guided investigators of childhood behavior disorders. Perspectives provide general assumptions that direct both researchers and practitioners. They help explain why a particular disorder may be seen differently or similarly by different investigators and why therapists may suggest different interventions. Later, as we look at particular disorders, it will become even more obvious how perspectives guide those interested in children's problems.

4

RESEARCH: ITS ROLE AND METHODS

THE NATURE OF SCIENCE

Observation and Measurement
Reliability
Validity

BASIC METHODS OF RESEARCH

Simple Descriptive Methods
Correlational Research
Experimental Research
Mixed Designs

LONGITUDINAL AND CROSS-SECTIONAL STRATEGIES

ETHICAL ISSUES IN RESEARCH WITH CHILDREN

SUMMARY

The developmental approach and various theoretical perspectives of psychopathology provide both a framework and an array of hypotheses that can be brought to bear on the genesis, maintenance, and treatment of children's problems. At first blush it might appear that the study of problem behavior could be handled with dispatch; after all, as humans, shouldn't we find it relatively easy to understand human behavior? But the phenomenon we are studying is extremely complex. Moreover, while speculation abounds as to the "what" and "how" of unusual or deficient behavior, our goal is to accumulate objective knowledge through scientific research.

THE NATURE OF SCIENCE

The word *science* comes from the Latin word for knowledge, or to know, but it specifically refers to knowledge gained by a particular method of inquiry. The application of the scientific method to human behavior is a relatively recent historical event. Humans have long considered themselves special creatures, too complicated and mysterious for scientific study. Even today we hear that scientific inquiry might be inappropriate or perhaps even dangerous when applied to humans. For the most part, though, psychology, the other social sciences, biology, and medicine are committed to the view that the scientific method can provide the most valid information about childhood disorders.

The overall purpose of science is to describe phenomena and to offer explanations for them. Investigators may wonder: How many parents use physical punishment as a means of disciplining their children? What will happen if a "slow" child is provided with an enriched school experience? Why are particular children withdrawn socially? Sometimes it is necessary only to describe, count, or measure a phenomenon in order to answer such questions. At other times it is necessary to determine the exact conditions under which a phenomenon occurs or its relationship to other variables.

Determining relationships increases our understanding of behavior, and this is especially true when cause-effect relationships can be demonstrated. In examining relationships among variables, researchers often try to test specific ideas or hypotheses. The advantage of hypothesis testing is that it tends to build knowledge systematically rather than haphazardly. For this reason, hypothesis testing is held in high esteem by scientists.

Theoretical concepts and assumptions are likely to guide the hypotheses forwarded as well as the research goals, choice of variables, procedures, analyses, and conclusions. In the early stage of research, theoretical concepts may be little more than hunches or guesses based on informal observations (Harrison, 1979). Later they may be more specific and more closely tied to a web of theorems. Whenever it occurs, the generation of ideas and hypotheses is a subjective, creative process. The scientific method demands that the hypotheses then be tested in order to establish whether they are genuine "discoveries" or incorrect guesses (Achenbach, 1978b). However, the results of any one investigation rarely prove that a hypothesis is correct or incorrect; instead, they provide evidence for or against the hypothesis. In turn, a hypothesis that is supported serves as evidence for the accuracy and power of the theoretical underpinnings. A failed hypothesis, in contrast, serves to disprove or limit the theory. As Harrison notes:

Thus science progresses through a combination of observations and theories. The observations form the basis of the theories. The theories summarize the observations, and direct researchers' attention to new observations by making predictions. The new observations test the accuracy of the theories and may require new theories if they disagree with the predictions. (1979, p. 7)

As researchers seek to refine theoretical concepts of human behavior, they are likely to ask a variety of questions and employ a variety of methods. In behavioral research the diversity of theoretical frameworks and the enormous scope of the field itself calls for different subjects, in different settings. Subhuman animals may be studied because certain research procedures are ethically unacceptable with humans, or because there is an interest in cross-species comparisons. Cross-cultural investigations are helpful in discovering the entire range of human behaviors and in providing clues to the determinants of behavioral diversity. Age-related developmental studies shed light on the typical course of change over time. The subjects, settings, purposes of research, and practical considerations all play a part in the selection of the particular research method employed. Regardless of the method involved, however, observation and measurement, reliability, and validity are always important considerations.

Observation and Measurement

At the heart of all scientific endeavors are observation and measurement, and so the scientific method can be applied only to aspects of the world for which these processes can be used. Both observation and measurement have been troublesome but not unachievable for behavioral scientists. It is relatively simple to observe and measure overt action, but thought and emotion, which are intricately entwined with action, are more elusive. In the attempt to tap all sources of information, behavioral scientists make many kinds of observations and measurements: They directly observe overt behavior with or without special apparatus; record physiological functioning of the heart, skin, brain, sense organs, muscles, and so on; ask persons to report or rate their own behavior, feelings, and thoughts; and collect the reports of other people about the subject of investigation. Such endeavors may be conducted in the laboratory or in natural settings, and they vary in the confidence and importance given to them.

Reliability

In addition to assuming that knowledge can be gained by observation, the scientific method also assumes that events repeat themselves, given identical or similar conditions. Thus, they can be observed again by others. If the same events are not reported under similar conditions, the original finding is considered unreliable, or inconsistent, and remains questionable. The need for reliability of results places a burden on researchers to clearly and concisely conceptualize, observe, measure, and communicate their findings so that others may replicate and judge their work. Science is a public endeavor that must be open to the scrutiny and evaluations of others.

Validity

While reliability refers to the repeatability, or consistency, of scientific results, validity directs attention to the correctness, soundness, or appropriateness of scientific findings. Although the term *validity* is used in different ways, when applied to conclusions drawn from research, the main concern is with internal and external validity.

Internal validity refers to the extent to which alternative explanations for a scientific result can be ruled out. Obviously, it is not an issue when explanation is not offered, as when the purpose of research is simply to describe phenomena. In all other instances internal validity is of crucial importance (Campbell and Stanley, 1963). It is maximized by research designs and procedures that build in control over the variables that may affect the outcome of the experiment. By controlling the procedures, the investigator is able to speak confidently about the exact conditions to which the subjects had been exposed. By controlling the influence of extraneous variables, the researcher optimizes the likelihood of being able to attribute the results of the study to the experimental variable.

The use of control groups is virtually always required to control for the influence of extraneous variables. For example, an investigator who wishes to test the effectiveness of a certain drug could expose subjects to a trial test with the drug and measure their behavior in some way. However, any change in behavior that occurred could be attributed to the subjects' expectations that the drug might cause change. In order to control for this possible extraneous influence, the researcher would have to include a placebo group in the design of the study. Persons in the placebo group would receive some kind of pill consisting only of a chemically inert substance. Neither group of participants would be informed, however, as to whether it had received the drug or the inert substance. In analyzing the results, comparison of the groups would allow change in the drug group that was greater than change in the placebo group to be attributed to the effects of the drug.

External validity asks the question of generalizability: To what populations and situations can the results of an investigation be generalized (Campbell and Stanley, 1963)? Broad generalizability is of obvious advantage but, in fact, cannot be assumed. It cannot automatically be concluded, for example, that research findings based on a particular population of preschool girls hold for older girls or for boys. Similarly, the results of laboratory studies may or may not generalize to the world outside of the laboratory. The question of generalizability is rarely if ever completely answered, although evidence increases as various populations and settings are tested. It is ironic that attempts to increase internal validity may decrease external validity because the former requires controls that may create artificial situations. This dilemma is one of several that must be taken into account in the selection of a research method.

BASIC METHODS OF RESEARCH

Although all research methods involve some kind of observation, they nevertheless vary in important ways. In the following discussion several basic strategies are described. As will be obvious, each has its weaknesses and strengths in terms of appropriateness and the kinds of information that it can or cannot provide. The limitations of research methods make it virtually impossible to rely on one method to answer all our questions. For example, certain

types of research cannot be conducted for ethical reasons, while practical considerations preclude other kinds of investigations. Because behavior is complex and influenced by many variables, its description and causes are not easy to discern. Thus, the best research evidence usually is acquired by interpretation of the results from different methods of study. It is the *confluence of research strategies* that provides the most accurate and complete picture of behavior.

Simple Descriptive Methods

The descriptive strategy of research in childhood psychopathology is designed to describe events or phenomena in order to gain knowledge of the course, possible determinants, correlates, and outcome of behavior problems. Description is frequently offered in two ways: the clinical case study and systematic direct observation.

The Clinical Case Study. Perhaps the most common type of descriptive study is the case study, or case report, that recounts the history, problem, and often the treatment of an individual child. The following is part of a case history of an adolescent male who displayed forty-eight rather than the typical forty-six chromosomes, with one extra X and one extra Y (48, XXYY). The author's stated purpose was to elucidate the psychodynamics involved and to compare the adolescent's behavioral disabilities with those previously associated with other aberrant chromosome complements.

The boy is described as having been a "happy baby" who was somewhat slow in walking, and did not speak until age 4. During his earliest years, there were two 1-week separations from his mother. No problems related to the separations were reported by the parents. However, the boy was always afraid of the dark, and his insistence that someone else sleep in his room with him has continued up to his present age of 16.

His mother sought a diagnostic evaluation of him at age 4 because of his slow development.

Psychological testing revealed a full-scale IQ of 96, and a neurological examination revealed no demonstrable abnormalities. It was recommended that he be enrolled in nursery school. The nursery school teachers reported to the mother that the boy would not defend himself and could be easily victimized by other children.

At age 9, the boy began to roam out of class, and later to roam out of school. He complained that other students picked on him, although his teachers did not feel that this was different from what had gone before. The boy developed a fear of the school bus, and by the time he was 13, he was hiding when he knew the school bus was coming. He felt himself to be a failure in school, had many fears about being beaten at school, and often simply roamed the hallways on days when he actually did enter the school building.

Over the years, the parents made many attempts to obtain help for their son. When he was 7, his mother and father attended a mental health clinic with him for approximately a year, where they were seen by a psychiatric social worker. She recommended that the entire family of five be entered into family therapy, but they did not follow through.

From the age of 12 until 14, the boy was seen by a school psychologist. Presenting problems were fear in the school building, manifested by staying outside of the classroom or not attending school at all; low frustration tolerance and short attention span, manifested by destroying his school work when it became difficult for him; difficulty with other students, manifested by provoking them; and extreme anxiety, manifested by fleeing from any situation that was frustrating or difficult for him. Treatment techniques consisted largely of reward for doing what he was supposed to do in school. Although there was some improvement, inpatient psychiatric hospitalization was sought when he was 14, in order to clarify his diagnosis and to outline a treatment plan.

By this time, the boy's antisocial behavior had begun to include setting small fires, stealing money from home, or stealing objects from home and selling them. A week before hospitalization, he had been playing with a toy cap gun, which he pointed at a passing car. The driver of the car thought that the gun was real, and notified the police. When the police apprehended him, he falsely admitted to having committed burglaries and setting fires. As a result of this incident, his parents subsequently tended to say that he "will confess to anything" when they were informed that he was suspected of having been involved in some antisocial activity.

Several other curious symptoms were elicited during the hospitalization. It was learned that the boy had developed a habit of putting on layers of clothing which included underwear, pajamas, and several pairs of pants. He was extremely fearful of gym classes and the locker room. He had begun taking his mother's clothes out of her closet and smearing them with things from the kitchen, such as catsup and mayonnaise, and then hiding them. When confronted with these behaviors, he usually denied them. . . .

Upon admission to The Woods Schools, at age 14 years 10 months, the boy presented as a 6-ft. 4-inch youngster with a high-pitched voice and a rather awkward gait. Pertinent physical findings included a small amount of axillary, abdominal, and facial hair, and very small testes. His somewhat infantile presentation was accentuated by two missing side teeth and a slight lisp. Intelligence testing again showed him to be functioning in the mild range of mental retardation, with a mental age of 8 years, 10 months, or a full-scale IQ of 60, on the Slosson Intelligence Test. Academic achievement levels were at about the third-grade level in mathematics and reading. (Mansheim, 1979, pp. 366–367)

The case study continues to describe the adolescent's anxiety, somatic complaints, episodes of stealing, interpersonal reactions, and psychosexual behavior. The report also compares these behaviors with behaviors previously associated with the 47, XXY and 47, XYY chromosome complements and suggests a disturbance in early basic trust and family dynamics.

In presenting this case study the investigator has traced one individual's development in considerable detail—a contribution that is largely lacking in other research methods. The reader is thus given a clear example of the disabilities associated with the 48, XXYY chromosome complement. A major strength of the case study is its power to illustrate. It may also suggest hypotheses. Nevertheless, all case studies are limited in the conclusions that can be drawn (Liebert and Spiegler, 1978). The life events described go back in time and the accuracy and completeness of retrospective data are always difficult to determine. Indeed, another investigator, drawing on the same information base, could present a quite different picture. Moreover, almost any interpretation can be applied to the descriptions, with no guidelines to judge it. Finally, as in all single-subject research, the descriptions cannot be assumed to generalize to others. In this case there is as yet no reason to believe that all or even many individuals with the aberrant 48, XXYY chromosome complement will display similar disabilities.

Systematic Direct Observation. Another descriptive method is systematic direct observation of individuals in either the natural environment or a simulated laboratory setting. Such description of phenomena (and classification that may accompany it) is often considered a first step in the development of a science. In their book on direct observation and measurement of behavior, Hutt and Hutt (1970) have noted that psychology, in the attempt to become a respectable science, may have too rapidly jumped to manipulative research that examines the *whys* of behavior. They argue that it is crucial to understand *what* constitutes behavior.

An example of the direct observation approach is an investigation by Leach (1972) of eighteen normal preschoolers and six preschoolers who had been diagnosed as having

Direct observation allows the researcher to systematically measure behavior as it is occurring.

difficulty in separating from their mothers. The purpose of the study was to reveal the social interactions of the children. All the youngsters were observed, with and without their mothers, while at free play in the nursery school. Data were collected on child-children, child-mother, and child-teacher interactions. Observations were made for each child, using a running commentary that addressed numerous behavioral items (Table 4-1). The observation required a great deal of preparation in defining, recognizing, and accurately recording the behaviors. The investigator was able, then, to ask an array of questions about the "Bad Separators" as compared to the normal children. Among the findings was that the Bad Separators directed

Table 4-1   Examples of the Behavior Items Recorded from Direct Observations of Normal Children and Those Considered to Have Separation Problems

Approach—The child walks toward a person, or object. (If the child runs towards a person, it is recorded as *run*.)

Avoid (or side-step)—The child is moving in one direction, but is confronted by an object, or person, and steps to the side, and may also bend the body away from obstruction.

Bend over to—This action is most often performed by adults to children. The upper body is inclined towards the child, or overhangs it.

Dress—This is a general term to cover all alterations to the clothing, such as putting on jerseys, tying up shoes. The teacher usually does these things for the children.

Follow—The child *walks* (or *runs*) towards a person who is moving away from it.

Get object—This covers a variety of reaching gestures, to obtain an object.

Give—An object, held in the child's hand or hands, is held out for another person to grasp and is then released; or the object may be placed on the other person's lap (usually mother's).

Grab (or *snatch*)—The child reaches for an object and pulls it abruptly towards itself, often with the body twisted round so that the object is rendered out of reach of another person.

Help—This is a word which I use frequently, but think it should really be split into the component actions. One person (usually an adult) assists another to perform some manipulative game or task, by a complex array of actions: *showing,* taking from and doing for, *giving,* arranging furniture or small objects, etc., often accompanied by verbal instructions as well.

Hit—Blurton Jones (1967) described a hit, or beat, as 'an overarm blow with the palm side of the lightly clenched fist. The arm is sharply bent at the elbow and raised to a vertical position, then brought down with great force on the opponent, hitting any part of him that gets in the way.' (But in our nursery I have seldom seen a powerful hit of this kind.) Sometimes a child may try to hit a person, and miss; or obviously 'aim to miss'—and this I record as *tryhit*.

Avert—The eyes are cast down or sideways, and the head is usually tilted down and to the side, thus avoiding eye-contact with another person.

From Leach, 1972.

less behavior to and were less responsive to other children. Paradoxically, they did not interact more with their mothers, although they did stay more with them. These children apparently were quite deprived of the opportunity to become socially adept.

The Leach investigation is a sophisticated observational study; the techniques had been well worked out in advance, and statistical comparison was possible between the two groups of children. Even when only one group is involved, direct observation has the benefit of systematically measuring behavior as it is actually occurring. In this regard the method surpasses the clinical case study, which is a retrospective account of global behavior. On the other hand, since direct observation is confined to the par-

ticular behaviors selected for study, it sometimes lacks the richness of the case study.

Correlational Research

Correlational strategies go beyond simple description, by determining whether a relationship exists between or among variables. Researchers typically calculate a correlation coefficient, which is a quantitative measure of the existence, direction, and strength of the relationship. Correlational research is extremely useful in many instances. When ethical considerations preclude manipulation, it is frequently possible to do correlational research. Suppose, for example, that an investigator seeks knowledge about the impact of child abuse, poor nutrition, or family conflict on children's problems. It clearly would be ethically impossible to manipulate these factors by exposing children to them. However, unfortunate as it is, children are exposed to these situations in the naturally occurring environment, and correlational investigation allows us to examine whether these situations are related to children's behavior. Correlational strategies are also useful in cases in which initial exploration is the goal of research. Here the researcher may first want to determine whether any relationships exist among variables before specific hypotheses are advanced.

In its simplest form the question asked in correlational research is: Are factors X and Y related, and, if so, in what direction are they related, and how strongly? The first step is to select a sample of children that represents the population of interest. Next, two scores must be obtained from each child, one a measure of variable X and the other a measure of variable Y. Statistical analysis of these data must then be performed. In this case the Pearson product-moment coefficient, r, could be computed, and determination could be made that the finding is not simply a chance event.*

The value of Pearson r, which always ranges between $+1.00$ and -1.00, indicates the direction and the strength of the relationship. Direction is indicated by the sign of the coefficient. The positive sign $(+)$ means that high scores on the X variable tend to be associated with high scores on the Y variable, and that low scores on X tend to be related to low scores on Y. This is referred to as a *positive*, or direct, correlation. For example, a positive relationship exists between children's age and body weight: As children become older, they usually gain weight. The negative sign $(-)$ indicates that high scores on X tend to be related to low scores on Y, and low scores on X tend to be related to high scores on Y. An example of a *negative*

correlation (also labeled an indirect, or inverse, correlation) is adult age and lung capacity: As adults increase in age, their lung capacity decreases.

The strength or magnitude of a correlation is reflected in the absolute value of the coefficient. Thus a correlation of $+.55$ is equally as strong as one of $-.55$. The strongest relationship is expressed by an r of $+1.00$ or -1.00, both of which are considered perfect correlations. As the coefficient value decreases in absolute value, the relationship becomes weaker. A coefficient of 0.00 indicates that no relationship exists at all. In this case the score on one variable tells us nothing about the score on the other variable.

Let us consider a hypothetical example of correlational research. Suppose that an investigator suspected that children's self-concept and performance on a certain achievement test are positively related. After obtaining an appropriate sample of children to serve as subjects, the researcher would next obtain two scores for each child—one a measure of self-concept and one a score on the achievement test. The hypothetical data might appear as in Table 4-2. Pearson r for these data would be calculated and its value found to equal $+.82$. How would this finding be interpreted? Obviously, a correlation exists, and the positive sign indicates that children who scored high on the measure of self-concept tend to score high on the achievement test. Moreover, the magnitude of the coefficient indicates that the relationship is quite strong (since $+1.00$ is the strongest relationship). Thus, the researcher's hypothesis is supported by the correlational analysis.

Could this finding have occurred merely by chance; that is, is it possible that were the study repeated, the results would show no correlation or even a negative one? That possibility does exist. However, a test for statistical significance could provide information as to the likelihood of the finding being just a chance event. With this mathematical procedure we could determine if the correlation in this study is statistically significant. As a general rule, significance

---

*Pearson r is just one of several correlation coefficients that could be calculated, depending on the nature and complexity of the study. The general procedures and interpretations described above apply to these situations as well.

Table 4-2   Self-Concept and Achievement Scores

Data from a Hypothetical Study of Children's Self-Concept and Performance on an Achievement Test. The Pearson r value is +.82, which indicates a strong positive relationship between the variables.

Child	Variable X Self-concept Score	Variable Y Achievement Test Score
David	2	5
Nina	3	4
Sara	4	12
Michael	7	16
John	9	10
Jennifer	11	22
Timothy	13	18

is defined by the probability that the obtained association would occur by chance five times or less if the study were to be repeated one hundred times. (This level, the .05 level, is indicated in research by the term $p < .05$). Thus, we are reasonably sure that a statistically significant result is not a chance finding.*

The Problem of Directionality and of Other Variables.   It is important to note, however, that even when a statistically significant correlation has been established, causal connections cannot be inferred. We cannot conclude from our hypothetical research that self-concept causes achievement test performance or that achievement test performance causes self-concept. Two problems of interpretation exist. One is that cause could flow in either direction. The other is that some other variable(s)—such as general intelligence or amount of parental criticism to which the child had been exposed—is responsible for the association between self-concept and achievement scores. The logic of correlational research does not permit us to choose among these alternatives.

---

*Statistical significance has nothing to do with the *importance* of results, which must be judged on broad theoretical and practical grounds. When applied to research results, significance refers only to the statistical probability that the finding is a chance result.

There are, however, a few things that can be done to provide some indication of what causal relationship might exist. For one thing, the nature of the variables can be examined for a suggestion of cause-effect. If a positive correlation were found between diet and school performance in children, for example, it would seem more likely that diet influenced schoolwork than vice versa. Still, other variables could be responsible for the relationship between diet and school performance—perhaps social-class factors. If we had good reason to suspect some role for social class, we might decide to use a partial correlation statistical procedure. This method partials out, or removes, the effects of other variables, allowing the investigator to determine whether the two original variables are still correlated. In our example the effects of social class could be removed; if the correlation remained after this procedure, we could conclude that the social-class variable did not completely account for the association between diet and school performance. The partialing procedure might also be used to control for the effects of still other variables, so that the field of possible causative factors could be narrowed considerably. The trouble with partialing, however, is that we are never sure that all possible causative variables have been examined. In the final analysis, then, correlations may suggest causation but *cannot* be assumed to demonstrate it. To establish causal relationships the "true" experiment must be conducted.

Experimental Research

Experimental research comes closest to meeting the rigorous standards of the scientific method. Regardless of its particular purpose, it is characterized by the following:

1. An implicitly or explicitly stated hypothesis
2. Subjects appropriately selected and assigned to specific conditions or manipulations
3. Two or more conditions or manipulations selected by the investigator (the independent variables)
4. Observation and measurement (the dependent variables)
5. Control of the procedures by the investigator
6. Comparison of the effects of the manipulations

Central to the experiment is control by the investigator. The experiences of the subjects are meticulously preselected and presented, with different groups being exposed to different conditions. This permits final judgment about the causes of the results of the study.

To illustrate the experiment we draw on the work of White and Davis (1974), who were interested in the efficacy of treating dental phobic children by means of a modeling procedure. Specifically, these investigators noted that disruptive behavior of children in the dental office is a source of "frustration and urgency within the field of dentistry today." They conceptualized the problem not so much as anxiety itself but as the behaviors that children adopt to cope with anxiety; it is these that "are the primary reason for the dentist's inability to render effective treatment. . . ." (p. 25). Furthermore, they spoke out against the use of premedication and general anesthesia, since medication always has some possibility of side effects; also its use denies children the opportunity to develop strategies to cope with fear. In their introduction the investigators thus provided a

background for their interest in the chosen area of study. They then drew on previous research that hypothesized and demonstrated the efficacy of modeling as a treatment for children's aggression, delinquency, and fears. Finally, their aim to extend earlier research was explicitly stated: "The present study was designed to test the efficacy of modeling as a means of modifying the disruptive behavior of children under dental treatment" (p. 26).

To fulfill this purpose it was necessary to work with children who were both under dental care and exhibited disruptive behavior. Fifteen girls, age 4 to 8 years, were identified on the basis of avoidant responses (crying, screaming, and flailing of arms and legs) that had rendered examination and treatment impossible. The girls were randomly assigned to three groups of five subjects; that is, each participant had an equal chance of being placed in any of the groups. *Random assignment*, accomplished by pulling names out of a container or using a table of random numbers, is crucial to the experiment because it is a method of creating groups that are approximately equal in characteristics. The rationale for random assignment is not that the group members will exactly equal each other but that in the long run, differences in subjects will balance out across the groups.

The investigators divided the subjects into three groups because they had already decided that the effectiveness of modeling would be evaluated by exposing the girls to three different conditions and comparing the outcomes. The manipulation is referred to as the *independent variable*, and in this experiment it had three levels. Group 1 members were treated in this way:

...each subject was seated behind a one-way viewing screen in the presence of a dental student who informed the child that she was to observe a patient undergoing dental treatment. In order to maximize attentiveness, each child was told that a reward would be forthcoming if she could correctly answer four questions regarding each of six sessions involving (1) toothbrush instruction, (2) oral examination, (3) prophylaxis, (4) fluoride treatment, (5) injection, and (6) a restoration procedure. Each session was five minutes in duration. All sessions were completed over a three-week period. The dentist, his assistant, and the model interacted during each of the sessions. (p. 28)

Unknown to the subjects, the model, a white female of 8 years, was a confederate of the experimenters and had been rehearsed in the entire sequence of responses. Thus, each subject was exposed to exactly the same preselected procedure.

Group 2 subjects were individually seated behind the one-way mirror with the dental student for six sessions. However, no model was present, and the dentist and his assistant merely named and manipulated the same equipment used in the Group 1 procedure. Each child was questioned and received rewards for correct answers as in Group 1. The purpose of this condition was to examine the possible effects on dental fears of exposure to the "dental milieu" itself.

Group 3 subjects had no involvement with the dental situation or the model. This condition, a no-treatment control, served to evaluate the possible effects of the passage of time on dental fears. Thus, along with Group 2, it al-

lowed comparison that would help isolate the efficacy of the modeling procedure.

To assess the influence of the independent variable, three measures were devised. These are the *dependent variables*, so labeled because they potentially depend upon the manipulation, or independent variable. In this case they consisted of checklists of the subjects' dental behavior, to be completed by the dentist without his being aware of the experimental condition each child had experienced. The *simple approach behavior checklist* assigned one point for completion of each of seven approach behaviors (see Table 4-3). The *modified approach behavior checklist* rated the completion of the same behaviors but assigned one point for completion in the presence of a significant other (mother, sister, and so on, whose presence the subject could request) and two points for completion without a significant other. *Avoidance behaviors* were assigned points on the basis of absence, or of mild, moderate, or severe, manifestations. Each subject was thus rated in three different ways, and ratings occurred two times—once at three days following the experimental manipulation and again six months later.

The results of the experiment revealed no differences between the immediate and the six-month tests. With regard to simple approach behavior, children who viewed the model

Table 4-3   The Checklists Used as Dependent Variables
in the White and Davis Experiment

Approach Behaviors	Avoidance Behaviors
Walked down hall	Crying
Entered operatory	Continual request for bathroom
Was seated	Wants to see instruments
Opened mouth	Restless in chair
Allowed exam	Hiding
Allowed anesthetic	Flailing of arms and legs
Allowed operative	Won't allow treatment
	Wants significant other

Adapted from White and Davis, 1974.

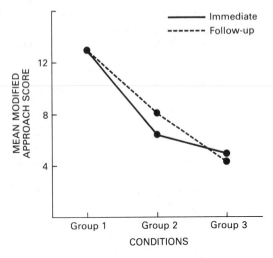

MEAN MODIFIED APPROACH SCORE

— Immediate
----- Follow-up

12

8

4

Group 1   Group 2   Group 3
CONDITIONS

Figure 4–1 Modified approach behavior immediately following treatments and on six-month follow-up. *Adapted from White and Davis, 1974.*

(Group 1) and those exposed to the dental milieu (Group 2) completed more of the dental procedures than children in the no-treatment control (Group 3). The average simple approach scores for Group 1 and Group 2 did not differ significantly; that is, although the scores were not identical, statistical analysis revealed that the difference could have been a chance event. However, for the modified approach behaviors, as shown in Figure 4-1, girls in the modeling group were rated higher than those in the other two groups. This indicates that Group 1 children completed more of the dental procedures without requesting the presence of a significant other. The data for avoidant behaviors revealed group differences for only three of the behaviors. Groups 1 and 2 emitted less hiding and refusal than Group 3, and Group 1 had less need for a significant other than either of the other groups. The other avoidant behaviors were displayed by all the children. From these data the investigators concluded that the experiment supported the hypothesis that modeling can be effective in curtailing disruptive behavior of children who are fearful of the dental situation. In particular, it resulted in the girls

cooperating with treatment independent of the support of others.

Is this conclusion justified? Yes, with certain limitations. Because a controlled manipulation was conducted and effects on behavior measured, explanatory or casual statements can be made with some degree of confidence. That is, it can be said that the manipulation was responsible for the differences in behavior among the differently treated groups of children. Due to random group assignment of subjects, there is no reason to attribute the outcome to differences in characteristics of the children. Moreover, possible systematic bias in measurement was precluded by the dentist being "blind" to each child's experimental condition. Statistical analysis indicates that important group differences were probably not due to chance rather than to the manipulation; differences most likely would appear again if the experiment were repeated. However, a limitation of the findings is that they apply to the population from which the subjects were selected—4 to 8 year-old girls who showed disruptive behaviors in the dental clinic. The results cannot with confidence be generalized to other populations such as adults, males, youngsters of different ages, and the like, although we may indeed be encouraged to extend the research to these populations.

The White and Davis experiment had one independent variable, but experiments may include more than one. For example, an investigator interested in determining the effects of two medications on hyperactive behavior may vary the type of medication and the dosage of the medications. Although the specific statistical analysis will be different for the more complex experiments, the purpose of the analysis will remain the same: to determine whether any group differences obtained go beyond what might be expected merely by chance. When a significant difference is found, and the experiment has been rigorously conducted, a causal connection between the independent and dependent variables can be assumed. Thus, the experiment is a powerful tool for scientific investigation and is often the method of choice (Kendall and Finch, 1979).

Single-subject Experiments. Frequently the experiment is conducted with groups of people, with one or more of the groups serving to help rule out alternative explanations of the findings. It is sometimes useful, however, to focus on an individual. A strategy akin to the experiment can be carried out with a single individual, provided that some control for alternative explanations is designed.

The single-subject experimental design is often employed to evaluate the influence of some environmental manipulation on problem behavior. Used by investigators with a bent toward operant conditioning, the context of the research is often clinical treatment. One method of controlling for alternative explanations is known as the ABA' design. The problem behavior is carefully defined and measured across time periods, during which the subject is exposed to different conditions. The first period (A) is devoted to measuring the frequency of the behavior as it occurs prior to any intervention. Referred to as baseline data, this information serves as a standard against which change can be evaluated. In period B the intervention is carried out while the behavior is measured in the identical way. The intervention is then removed for a period of time known as the reversal period (A').

This design is exemplified by the work of Koegel, Firestone, Kramme, and Dunlap (1974) with autistic children. The youngsters spent little time in appropriate, spontaneous play but often engaged in self-stimulatory behaviors such as hand and leg movements, repetitive vocalizations, facial grimacing, and mouthing objects. On the basis of previous research, the investigators believed that self-stimulation could be decreased by sharply telling the children "No" and slapping or immobilizing the body part involved. They also wished to demonstrate that reduction in self-stimulation would be accompanied by increases in spontaneous play. To test these ideas they worked with two children individually—one boy and one girl. The occurrence of both self-stimulatory and play behaviors was measured during three time periods: prior to intervention, during treatment by suppression techniques, and after intervention was removed. The pattern of results was the same for both subjects and is shown in Figure 4-2 by the data for one of the children. Here we see—as hypothesized by the researchers—that the behaviors changed in the expected directions. Because observation, measurement, and procedures were controlled and the intervention systematically made absent or present, it is likely that the behavioral change was caused by the intervention. Nevertheless, there is insufficient grounds on which to generalize the findings to other children. If the results were to be found repeatedly for many children, some confidence could be placed in their generality.

Figure 4–2 Percent of sampled time during which self-stimulatory and play behaviors occurred. *From Koegel, Firestone, Kamme, and Dunlap, 1974.*

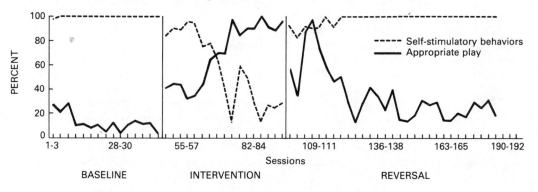

The ABA' design represents a genre of studies that employs a single subject who serves as his or her own control as systematic measurement occurs across time periods. In studies in which the intervention is shown to change behavior favorably, particularly if clinical treatment is the aim, a fourth period (B'), during which the successful intervention is reintroduced, must be added for ethical reasons. Typically the relevant behaviors show improvement again. Nevertheless, the reversal design is problematical in that the manipulation may make reversal unlikely; in this case the manipulation might be successful, but there would be no way to demonstrate its effects. The reversal design also has ethical problems in that a researcher/clinician may hesitate to return to baseline conditions once a manipulation is associated with positive change. And again, although the manipulation would appear responsible for the change, a definite demonstration of its effects would be lacking.

In some instances in which the ABA' design is inappropriate, the multiple baseline design may be employed. In this method two behaviors are recorded across time. After baselines are established for both, the intervention is made for only one of the behaviors. During the next phase intervention is applied to the other behavior as well. For example, in working with a behaviorally disturbed child, an experimenter may hypothesize that attention given to tantrums and to the throwing of objects reinforces these inappropriate behaviors. Withdrawal of attention thus may result in their reduction. Support for the hypothesis can be seen in Figure 4-3, a hypothetical graph of the frequency of both behaviors across time. Since behavior change follows the pattern of the treatment procedure, it is likely that withdrawal of attention and not some other variable caused the change. Thus, the multiple baseline procedure, like the reversal and other single-subject methods (cf. Hersen and Barlow, 1976), permits the researcher to test hypotheses while working with only a few subjects and, in the case of treatment, focusing on the child of immediate concern.

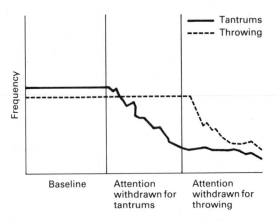

Figure 4–3   Frequency of tantrums and throwing across the phases of a hypothetical multiple baseline, single-subject experiment.

Mixed Designs

In the study of development and of psychopathology, it is common to find the correlational and experimental methods combined in a mixed design (Achenbach, 1978b; Davison and Neale, 1982). In this method two or more groups differing on what is believed to be a relevant variable are measured on some dependent variable. The groups may differ in diagnostic label, age, sex, social class, and the like. It is assumed that these variables might be differentially related to the dependent variable. However, the variables are not manipulations by the experimenter but merely ways in which persons are classified. Thus, they are called classificatory variables rather than true experimental variables, and they are only associated (correlated) with the dependent measure. Interpretation of mixed designs must be made cautiously.

For example, consider the investigation of Goldberg and Konstantareas (1981), who were interested in establishing that attentional processes may be central in childhood hyperactivity. They chose to examine performance on a self-paced vigilance task because little was known about it. Ten hyperactive and ten normal boys participated in the research. The former were enrolled in day-treatment programs, having been removed from the regular school setting due to their difficulties. The ten normal boys, who served as a comparison group, attended a local public school, where they were considered to be functioning in a typical manner. There were no statistical differences between the groups in age range and intellectual level.

Each boy was individually tested on the vigilance task. The apparatus consisted of a televisionlike box and a pair of keys that controlled, in part, the stimuli on the screen. One dependent measure was the rate of the observing response; that is, the rate at which each boy pressed the left key to bring a clown's face into view. The other dependent measure concerned signal detection. The boys were told that every time the clown's nose lit up (the signal), they were to let the clown know by pressing the right key. Based on past research it was hypothesized that the hyperactive children, as compared to the control group, would (1) emit lower observing response rates and (2) make more errors on the signal detection task. Group means on the dependent measures were statistically compared, and the hypotheses were borne out. It was thus concluded that hyperactive boys were shown to have deficits in attending to stimuli.

While the conclusion is warranted, interpretation may extend to the assumption that the condition of hyperactivity as an attention deficit somehow caused differential group performance. In fact, there is no clear way to rule out the possibility that other factors associated with hyperactivity may have produced the outcome. Perhaps the hyperactive children held lower self-expectation or were overly anxious in the situation. Lack of experimental control precludes our knowing exactly what it was about the hyperactive boys that led to the findings. Whenever classificatory variables are employed as the "independent" variable, interpretation is limited in this way.

As difficult as it is to interpret mixed designs, as well as standard correlational research, these methods are frequently employed in investigations of psychopathology. Typically groups of people who had previously been as-signed to diagnostic categories are compared with each other. While certain kinds of information are forthcoming from these studies, it should be noted that the power of the true experiment to draw firm conclusions about causation is lacking in these methods.

LONGITUDINAL AND CROSS-SECTIONAL STRATEGIES

In addition to the distinction already made among research methods, investigations can also be categorized as either longitudinal or cross-sectional. Both of these strategies may incorporate descriptive, correlational, experimental, or mixed designs.

Longitudinal research involves studying subjects over some length of time, repeatedly observing or testing them at various intervals. Longitudinal study is an old method, aimed at "seeing" development as it occurs. Among the first longitudinal investigations was Lewis Terman's study of the gifted in which, beginning in 1921, a population selected on the basis of high intelligence was examined at certain times during several decades (Sears, 1975). Terman's research was followed by several other studies designed to trace the growth of intellectual, social, and physical abilities.

The longitudinal strategy is unique in its capacity to answer questions about the nature and course of development. Does an early traumatic event, such as the death of a parent, play a role in the genesis of childhood depression? Does preschool intervention for poor children overcome the later academic deficits so often found among low SES children? Does aggression in early life predict aggression in adulthood? The longitudinal strategy can be extremely helpful in answering these kinds of questions.

Still, it has serious drawbacks. From a practical point of view, longitudinal studies are extremely expensive and require that investigators commit themselves to a project for several years. Also it is sometimes difficult to retain the subjects over many years, and "dropouts" may have certain characteristics. For example, they may be more transient, less psychologically oriented, or less healthy than the subjects who continue. There is the possibility, then, that subject loss systematically biases the results. Repeated testing may also be problematical: Subjects become test-wise, and efforts to change or improve the testing instruments make it difficult to compare earlier and later findings. Finally, subjects are not the only ones who change over time; society may also. So, for example, if several individuals were followed from 1920 to 1950, their development might be quite different from that of persons of the same age followed from 1950 to 1980, due to historical variables. The 1920–1950 group certainly might have had different experiences than the 1950–1980 group (for example, in diet, health care, educational environments). The possibility of such generational or cohort effects must be considered in interpreting longitudinal studies.

In contrast to longitudinal research, the cross-sectional strategy focuses on different subjects at one point in time. Its main thrust is to test across different groups of people at a particular period. In this sense the cross-sectional approach can be thought of as slicing across time rather than following time, as in longitudinal study. Although cross-sectional research is often experimental in design, same-age or different-age children may be described, measured, or differentially treated, depending on whether description, correlation, or manipulation is intended. With this method expense is minimized, subject loss can be controlled, repeated measurement is not a problem, and researchers are not compelled to commit themselves to a project for several years.

On the other hand, tracing developmental change with the cross-sectional strategy is quite problematic. Researchers attempt this goal by examining the performance of different-age children and then comparing the results. For example, someone interested in whether the rate of aggression changes with age may measure aggressive behaviors in 5-, 10-, and 15-year olds. If the younger children displayed more aggression, could it legitimately be concluded that aggression decreases with age? Not without

serious reservation. *Age difference* is not necessarily *age or developmental change*. Since age is a classificatory variable, one alternative hypothesis is that specific experiences of the different age groups is responsible for the differential results. Perhaps the younger children watched more violent television or received greater amounts of positive reinforcement for aggression, due to changes in this direction in societal values. Changing social conditions can influence different age groups differently, making it difficult to interpret cross-sectional data.

To overcome some of the weaknesses of the longitudinal and cross-sectional strategies while retaining some of their strengths, researchers combine the two approaches in a variety of sequential designs. Here we mention only one of these, in which groups of children of different ages are studied over some relatively short time span. For example, at Time I children at ages 3, 6, and 9 years may be examined in a cross-sectional study. Similar examination of the same groups of children may occur again at Time II, three years later, and at Time III, still another three years later. Figure 4-4 is a schema of this hypothetical design. As can be seen, reading down the columns of the schema, cross-sectional comparisons are made at three different times. In addition, reading from left to right on the schema, three groups of children (A, B, and C) are studied longitudinally over a six-year span (1984–1990). The age range in the investigation is from 3 to 15 years.

Various comparisons can provide a wealth of information from such a sequential design. To take a simple case, if aggression were found to decrease with age at Time I, and II, and III (cross-sectional analyses) and also across time for each of the groups of children (the longitudinal analyses), evidence would be strong for developmental change over the entire age range covered in the study. Moreover, by comparing aggression at age 6, or 9, or 12 (as boxed on the schema), the possible impact of societal conditions could also be obtained. It might be found, for example, that aggression at age 9 increased from 1984 to 1987 to 1990. Since only one age is involved, this increase is not devel-

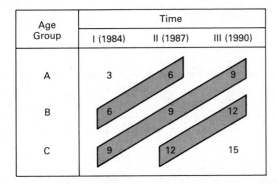

Age Group	Time		
	I (1984)	II (1987)	III (1990)
A	3	6	9
B	6	9	12
C	9	12	15

Figure 4–4 Schema of a sequential research design in which children of different ages are examined cross-sectionally and longitudinally.

opmental and thus indicates a change in societal conditions during the particular years under investigation. Thus, sequential designs can be powerful research tools that permit the researcher to separately examine age differences and developmental changes while taking generational or cohort effects into consideration.*

ETHICAL ISSUES IN RESEARCH WITH CHILDREN

Although it is widely agreed that scientific research brings potential benefits through better understanding of human behavior, we are presently witnessing great concern for the rights and welfare of participants in research. This is due, in part, to a current emphasis on individual rights: but it is also due to past, documented abuse of research subjects. One well-known instance involves a study, begun in 1932, of the natural course of syphilis. The investigation was continued into the early 1970s, even though the development of antibiotics could have provided treatment for the subjects long before then (Kelty, 1981). It could be argued that abuse in

*The varied designs and interpretations of sequential investigations are quite complex. For a more complete discussion of this topic, the reader is referred to Achenbach, 1978b.

social science research has not been as dramatic as that in biomedical research; nevertheless, there is legitimate cause for concern. In the widely discussed Milgram (1963) study, for example, subjects were deceptively informed that the research procedure necessitated their administering electric shocks to another participant who was engaged in a learning task. In fact, no electric shock was possible with the rigged procedures but the subjects were unaware of this. The study was designed to evaluate the degree to which the subjects were willing to bring harm to other human beings in the particular context in which they were placed. Many of the subjects did indeed follow the procedure, albeit with great discomfort, believing that they were shocking their partners. The Milgram study included a postexperimental interview aimed at alleviating any guilt or anxiety that the subjects might have experienced. Nevertheless, the experiment raised much controversy about the ethics of researchers in deceptively setting up a situation that might bring later guilt, anxiety, or embarrassment to the subjects (e.g., Baumrind, 1964).

Not surprisingly, ethical considerations about research virtually always raise the question of possible harm and discomfort to participants. As shown in Table 4-4, several other concerns have also been expressed. The use of deception was criticized by Kelman (1967), among others, on the grounds that researchers may not have the right to ''add to life's little anxieties'' or to expose research subjects to lies and tricks that would be unacceptable in most human relationships. The individual's right to confidentiality must be continuously guarded. Participation without consent and knowledge of the purpose and procedures of the study is now considered unacceptable, as is participation under coercion. All these issues are complex, and perhaps no perfect solution exists for safeguarding research participants. For example, as troublesome as the issue of deception may be, biasing of results may occur if a subject is informed that he or she has been assigned to the placebo group in reseach comparing the effects of medication on a particular disorder. Never-

Table 4-4   Some Ethical Issues in Research and Suggested Resolutions

Issues	Suggested Resolutions
Risk and discomfort to the participant	Attempt to minimize. Balance risk, discomfort, gain to the participant, and the significance of the research. Do not go beyond a certain level of risk/discomfort. Seek consultation and approval of review committees.
Deception	Use only when necessary to the research question, and balance against amount of gain. Counteract by excluding vulnerable participants, minimizing degree of deception, and using postexperimental feedback to enhance the subjects' positive self-regard and educational experience in the research.
Confidentiality	Avoid use of names. When identification by name is necessary, use a code number with matching name kept under lock and key. Avoid unnecessary personal discussion of the participant.
Participation without consent or knowledge	Consent should always be obtained. When the subject is young or is disabled in a way that precludes understanding, consent of parent, guardian, or social agency is necessary. Purposes and procedures should be explained as clearly and as accurately as possible.
Participation under coercion	Unacceptable. Sensitivity to subtle coercion is a must. For example, children may feel they should go along with adult requests; institutionalized subjects similarly may believe that participation is required or needed to put them in good stead with those in power. The right of refusal must be made clear. If subjects desire to stop in the middle of the procedure, they may do so without negative consequences.

theless, guidelines such as those suggested in Table 4-4 can go a long way toward alleviating potential abuse. Thus, for many years the American Psychological Association has published a manual of ethical guidelines for research. Social science research more recently has come under the aegis of the National Committee for the Protection of Human Subjects of Biomedical and Behavioral Research. It is now common practice for review committees to pass judgment on the ethics of proposed research before any investigation is initiated.

Even more complex is the issue of ethics where children are used as subjects. To a large extent the ethics of research revolves around the idea of informed consent of the participant, which, in turn, requires that the participant be free of coercion and have reasonable knowledge of the risks and benefits entailed (Frankel, 1978). For adults, knowledge of the research

situation includes understanding its purpose, the role of the subject, reasons for subject selection, procedures, discomforts and risks, benefits, and alternatives (Ferguson, 1978). Adult subjects also may give permission to the researcher to withhold information about the study. What constitutes informed consent for the child? Surely, very young children are not capable of truly understanding the nuances of all these elements.

Ferguson (1978) has provided a rough sketch of children's ability to understand a situation sufficiently well to give informed consent. She suggests that adolescents be accorded the adult role; that is, be given the same information an adult would be given and then be asked to sign a consent form. Since the adolescent may be a minor in the eyes of the law, however, the parent must also sign, just as with young children. The same procedure is suggested for the school-

Informed consent by a parent or guardian should be obtained when a child participates in research. The problem of what constitutes informed consent by the child participant is a complex, but important, issue.

age child. However, preschool and primary-age youngsters are limited cognitively and require that explanation be in more concrete, immediate terms, with personal consequences clearly spelled out. It is often appropriate to indicate to the child that his or her help is needed by the investigator. Some researchers feel more comfortable, even with children as young as 7 years, in obtaining their signed consent. With infants and toddlers, informed consent is not a reasonable expectation, and thus parental consent may be sufficient for the child's participation.

Proxy consent is not without its problems, nevertheless. Society allows parents to make decisions for children, based on the assumption that parental and child needs coincide and that when they do not, parents will place the child's needs first (Frankel, 1978). This is not always the case. Moreover, parents may feel coerced by social or economic pressures into permitting their child's participation. For example, if research participation is desired by an agency that

offers therapeutic care, the parents of a child in need of such care may be afraid to challenge the agency. Similarly, parents of children who are being treated by an institution may confuse the need for research with the actual care of their child. All these considerations raise doubts about the unqualified use of proxy consent. Contemporary opinion appears to accept proxy consent when nontherapeutic research carries little or no risk to the child. Nontherapeutic research of greater risk, even with proxy consent, is generally not acceptable.

In the final analysis, the ethics of research, like other ethical issues, can never be a completely settled question. Ongoing discussion and tension are appropriate. The prevailing emphasis on human rights and recognition of past abuse has led to stringent surveillance and guidelines for participation in research. At the same time, children would pay a high price were society to give up its efforts altogether to increase understanding of human behavior.

SUMMARY

Knowledge of human behavior is gained by scientific methods that vary with regard to subjects, settings, procedures, and designs. The purpose of science is to describe phenomena and offer explanations for them. Explanation is facilitated considerably by explication of relationships, especially cause-effect relationships. Theoretical concepts guide all aspects of research, including the hypotheses advanced. Hypotheses may be little more than hunches, or they may be quite sophisticated conceptual statements. In either case, hypothesis testing builds knowledge systematically and is intricately tied to the advancement of theory.

Observation and measurement are at the heart of science. They may focus on overt behavior; physiological systems; self-reporting of emotions, thoughts, and behavior; and reports of others about the subject of the research. The scientific assumption that events repeat themselves, given the same or identical conditions, places importance on the reliability, or consistency, of findings. Researchers thus must clearly describe their work and make it accessible for replication by others. Research must also address issues of validity; that is, the soundness and appropriateness of scientific results. Internal validity refers to the degree to which alternative explanations for results can be ruled out with confidence. External validity is the issue of generalizability of scientific findings to populations and settings other than those of the original study.

All the various research methods have weaknesses and strengths. Simple descriptive procedures fulfill the basic purpose of science: to paint a picture of phenomena. The case study can provide a particularly rich picture of phenomena, and hypotheses can readily be generated from this pool of description. However, the accuracy and completeness of retrospective data cannot easily be verified, case study descriptions tend to be imprecise, and guidelines for interpretation are nonexistent. Case studies do not lend themselves to replication, and they cannot be generalized with any confidence.

Systematic direct observation can provide more precise, accurate, and current details of behavior but may lose some of the richness of the case study. Depending on the specific procedure (for example, group versus individual recordings), the information gathered may or may not be replicated and generalized.

The primary purpose of correlational research is to determine the existence of relationships, or associations, between and among variables, as well as the direction and strength of the relationships. It is an excellent method for initial exploration and for when experimental manipulation is impossible. An advantage of the correlational method is its suitability for analyzing relationships as they occur naturally rather than in the confines of the laboratory. However, cause-effect cannot be definitively established, thereby limiting explanation of the findings.

To determine causal relationships the true experiment must be conducted. Here the independent variable is manipulated and controlled by the researcher to test its possible influence on the dependent variable. With careful research design and control, internal validity can be quite high. As with other methods, the question of generalization must always be considered. One of the weaknesses of the experiment is that it requires a degree of control that may bring artificiality to the situation.

The single-subject experiment, which also permits cause-effect inferences, is especially weak in external validity. However, the reversal and multiple-baseline designs, along with other single-subject designs not described in this chapter, have the advantage of economy and of focusing on the individual when this is appropriate.

The mixed design superficially resembles the true experiment, but the independent variable is actually a classificatory variable rather than a true experimental variable. For this reason the results are difficult to interpret, limiting internal validity. Generalizability is an issue, but it is possible to some extent.

In addition to the distinctions already drawn among research methods, longitudinal and cross-sectional strategies also may be adopted. The longitudinal strategy does a superb job of looking at development as it occurs across a long time span. Nevertheless, it is expensive, requires a lengthy commitment from investigators, and may suffer from biased subject loss and repeated measurement. The cross-sectional strategy, which focuses on different people at one point in time, circumvents many of the weaknesses of longitudinal study. However, cross-sectional research cannot trace developmental change, since it examines age differences rather than developmental changes.

Researchers combine the longitudinal and cross-sectional strategies to retain their strengths and overcome some of their weaknesses. Such sequential designs permit separate examination of age differences, age changes, and the possible influence of variables that may be associated historically with age groups.

Regardless of the specific method employed in research today, considerable concern is being voiced about the rights of participants. Questions about possible harm and discomfort, deception, confidentiality, informed consent and knowledge, and coercion are of utmost importance. Children's participation in research raises ethical concerns over and above those expressed for adult subjects. The ethics of research primarily revolve around the idea of informed consent, which, in turn, requires freedom from coercion to participate and sufficient knowledge of the risks and benefits. Both are a problem in situations in which children are the main actors. It is advisable for the investigator to take the age of the subjects into consideration in deciding how best to protect their rights. Proxy consent is acceptable for the very young child when nontherapeutic research carries little or no risk. In the final analysis, concern about rights for research participants is appropriate, but specific guidelines are best reached by weighing individual rights and the potential benefits derived from studying human behavior.

5

CLASSIFICATION AND ASSESSMENT

CLASSIFICATION AND DIAGNOSIS

Clinically Derived Classification Systems
Empirical Approaches to Classification
The Similarity of Derived Syndromes
The Dangers of Labeling

ASSESSMENT

Assessment of Physical Functioning
Personality-Behavior Assessment
Intellectual-Educational Assessment
Doing a Comprehensive Assessment

SUMMARY

This chapter is concerned with classification, diagnosis, and the related process of assessment as they apply to behavior disorders of children. Although the terms *classification* and *diagnosis* are often used interchangeably here and elsewhere, the former emphasizes description and grouping for scientific study, while the latter involves grouping for clinical purposes. *Assessment* refers to the process of evaluating the phenomenon to be classified or diagnosed.

CLASSIFICATION AND DIAGNOSIS

What is a good system of classification? Before we examine current systems for classifying children's disordered behavior, we need to examine the criteria by which any system's adequacy will be judged. First and foremost, the categories of the system must be clearly defined. This means explicitly stating the criteria for determining if a particular case fits a category. After this it must be demonstrated that the category exists. This means that features used to describe a category tend to occur together regularly—in one or more situations or as measured by one or more methods. A system composed of categories that are either poorly defined or that do not exist is doomed to failure.

Secondly, the system must be reliable. In a general way reliability refers to consistency or stability. *Interrater reliability* refers to agreement, or the consistency with which diagnosticians use the same category to describe a child's behavior. It addresses the question, for example: Is Billy's behavior called hyperactivity by two or more professionals who observe it? *Test-retest reliability* evaluates whether assignment of a category is stable over some reasonable period of time. Is Mary's problem diagnosed as learning disability again when she returns to the clinic for a second evaluation? The degree of reliability in a system sets a limit on the validity of that system.

A system must also be *valid*. To have validity, diagnoses must be clearly discriminable from one another. Also, a diagnosis must provide us with more information than we had when we originally defined the category. Thus, diagnoses should give us information about the etiology of a disorder, the course of development the disorder is expected to take, response to treatment, or some additional clinical features of the problem. Does the diagnosis of Conduct Disorder, for example, tell us something about this disorder that is different from other disorders? Does it tell us something about what causes this problem? What is likely to happen to children who are viewed as having this disorder? What treatments are likely to help them? Does it tell us additional things about these children or their backgrounds? Information concerning causes is often referred to as *etiological validity*. Information about how the disorder might develop or what treatments will be successful is usually referred to as *predictive validity*. *Concurrent validity* is usually evaluated by whether or not the diagnosis suggests additional features of the disorder. The question of validity is thus largely one of whether we know anything we did not already know when we defined the category.

Finally, the adequacy of a classification system is judged by its *clinical utility*; that is, by how complete and useful it is. A diagnostic system that describes all the behavioral disorders that come to the attention of clinicians in a manner that is useful to them is more likely to be employed. Clinically derived classification systems have clinical utility as one of their primary goals.

Clinically Derived Classification Systems

The consensus of clinicians that certain characteristics occur together is the basis for clinically derived classification systems. Historically the classification of abnormal behavior has focused primarily on adult disorders. Until recently there has not been any extensive classification scheme for childhood psychopathology.

DSM. The most widely used classification system in the United States is the American

Psychiatric Association's *Diagnostic and Statistical Manual of Mental Disorders (DSM)*. This classification system is an outgrowth of the original psychiatric taxonomy developed by Kraeplin in 1883, from which children's disorders were omitted. DSM-I (American Psychiatric Association, 1952) contained only two categories of childhood disorders: Adjustment Reaction and Childhood Schizophrenia. Children also could be diagnosed in the adult categories. However, a national survey indicated that 70 percent of the children seen in psychiatric clinics were classified under Adjustment Reaction or received no diagnosis at all (Rosen, Bahn, and Kramer, 1964).

By the 1960s it had become obvious that a more extensive system was needed. The 1968 revision, DSM-II (American Psychiatric Association, 1968), added the category of Behavior Disorders of Childhood and Adolescence, which was subdivided into six kinds of disorders. This appeared to permit clinicians to more finely discriminate their cases (Cerreto and Tuma, 1977).

A third version, DSM-III (American Psychiatric Association, 1980), has been issued, which further expands the number of categories specific to children. DSM-III also involves some changes in the organization of particular categories. Table 5–1 presents the major diagnostic categories specific to children. As in the past, some adult diagnoses may also be used for children. In fact, for certain disorders (for example, depression), no diagnostic distinction is made between children and adults. In addition, DSM-III recommends that each individual be evaluated along five dimensions, or axes, so that a fuller picture of the child is created. On Axis I the clinician indicates any existing mental disorder except those under the categories of Specific Developmental Disorders or Personality Disorders. Any condition not attributable to a mental disorder but that, nevertheless, will be focused on in treatment (for example, an academic problem) is also listed on this axis. Specific Developmental Disorders and Personality Disorders are indicated on Axis II. If there are any current physical conditions that are relevant to understanding or treating the child, these are indicated on Axis III. Axes IV and V, respectively, are used to indicate the severity of psychosocial stressors in the child's life and the highest level of adaptive functioning achieved by the child during the past year. Table 5–2 illustrates how these two axes might be used in diagnosing a child. Whether clinicians will use this system, whether it will be reliable, and whether it will have any clinical utility remain to be demonstrated at this time.

DSM-III's handling of childhood disorders is considerably more complex and provides more specific categories than did earlier versions. However, the actual existence of categories this specific is not well supported by empirical studies. Moreover, specific categories may threaten the reliability of a system. For example, in earlier attempts at diagnosing adult disorders, about 60 percent agreement among diagnosticians could be achieved for major categories, such as psychotic versus neurotic disorders. However, this figure dropped considerably for subgroups within the larger categories (e.g., Beck, Ward, Mendelson, Mock, and Erbaugh, 1962). Ward and his colleagues (1962) found that two-thirds of these disagreements between diagnosticians resulted from inadequate criteria for making a diagnosis. DSM-III has attempted to improve this situation by providing operational diagnostic criteria rather than just general descriptions of disorders.

The reliability of the childhood categories of DSM-III has not yet been evaluated. However, in field studies conducted prior to the final draft of DSM-III, twenty raters made diagnoses based upon twenty-four actual case histories (Cantwell, Russell, Mattison, and Will, 1979; Mattison, Cantwell, Russell, and Will, 1979). As in the adult studies described above, good agreement existed among raters for the broad groupings, but poor reliability was obtained for subgroups. Similar conclusions have been reached concerning the childhood categories of the World Health Organization's classification system (Rutter and Shaffer, 1980).

With regard to the validity of DSM-III, Rutter and Shaffer (1980) suggest that available

Table 5-1   DSM-III Diagnostic Categories of Disorders Usually First Evident in Infancy, Childhood, or Adolescence

Mental Retardation
  Mild
  Moderate
  Profound
  Unspecified
Attention Deficit Disorder
  With hyperactivity
  Without hyperactivity
  Residual type
Conduct Disorder
  Undersocialized, aggressive
  Undersocialized, nonaggressive
  Socialized, aggressive
  Socialized, nonaggressive
  Atypical conduct disorder
Anxiety Disorders
  Separation anxiety disorder
  Avoidant disorder
  Overanxious disorder
Other Disorders
  Reactive attachment disorder of infancy
  Schizoid disorder of childhood or adolescence
  Elective mutism
  Oppositional disorder
  Identity disorder
Eating Disorders
  Anorexia nervosa
  Bulimia
  Pica
  Rumination disorder of infancy
  Atypical eating disorder
	Stereotyped Movement Disorders
	  Transient tic disorder
	  Chronic motor tic disorder
	  Tourette's disorder
	  Atypical tic disorder
	  Atypical stereotyped movement disorder
	Other Disorders with Physical Manifestations
	  Stuttering
	  Functional enuresis
	  Functional encopresis
	  Sleepwalking disorder
	  Sleep terror disorder
	Pervasive Developmental Disorders
	  Infantile autism
	  Childhood onset pervasive developmental disorder
	  Atypical pervasive developmental disorder
	Specific Developmental Disorders
	(coded on Axis II)
	  Developmental reading disorder
	  Developmental arithmetic disorder
	  Developmental language disorder
	  Developmental articulation disorder
	  Mixed specific developmental disorder
	  Atypical specific developmental disorder

American Psychiatric Association, 1980.

evidence does not support the validity of many of the categories that have been created. Indeed, those who were instrumental in developing this revision of DSM acknowledge that many of the categories do not have established validity (Spitzer and Cantwell, 1980). Concern has been expressed about the very comprehensiveness of this system. For example, the motivation for and wisdom of making such a wide variety of children's behaviors classifiable as mental disorders has been questioned (e.g. Harris, 1979; Schacht and Nathan, 1977). Nevertheless, as Rutter and Shaffer (1980) suggest, despite several concerns about DSM-III, many positive directions have been taken: the increased use of a structured set of rules for diagnosis, greater comprehensiveness, and the use of a multiaxial system.

GAP and ICD-9.   Two other widely recognized systems for classification exist. The classification system of the Group for the Advancement of Psychiatry (GAP, 1966) was developed prior to DSM-III because of dissatisfaction with earlier versions of the DSM system. The *Ninth Revision of the International*

Table 5-2   Examples of the Use of Axes IV and V of DSM-III

Axis IV—Severity of Psychosocial Stressors

Rating	Example
1—None	No apparent psychosocial stressor
2—Minimal	Vacation with family
3—Mild	Change in school teacher; new school year
4—Moderate	Chronic parental fighting; new school; illness of close relative, birth of sibling
5—Severe	Death of peer; divorce of parents; arrest; hospitalization; persistent and harsh parental discipline
6—Extreme	Death of parent or sibling; repeated physical or sexual abuse
7—Catastrophic	Multiple family deaths

Axis V—Highest Level of Adaptive Functioning Past Year

Rating	Example
1—Superior	A 12-year-old girl gets superior grades, is extremely popular among her peers, and excels in sports.
2—Very Good	An adolescent boy gets excellent grades, works part-time, has several close friends, and plays banjo in a jazz band. He admits to some distress in "keeping up with everything."
3—Good	An 8-year-old boy does well in school, has several friends, but bullies younger children.
4—Fair	A 10-year-old girl does poorly in school, but has adequate peer and family relations.
5—Poor	A 14-year-old boy almost fails in school and has trouble getting along with peers.

Adapted from American Psychiatric Association, 1980.

Classification of Diseases (ICD-9) is a broad classification system developed by the World Health Organization (WHO, 1977). It devotes one section to mental disorders but does not provide a separate section on the disorders of childhood. A number of specific classifications, however, occur only in childhood. The ICD-9 is the classification system most likely to be employed outside the United States.

It is likely that DSM-III will be the dominant system in this country. However, we think it is important to note one innovation of the GAP system that did not find its way into DSM-III—the category of Healthy Responses. The GAP committee intentionally placed this category first to emphasize the importance of assessing a child's strengths rather than simply defining mental health as the absence of pathology. Moreover, the GAP system recognizes that behavior that may seem abnormal is often a normal reaction. The anxiety that infants commonly exhibit at around 6 to 8 months when their mothers are not present is one example offered. The group responsible for the childhood disorders section of ICD-9 made a similar recommendation for the inclusion of a category of Normal Variation. Although not acted on, the recommendation acknowledged the variability in children's development and the occurrence of transient problems that cause parental concern but are compatible with normal development (Rutter, Lebovici, Eisenberg, Sneznevskij, Sadoun, Brooke, and Lin, 1969).

Empirical Approaches to Classification

The 1960s and 1970s witnessed a number of attempts to use an empirical rather than clinical approach to identifying childhood syndromes. This approach to the classification of childhood behavioral disorders, unlike the situation with adults, did not have to contend with an elaborate and entrenched clinical classification system. Empirical approaches were also facilitated by the development of computers and sophisticated statistical techniques.

The empirical approach to classification uses statistical techniques to identify patterns of behavior which are interrelated. Since children rarely seek treatment for themselves, the information used in empirical approaches is usually provided by adults. The general procedure is for the adult to indicate the presence or absence of specific behaviors in the child. The information is quantified in some way. For example, a 0 is marked if the child does not exhibit a certain characteristic, a 1 is given if a moderate degree of the characteristic is displayed, and a 2 is indicated if the characteristic is clearly present. Similar information is obtained for a large number of children. Statistical techniques are then employed to indicate which behaviors tend to occur together. This cluster of behaviors constitutes a syndrome. Thus, rather than relying on clinicians' memories and impressions as to what behaviors tend to occur together, empirical and statistical procedures are employed as the basis for developing a classification scheme.

Factor analysis is the primary statistical technique employed in these studies. Factor analysis is based on correlations among items. The correlation of every item with the others is calculated, and groups of items that tend to occur together are identified. These are referred to as factors or clusters. The following example illustrates this procedure in fairly simple form:

. . . . a look at the correlations among individual items might show that *phobias* and *stomachaches* correlate .60; *phobias* and general *fearfulness* correlate .49; *stomachaches* and *fearfulness* correlate .47; *phobias* and *pains* (other than stomachaches) correlate .32; *stomachaches* and *pains* correlate .41; *fearfulness* and *pains* correlate .27; *phobias* and *disobedience* correlate —.65; *stomachaches* and *disobedience* correlate —.43; *fearfulness* and *disobedience* correlate —.51; and *pains* and *disobedience* correlate —.27.

From the preceding correlations we could conclude that phobias, stomachaches, fearfulness, and pains all tend to occur together, whereas disobedience tends not to be reported for children who show the other symptoms. Thus, a rough approximation to a descriptive category might be the combination of phobias, stomachaches, fearfulness, and pains, in the *absence* of disobedience (Achenbach, 1974, p. 552).

The earliest reports on empirically derived syndromes were based on the observations of clinicians (e.g., Ackerson, 1942; Lorr and Jenkins, 1953). However, most of the widely cited empirically developed syndromes were originally derived from ratings by teachers of children in regular school classes. The Behavior Problem Checklist developed by Peterson (1961) and revised by Quay and Peterson (1975), and the Pittsburgh Adjustment Survey Scales (Ross, Lacey and Parton, 1965), are two examples of general purpose checklists. Parental reports have also been employed. Some investigators have used the same instruments that were employed by teachers (e.g., Conners, 1970; Quay and Peterson, 1975), while others have developed instruments based on reports by parents of clinic children. Achenbach's Child Behavior Checklist (1979) is one such example.

The Similarity of Derived Syndromes

Do different investigators, employing different instruments, completed by different kinds of adult caregivers, evaluating different populations of children, in different settings, produce a similar set of factors or syndromes? This already-complex question is made even more difficult to answer because studies vary considerably in methodology and data analysis procedures. However, the results available do suggest some consistency. For example, Achenbach and Edelbrock (1978), after judging syndrome similarity across studies, established categories of syndromes and assigned syndromes derived from various studies to these categories. Two independent judges also made these assignments and agreed in 95 percent and

88 percent of the cases. The resulting categories were then given names intended to reflect common elements in syndromes that appear similar. From the results of this analysis it seems clear that there is substantial evidence for the existence of the two broad-band, or general, syndromes labeled Undercontrolled and Overcontrolled. These syndromes are evident in data derived from a variety of instruments completed by various categories of adults (clinicians, teachers, and parents) who interact with children in a variety of settings (clinics, school, home).

Quay (1979) also found evidence for the *Undercontrolled* syndrome in all of the thirty-seven studies he reviewed. Quay chose to label this syndrome Conduct Disorder. Fighting, temper tantrums, disobedience, and destructiveness are some of the characteristics most frequently associated with this pattern. This syndrome again emerged in a variety of settings and with varied populations of children. It was also evident in information obtained from different kinds of caretakers as well as from the children themselves. Thus, the concept of an Undercontrolled-Conduct Disorder Syndrome would appear to be a highly robust and viable one. The *Overcontrolled* syndrome, which Quay (1979) labels Anxiety-Withdrawal, was almost as frequent in its appearance. Descriptions such as anxious, shy, withdrawn, and depressed are some of the characteristics associated with this syndrome. It is found in the same broad range of children and settings and reported by the same variety of observers as is the undercontrolled pattern.

Syndromes According to Age and Sex. Achenbach (1979) found specific subcategories called narrow-band factors within the broad internalizing and externalizing factors (Achenbach's terms for the overcontrolled and undercontrolled categories, respectively). However, different subcategories were found for different age-sex groups. Table 5–3 illustrates the different narrow-band factors found for boys

Table 5–3   Syndromes Found for Boys and Girls of Different Ages

Group	Internalizing Syndromes	Mixed Syndromes	Externalizing Syndromes
Boys 6–11	Schizoid Depressed Uncommunicative Somatic complaints	Social-withdrawal	Hyperactive Aggressive Delinquent
Boys 12–16	Somatic complaints Schizoid Uncommunicative Immature Obsessive-compulsive	Hostile-withdrawal	Delinquent Aggressive Hyperactive
Girls 6–11	Depressed Social-withdrawal Somatic complaints Schizoid-obsessive		Hyperactive Sex problems Delinquent Aggressive Cruel
Girls 12–16	Anxious-obsessive Somatic complaints Schizoid Depressed-withdrawal	Immature-hyperactive	Delinquent Aggressive Cruel

Adapted from Edelbrock and Achenbach, 1980.

and girls in age groups 6 to 11 and 12 to 16. Thus, it would appear that general Internalizer and Externalizer categories exist for both sexes at all ages. However, more specific problems within these syndromes differ, depending upon the age and sex of the child.

Interestingly, Edelbrock and Achenbach (1980) suggest that in contrast to describing the multiple characteristics of a single child, the Child Behavior Checklist can be employed to assign children to categories. A profile of scores on the subscales is prepared for each child. By statistically analyzing large samples of profiles of disturbed children and putting them into groups of similar profiles, a typology of profiles can be formed. An individual child may then be assigned to the group which his or her profile most closely resembles. Agreements ranging from 70 percent to 95 percent in assigning profile types have been reported by these authors. This development is of concern, since it represents a shift from classifying behaviors or problems to classifying children. The problems that result from such categorization and the related use of labels are discussed later in this chapter.

Reliability and Validity. The reliability of empirically derived classification systems has received far greater attention than has the reliability of their clinically derived counterparts. Available reports indicate high test-retest reliability. For both broad-band (general) and narrow-band (more specific) syndromes, reliabilities were .82 or better when test and retest were conducted within one week to one month (Achenbach and Edelbrock, 1978). With increasing time intervals the stability was reduced considerably (Achenbach and Edelbrock, 1978; Quay, 1979). Changes over longer periods of time, however, may have more to do with how stable childhood behavior disorders are than with the reliability of empirically derived classification systems. Low stability of scores may suggest that at least some childhood behavior disorders may not be expected to persist over time.

Agreement between raters observing the child in the same situation is also quite good. For example, Achenbach (1978a) reported interrater reliability between parents to be .76, and Peterson (1961) reported the same figure for interrater agreement between teachers. Agreements are lowest between raters who observe children in distinctly different situations. For example, Quay, Sprague, Shulman, and Miller (1966) report correlations of .37 between the ratings of mothers and teachers. This suggests that attention be paid to the possible bias of a rater's perspective and to the importance of situational determinants of children's behavioral disorders.

The validity of empirically derived classification systems is indicated by a variety of studies. The internalizer-externalizer distinction is supported by studies which report differences between children classified into these two categories. For example, externalizers outnumbered internalizers by about 2 to 1 among boys, but the ratio was reversed for girls (Achenbach, 1966). This suggests that the classifications are related to characteristics other than those employed to define them. Internalizers and externalizers also appear to differ on a number of qualities related to etiology, prognosis, and response to treatment. For example, parents of internalizers are reported to be stricter and more concerned about their children's problems; also, they have different clinical profiles than parents of externalizers (Achenbach and Edelbrock, 1978). Further, among individuals labeled as delinquent, internalizers and externalizers were found to differ in moral and cognitive development, ability to attend to a task, and the need to seek stimulation (Jurkovic and Prentice, 1977; Skrzypek, 1969). This suggests differing etiologies for the two syndromes. Clearly, however, these findings are only suggestive—cause and effect are not clear from these studies. Differential prognosis is also suggested by a number of studies. For example, internalizers in general have been reported to be better adapted than externalizers (Achenbach and Edelbrock, 1978) However, among men classified as schizophrenic, those classified as internalizers as children had poorer outcomes (Roff, Knight, and Wertheim, 1976). Finally, internalizers are also reported to respond better to psychotherapy and to benefit more from therapy programs for delinquents (Achenbach and Lewis, 1971; Quay, 1979; Quay and Love, 1977).

While available literature supports the broad internalizer-externalizer distinction, additional information concerning the validity of the narrow-band syndromes needs to be obtained. At this point the usefulness of these more specific categories remains unclear.

The Dangers of Labeling

For many professionals involved in the welfare of children, the impact of labeling a child by any classification system is of concern. Before examining criticisms of labeling let us briefly look at the major reasons for using categories or labels. As we noted in Chapter 3, all people form categories or concepts which help them organize their world. In this way we attempt to deal with and make sense of the variety of experiences which confront us. Without such concepts we would be less effective in dealing with new situations. Thus, forming categories is part of the way we think about all things. As we indicated above, from a scientific or professional point of view, forming categories of classification or diagnosis has a similar purpose. It is intended to facilitate our understanding and treatment of childhood behavior disorders. As scientists, we can study groups of children to seek common etiologies. As clinicians, we can benefit from previous knowledge in our approach to new cases. However, as with perspectives, categories may also limit the information we seek or the interpretations we make of events. It is this aspect of classification—when it is applied to an individual child and becomes a label—that causes concern. Although classification is intended as a scientific and clinical enterprise, it can be seen as a social process as well. The diagnostic label becomes a social status. This social label carries with it implications for how children are thought of and treated. If this impact is negative, it in effect detracts from the original purpose of categorizing—helping children.

From the start, formal classification has had the categorization of disorders, not persons, as its stated intent. Indeed, Cantwell—one of the creators of DSM-III—has noted: "Any classification system classifies psychiatric *disorders* of childhood; it does *not* classify *children*. Thus it is correct to say, 'Tommy Jones has infantile autism.' It is incorrect to say 'Tommy Jones, the autistic' . . . " (Cantwell, 1980a, p. 350). Despite this stated intent, it is a common observation that the label is applied to the child rather than to the disorder. Indeed, the attempt to classify children is sometimes explicit, as is evident in the work of Edelbrock and Achenbach, described on page 97. One of the dangers inherent in this "misplacement" of classification, only "noticing" information consistent with a label, is illustrated in a study by Foster and Salvia (1977). Teachers were asked to view a videotape of a boy and rate his academic work and social behavior. The tape displayed age- and grade-appropriate behavior in all cases, but some teachers were told that the boy was learning disabled, while others were told that he was normal. Teachers watching the "learning disabled" boy rated him as less academically able and his behavior as more socially undesirable than did teachers watching the "normal" child.

The use of labels also invites a number of other difficulties. The danger of overgeneralization is one concern—assuming that all children labeled Attention Deficit Disorder, for example, are alike. Such overgeneralization may occur even in the face of contradictory evidence. Critics also point to the logical fallacy that often results from the use of labels. A label originally used to describe a behavioral pattern may then be stated as the cause of the same observed behavior. For example, a clinician who observes a pattern of restlessness, high levels of active behavior, and poor attention may describe this behavior as hyperactivity. In a subsequent conference with the child's parents, the clinician may then state that the child's problem behavior is caused by hyperactivity. A related danger is the process of reification. A label originally intended as an aid to explanation soon becomes a "real" thing and is viewed as a stable attribute of the child. People react to the child as a member of a category, and the child is likely to behave so as to be consistent with the expectations of the label. There is the further danger that such a label is likely to be retained despite changes in behavior (cf. Rosenhan, 1973).

Lilly (1979) and others have also suggested that traditional categories ignore the fact that a child's problems "belong" to at least one other person—the one identifying or reporting them. As Algozzinne (1977) has noted, the child may not be inherently "disturbed," but is labeled deviant because of the reactions of others to his or her behavior. Algozzinne modified the instructions for the Behavior Problem Checklist (Quay and Peterson, 1975) so that adults were asked to indicate "how disturbing" a particular item would be in working with children. The responses of adults to this Disturbing Behavior Checklist were submitted to a factor analysis. Interestingly, behavior rated as to *disturbingness* seemed to cluster in much the same way as it did in previous studies to determine *disturbed* behavior. Algozzinne also reported that behavior represented by the factor which he labels social defiance was significantly more disturbing than other behaviors (for example, general social immaturity). These results suggest the importance of attending to environmental responses in understanding children's problem behavior. Lilly (1979) has suggested that instead of describing exceptional children, we should begin defining exceptional situations.

In response to widespread concern with the classification of exceptional children, ten federal agencies joined together to sponsor the Project on the Classification of Exceptional Children (Hobbs, 1975). Many of the experts involved expressed concern regarding the problems inherent in the use of categorical labels and advocated concerted attempts to reduce the harmful effects of categories and labels. It was also recommended that services be provided to children, without inflexible references to categories. However, it was acknowledged that cat-

egorization is so embedded in our thinking and problem solving that completely discarding it is probably impossible. Thus, it is both valuable and necessary to be sensitive to social factors inherent in the use of categories, the social status imparted by a label, and the impact of labels on the child and others (Rains, Kitsuse, Duster, and Freidson, 1975).

ASSESSMENT

Evaluating children's problems is a complex process. Most often it will involve assessing multiple aspects of a child's functioning. Assessment is also a process that requires considerable skill and sensitivity. It is best accomplished by a team of clinicians carefully trained in the administration and interpretation of specific procedures and instruments. Assessment is usually conducted immediately upon contact with the child or family; thus, it demands special sensitivity to anxiety, fear, shyness, manipulativeness, and the like. If treatment ensues, assessment should be a continuous process, so that new information can be gleaned and the ongoing effects of treatment can be ascertained. In this way the clinician remains open to nuances and can avoid rigid judgments concerning what is a multifaceted and complex phenomenon.

Assessment of Physical Functioning

Assessment of physical functioning can provide several kinds of information valuable to understanding disordered behavior. Family and child histories and physical examinations may reveal genetic problems, such as phenylketonuria (p. 21). Diseases and defects may be diagnosed that directly (for example, urinary tract infection causing problems in toilet training) or indirectly (for example, a sickly child being overprotected by parents) affect important areas of functioning. Signs of atypical or lagging physical development may be an early indication of pervasive developmental disorders that eventually influence many aspects of behavior.

The assessment of the nervous system is considered particularly important to understanding a variety of problem behaviors, but especially mental retardation, learning disability, and hyperactivity. Brain and other neurological dysfunction is thought to be associated with abnormal physical reflexes, sensory and perceptual defects, and various neurophysiological and neuropsychological measures. The recent popularity of the concept of minimal brain dysfunction (MBD) to describe learning and behavioral problems has contributed to increased interest in neurophysiological and neuropsychological assessment.

Neurophysiological Assessment. Neurophysiological assessment refers to attempts to directly evaluate the physiological integrity of the nervous system. The primary measures employed in the assessment of presumed dysfunction in children are presented in Table 5-4. The most well known procedure is the electroencephalograph (EEG); its use in the assessment of hyperactivity, for example, dates back to 1934 (Kahn and Cohen, 1934).

The EEG consists of electrodes placed on the scalp, which record activity of the brain cortex. It is assumed that learning and behavioral problems may be due to brain dysfunctions that can be measured in this manner. However, available research suggests that EEG evaluation in children with learning disabilities and behavioral problems is of questionable value (Feuerstein, Ward, and LeBaron, 1979). When EEG abnormalities are found in children identified as having a particular disorder, scores on measures of intellectual and behavioral functioning raise questions about the significance of these findings. Satterfield, Cantwell, Saul, and Yusin (1974) found that hyperactive children with EEG abnormalities scored significantly *higher* on several measures of intellectual functioning and achievement than hyperactive children with normal EEG patterns. In addition, behavioral ratings by parents and teachers did not differ for the two groups. As Satterfield and his associates indicate, if abnormal EEG had been used to determine the need for special ser-

vices, those with the least need would have qualified.

The use of clinical EEGs is thus quite controversial. More recent, sophisticated procedures for analyzing EEGs may prove useful in differentiating normal and problem children (Feuerstein et al., 1979). These analyses make use of various computer techniques. Rather than evaluating brain activity in a static test environment, measurement is made of cortical responses of children engaged in some task requiring processing of information.

Probably the most controversial procedure for assessing neurological damage is the use of what are frequently referred to as equivocal, or soft, neurological signs. Assessing the development of hand preference (laterality), the ability to cross the midline of the body, muscle tone, and the use of the ''whirling'' test are common examples of evaluating soft signs. Table 5-5 presents some examples of the assessment of these signs. At present there is little standardization of measurement procedures, a lack of knowledge concerning reliability and validity, and a need for norms with a general population. Thus, the significance of soft signs must be considered with extreme caution (Werry, 1979b).

Neuropsychological Assessment. Neuropsychological assessment makes use of a variety of standardized tests to measure behavioral and psychological processes in the performance of learning, sensorimotor, perceptual, verbal, and memory tasks. From the individual's performance inferences are made about neurological deficits and the likely location of any brain lesions. Neuropsychological assessment is thus an *indirect* means of assessing brain function; no direct examination of physiological functioning is made. Knowledge or theories of brain-behavior relationships are used as the basis for translating observed behavior into inferences concerning actual neurological functioning.

The tests most commonly used to assess brain damage in children are the Bender Visual-Motor Gestalt Test (Bender, 1946; Koppitz, 1964), the revised version of the Wechsler

Table 5-4   Physiological Measures for the Assessment of Nervous System Dysfunction

Measures	Description	Behavioral Significance
Electroencephalograph (EEG)	Scalp recording of gross cortical activity with frequency and amplitude parameters	Frequency-amplitudes are related to various states of consciousness. Lower frequency-higher amplitude activity indicative of less alert/attentive states, while high frequency-low amplitude activity correlates with attention and high arousal.
40-Hz EEG	Specific frequency of EEG activity (i.e., 40 cycles per second)	Increases in this response occur during periods of focused arousal/attention. It has been suggested that this response is related to short-term memory prior to consolidation in long-term store.
Sensory averaged evoked response (AER)	Measure of cortical responsiveness to sensory stimuli	Various components in the total response are measures of the degree of cortical responsivity to a stimulus. Latency and amplitude measures are related to attention and other components of information processing.
Skin conductance	Electrical activity of the skin	High levels of skin conductance indicate autonomic nervous system activation and its psychological concomitants (i.e., increased cognitive and/or emotional activity).
Heart rate	Rate of heart muscle contraction	Deceleration often observed during periods of attentiveness.

Adapted from Feuerstein, Ward, and LeBaron, 1979.

Intelligence Scale for Children (WISC-R) (Wechsler, 1974), and the Reitan-Indiana and Halstead Neuropsychological Test Batteries for Children (Reitan, 1969; Reitan and Davison, 1974).

The Bender-Gestalt Test consists of a set of designs (Figure 5-1) which the child is asked to copy. The system of thirty possible errors developed by Koppitz (1964) is the most common scoring method. The test is quick and easy to administer and thus is probably the most frequently employed. Nevertheless, its use to assess neurological dysfunction in individual children is problematical (Buckley, 1978; Feuerstein et al., 1979). For example, Ackerman, Peters, and Dykman (1971) found, as might be expected, that significantly more learning disabled (LD) children than normal controls scored above the mean number of errors for their age. There were, however, many false positives (normals who scored as brain damaged) and false negatives (LDs who scored as normal). Furthermore, the number of scores indicating marked impairment did not differ significantly for the groups. Palkes and Stewart (1972) also found that when Bender-Gestalt scores were adjusted for IQ differences, there was no significant difference between hyperactive children and normal controls matched for sex, age, grade, race, and socioeconomic status.

The WISC-R, primarily employed as a measure of intellectual development, is sometimes used to assess the presence of brain damage. Scores on particular subtests, and subtest patterns or scatter (the variability between subtest scores), are the most frequent basis for judgment. The available literature does not support the use of the WISC-R in this manner. Studies

Table 5-5   Examples of Assessment of "Soft" Neurological Signs

Hand-Foot-Eye Preference (Lateral Dominance)

    a. Show me which hand you throw with.

    b. Show me which hand you write with.

    c. Show me which foot you kick with.

    d. Look through telescope.

    A soft sign is indicated if the child performs less than three of the responses with the limb (or eye) on the same side of the body.

Crossing Midline

Evaluated with child's eyes open, then with eyes closed.

    a. Touch your left ear with your right hand.

    b. Touch your left eye with your left hand.

    c. Touch your right knee with your right hand.

    d. Touch your right shoulder with your left hand.

    A soft sign is indicated if one-half or fewer of the responses is correct.

"Whirling" Test

    The child stands with arms extended, parallel to each other, and with eyes closed. The head is passively rotated to one side as far as possible without discomfort. This is repeated to opposite side. The positive response of whirling (a soft sign of damage or immaturity) consists of the child turning the entire body as long as the examiner turns the head.

Adapted from Shapiro, Burkes, Petti, and Ranz, 1978.

employing clinical and normal control groups matched for IQ fail to find differences (Feuerstein et al., 1979), and considerable profile scatter has been found to be characteristic of normal children (Kaufman, 1980).

The Reitan-Indiana Neuropsychological Test Battery has been employed to evaluate differences among children with learning and behavioral problems suspected of having minimal brain damage, children with known brain damage, and normal controls. It appears that no items consistently differentiate children with problems from normal controls (Feuerstein et al., 1979). Furthermore, in a study of normal controls, brain-damaged, MBD-academic difficulty, and MBD-behavioral problem children, although the brain-damaged group did perform significantly worse than the other three groups, the MBD children's performance did not differ from that of the normal children (Reitan and Boll, 1973). This study would suggest either that the Reitan Test Battery cannot detect minimal brain damage or perhaps that no such damage exists.

Overall, it appears that current assessment of brain damage or dysfunction in most children with behavioral or learning disorders is probably no more than enlightened guesswork (Werry, 1979b). It is often difficult, if not impossible, to determine the actual existence of brain damage and to discern its relationship to observed behavior. Brain damage, for example, is correlated with a variety of sociofamilial variables that have been shown to be disadvantageous to social adjustment and physical health (Rutter, Graham, and Yule, 1970; Sameroff and Chandler, 1975). These sociofamilial variables may themselves underlie *both* the brain damage and the observed behavioral or learning problems.

Personality-Behavior Assessment

The Interview.   The most common form of personality-behavior assessment is the interview. Regardless of the theoretical orientation of the clinician and other assessment instruments employed, it is almost certain that an interview will be conducted. The nature of the questions asked and the information sought in the interview, however, will probably vary, depending upon the orientation of the clinician. The clinician will seek to obtain information concerning the nature of the problem, past and recent history, present conditions, feelings and perceptions, attempts to solve the problem, and expectations concerning treatment. This information may be sought from the child or from parents, other family members, or other individuals having contact with the child. Who is interviewed may depend on the problem, the clinician's theoretical orientation, and the anticipated modes of intervention.

Hetherington and Martin (1979) have criticized the interview as a method for obtaining information from parents concerning child-rearing practices and past behaviors of the child. They suggest that such interviews yield information that shows little stability over time and is distorted in the direction of precocity, idealized expectations, and cultural stereotypes. Although this is a serious criticism, it should be noted that Rutter, Tizard, and Whitmore (1970) found the parental interview to be the single best indicator of disorders in the child. Achenbach and Edelbrock (1978) also suggest that parents may be the most reliable source of information and that their reports include observations of behavior that is less likely to be seen in the clinic.

Whether the child will be interviewed alone probably varies with the age of the client. The older child generally is more capable and is more likely to provide valuable information. Nevertheless, clinicians often elect to interview even the very young child in order to obtain their own impressions. The fact that the child's behavior is likely to vary in different situations argues for the value of interviewing a variety of individuals who have contact with the child (for example, siblings, teachers).

Psychological Tests. The most common form of psychological test employed to assess childhood personality is the projective test. The development of this tool derived from the conceptualization of projection as a defense mech-

Figure 5-1 The Bender-Gestalt consists of designs, similar to those below, which the child is asked to copy.

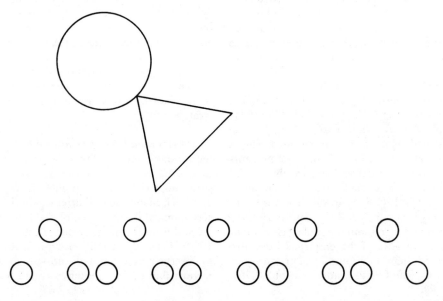

anism. This hypothesis is based upon the psychodynamic notion that one of the ways the ego deals with impulses that it finds unacceptable is to project them onto some external object. Thus, it is assumed that when the child is exposed to an ambiguous stimulus, the child's interpretation of the stimulus will reveal aspects of psychic functioning that cannot be consciously expressed. The projective test is thus used as a way of assessing the individual's ''unacceptable'' thoughts and impulses, as well as the defenses against them. Projective tests are also used by some clinicians in a manner that involves less psychodynamic inference. This type of analysis examines formal aspects of the test response; for example, does the child describe the entire stimulus or just part of it? Interpretations are then made based upon this response style rather than on the content of the response.

Several projective tests are commonly employed by child clinicians. In the Rorschach the child is simply asked what he or she sees in each of ten ink blots. The child's protocol is scored by one of a number of systems (Exner, 1974; Klopfer and Kelly, 1942; Piotrowski, 1957), based on characteristics of the response such as the portion of the blot responded to (location), factors such as color and shading (determinants), and the nature of what is seen in the blot (content). The Human Figure Drawing or Draw-a-Person test (Machover, 1949) requires that the child draw a picture of a person and then a second person of the opposite sex. Typically the clinician then asks the child questions about the drawings. Murray's (1943) Thematic Apperception Test (TAT) and Bellak's (1971) Children's Apperception Test (CAT) provide the child with pictures for which he or she is asked to make up a story. Figure 5–2 presents pictures similar to those used in the CAT. Some clinicians also make use of the Bender-Gestalt and WISC-R as projective tests, although this is certainly not their primary use.

Projective tests remain a popular assessment device, but reviews of the empirical literature have faulted them on a number of grounds (cf. Gittelman, 1980; O'Leary and Johnson, 1979).

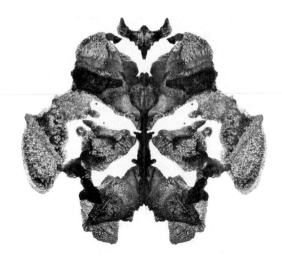

Inkblot designs, similar to the one pictured above, are employed in the Rorschach.

Overall, they appear to lack adequate test-retest reliability, fail to provide valid estimates of personality characteristics, and do not differentiate between diagnostic groups. In addition, the vast majority of studies of projective tests fail to control for factors such as IQ. Also, these studies often employ raters who are not ''blind'' to the child's condition or history, and thus it is difficult to know whether their judgments are based on test responses alone (Gittelman, 1980). As O'Leary and Johnson (1979) indicate, significant training and substantial time is required to learn to administer and score projective tests. Given the weaknesses of these tests, their clinical utility remains to be demonstrated.

Observational Assessment.   The earliest attempts at systematic direct observations of children's behavior were associated with the child study approach described in Chapter 1. This approach made use of diaries or continuous observations and narrations of the child's behavior and were deliberately nonselective (Wright, 1960). From this tradition evolved an attempt to observe a more limited, pinpointed set of behaviors that could be reliably coded by observ-

Figure 5–2. Drawings similar to those employed in the CAT.

ers (Bijou, Peterson, Harris, Allen, and Johnston, 1969). Recent observational methods have come largely from workers with a behavioral/social learning perspective. The observations are most frequently made in the child's natural environment. They range from observations of single, relatively simple behaviors of the child, such as selection of play material, to observations of the child and peers, to complex systems of interactions of family members (e.g., Israel and O'Leary, 1973; Israel, Pravder, and Knights, 1980; Patterson, 1977). Clearly, ongoing interactions are more difficult to observe and code than are the behaviors of a single individual. Table 5-6 shows some of the behaviors coded in Patterson's work on parent-child interactions in the home.

The first step in any behavioral observation system involves explicitly pinpointing and defining the behaviors of interest. Observers who are trained to use the system then note whether a particular behavior occurs during a designated time interval. Most coding systems have been inspected for reliability and validity; indeed, behavioral/social learning studies commonly report on the reliability of the observations employed, even if a reliability check is not the major purpose of the research.

The most frequent aspect of reliability reported is interrater reliability. Two or more observers independently observe the same behavior, and the degree of agreement is calculated. A variety of behaviors have been reliably recorded. Research indicates that a number of factors, such as the complexity of the system, changes in the observers' use of the system, and knowledge that reliability is being checked, affect the degree of reliability (Johnson and Bolstad, 1973). The reliability of observers must be checked periodically to assure consistently accurate measurement. Taplin and Reid (1973) demonstrated that informing observers that they will be unknowingly checked for agreement produces improved reliability.

The validity of observational systems has also received some attention. Content validity refers to whether observations are representative of actual behavior. Researchers have focused on two threats to the content validity of observational systems: observer bias and reactivity. Observer bias addresses the question of whether observer expectations of how children will behave distort the observations to fit the expectations. To examine this issue Kent, O'Leary, Diament, and Dietz (1974) gave clear expectations to observers as to what they might see

Table 5-6   Some of the Twenty-Eight Behavioral Categories of Patterson's Behavior Coding System Designed to Evaluate Parent-Child Interactions in the Home

Verbal
CM (Command): This category is used when an immediate and clearly stated request or command is made to another person.
CN (Command negative): A command which is very different in "attitude" from a reasonable command or request (CM): (1) immediate compliance is demanded; (2) aversive consequences are threatened if compliance is not immediate; (3) a kind of sarcasm or humiliation directed to the receiver.
CR (Cry): Whenever a person cries, with no exceptions.

Nonverbal
DS (Destructiveness): The person destroys, damages, or attempts to damage any (nonhuman) object; the damage need not actually occur, but the potential for damage must exist.
HR (High-rate): A repetitive behavior *not covered by other categories* that if carried on for a long period of time would be aversive or annoying.

Adapted from Patterson, 1977.

on videotapes they were coding. There were no effects of expectations on the direct behavior observations. However, subjective ratings of general impressions were affected by the expectations. This suggests that behavioral observation systems are more resistant to observer bias than are subjective impressions and global ratings.

The second threat to content validity—reactivity—involves the issue of whether the knowledge that one is being observed changes one's behavior. Zegiob, Arnold, and Forehand (1975) observed mother-child interactions and reported that such knowledge had a significant effect on a number of the categories observed, tending to increase positive behaviors. It has also been demonstrated that parents are capable of making their children look good or bad if they so desire. When parents were told to make their children look good on some days and bad on other days of home observation, target behaviors were clearly affected by these instructions (Johnson and Lobitz, 1974a; Lobitz and Johnson, 1975b). The question of whether reactivity is only a temporary adjustment to a novel situation has also been addressed. A number of studies conducted over relatively long time intervals (e.g., Dubey, Kent, O'Leary, Broderick, and O'Leary, 1977; Mercatoris and Craighead, 1974) compared target behaviors of children and their teachers under two conditions. Observations were done both with observers in the classroom and unobtrusively, with no observers in the classroom. These investigators found no systematic effects of observer presence or absence on the behavior of the children or their teachers. It would thus appear that reactivity probably abates over periods of time.

Some researchers have also attempted to evaluate the validity of observational systems by asking whether they discriminate between deviant and nondeviant groups. For example, Lobitz and Johnson (1975a) compared observations of children referred to a clinic for conduct disorder to observations made of normal, nonreferred children. Referred children showed more deviant behavior in their home than did nonreferred children, thus validating the observational system. Interestingly, though, parental attitude questionnaires were more successful in classifying the children than were the observational measures. Perhaps parental attitude is more important than the child's actual behavior in determining whether a child will be brought to the clinic.

While available information suggests that observational systems are valid assessment devices, certain aspects of validity remain largely undetermined. Particularly lacking is information on whether behavioral observations can predict other present and future behaviors or outcomes (concurrent and predictive validity).

Problem Checklists and Dimensional Rating Scales. The problem checklists and rating scales described in the section on empirical approaches to classification are also employed as assessment devices. These instruments, which provide information on parent, teacher, and clinician perceptions of the child's behavior, are available for both general use (for example, the Behavior Problem Checklist and the Child Behavior Checklist) and for use with restricted populations (for example, Conners's Teacher Rating Scale, 1969). The considerable empirical literature described (pp. 95–98) suggests that these instruments are valuable assessment devices for clinicians holding a variety of perspectives.

For example, parents of 1,300 children referred for mental health services and 1,300 parents of randomly selected nonreferred children completed the Child Behavior Checklist (Achenbach and Edelbrock, 1981). High levels (in the .90s) of test-retest and interparent reliabilities were obtained for the checklist measures. The validity of this assessment device seems supported as well. The Child Behavior Checklist clearly discriminated between the clinic and nonreferred children on both behavior problem and social competence scores. Furthermore, referral status accounted for greater differences than did factors such as age, SES, and gender. Figure 5-3 illustrates the differences between clinic and nonreferred children.

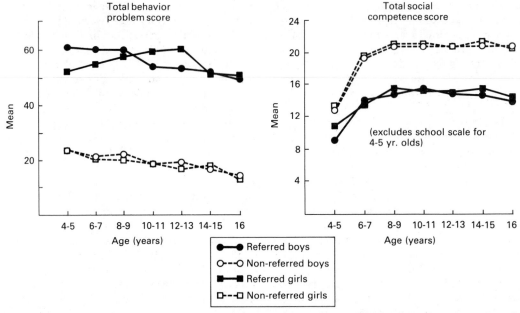

Figure 5–3.   The behavior problem and social competence scores of clinic-referred and nonreferred children were significantly different for both boys and girls at all ages. *From Achenbach and Edelbrock, 1981.*

Intellectual-Educational Assessment

The assessment of a child's functioning in the intellectual-academic sphere is an important part of almost all clinical assessments. Intellectual functioning is of central importance in disorders such as retardation and learning disabilities, but it may also contribute to and be affected by a wide variety of behavioral problems. In contrast to most other assessment instruments, tests of intellectual functioning tend to have better established normative data, reliability, and validity. While our present discussion of these instruments is brief, additional information will be presented in later chapters.

Intelligence Tests.   By far the most commonly employed assessment devices for evaluating intellectual functioning are intelligence tests. In fact, they probably constitute the most frequently employed assessment device other than the interview. The Stanford-Binet (Ter-

man and Merrill, 1960) and the Wechsler tests—the Wechsler Preschool and Primary Scale of Intelligence (Wechsler, 1967); the Wechsler Intelligence Scale for Children (Wechsler, 1974); and the Wechsler Adult Intelligence Scale (Wechsler, 1981)—are the intelligence tests most widely used in clinical settings. All are individually administered and yield an intelligence quotient (IQ) score. The average IQ score is 100, and an individual IQ score reflects how far above or below the average person of his or her age an individual has scored.

IQ tests have long been the subject of heated controversy. Critics have argued that the use of IQ scores has resulted in a reification of the concept of intelligence and a view of intelligence as a rigid and fixed attribute. Moreover, they claim that intelligence tests are culturally biased and have led to social injustice (cf. Kamin, 1974; Zigler and Trickett, 1978). Although IQ tests are popular and have proven useful in predicting a variety of outcomes, these criticisms demand caution in the administration and interpretation of such tests.

Developmental Scales. Assessment of intellectual functioning in very young children, and particularly in infants, requires a special kind of assessment instrument. Several have been developed: the Gesell Developmental Schedules (Gesell and Amatruda, 1947), the Cattell Intelligence Tests for Infants and Young Children (Cattell, 1960), and the Bayley Scales of Infant Development (Bayley, 1969). Performance on these tests yields a developmental quotient (DQ) rather then an IQ. Unlike intelligence tests, developmental scales rely heavily on sensorimotor skills and simple social skills rather than on language and abstract reasoning abilities. For example, the Bayley examines the ability to sit, walk, place objects, attend to visual and auditory stimuli, smile, and imitate adults. Perhaps because intelligence tests and developmental scales tap different abilities, there is only a low correlation between performance on them (Pease, Wolens, and Stockdale, 1973; Rubin and Balow, 1979).

Ability and Achievement Tests. In addition to assessing general level of intellectual functioning, it is often necessary or helpful to be able to assess the level of functioning in a particular area. A variety of tests has been developed for this purpose. The Frostig Developmental Test of Visual Perception (Frostig, Lefever, and Whittlesey, 1966) and the Illinois Test of Psycholinguistic Abilities (Kirk, McCarthy, and Kirk, 1968) evaluate visual-motor and language ability, respectively. The Wide Range Achievement Test (Jastak and Jastak, 1965) and the Spache Diagnostic Reading Scales (Spache, 1963) are administered individually and measure academic achievement. Tests such as the Iowa Test of Basic Skills (Lindquist and Hieronymous, 1955–56) and the Stanford Achievement Test (Kelley, Madden, Gardner, and Rudman, 1964) are group-administered achievement tests employed in many school settings. Specific ability and achievement tests are

particularly important in working with children with learning and school-related problems, and they will be further discussed in later chapters.

Doing a Comprehensive Assessment

As we indicated in starting our discussion of assessment, evaluating children's problems is a complex process. By the time a child comes to the attention of a clinician, the presenting problem is usually, if not always, multifaceted. Also, since assessment is the first part of any contact, the professional's knowledge of the problem will be limited. Both of these factors, as well as common sense and caution, argue for a broad and comprehensive assessment process. Thus, the clinician will likely evaluate multiple areas of functioning and make use of a variety of assessment procedures. The particular device chosen may depend, in part, on the assessor's perspective. For example, projective tests are more likely to be employed by clinicians who place heavy emphasis on unconscious influences. However, whatever the clinician's perspective, the best interests of the child are most likely to be served by a comprehensive assessment of multiple facets of the child and his or her environment.

SUMMARY

DSM-III is the most recent version of the classification system of the American Psychiatric Association. It is the clinically derived classification system most likely to be employed in the United States. The number of categories of childhood disorders in DSM-III represents a considerable increase over previous versions. The current system also provides more highly structured rules for diagnosis, and through a multiaxial system it attempts to ensure that the diagnostic process includes various aspects of functioning. At present there is not much information about the reliability and validity of DSM-III. The greater precision of diagnostic rules is likely to produce greater reliability; however, the increased number of specific categories is likely to work against reliability.

Empirical approaches to classification rely on the use of behavior checklists and statistical analyses rather than on clinicians' judgments. There is fairly good support, across a number of studies, for two broad syndromes—an Undercontrolled, Externalizing, Conduct Disorder syndrome and an Overcontrolled, Internalizing, Anxiety-Withdrawal syndrome. There is also some support for subcategories within each general syndrome that probably differ depending on the age and gender of the child.

A number of critics of diagnostic systems have reminded us that we need to be sensitive to the possible dangers of labeling children. To the extent that such labels reduce our effectiveness as scientists and clinicians, they do not serve the child's best interest.

Whatever approach one takes to classification and diagnosis, it is necessary to conduct some form of assessment. There is fairly broad consensus that the complex process of assessment requires a multifaceted and comprehensive approach. Methods for evaluating the physical, personality-behavioral, and intellectual-educational functioning of the child are available. There is considerable variability regarding both the frequency with which different assessment procedures are employed and the empirical support for their use.

6

DISORDERS OF EATING, ELIMINATION, AND SLEEP

DISORDERS OF EATING

Rumination
Pica
Obesity
Anorexia Nervosa

DISORDERS OF ELIMINATION

Enuresis
Encopresis

SLEEP DISORDERS

Sleepwalking
Nightmares and Night Terrors
Causes and Treatment of Sleep Disorders

SUMMARY

In this chapter we will examine disturbances in the basic physiological functions of eating, elimination, and sleep. Developing control of these functions is a goal of child rearing in all societies. But while every culture deals with each of these issues, there is appreciable variability in the goals of socialization and the manner in which they are attained (Whiting and Child, 1953). All cultures and all families must, for example, establish feeding and weaning practices. Some cultures and families expect early weaning and may be quite severe in their practices, while others may approach the task far more gradually and be quite indulgent. What is evident in all instances is that the child's ability to master these relevant tasks, and the parents' ability to train the child, are important to the immediate well-being of both children and adults.

Perhaps even more important than the immediate effects, however, is the role these tasks play in providing an arena for broader issues of development. How they are handled may help set the stage for the child's style of interacting with others and contribute to overall personality development. Thus, early parent-child interaction concerning these functions can set the foundation for later difficulties, either in the same area (for example, the later eating disorder of anorexia nervosa) or in more general ways (for example, problems with authority figures).

It is common for children to exhibit some difficulty in acquiring appropriate habits of eating, elimination, and sleeping. While parents often solve these difficulties themselves, professional assistance is also frequently sought (Routh, Schroeder, and Koocher, 1983). This chapter looks at problems that are serious enough to make them of clinical concern.

DISORDERS OF EATING

A wide range of problems having to do with eating and feeding are commonly reported, including those of undereating, selective eating, overeating, problems in chewing and swallowing, bizarre eating habits, annoying mealtime behaviors, and delays in self-feeding. Some eating problems may actually endanger the physical health of the child; virtually all have varying degrees of psychological and social consequences. The clinical disorders discussed below are those that have attracted a good deal of attention from researchers and clinicians.

Rumination

Rumination (or mercyism) is characterized by the voluntary regurgitation of food or liquid. First described in 1687, it is a fascinating syndrome with a long history (Kanner, 1972). When infants ruminate, they appear to deliberately initiate regurgitation. The child throws its head back, and chewing and swallowing movements are made until food is brought up. In many instances the infant initiates rumination by placing his or her fingers down the throat or by chewing on objects. The child exhibits little distress; rather, pleasure appears to result from the activity. If rumination continues, serious medical complications can result, with death being the outcome in extreme cases. Kanner (1972) reported that in fifty-two cases of rumination, "not less" than eleven children died. In all of the cases rumination was noticed during the first year of life, and medical complications frequently were observed. Kanner's observations and other subsequent reports (Linscheid, 1978) indicate no apparent sex or race differences in the incidence of this disorder.

Etiology and Treatment. Psychoanalytic and behavioral perspectives offer the major etiological explanations of rumination. Richmond, Eddy, and Green's (1958) psychoanalytic hypothesis is that rumination is caused by a mother who is psychologically incapable of providing a warm, physically intimate relationship. Rumination is the infant's attempt to provide this missing gratification. The behavioral explanation is more in line with Kanner's (1972) conclusion that the act is clearly habitual in nature. He and others view rumination as being acquired incidentally and then taken up as a voluntary, pleasurable habit. This pattern may start, for example, with the normal occurrence of spitting up by the infant. The rumination is then reinforced by a combination of pleasurable self-stimulation and increased attention from adults (e.g., Linscheid, 1978). It should be noted that both the psychoanalytic and behavioral explanations propose that pleasure and attention received by the infant maintain rumination. However, the behavioral explanation recognizes many reasons why a mother may give her infant inadequate attention. For example, a working mother with several other children may be too busy to give a great deal of attention. She most likely would nevertheless clean the infant following vomiting, thereby reinforcing the behavior. The behavioral explanation also focuses on self-stimulation rather than symbolic substitution as the major source of gratification.

A wide variety of treatments has been suggested for infant rumination. Restraining the infant and providing thick feedings (for example, thickened farina) are often recommended, the latter being used as an adjunct to other forms of intervention. Clinical reports suggest that the provision of affection and attention, combined with aids such as thick feedings and restraint, is successful in treating the problem (e.g., Kanner, 1972; Bakwin and Bakwin, 1972). However, sufficiently controlled evaluations of these procedures are lacking.

A number of controlled investigations have been conducted from a behavioral perspective with infants for whom other treatments had failed. In these cases an aversive or unpleasant stimulus is administered to the infant as it begins rumination. In an early report of this procedure, a 9-month-old male infant was given brief electric shocks contingent upon vomiting (Lang and Melamed, 1969). Within a few days of treatment the rumination ceased; it had not returned at the one-year follow-up, and the child was developing normally. Other similar treatments have proven equally successful. The shock levels employed in these procedures

caused the infant to startle but were not necessarily painful. Sajwaj, Libet, and Agras (1974) used lemon juice squirted into the infant's mouth, rather than shock, as the aversive stimulus. The mild level of aversive stimulation employed in these studies raises the question of whether their success is due to the aversive properties of the stimuli or to distraction. Procedures that avoid aversive stimuli altogether therefore deserve research attention.

Pica

Pica is the Latin term for magpie, a bird known for the diversity of objects it eats. This disorder is thus characterized by the habitual eating of substances usually considered inedible, such as paint, dirt, papers, fabric, hair, and bugs.

During the first year of life, most infants put a variety of objects into their mouths, partly as a way of exploring the environment. Within the next year they typically learn to explore in other ways, and come to discriminate between edible and inedible materials (Doll, 1965). The diagnosis of pica is therefore usually made when there is a persistent eating of inedibles beyond this age, and pica is most common in 2- and 3-year-olds.

Pica has been observed in children from all backgrounds, but the problem may be more common among low-income and black populations. Cooper (1957) reported that in her sample of children referred for mental health guidance, pica occurred in 27 percent of the black children and in 17 percent of the white children. It was also slightly more frequent for boys than for girls. Among a nonreferred sample, 32 percent of 486 children from low-income families ate inedible substances, as compared to only 10 percent of 294 children from middle- and upper-income families. Based on similar samples, it also seemed that the rates of pica in white low-income and black middle-income children were comparable to those in black low-income populations (Millican and Lourie, 1970).

Pica can lead to a variety of damage, in-

Children who reside in older, deteriorating neighborhoods may be at risk for accidental lead poisoning.

cluding dental problems and intestinal obstruction due to the accumulation of hair and other materials. It also appears related to accidental poisoning. Millican and Lourie (1970) noted that in their sample of children hospitalized for poison ingestion over a specific time period, 55 percent exhibited pica. Perhaps most serious is lead poisoning. The child who lives in an old house is at particular risk because lead-based paint was used almost exclusively prior to the 1940s. In the United States the annual incidence of poisoning by paint is estimated to be 400,000 cases (Wright, Schaefer, and Solomons, 1979). As many as 2,000 of the cases result in death, about 4,000 in serious neurological damage, and about 200,000 in possible subclinical neurological injury.

Etiology and Treatment. A number of causes for pica have been postulated. Because

youngsters have been observed eating strange substances when food is unavailable, it has been suggested that pica is an attempt to satisfy nutritional deficits. However, several investigators have found no nutrient deficiency associated with pica (e.g., Kanner, 1972; Millican and Lourie, 1970).

Clinical reports often cite parental inattention and lack of supervision as causes of pica (Kanner, 1972). The behavior may occur because the child substitutes the satisfaction derived from overeating for parental affection, or because lack of supervision fails to discourage the behavior.

Several findings also suggest cultural influences. For the black children studied by Millican and Lourie (1970), culture seems to have been an important factor. Most of the families involved had migrated from the southeastern United States, where eating of earth containing clay and laundry starch is a frequent custom. Certain superstitions are reported to govern this behavior. Eating clay and other nonfood substances is believed to prevent a curse on the fetus, reduce the side effects of pregnancy, produce good blood in the unborn child, and eliminate the possibility of syphilis. Interestingly, the mothers of children with pica were found to have a higher frequency of the behavior than mothers of children without pica. Sixty-three percent of children with pica in this sample had mothers who also exhibited pica. Some mothers directly taught their children to eat nonfood substances; others presumably served as models for their children's behavior. The cultural explanation is consistent with explanations of pica as a learned habit that is reinforced through satisfaction associated with chewing or inadvertently reinforced by parental attention (e.g., Wright et al., 1979). Interestingly, young black children, who might be strongly affected by cultural acceptance of pica, exhibited a lower rate of psychological difficulties than did older and white children displaying pica.

Educational approaches aimed at informing mothers of the dangers of pica and encouraging them to discourage the behavior may be somewhat successful (e.g., Millican & Lourie, 1970). However, even reports of successful programs indicate a need to supplement the interventions with more intensive therapeutic endeavors in some cases. The success of behavioral interventions with other eating disorders suggests that such interventions might be useful in treating pica (Finney, Russo, and Cataldo, 1982).

Obesity

The popularity of new weight-loss diets, best-selling diet books, commercial weight-loss programs, and over-the-counter diet pills all attest to the significance of the problem of overweight in our society. Through the popular media increasing numbers of people have become aware of the health and personal difficulties associated with being overweight. In addition, mass advertising reminds us of the slender, trim ideal.

The number of individuals who are considered obese is difficult to establish due to variability in both the measures (for example, weight, proportion of body fat) and criteria (for example, 15 percent or 20 percent overweight) employed. In addition, prevalence rates vary with factors such as sex, socioeconomic status, and age. Available data suggest, however, that about 20 to 30 percent of the population is obese and that prevalence increases with age (e.g., Lauer, Conner, Leaverton, Reiter, and Clarke, 1975; Stunkard, D'Aquili, Fox, and Filion, 1972).

Regardless of the specific criterion, it is clear that obese children are likely to continue to be obese. Miller, Billewicz, and Thomson (1972) reported small but statistically significant correlations between birth weight and weight-for-height ratios at age 5. An even stronger association has been found between obesity during infancy and obesity in later childhood (Eid, 1970). Overweight in childhood is also related to overweight in later life. Miller and associates (1972) reported highly significant correlations between weight-for-height ratios at age 5 and at age 22. Eighty percent of the sample of overweight children, 10 to 13 years old, examined by Abraham and Nordsieck (1960) were still overweight at 26 to 35 years of age.

In addition, overweight parents are more likely to have overweight children (Charney, Goodman, McBride, Lyon, and Pratt, 1976). This relationship does not seem attributable to genetic factors only, since it appears to hold for adoptive children as well (Garn, Cole, and Baily, 1976). And interestingly, Mason (1970) reported that when dog owners have a normal physique, the incidence of obesity in their pets is 25 percent while for owners who are obese the incidence rises to 45 percent! These data certainly argue for the importance of environmental factors.

Accumulating evidence suggests that obesity in childhood is associated with numerous health problems and social and psychological consequences (Israel and Stolmaker, 1980). Obesity may contribute to orthopedic disorders, inadequate circulation, and a number of factors thought to be associated with later cardiovascular disease. The obese child may be devalued by peers as well. Kindergarten children have been found to prefer figures of average physique and dislike those of fat physique (Lerner and Schroeder, 1971). When children were asked to rank pictures of other children in terms of their likeability, obese children were ranked as less liked than those with recognized physical handicaps (Maddox, Back, and Liederman, 1968). Evidence regarding the psychological effects of obesity on children is somewhat contradictory, however. Some investigators have found no differences in psychological adjustment between obese and normal subjects (Sallade, 1973; Stunkard, 1959). Others indicate that obese children have poor self-concepts and report more psychological problems than do control children (e.g., Held and Snow, 1972).

In a recent study parents of each overweight child enrolled in a weight-loss program completed Achenbach's Child Behavior Checklist prior to treatment (Israel and Simon, 1983). The advantage of this instrument (described in Chapter 5) is that norms exist both for a general population and for a population of children receiving services for psychological problems (clinic-referred children). The Internalizing, Externalizing, and total behavior problem scores of children in this study were significantly higher than the norms for the general population. However, they were significantly lower than the norms reported for clinic children. These findings are illustrated in Figure 6-1. Overweight boys also had higher scores than the "general" norms on six of the nine behavior problem subscales and lower scores than the clinic-referred norms on seven of the nine subscales. Overweight girls' scores were higher than the general norm on seven of the nine subscales and lower than the clinic-referred norms on eight of the nine subscales. Thus, it would appear that overweight children attending a weight-loss program experience psychological difficulties to a greater extent than do members of the "general" population, but that their problems are not as severe as those exhibited

by children receiving psychological assistance for other behavioral problems. Clearly, it cannot be determined from this study whether these problems contribute to or result from being overweight.

Nevertheless, for the obese child interaction with peers and adults is likely to be adversely affected by negative evaluations. The reduction of activity and dexterity that often accompanies obesity makes social isolation and rejection even more likely. It thus seems likely, but not inevitable, that obese children may experience significant psychological difficulty.

Eating Patterns and Activity Levels of Obese Children. Since weight gain is due to excessive caloric intake and/or inadequate calorie expenditure, investigators have looked for differences in the eating and activity behaviors between overweight and nonoverweight children. Observations of school-age children suggest that overweight children exhibit a number of eating behaviors that are different from those of their normal-weight peers. Overweight children have been reported to interrupt their eating less and take more bites per interval of time, but with fewer chews per bite—thus, they eat faster (Drabman, Hammer, and Jarvie, 1977; Marston, London, and Cooper, 1976). Similar results have been found among preschoolers, some as young as 1½ years of age (Drabman, Cordua, Hammer, Jarvie, and Horton, 1979). Thus, rapid eating may occur in obese children almost as soon as they first attempt to feed themselves.

There is some evidence that lack of self-control is related to these eating patterns. For example, Israel, Stolmaker, and Prince (in press) found that children rated low on self-control interrupted their eating less than children rated higher in self-control. Moreover, Lewittes and Israel (1978) found a relationship among kindergarten children between how overweight they were and their ability to delay gratification. In this study children could earn a desired food reward either for themselves or for themselves and other children if they were able to

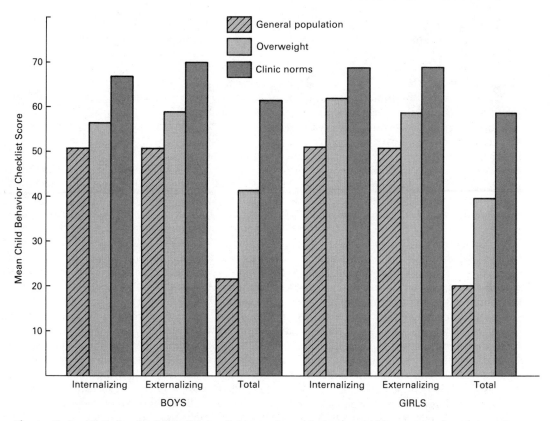

Figure 6–1 Mean Internalizing, Externalizing, and total behavior problem scores for overweight children, clinic norms and general population norms. *Adapted from Israel and Simon, 1983.*

wait alone in a room until an experimenter returned. If the child could not wait the entire delay period, a less preferred food was given. Overweight children were able to delay less well than normal-weight children when they earned the reward *only* for themselves. However, no such relationship between overweight and ability to delay existed when the children earned the reward for themselves and other children. These results suggest that there may indeed be some relationship between overweight and self-control, although, not surprisingly, this relationship can be affected by environmental conditions.

Overweight children may also have different activity levels. Rose and Mayer (1968) me-

chanically recorded the movements of infants. They found that overweight infants were less active than those of normal weight. However, most of the studies on activity level have been conducted with adolescents, and results are inconsistent. When the adolescents themselves, or their parents, were asked to report on their activity levels, obese adolescents were found to be less active than their normal-weight peers (Johnson, Burke, and Mayer, 1956; Stephanic, Heald, and Mayer, 1959). Motion pictures of obese adolescent girls also showed them to be relatively inactive (Bullen, Reed, and Mayer 1964). In contrast, studies employing other objective measures of activity, such as pedometers and heart rate, have found no differences between obese and nonobese children (e.g., Brad-field, Paulos, and Grossman, 1971; Stunkard and Pestka, 1962).

The Etiology of Obesity. The causes of obesity are probably multiple and complex. Much of the experimental work on hunger, satiety, and obesity has been conducted with animals because of the practical and ethical difficulties involved in conducting such research with humans. Any conclusions regarding the causes of human obesity are best thought of as tentative, and many possible determinants and explanations (biological, psychological, social) exist.

Two of the most prominent biological explanations are the set point and adipose cellularity theories. *Set point theory* is based on the general observation that organisms maintain remarkable consistency in their internal environments. There is some evidence that humans have a point at which body weight is set and that changes away from this set point result in psychological and metabolic changes intended to defend the "ideal" body weight (Nisbett, 1972). It is presumed that obese individuals have a high set point. Support for this theory comes from research on laboratory animals with lesions of the hypothalamus (a part of the brain involved in food regulation) and observations of humans under circumstances of experimental starvation and excessive feeding (Brownell and Venditti, 1982).

The *adipose cellularity (fat cell) theory* is based on the fact that adipose tissue is central in determining body weight. There are two ways in which changes in adipose tissue can influence body weight: increases in cell number or increases in cell size. The fat cell theory assumes that for any individual the size of fat cells can change, but the number of cells is stable from early in life. Dieting can reduce the size of fat cells but not their number. Data from weight-loss programs are both supportive of and inconsistent with this theory (Bjorntorp et al., 1975; Jeffrey, Wing, and Stunkard, 1978).

Another biological theory comes from a study by DeLuise, Blackburn, and Flier (1980), who suggest that obese persons have lower levels of an enzyme involved in the pumping of sodium and potassium across cell membranes. This results in lower energy use in the cells of obese persons. Thus, in obese persons fewer calories are burned up as heat, and more are stored as fat.

Each of these theories is controversial or based upon limited data. It is thus premature to presume any particular predisposing biological mechanism for obesity. The danger in doing so is that obesity may be viewed as inevitable for a particular individual.

The significant influence of psychosocial factors on the development of obesity is acknowledged by most major workers in the field. Social learning theory, probably the most influential of the psychosocial theories, recognizes biological influence but views social learning as more central. Problematic food intake and inactivity are presumed to be learned in the same manner as any other behavior. Children observe and imitate the eating behavior of their parents and others around them and are reinforced for engaging in that style of eating. Eating is also reinforced by immediate pleasurable consequences, while the negative consequences of gaining weight are more delayed. Eating may become strongly associated with physical and social stimuli, so that it becomes almost automatic in some circumstances. Moreover, some people learn to use food to overcome negative mood states such as boredom and anxiety. The treatment of obesity developed from a social learning perspective seeks to break these learned patterns and develop more adaptive ones.

Television provides a striking example of how the larger society might contribute to the development of weight problems in children (Jeffrey and Krauss, 1981). On average, American children watch between two and three hours of television each day throughout their entire childhood (Liebert and Schwartzberg, 1977; Poulos, Harvey, and Liebert, 1976). In addition to the negative effects of inactivity associated with television watching, children's diets are probably adversely influenced. For example, Masover and Strampler (1977) found that approximately 70 percent of advertising time on four Chicago channels was devoted to promoting food generally high in fat, saturated fat, cholesterol, sugar, or salt, and that only 3 percent of the time was devoted to fruit and vegetables. Direct support for the negative effects of such advertising is provided in a study by Jeffrey and his colleagues, in which children viewed commercials edited from typical Saturday morning programming (Jeffrey, Lemnitzer, Hess, Hickey, McLellarn, and Stroud, 1979). Results of a behavioral eating test indicated that low-nutritional advertising was more effective than pronutritional advertising.

Behavioral Treatment. As with adult obesity, the treatment of childhood obesity by traditional methods (diets, medication, hormones, therapeutic starvation) has been found to be relatively ineffective (cf. Coates and Thoresen, 1978). The success of behavioral programs for adult weight reduction has recently led a number of investigators to implement similar programs with overweight children. The approach presumes that modification of the child's eating and activity patterns is necessary for long-term weight change. Thus, rather than recommending a specific diet or rapid weight loss, behavioral treatments have tended to focus on slower—and presumably more long-lasting—changes in the child's habits.

The work of Israel and his colleagues illustrates the general approach. Children and parents attend eight to twelve weekly therapy meetings, during which four areas are regularly addressed: *Intake*, which includes nutritional information, caloric restriction, and changes in actual eating and food preparation behaviors; *Activity*, which includes both specific exercise programs and increasing the energy expended in daily activities, for example, walking to a friend's house rather than being driven; *Cues*, which seeks to identify the external stimuli and internal cues associated with excessive eating or inadequate activity; and *Rewards*, which provides positive consequences for progress by both the child and parent. Homework assignments are employed to encourage the families to

Behavioral treatment programs for overweight children attempt to change child and family habits so as to reduce caloric intake and increase energy expenditure.

change their environments and to practice more appropriate behavior. Following the initial eight- to twelve-week period, phone contact and periodic visits are maintained in order to assist the family in problem solving. The frequency of these contacts is reduced gradually over time (Israel, Stolmaker, Sharp, Silverman, and Simon, 1983).

A number of studies support the effectiveness of the behavioral approach to children's weight reduction (e.g., Aragona, Cassady, and Drabman, 1975; Epstein, Wing, Koeske, Andrasik, and Ossip, 1981). These studies also suggest that weight losses can be maintained over periods of three months to a year. Even more promising are the results of Rivinus, Drummond, and Combrinck-Graham (1976), which indicate that more than two years following treatment, children had reduced from an average of 72 percent overweight to 21 percent overweight. One-third of the children were normal weight. Improvement continued to a point five years after treatment (Rivinus, 1979). Although this is an uncontrolled study and therefore must be judged cautiously, both the impressive degree of weight loss obtained in this study and the persistence of the changes are encouraging.

A number of controlled investigations have suggested factors that may enhance the effectiveness of behavioral programs. The importance of positively reinforcing changes in the child's behavior and attending to parental behavioral change have both been emphasized (e.g., Aragona, Cassady, and Drabman, 1975; Israel, et al., 1983). Israel, Stolmaker, and Guile (1983) investigated the contribution of training in parenting skills to successful weight reduction. Parents of overweight children were given a three-week course in the general principles of child management. They then participated with their children in a behavioral weight-reduction program similar to the one by Israel, Stolmaker, Sharp, Silverman, and Simon described above. Throughout these sessions the application of the general parenting skills to weight reduction was emphasized. Another group of parents and children received the usual behavioral weight-reduction program alone—which does focus on parental behavior but does not include separate parent training. At the end of treatment both groups achieved a significantly greater weight loss than control children. A measure of change in eating habits also indicated changes for treated children but not for controls. Parents who received child-management training scored higher on a test of knowledge of behavioral change principles than did parents who participated only in the behavioral weight-reduction group. One year following treatment, children whose parents had received separate child-management training maintained their weight losses better than did

other treated children (see Figure 6-2). These results suggest the importance of providing parents with the skills to maintain appropriate behavior once the treatment program has ended. This is a particularly important issue in light of repeated evidence that individuals frequently regain the weight they have lost.

Anorexia Nervosa

Anorexia nervosa refers to a persistent refusal to eat, which appears to be motivated by the pursuit of extreme thinness and a fear of gaining weight rather than by a genuine lack of hunger. It is found primarily in young females, with onset often in adolescence. Males are estimated to account for only 5 to 15 percent of reported cases. Once rare, the incidence of anorexia nervosa appears to have increased dramatically over the past twenty years. It is now estimated at between .24 and 1.6 per 100,000 of the population (Bemis, 1978). Precise statistics are not available, however, because of inconsistencies in criteria and inadequate records. Moreover, reports of rising incidence (e.g., Bruch, 1973) may be due to heightened awareness of the disorder rather than actual increases in frequency.

Table 6-1 presents the set of diagnostic criteria employed by DSM-III. The major symptom of anorexia nervosa is substantial loss of body weight due to extreme caloric restriction. Although approximately two-thirds of all anorexics recover or improve, the others remain chronically ill or die (Bliss and Branch, 1960). Estimated mortality rates range from 3 to 25 percent (Bemis, 1978). The seriousness of extreme weight loss can be seen in Bruch's (1979) description of one of her clients:

. . . she looked like a walking skeleton, with her legs sticking out like broomsticks, every rib showing, and her shoulder blades standing up like little wings. Her mother mentioned, "When I put my arms around her I feel nothing but bones, like a frightened little bird." Alma's arms and legs were covered with soft hair, her complexion had a yellowish tint, and her

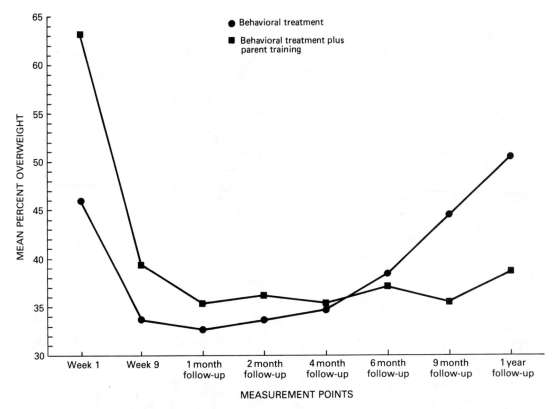

Figure 6-2 Changes in percent overweight for children in the behavioral treatment alone and children in the behavioral treatment plus parent training condition. *Adapted from Israel, Stolmaker, and Guile, 1983.*

dry hair hung down in strings. Most striking was the face—hollow like that of a shriveled-up old woman with a wasting disease, . . . Alma insisted that she looked fine and that there was nothing wrong with her being so skinny. "I enjoy having this disease and I want it." (pp. 2–3)

In addition to extreme weight loss, alternating periods of bulimia (uncontrolled excessive

Table 6-1 DSM-III Diagnostic Criteria for Anorexia Nervosa

A. Intense fear of becoming obese, which does not diminish as weight loss progresses.

B. Disturbance of body image, e.g., claiming to "feel fat" even when emaciated.

C. Weight loss of at least 25% of original body weight or, if under 18 years of age, weight loss from original body weight plus projected weight gain expected from growth charts may be combined to make the 25%.

D. Refusal to maintain body weight over a minimal normal weight for age and height.

E. No known physical illness that would account for the weight loss.

American Psychiatric Association, 1980.

eating), often followed by self-induced vomiting or laxative abuse, may occur. Other unusual eating habits, such as monotonous eccentric diets, hoarding food, and obsessive preoccupation with food and cooking, are also common. A frequent symptom in anorexic females is amenorrhea, absence or suppression of menstruation. Many other physical problems are typically present as well (for example, vomiting, low blood pressure, infantile uterus). The individual frequently has a distorted body image—insisting that she is overweight and overestimating her physical dimension on a variety of measures (Bemis, 1978).

Predisposing Variables. Deliberate self-starvation is clearly a puzzling and bizarre phenomenon. In an attempt to understand anorexia nervosa, researchers and clinicians have sought to identify preexisting conditions and personality patterns. The typical clinical report is of a good student who is a well-behaved, introverted, and conscientious child. Although clinical reports mention early feeding difficulties, it is not clear that early eating problems are more frequent in these children. Much debated is the idea that self-starvation begins as an attempt to control genuine obesity. Comments that the young girl is "getting plump" may stimulate normal dieting, which evolves into anorexic refusal to eat. The frequency of dieting among adolescent girls, however, raises the question of why some girls who begin this common social ritual persist well beyond the point of socially desired slimness. Numerous clinical reports suggest that anorexia nervosa is a response to stress, often the onset of puberty itself, for which existing skills seem inadequate (Bruch, 1973; Katz, 1975; Rollins and Blackwell, 1968).

The family dynamics of anorexics have received a great deal of attention. Mothers are most commonly described as intrusive and dominant, and a "peculiar relationship" and "ambivalence" between mother and child are often noted (e.g., Bruch, 1973). Fathers, on the other hand, are frequently characterized as playing a minor role in the family structure and

Schiffman/Gamma-Liason

Grammy award singer Karen Carpenter, who died at age 32 of heart failure, had suffered from the effects of anorexia nervosa for many years.

as being passive and ineffectual (e.g., Sours, 1974). Nevertheless, a number of writers dissent from these descriptions, which are based on clinical reports rather than controlled studies (e.g., Dally, 1969). Moreover, it is difficult to determine whether any pattern observed in a family subsequent to the onset of a disturbance is a cause or effect. This is especially the case in anorexia, in which family observations have frequently followed the offspring's sustained life-threatening refusal to eat.

Biological Model. Given the striking somatic components of anorexia nervosa, it is not surprising that some investigators believe that biological disturbance is primary in the etiology of the disorder. The most frequently cited cause is a fundamental malfunctioning of the hypothalamus (Lundberg and Walinder, 1967; Russell, 1970). Indeed, many of the processes known to be regulated by the hypothalamus are disturbed in anorexia nervosa (for example, eating, activity level). Moreover, animals who have received hypothalamic lesions for experimental purposes exhibit behavior similar to the symptoms of anorexia nervosa (Templer, 1971).

Those who argue against a primary biological etiology note that the hypothalamus contains both ascending and descending pathways to the higher centers of the brain cortex, therefore making it difficult to establish the directionality of causation. Perhaps self-induced starvation by the anorexic damages the hypothalamus, or psychological stress interferes with its functioning. In either of these cases biological disturbance would be secondary to psychogenic variables.

Critics of the biological model also argue that starvation itself may be responsible for the other symptoms. They note that most anorexics return to regular hormonal and menstrual functioning following weight gain (e.g., Crisp, 1970; Sherman, Halmi, and Zamudio, 1975). They also point out that some of the physical and psychological symptoms of anorexia nervosa occur in individuals who have experienced prolonged food deprivation but are otherwise normal. For example, high rates of menstrual disturbance in concentration camp prisoners are often cited as evidence that amenorrhea results from starvation. However, amenorrhea sometimes occurs before severe food restriction, and some female prisoners resumed normal menstruation prior to their release, despite continued aversive conditions (Williams, 1974; Halmi, 1974). Thus, starvation itself does not appear to be an adequate explanation of amenorrhea.

It could be argued that the "classic" premorbid personality profile (that is, the introverted, conscientious child) exhibited by anorexics is evidence for a nonorganic conceptualization. There is disagreement, however, as

to whether this personality profile exists in all anorexics and, if it does, whether it is actually a byproduct of starvation. Some writers (e.g., Bruch, 1973; Dally, 1969) note that the over-representation of anorexics in the middle and upper classes also suggests a nonorganic etiology. Inconsistencies in these social-class data and the possibility that the findings are due to selection factors rather than to actual prevalence makes this criticism problematic. Finally, it appears that anorexia nervosa is not associated with genetic transmission (e.g., Bruch, 1969; Halmi and Brodland, 1973), ruling out inheritance of organic disturbance.

It seems that none of the arguments refuting the biological model are sufficient to disprove it. Nevertheless, they suggest that an interaction of organic and psychological variables is the most likely explanation of anorexia nervosa.

Psychodynamic Model. The psychodynamic perspective on anorexia nervosa has its origins in the early psychoanalytic proposition that equated eating behavior with sexual instinct (S. Freud, 1918/1959). It was suggested that the adolescent is unable to meet the demands of mature genitality and regresses to a more primitive level, at which oral gratification is associated with sexual pleasure. From this perspective the symptoms of anorexia nervosa can be viewed in the following manner: Refusal to eat is viewed as a defense against oral impregnation fantasies (A. Freud, 1958), bulimia is seen as an expression of unconscious desires for sexual gratification (Kaufman and Heiman, 1964), and amenorrhea is viewed as a symbol of pregnancy (Kaufman and Heiman, 1964) and a denial of femininity (Lorand, 1964).

The classical psychodynamic perspective has been expanded to include aggression and guilt in the formation of the anorexic symptoms, giving many possible meanings to food and eating. For example, according to Falstein, Feinstein, and Judas (1956), "Eating may be equated with gratification, impregnation, intercourse, performance, pleasing the mother, growing; or it may represent castrating, destroying, engulfing, killing, cannibalism. Food may symbolize the breast, the genitals, feces, poison, a parent or a sibling'' (p. 765).

The classical psychodynamic interpretation of anorexia nervosa can be criticized on a number of grounds (cf. Bemis, 1978). Most accounts rest entirely on clinical inference, and many are based on a single case. Some of the basic assumptions have failed to receive support; for example, the existence of oral impregnation fears has not been supported in large samples. Also, the dynamic significance of symptoms is at least questionable, given similar symptoms in normal individuals undergoing starvation. Furthermore, it appears that psychoanalytic therapy has been ineffective in the treatment of anorexia nervosa.

It is noteworthy that clinicians working within the psychodynamic tradition, but from the perspective of ego psychology, have shifted their focus from oral drives to disorders of the mother-child relationship. Early maternal deprivations are thought to produce defects in the child's ego and ambivalence toward the mother. This, in turn, results in the anorexic symptoms. The anorexic is ill prepared to face adulthood and rejects food (the maternal substitute) and the feminine role. Writers such as Bruch (1973) and Selvini (1971) describe the mother as putting aside the needs of the developing child in order to satisfy her own need for what she thinks is appropriate behavior. Bruch (1979) has also described the anorexic girl as the object of much family attention and control who is trapped by a need to please and a feeling of inadequacy:

She enjoyed being home but missed the fuss they had made about her in the past, when everybody was acutely concerned about her . . . .

Even as a child Ida had considered herself not worthy of all the privileges and benefits that her family offered her, because she felt she was not brilliant enough. An image came to her, that she was like a sparrow in a golden cage, too plain and simple for the luxuries of her home, but also deprived of the freedom of doing what she truly wanted to do. (pp. 23–24)

The anorexic symptom is then seen as a desperate attempt by the child to express an individual identity.

Bruch (1973) has presented information on the long-term outcome of a number of cases she has treated. However, it is difficult to attribute various outcomes to specific therapeutic procedures. Length of contact varied from brief consultation to long-term psychotherapy, and the mode and length of treatment in each case are not sufficiently detailed. Thus, conclusions regarding the efficacy of psychodynamically oriented treatments also appear to rest heavily on clinical observation and inference.

The Behavioral Model. The behavioral perspective has contributed relatively little to explaining the etiology of anorexia nervosa. Refusal to eat is usually conceptualized as a form of avoidance or as a learned response that is reinforced by attention (Ayllon, Haughton, and Osmond, 1964; Leitenberg, Agras, and Thomson, 1968). These conceptualizations parallel those of other perspectives that emphasize fear of fatness and complex family dynamics; but they are far less elaborated by behavioral writers. Attention is given instead to treatment procedures.

Treatment can be conceptualized as consisting of two phases: intervention to restore body weight and save the patient's life, and subsequent extended intervention to ameliorate long-standing adjustment difficulties and maintain normal weight. Behavioral interventions have tended to focus on the first phase and to rely almost exclusively on operant learning principles. One of the strengths of this approach has been relatively precise experimental control.

In an attempt to determine what aspects of earlier programs were responsible for successful treatment, Agras, Barlow, Chapin, Abel, and Leitenberg (1974) examined separately the effects of positive reinforcement, negative reinforcement, informational feedback, and the size of meals. In a series of single-case experiments with nine patients, the authors demonstrated that all four variables contributed to increased food intake and weight gain. Information given to the patient about the number of mouthfuls eaten, calories consumed, and weight change was the most potent variable. Without such feedback positive reinforcement seemed relatively ineffective. Furthermore, patients appeared to be eating more and gaining weight in order to leave the hospital (negative reinforcement) rather than for praise and access to activities (positive reinforcement). However, like positive reinforcement, negative reinforcement was not as important as feedback about caloric intake and weight gain. Size of meal was the least significant factor, although patients ate more when larger meals were served.

Behavioral interventions have proven reasonably successful at producing weight gain in a relatively brief period of time. Most interventions have focused on treating hospitalized patients at a fairly critical point in their illness, and their effectiveness at this life-threatening point is an obvious contribution. However, long-term weight maintenance is still an issue that needs attention, as is the social-emotional adjustment of patients after they leave the hospital. Behavioral investigators themselves (e.g., Stunkard and Mahoney, 1976) have called for placing increased emphasis on continued treatment and family therapy to maintain the behavior reinforced during the period of hospitalization. Behavioral problems other than weight loss that may be associated with anorexia nervosa also need to be addressed.

Family Systems Approach. The provision of family therapy derives from the observation by clinicians of varying persuasions that the families of anorexic patients are intimately involved in the maintenance of anorexic behavior. The family systems approach, represented by Minuchin and his colleagues, views the family context as central to many disorders involving somatic symptoms, including anorexia nervosa (Minuchin, Rosman, and Baker, 1978). These investigators criticize other perspectives for continuing to view the locus of pathology as within the individual and for

emphasizing the past. Minuchin does employ behavioral procedures, however, to produce weight gain during brief hospitalization or on an outpatient basis.

The families of anorexics, according to Minuchin, can be described as enmeshed. The members of the family do not have distinct identities. Rather, there are diffuse boundaries among family members—they are highly involved in each other's lives. These families also exhibit a high degree of communication and concern. In this kind of family the child learns to subordinate the self (individuality) to family loyalty. In turn, the child is protected by the family, and this further subverts the child's autonomy. Goal-directed behavior, for example, is not engaged in for the sake of competence but for family approval. This highly enmeshed family is a tightly woven system in which questioning of the system is not permitted. Even the usual kind of individual life change threatens the family's equilibrium. Adolescence may produce a particularly difficult crisis in such a family. The child's overinvolvement with the family prevents the individualization that is necessary at this time of life; the view of one's self as independent of the family is blurred at best, and peer experience is lacking.

Anorexic families are enmeshed families in which there has always been a special concern with eating, diet, and rituals pertaining to food. The anorexic adolescent begins to challenge the family system, and rebellion is exhibited through refusal to eat. The family comes to the "protection" of the child—and maintains its stability—by making the child a sick, incompetent person who requires care. The sick role is reinforced, and the child is both protected and scapegoated.

It follows from this conceptualization that the entire family system must be treated. Therapy begins around a family lunch session, where the goal is to enact family issues rather than just talk about them. The specific techniques employed vary with the age of the identified patient and the structural characteristics of the family. Minuchin and his colleagues (1978) report that 86 percent of the fifty-three cases they treated recovered from both the anorexia and its psychosocial components. Although controlled research is lacking, these early results seem promising, and the logic of family systems therapy seems compelling.

DISORDERS OF ELIMINATION

Like eating and feeding, the process of toilet training is one of the major early child-rearing tasks faced by parents. Perhaps more than feeding, toilet training is likely to be an area of difficulty. Parental concern is reflected in a survey which revealed that of twenty-two categories of preschool problems, parents rated difficulties in toilet training second in importance (Mesibov, Schroeder, and Wesson, 1977). The high value placed on cleanliness in our society plus the frequency with which toilet training is used as a developmental milestone results in frequent pressure for early toilet training.

The usual sequence of acquisition of control over elimination is nighttime bowel control, daytime bowel control, daytime bladder control, and finally, nighttime bladder control. While there is considerable variation in children's developmental readiness, most middle-class American parents begin toilet training sometime between 12 and 18 months of age. Training usually is completed between the ages of 18 and 30 months.

As with other central socialization experiences, toilet training is of obvious importance to the child's overall development. The major focus of this section, however, is on enuresis and encopresis, the failure to achieve appropriate control over elimination.

Enuresis

The term *enuresis* comes from the Greek word meaning "I make water" and refers to the involuntary voiding of urine, after an age at which toilet training is expected to have been completed. About 50 percent of 2-year-olds in the United States display daytime bladder control;

this figure rises to 85 percent for 3-year-olds and 90 percent for 4-year-olds (Erickson, 1978; Walker, 1978). Nighttime bladder control is achieved more slowly. According to one investigator, it is reported in 67 percent of 3-year-olds, 75 percent of 4-year-olds, 80 percent of 5-year-olds, and 90 percent of 8½-year-olds (Harper 1962, cited by Walker, 1978). The comparison between daytime and nighttime control is shown in Figure 6-3.

Disagreement exists as to the precise definition of enuresis. The most obvious question is the *age* at which lack of urinary control should be diagnosed as enuresis. The diagnosis is applied variously after age 3 (e.g., Kanner, 1972; Wright, Schaefer, and Solomons, 1979) to after age 5 (Gerard, 1939). A second issue is the *frequency of lack of control* necessary for diagnosis. DSM-III sets a criterion of at least two such events per month for children of ages 5 and 6, and at least once a month for older children. Other authors set a more stringent standard, requiring regular wetting an average of three or more times a week (e.g., Doleys, 1979b). Clearly, the criterion for frequency is likely to be tied to age, with less frequent wetting required for the diagnosis of enuresis in older children.

No matter which definition is employed, the incidence of enuresis in boys is about twice as

Figure 6-3 Percentage of children of various ages achieving daytime and nighttime bladder control. *From Liebert and Wicks-Nelson, 1981.*

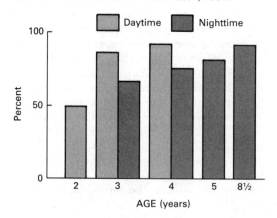

great as that in girls. It is frequently stated that the prevalence of enuresis is greater in lower socioeconomic groups. However, inconsistencies in the data and methodological concerns suggest caution in this conclusion. Enuresis is often classified into subtypes. One distinction is that between the more common nocturnal enuresis (nighttime bed-wetting) and diurnal (daytime) enuresis. Kanner (1972) indicated that of the cases seen at his clinic, 63 percent were nocturnal, 30 percent were both nocturnal and diurnal, and only 7 percent were diurnal alone. A second distinction exists between primary and secondary enuresis. Primary enuresis refers to instances in which the child has never demonstrated bladder control. Secondary enuresis is diagnosed if the problem is preceded by a period of urinary continence. About 85 percent of all cases of enuresis are of the primary type (de Jonge, 1973).

According to Glicklich (1951), enuresis was recognized as a problem as early as 1550 B.C. Numerous causes and treatments have been suggested, reflecting the existing *zeitgeist*. Recommended treatments have included wood lice and swine's urine and, as late as the eighteenth and nineteenth centuries, burning of the sacrum for boys and insertion of inflated rubber bags into the vagina for girls (Anders and Freeman, 1979; Sours, 1978).

Enuresis is often regarded as a sign of emotional or psychiatric disturbance. Gerard (1939), in a frequently cited paper, suggested that in a majority of cases enuresis was a symptom of a clear-cut neurotic syndrome, arising out of a fear of harm from persons of the opposite sex. A similar position is advocated by some contemporary authors, largely of psychoanalytic orientation (e.g., Pierce, 1975; Sperling, 1965).

Other clinical reports suggest that enuresis is rarely an isolated symptom. Reports of thumb sucking and temper tantrums, as well as other problem behaviors, and suggestions of general immaturity are common in the clinical literature (e.g., Kanner, 1972; Kessler, 1966). Nevertheless, Schaffer (1973) and Rutter, Yule, and Graham (1973), in summarizing much of the earlier work, indicate that there is little consistent evidence that enuresis is correlated with either a specific psychiatric syndrome or a specific behavioral problem (for example, thumb sucking). Also, we can not tell from available reports whether behavioral problems were present prior to the enuresis, and thus may have been precipitating factors, or whether they developed as a result of the enuresis. A majority of contemporary writers, in fact, tend to focus on the social and emotional consequences of enuresis. Enuretic children, especially as they become older, are very likely to experience difficulties with peers and other family members. It would also not be surprising if the child's self-image suffered.

The Causes of Enuresis. Many explanations of why enuresis occurs include some physical factor. Involuntary urination clearly caused by physical disorders such as diabetes or a seizure disorder are not considered instances of the problem. However, several other physical factors are thought to account for "functional" enuresis or to predispose the child to develop the disorder via some other mechanism, such as learning.

It is frequently suggested that differences in sleep and arousal contribute to the development of enuresis. Many parents and professionals, for example, assume that nocturnal enuresis occurs because the child is an unusually deep sleeper. Indeed, parents often spontaneously report difficulty in arousing their enuretic children during the night. However, research findings regarding the role of sleep and arousal are inconsistent. It appears that wetting can occur in any of the stages of sleep, not just in "deep sleep." Wetting does not, however, typically occur in REM (rapid eye movement) sleep, which is associated with dreaming. On the other hand, Finley (1971) observed that wetting does tend to occur in lighter sleep as the child gets older. If the urge to void occurs in increasingly lighter periods of sleep, the child is increasingly likely to wake. Thus, children would be expected to "outgrow" wetting, as indeed they do.

Do enuretic children exhibit EEG patterns indicating that they may be more difficult to arouse than nonenuretic children? The findings are inconsistent, with some authors noting differences in the EEG patterns of enuretic children while other investigators do not (Wright, Schaefer, and Solomons, 1979). Finley and Perry (1973) have asked the question about EEG patterns somewhat differently: Are there different kinds of enuretics, some of whom have normal EEG patterns and some who do not? They conclude from their findings that this is the case and that enuretics with abnormal EEG patterns also exhibit emotional disturbances. Another group of investigators agree that enuretics may or may not have arousal disorders (Ritvo, Ornitz, Gottlieb, Poussaint, Maron, Ditman, and Blinn, 1969). However, in contrast, they suggest that children with no arousal (EEG) deficit are more likely to have emotional problems.

It is a common observation that the family histories of enuretics frequently reveal a number of relatives with the same problem. Kanner (1972) indicated that in 52 percent of the cases seen in his clinic, one or more members of the family were or had been enuretic. Some authors view this as a strong indication of a hereditary basis for enuresis. Bakwin (1971), who favors such an explanation, also presented data on 146 twin pairs, at least one of whom was enuretic after the fourth birthday. Sixty-eight percent of the monozygotic twins, but only 36 percent of the dizygotic twins, were concordant for enuresis. Kaffman and Elizur (1977) studied 114 4-year-old kibbutz children who had siblings at least 5 years old. There was a markedly greater incidence of bed-wetting among the siblings of enuretic children than among siblings of dry children, even though each kibbutz sibling had been toilet trained by a separate caretaker in a different child's communal house. While all these results can be interpreted in terms of family attitudes and child-rearing practices rather than family genes, the results strongly suggest that at least some portion of enuretic children have an organic predisposition toward enuresis. This as yet unspecified

risk factor may or may not result in the development of enuresis, depending upon various experiential factors, such as parental attitude and training procedures.

The central tenet of behavioral theories of enuresis is that wetting results from a failure to learn control over reflexive wetting. This failure can result from either faulty training itself or other environmental influences that interfere with learning. Many behavioral theories incorporate some physical difficulty (for example, arousal deficit) into their explanation. Individual theories differ in the extent to which they emphasize the physical system or the learning process in their explanations (Lovibond and Coote, 1970).

In contrast to behavioristic-physiological theories, the psychodynamic explanation of enuresis tends to view wetting as a symptom of some underlying emotional disorder. Gerard (1939) traced the sexual significance of enuresis to Freud's original view that when bed-wetting was not the result of an epileptic attack, it was a "pollution" (ejaculation). On the basis of psychoanalysis and unspecified other methods, Gerard concluded that most cases were "true enuresis"—due to "psychogenic" causes. In these cases wetting was viewed as a substitute for masturbation. She also noted that this explanation is consistent with the frequent cessation of enuresis during puberty, when increased sexual stimulation may provoke the child to masturbate, despite anxiety and guilt. Wetting, as a substitute for masturbation, would thus no longer be necessary. In a small portion of the cases discussed by Gerard, wetting was viewed as the result of a conscious attitude rather than an unconscious conflict. In these cases enuresis might be due to jealousy of a new sibling or revenge against the person conducting bladder training.

Other psychodynamic authors have taken a somewhat modified position. Sours (1978) suggests that primary enuresis caused by psychogenic (as opposed to organic) factors falls into two distinct categories. The first is "conditioning failure"—caused mostly by the deprivations of low socioeconomic class and to a lesser extent by parental permissiveness in children of higher SES. The second category of primary enuresis is due to difficulties in dissolution of a symbiotic mother-child relationship. Sours describes secondary enuresis as a neurotic reaction to either external stress (for example, birth of a sibling) or internal stress, often of a psychosexual or Oedipal nature. This description of secondary enuresis bears close resemblance to Gerard's largest category of "true enuresis."

Psychodynamic explanations are based almost entirely on clinical impressions of cases seen in psychiatric settings. Perhaps this represents a biased sample of cases of enuresis. Most current explanations of enuresis do not stress psychodynamics. Rather, the problem is most frequently viewed as arising out of physical-developmental and/or environmental-learning factors.

Treatment approaches.   Although a variety of drugs have been used in the treatment of enuresis, imipramine hydrochloride (Tofranil), a tricyclic antidepressant, is probably the most commonly employed. Imipramine is believed to influence the muscles surrounding the bladder so that urine can be retained while the child sleeps through the night. Although a number of studies have demonstrated that imipramine is superior to placebos (Stewart, 1975), it appears that it is not as successful as the urine-alarm procedure, which is described below. Moreover, the use of any pharmacological agent should be approached with caution.

Behavioral treatments for nocturnal enuresis have been classified into three categories: those that employ a urine alarm, those that employ retention control training, and those that modify stimulus or consequent events but do not employ either of the first two methods as the primary mode of treatment (Doleys, 1977).

The most popular and carefully researched of these methods is the urine-alarm system. This procedure was originally introduced by the German pediatrician Pflaunder in 1904 and was adapted and systematically applied by Mowrer and Mowrer (1938). Since then the device and the procedures have been refined by a number of investigators. The basic device consists of an absorbent bed sheet between two foil pads (Figure 6-4). When urine is absorbed by the sheet, an electric circuit is completed that activates an alarm. The awakened child is taught to turn off the alarm and go to the bathroom to finish voiding. The bedding is then changed, and the child returns to sleep. Usually records of dry and wet nights are kept, and after fourteen consecutive nights of dryness, the device is removed. According to the Mowrers, the procedure is based upon classical conditioning. Tension of the full bladder (the conditioned stimulus) is paired with the alarm (the unconditioned stimulus) to produce awakening (the conditioned response) and inhibition of urination. Eventually the child wakens in response to a full bladder prior to wetting and setting off the alarm. Lovibond (1964) has proposed an alternative theoretical explanation—avoidance learning. He suggests

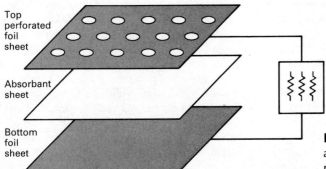

Top perforated foil sheet

Absorbant sheet

Bottom foil sheet

Figure 6-4   The urine alarm apparatus has become one of the most popular methods for treating enuresis.

that the child learns to inhibit urination in order to avoid the aversive consequence of being awakened by the alarm.

Doleys (1977) examined the research conducted on the urine-alarm system over a fifteen-year period ending in 1975. Of the 628 cases reported, 75 percent were successfully treated. Treatment duration was between five and twelve weeks. For studies in which adequate follow-up data were available, it was found that in 41 percent of the cases, relapses occurred. Some of the relapsed subjects were retreated, and 68 percent of them achieved dryness. In comparison with placebo, no-treatment, and verbal psychotherapy groups, the urine alarm has been found to be superior (Baker, 1969; DeLeon and Mandell, 1966; Werry and Cohrssen, 1965; White, 1968). As previously noted, the success rates reported for imipramine are not as good as those reported for the urine alarm. Furthermore, Doleys (1977) concluded that imipramine and amphetamines used as adjuncts to the urine alarm do not improve treatment effectiveness.

Two modifications of the standard urine-alarm procedures have been found to reduce relapses. In the *intermittent alarm procedure* the alarm sounds subsequent to some percentage of wettings rather than to each wetting (continuous alarm procedure). Relapse rates of only 15 percent for an intermittent condition as compared to 44 percent with a continuous condition have been reported (Finley, Besserman, Bennett, Clapp, and Finley, 1973).

The second modification of the standard urine-alarm procedures is the use of *overlearning*. Once the initial criterion for dryness is met, the child's intake of liquids prior to bedtime is increased, and the urine-alarm procedure is continued for some period of time. Fewer relapses have been reported for those children for whom overlearning was added (Jehu, Morgan, Turner, and Jones, 1977; Young and Morgan, 1972). It is unclear at this time whether overlearning is effective because the child learns to generalize dryness to fuller bladder levels or because of the extended training period. A number of authors (e.g., Doleys, 1979b) have

suggested a period of extended training prior to increases in fluid intake and then a gradual increase in fluid level. The procedure may help avoid possible relapse.

The behavioral technique of *retention control training* is based on the assumption that enuretic children have a smaller bladder capacity than normal children. This assumption has received some experimental support (Zaleski, Garrard, and Shokier, 1973) and, along with the desire to find a daytime training procedure, has provided the impetus for retention control training.

Retention control training was first introduced by Kimmel and Kimmel (1970). During the day the child is required to refrain from voiding for gradually increasing periods of time, up to thirty minutes. Positive reinforcement is given for successful retention. However, Doleys (1979b) indicates that early positive results (Paschalis, Kimmel, and Kimmel, 1972) have not been replicated in other studies. The possibility of employing retention control training for that subpopulation of enuretics with demonstrated small bladder capacity (Hunsaker, 1976), or in combination with the urine-alarm approach (Doleys, 1979b), has been suggested.

Azrin and his co-workers (Azrin, Sneed, and Foxx, 1974) combined a number of procedures for nighttime treatment into a program referred to as *dry-bed training*. A urine alarm is placed only in the parents' bedroom so as to wake the parents to any wetting episode. On the first night trained therapists come into the home and explain the procedures to the child and parents. Prior to going to bed the child engages in a series of positive practice trials (practicing the appropriate series of toileting behaviors). Each hour the child is awakened, praised for a dry bed, and given more liquid. Each wetting episode is followed by cleanliness training and twenty positive practice trials. Cleanliness training consists of the child changing his or her bed and nightclothes. On the second and subsequent nights, the child is aroused by the parents and given cleanliness training and positive practice following each wetting episode. Positive reinforcement is given following each dry night. After seven consecutive dry nights the alarm is taken off the bed. Cleanliness training and positive practice continue to be administered following each wetting episode. Posttraining supervision by the therapist is reintroduced if two wettings occur within a seven-day period.

In analyzing dry-bed training, where the alarm does not sound in the child's room at all, Azrin and Thienes (1978) called into question the classical conditioning explanation of the urine-alarm procedure. They suggested that the social consequences of wetting were more important than the pairing of the bell with urination. A modification of dry-bed training was therefore proposed which eliminated the urine alarm entirely. Added to the program were daytime procedures similar to Kimmel and Kimmel's retention control training. The elimination of some of the aversive nighttime procedures for the parents, and the substitution of daytime training, were also intended to reduce dropout rates.

Azrin and Thiens tested their ideas by randomly assigning fifty-five children to either the revised dry-bed or the standard urine-alarm treatment. Parents were told that they could transfer their child to the other procedure if they were not satisfied with progress after two weeks. Figure 6–5 presents the percentage of wet nights prior to training and after two weeks of treatment. The new dry-bed procedure was clearly superior to the urine-alarm system. In fact, parents of most of the children assigned to the urine-alarm method requested to be switched to the other method after two weeks. Of the fifty-one children who began dry-bed training, all but four completed training. All achieved the criterion of fourteen consecutive dry nights, with the average child having only four accidents before achieving the desired goal. Relapses occurred in 20 percent of the cases, but reinstitution of the procedures resulted in the child regaining control in all instances. At the end of one year, wetting occurred on less than 2 percent of the nights.

Treatments derived from a behavioral perspective have been demonstrated to be quite successful in eliminating wetting. Nevertheless,

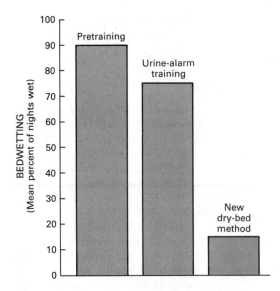

Figure 6–5 Comparison of bedwetting prior to training and after the first two weeks of either urine-alarm or revised dry-bed treatment.

Adapted from Azrin and Thienes, 1978. Reprinted by permission of the publisher and the author.

several workers—primarily from a psychodynamic perspective (e.g., Sperling, 1965)—have argued that the behavioral procedures, as well as medical procedures, treat only the overt symptom of wetting and fail to deal with the underlying problems that are the core of enuresis. They argue that such treatment will result in new symptoms as substitutes for wetting. A number of studies have addressed this issue. In general, they have revealed an absence of any new symptoms following the elimination of wetting. Baker (1969) found that prior to treatment enuretic and control children did not differ significantly on any of a number of adjustment measures. Furthermore, after behavioral intervention the treated children still measured the same as the controls or actually showed improvement. Sachs, DeLeon, and Blackman (1974) evaluated fifty-one children treated by conditioning or psychotherapy-counseling methods (control group). Their results indicate that in both groups children's adjustment improved following treatment and that these improvements remained at the one-year follow-up. Thus, there seems little support for the argument of symptom substitution.

Encopresis

Functional encopresis refers to the passage of feces into the clothing or other unacceptable area, in the absence of any organic pathology. As with enuresis, there is some disagreement as to the age at which encopresis should be diagnosed. The usual range is from 2 (e.g., Bakwin and Bakwin, 1972) to 4 years of age (e.g., DSM-III; Werry, 1979c). The later age criterion is based on a number of studies that indicate that 50 percent of children achieve bowel control by age 2, while 100 percent do by age 4 (Bellman, 1966; Stein and Susser, 1967). The significance of deciding when to acknowledge the problem and intervene lies in the fact that in retentive encopresis (described below) the longer one waits to intervene, the more distended the child's colon becomes. This consideration suggests that perhaps Doley's (1979a) recommendation of a criterion of 3 years of age is a reasonable one.

Several subcategories of encopresis are usually suggested. The primary-secondary distinction, similar to the distinction made for enuresis, refers to whether or not the child exhibited a previous period of bowel control. The other major distinction is between retentive and nonretentive encopresis. Encopretic children who produce normal stools, which are passed into clothing or some other inappropriate place, are described as nonretentive. The retentive type refers to the child who retains feces in the bowel, resulting in the rectum and colon being distended by hard feces (a condition often referred to as megacolon). The bowel then becomes incapable of responding with a defecation reflex when filled with normal amounts of fecal matter. Children exhibiting retentive encopresis may demonstrate overflow incontinence, the leakage of fecal matter around the impacted material. Retentive encopresis is usually estimated to account for approximately 80 percent of all cases. A third distinction made with regard to encopresis is based on whether or not

the child seems to exhibit a fear of the toilet itself.

Less writing and research have been done concerning encopresis than concerning enuresis. Estimates of the incidence of encopresis range from 1.5 to 5 percent (Wright et al., 1979). The higher figures are usually cited by authors whose estimates are based on children attending psychiatric or general pediatric clinics (e.g., Levine, 1975). The figure of 1.5 percent is most frequently cited for the incidence of encopresis in the general population (e.g., Bellman, 1966). The problem occurs more frequently in males and is reported to be rare in adolescents and adults.

The Causes of Encopresis. Three categories of theories concerning the etiology of encopresis are dominant: These include medical, psychodynamic, and learning-behavioral theories. Regardless of the approach, most theories acknowledge the possibility that different types of encopresis may result from different causative mechanisms.

The medical perspective tends to take a neurodevelopmental approach. Encopresis is viewed as resulting from developmental inadequacies in the structure and functioning of the physiological and anatomical mechanisms required for bowel control. These organic inadequacies are viewed as temporary.

As is the case in enuresis, psychodynamically oriented theorists tend to view encopresis as a sign of some deeper conflict. Much of early psychoanalytic thinking relied heavily on Freud's description of the anal character as exhibiting the triad of obstinacy, parsimony, and orderliness. Bemporad's (1978) perspective is representative of more recent psychodynamic explanations in that it places more emphasis on family and social context. This viewpoint is derived from Anna Freud's (1965) model of developmental lines, in which the child is seen as progressing from giving or retaining feces as a sign of love or anger, to independent control. A disruption in the mother-child relationship may therefore result in the child losing any internalized urge to be clean or perhaps never progressing to that point. The initial selection of the symptom is maintained, according to Bemporad, by particular types of family processes. For example, the child's continuing need for structure and security produced by a perfectionistic-sterile home environment may help maintain the encopresis.

The behavioral perspective on encopresis stresses faulty toilet training procedures. Primary encopresis is largely explained by a failure to apply appropriate training methods consistently. Secondary encopresis is said to occur because positive consequences maintain soiling, and inadequate reinforcement is given for appropriate toileting (Doleys, 1979a). Fear arising out of initially painful defecation caused by constipation has also been offered as an explanation (Doleys, 1979a; Wright et al., 1979). These various learning explanations are not incompatible with physiological explanations. For example, insufficient physiological-neurological mechanisms may be compounded by poor parental training.

Treatment Approaches. The treatment of encopresis has also received less research attention than has enuresis. Medical treatments of encopresis tend to rely on the use of laxatives and enemas, usually combined with manipulation of diet. Davidson, Kugler, and Bauer (1963) describe a successful three-phrase program employed with 119 encopretics. The first phase consisted of the use of enemas to eliminate fecal impactions and mineral oil to induce regular bowel movements. The second phase was begun after one month and consisted of the gradual removal of laxatives so as to develop regular nonlaxative bowel movements. This phase lasted three months. The final phase consisted of maintaining and monitoring the habits established during the program. Doleys (1979a), in reviewing reports of medical treatment, found a number of consistent problems—absence of controlled studies, inadequate descriptions of procedures, inadequate data collection, and an absence of information on the establishment of appropriate toileting behaviors.

The use of psychoanalysis or some other form of verbal psychotherapy has often been advocated for the treatment of encopresis. However, most of the available information is based on clinical case reports (e.g., Bemporad, 1978; Pinkerton, 1958), controlled studies are lacking, and treatment procedures are only vaguely described. Furthermore, reported success rates fall below those for other methods. This may, in part, be due to highly selected, more severe samples (Werry, 1979c).

Most current behavioral reports advocate using a combination of both medical, reinforcement, and punishment procedures. One such program has been described by Wright and his co-workers (Wright, 1973, 1975; Wright and Walker, 1976). Positive reinforcement is delivered both for appropriate toileting behavior and for having clean pants. Loss of privileges, fines, and the like are given as punishments for soiling. Enemas and suppositories are used to induce defecation on days when it does not occur, but these artificially induced bowel movements are not reinforced. The program is withdrawn gradually and discontinued following one week of continence. Wright (1975) reported a 100 percent success rate for fourteen children in an average treatment period of about seventeen weeks. Only one child relapsed during a six-month follow-up period. As we might expect, program success and duration were related to parental consistency in carrying out the program. Though reports of behavioral programs suggest good success rates there is a clear need for well-controlled group studies.

SLEEP DISORDERS

Parents commonly complain of sleep problems in their offspring. During the child's first year of life, the parents' most frequent complaint is that the child does not sleep through the night. A reluctance to go to sleep, and nightmares, often occur during the second year, and the 3- to 5-year old presents a variety of problems, including difficulty in going to sleep, nighttime wakenings, and nightmares. Parents seek psychological assistance only when these problems become severe or chronic. Some professionals may view the difficulties as indicative of more extensive disturbance, perhaps excessive fear of separation from the parents. Of possibly greater concern to both parents and professionals, however, are the disturbances labeled *Sleepwalking Disorder* and *Sleep Terror Disorder*.

Sleepwalking

Sleepwalking (somnambulism) begins with the child sitting upright in bed. The eyes are open but appear "unseeing." Usually the child leaves the bed and walks around, but the episode may end before the walking stage is reached. This sequence occurs without the child achieving full consciousness, and there is no later memory of the episode. During the episode the sleepwalker is often remarkably unresponsive to communication and to being awakened. The child may then wake and experience several minutes of disorientation, or may return to bed without gaining consciousness. It was once believed that the sleepwalking child was exceptionally well coordinated and safe. This has proven to be a myth, and, indeed, physical danger may be one of the serious consequences of the disorder.

Approximately 15 percent of children between the ages of 5 and 12 have isolated experiences of walking in their sleep. Sleepwalking disorder, that is, persistent sleeping-walking, is estimated to occur in 1 to 6 percent of the population and to be more frequent in boys than in girls (Anders and Weinstein, 1972). Somnambulism usually persists for a number of years but then disappears by adolescence.

The vast majority of sleepwalking episodes occur in the first one to three hours following sleep onset, and they last from a few minutes to half an hour. Sleepwalking occurs exclusively in non-REM sleep. This appears to invalidate the idea that sleepwalking is the acting out of a dream. A characteristic EEG pattern has been found to precede each episode (Kales, Jacobson, Paulson, Kales, and Walter, 1966). The fact that this pattern exists in 85 percent of children during the first year of life but is present in only 3 percent of 7- to 9-year-olds has led

Kales and his colleagues to suggest that central nervous system immaturity is of significance in sleepwalking disorder. This does not, however, rule out psychological or environmental factors. Frequency of sleepwalking has been reported to be influenced by the specific setting, stress, and fatigue (Ablon and Mack, 1979; Anders and Weinstein, 1972). Greater concordance rates for sleepwalking among monozygotic twins than among dizygotic twins (40 percent versus 9 percent) and family patterns of sleepwalking have also been reported (Bakwin and Bakwin, 1972; DSM-III, 1980).

Nightmares and Night Terrors

Both nightmares and night terrors are fright reactions that occur during sleep. Night terrors is recognized by DSM-III as a diagnostic category and is labeled Sleep Terror Disorder. It has also been referred to as *Pavor Nocturnus*. Nightmares and night terrors have been distinguished on several grounds. Nightmares occur during REM sleep, while night terrors occur during non-REM sleep arousal. Table 6-2 presents Kanner's clinical differentiation between these disorders.

Night terror is quite striking in that the still-sleeping child suddenly sits upright in bed and screams. The face shows obvious distress, and there are signs of autonomic arousal, such as rapid breathing and dilated pupils. In addition, repetitive motor movements may occur, and the child appears disoriented and confused. Attempts to comfort the child are largely unsuccessful. Later recall of the episode or its contents is lacking. Night terrors are most common in preschool children, although they occur in older children as well.

Causes and Treatment of Sleep Disorders

Children's sleep disorders have received very little attention from social learning-behaviorally oriented investigators. Clement's (1970) successful treatment of a 7-year-old boy for somnambulism by wakenings similar to those

Table 6-2 Characteristics Differentiating Nightmares and Night Terrors

Nightmare	Night Terror
Fearful sleep experience after which the child wakes. The fear then gives way to good orientation and clear realization.	Fearful experience taking place in the sleep, not followed by waking.
Slight defensive movements or moaning immediately before waking are the only noticeable activities.	The features are distorted and express terror. The eyes stare, wide open. The child sits up in bed or even jumps to the floor in great agitation, runs helplessly about, clutches at persons or objects, implores an imaginary dog or burglar to leave, shouts for help, or screams inarticulately.
The child is already awake when the parents notice distress. After being calmed, the child is able to give a coherent account of what has happened.	The child, sleeping through the episode, is unable to give any account of the distress, which is being lived out in all details while the parents look on and infer from shouts and actions what might go on within the child. The attack cannot be cut short by any amount of calming and reassurance.
The child, after waking, knows all the persons and objects of the surroundings.	The persons and objects of the environment are often not recognized and may be mistaken for others and woven into the dream content.
No hallucinations ever occur.	The child hallucinates the frightening dream objects into the room.
No perspiration occurs.	Perspiration occurs.
A long period of waking and consciously going over the dream situation may follow.	Peaceful sleep instantly follows the termination of the reaction.
The entire episode rarely lasts longer than one or two minutes.	The terror may last for some time, up to fifteen or twenty minutes.
The contents are remembered more or less clearly. The incident itself is always recalled.	There is complete amnesia for the contents as well as for the occurrence of the episode.

Adapted from Kanner, 1972.

employed in the treatment of enuretics is one exception. The milder, more common, problems, such as refusal to sleep, are usually attributed to the parental attention they receive. Suggestions for treatment frequently involve giving the child attention prior to bedtime, not attending to the child after bedtime, and providing attention the next day as a reward for good behavior the previous night (Wright et al., 1979; Yen, McIntire, and Berkowitz, 1972).

With advances in EEG technology, biologically oriented investigators have begun to attend to children's sleep disorders. Most etiological explanations involve central nervous system immaturity. From this perspective it is assumed that maturation will likely result in disappearance of the problem (Ablon and Mack, 1979; Anders and Weinstein, 1972). This of course does not preclude the possibility of intervention in cases where it is unwise to wait for normal maturation to occur. Drug treatment has frequently been suggested, but there is little empirical evidence to support its efficacy and some concern for side effects (Ablon and Mack, 1979; Wright et al., 1979).

The most extensive (albeit still-limited) writings concerning the etiology of childhood sleep disorders have come from the psychodynamic perspective. Fraiberg (1950), for example, notes that sleep disturbances begin in the second year. The psychodynamic perspective views this as a time when the child's immature ego has difficulty handling anal conflicts. The child's dreams are believed to be symbolic substitutes for the pleasures of soiling, but the fear of loss of the mother is great and awakens the child. Similarly, reluctance to go to sleep may be viewed as resulting from separation anxiety and the young child's fear of loss of control regarding toilet training or aggressive wishes (Kessler, 1966). Psychoanalytic theorists also note that sleep disturbances are particularly common between the ages of 4 and 6. Night fears, in this age group, are postulated to result from a fear of loss of control over masturbation and Oedipal anxieties. The male child is said to project his fear of his father, and this anxiety is transformed into fear of some other object, such as a skeleton. In night terrors the child is reliving some traumatic event—most likely the witnessing of parental sex relations (Fraiberg, 1950; Kessler, 1966). The psychodynamic interpretation of childhood sleep disturbances should be viewed with caution, since it is based almost exclusively on clinical reports. Indeed, much progress regarding our knowledge of children's sleep disorders and their treatment remains to be made (Anders, 1982).

SUMMARY

Establishing patterns of eating, elimination, and sleep are important developmental tasks in all cultures. A variety of psychological perspectives acknowledge that these developmental tasks have important implications for broadly based adjustment issues. This chapter, however, discusses problems specific to each of these areas of functioning.

A number of eating disorders have received attention from researchers and clinicians. Of these, obesity and anorexia have probably generated the most interest. Behavioral and biological explanations of the etiology of obesity

have probably received the greatest support. The learning of eating and activity patterns have formed the basis of behavioral treatment programs. This approach to altering food-related lifestyle is the intervention with the most empirical support. However, behavioral psychologists themselves agree that greater weight loss and better maintenance results still need to be achieved. Although a number of biological theories of obesity—such as fat cell and set point explanations—have received support, they remain controversial. The contribution of biology is not questioned; however, its exact role and treatment implications remain unclear.

Anorexia nervosa is a serious, life-threatening disorder characterized by extreme weight loss. A number of other physical and psychological problems are present as well. Psychodynamic, behavioral, biological, and family systems theorists have all offered explanations for this puzzling phenomenon. An explanation that incorporates organic and psychological influences is most likely, but no particular explanation is clearly supported. Nonetheless, most perspectives agree on the importance of family influences. The treatment of anorexia has been conceptualized as a two-phase process—resumption of eating with associated weight gain, and maintenance of improvement and treatment of associated problems. Behavioral interventions have exhibited reasonable success during the first, life-saving, phase. They have attended less to the second part of the treatment. Family systems theorists have employed behavioral procedures and also have addressed the family process that maintains weight loss and the other problems associated with anorexia.

Enuresis and encopresis are disorders of elimination that seem best explained by a combination of biological predisposition and failure to train-learn. The use of imipramine is the most popular and best-supported medically oriented procedure for treating enuresis. Behavioral interventions based on classical conditioning and operant learning theories (for example, bell and pad method and dry-bed training) have reported high success rates and low rates of remission and seem to be the treatments of choice at present. Encopresis, which has received considerably less attention, is probably best dealt with through a combination of medical (for example, enemas) and behavioral (for example, reinforcement) procedures.

Sleep disorders such as sleepwalking, nightmares, and night terrors are probably best conceptualized as resulting from a combination of nervous system immaturity and environmental factors (for example, stress and fatigue). At present the effectiveness of various treatments remains unclear.

7

INTERNALIZING DISORDERS

FEARS AND PHOBIAS

Clinical Description and Classification
Developmental Characteristics
  of Children's Fears
Etiological Paradigms
Treatment of Childhood Phobias
School Phobia

OTHER ANXIETY DISORDERS

The Overanxious Child
Obsessive-Compulsive Disorder

THE SOCIALLY WITHDRAWN CHILD

Peer Relations and Development
Peer Relations and Adjustment
Behaviors Related to Peer Status
  and Social Competence
Treatment of the Withdrawn Child

CHILDHOOD DEPRESSION

Prevalence
Classification of Childhood Depression
Is Childhood Depression a Distinct
  Disorder?
Theories of Depression
Assessment and Treatment

SUMMARY

As we already have seen, behavioral problems of childhood can be grouped into two broad categories: externalizing and internalizing disorders. The present chapter deals with the latter category. Historically the problems now under discussion have been referred to as neuroses, a term that is becoming controversial. However, the traditional labels of phobias, obsessions and compulsions, anxiety neurosis, and depression continue to appear in most of the literature and current clinical practice. Recent empirical analyses reveal that many of the behaviors subsumed by these labels tend to occur together (see Table 7-1). This cluster of behaviors has variously been designated as the internalizing, overcontrolled, or anxiety-withdrawal dimension or syndrome.

Whether or not they employ traditional terms such as *neurosis,* clinicians of varying persuasions appear to agree that there is a cluster of childhood behavioral problems that tend to occur together and that can be characterized in certain ways. For example, we might observe that the problems exhibited seem to be directed more at the self than at others. Of course, this distinction is not clear-cut. It is true that these problems often do not create as much disruption as do many of the other disorders we will discuss. However, parents or other adults can become upset if a child is excessively fearful, withdrawn, or sad. Also, the child's own distress and the obstacles to normal development which may be created are cause for concern. It is also the case that these problems may arise, at least in part, because of the reactions they create in others. Nonetheless, the disorders described in this chapter do more clearly appear to cause the child distress than do those described as externalizing disorders (see Chapter 11). They are also less severe and incapacitating than those disorders often labeled psychotic, which are described in Chapter 8. Finally, most clinicians would agree that many of these disorders are characterized by a high level of anxiety.

FEARS AND PHOBIAS

Children's fears have played a major historical role in the development of modern theories of behavior (Barrios, Hartmann, and Shigetomi, 1981). Freud's (1909, 1953) case of Little Hans served as the basis for much of the psychoanalytic conceptualization of phobias. It also marked the beginning of child psychoanalysis and supported several aspects of psychoanalytic theory. Watson's case of Little Albert followed shortly thereafter (Watson and Rayner, 1920). It not only demonstrated the conditioning of fear but was one of the early tests of behaviorism. Finally, Jones (1924) provided one of the first interventions based on behavioral principles in her treatment of Peter's fear of white furry objects. Given this early history, one would expect a well-developed literature concerning the genesis and treatment of children's fears. Nevertheless, much is yet to be discovered (cf. Berecz, 1968; Graziano, DiGiovanni, and Garcia, 1979).

Table 7-1 Characteristics Associated with the Internalizing, Overcontrolled, or Anxiety-Withdrawal Syndrome

Anxious, fearful, tense
Shy, timid, bashful
Withdrawn, seclusive, friendless
Depressed, sad, disturbed
Hypersensitive, easily hurt
Self-conscious, easily embarrassed
Feels inferior, worthless
Lacks self-confidence
Easily flustered
Aloof
Cries frequently
Reticent, secretive

Adapted from Quay, 1979 by permission of John Wiley & Sons, Inc.

Clinical Description and Classification

Phobias, as distinguished from normal fears, are judged to be excessive, persistent, or unadaptive. Children with phobias try to avoid the situation or object they fear. When confronted with the threatening stimulus, they "freeze" and become immobile. In crying out for help, the child may describe feelings of tension, panic, or even fear of death. Nausea, palpitations, and difficulty in breathing may also occur. A reaction may also be judged phobic when the threatening stimulus is benign, and fear is thus inappropriate. Finally, fears that may be appropriate or normal at one age may be judged to be clinically significant if exhibited by an older child.

There is no well-established system of classification for children's fears. At one time it was fashionable to enumerate long lists of phobias including pyrophobia (fear of causing fire), taphephobia (fear of being buried alive), ergasiophobia (fear of activity), and even phobophobia—the fear of phobias (Berecz, 1968). The possibilities were endless, as, indeed, were the lists generated. This method of classification did not prove useful, and more recent attempts have tended to group phobias into broader categories.

Miller and his colleagues (1974) have proposed a classification system which divides phobic reactions into fears of physical injury, natural events, social anxiety, and miscellaneous (Table 7-2). The results of several studies applying factor analysis to reports of children's fears served as the primary basis for this proposed classification. Conventional wisdom and considerations of treatment and assessment also contributed to the schema. For example, physical injury is subdivided into concrete and abstract objects, since the former—but not the latter—may be more amenable to *in vivo* treatment. Miller et al. view their schema as tentative, since little reliable research is available.

There is no category for childhood fears in DSM-III. The adult category of Phobic Disorder (or Phobic Neurosis) may be applied to children. One problem that exists in employing this diagnosis, especially with younger children, is that the client presumably is aware that the fear is excessive or unreasonable. It is not clear that all children showing phobic behavior are capable of this perspective.

Developmental Characteristics of Children's Fears

Knowing about the development of normal fears is important for understanding fears that require clinical attention. Many investigators over the last half century have attempted to explore the development of fears, and a number of trends are suggested.

The General Incidence of Fears. Several classic studies indicate that normal children exhibit a surprisingly large number of fears. Jersild and Holmes (1935) reported that children aged 2 to 6 years averaged between four and five fears and exhibited fearful reactions once every 4½ days. MacFarlane, Allen, and Honzik (1954), in their longitudinal study of children from 2 through 14 years, found that specific fears were reported in 90 percent of the sample. Forty-three percent of the 6- to 12-year-olds studied by Lapouse and Monk (1959) had seven or more fears. An interesting aspect of the latter study is the suggestion that mothers may underestimate the prevalence of fears in their children. Mothers reported 41 percent fewer fears than indicated by the children's own reports.

It appears, though, that while fears among children are quite common, intense fears may not be quite so prevalent. In one investigation in the United States, less than 5 percent of mothers indicated that their children exhibited extreme fear, as opposed to normal (5 to 15 percent) or no (84 percent) fear reactions (Miller et al., 1974). This is consistent with Rutter, Tizard, and Whitmore's (1970) Isle of Wight study, in which serious fears were reported in only 7 per 1,000 of the 10- and 11-year-olds studied.

Sex Differences. Girls exhibit a greater number of fears than boys. Their fears are also

Table 7-2 Proposed Classification of Childhood Phobias

I. Physical Injury	II. Natural Events	III. Social Anxiety	IV. Miscellaneous

A. Abstract
  1. War
  2. Riots
  3. Poisoned food
  4. Specific foods
  5. Dying
  6. Someone in family dying
  7. Seeing someone wounded
  8. Being wounded
  9. Someone in family getting ill
  10. Becoming ill
  11. Germs
  12. Choking
  13. Having an operation
  14. Hospitals
  15. Hell
  16. The devil
  17. Breaking a religious law
  18. Being kidnapped
  19. Getting lost
  20. Being adopted
  21. Parents getting a divorce
  22. Going crazy
B. Concrete
  1. Flying in airplane
  2. High places
  3. Deep water
  4. Strangers
  5. Being seen naked
	A. Storms
	  1. Tornadoes, floods, earthquakes
	  2. Lightning
	  3. Thunder
	B. Dark
	C. Enclosed places
	  1. Bathrooms
	  2. Closets
	  3. Elevators
	  4. Confined or locked up
	  5. Strange rooms
	D. Animals
	  1. Snakes
	  2. Insects, spiders
	  3. Rats or mice
	  4. Frogs or lizards
	  5. Dogs or cats
	  6. Horses or cows
	E. Other
	  1. Fire
	  2. Frightening thoughts or daydreams
	  3. Ghosts
	  4. Being alone
	  5. Nightmares
	  6. Space creatures or monsters
	  7. Faces at window
	  8. Masks or puppets
	  9. Sight of blood
	  10. People with deformities
	  11. Toilets
		A. School
		  1. Young (Age 3–10)
		    (a) Type I
		    (b) Type II
		  2. Old (Age 11–22)
		    (a) Type I
		    (b) Type II
		B. Separation
		  1. Separation from parents
		  2. Parts of house
		  3. Going to sleep at night
		C. Performance
		  1. Tests or examinations
		  2. Being criticized
		  3. Making mistakes
		  4. Reciting in class
		D. Social Interactions
		  1. Attending social events
		  2. Making another person angry
		  3. Crowds
		  4. Being touched by others
		E. Medical Procedures
		  1. Doctors or dentists
		  2. Getting a shot
		F. Other
		  1. Riding in a car or bus
			1. Dirt
			2. Furry toys
			3. Sirens
			4. People who are old
			5. Crossing a street
			6. People who are ugly
			7. Loud sounds, as caps, firecrackers, explosions
			8. People in uniforms, a policeman, mailmen, etc.
			9. People of the opposite sex
			10. Having bowel movements
			11. Members of another race

From Miller, Barrett, and Hampe, 1974 by permission of John Wiley & Sons, Inc.

likely to be of snakes and mice, while boys are more likely to exhibit excessive fear of being criticized (Lapouse and Monk, 1959; Miller et al., 1974). Some studies suggest a greater fear intensity in girls as well (Graziano et al., 1979). Findings of sex differences probably should be interpreted with caution, since it is quite possible that sex-role expectations influence the displaying and reporting of fear.

Age Trends.   The number of children who report one or more fears, and the number of fears reported, seem to decline with age. The relationship may not be a linear one, however, since there seems to be a sharp increase at about 11 years of age (Graziano et al., 1979). In addition, certain fears appear to be common at particular ages (Table 7-3). Most authorities would not classify such age-appropriate fears as phobias unless they are exaggerated or continue longer than expected.

Childhood fears also seem to be relatively short-lived. Mild fear reactions and those specific to a developmental period might be expected to dissipate quickly (Barrios et al., 1981). But even serious childhood phobic reactions may disappear in a relatively short period of time. It has been suggested that fears that persist beyond two years be considered of clinical duration (e.g., Graziano et al., 1979). How-

ever, if the fear—though short-lived—creates sufficient discomfort or interferes with functioning, intervention may be justified.

A developmental perspective is helpful in evaluating children's fears (Harris and Ferrari, 1983). The age-specific and transitory nature of many fears is important in judging the seriousness of this behavior. Developmental changes in children's perception also bear on our understanding of their fears. For example, increasing differentiation of internal reality from objective reality may help explain why younger children fear ghosts and monsters, while older children have more realistic fears of physical danger or injury. Social expectations and the acceptability of expressing certain fears at a particular age must also be considered. Older children, for example, may be socialized to believe that bedtime fears are inappropriate, and they therefore may not express them. Age combined with sex-role expectations may produce similar effects. For example, while equal proportions of younger boys and girls indicate that they have frightening dreams, 10 percent of sixth-grade boys as opposed to 70 percent of same-age girls report this experience (Bauer, 1976).

Some fears may be short-lived, and childhood fears may not be the precursors of those experienced by adult phobics (Marks and Gelder, 1966); however, childhood fears may have long-range implications. Adult phobics report having more phobias as children than do nonphobics (Solyom, Beck, Solyom, and Hugel, 1974). Although this is retrospective data, a developmental perspective might also suggest that the expression of a fearful style may change with age rather than disappear.

Etiological Paradigms

The two dominant perspectives regarding the etiology of fears are the psychoanalytic and the behavioral paradigms. As mentioned earlier, the conceptualization of fear played a central role in the general development of both these perspectives. Thus, each viewpoint's explanation of the development of phobias is prototypal of its general etiological perspective.

Table 7-3   Common Fears at Different Age Levels

Age	Fears
0–6 Months	Loud noises, loss of support
6–9 Months	Strangers
1st Year	Separation, injury, toilet
2nd Year	Imaginary creatures, death, robbers
3rd Year	Dogs, being alone
4th Year	Dark
6–12 Years	School, injury, natural events, social
13–18 Years	Injury, social
19 + Years	Injury, natural events, sexual

From Miller et al., 1974 by permission of John Wiley & Sons, Inc.

The Psychoanalytic View. In Freud's case study of Little Hans (p. 57), phobias were viewed as arising from unresolved Oedipal conflicts—demonstrated by Hans's desire for his mother and fear of his father and castration. The unacceptable idea of possessing mother and displacing father (and the anxiety associated with it) was repressed. This was followed by projection—Hans believed that his father wanted to be rid of or harm him. The final step, and the essence of the phobia, was displacement. The unconscious anxiety was displaced onto some external object which in some way was related to or symbolic of the unconscious wish. For Hans the horse was related to, among other things, playing horsie with his father, his father's appearance (the horse's muzzle symbolized his father's mustache), and castration (symbolized by the horse's biting). Displacement allowed Hans to avoid the phobic object—the horse—whereas he could not avoid his father. Moreover, displacement eliminated Han's ambivalent feelings toward his father.

Psychoanalytic theorists have changed and extended Freud's theory, but the basic structure has not been altered. The primary changes allow that affect arising from aggression, separation anxiety, and non-Oedipal sexuality may also serve as the basis for phobia development (cf. Nemiah, 1980). For example, Berecz (1968) cites Pinchon and Arminda's (1950) case of a balloon phobia in an 11-month-old girl. The phobia, developed during her mother's second pregnancy, was conceptualized as resulting from the child's destructive impulses toward the content of her mother's rounded abdomen.

As in other instances, the psychoanalytic framework for childhood phobias is based almost exclusively on interpretation of case material. Although the clinical detail is rich, generalizations cannot easily be made. Also, the concepts employed are difficult to operationalize and therefore difficult to evaluate or refute.

Behavioral Paradigms. Behavioral theories have taken a number of different forms. Classical conditioning, operant conditioning, and observational learning explanations have all been offered.

CLASSICAL CONDITIONING. Watson and Rayner's (1920) case of Little Albert, described earlier (p. 59), served as the prototype for classical conditioning explanations. A neutral stimulus present during a high-intensity fear response or repeatedly paired with a fear-evoking stimulus comes to evoke anxiety or fear. The acquired response may persist without additional pairings (reinforcement). Moreover, generalization to stimuli perceived as similar to the original phobic stimulus can also occur. Extinction does not take place, since the child avoids the conditioned stimulus and thus never learns that it is no longer followed by the unconditioned stimulus.

OPERANT CONDITIONING. The operant perspective suggests that reinforcement, primarily social reinforcement in the form of attention, is the central etiological mechanism in phobias. According to this viewpoint, children are taught to be afraid by parents or others who selectively attend to and reward fearful behavior, perhaps unintentionally. Withdrawal from social situations and accompanying "fearful" behavior may allow the child to stay with the mother, who out of sympathy soothes the child, offers favorite foods, and plays the child's favorite game. The child's fear or anxiety is not posited as a mediator in this model. A set of behaviors is maintained by its consequences.

TWO-FACTOR THEORY. Originally proposed by Mowrer (1939), two-factor theory incorporates both classical and operant concepts. Phobias are thought to originate through classical conditioning and to be subsequently maintained through operant conditioning. The pairing of a neutral (conditioned) stimulus with an aversive unconditioned stimulus produces the initial fear or anxiety. Subsequently, avoiding the conditioned phobic stimulus produces a reduction in anxiety or fear—which then maintains the avoidant behavior.

OBSERVATIONAL LEARNING. Phobic responses may also be learned when children observe and imitate the phobic responses of others. For example, a little girl who observes her mother's fear of dogs may imitate this reaction. Children can also learn vicariously through another's repeated descriptions. That children often exhibit the same kinds of fears as their parents is consistent with an observational learning explanation (e.g., Bandura and Menlove, 1968).

EVALUATION. Learning theory explanations have been criticized on a number of grounds. Some attempts to classically condition fears have not been successful (e.g., Bregman, 1934; English, 1929), although the methodological adequacy of these studies has been questioned (cf. Delprato, 1980). Classically conditioned fear responses in humans also seem to extinguish rather quickly (e.g., Bridger and Mandel, 1965). Ethical considerations have restrained researchers from employing highly aversive stimuli in these studies. Nonetheless, rapid extinction is not consistent with the observed persistence of phobic behavior. Also, clinical reports suggest that a large proportion of phobic cases occur with no evidence of the frightening-traumatic event assumed in the classical conditioning model. For example, snake phobics often report that they cannot recall any frightening experiences with snakes. Similarly, phobic patients often fail to report observations of fearful models. Since both criticisms are based on retrospective reports, the possibility exists that these experiences did occur and that memory is distorted. On the other hand, people who have traumatic experiences or observe frightening situations do not usually become phobic. Also, some stimuli (for example, snakes) are more likely than others to become conditioned fear stimuli. Some explanation of these differences is necessary for an adequate understanding of how phobias are acquired.

Criticisms of the operant model have ques-

By observing the reactions of adults, children may learn to become fearful—even of objects or situations that others might consider harmless.

tioned the lack of attention given to thoughts and subjective feelings of fear. Furthermore, critics point out that phobic individuals often suffer considerably as the result of their behavior. They also avoid harmless situations that might provide considerable pleasure. Why do the positive consequences—attention or anxiety relief—continue, over long periods, to outweigh the negative consequences? While it is possible to argue that the positive rewards are more powerful consequences, this question places some strain on the operant explanation.

Despite these criticisms, some evidence does exist supporting a behavioral conceptualization. It is probably the case that classical conditioning of fear, imitation, and the consequences of avoidant behavior do contribute significantly to the development of phobias. Thus, these paradigms may not be so much incorrect as incomplete.

A Biological Perspective. The failure of some attempts to replicate Watson and Rayner's (1920) classical conditioning of fear, along with the observation that phobias seem to develop more readily to some stimuli than others, led some workers to posit an innate basis for fears. Seligman (1971), following ideas expressed earlier by Thorndike (1935), suggested the notion of preparedness to account for the fact that phobias are more likely to occur to some stimuli. It is postulated that organisms are genetically prepared to acquire fear responses to stimuli that posed threats to their ancestors and were, thus, of evolutionary significance.

The work of Garcia and his associates is one of the lines of research on which the preparedness notion is based (e.g., Garcia, McGowan, and Green, 1972). For example, it was discovered that rats could learn to avoid a previously neutral taste (CS) if they were nauseated by an aversive UCS (for example, lithium chloride) following ingestion of food. The repeated pairing of the neutral taste with lithium chloride resulted in nausea occurring to the neutral taste alone. In contrast, a taste aversion was not developed to just the sight of food (without tasting). Similarly, Öhman and his colleagues (e.g., Öhman, Erixon, and Löfberg, 1975) found that human subjects who saw slides of stimuli such as snakes paired with shock exhibited fears that were more resistant to extinction than were those of subjects receiving pairings of other slides (for example, houses) and shock.

A number of criticisms of this and similar research (cf. Delprato, 1980) suggests caution in drawing conclusions regarding evolutionary preparedness. Investigators have often failed to equate stimuli for their novelty or to consider what features of stimuli produce fear. Also, researchers often ignore the developmental histories of the organisms they study. For example, individuals may have neutral, positive, or negative experiences correlated with houses. In contrast, previous associations or references to snakes are likely to have been consistently negative.

Delprato (1980) also offers a good example of the logical problems involved in deciding on the preexisting evolutionary potential of stimuli. Mushrooms have been employed as an example of a neutral stimulus in fear-conditioning studies such as those described above. Yet the large variety of poisonous mushrooms that exist suggest that mushrooms have posed a greater threat to survival and are thus a more likely phobic stimulus than spiders and snakes.

Examination of clinical cases provides evidence that conflicts with the evolutionary hypothesis. Seligman (1971) has described phobias to stimuli that threatened survival as "prepared." It would be predicted that prepared phobias would be more easily acquired than others but more difficult to treat. However, deSilva, Rachman, and Seligman (1977) retrospectively examined a large number of phobia cases seen over a five-year period and found that acquisition rate and therapeutic outcome were unrelated to preparedness.

Although there may be difficulties with conditioning models of phobias, the innate versus learned dichotomy that is characteristic of much of the literature does not seem necessary. For example, fears need not be innate to be influenced by biology. A child whose autonomic nervous system is very reactive may be more likely to develop phobic behavior. Fear, like any other behavior, can be viewed from a developmental perspective in which a continuing interchange between the organism (upon which genetics has had its impact) and its environment results in particular behaviors at a given point in time (Delprato, 1980).

Treatment of Childhood Phobias

There are numerous case studies of psychodynamic treatment of childhood phobias (e.g., Bornstein, 1949; Sperling, 1952) but little systematic research. Phobias are viewed as part of a larger symptom picture involving various defenses of dependency and avoidance. Treatment often involves interpretation, explanation, and suggestion.

Although many early reports of behavioral treatment are also case studies, there has more recently been an attempt to conduct controlled outcome research. These investigations suffer from a number of limitations (Graziano et al., 1979; Morris and Kratochwill, 1983). The vast majority deal with the treatment of fears of mild to moderate intensity, leaving the effectiveness of treatment of severe fears largely unexplored. In addition, most studies combine a number of different techniques, making it difficult to evaluate the efficacy of individual procedures.

One of the most widely used behavioral treatments for phobias is *systematic desensitization*. A hierarchy of fear-provoking situations is constructed, and the person is asked to visualize scenes of increasing fearfulness. These visualizations are paired with relaxation or some other response which is incompatible with fear, until the most fear-provoking scene can be comfortably visualized. Behavioral tests of the ability to approach the feared object (for example, a snake) are usually included in the evaluation of treatment effectiveness. Systematic desensitization has been shown to be effective in reducing adults' fears, but support for its use with children, while encouraging, is not overwhelming. Support for the use of systematic desensitization is greatest for older phobic children

(ages 11 to 16), but even here few methodologically adequate studies exist (Ollendick, 1979).

The Use of Therapeutic Models. The most commonly employed behavioral procedure is modeling. Of the twenty-eight controlled studies reviewed by Graziano et al. (1979), twenty involved the use of modeling. Jones's (1924) treatment of Peter's fear of furry objects is probably the earliest report of the therapeutic use of modeling. More recently the work of Bandura and his colleagues (e.g., Bandura and Menlove, 1968) has served as the impetus for controlled research. Modeling procedures have been demonstrated to be superior to control conditions and to be effective over a fairly wide age range. While observation of a single model seems effective in reducing fears, observation of multiple models and the use of varied fear stimuli in training probably enhance efficacy. *Participant modeling,* in which observation is followed by the fearful child joining the model in making gradual approaches to the feared object, is one of the most potent treatments (Rosenthal and Bandura, 1978). Several workers (e.g., Meichenbaum, 1971) have also suggested that effectiveness can be increased by the use of *coping models,* who initially exhibit fearful behavior and then eventually cope with the situation, rather than those who master the situation from the start.

Lewis's (1974) treatment of fear of the water illustrates the use of modeling, and participant modeling in particular. Forty boys between the ages of 5 and 12 were assigned to one of four treatment conditions. Children in the *modeling-plus-participation* condition observed a film of three boys of similar age performing tasks such as those in a swimming test. The coping models initially exhibited fear but gradually increased their competency in dealing with the tasks; eventually they were shown playing together happily in the water. Immediately following observation of the film, the children were taken by a second experimenter to the pool for a ten-minute participation phase. They were encouraged to engage in the activities involved in the swimming test and were given social reinforce-

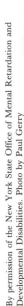

Observation of peers interacting with a feared object can be employed to help a child overcome a phobia.

ments for attempting these activities. Boys in the *modeling only* condition observed the film and then played a game at poolside for ten minutes; those in the *participation only* condition saw a neutral cartoon and then completed the ten-minute participation phase; and those in the *control* condition saw the cartoon and played the poolside game. When the behavioral swimming test was repeated the next day, the control group showed no change. Boys who had experienced participation exhibited significant improvement, greater than that provided by modeling alone. The most effective treatment was the combination of modeling and participation. A follow-up evaluation of twenty-five of the boys five days later suggested that the gains had been maintained and had generalized to a different pool and different swimming instructor. Once again the modeling plus participation boys seem to have fared the best.

These findings and others indicate that modeling treatments can be highly effective. How-

ever, it is not clear what is responsible for the success of modeling. Treatments such as Lewis's (1974) often involve other components, such as the social reinforcement given to the boys for swimming activities. The mechanism for change is also unclear. Is the child's fear actually being reduced? Or alternatively, are coping skills being improved? Bandura (1977) suggests that the child's expectations of personal efficacy may be increased by the modeling procedure.

Cognitive Treatments. Some investigators have begun to examine the role of beliefs or cognitions in eliminating children's fears. Kanfer's cognitive self-control approach is one example (Kanfer, Karoly, and Newman, 1975). Kindergarten childen who were afraid of the dark—defined by being unable to remain alone in a dark room for three minutes—experienced one of three conditions. The children were taken individually into a room by a familiar experimenter. The room was equipped with a rheostat that enabled the child to control the illumination and an intercom to call for the return of the experimenter. The experimenter left the room and timed how long the child was able to tolerate the dark. Following this pretest children in the *competence* condition were taught self-statements such as "I am a brave girl (boy). I can take care of myself." Children in the *stimulus* group were taught self-statements intended to reduce the fear-evoking potential of the dark, such as, "The dark is a fun place to be." Those in the *control* condition were taught to use neutral self-statements, such as "Mary had a little lamb." At a post-test immediately following training, children who learned competence self-statements exhibited the most improvement. All verbalization groups showed improvement, however, and this suggests that some adaptation had occurred from exposure to the feared stimulus. It is also difficult to generalize from these findings to clinical phobias, since the original intensity of the fear was not great; indeed, intensely fearful children were specifically excluded. Finally, children in the study had clear control of the feared stimulus, a situation very different from one in which the child feels helpless and lacking control (Ross, 1981).

Some studies have explored the treatment of fears of a clinical magnitude and have employed cognitive strategies as part of the treatment program (e.g., Graziano, Mooney, Huber, and Ignasiak, 1979). Although these treatments appear to be successful, it is not possible at present to evaluate the specific contribution of cognitive procedures.

School Phobia

School phobia refers to an extreme reluctance to go to school. Severe anxiety and somatic symptoms such as dizziness, stomachaches, and nausea "keep" the child at home. The parents, concerned with the child's health and anxiety, are often reluctant to force attendance. Since it is not clear that in all cases the child actually fears the school situation, some workers question the use of the term *school phobia* to describe the disorder. Hersov (1960b) found that fears either of academic performance or of some aspect of the school situation were present in 50 percent of such cases. Some cases, however, seem to be based primarily on a reluctance to leave the mother and home. Avoidance of school may be just one manifestation of the fear of separation. Thus, some workers prefer the term *school refusal* (e.g., Hersov, 1960a) to the more popular term *school phobia*.

School phobia is not the equivalent of truancy. Truants are usually absent on an intermittent basis, often without parental knowledge. The school phobic, in contrast, is usually absent for continuous extended periods, during which time the parents are aware of the child's being at home. Also, truants—unlike the school-phobic child—are often described as poor students who exhibit other conduct problems such as stealing and lying.

Prevalence. School phobia is usually estimated to occur in less than 1 percent of the population (e.g., Kennedy, 1965) and seems less prevalent than other phobias. Interestingly, however, 69 percent of referrals for any kind of child phobia were for school phobia (Miller, Barrett, Hampe, and Noble, 1972), and the ratio of professional papers on school phobia versus all other phobias is at least 25 to 1 (Miller et al., 1974). Miller and others have suggested that this greater attention is due to the fact that this phobia creates the most problems for parents and school personnel.

School phobia can be found in children of all ages and intelligence levels. Prognosis seems best for children under the age of 10 years (Miller et al., 1974). It is recognized that school phobics are not a homogeneous group. Many investigators distinguish Types I and II, usually referred to as acute or neurotic versus chronic or characterological (e.g., Berg, Nichols, and Pritchard, 1969; Coolidge, Hahn, and Peck, 1957). Preliminary evidence suggests that the types differ in terms of family background, with acute school phobics faring better in degree of parental disturbance, prognosis, and response to treatment (Baker and Wills,

1978; Kennedy, 1965). The problem may be slightly more frequent among girls and in higher socioeconomic groups (Gordon and Young, 1976).

Theoretical Viewpoints. The most common conceptualization of school phobia attributes the problem to separation anxiety. Indeed, DSM- III provides for the diagnosis of school refusal under the category of Separation Anxiety Disorder. Both psychodynamic and behavioral perspectives have offered variations on this hypothesis. The basic notion is that a mutual and excessive dependency exists between the mother and child. Strong attachment on the child's part leads to fear that something

Ed Lettau, Photo Researchers, Inc.

Many cases of school refusal are considered to arise from separation anxiety.

may happen either to the self or to the mother. The child's insistence on remaining at home satisfies both the mother's and child's needs and anxieties. There is little information available about the father's role in this process.

Psychodynamic views suggest that the mothers of school-phobic children often have poorly resolved dependence relationships with their own mothers, identify closely with the child, are overprotective, indulge the child's every need, and have unresolved neurotic conflicts concerning aggression that make discipline difficult. The father's role is a negative one—failure to counteract the mother's overprotectiveness (Davids, 1973; Kessler, 1966). There are problems with the assumption that school phobia is always accompanied by some neurosis in the mother. The same conflicts have been described in mothers of children with other problems, and it is not known whether some mothers with the same conflicts rear children free of phobias. Moreover, the research has been conducted after the child has already experienced the problem, making cause and effect extremely difficult to separate.

Psychodynamic explanations also often describe the child as having aggressive wishes toward the parent that cannot be expressed for fear of abandonment. The child defends against these wishes by regressing to an earlier dependency and displacing anger to the outside world and the school in particular. However, psychodynamic explanations acknowledge that school attendance may constitute an actual and direct expression of separation anxiety rather than school refusal resulting from displaced anger.

Behavioral theorists also often view separation anxiety as the central problem in school phobia, but they do not rely on hypothesized psychodynamics. Rather, it is presumed that the child has learned an avoidance response because of some association of school with an existing intense fear of losing the mother. For example, the mother may have threatened that she will not be home when the child returns from school (Garvey and Hegreves, 1966). Once avoidance behavior occurs, it may be reinforced by attention and other rewards, such as toys and special foods, that the child receives while at home.

While separation anxiety is the most prevalent explanation for school phobia, it is probably unwise to consider it the basis for all cases. Some authors have emphasized a true "fear of school." Leventhal and Sills (1964), for example, offer a psychodynamic interpretation that describes the school phobic as a child with an inflated self-image. When this self-image is threatened in some way in the school situation, the child develops an avoidance pattern, preferring to remain at home where power is not threatened. Behavioral explanations of actual fear of school are likely to posit that anxiety is conditioned through actual upsetting or traumatic experiences in the school situation. Like behavioral "separation anxiety" views, the attention the conditioned fear receives contributes to its maintenance.

Treatment.   The majority of clinicians of all orientations stress the importance of getting the child back to school quickly. Psychodynamic approaches tend to recommend insight-oriented therapy to strengthen the child's ego. The need for the mother to receive therapy may also be emphasized. Behaviorally oriented treatments emphasize (1) the reduction of anxiety about leaving the mother or about the actual school situation and (2) the alteration of contingencies applied to the avoidant behavior. Anxiety-reduction procedures employed with other phobias, such as systematic desensitization and guided exposure, have been used with school phobics (e.g., Garvey and Hegreves, 1966). Contingency management involves eliminating the positive consequences of staying at home (for example, attention and access to favorite things) and providing rewards for increased school attendance.

Most workers agree that the prognosis is quite good for the Type I or acute school phobic. Indeed, a frequently cited method used by Kennedy (1965) suggests that successful treatment can be rapid. At an initial meeting the father is instructed to take the child to school the following Monday, and school personnel are instructed to keep the child in school all day. No excuse is to be accepted for altering this plan, and physical complaints are dealt with by after-school visits to the pediatrician. An expectation is created that the symptoms will be absent by Wednesday, and lengthy discussions about school are not permitted. School attendance is praised, even when involuntary. The child is seen briefly by the therapist after school hours. Stories illustrating the transitory nature of fears and the "need to get back on the horse after a fall" are relayed to the child. On Wednesday a party is held to celebrate the child's having overcome the difficulty. Kennedy reports success in 100 percent of the fifty cases treated in this manner. Follow-ups of the subjects of no less than two years and up to eight years later indicate no recurrence of the problem. The absence of controlled comparison studies, however, suggests caution in drawing firm conclusions.

OTHER ANXIETY DISORDERS

The Overanxious Child

Clinical Description.   Clinicians frequently describe children who worry excessively and exhibit extensive fearful behavior. These disturbances are not focused on any particular object or situation and are not due to a specific recent stress. The children seem excessively concerned with their competence and performance, and they exhibit nervous habits (for example, nail biting), sleep disturbances, and physical complaints such as stomachaches. Current knowledge concerning the overanxious child is based almost entirely on clinical reports, as in the case of the 9-year-old boy described by Anthony (1981).

Like his mother, John had a very low opinion of himself and his abilities . . . and found it difficult to cope with the "scary things" inside himself. His main problem had to do with the numerous fears that he had and the panic attacks that overtook him from time to time. He was afraid of the dark, of ghosts, of monsters, of being abandoned, of being alone, of strangers, of war, of guns, of knives, of loud noises, and of snakes. . . . Like his mother again, he had many psychosomatic complaints involving his bladder, his bowels, his kidneys, his intestines and his blood. . . . He also suffered from insomnia and would not or could not go to sleep until his mother did. . . . He was also afraid to sleep alone or to sleep without a light, and regularly wet and soiled himself. He was often afraid but could not say why and was also fearful of contact with others. (pp. 163–164)

DSM-III recognizes this clinical entity by providing the diagnosis Overanxious Disorder within the category of Anxiety Disorders of Childhood or Adolescence. This diagnosis is used when anxiety is not due to another disorder (for example, Obsessive-Compulsive or Phobic Disorder).

Prevalence and Predisposing Factors. There is little information available regarding the prevalence of this disorder beyond the DSM-III statement that Overanxious Disorder is "apparently common." This is due, in part, to the vague description of this syndrome in the literature. What evidence is available suggests that the disorder occurs in 2 to 3 percent of the population (Yule, 1981).

Clinical reports describe the disorder as being most common among small families, higher socioeconomic groups, eldest children, and families in which there is unusual concern about performance, even when the child is functioning at an adequate or superior level (Werkman, 1980). Onset is usually described as gradual, and diagnosis before the age of 3 is not recommended. Disagreement exists as to whether the disorder is more common in boys (DSM-III) or in girls (Werkman, 1980).

Obsessive-Compulsive Disorder

Obsessions are unwanted repetitive, intrusive thoughts or ideas, while compulsions involve stereotyped behaviors the child feels compelled to perform. The disorder involves either obsessions or compulsions or, usually, a combination of the two. The child probably recognizes that the ideas or behaviors involved are unreasonable but feels the need to repeat them nevertheless. Obsessive-Compulsive Disorder appears to be quite rare in children, and there are relatively few reports and even less research on the topic.

Description and Prevalence. Available information suggests that less than 2 percent of the child clinical population exhibits this disorder, although a larger number shows some obsessive or compulsive behaviors (Adams, 1973; Judd, 1965). In a recent study of 8,367 children and adolescents seen at UCLA Neuropsychiatric Institute between 1959 and 1975, only 50 showed appreciable signs of obsessive-compulsive qualities (Hollingsworth, Tanguay, Grossman, and Pabst, 1980). Of these, only 17 actually met a stringent criteria suggested by Judd (1965). The mean age of onset was 9.6 years. Most workers indicate that boys and girls are equally represented, although 14 of the 17 cases identified by Hollingsworth et al. (1980) were boys.

A number of authors (e.g., Kessler, 1966) point out that severe obsessive-compulsive qualities exist in a number of other diagnostic groups, including schizophrenia. For example, of twenty-nine children with obsessive symptoms who Judd (1965) did not diagnose as Obsessive-Compulsive, twenty-five were labeled Schizophrenic. There does not appear to be any information regarding the prevalence of Obsessive-Compulsive Disorder in the general population.

Behavior with obsessive-compulsive qualities occurs in various stages of normal development. The feeding and bedtime rituals of very young children are examples; disruption of these routines often leads to distress. Also, young children are often observed to engage in repetitive play and to show a distinct preference for sameness. Benjamin Spock (1974), in his widely read book for parents, notes that mild compulsions—such as stepping over cracks in the sidewalk or touching every third picket in a fence—are quite common in 8-, 9-, and 10-year-olds. Such behaviors, common to the child's peer group, are probably best viewed as games. Only when they dominate the child's life and interfere with normal functioning is there cause for concern.

Treatment.   There are relatively few published reports on the treatment of obsessive-compulsive children. The follow-up results of Hollingsworth et al. (1980) are not encouraging, at least with respect to insight-oriented psychotherapy. Ten children were followed an average of 6.5 years (range: 1½ to 14 years). Despite an average of 17.7 months of intensive insight-oriented psychotherapy, most of them continued to exhibit some obsessive-compulsive behavior, and all reported serious problems with social life and peer relationships.

Behavioral procedures such as systematic desensitization and the use of aversive consequences have been employed primarily with adults, and there is insufficient evidence to support their use. The behavioral procedure that has been most successful with compulsive behavior in adults is response prevention (Gelder, 1979). Stanley's (1980) clinical report describes response prevention in the treatment of an 8-year-old girl and her family:

Amanda was referred by her G.P. because of her excessive checking behaviour. Three months prior to this referral Amanda's parents became increasingly worried as more and more of her time was involved in carrying out her rituals, e.g., she was taking at least 20 minutes to dress in the morning instead of the 5 minutes which had been more than ample previously. The symptoms had first become noticeable 6 months before.

The rituals had begun slowly following the family's move to their present home. This had been the second major move made by the family in three years involving a change of house, school, geographic area and father's job. . . . both Amanda and her younger sister had coped reasonably well with the moves, and the parents

did not think these had any connection with Amanda's symptomatology. No satisfactory reason for the development of the symptoms was identified. . . .

At interview Amanda presented as an alert, bright eight-year-old whose face fell at the mention of her "fussiness." . . . There was no evidence of obsessional symptoms in her school work and the teacher had not noticed anything unusual in her affect or behaviour.

Amanda was able to talk about her symptomatology as though it were a thing apart from herself. She saw it as an intrusion on her previously happy life and felt depressed by the restrictive elements of her ritual. She found her peer relationships were affected by no longer being able to invite friends home in case they disturbed her ornaments, toys, etc. . . . The family appeared to be functioning very cohesively which may explain how each person had become involved in Amanda's symptomatology.

At the time of referral Amanda's symptoms included the following. . . .

(1) Every night she closed the curtains, turned down the bed and fluffed up her pillow three times before beginning to undress. Any disruption of this routine caused great distress.

(2) The top bedcover had to be placed with the fringes only just touching the floor all around.

(3) At night Amanda removed her slippers slowly and carefully, she then banged them on the floor upside-down, then the right-way-up, three times and nudged them gently and in parallel under the bed.

(4) Before going to sleep Amanda had to go to the toilet three times. She often woke up in the middle of the night and carried out the same performance.

(5) Before carrying out a ritual Amanda sang:

> "One, two, three,
> Come dance with me
> Tra la la, Tra, la, la."

(6) All dressing and undressing had to be done three times. This included pulling up her pants three times after every visit to the toilet.

(7) All Amanda's toys had special places which had to be checked and rechecked before leaving the bedroom.

(8) The ornaments on top of the piano had special places. These positions were so precise that Amanda's mother found dusting and polishing almost impossible. (p. 86–87)

The family was instructed not to give Amanda special attention and to treat her as a girl who did not have compulsive urges. The parents were also trained to initiate response prevention procedures. Starting with the least upsetting situation, the parent's prevented Amanda from engaging in her rituals. Once she coped with a situation, the next step up the hierarchy was taken. After the first two days in which Amanda experienced considerable anxiety, she gradually began to relax. After two weeks all her symptoms had disappeared. No new or additional problems arose, and Amanda was still symptom free at the one-year follow-up.

THE SOCIALLY WITHDRAWN CHILD

For the first time the DSM system has officially noticed the problem of social withdrawal. As a result, DSM-III includes the diagnoses of Avoidant Disorder of Childhood or Adolescence and Schizoid Disorder of Childhood or Adolescence.

Avoidant Disorder and Schizoid Disorder are distinguished by the nature of the social isolation. The avoidant child is inhibited by anxiety from making friends but enjoys peer relations, once established. The schizoid child is viewed as having no desire for social contact.

Information concerning the prevalence of withdrawn-isolate behavior is either not readily available or is difficult to interpret because of definitional problems. From 5 to 28 percent of preschoolers have been designated as isolates with a mean of 25 percent in the seven preschool studies reviewed by Hops and Greenwood (1981). These same authors report that in their primary-grade studies, 1 to 3 percent of the population is designated as withdrawn.

Peer Relations and Development

Social behavior directed toward peers has been observed as early as age 2 to 3 months. At this time the social smile, vocalizations, and head control emerge. Infants can be observed taking long looks at their peers and cooing and smiling. They seem more interested in peers than in their own reflection in a mirror. As development proceeds, changes occur in the quality and extent of social behavior. From 12 months of age through the preschool period, increases in prosocial initiations, a general increase in peer interactions, and a parallel decrease in adult interactions occur (Field, 1981).

Peer interactions and influence are different than those associated with child-adult interactions. Whereas infants touch and hug adults more frequently, they look more often at peers. Different affective and play behaviors are also exhibited in response to peers versus adults, and these differences occur in a variety of cultures (Field, 1981; Whiting and Whiting, 1975). Hartup (1976, 1979) has enumerated some of the ways in which peer interactions play a unique and essential role, including the development of sociability and attachment, the control of aggression, socialization of sexuality and sex roles, moral development, and the development of empathy. Of course, this does not mean that peer social development is independent of child-adult interactions. Indeed, early parent-child socialization seems to predict later peer interactions (e.g., Waters, Whippman, and Sroufe, 1980).

Peer Relations and Adjustment

Early isolation from peers places the child at risk for later adjustment problems (Hartup, 1980; Ziv, 1970). Children with poor peer relationships are at risk for a variety of social and emotional problems. Social withdrawal is a

Interactions with peers provide the opportunity to learn cooperation and control of aggression, to develop effective communication, and to practice adult roles.

common feature of childhood schizophrenia and autism. Poor peer relations are also reported to be associated with high rates of juvenile delinquency (Roff, Sells, and Golden, 1972), dropping out of school (Ullmann, 1957), and bad conduct discharges from the army (Roff, 1961). Cowen and his colleagues have found an association with later psychiatric referrals (Cowen, Pederson, Babigian, Izzo, and Trost, 1973). In a series of studies they screened large numbers of children for signs of disturbance. A variety of measures was obtained, including days absent, grades, achievement and IQ test scores, child and teacher measures of adjustment, and

a sociometric measure of peer acceptance. Of all the measures, low peer status in the third grade was the best predictor of later appearance on a communitywide psychiatric register.

The relationship among interaction with peers, popularity, social competence, development, and adjustment is clearly complex (Hops, 1983). Problems with definition and methodology are appreciable. For example, all unpopular children may not be socially withdrawn, and adequate peer-related behavior is probably not the same at ages 4 and 10. Thus, much of the available information needs to be viewed with caution. Nonetheless, peer relations are a

Ken Karp

By permission of the New York State Department of Education

powerful influence on the socialization of children (Field, 1981). Isolation of a child from his or her peers will likely have widespread impact.

Behaviors Related to Peer Status and Social Competence

The question of which social skills differentiate between popular and unpopular children has been the subject of a number of studies (e.g., Gottman, Gonso, and Rasmussen, 1975). Distributing and receiving positive reinforcement, the ability to take another's perspective and communicate clearly, and knowledge of how to make friends have emerged as significant skills.

Responding Positively to Peers.   Global characteristics—friendliness and outgoingness—and certain specific behaviors—giving attention and approval, submitting to another's wishes, and giving things to others—have consistently been associated with peer acceptance (Combs and Slaby, 1977). Children who are less popular spend more time daydreaming or "tuned out" (Charlesworth and Hartup, 1967; Gottman et al., 1975). Interactions with a peer specifically chosen as a friend, as well as general peer acceptance, are characterized by high rates of positive behaviors. Interestingly, levels of positive behavior directed at disliked children and children neither liked nor disliked do not seem to differ (Masters and Furman, 1981).

Perspective Taking and Accurate Communication. The ability to judge another's perspective and communicate accurately is experimentally assessed by asking the child to give appropriate clues in a password-type game or to give descriptions of something from another person's perspective (for example, how a mountain of blocks appears to another person). The child's ability to give helpful clues is assumed to reflect the child's referential communication ability—that is, his or her ability to adopt another person's perspective and communicate accurately from that perspective. This skill is an important aspect of social development (Selman, 1976; Shantz, 1975).

Gottman et al. (1975) found that popular children give more good clue words or helpful descriptions. Also, among fifth- and sixth-grade boys in a special class for the emotionally disturbed, social withdrawal was found to be associated with poor perspective-taking ability (Waterman, Sobesky, Silvern, Aoki, and McCaulay, 1981). Interventions aimed at training perspective taking have generally been successful in improving this ability. There is also some suggestion that such improvement may be related to improvement in overall adjustment (Urbain and Kendall, 1980).

Initiating Interactions. Popular and unpopular children have also been found to differ when asked to role play making a friend (Gottman et al., 1975). Third and fourth graders who were more popular with their peers were more likely to perform certain initiation behaviors—

greeting, offering information, extending offers of inclusion, and asking for information. On the other hand, Greenwood and his colleagues have reported that socially withdrawn children are not as likely to respond to other children's initiation, and when they do respond, most often their responses are nonverbal (Hops and Greenwood, 1981).

Treatment of the Withdrawn Child

Recent years have witnessed a burst of programs designed to improve the social skills of children. A thorough review of this material is beyond the scope of this section. Several recent reviews provide a good summary and critique of this literature and of interventions with withdrawn children in particular (cf. Combs and Slaby, 1977; Conger and Keane, 1981; Furman, 1980; Kendall, 1981; Strain and Fox, 1981). Differences in definition of the withdrawn, isolated, shy, socially unskilled, unpopular child has led to a diversity of recommended interventions.

Some workers have focused on the antecedents and consequences of low rates of peer interaction. The effectiveness of reinforcement in increasing peer contact has been demonstrated (e.g., Allen, Hart, Buell, Harris, and Wolf, 1964; Walker, Greenwood, Hops, and Todd, 1979). However, reinforcement of high rates of interaction may also lead to unacceptable rates of aggressive behavior (Kirby and Toler, 1970) and thereby to being unpopular (Conger and Keane, 1981).

Exposure to filmed models has also been shown to positively affect the behavior of preschool isolates (e.g., O'Connor, 1969, 1972). However, a number of methodological concerns with this research have been raised, and it is unclear whether the effects are due to observation of a model or to other variables, such as coaching and instruction (Conger and Keane, 1981).

Several investigators have explicitly employed coaching-instructional techniques. These interventions use a variety of procedures, including instruction, modeling, and reinforcement (e.g., Bornstein, Bellack, and Hersen, 1977; Gottman, Gonso, and Schuler, 1976; LaGreca and Santogrossi, 1980; Oden and Asher, 1977). Ladd (1981), for example, assigned third-grade children low on peer acceptance to either a skill training treatment, attention control, or nontreatment control condition. Training consisted of instructions, guided and self-directed rehearsal, and feedback plus training in self-evaluation. Three verbal skills were targeted: asking questions, leading (offering useful suggestions and directions), and offering support to peers. Differences in both behavioral observations and sociometric ratings in favor of the treatment condition were obtained.

While most interventions for improving children's social skills are implemented by adults, an interesting approach is the use of peers as helping agents. Peers can provide appropriate models for desired behavior. They are also already present in the setting where the relevant behavior occurs and can provide natural consequences that continue to maintain behavior over time. Strain and Fox (1981) have reviewed the literature on the use of peers as change agents for withdrawn children. Peers have been successfully trained to prompt and reinforce appropriate behavior in social isolates, to increase social initiations with withdrawn peers, and to serve as live peer models. Some less direct interventions have also been effective. For example, intervention with one withdrawn child has been shown to produce "spillover" effects; that is, improvement in other withdrawn children in the classroom. Group contingencies where, for example, rewards earned by an isolate child are given to the entire peer group, have also been employed successfully. While peer-mediated techniques produce positive results, there is evidence that they are not equally effective with all withdrawn children. For example, children who exhibit lower levels of social behavior have been shown to respond less well to increased peer initiations than socially withdrawn children with relatively higher initial levels (Strain, 1977).

Furman, Rahe, and Hartup's (1979) pro-gram employing peers to assist socially withdrawn children is particularly intriguing because of its use of basic research to suggest clinical interventions. A fascinating series of laboratory and naturalistic observations have indicated the importance of peer relations for monkeys. For example, it has been shown that infant monkeys reared by several peers in the absence of a mother show no later disturbances. However, those raised by a mother in the absence of peers show both short- and long-term disturbances in play and affective development (e.g., Harlow and Harlow, 1965). Perhaps most intriguing is the use of peers as "therapists" for young socially withdrawn monkeys (e.g., Suomi and Harlow, 1972). Adult monkey "therapists" were not effective in getting young monkeys to overcome their social withdrawal. However, infant monkeys, three months younger, were able to effectively "treat" their withdrawn peers.

Drawing on this research, Furman et al. had identified preschool children who engaged in peer interactions during less than 33 percent of observations and who were at least 10 percentage points below their class means. Twenty-four such social isolates were assigned to unstructured play sessions with a "therapist" twelve to eighteen months younger, to play sessions with a same-age "therapist," or to no treatment. As Figure 7-1 illustrates, exposure to a younger peer was highly effective in increasing the social activity of withdrawn children. Both groups of children exposed to "therapists" showed improvement, while the control group did not. However, seven of the eight isolates exposed to a younger partner increased their social behavior at least 50 percent, while only three of the eight withdrawn youngsters exposed to a same-age partner exhibited comparable increases. The principal effect of the treatments was to increase rates of positive behaviors but not of neutral and punishing acts. The authors hypothesize that the effectiveness of the peer play sessions, particularly with younger children, was due to an increased opportunity to successfully practice initiating and directing social activity.

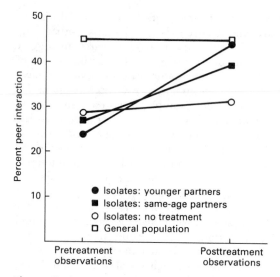

Figure 7–1 Pre- and post-treatment rates of peer interaction in the classroom. *From Furman, Rahe, and Hartup, 1979.*

As our understanding of the socially withdrawn child increases, we will be able to develop increasingly successful ways of working with these children. Responding positively to peers, ability to take another's perspective, and skill at initiating interactions differentiate popular from unpopular children. Other attributes that distinguish children who successfully interact with peers from those who do not remain to be uncovered. In addition, distinctions among different types of social withdrawal need to be made—the rejected child versus the ignored child; the child who lacks appropriate skills versus the child whose fears prevent interaction (Dodge, Cole, and Brakke, 1982). The importance of peer interactions to normal development make this an important task. Hopefully, refinements in our understanding will lead to improvements in our interventions.

CHILDHOOD DEPRESSION

In everyday usage the term *depression* refers to the experience of an unhappy mood that is difficult to bear. This subjective experience of dysphoria is also a central feature of the clinical definition of depression. Descriptions of children diagnosed as depressed suggest that they also exhibit a number of other problems. Loss of the experience of pleasure, as well as social withdrawal, lowered self-esteem, inability to concentrate, poor schoolwork, alterations of biological functions (sleeping, eating, elimination), and somatic complaints are often noted. In some cases it is believed that severe depression may lead the youngster to attempt suicide. However, the link between depression and suicide is not clear (see Box 7–1).

Disagreements in the literature regarding diagnosis and, indeed, the existence of a childhood depressive disorder make it difficult to estimate prevalence.

Prevalence

Estimates of the prevalence of childhood depression in the general population vary considerably. Kovacs and Beck (1977) report that approximately one-third of the 63 children in seventh and eighth grade who completed their depression inventory fell into the "moderate" or "severe depression" categories. Kashani and Simonds (1979), however, found that among 103 children aged 7 to 11, 18 percent exhibited depressive affect and only 1.9 percent met the DSM-III criteria.

Pearce (1977) suggests that a depressive disorder will occur in somewhere between 15 and 20 percent of children referred for psychiatric help. Kashani and Simonds (1979) found reports from other studies that ranged from 2.3 to 59 percent. A recent study by Carlson and Cantwell (1980) indicates that much of the discrepancy may be due to differing assessment methods and criteria. A sample of 210 children was selected at random from over 1,000 children between the ages of 7 and 17 seen at the UCLA-Neuropsychiatric Institute. At intake the presence of depressive symptoms among the presenting problems was noted. The children were also administered the Short Children's Depression Inventory (SCDI) (Kovacs and Beck, 1977). Separate interviews with 102 of the

Box 7-1   Child and Adolescent Suicide

The death by suicide of a child or adolescent is a shocking event. It is probably more disturbing than adult suicide or even the great sadness we feel at a child's death from cancer or a traffic accident. Fortunately, suicide is a relatively rare event, particularly among younger children.

Self-inflicted death occurring before the fifteenth birthday is usually termed childhood suicide, and such a death between the ages of 15 and 19 is called adolescent suicide. Very few children under the age of 12 commit suicide, but there is a general increase in the suicide rate between the ages of 12 and 19. Rates of actual suicide are probably underestimated, since many are probably viewed as accidents. Nonetheless, available national statistics indicate that only two children under 10 years of age committed suicide in 1978. The suicide rate for children between the ages of 10 and 14 in that same year was 0.81 per 100,000; for adolescents 15 to 19 years old, it was 7.64 per 100,000. These rates are appreciably lower than the rate in the adult population—about 174 per 100,000 (Shaffer and Fisher, 1981).

Suicide attempts are more frequent than completed suicides. Moreover, the intent to actually kill oneself is usually thought to be quite low in juvenile suicide attempts. Ingestion of drugs or pills is the most frequent method of attempted suicide, especially for older children (Hawton, 1982). Even if it is not intended, there is always the risk that the child's misjudgment will result in death. Clinician's are therefore likely to take suicide attempts quite seriously. Furthermore, there may be serious risk of later psychological disturbance or future suicide attempts unless there is some attempt to understand the problem and assist the child.

Suicide is frequently viewed as a "cry for help." The appeal is thought to be directed to family and friends rather than to some outside helping agency. The suicide attempts of adolescents appear to be motivated by one or more factors—relief from a feeling of stress or from a stressful situation, a way of showing others their desperation, an attempt to get back at others, or a dramatic effort to get others to change. If the suicide is not an appeal for outside help, this may help explain why later treatment participation is frequently poor and why these youths

often deny the seriousness of their attempts (Toolan, 1981).

What factors lead a child to reach the point where he or she attempts suicide? As with adults, it would appear that suicide is not always associated with depression and feelings of hopelessness. Indeed, among those who attempt suicide depressed youngsters are barely more common than nondepressed youngsters. Duration of psychopathology also does not appear to play a role in suicidal behavior (Carlson and Cantwell, 1982).

A number of factors, however, may distinguish children who attempt suicide. Seventy-six children between the ages of 5 and 14 discharged from an inpatient psychiatric unit were designated as either (a) suicidal, (b) depressed nonsuicidal, or (c) psychiatric controls—patients who did not fit the other two categories (Sandler-Cohen, Berman, and King, 1982). Children were classified as suicidal if they had engaged in overt, potentially self-destructive behavior and verbalized an intent to harm themselves. Suicidal children did not differ from either depressed (D) or psychiatric controls (P) in terms of age, sex, race, treatment history, family size, or family psychiatric and suicide history. Suicidal children were, however, more frequently firstborns, and their parents more frequently abused alcohol and drugs. Perhaps most interesting is the finding that compared to nonsuicidal children (D and P), those classified as suicidal seem to have experienced significant and increasing amounts of stress, particularly during the period of later childhood and early adolescence (8½–14+ years of age) and in the prior twelve months. Life events such as death of a grandparent, hospitalization of a parent, a broken home, or separation, divorce, or remarriage of parents seemed to best discriminate between the suicidal and nonsuicidal children. It would thus appear that in the context of longstanding chaotic and disruptive environments, losses and separations from important people may precipitate suicidal attempts.

While it is true that death by suicide is rare, particularly among younger children, reports such as those of a 6-year-old boy who made several attempts to hang himself (Morrison and Collier, 1969) remind us of the importance of understanding this rare, but serious problem.

children and their parents were conducted to assess the presence of affective disorder, according to DSM-III criteria. The use of depressive symptoms as the criterion for diagnosis led to the largest number of positive diagnoses; SCDI led to fewer, and DSM-III criteria led to the least. However, the results also make it clear that this was not simply a matter of more or less stringent criteria but rather of some differences in definition. For example, not all SCDI depressed children were symptom depressed, and not all DSM-III Affective Disorder children were SCDI depressed.

Classification of Childhood Depression

Depression in childhood is often described as taking several forms (e.g., Cytryn and Mc-Knew, 1972). Acute depressive reactions are thought to be displayed by children with a good premorbid history. Depression occurs in response to some precipitating life event, such as parental loss. In contrast, chronic depressive reactions are believed to occur in children with a poor premorbid history. Manifestations of depression become evident gradually over some period of time. Children in this category are described as experiencing a long history of frequent losses or separations rather than a single precipitating event.

The term *masked depressive reactions* refers to cases in which the child's depression is "masked" by other problems (depressive equivalents), such as hyperactivity or delinquency. The "underlying" depression, while not clearly displayed, is detected by the clinician through interview or testing. Some workers suggest that masked depressions are quite common and may result in depression being underdiagnosed (Cytryn and McKnew, 1974; Malmquist, 1977). However, the concept of masked depression is quite controversial. Indeed, even some of its advocates seem to view it as less important than once thought (Cytryn, McKnew, and Bunney, 1980). Perhaps the phenomenon can be explained without reliance on the notion of "masked depression." It could be argued that children at different developmental stages dis-

play their sadness (depression) in different ways. Alternatively, it might be argued that children display a diversity of "symptoms" until they learn a consistent depressed style (cf. Leon, Kendall, and Garber, 1980).

DSM-III does not provide for a separate diagnosis of childhood depression. The diagnosis of depression may be given to children, but the criteria employed are the same ones used for adults. These include dysphoric mood or loss of interest in usual activities; changes in eating, sleeping, or motor activity; fatigue; feelings of worthlessness; poor concentration; and suicidal thoughts. However, differences in age-specific associated features are acknowledged. For example, in prepubertal children depression is thought to be associated with repeated separation anxiety experiences. Depressed adolescent boys are thought likely to display negativistic and antisocial behavior.

There is also one DSM-III diagnosis that is specific to childhood and is related to other descriptions of depression. Reactive Attachment Disorder of Infancy is diagnosed if there is a lack of age-appropriate social responsiveness, apathetic mood, and poor physical development in response to inadequate caretaking. Onset occurs before 8 months of age, and extreme cases are often referred to as "failure to thrive" or "hospitalism."

Is Childhood Depression a Distinct Disorder?

Both the existence of childhood depression as a diagnostic category and its definition are controversial on a number of counts (cf. Gittleman-Klein, 1977; Lefkowitz and Burton, 1978). There appear to be two opposing points of view. The first, based mostly on clinical literature, is that childhood depression is a genuine and distinct clinical entity. This viewpoint is probably held by the majority (Schulterbrandt and Raskin, 1977), and many of its advocates argue that the disorder is underdiagnosed. At the other pole is the position, based largely on studies of normal children (and a developmental perspective), that childhood depression may not be a distinct clinical syndrome. Rather, it is a transient developmental phenomenon present in normal children. Still other critics argue that the existence of the disorder in childhood is inconsistent with theoretical conceptions of depression (e.g., Mahler, 1961; Rie, 1966). Some psychoanalytic theorists, for example, hold that in depression the superego acts as a punisher of the ego. It is argued that a child's superego is not sufficiently developed to play this role.

The question of whether childhood depression exists as a distinct disorder has begun to receive the attention of researchers. Leon, Kendall, and Garber (1980) identified children in grades three to six as depressed or nondepressed, based on their scores on a depression scale completed by parents. The study is interesting because it assessed whether manifestations of depression were present across situations (home and school) and from the perspectives of several individuals (parent, teacher, and the child). There was a significant, but only moderate, consistency between parental and child ratings of depression. Interestingly, children designated by their parents as depressed were also rated by their parents as exhibiting significantly more conduct problems, anxiety, impulsive hyperactivity, learning problems, psychosomatic problems, perfectionism, and muscular tension than children rated as nondepressed. Teachers, however, rated these same depressed children as displaying more inattention-passivity but did not rate the children differently on other behavior problems.

How similar was childhood depression in this study to the adult disorder? As with findings in the adult literature (e.g., Seligman, Abramson, Semmel, and Von Baeyer, 1979), depressed children attributed positive events to external causes and negative events to internal causes significantly more than did nondepressed children. However, unlike depressed adults, the children did not seem to have motivational deficits or psychomotor retardation.

The lack of consistency of behavior across settings is also different from the generalized syndrome described in adults. The discrepancy apparent in parent and teacher reports may be due to actual variations in behavior in these different settings, but another interpretation is possible. Perhaps parents who rate their children as depressed are generally inclined to see behavioral problems in their offspring. Alternatively, the variety of behavioral problems displayed at home by depressed children may suggest a more general difficulty rather than a specific depressive syndrome. In contrast, children in this sample who were rated by their parents as hyperactive did not display this same variety of problems.

It would appear that the existence of a distinct syndrome of childhood depression is still controversial. Manifestations of depression in children do seem in some ways to be different from the adult disorder, and the problems of situational specificity and developmental considerations must be incorporated into any explanation.

A Developmental Perspective. The phenomenon of depression in childhood is another good example of the importance of normative data and the possible implications of a developmental perspective. Some workers (e.g., Lefkowitz and Burton, 1978) suggest that the behaviors that lead to the diagnosis of depression are only transitory developmental phenomena common among children in certain age groups.

How common are the behaviors symptomatic of depression, and what is their prevalence in particular age groups? Although adequate longitudinal or epidemiological studies are lacking, it seems that some of the behaviors are fairly typical of young children but are short-lived and far less common in older children. For example, the Berkeley survey found that 37 percent of girls and 29 percent of boys at age 6 exhibited insufficient appetite. By age 9 these figures had dropped to 9 percent and 6 percent, respectively, and 14 percent of both sexes at age 14 had insufficient appetites (Macfarlane, Allen, and Honzik, 1954). Thus, insufficient appetite should probably not be considered a deviant behavior among 6-year-olds. However, if it is present at age 9, especially in boys, it might be considered atypical. Other behaviors, such as "excessive reserve," occur too often in children of all ages to be considered abnormal.

Lefkowitz's (1977) reexamination of Werry and Quay's epidemiological study of behavior symptoms in a general population of 1,753 kindergarten through second-grade children also sheds light on the question. Sixteen of the fifty-five behaviors surveyed were judged to be those commonly associated with depression. The range of prevalence of these behaviors was 7.2 to 46.3 percent (mean = 22 percent) for boys and 6.4 to 41.4 percent (mean = 18 percent) for girls. This suggests that about 20 percent of the normal population may possess symptoms judged characteristic of depressive disorder in clinical samples.

Thus, depression in childhood may not exist as a clinical entity different from common and transient developmental phenomena. Lefkowitz and Burton (1978) indicate that perhaps one of the reasons why clinicians give the diagnosis of childhood depression is the belief that these behaviors (symptoms) are rare and therefore important when manifested. Awareness of normative and developmental patterns might change this impression, leading to changes in diagnostic practices.

Theories of Depression

Separation-loss. Despite increased interest in recent years, much of the thinking regarding childhood depression is based on theories and information derived from adults. Probably the most common psychological explanation of depression is separation or loss. Psychoanalytic explanations of depression emphasize the notion of object loss. The loss may be real (parental death, divorce) or symbolic. Individuals who are fixated at the oral stage of development, and thus are highly dependent, are likely to experience depression. Identification with and ambivalent feelings toward the lost love object result in the person directing hostile feelings concerning the love object toward the self. Some behaviorally oriented explanations also involve separation and loss. Both Ferster (1974) and Lewinsohn (1974) emphasize the role of inadequate positive reinforcement in the development of depression. Loss of or separation from a loved one is likely to result in a decrease in the child's sources of positive reinforcement. However, inadequate reinforcement may also result from factors such as not having adequate social and vocational skills to obtain desired rewards.

Support for the role of separation in the genesis of depression comes from a number of different efforts. A fairly typical sequence of reactions to prolonged separation of young children from their parents has been described by a number of investigators (e.g., Bowlby, 1960; Spitz, 1946). In this so-called anaclitic depression, the child initially goes through a period of "protest" characterized by crying, asking for the parents, and restlessness. This is followed shortly by a period of depression and withdrawal. Most children begin to recover after several weeks. Interestingly, separation has been shown to produce similar responses in infant monkeys (e.g., Kaufman and Rosenblum, 1967).

There is also evidence of high rates of early parental loss or separation among children referred for treatment of a variety of psychological problems. Seligman, Gleser, Rauh, and Harris (1974) report that among one hundred consecutive adolescent referrals, 36.4 percent had experienced loss of one or both parents. In contrast, in public school and medical clinic control samples, only 11.7 percent and 16.6 percent, respectively, had experienced such loss. Differences between the treatment and control samples were particularly high for parental loss between 3 to 6 years of age and 12 to 15 years of age. The general relationship between parental loss and behavior disorders appears to apply to depression as well. For example, a comparison of depressed and nondepressed neurotic children between the ages of 5 and 16 indicated that the depressed group was more likely to have experienced parental separation prior to the age of 8—50.7 percent versus 23.2 percent (Caplan and Douglas, 1969).

Although there does seem to be appreciable support for the role of separation-loss, it should be noted that not all the depressed children in the studies cited above experienced such separation. Perhaps parental withholding of reinforcers in subtle ways accounts for some of this discrepancy. Separation does not always result in depression either (Rutter, 1971). Perhaps the presence of alternative "parenting," affection, and support are related to the rapidity of the child's recovery from loss or separation (Hetherington and Martin, 1979).

Other Psychological Theories. A learned helplessness explanation of depression is offered by Seligman (1974). It is suggested that some individuals, due to their learning histories, have come to perceive themselves as having little control of their environment. Seligman's theory thus emphasizes how the person thinks about activity and outcome. Learned helplessness is associated with mood and behavior characteristic of depression. Separation may be a special case of learned helplessness: The child's attempts to bring the parent back may result in the child's thinking that personal action and positive outcome are independent of each other.

The role of cognitive factors in depression is also the major emphasis of other theorists. Beck (1967), for example, assumes that depression results from the way individuals interpret events. Depressed individuals, Beck hypothesizes, have developed certain errors in thinking that result in their distorting even mildly annoying events into opportunities for self-blame and failure.

It is difficult to evaluate how applicable Seligman's and Beck's theories are to childhood depression. Although adequate studies have yet to be conducted, some workers believe that these theories will prove useful in understanding and treating the disorder (Dweck, 1977; Kovacs and Beck, 1977).

Biological Theories. There is no convincing evidence at present for a biochemical deficit or for genetic transmission in the etiology of childhood depression. This is not to say that alterations in mood are not accompanied by biochemical changes. Few workers would make such a contention. Rather, it is assumed that there is an ongoing interaction between psychological and biological influences, and it is unclear at present whether biochemical factors play an etiological role or are simply correlates of depressed mood and inactivity.

Much of the speculation concerning the role of biochemical factors comes from clinical reports on the use of drugs in the treatment of childhood depression. Such treatment is probably quite common, despite the fact that there is little research support for its efficacy (Rapaport, 1977a). In fact, no relationship between the use of pharmacological agents and changes in mood has been established. Conners (1977) also makes the important point that improvement following the administration of a certain drug does not mean that the child has a biological deficit specific to that drug. Methodological difficulties with available research and the failure to obtain convincing support suggests that at present there is little evidence either for the efficacy of drug treatment or for the role of psychopharmacology in understanding childhood depression (Schulterbrandt and Raskin, 1977).

The role of genetic factors in childhood depression is unknown. Data regarding adult depressive disorders and studies reporting a history of depression in relatives of depressed children (e.g., Brumback, Jackoway, and Weinberg, 1980) serve as the principal basis for speculations. However, it has not been demonstrated that rates of parental depression are higher among depressed children than among children with other disorders. Also, findings of high rates of depression in family members does not necessarily imply hereditary mechanisms.

Assessment and Treatment

A variety of instruments have been employed to assess childhood depression—self-report scales, interviews, projective techniques, peer ratings, behavior checklists (Kazdin, 1981). Other procedures, such as observation of overt behavior (for example, activity level), that have been employed with adult depressives may also be useful. However, the technology for assessing childhood depression is not well developed. Evaluation of several aspects of the problem have not yet been attempted. For example, Costello (1981) suggests the assessment of family interactions and the impact of larger social systems. In addition, further information regarding the reliability and validity of assessment procedures is needed (Kazdin and Petti, 1982).

Lefkowitz and Tesiny's (1980) development of a peer nomination measure serves as an example of the kind of research that is needed. The Peer Nomination Inventory for Depression (PNID) asks children to nominate peers who fit certain descriptions. Table 7–4 presents the

Table 7–4   Peer Nomination Inventory for Depression Items

Who often plays alone? (D)
Who thinks they are bad? (D)
Who doesn't try again when they lose? (D)
Who often sleeps in class? (D)
Who often looks lonely? (D)
Who often says they don't feel well? (D)
Who says they can't do things? (D)
Who often cries? (D)
Who often looks happy? (H)
Who likes to do a lot of things? (H)
Who worries a lot? (D)
Who doesn't play? (D)
Who often smiles? (H)
Who doesn't take part in things? (D)
Who doesn't have much fun? (D)
Who is often cheerful? (H)
Who thinks others don't like them? (D)
Who often looks sad? (D)
Who would you like to sit next to in class? (P)
Who are the children you would like to have for your best friends? (P)

Note: D = items that are included in depressed score
H = items in happiness score
P = items in popularity score

Adapted from Lefkowitz and Tesiny, 1980.

characteristics of depression, happiness, and popularity to which the children are asked to respond. A child's score is the sum of the nominations received for all the depression items. Based on the scores of 944 fourth and fifth graders, the authors were able to establish the reliability of this measure of depression. The validity of the instrument was assessed by correlating PNID scores with a variety of other measures.

Scores on the inventory correlated moderately both with teacher ratings of depression and with self-ratings as assessed by two other instruments—a modified Zung Self-Rating Depression Scale (Zung, 1965) and a modified Children's Depression Inventory (Kovacs and Beck, 1977). In addition, high ratings on the PNID were significantly correlated with reduced intellectual functioning, poor social behavior, poor self-esteem, low peer ratings for happiness and popularity, poor school attendance, and the perception of external control over events. These results are promising and the study exemplary. However, the clinical utility of a peer nomination instrument is limited to the existence of a stable peer group that can be called upon to complete the instrument.

Information concerning the treatment of childhood depression is based almost exclusively on clinical reports. Interventions are derived from the clinicians' perspective on the etiology of the disorder—psychodynamic clinicians usually employ an insight-oriented approach, and biological theorists are likely to use medication. Behavioral clinicians can be expected to emphasize reinforcement of activity and cognitive strategies. However, treatment recommendations await further research.

SUMMARY

At present it is probably best to think of the problems described in this chapter as a single internalizing syndrome characterized by anxious and withdrawn behavior. This viewpoint is supported by empirical research and clinical reports stating that children frequently display a number of problems rather than a "single disorder." Subtypes are not necessarily ruled out, but their reliability and validity need to be established.

Available literature and clinical practice, however, are characterized by discussions of separate disorders. Childhood phobias have probably received the most attention. Studies of large numbers of normal children indicate that fears are common among children and that many children exhibit a large number of fears. Therefore, it is important to maintain a developmental perspective in judging the clinical importance of childhood fears. Several reports suggest that children's fears are relatively short-lived. This does not necessarily suggest that they need not be treated. The problem may be sufficiently disturbing and disruptive to warrant intervention, and as of yet we cannot be certain that some "fearful style" does not persist even if the specific fear itself is short-lived.

The etiology of childhood phobias has received the attention of each of the major perspectives. None seems to offer a complete explanation. Psychodynamic explanations rest almost exclusively on case material. An explanation that incorporates several learning mechanisms, perhaps combined with a biological predisposition, seems most viable at present. Other anxiety disorders have received considerably less attention.

An appreciable degree of attention has recently been focused on the socially withdrawn child. This has arisen, in part, from an acknowledgment of the importance of peer relations to normal development. Also, an association between poor peer relations and later adjustment has been reported.

Popularity with peers has been shown to be related to distributing and receiving positive reinforcement, ability to take another's perspective and communicate clearly, and knowledge of how to make friends. Reinforcement has been successfully employed to increase the rate of peer interactions. Caution needs to be exercised so that aggressive behaviors are not increased, thereby defeating the goal of improving peer acceptance. Programs which incorporate reinforcement, modeling, coaching, and instruction would seem most likely to be successful. The use of peers as helping agents is an important innovation in this area.

The concept of childhood depression is a controversial notion that is receiving increased attention. There is no separate DSM-III category for childhood depression, and the adult diagnostic criteria must be employed. Considerable disagreement exists as to whether there is a specific, distinct syndrome of childhood depression and, if so, whether it is like the adult category. Awareness of the high frequency of many "depressed" behaviors among the general population at certain ages also has important implications for diagnostic practice.

Both behavioral and psychodynamic theories stress the concepts of separation and loss in the etiology of depressed behavior. Other psychological theories may have implications for depression in children but, to date, have largely concentrated on adults. At present the role of biological factors remains unclear. Also, little information is available regarding treatment.

8

CHILDHOOD PSYCHOSES: PERVASIVE DEVELOPMENTAL DISORDERS

THE PROBLEM OF DEFINITION

EARLY ONSET: INFANTILE AUTISM

What is the Basic Defect?
Etiology

LATER ONSET PSYCHOSES

Clinical Features
Etiology

WHAT HAPPENS TO PSYCHOTIC CHILDREN?

HELPING THE PSYCHOTIC CHILD

PHYSICAL METHODS OF TREATMENT

TRADITIONAL THERAPIES

BEHAVIOR MODIFICATION

Language Training
Self-injurious Behavior
Training Parents as Therapists
Efficacy

SUMMARY

Some of the most strikingly tragic behavioral deficits are displayed by children who suffer pervasive developmental disorders. Historically referred to as childhood psychoses, pervasive developmental disorders are characterized by severe distortions in the development of social, emotional, and cognitive growth. These fundamental areas are affected in such a way that the psychotic child appears qualitatively different than other children. Fortunately, the conditions are quite rare in the general population, occurring in no more than four children in every ten thousand, in more boys than girls (Goldfarb, 1980; Lotter, 1966).

THE PROBLEM OF DEFINITION

Psychotic disturbances of adulthood were noted in the early modern classifications of mental disorders. Kraepelin, when setting the basis for modern classification, labeled various psychotic syndromes dementia praecox and attributed them to biological determinants. *Dementia* reflected his belief that the disorders involved progressive deterioration, while *praecox* indicated that they began early—usually in adolescence or early adulthood. Bleuler later applied the term *schizophrenia* to these syndromes—arguing, however, that deterioration was not inevitable, that biological factors did not completely account for etiology, and that adolescence and early adulthood were not always the time of origin. In fact, both Kraepelin and Bleuler recognized a small number of cases that were traceable to childhood, and the first efforts to label and diagnose psychotic behavior in children were rooted in the work of these men. Early labels for childhood psychoses—dementia praecocissima, dementia infantilis, and childhood schizophrenia—were undoubtedly derived from terminology employed by these investigators (Goldfarb, 1970). General acceptance of childhood psychoses occurred in the third decade of this century, but even today many questions remain.

One such question involves the relationship of childhood psychoses to disturbances of adulthood labeled schizophrenia. In adults schizophrenia is considered a pervasive functional deterioration marked variously by delusions, hallucinations, incoherence, loose associations, and inappropriate affect. At one time it was commonly assumed that severe developmental disorders in children represented the identical pathological processes of schizophrenia, with different manifestations due to the immaturity of youth. Although this view still exists, the trend is to distinguish psychoses that appear in childhood from those that appear in adulthood. DSM-III and ICD-9 still permit children to be classified under schizophrenia that typically occurs in adulthood, but both systems now also include categories of disorders that originate only during childhood. DSM-III calls its new category *Pervasive Developmental Disorders* and states that it bears "little relationship to the psychotic disorders of adult life" (American Psychiatric Association, 1980, p. 86). Historically, though, children who fit the new category have been widely described as schizophrenic and psychotic.

Although most investigators agree that some disturbed children can be called psychotic (or can be said to be suffering from pervasive developmental disorders), they agree less on specific diagnostic subcategories and the criteria to be used (Werry, 1979a). Age of onset has become an increasingly crucial consideration (Kolvin, 1971b). Studies conducted in Britain, Japan, and the Soviet Union all indicate a bimodal distribution of age of onset (Kolvin, 1971a; Rutter, 1974a, 1978b). Figure 8–1 shows the large peak that occurs very early in life and the smaller one that is evident for late childhood/early adolescence. Remarkably few cases are noted for the age range of 3 to 6 years, even though the severity of psychotic disorders makes it unlikely that they go unreported. Early onset disorder is widely recognized and is labeled as infantile autism. Later onset disorders are marked by ambiguous conceptualization and labeling. When originating near puberty, the disorders are considered more similar to

167

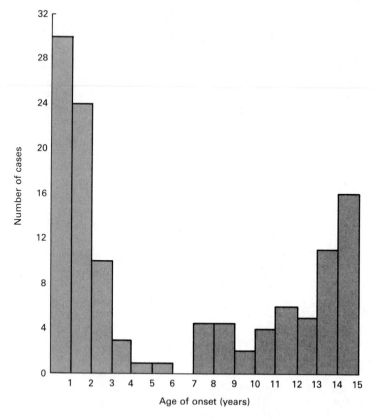

Figure 8–1 Cases of childhood psychoses according to age of onset. *From Rutter, 1974.*

adult schizophrenia than when they arise earlier (Eggers, 1978; Ross and Pelham, 1981).

The present chapter is devoted to the severe disturbances that originate in infancy and childhood that are variously known as psychoses and pervasive developmental disorders. Clinical features and etiological hypotheses are presented separately for early and later onset disorders. The chapter then moves on to prognosis and treatment. A word of caution is necessary at the outset, though: Researchers and clinicians have often lumped children together regardless of age of onset and have inconsistently used different labels and criteria for classification.

EARLY ONSET: INFANTILE AUTISM

Infantile autism was first described by Leo Kanner (1943) when he documented the his-

tories of eleven children who, he argued, were different from other severely disturbed youngsters. The following is his description of one of these children, Paul, who was referred at age 5 for suspected intellectual deficiency:

Paul was a slender, well built, attractive child, whose face looked intelligent and animated. He had good manual dexterity. He rarely responded to any form of address, even to the calling of his name. . . . Yet one never had the feeling that he was willingly disobedient or contrary. He was obviously so remote that the remarks did not reach him. He was always vivaciously occupied with something and seemed to be highly satisfied, unless someone made a persistent attempt to interfere with his self-chosen actions. Then he first tried impatiently to get out of the way and, when this met with no success, screamed and kicked in a full-fledged tantrum.

There was a marked contrast between his relations to people and to objects. Upon entering the room, he instantly went after objects and used them correctly. He was not destructive and treated the objects with care and even affection. . . . He got hold of a pair of scissors and patiently and skillfully cut a sheet of paper into small bits, singing the phrase "Cutting paper," many times. He helped himself to a toy engine, ran around the room holding it up high and singing over and over again, "The engine is flying." While these utterances, made always with the same inflection, were clearly connected with his actions, he ejaculated others that could not be linked up with immediate situations. These are a few examples: "The people in the hotel"; "Did you hurt your leg?" "Candy is all gone, candy is empty"; "You'll fall off the bicycle and bump your head." However, some of those exclamations could be definitely traced to previous experiences. He was in the habit of saying almost every day, "Don't throw the dog off the balcony." His mother recalled that she had said those words to him about a toy dog while they were still in England. At the sight of a saucepan he would invariably exclaim, "Peter-eater." The mother remembered that this particular association had begun when he was 2 years old and she happened to drop a saucepan while reciting to him the nursery rhyme about "Peter, Peter, pumpkin eater." Reproductions of warnings of bodily injury constituted a major portion of his utterances.

None of these remarks was meant to have communicative value. There was, on his side, no affective tie to people. He behaved as if people as such did not matter or even exist. It made no difference whether one spoke to him in a friendly or a harsh way. He never looked up at people's faces. When he had any dealing with persons at all, he treated them, or rather parts of them, as if they were objects. He would use a hand to lead him. He would, in playing, butt his head against his mother as at other times he did against a pillow. He allowed his boarding mother's hands to dress him, paying not the slightest attention to her. When with other children, he ignored them and went after their toys.

The Johns-Hopkins Medical Institutions

Leo Kanner, who offered the first description of infantile autism, is considered a pioneer in the study of childhood psychoses.

His enunciation was clear and he had a good vocabulary. His sentence construction was satisfactory, with one significant exception. He never used the pronoun of the first person, nor did he refer to himself as Paul. All statements pertaining to himself were made in the second person, as literal repetitions of things that had been said to him before. He would express his desire for candy by saying, "*You* want candy." He would pull his hand away from a hot radiator and say "*You* get hurt." Occasionally there were parrot-like repetitions of things said to him.

Formal testing could not be carried out, but he certainly could not be regarded as feebleminded in the ordinary sense. After hearing his boarding mother say grace three times, he repeated it without a flaw and has retained it since then. He could count and name colors. He learned quickly to identify his favorite victrola records from a large stack and knew how to mount and play them.

His boarding mother reported a number of observations that indicated compulsive behavior. He often masturbated with complete abandon. He ran around in circles emitting phrases in an ecstatic-like fashion. He took a small blanket and kept shaking it, delightedly shouting. ''Ee! Ee!'' He could continue in this manner for a long time and showed great irritation when he was interfered with. All these and many other things were not only repetitions but recurred day after day with almost photographic sameness. (Kanner, 1943, reprinted in Kanner, 1973, pp. 14–15)

On the basis of the eleven case histories, Kanner induced that the fundamental disorder was an inability to relate to people and situations from the beginning of life. He quoted parents as referring to their disturbed offspring as ''self-sufficient,'' ''like in a shell,'' ''happiest when left alone,'' ''acting as if people weren't there,'' and ''failing to develop the usual amount of social awareness'' (1973, p. 33). To this extreme aloneness Kanner applied the term *autistic*, which denotes an absorption in the self

or subjective mental activity. Kanner noted several other features. The children often developed unusual communication patterns, were delayed in speech, or failed to develop any speech. Another feature was an obsessive desire for sameness in the environment. One of the children, for instance, was driven to despair by changes in routine and in furniture placement. Finally, it was noted that the children displayed unusually strong fascination for inanimate objects and that they possessed good, albeit atypical, cognitive potential in isolated areas.

Thirteen years later Kanner and Eisenberg (1956), after observing over 120 children diagnosed as autistic, concluded that the two distinctive features of the syndrome were extreme self-isolation and insistence on sameness in the environment. Nevertheless, all the characteristics originally described have been widely recognized along with several others, including self-stimulatory and self-injurious behaviors (e.g., Lovaas, Young, and Newsom, 1978). Inconsistency in diagnostic criteria has been dominant, but recently some accord is apparent, as reflected in DSM-III and ICD-9 categories (Table 8-1). Research continues to be hindered to the extent that a common definition is not employed (Newsom and Rincover, 1981; Ross and Pelham, 1981; Rutter, 1978b). In addition, there is a dire need for subclassification. For example, autism has been found at IQ levels ranging from severely retarded to superior,

Table 8-1   DSM-III and ICD-9 Criteria For Infantile Autism

DSM-III	ICD-9
Onset before 30 months	Onset in the first 30 months
Lack of social responsiveness	Abnormal responses to auditory and visual stimuli
Gross language deficits	Delayed and abnormal speech
Peculiar language, e.g., echolalia, pronoun reversal	Problems in social relationships, e.g., impairment in eye-to-eye gaze, attachment, social play
Bizarre responses, e.g., resistance to change, interest in inanimate objects	Ritualistic behavior: abnormal routines, resistance to change, stereotyped patterns
Absence of delusions, hallucinations, loosening of associations	Diminished capacity for abstract thought with intelligence ranging from subnormal to above normal

American Psychiatric Association, 1980, and World Health Organization, 1977.

but these conditions are probably different in symptomatology, etiology, prognosis, and treatment (Rutter, 1978b). Valid subclassification would allow children to be grouped in ways meaningful for both research and treatment.

What Is the Basic Defect?

As the study of autism has proceeded, a common question has been: What is the core defect in the disorder? Initially it was seen as a disturbance in affective contact, an inability to relate to others almost from the beginning of life. This view has been upheld by Des-Lauriers's (1978) study of Clarence, one of Kanner's original autistic children. Descriptions of Clarence's attempts to form heterosexual relationships and to marry give clear evidence of his difficulties. So too does the case study of 31-year-old Jerry, who was diagnosed by Kanner at age 4 (Bemporad, 1979). Nevertheless, these descriptions do not establish that affective disturbance is the central defect in au-

tism from which other deficiencies spring. It is possible, of course, that disturbed relationships deleteriously affect the development of language and social behavior (Bemporad, 1979). But the more accepted view today is that some perceptual or cognitive defect is at the heart of the disorder, leading to affective and social disturbance. Investigators are exploring a variety of functions; however, no specific defect has been convincingly shown to be central. Indeed, the research is quite complex and conceptually scattered. The following examples demonstrate the variety of functions being explored.

Perceptual Disturbances. Certain characteristics of autism have led many researchers to hypothesize that faulty perception is a prominent feature of the syndrome. Ornitz and Ritvo are foremost among these (Hagamen, 1980a; Ornitz, 1978; Ornitz and Ritvo, 1968; Tanguay, 1976). As the information presented in Table 8–2 indicates, large percentages of autistic children are reported to engage in behaviors that suggest disturbance in sensory input or

Table 8–2 Percentages of Autistic Children with Disturbances of Sensory Input or Motor Output As Reported by One Sample of Parents

Disturbance	Percentage
Ignored or failed to respond to sounds	71
Excessively watched the motion of own hands or fingers	71
Stared into space as if seeing something that was not there	64
Preoccupied with things that spin	57
Preoccupied with minor visual details	57
Preoccupied with the feel of things	53
Let objects fall out of hands as if they did not exist	53
Preoccupied with scratching surfaces and listening to the sound	50
Agitated at being taken to new places	48
Agitated by loud noises	42
Flapped arms or hands in repetitive way	76
Whirled around without apparent reason	59
Rocked head or body	51
Ran or walked on toes	40

From Ornitz, 1978.

sensorimotor behavior. They may fail to respond to sound, stare into space, display a bizarre preoccupation with moving objects, flap their limbs, whirl, and rock. Ornitz and Ritvo attribute these disturbances to a defect in the regulation and integration of sensory input and motor output. They argue that perceptual inconstancy prevents the child from constructing a stable representation of the world. In turn, the environment is so little comprehended that appropriate social interaction and language have no basis for development.

Selective Attention and Learning. Lovaas and his colleagues are among those who have demonstrated that attentional processes may be disturbed in autism. They conducted a series of experiments on autistic children's attention to multiple cues. In one widely cited study autistic, retarded, and normal children were presented with a complex stimulus consisting of a light, white noise, and tactile pressure. In subsequent testing the normal children responded to all components of the stimulus, the retarded responded to some of them, and the autistic responded to only a single component (Lovaas, Koegel, and Schreibman, 1979; Lovaas, Young, and Newsom, 1978). This experiment and others show that autistic youngsters selectively attend to particular stimulus events while seemingly ignoring others. Such overselectivity is not due to specific sensory defects, because the children can be trained to respond to the stimuli they initially ignore. They may have idiosyncratic preferences for modes of stimuli, for example, for auditory over visual material (Kolko, Anderson, and Campbell, 1980). However, overselectivity occurs even when all components of the complex stimulus are in one modality (for example, all are visual).

Stimulus overselectivity may have a wide range of effects on learning, and thus on language and social development (Rincover and Koegel, 1977; Schreibman, Koegel, Charlop, and Egel, 1982). Much basic learning depends on the association of various cues or events—whether it is the UCS and CS in classical conditioning, a given response and its consequence in operant learning, or the contiguous cues in observational learning. If autistic children "hook" on to an irrelevant stimulus, their learning is impeded. Rincover and Koegel (1977) have provided telling examples of this. In one study they taught autistic children a new behavior in one setting and recorded this behavior in a different setting. Four of the ten subjects showed no generalization to the different setting. It was discovered that each of these children had been responding to an incidental stimulus during training, in one case to the hand movement of the teacher that inadvertantly coincided with the training trials. When the incidental stimulus of the training setting was introduced into the new setting, all of the children responded correctly!

It should be noted that stimulus overselectivity is not unique to autistic children; it occurs in retarded persons and in the very young (Lovaas, Young, and Newsom, 1978; Ross and Pelham, 1981). However, it alerts us to attentional and learning deficits.

Communication. Communication difficulties appear critical in autism. In one study at Maudsley Hospital (Britain), all the autistic children studied displayed some language delay or regression. Half were without speech at 5 years of age, and over three-quarters of those

Extreme "aloneness" and a lack of awareness or interest in social interactions is a common characteristic of children described as autistic.

By permission of Sagamore Children's Center, Melville, NY. Courtesy of Kenneth F. Kaufman, Ph.D.

who had acquired speech showed abnormal features (Rutter, 1978c). Although no one aspect of language signifies autism, several characteristics are commonly observed. One is *echolalia*—the repetition or echoing back, immediately or after various delays—of the speech of others. Another is *pronoun reversals*: Many autistic children refer to themselves as "you" or "he," as did Paul in our early example. Diminished vocabulary, comprehension problems, inappropriate remarks, unusual expressions, and deviations in articulation, pitch, rhythm, and inflection all have been noted (Baker, Cantwell, Rutter, and Bartak, 1976). Impairments may also exist in skills thought to precede language; for example, patterns of babbling may be unusual and social imitation, gesture, and mime may be lacking.

From these descriptions Rutter (1978c) has concluded that language deficits in autistic children are severe and extensive and are a true cognitive incapacity rather than simply the results of disturbed social relationships that prevent the use and development of language. As evidence, Rutter points out that autistic children do relatively poorly on tasks that require no actual speech but that do require verbal sequencing and abstraction skills. (One example of such a task is the Picture Arrangement on the Wechsler Intelligence Scale for Children; it requires that the child arrange a set of jumbled pictures so that a story is properly sequenced.) It has also been demonstrated that autistic children make relatively little use of meaning in language (Hermelin and O'Conner, 1970). While normal children remember sentences better than they do random words, the meaning in sentences does not help autistic children. From a review of studies on linguistic functioning, Tager-Flusberg (1981) has concluded that semantics (the meaning of language) and pragmatics (the social context of language) appear more disturbed in autism than either phonology (the sound system) or syntax (how words are combined into phrases or sentences). All these findings support the idea that basic cognitive deficits, with language as a central aspect, exist in autism.

Etiology

The causes of autism are unknown, but many ideas about etiology exist. Just as a shift has occurred toward conceptualizing the disorder in terms of cognitive instead of affective deficits, so too has there been movement from psychogenic toward biological etiologies.

Psychogenic Determinants. Those who look to psychogenic factors as primary in the etiology of autism emphasize the role of parental interaction and psychopathology. At the extreme, parents are viewed as causing a biologically normal child to become autistic by means of their own deviant personalities or interactions. Less extreme is the view that parents exacerbate abnormalities in children who are already biologically vulnerable (McAdoo and DeMyer, 1978).

In his classic 1943 publication Kanner described the families of his autistic sample as highly intelligent and professionally accomplished. Subsequent research has revealed that parents of autistic children tend toward high IQ and social class—but that autistic children come from parents of all intelligence and social levels (Cantwell, Baker, and Rutter, 1978; Schopler, Andrews, and Strupp, 1979). Kanner also noted that the families were strongly preoccupied with scientific, literary, and artistic abstractions and lacked genuine interest in people. He later noted that most of the children had been exposed from the beginning of their lives to a mechanical, cold, and obsessive attention to material needs (Kanner, 1949). Kanner was interested in whether and how these factors contributed to the condition of the children, but he did not believe that "refrigerator parents" were sufficient to explain the appearance of autism (Kanner, 1943; Kanner and Eisenberg, 1956). Nevertheless, the idea grew that mechanical parenting might be the cause of the condition. This was due, in part, to the *zeitgeist*, which from about 1945 to 1965 emphasized the psychoanalytic view that parents could be causal agents of psychopathology in their offspring (Schopler, 1978).

Today Bruno Bettleheim's conceptualizations are foremost among psychogenic theories of autism. In his book *The Empty Fortress*, and other works, Bettleheim (1967a,b) hypothesized that autism results from early unsatisfactory and threatening experiences. According to Bettleheim, normal personality and ego development critically depend on the child's acting successfully on the environment to fulfill needs and on communicating emotions to others and receiving a fitting reply. This process begins very early and requires minute adaptations on the part of caretakers. If mutuality develops as it should, the infant's cries, smiles, and other signals are validated by appropriate responses from others. The child then continues to act on the world and develop a sense of self. However, if the environment is unresponsive during the first two years of life, the child may perceive the world as frustrating, threatening, and destructive, and withdraw from it. The will to act is relinquished, learning may stop or regress, and reality may be left behind. In short, the child retreats to an empty fortress. Parental interaction, particularly that of the mother, is crucial in this process because it is the center of the child's experience. Thus, according to Bettleheim, the mother's response to the infant's strivings—whether during nursing, diapering, or bathing—significantly shapes all later self-motivated action. Damage clearly can result from outright maternal rejection, but any handling that ignores the infant's attempt to act on its own behalf also may be detrimental. The child who becomes autistic has not necessarily been neglected and deprived of food and care; rather, it has been robbed of the conviction that its action has influence.

Another analysis that focuses on psychogenic factors is that of Charles Ferster (1961, 1966). While Bettleheim's work stems from psychodynamic formulations, Ferster's proposal is based on a learning framework. The development of behavior is explained largely in terms of operant learning. Accordingly, behavioral repertoires are shaped by reinforcing and punishing contingencies, which are primarily controlled by parents. Parents themselves are conditioned reinforcers; that is, because they are paired very early in life with primary reinforcers such as food and comfort, they become reinforcing in themselves. Therefore, they are crucial in the shaping of all subsequent behavior. According to Ferster, parents of autistic children have somehow failed in this role. Having never acquired adequate conditioned reinforcers, the autistic child lacks support for the development of a normal repertoire of social behaviors. Furthermore, it is suggested that self-stimulatory and other primitive behaviors are strengthened by the reinforcement they garner. It is unresponsive parents who are most likely not to become reinforcers, due to their preoccupation with other activities, rejection of the child, depression, and the like. Thus, it can readily be seen that although Ferster's analysis is clearly different than that of Bettleheim, the two theorists share the view that early parental interaction plays a central role in bringing about the autistic syndrome.

The theories just described are examples of the psychogenic viewpoint that has waned in influence (although we shall see that Ferster's proposals fostered the current behavioral approach to treatment). One reason for the decline of psychogenic theories is the very nature of autism. The severity and bizarreness of some of the symptoms—displayed so early in life—intuitively seem unexplainable solely, or even primarily, by environmental factors. Another reason is the lack of empirical support. Recent reviews of research have not, on the whole, substantiated a primary etiological role for parents (Cantwell, Baker, and Rutter, 1978; McAdoo and DeMyer, 1978; Werry, 1979a). It appears that autistic children do not tend to come from broken homes, do not suffer early family stress, and are not exposed to exceptional parental attitudes and child-rearing practices. Moreover, the weight of the evidence is that parents of autistic youngsters display no definitive tendency toward schizophrenia, thought disorders, lack of empathy, extroversion, obsessionality, or deviant personalities (e.g., McAdoo and DeMyer, 1978). Occasionally they have been shown to be different than parents of normal children, but this only raises the question of which came first, the chicken or the egg. It would not be surprising if disturbance in the young gives rise to parental problems rather than the other way around. Indeed, studies indicate that parents of brain-damaged and retarded children frequently are tense and domineering, but it is unlikely that these behaviors initially caused the youngsters' disorders (Ross, 1974). Adequate research minimally requires a comparison group of parents whose children display some kind of behavior problems other than autism. When this requirement is met, it appears that parents of autistic children do not differ from parents of other disturbed youth, thereby supporting the idea that parental behavior may well be the result of the children's disturbance (Cantwell, Baker, and Rutter, 1978).

Biological Factors. Evidence for biological determinants has gradually been accumulating, with research moving forward rapidly (Cohen and Shaywitz, 1982). It has been shown that women who contract rubella during the first trimester of pregnancy are at risk for producing autistic offspring (Chess, 1971). The syndrome has also been associated with physical conditions such as tuberose sclerosis (an inherited disorder manifested by mental retardation and small tumors) and congential syphilis (Lotter, 1974a; Rutter, 1978a). Autistic children appear to experience a higher incidence of adverse prenatal and perinatal conditions (Campbell, Geller, and Cohen, 1977), and they have more physical anomalies than their siblings (Links, Stockwell, Abichandani, and Simeon, 1980). Neurological signs such as abnormal EEG recordings and the occurrence of seizures also have been observed (e.g., Lotter, 1974a). Researchers have implicated different parts of the brain—the left temporal lobe, reticular system, and vestibular system, for example (DeLong, 1978; Ornitz, 1978; Rimland, 1964). No evidence to date, however, establishes a specific anatomical site of defect.

Investigators have also looked to biochemistry as the locus of disturbance. Considerable research is being directed at the role of serotonin, the central nervous system neurotransmitter. Although some studies indicate that autistic subjects have elevated blood levels of serotonin, the findings are discrepant (Ritvo and Freeman, 1977). Other neurotransmitters, amino acids, and enzymes are also being examined. Thus far biochemical abnormalities have not been clearly established. Moreover, this area of research has been marred by serious difficulties (Ritvo and Freeman, 1977; Ritvo, Rabin, Yuwiler, Freeman, and Geller, 1978). First, because different investigators have used different criteria to diagnose their subjects, interpretation and generalization of results are problematical. Second, nonstandard biochemical methods have frequently been employed. Third, for most of the biochemical analyses conducted, lack of normative and developmental data hinders interpretation of the findings. If, for example, the normal range of values for the blood level of a particular biochemical—or the way in which blood level might change with age—is unknown, no basis for comparison exists. In addition to methodological problems, biochemical assay of the brain and nervous system is made difficult by the nature of the biological systems. Cerebrospinal fluid, blood, urine, and other tissue are examined, but they are far removed from the brain. Blood contains nutrients and metabolites from all over the body, while urine is the repository of metabolic wastes from the entire body. The task of establishing biochemical abnormalities that are related to autism or to any other behavioral disturbance is thus an arduous one.

Finally, genetic factors have been examined. Chromosome analyses have so far failed to detect any gross abnormalities. There is also no substantial evidence for the family patterns of single-gene inheritance; that is, for sex-linked, recessive, and dominant genes (Spence, 1976). It would be difficult to establish these patterns, however, because the syndrome is so rare. Then too, an autistic child with an autistic parent is hardly ever seen, since these individuals usually do not marry and have children (Folstein and

Rutter, 1978). Nevertheless, two findings from family history studies suggest hereditary influence. About 2 percent of the siblings of autistic children display the syndrome. Although this is a small percentage, it is fifty times that expected in the general population. Furthermore, in about 25 percent of the cases, there is a family history of speech delay, raising the possibility that some broad linguistic or cognitive deficiency may be inherited.

Support for hereditary influence also comes from twin studies, particularly from the work of Folstein and Rutter (1978). Twenty-one pairs of same-sex twins were located in which one of each pair met a stringent definition of autism (that is, serious impairment in social relationships, language delay or deviance, stereotyped or ritualistic activities, onset at 5 years of age or earlier, no known neurological disorder). The twins ranged in age from 5 to 23 years and, on the basis of careful zygosity tests, were classified as eleven monozygotic and ten dizygotic pairs. In line with other studies, the male-female ratio was 3.2 to 1, none of the parents were schizophrenic, and only one of the nontwin siblings was autistic. About one-half of the autistic children were retarded, but almost one-third had average IQs on nonverbal tests of intelligence.

Information about the twin pairs came from interviews with the twins and their parents, examination of the subjects, and detailed descriptions that had been collected previously. The results showed that none of the dizygotic, but 36 percent of the monozygotic, pairs were concordant for autism. Interestingly, 10 percent of the dizygotic and 82 percent of the monozygotic pairs were concordant for various cognitive/linguistic problems. These DZ-MZ differences suggest the influence of inheritance, although damage to genetic material very early in development could also result in such differences (Ornitz, 1978, cited by Ross and Pelham, 1981). Folstein and Rutter ruled out the likelihood that perinatal complications accounted for the concordance findings: In no twin pairs concordant for autism or for cognitive/linguistic deficits did both twins suffer biological hazards associated with birth.

Nevertheless, these investigators concluded that environmental events involving the risk of brain damage play a part in the etiology of autism. Of the seventeen pairs of twins in their sample who were discordant for autism, there were twelve in which the autistic child, but not the cotwin, had suffered biological hazard, mostly prenatal in origin. Thus, it was noted that while hereditary transmission may be sufficient to cause autism in some cases, brain injury alone or in combination with inherited cognitive abnormalities may also be sufficient.

Summary. From all the evidence it appears that autism has multiple biological etiologies. It may be viewed as a final common pathway, a syndrome that can be caused by any one of a variety of central nervous insults occurring between conception and the first few years of life (Hagamen, 1980). This does not necessarily mean tht psychogenic factors have no role in the appearance or shaping of autism. Cantwell, Baker, and Rutter (1978) suggest that the environment could act in several ways:

1. Perhaps some kinds of autism are primarily determined by psychogenic influences.
2. Although organic impairment may be necessary, perhaps it is not sufficient; that is, an interaction with an environmental stress may be required for the syndrome to appear.
3. Perhaps the child's biological deficits lead to damage by even quite ordinary family influences that would not adversely affect most children.
4. Environmental factors perhaps play no part in the etiology of autism but may influence its development and prognosis. Educational experiences and home interventions have indeed been shown to alter autistic behaviors.

All of these alternatives are still worthy of consideration.

LATER ONSET PSYCHOSES

The array of psychoses that are recognized as originating from approximately age 3 to early adolescence have not been consistently conceptualized. Normal or near-normal development prior to the occurrence of symptoms is widely agreed upon. The question of how and why development goes awry has received more attention than would be expected based on the frequency of the disorders, but consensus is still lacking. Agreement is also lacking with regard to diagnosis and description. Table 8–3 shows the diagnostic categories employed by DSM-III, including the category of schizophrenia that can be used for children and adults. Later onset disorders have received other labels as well; for example, symbiotic psychosis, disintegrative psychosis, and most frequently, childhood schizophrenia. Let us examine some of the clinical descriptions provided by various investigators, beginning with the historically important work of Lauretta Bender.

Clinical Features

Bender's Descriptions. Along with Kanner, Bender is considered a pioneer in the study of childhood psychoses. Working at New York City's Bellevue Hospital for many years, she described, treated, and followed the progress of a group of severely disturbed children she labeled schizophrenic (Bender, 1947, 1972, 1974). Although some of Bender's observations are disputed today, their influence has been strong.

According to Bender, childhood schizophrenia reveals itself in uneven development in

Table 8-3   DSM-III Categories for Late Onset Disturbances

Along with Infantile Autism, the following two categories are listed under Disorders Usually First Evident in Infancy, Childhood, or Adolescence: Pervasive Developmental Disorders

1. *Childhood onset pervasive developmental disorders*
   Gross and sustained impairment in social relationships
   At least three of the following: sudden excessive anxiety; constricted or inappropriate affect; resistance to change or insistence on sameness; odd motor movements; abnormalities of speech; hyper- or hyposensitivity to sensory stimuli; self-mutilation
   Onset after 30 months and before 12 years
   Absence of delusions, hallucinations, loosening of associations

2. *Atypical pervasive developmental disorders*
   Distortions in the development of multiple basic psychological functions involved in language and social skills that cannot be classified as Infantile Autism or Childhood Onset Pervasive Developmental Disorders

Criteria for Schizophrenic Disorders, which are identical for children and adults

At least one of the following symptoms must be present during a phase of the illness: some type of delusion (bizarre, grandiose, etc.); hallucination (auditory, etc.); loosening of associations, illogical thinking; or poverty of content of speech
Deterioration from a previous level of functioning
Continuous signs of the illness at least six months, during which the above signs are apparent. Some residual symptoms may also appear: social isolation; peculiar behavior; impairment in grooming; inappropriate affect; digressive, vague, or otherwise unusual speech; unusual perceptual experiences; etc.
Onset before 45 years of age
Not due to known organic mental disorder or to mental retardation

American Psychiatric Association, 1980.

every area of central nervous system functioning: vegetative, motor, perceptual, intellectual, emotional, and social. With regard to vegetative symptoms, sleeping, eating, and elimination are disturbed, as are growth patterns and the timing of puberty. The children are motorically awkward, and primitive reflexes such as the whirling response may persist for an unusually long time (see p. 102). Bender related motor problems to more general psychological difficulties such as the inability to determine the periphery of the body and the personality, as well as failure to draw relationships to time and space. She also described intellectual retardation, language problems, distorted thinking, and disturbed interpersonal relationships. The essential psychological problem, according to Bender, is "difficulties in identifying one's self and thereby relating to the rest of the world" (1972, p. 639).

An advocate of the position that childhood psychosis is a single entity that manifests itself according to developmental status, Bender differentiated the clinical picture by age of onset. The first critical period is early onset—up to two years of life—when the child manifests a "mental illness" that "subsequently proves to be schizophrenia" (1972, p. 643). Today many of these children would receive the label of infantile autism, and Bender herself used this term. A second critical age of onset, 3 to 4 ½ years, involves either insidious and slow or abrupt and rapid regression. The third critical age is prepubertal, from about 10 to 11½ years. Children with such late onset may display high anxiety, obsessive-compulsive behavior, delusions, hallucinations, and suicidal tendencies.

Char and Lubetsky's Descriptions. Although it is rare for pervasive developmental disorders to appear between 3 and 6 years of age, some recognition has been given to this age of onset as a distinct entity. As we have seen, Bender (1972) delineated both rapid and gradual change from normalcy. Using the psychodynamic model, Mahler (1952) proposed that manifestations of "symbiotic psychosis" usually appear in the third or fourth year of life,

when the child is psychologically unable to separate itself from its mother. Primary process thinking, hallucinations, panic, rage, and low frustration tolerance were all noted by Mahler.

More recently Char and Lubetsky (1979) have provided case descriptions of children who began to show behavioral disturbance during the preschool years. Treated in a small therapeutic nursery, three of the youngsters were eventually able to attend regular kindergarten. The following is a description of one of these children:

B. T., a boy of 3 years 11 months of age, was referred with the chief complaint of behavior difficulties at nursery school and at home. . . . He suddenly and persistently began refusing to go to school, and to cry inconsolably there for no apparent reason. He stopped playing with other children with whom he had previously played. No precipitating event could be discovered to account for this sudden change in behavior.

About 9 months prior to referral, when B. T. was just over 3 years of age, the parents noted an inordinate fear of rain and an intense fear of the toilet flushing, the electric garage door opener, and windshield wipers. He would often have tantrums in the face of these fears. He developed a ritual following a tantrum, wherein he had to be kissed exactly four times and then would kiss the other members of the family in a particular order, which at his insistence always remained the same.

History revealed that B. T. was the product of an uncomplicated pregnancy and delivery with a birth weight of 8 pounds and 2 ounces. No feeding or sleeping problems were noted during the first year of life. He was described as an affectionate, responsive infant. He crawled at 6 months and walked at 15 months of age. He began to use words at about 18 months of age. At about 36 months of age, it was noted that B. T. knew all the letters of the alphabet and that he could read simple words. The parents noted that B. T. persistently used the pronoun *you* when referring to himself and the pronoun *I* when referring to another person. The rest of his language was reported to be normal.

. . . Pediatric examination, including the neurological, was within normal limits. Psychiatric evaluation, when B. T. was 4 years of age, revealed that he showed little if any appropriate separation anxiety. He would laugh and giggle to himself for no apparent reason. He avoided eye contact and could not be engaged in play. . . .

Psychological testing at age 4 years revealed that B. T. had an IQ of 70 as tested with the Stanford-Binet, with a few test items as much as 2 years above his chronological age. Visual-motor skills were found to be at age level. Much of his language was age-appropriate, but he tended to use idiosyncratic language. For example, he referred to a chicken as a "sousa," an arm as a "kock," and a cow and a horse were both called a "camel," even though he demonstrated that he knew common farmyard animals.

Prior to his entering kindergarten, psychological retesting, when B. T. was 5 years of age, revealed an increase of 22 points in IQ on the Stanford-Binet so that his IQ then measured 92. . . . He was found to be reading at the second-grade level, to be spelling at the 1.6-grade level, and to be doing arithmetic at the 1.8-grade level.

Projective testing revealed a breakdown in logical thinking and a misperception of reality, so that an arm was described as a "boy sitting," and the ear's function was described as "my ears wouldn't see anything, we look with our mouth and smell with our nose." Another card was responded to with "that's a scary big snake that looks like a dog, going to get hurt the Six Million Dollar Man, a monkey I mean." Note was made that these responses were not offered playfully.

Psychiatric reevaluation revealed that much of the isolated behavior and some of the inappropriate laughing remained. The intellectual gains

were noted, and B. T. now used pronouns correctly. (pp. 272–275)

Eggers's Descriptions. Eggers (1978) has described a sample of fifty-seven children, ages 7 to 13, who are said to be suffering from childhood schizophrenia. This investigator recognizes a clear distinction between infantile psychosis and late onset psychosis. The term *childhood schizophrenia* is applied to late onset, but only when the symptoms of adult schizophrenia are identified. Childhood and adult schizophrenia are considered the same process.

In Eggers's sample of schizophrenic children, the behaviors of youngsters under 10 are distinguished from those over 10. The former showed sudden personality changes that included increasing loss of contact with reality, reduced activity, narrowing of interests, negativism, disturbed motility (for example, stereotypy, hyperactivity, peculiar posture and mannerisms), and speech disturbances (for example, echolalia, neologisms*). They exhibited emotional changes that included coldness toward loved ones, and even brutality; for example, to their pets. Some of the children were anxious, stubborn, and distrustful. Some showed aimless destruction of objects, as well as self-injury that endangered their lives. Delusions and hallucinations were displayed. One form of delusions involved loss of identity: The children identified themselves as other persons or as animals or inanimate objects. Delusional symptoms appeared as irrational, diffused fears or perhaps as cosmic threats, as in "The sun is falling from the sky." Sometimes transitory paranoid ideas were also exhibited, in one case delusions of being poisoned.

With increasing age, symptoms more closely resembled those of the adult schizophrenic. Specifically, children between 10 and 13 years of age commonly reported auditory and, to a lesser extent, visual hallucinations, as well as more persistent delusions. Consistent with the growth in cognitive ability, delusions became

---

*Neologisms are words of one's own making that others do not usually understand.

more abstract, precise, and systematized. Unlike those under 10 years of age, the prepubertal children more frequently had acute rather than chronic episodes of disturbance. They also showed more favorable outcome.

Etiology

Psychogenic Variables. As with early onset pervasive developmental disorders, psychogenic hypotheses stress family and, to a lesser extent, social-class factors. Here we find that childhood schizophrenia, unlike infantile autism but similar to adult schizophrenia, appears inversely related to social class (Werry, 1979a). Moreover, families of schizophrenic children often display diverse psychopathology, more so than families of children diagnosed as autistic (Hagamen, 1980a; Wing, 1970).

Among the strong advocates of a psychogenic explanation is Szurek (1956), who attributed childhood schizophrenia almost exclusively to the child's unconscious conflict with parents who themselves are in conflict. Other psychogenic views, especially those of a psychoanalytic bent, have focused on identification with abnormal parents, pathological role taking, and reactions to pathological family dynamics (Alanen, 1960). Unfortunately, both the theoretical conceptualizations and the relevant research, if any, have often been lacking in clarity and precision.

Mahler and Rank have been influential, particularly with psychodynamically oriented clinicians, in explaining the occurrence of psychoses in the preschool child. Although both recognized constitutional factors, they focused on the mother-child relationship. Rank and her colleagues referred to the young psychotic child as "atypical." They depicted varieties of mothers who are incapable of maternal impulses and functions (Rank, 1949, 1955; Goldfarb, 1970). Some are overtly psychotic themselves, while others are emotionally immature and lacking in spontaneous affection for their offspring. Fathers in these families are considered too passive to counteract the negative influences of the mothers. Also contributing to the development

of the atypical child are traumatic events such as physical illness, birth of a sibling, and separation from parents.

Mahler (1952) hypothesized that the source of disturbance in some psychotic youngsters is the child's inability to separate itself from the mother—thus the term *symbiotic psychosis*. The child is unable to develop self-boundaries and clings to adults, especially the mother. Mahler suggested that children who experience symbiotic psychosis are constitutionally predisposed to have a defective ego and that this, in turn, causes the mother to act in ways that damage the child's efforts toward separation.

The work of Goldfarb and his colleagues is noteworthy as an extensive effort to evaluate the psychological climate of the family of psychotic children both by interview and by direct observation (Goldfarb, 1970; Goldfarb, Spitzer, and Endicott, 1976). These investigators found that parents of schizophrenic children were considered schizophrenic more often than would be expected in the population at large, the specific incidence varying across studies. In one investigation that exemplifies their work, parents of schizophrenic youngsters treated at the Ittleson Center were compared through a structured interview both with adults who had attended a psychiatric clinic and with a cross-section of adults living in upper Manhattan (Goldfarb, Spitzer, and Endicott, 1976). As shown in Figure 8–2, the parents of schizophrenic youngsters tended to fall between the two contrast groups on measures of psychopathological expression. It cannot be concluded, of course, that parental psychopathology caused schizophrenia in the offspring; perhaps causation was in the other direction, or perhaps other variables were responsible for both parental and child problems. In another part of the same study, judgments of psychopathology in the parents from the time they were 12 years old to the birth of the psychotic child were compared to similar judgments about nonpatient adults. The parents of schizophrenic children appeared more impaired. This comparison precludes the possibility that parental psychopathology was a reaction to the disturbed offspring. However, it

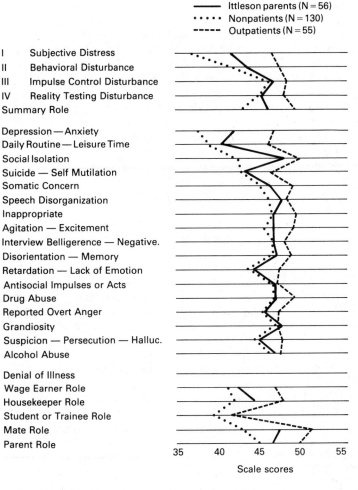

——— Ittleson parents (N = 56)
• • • • Nonpatients (N = 130)
- - - - Outpatients (N = 55)

I   Subjective Distress
II   Behavioral Disturbance
III   Impulse Control Disturbance
IV   Reality Testing Disturbance
Summary Role

Depression — Anxiety
Daily Routine — Leisure Time
Social Isolation
Suicide — Self Mutilation
Somatic Concern
Speech Disorganization
Inappropriate
Agitation — Excitement
Interview Belligerence — Negative.
Disorientation — Memory
Retardation — Lack of Emotion
Antisocial Impulses or Acts
Drug Abuse
Reported Overt Anger
Grandiosity
Suspicion — Persecution — Halluc.
Alcohol Abuse

Denial of Illness
Wage Earner Role
Housekeeper Role
Student or Trainee Role
Mate Role
Parent Role

35   40   45   50   55
Scale scores

Figure 8–2 Mean psychiatric scores of Ittleson parents, adult nonpatients, and adult outpatients. *From Goldfarb, Spitzer, and Endicott, 1976.*

rests on reports about a much earlier time of life, the memory of which could be systematically biased by the later experience of having a disturbed child. Thus, the Goldfarb work, despite much effort on the part of the investigators, exemplifies some of the difficulties of conducting research into family influences on etiology.

Despite these difficulties, no discussion of psychogenic variables in childhood psychoses would be complete without mentioning research into specific parent-child interactions. Myers and Goldfarb (1961), for example, found that mothers of schizophrenic children were more perplexed than mothers of normal youngsters. They exhibited greater indecisiveness, lack of control, and lack of authority, but less spontaneity, empathy, and sensitivity to their children's needs. Goldfarb, Goldfarb, and Scholl (1966) suggested that maternal communication with offspring was deficient in several ways. For example, it failed to stimulate interest in communication, to reinforce acceptable communication, and to cope with the child's deviant communications.

The studies just noted represent innumerable investigations designed to determine whether and how families with a psychotic child interact in a way that is harmful to their offspring. This effort runs parallel to the wide-scale attempt to identify deviant interactional patterns in families with an adult schizophrenic (e.g., Bateson, Jackson, Haley, and Weakland, 1956; Brodkin, 1980; Mishler and Waxler, 1965). Although the hypotheses and findings have frequently been challenging, so far this line of research has not delineated any interactional pattern that is specific to families with a psychotic member. Indeed, agreement is still lacking on the basic question of whether interaction is deviant at all (Goldfarb, 1970; Werry, 1979a). Severe methodological problems and the complexity of the phenomena have yet to be adequately dealt with (Hetherington and Martin, 1979).

Organic Factors. Many of the disturbances displayed by psychotic children have led investigators to implicate organic factors in etiology. Goldfarb (1970), for example, differentiated two groups of schizophrenic children, "organics" and "nonorganics." The former showed greater intellectual deficits as well as neurological signs. Bender considered childhood schizophrenia "a psychobiological entity determined by inherited predisposition and precipitated by an early physiological and organic crisis" (1974, p. 280).

Research has linked childhood schizophrenia with pregnancy complications, particularly toxemia, vaginal bleeding, and severe maternal illness (Pollack and Woerner, 1966; Rieder, Broman, and Rosenthal, 1977). Impaired integrity of the child's central nervous system has been inferred from abnormalities in posture, gait, muscle tone, motor coordination, and sensory integrations. Both a high incidence of abnormal EEG recordings and reports of convulsions tend to support this inference (Davison and Neale, 1978; Goldfarb, 1970). Biochemical studies continue, but so far they have produced little unequivocal information. While adequate investigation into the role of genetic factors is still lacking, some data are available.

Genetic Influence. Among the most relevant research is Kallmann and Roth's (1956)

study of preadolescent twins. Average age of onset was 8.8 for the males and 11.1 for females. The sample excluded mentally deficient youngsters, although many schizophrenic children display mental deficiency. There was a 70.6 percent concordance for psychoses in monozygotic twin pairs compared to a 17.1 percent concordance for dizygotic twins. (The figures rose to 88.2 and 22.9 percent, respectively, when the subjects were evaluated in later years.) Other research indicates that the incidence of schizophrenia in parents of schizophrenic children is greater than would be expected in the population at large (Goldfarb, 1970; Fish and Ritvo, 1979).

Less direct evidence comes from a variety of studies of adult schizophrenia. The incidence of schizophrenia in the general population is about 1 percent, but for parents of adult schizophrenics it has been estimated to range from 5 percent to 10 percent. The incidence in siblings of schizophrenics ranges from 8 to 14 percent (Davison and Neale, 1982). Overall, the closer the relationship to a schizophrenic adult, the greater the risk of a relative being labeled schizophrenic. It has also been shown that 16 percent of the children of schizophrenic mothers develop schizophrenia by adulthood (Heston, 1966). On the other hand, being reared with a schizophrenic adoptive parent does not increase the risk of schizophrenia in individuals who have normal biological parents (Davison and Neale, 1978). Finally, concordance for the disorder is greater in monozygotic than in dizygotic twin pairs. Based on this evidence, it is widely accepted today that heredity has some influence on schizophrenia that develops during adulthood (Davison and Neale, 1982; Fish and Ritvo, 1979; Rosenthal, 1970). Although the data do not directly apply to childhood psychoses, they are of interest, particularly to those who view childhood and adulthood schizophrenia as the same entity.

Summary. It appears likely that biological factors are important in the etiology of later onset psychotic disorders. They may range from overt, recognizable syndromes (for example, tuberose sclerosis, lead encephalopathy, Heller's disease) to elusive organic predispositions that increase vulnerability. Hereditary influence is likely to be involved in some instances, but further research is needed to establish the mechanisms, strength, and specific ways in which it operates. Moreover, as in infantile autism, environmental variables are expected to play some role. Considering the enormous effort to establish the impact of family and social variables on etiology, it is disappointing that our knowledge remains quite limited. The weight of the evidence suggests, however, that later onset is associated with low social-class status and parental psychopathology. This picture is different than that for infantile autism and argues for the dichotomy between early and later onset. Since later onset disorders encompass all the years from 3 to early adolescence, environmental variables may be increasingly influential, if for no other reason than that they have much opportunity to operate. In the final analysis, it is important to note that later onset disorders consist of a variety of severe disturbances that manifest themselves in similar—but not identical—ways. It is probable that these disorders stem from different causes and transactions.

WHAT HAPPENS TO PSYCHOTIC CHILDREN?

With few exceptions, investigations that have followed the progress of psychotic children give little reason for complacency about outcome. Bender (1974) followed one hundred children observed at Bellevue Hospital, whose onset varied from the first to twelfth year of life. At follow-up they ranged from 22 to 46 years. Bender reported that 63 percent had been placed in institutions for the mentally ill or retarded, while the remaining 37 percent were in the community. Kanner (1973) revealed that only eleven of the ninety-six autistic children he examined were maintaining themselves in the second and third decades of life. The eleven were doing moderately well: Several had achieved a college education; their jobs included bank teller, accountant, and truck-loading supervisor; they had hobbies; and most were

living alone with few friendships or romantic relationships. Lotter (1974a) reviewed three independent studies of autistic children in England and the United States. In two of the studies the subjects were 16 to 18 years at follow-up, and in the other they were 12 years old. As Figure 8–3 shows, 61 to 74 percent were judged as having poor or very poor status. They were rated as severely handicapped and unable to lead independent lives, as compared to the relatively few who were functioning educationally and socially or making progress despite some behavioral abnormalities. More extensive reviews of psychotic children that included follow-up into early adulthood essentially confirmed this finding (Goldfarb, 1980; Lockyer and Rutter, 1969; Lotter, 1978). These studies allow only superficial and uncertain generalities because they vary in diagnostic criteria and method (Lotter, 1978), but it does appear that the outlook for many severely disturbed children is unfortunate, if not tragic.

At the same time, prognosis can be quite variable. Lotter (1978) found that approximately half of the children in his study who were severely disturbed remained that way, while the other half progressed to different levels. Can outcome be predicted on the basis of the clinical profile? To some extent it can, although most follow-up studies pertain to infantile autism. Here, of the many variables that have been examined, the most clearly implicated are language development and performance on tests of intelligence (Kanner, 1973; Lotter, 1978; Rutter, 1978a). All of Kanner's eleven "emergers" had been able to speak before the age of 5. The best outcomes in Rutter's studies were for children who spoke before age 5, never showed a profound lack of response to sounds, and passed easily through a phase of echolalia. Autistic children of *normal* nonverbal intelligence have been found to make educational progress, become reasonably proficient in speech, and function productively in employment (Rutter, 1978a). These children respond to treatment; but interestingly, cognitive development and language do not improve as much as socialization, communication, behavior, and scholastic achievement. Improvement may continue

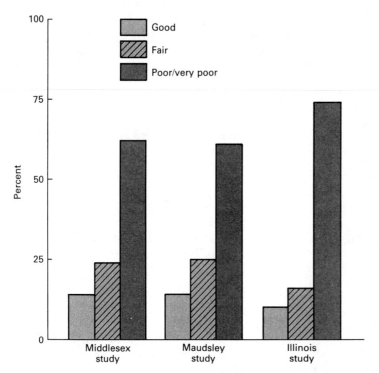

Figure 8-3 Percent of psychotic children judged good, fair, or poor/very poor several years after initial contact. *Adapted from Lotter, 1974a.*

into adolescence and even into early adulthood, but often social relationships are still qualitatively lacking.

Eggers's (1978) study stands out as a follow-up of children whose relatively clear manifestations of "childhood schizophrenia" occurred only after the age of 7 years. Half showed good improvement, with some considered fully recovered. About one-third showed very poor status, and the remainder fell into fair to poor status. Eggers found that all the children who had become psychotic before age 10 had poor outcome. Above average intelligence was associated with favorable outcome. Premorbid personality was also predictive of later status. Children had a better chance of recovery if they had once been well-adapted, kind, warm-hearted, and capable of making friends and having interests. Less favorable outcome accrued to those who had been insecure, inhibited, shy, and introverted. Interestingly, family mental disorders and family atmosphere did not predict outcome. Although Eggers noted that

prognosis in his sample was better than that usually assumed for the psychotic child, the overall poor outcome for these children makes it clear that research and treatment efforts are of the utmost importance.

HELPING THE PSYCHOTIC CHILD

Providing help to the psychotic child requires a great deal of patience and perseverance. As with all disorders, the child's behavior must first be judged according to a set of criteria. But adequate assessment not only serves the task of diagnosis—it also points the way to treatment.

Newsom and Rincover (1981), in discussing infantile autism, have provided an outline of methods for sampling a broad spectrum of behaviors that describe the "whole child." These methods could be used when the child is being evaluated for initial placement in school or other settings, for periodic progress, to meet legal requirements, or for ongoing research.

Informal observations can be made in the classroom or at home and during screening interviews that usually involve the parents. The following can be examined: activity level, self-stimulation, self-injurious behavior, self-care skills, functional reinforcers, special diet and medication, and unique features and skills. Child-management practices and parental ability to follow through in home interventions can also be evaluated. Warnings of potential difficulty may be given by parents who emphasize financial or work-related burdens, indicate depression or severe marital conflict, or discuss medical approaches (for example, diet, medication) that require little effort on their part.

It is also helpful to employ *standard tests* and *checklists*. General intelligence or developmental tests, often required by law, are limited in value because they sample a small range of intellective behaviors. However, they can provide some impression of language, motor, or intellectual skills and aid in evaluating placement of the nonretarded autistic child in regular classrooms. The primary usefulness of *educational tests* is for individual program planning and evaluation of progress. *Behavioral checklists* are sometimes helpful in distinguishing psychotic, retarded, and brain-damaged children. One example is Rimland's Diagnostic Checklist for Behavior Disturbed Children, which is designed to discriminate autistic children from other psychotic children (Rimland, 1964, 1971, 1974). Table 8-4 shows several items from the checklist. We note for instance, that parents of autistic children, more than parents of nonautistic psychotic children, had suspected deafness in their offspring and had noted awkward body posture.

Structured observational procedures involve direct observation and recording of behaviors in controlled situations, often with standard presentations of stimuli. For example, the Multiple-Response Recording procedure of Lovaas and his colleagues consists of continuous recordings of self-stimulation, echolalic and bizarre speech, appropriate speech, nonverbal social behavior, and appropriate play (Lovaas, Freitag, Gold, and Kassorla, 1965). This procedure has been used to measure behavior over time in conjunction with treatment programs. Its major

Table 8-4 Percentage of Parents of Autistic and Nonautistic Psychotic Children Rating Their Offspring on Certain Items on Rimland's Checklist

Description	Autistic		Nonautistic
	Speaking	*Mute*	
It was suspected at some time that child was nearly deaf.	77	94	54
Child rather stiff and awkward to hold, age 2–5.	90	88	56
Child exceptionally skillful in doing fine work with fingers or play with small objects, age 3–5.	71	75	33
Child fascinated by certain mechanical things, such as the stove or vacuum cleaner, age 3–5.	77	92	56
Child definitely gets upset if certain things he is used to are changed, age 3–5.	87	86	41
Child says "Yes" by repeating the same question he has been asked, age 3–5. (Example: If parent asks, "Shall we go for a walk, Honey?" child says yes by repeating, "Shall we go for a walk, Honey?")	94	12 (item not applicable to mute children)	22

From Rimland, B. Infantile autism: Status and research. In A. Davids (Ed.) *Child Personality and Psychopathology: Current Topics* N.Y.: Wiley Interscience, 1974. Copyright © 1974 and reprinted by permission of John Wiley & Sons, Inc.

strength is the direct recording of actual behaviors outside of the treatment environment.

Treatment of pervasive developmental disorders may come in many different ways, depending on the severity of the behavioral deficits, opportunity for treatment, and community/family support. Some severely disturbed children remain at home and attend special schools; others are placed in residential settings for various lengths of time. Therapeutic methods run the entire gamut of medical and psychotherapeutic approaches.

PHYSICAL METHODS OF TREATMENT

Electroconvulsive shock and medication are the best-known physical methods of treatment of childhood psychoses. Shock treatment was recommended by Bender (1947), who claimed it was effective with at least some of her patients. Nevertheless, it is not accepted today. Systematic study of drug use with children goes back to the early 1930s, but the method has grown in popularity only during the last two decades (Conners, 1978).

Several classes of medications have been tried. Table 8-5 summarizes the major types and their effects. The most positive finding is that some of the antipsychotic medications appear to reduce withdrawal, hyperactivity, and stereotyped behavior. Efficacy may be enhanced by concurrent behavioral treatment (Campbell et al., 1978). The overall picture is complex, however. Methodological flaws in studies of drug effectiveness are pervasive (Campbell, Geller, and Cohen, 1977). Moreover, specific diagnosis, age of the subject, drug dosage, and the behaviors being measured all play a role in outcome. The complexity of the situation, along with possible negative side effects, undoubtedly contributes to the sometimes cautious attitudes toward pharmacological intervention. Campbell and her colleagues note that under careful monitoring of medication, serious side effects are rare. Still, long-term side effects on cognition and physical growth, along with motor symptoms following drug withdrawal, require a greater research effort.

Table 8-5   Classes of Drugs Commonly Discussed in Relation to Childhood Psychoses

Class	Effect
Stimulants, e.g., benzedrine, dextro-amphetamine	May worsen psychoses, even in low dosages.
Tricyclic Antidepressants, e.g., imipramine	The few trials conducted suggest that further study is warranted. May help severely retarded autistic children.
Antipsychotics, e.g., phenothiazines, butyrophenones, thioxantheses	Some of these most widely used drugs help reduce withdrawal, hyperactivity, and stereotyped behaviors. Some may cause excessive sedation in young children. True antipsychotic effects (dissipation of thought disorders, hallucinations, delusions) are likely to be seen in older children or when onset is acute.
Hallucinogens, e.g., LSD	Some studies show decreases in withdrawal; others show the opposite.
Lithium	The few trials suggest that further research is warranted with children who are aggressive or show explosive affect.
Megavitamins	Widely used, but research evidence is unsound.

Adapted from Campbell, Geller, and Cohen, 1977; and Conners and Werry, 1979.

TRADITIONAL THERAPIES

Although traditional views of childhood psychoses sometimes recognize a possible role for biological factors, they emphasize intrapsychic, dynamic phenomena. Treatment thus focuses on aspects such as primary process thinking, the task of separation from parents, and ego development. A firm distinction is often not drawn between early autism and later onset disorders.

Ekstein, Friedman, and Caruth's (1972) approach serves as an example of traditional, analytical treatment. They view the psychotic child as suffering from a personality organization that is fragmented and disassociated. The disturbance has its origin in the failure of the child to progress from early mother-child fusion to normal object relatedness. The infant struggles unsuccessfully and retreats into autistic withdrawal (much like Mahler described symbiotic psychosis). Due to this basic flaw, development proceeds abnormally and results in the fixation of thinking at the primary process level. Psychotic children thus live in a world in which inner and outer reality is not distinguished, in which instinctual impulses reign, in which knowledge and trust of the future does not exist. Ego functions that control, integrate, and synthesize do not develop. According to Ekstein, Friedman, and Caruth, the task of the therapist is to aid in the development of a stable ego structure that will permit predictable and self-controlled choices. This is accomplished by building bridges from primitive structures to more advanced ones. The therapeutic tools employed are the usual psychoanalytic tools of the therapeutic relationship (transference) and interpretation. The therapist must be willing and able to use the psychotic thinking of the child while retaining one foot in the world of reality. Success is marked by the child giving up the psychotic retreat and developing the capacity to master reality.

Bettleheim's residential treatment program at the Orthogenic School in Chicago is an example of the combination of a general psychoanalytic framework with milieu therapy (Bettleheim, 1967a; Ekstein, Friedman, and Caruth, 1972). As we have already seen, Bettleheim attributes autism to failed parenting that involves outright emotional rejection and/or lack of mutual interaction. Treatment consists of creating a complete environment away from the parents in which the child can, for the first time, develop an autonomous existence as a person. The milieu includes a therapist—a steady, ever-present object—around which the newly forming personality can be unified. It must also permit the child to freely and safely explore, to experiment with letting go of the autistic defenses that had been constructed. In doing so, the child gradually gives up the world of fantasy and achieves more normal affective relationships.

Is traditionally oriented therapy effective with psychotic children? In evaluating his own treatment procedures, Bettleheim (1967a) noted that success was directly related to the child's original language ability and that ego functions (that is, reasoning, mastering of nonaffective reality, reading comprehension) often never reached normal developmental levels. Nevertheless, he claimed a high rate of success—79 percent of the outcomes were judged "good" or "fair." This favorable rate is so out of keeping with most evaluations of therapy that it raises questions about the criteria for success (Werry, 1979a). Moreover, several investigators have reported that psychodynamically treated psychotic children do not appear to prosper from treatment (Kozloff, 1973; Rutter, 1966; Schopler, 1974). Since adequately controlled studies are lacking, traditional therapies are of uncertain value (Werry, 1979a).

BEHAVIOR MODIFICATION

A few decades ago Ferster (1961) offered the conceptualization of infantile autism that heralded the behavioral treatment of the many problems displayed by psychotic children. Behavior modification encompasses extensive training for parents and teachers as well as direct applications to the client. The following examples describe the rationale and some of the procedures that have been applied to pervasive developmental disorders.

Language Training

Autistic children are often either mute or echolalic; they seem able to understand little of what is being said to them and are unable to express their needs to others. A number of behavioral researchers have analyzed language acquisition into specific learning variables that may be manipulated to produce language (e.g., Hewett, 1965; Lovaas, 1977; Risley and Wolf, 1967). Here the work of Lovaas and his colleagues will be considered.

Lovaas, Young, and Newsom (1978) conceptualize language acquisition as the learning of two fundamental events. First, children must acquire verbal responses of increasing complexity: basic speech sounds (phonics); words and parts of words (morphemes); and the arrangement of words into phrases and sentences (syntax). Second, they must acquire an appropriate context for verbal responses; that is, assign meanings and anticipate further responses.

In working with autistic children it is frequently necessary to prepare them for the training situation. This may include techniques that suppress self-stimulatory (p. 81) and self-injurious behaviors that interfere with learning. Procedures that achieve this have been developed. It may also be necessary to establish generalized imitation—that is, to teach the child to do what the therapist (model) is doing (Baer and Sherman, 1964). Autistic children show deficits in observational learning (Varni, Lovaas, Koegel, and Everett, 1979), but those who do not imitate may be taught to do so by reinforcement. For example, the therapist may at first clap hands and reinforce the child for copying this action. When consistent imitation is established, the therapist may then switch to a different motor behavior—perhaps opening the mouth—and eventually to uttering a sound. The child is reinforced in turn for each of these different imitations and gradually comes to copy

Language training with autistic children requires the use of frequent reinforcement. Often the child must first be taught to imitate.

the therapist's novel action on the first trial. Imitation of new language is now possible.

The acquisition of verbal responses is a four-step process (Lovaas and Newsom, 1976). In Step 1 the therapist rewards the child with food for any vocalizations. In Step 2 reward is given only if the response occurs within about three seconds of the therapist's prompt. In Step 3 the child is rewarded for closer and closer approximations to the verbal stimulus given by the therapist, until the child matches the stimulus. In Step 4 the therapist introduces other, dissimilar sounds and reinforces only correct responses. Speech sounds, words, and phrases are painstakingly programmed so that the child gradually acquires a repertoire of language through modeling and reinforcement.

The ability to use language in a meaningful way involves both expressive and receptive discriminations. *Expressive discrimination* occurs when the child is presented with a nonverbal stimulus and is required to make a verbal response that labels or describes it. For example, a cup is presented and the child must label it *cup.* Labeling of objects is made functional as soon as possible. *Receptive discrimination* occurs when the stimulus is verbal and the desired response is nonverbal, as in the command "Touch the cup." Training becomes more complex as both expressive and receptive discriminations are required. Sequences are carefully presented so that new discriminations are based on already-mastered material. As the child progresses, language becomes rewarding in itself, and external reinforcers and prompts are eliminated. The program gradually incorporates more abstract terms (pronouns, adjectives, verb tenses). The Lovaas program requires an enormous amount of meticulously planned training, but it enables some children to progress to the point where they can generate sentences and respond to an array of verbal stimuli.

Self-injurious Behavior

Self-injurious behavior (SIB) is behavior that results in damage to the individual's own body (Tate and Baroff, 1966). Its most common forms appear to be head banging, biting, scratching, gouging, and pinching. SIB tends to be chronic and repetitive, with frequency varying from a few times a day to several times a second. Damage is usually quite minor, but SIB can be life threatening due to possible concussion and the like or to recurrent infection associated with repeated injury (Russo, Carr, and Lovaas, 1980). On the basis of an earlier review, Schroeder, Mulick, and Rojahn (1980) drew the following tentative conclusions about self-injurious behavior:

1. Among the general population of babies and children, the prevalence of SIB is between 7 and 17 percent.
2. If it occurs in normal children, it usually appears between 7 and 8 months and disappears by age 5.
3. Self-injurious behaviors are much more prevalent in psychotic and retarded children. They may be emitted by as many as 40 percent of severely schizophrenic children. Prevalence among institutionalized retarded children is between 8 and 14 percent.
4. SIB is often accompanied by stereotyped movements, aggression, communication deficits, and neuropathology.

5. Sex differences may appear in the topography of SIB, with head banging more prevalent among boys and biting more common among girls.

The considerable effort to understand and treat self-injurious behavior is aimed at avoiding the appreciable physical harm that may be done. But treatment is important, too, because SIB interferes markedly with learning. Hypotheses concerning self-injurious behavior come from various perspectives, and it is impossible to completely separate etiology and maintenance. As shown in Table 8–6, these hypotheses have been categorized by Carr (1977) as organic, behavioral, self-stimulation, and psychodynamic. Carr considers the psychodynamic hypothesis moot because concepts such as "ego boundaries" have not been satisfactorily operationalized and tested. Utilizing the remaining hypotheses, he suggests a screening sequence for determining the possible motivation for self-injury. First, the possibility of organic abnormalities should be investigated. Second, the immediate consequences of SIB should be analyzed to ascertain whether the behavior is being controlled by external contingencies. If neither of these appears to be operating, the possibility of self-stimulation should be evaluated.

Treatment does not necessarily proceed from such a screening, however. Even if organic conditions are established, they cannot always be treated. Drug treatment seems plausible, but so far it has been largely unsuccessful. Overall, behavior modification has proven somewhat more helpful in controlling self-injurious behavior. One group of behavioral procedures involves placing specific contingencies on SIB; the other seeks to reduce self-injury by focusing on antecedents to the behavior and by training alternative responses (Russo, Carr, and Lovaas, 1980).

It has been assumed that SIB is often reinforced by attention from others. Caretakers indeed might attempt to comfort, distract, or verbally persuade the child to stop self-injury. These attentive behaviors have been shown to

Table 8-6 Motivation for Self-injurious Behavior

Hypothesis	Related Treatment Procedures
Organic: SIB results from an aberrant organic process (e.g., Lesch-Nyhan syndrome, middle-ear infection, abnormal pain thresholds)	Medical Intervention
Behavioral: SIB is a learned operant maintained by positive or negative social reinforcement	Extinction Time-out Punishment Prevent escape Reinforcement of other behaviors Control antecedents
Self-stimulation: SIB occurs because it provides sensory stimulation in the absence of adequate sensory input	Provide an enriching environment
Psychodynamic: SIB is an attempt to establish ego boundaries or reduce guilt, etc.	Verbal, supportive therapy

Adapted from Carr, 1977.

actually increase SIB, whereas withholding attention can reduce it (Lovaas and Simmons, 1969; Russo, Carr, and Lovaas, 1980). Nevertheless, such an extinction procedure is not always successful and has definite drawbacks. Extinction can be lengthy and commonly results in an increase in the behavior before an eventual decrease. This can be a serious problem when self-injurious behavior is involved. In one case the subject of extinction hit himself almost 9,000 times before the behavior was eliminated (Lovaas and Simmons, 1969). Similarly, a period in an isolated room with time-out from any positive reinforcement could also be dangerous if SIB continues. Additionally, extinction and time-out simply do not apply when positive reinforcement is not the motivation for SIB. Sometimes self-injury appears to be negatively reinforced as, for example, when some kind of performance is expected from the child. In this situation SIB may operate so as to eliminate the demands. Carr, Newsom, and Binkoff (1976) described negative reinforcement of SIB in an 8-year-old psychotic boy. When he was alone, self-injury was negligible. When an adult made demands, the rate of punching and slapping himself immediately escalated to a high level. When confronted with this pattern, adults may readily allow the child to leave the demand situation, thereby negatively reinforcing the be-

havior by escape. Negative reinforcement may actually increase SIB over time (Russo, Carr, and Lovaas, 1980).

Physical punishment is probably the most widely used and successful contingency for the management of self-injurious behavior. One prevailing procedure is the application of a noxious but harmless electrical stimulus, paired with a verbal reprimand such as "No." Although no other method is as successful in immediately suppressing SIB, the effects tend not to generalize to other situations (Lovaas, Young, and Newsom, 1978). The use of shock and other physical punishers also raises ethical questions. Punishment is thus used only as a last resort. In the words of Lovaas, Young, and Newsom:

In situations where one does use pain therapeutically, it has to be a last resort, and justified on the basis that a relatively small pain in the present can be used to prevent a relatively large and enduring pain in the future. The large pain we are referring to could include a lifetime spent in full bodily restraints as well as self-destructive acts leading to permanent tissue damage (1978, p. 393).

More recently a punishment procedure known as *overcorrection* has received consider-

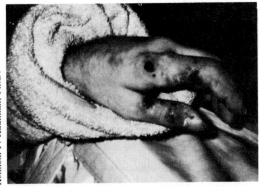

By permission of Sagamore Children's Center, Melville, NY. Courtesy of Kenneth F. Kaufman, Ph.D.

Self-injurious behavior can often result in appreciable harm and may necessitate placing the individual in some form of physical restraint.

able attention. Overcorrection is geared to the specific SIB and always involves repeated responses that are incompatible with the self-injurious behavior. A simple example is making a girl who slaps herself hold her hands by her sides for several minutes following self-slapping. Overcorrection can be quite effective, although it requires much effort on the part of caretakers (e.g., Foxx and Martin, 1975; Kelly and Drabman, 1977; Marholin, Luiselli, and Townsend, 1980; Ollendick and Matson, 1978).

So far, discussion has focused on behavioral methods that place contingencies directly on SIB. Other procedures try to decrease the probability that SIB will occur at all. One involves the reinforcement of other behaviors (DRO) that help decrease SIB, perhaps by distraction or incompatibility. The child may be praised for appropriate play, compliance, and the like. DRO is probably most effective when it is used in conjunction with direct contingencies for self-injury. Finally, researchers are beginning to target the settings and antecedent conditions that may control SIB. A number of environmental conditions, including space per person, diet, climate control, peer communication skills, clothing, and noise, can dramatically affect the rate and topography of self-injurious behavior

(Schroeder, Mulick, and Rojahn, 1980). The implications of these findings are still unexplored, but the benefits of a preventive strategy are obvious.

Training Parents as Therapists

The training of parents as therapists is not unique to the behavioral approach, but behavior therapists have integrated parent training into their practice more than clinicians of other persuasions (Harris and Milch, 1981). Most parents are able to learn virtually any behavior modification skill for which training is available.

Kozloff's training program was one of the early efforts to teach parents to deal effectively with their disturbed children. In *Reaching the Autistic Child* (1973), Kozloff provides a rationale for his work. First, there is the matter of economics. There are simply not enough professionals to care for the needs of disturbed children. A second factor is the problem of generalization. Researchers have determined that training effects do not easily generalize across situations and persons. Since the home is the setting for most of the child's behavior, and since the parents are the most natural observers, training in the home should be more easily maintained and generalized to other similar situations than training obtained in less natural surroundings. A third factor is the apparent weakness of other approaches to treatment.

The approach outlined by Kozloff emphasizes an educational process. Treatment is designed to teach the child behavioral patterns necessary for participation in various social environments. The program is based on operant conditioning and social exchange theory. Disturbed behaviors are targeted for change through the application of reinforcement, punishment, and extinction. Antecedent events are also carefully structured. Stimulus-response relationships are viewed, according to social exchange theory, as reciprocal exchanges between the participants of an interaction. It is not only responses that are shaped but also patterns of behavior. For example, if an autistic boy bangs his head and the parents respond with attention to stop the banging, the child may repeat the head banging in the future in order to produce attention, and the parents may repeat giving attention because in the past it enabled them to escape the noxious head banging. Such reciprocal exchanges encourage the adaptive and maladaptive acts of its participants, whether children, parents, or other adults.

Kozloff notes that in social systems comprised of autistic children and their parents, most exchanges follow the pattern of negative reinforcement described in the above example. Parents attempt to escape or avoid the disruptive behavior of their autistic children. Furthermore, they tend to ignore appropriate behaviors. This pattern may occur because (1) parents are so overwhelmed by the child's disruptive actions that they do not even notice the few instances of appropriate behavior; (2) the child's approximations to appropriate behavior may be so primitive that the parents do not recognize them as approximations or do not realize that approximations should be reinforced; (3) the parents' efforts to interact with the child may have been so effectively punished by the child's disruptive and unresponsive behavior that they no longer try to teach the child to play, speak, or perform simple tasks; (4) the parents may not see the child as capable of learning to behave differently. Both the parents and the child are trapped. The more the parents try to terminate the child's inappropriate behavior, the stronger it becomes. And the less often parents try to teach the child, the fewer opportunities the child has for learning appropriate behaviors.

The social exchange approach to the treatment of autistic children attempts to disrupt maladaptive components of the family's social system and replace them with adaptive exchanges. Parents must learn which responses to require of their child and which responses are unacceptable; how to initiate exchanges with the child so that positive exchanges result; how to teach the child new behaviors; how to reward appropriate behavior and respond to inappropriate behavior; and how to maintain positive change. The program is adapted to the needs of each individual family, and progress is evaluated with the ABA' experimental design.

Efficacy

Behavioral treatment of psychotic children is widely recognized today as having substantial merit. Effectiveness has been demonstrated in changing patterns of communication, self-injury, self-stimulation, classroom learning, social behavior, and parent-child interaction (Goldfarb, 1980; Leff, 1968; Rincover and Koegel, 1977). Treating "psychosis" as inappropriate behaviors rather than as a disease has resulted in a powerful intervention for children formerly considered nontreatable. There is little doubt that the psychotic child can be helped, and families have been given new hope. On the other hand, the end result often falls short of bringing the child to a level of functioning that might be called normal. To paraphrase one group of investigators, improvement is like taking ten to twenty steps on a ladder having one hundred steps (Lovaas, Koegel, Simmons, and Long, 1973). Enormous effort is required to plan and augment a behavioral program for an individual child or family. Even then, the problem of generalization remains. When the child is trained to respond in a new way, the response does not appear to generalize in topography or over situations and time (Rincover and Koegel, 1977). Since the psychotic child has extensive deficits, this is a serious problem. Finally, little is known about teaching certain social behaviors. For example, many psychotic children lack appropriate play, emotional expression, and humor (Lovaas, 1979). Increased understanding of these facets of human behavior can lead to enriching the repertoire of the pervasively disturbed child.

SUMMARY

Psychoses in adults were recognized long before the term became applicable to the young. Today such severe disorders in children are increasingly referred to as *pervasive developmental disorders*, and the tendency is to distinguish between childhood and adulthood disturbance. Age of onset in children has become crucial in distinguishing subtypes. Several studies of prevalence indicate a large peak early in life and a small peak for late childhood-adolescence. The dichotomy of early onset versus later onset is widely accepted, although there is still a need for definitional clarity.

Early infantile autism was first described by Kanner in 1943. It is characterized by onset before 30 months of age, social isolation, language deficiencies and peculiarities, ritualistic and stereotyped motor movements, and resistance to environmental change. Affective and social dysfunction were once emphasized as central in infantile autism; today there is greater interest in perceptual and cognitive deficits. Etiological hypotheses concerning infantile autism are quite varied. Although parental practices and psychopathology have been implicated by diverse theorists, research has not substantiated a primary etiological role for parents. The search for causal factors has shifted somewhat to biological factors. Infantile autism has been associated with inherited disease, prenatal and perinatal misfortune, and neurological signs. No evidence to date, however, has established either a specific brain dysfunction or biochemical imbalance. Turning to genetic variables, so far no gross chromosome aberrations have been detected, nor any evidence of single-gene inheritance. Nevertheless, there is some evidence that infantile autism occurs in siblings of autistic children with greater frequency than it appears in the general population. Twin studies also indicate higher concordance for monozygotic than for dizygotic pairs. From all the evidence, it is likely that the disorder can be caused by any one of several central nervous insults occurring very early in life. However, the possible role of environmental factors is still worthy of investigation.

Later onset psychoses, those that occur from about age 3 to early adolescence, have not been consistently conceptualized or classified. They receive labels such as childhood schizophrenia, symbiotic psychosis, disintegrative psychosis, and childhood onset pervasive developmental disorders. The older the child at onset of the disorder, the more likely is the condition to be considered similar to adult schizophrenia. Later onset disorders have garnered an enormous variety of clinical descriptions, including vegetative, motor, language, perceptual, affective, thought, and social dysfunctions. Etiology has focused on family environmental and biological variables. Although the families show more psychopathology than do families of autistic children, studies have not verified any specific detrimental parent-child interactions. On the other hand, research has linked childhood schizophrenia with pregnancy complications, maternal illness, abnormal EEGs, convulsions, and abnormalities in motor coordination, posture, and sensory integration. There is some direct and indirect evidence for the role of inheritance. Later onset disorders are linked to low social class as well.

The severity of pervasive developmental disorders is indicated in studies that have followed children over some length of time. Although the exact outcomes vary somewhat from study to study, it appears that most of the children do not function well in later life. This is particularly true when the disorder arises early and is associated with language deficits and low intelligence.

Treatment approaches to childhood psychoses involve different settings and techniques. Several classes of medications have been tried; the antipsychotics are most widely employed to reduce withdrawal, hyperactivity, and stereotyped behavior. Psychodynamically oriented therapists view the child as operating at primitive levels; thus, they seek to help the child give up this psychotic retreat by strengthening ego functions. Behavior modification has enjoyed some success in training psychotic children and their parents. For example, Lovaas and his colleagues have been able to establish some speech in quite disturbed children. Self-injurious behavior, which is relatively common in psychotic and retarded individuals, has been treated by placing contingencies on the behavior, training alternative responses, and focusing on antecedent events. Kozloff's program aims at bettering child-parent interaction through contingency management. Behavioral methods have helped severely disturbed children function better, but treatment requires enormous effort and does not easily generalize. The need for continued research into etiology and treatment is obvious.

9

MENTAL RETARDATION

HOW IS MENTAL RETARDATION DEFINED?

THE NATURE AND MEASUREMENT OF INTELLIGENCE

Conceptualizing Intelligence
  Tests of Intelligence: The Binet
  and Wechsler Scales
Infant Tests of Intelligence
Interpretation of IQ

ADAPTIVE BEHAVIOR

Vineland Social Maturity Scale
AAMD'S Adaptive Behavior Scale

LEVELS OF RETARDATION

EPIDEMIOLOGY

ETIOLOGY

Chromosome Aberrations
Mendelian Inheritance
Prenatal, Perinatal, and Postnatal
  Variables
Family and Sociocultural Factors

COGNITION AND LEARNING

Piagetian Theory
Learning and Information Processing

PERSONALITY AND MOTIVATIONAL VARIABLES

Effects of Social Deprivation
Effectiveness of Reinforcers
Expectations for Failure and Success

FAMILY ADJUSTMENT

ISSUES IN TREATMENT AND EDUCATION

The Right to Education and the Least
  Restrictive Environment
Deinstitutionalization
Behavior Modification

SUMMARY

The saga of the "Wild Boy of Aveyron," otherwise known as Victor, began around 1800 and was to have far-reaching implications for the conceptualization and treatment of childhood dysfunctions. Although different versions exist, it appears that Victor was first seen running through the woods in France, naked, searching for roots and acorns to eat. He was caught but escaped more than once before his final capture and assignment to a medical officer, Jean M. Itard, at the National Institute for the Deaf and Dumb in Paris. Irrational expectations were rampant: The wild boy would be astonished at the sights of Paris; he would soon be educated; he would be able to recount his fascinating existence in the forest. When he arrived in the capital city, however, Victor was

. . . a disgusting dirty child affected with spasmodic movements and often convulsions who swayed back and forth ceaselessly like certain animals in the menagerie, who bit and scratched those who opposed him, who showed no sort of affection for those who attended him; and who was in short, indifferent to everything and attentive to nothing. (Itard, as cited in Harrison and McDermott, 1972, p. 727)

Victor's senses were reportedly primitive; his memory, attention, judgment, and reasoning destitute; and his ability to communicate almost nil. Itard believed that Victor had existed alone in the woods from at least age 4 or 5, and he attributed the cause of the deficiencies to lack of contact with civilized people. Others, including Pinel, who was influential in treatment of the mentally ill, drew a parallel between Victor and children considered incurably affected with "idiocy."

Itard attempted to reconstitute the Wild Boy of Aveyron. He was largely unsuccessful, much to his discouragement, and Victor lived in custodial care until his death in 1828. But Itard's five-year celebrated endeavor is considered among the first systematic efforts to treat mental deficiency, and it did much to stimulate interest in the "feebleminded" or "retarded"

(Rie, 1971). In its long history the field has witnessed many changes, including the manner in which mental deficiency is labeled, defined, and diagnosed.

HOW IS MENTAL RETARDATION DEFINED?

Scant references to the mentally retarded in the religious and medical writings of antiquity and medieval times show some early awareness of the problem but give only limited information (Cytryn and Lourie, 1980). It is known that ancient Roman and Spartan law included provisions for exterminating mentally retarded persons and that medieval Europe often looked upon them as jesters, freaks, and creatures of the devil. The condition was considered a variation of insanity until 1689, when Locke drew a distinction between the two.

In modern times the term *feebleminded* appeared in the literature during the latter half of the nineteenth century, simultaneously with the establishment of several institutions for "idiots" and "imbeciles" (Potter, 1972). The latter terms, the first from the Greek meaning "uncouthness" and the second from the Latin meaning "weakness of mind and body," were used in medical writings since antiquity to signify gross pathology in body and behavior. During the 1920s *mental deficiency* became the more popular label, but it too was replaced, in the 1950s, by the term *mental retardation*.

Today, although mental retardation may be variously defined, the definition set by the American Association on Mental Deficiency (AAMD) is widely employed and is followed by the major classification systems. According to AAMD: "Mental retardation refers to significantly subaverage general intellectual functioning existing concurrently with deficits in adaptive behavior, and manifested during the developmental period" (Grossman, 1977, p. 11). *General intellectual functioning* is defined in terms of performance on a standard individual test of intelligence, such as the Stanford-Binet or Wechsler scales. *Subaverage* refers to an IQ that falls more than two standard deviations below the mean for the test. *Adaptive behavior* is the degree to which an individual meets standards for personal independence and social responsibility considered appropriate for age and social group. It may be measured by particular scales designed for that purpose. *Developmental period* is specified as the time between birth and the eighteenth birthday. Older persons who display mental deficiency for the first time are thus not considered mentally retarded.

On the surface the AAMD definition may appear quite simple and ordinary by today's standards. In fact, it reflects several changes in how mental deficiency has been viewed. First, reliance on intelligence tests is a clear indication of progress in assessment of intellectual functioning. Second, importance is given to the idea that adaptation to the everyday environment is as critical as performance on a test of intelligence. Third, the definition is specifically developmental, tying the beginnings of mental deficiency to the early years and evaluating performance with reference to age norms (Robinson and Robinson, 1976). Fourth, mental retardation is viewed as a current condition that may change over time.

THE NATURE AND MEASUREMENT OF INTELLIGENCE

Conceptualizing Intelligence

What is intelligence? Despite the fact that people seem to have an intuitive idea about the nature of intelligence, it has been difficult to conceptualize precisely. An array of definitions have been offered, with a few themes commonly expressed (Robinson and Robinson, 1976). Intelligence has often been seen as the totality of accumulated knowledge, the ability to learn, and the capacity to adapt to the environment—especially to new situations.

Many theorists have assumed that the individual differences displayed vis-à-vis these commonalities represent a general ability that can

be termed intelligence. Others have argued that intelligence is best conceptualized as several separate abilities. Thurstone and Thurstone (1941), for example, concluded that intelligence consists of seven primary factors: word comprehension, word fluency, perceptual speed, memory, space, number, and induction.

Intrinsic to many theoretical accounts of intelligence is the tendency to assume that it is an attribute of the individual—much as brown eyes and black hair are considered attributes. Until the late 1940s it was believed that intelligence is *fixed* at a particular level that is *predetermined* by heredity (Hunt, 1961). This strong biological focus began to weaken as data accumulated that intelligence, as measured on IQ tests, could change—sometimes dramatically—with environmental events. Moreover, many of those employing tests of intelligence began to argue strenuously that measured intelligence is not a fixed entity within the individual but is a hypothetical construct—a concept that enables us to explain and predict behavior. From this point of view measures of intelligence and their applications in various settings need to be critically examined.

Tests of Intelligence: The Binet and Wechsler Scales

Although many tests of intelligence exist, only those meeting certain criteria are considered adequate to judge mental deficiency. Among these the Stanford-Binet (S-B) and Wechsler scales, both of which are individually administered, have earned confidence and popularity.

The Binet Scales. Alfred Binet and Theophile Simon are credited with construction of the first successful test of intelligence. Their work was the result of a request from the Minister of Public Instruction in Paris, who wished to assure the benefits of education to mentally deficient children (Tuddenham, 1963). The original 1905 scale consisted of thirty tests of diverse content that became progressively more difficult. In a revision the Binet-Simon scale was ordered according to age; that is, all the tests

New York Public Library Picture Collection

Alfred Binet (1856–1911), a French psychologist, helped develop the first intelligence test.

of an individual's mental age to chronological age, multiplied by 100 to avoid decimals. The ratio IQ enabled direct comparison of the performance of children of different ages. A girl of 8 who attains a mental age of 6 will have an IQ of 75 (6/8 × 100 = 75), as will a girl of 12 who attains a mental age of 9 (9/12 × 100 = 75).

The Stanford-Binet has been revised and updated several times. It still consists of many different kinds of cognitive and motor tasks, which range from easy to difficult. Designed for 2 years of age to adulthood, younger examinees start with the easier tasks, such as stringing beads, folding paper into specified shapes, and identifying pictures of common objects. Higher-age tasks involve vocabulary and abstract problems. Since the 1960 revision the concept of deviation IQ has been employed; this allows the individual to be compared with the average IQ earned by those of the same chronological age. The average IQ for each age group is set at 100 by statistical procedures. An attained IQ higher than 100 means that the person has performed better than average for his or her age; an IQ less than 100 means a less-than-average performance. Table 9–1 summarizes the various measures we have mentioned so far with regard to tests of intelligence.

passed by normal 4-year-olds, for example, were placed together, and so on. On the basis of their performance, children were assigned a *mental age* (MA), the age corresponding to the *chronological* age (CA) of children whose performance they equaled. Thus, a 7-year-old who passed the tests that the average 8-year-old could pass obtained a mental age of 8. MA is a concept that is still used today, partly because it is readily understood.

The testing movement began in the United States when Henry Goddard translated the Binet test for use with residents of the Vineland Training School in New Jersey (Cushna, 1980). Then, in 1916, Lewis Terman—working at Stanford University—revised the early scales into the Stanford-Binet. He adapted the items to the new population and tested a relatively large number of American children with them. Terman and his associates also adopted the idea of the *intelligence quotient* (IQ), which is the ratio

Wechsler Scales.   The Wechsler scales compete in popularity with the Stanford-Binet. Based on the work of David Wechsler, the original scale, the Wechsler-Bellevue, was constructed in 1939. Presently there are three instruments designed for different age groups: the Wechsler Adult Intelligence Scale (WAIS or WAIS-R), the Wechsler Intelligence Scale for Children (WISC or WISC-R), and the Wechsler Preschool and Primary Scale of Intelligence (WPPSI). All these tests follow the same format. Like the Stanford-Binet, they consist of different kinds of tasks, but the tasks themselves are not arranged by age level. Instead, each of 10 tasks begins with an easy item and becomes progressively more difficult. Every examinee works at every task until failure or completion occurs. The tasks are considered either verbal or performance tasks. The former emphasize

Table 9-1 Measures Relevant to Tests of Intelligence

CA	Chronological Age.
MA	Mental Age. The age score corresponding to the chronological age of children whose performance the examinee equals. For the average child, MA = CA.
IQ (ratio)	The ratio of mental age to chronological age multiplied by 100. $IQ = MA/CA \times 100$.
IQ (deviation)	A standard score derived from statistical procedures that reflects the direction and degree to which an individual's performance deviates from the average score of the age group.

verbal skill, knowledge of the environment, and social understanding. Performance tasks emphasize perceptual-motor skills, speed, and nonverbal abstraction. Deviation IQs are calculated separately for the verbal and performance scales as well as for the entire test.

Infant Tests of Intelligence

Because it is believed that early identification is beneficial, efforts have been made to evaluate the intellectual status of very young children. The Gesell Development Schedules, the Cattell Intelligence Tests for Infants and Young Children, and the Bayley Scales of Infant Development are widely known today. Performance on these individually administered instruments is termed *developmental quotient* (DQ), rather than IQ.

The Bayley Scales of Infant Development serves as an example of these tests (Bayley, 1970). It is constructed for infants from 2 to 30 months of age and consists of a mental and motor scale and a behavior record. The Mental Scale is designed to evaluate adaptive functioning. It includes tasks such as responding to visual and auditory stimuli, manual manipulation of objects, imitation, and vocalization. The Motor Scale assesses behaviors such as lifting the head, sitting, throwing a ball, and walking up stairs. The Infant Behavior Record rates behavior indicative of social orientation, cooperativeness, fearfulness, attention span, activity, and the like.

Infant tests of intelligence differ from those designed for older children in that they give greater emphasis to sensorimotor functioning and less emphasis to language and abstraction.

At least in part this accounts for the low correlations found between scores on infant tests and later IQs (Anderson, 1939; Bayley, 1955; Rubin and Balow, 1979). Overall, prediction from tests given during the first few years of life cannot be heavily relied upon. It appears, however, that early judgment of mental deficiency is more accurate than judgment of average and superior performance, particularly if it includes additional information such as histories and clinical impressions (Illingworth, 1961; MacRae, 1955). However, caution is suggested by the finding that one out of every four or five children who are judged mentally retarded before the age of 2 or 3 will not be judged so later on (Robinson and Robinson, 1976). It seems most reasonable, then, that early indications of mental retardation be followed with regular examinations and efforts to provide an optimal environment.

Interpretation of IQ

Since performance on intelligence tests is critical in judging mental retardation, it is important to examine the many issues that enter into the interpretation of an IQ score. In one way or another interpretation is intricately tied to the way in which intelligence tests have been conceived and constructed.

What Does IQ Measure? Perhaps the most central concern is the question of what IQ tells us about a person. Recall that Binet and Simon set about to determine which youngsters might benefit from special education rather than the usual classroom setting. They used a direct approach to this practical problem: They selected tasks which, they reasoned, would be relevant to learning in school. They subsequently confirmed their impressions by determining if performance on their scale was correlated with measures of academic performance such as teachers' ratings and actual school grades. This was an examination of *validity,* or whether a test actually measures what it is designed to measure. The comparison measures (for example, teachers' ratings and grades) are called the criterion measures.

The most widely used tests of intelligence are considered valid measures of academic achievement. Correlations between test scores and criterion measures are typically in the range of .40 to .75. It is also widely agreed that most IQ tests emphasize verbal abilities (Matarazzo, 1972; Robinson and Robinson, 1976). Even many of the so-called performance tasks are probably facilitated by verbal mediation. While IQ tests predict academic performance quite well, no claim is made, however, that they assess attitudes, persistence, and the like, which may contribute to general intelligence (Wechsler, 1974).

Is IQ Constant? The constancy of measured intelligence has been a much-argued issue. Before any conclusions can be reached about constancy, however, it is necessary to establish the reliability of IQ tests. Reliability refers to how accurately or consistently a test measures whatever it is measuring (Tyler, 1963). When an individual takes a test, the score may be influenced by factors other than ability—perhaps by guessing, discomfort with the room conditions, and worry over some extraneous matter. These chance factors may not affect all examinees in the same way or to the same degree and are quite unpredictable. Thus, to the extent that a test is sensitive to these chance factors, it will provide inconsistent and misleading results. Fortunately, several methods are known that allow the test constructor to analyze reliability. One commonly used method is to administer the test on several occasions to a group of individuals and determine the correlation between the different sets of scores. The higher the correlations, the higher the reliability. Based on this method and other procedures, quite high reliability has been established for tests such as the S-B and the Wechsler scales.

However, the constancy of IQ is a complex issue that necessitates examination of several findings. First, it appears that for groups of people, IQ scores are relatively constant when measurement is made after the period of infancy. Table 9–2 shows data from a study that involved repeated testing over thirty-eight years, beginning when the examinees were preschool age. These findings, which are similar to those of other studies (cf. Bloom, 1964), also indicate that the correlations between tests given at various time intervals increase as the intervals decrease. Several other investigations suggest that the IQ of the mentally retarded, especially for those with very low scores, is even more constant than for children with average or superior intelligence (Robinson and Robinson, 1976).

Despite demonstrated constancy of IQ for *groups* of individuals, it cannot be assumed that tested intelligence can not change. Historically this assumption was the basis for one of the fiercest controversies in the field. Earlier in this century the belief that IQ scores could be modified was unpopular. Then, around 1930, Wellman reported that tested intelligence of preschool children substantially increased dur-

Table 9–2 Correlation Between IQ Scores Attained at Different Times by a Group of Individuals

	1941	1956		1969	
S-B	*S-B*	*S-B*	*WAIS*	*S-B*	*WAIS*
1931	.65	.59	.64	.41	.39
1941		.85	.80	.68	.53
1956			.83	.77	.58
1969					.77

From Kangas J., and Bradway, K., 1971. 5. Copyright 1971 by the American Psychological Association. Adapted by permission of the author.

ing their attendance at the Iowa Child Welfare Station (Stott and Ball, 1965). Gradually information emerged to suggest that IQ change is indeed possible. In the Child Guidance Study, for example, 252 children were tested several times between the ages of 6 and 18 (Honzik, MacFarland, and Allen, 1948). Sixty percent of them showed an IQ change of fifteen or more points. McCall, Applebaum, and Hogarty (1973) concluded from their own and other data that IQ changes of thirty and forty points occur fairly often, that boys' scores are more likely than girls' to increase, that the scores of children of low SES are less likely to change, and that personality variables are associated with the direction of shift. Transient conditions such as illness, fatigue, change in the family situation, educational opportunity, social adjustment, and mental health have all been associated with change in individual IQ (Robinson and Robinson, 1976). Caution is necessary, then, in interpreting measured intelligence and in using it to label a child mentally retarded. Although individual IQ scores are relatively constant, they can change.

Are Intelligence Tests Biased? The ongoing, heated debate over possible bias in intelligence testing centers on whether IQ tests are constructed and administered so that they disadvantage certain groups of people, namely those of low SES and certain racial/ethnic backgrounds. In fact, it is by now well established that a positive relationship exists between SES and IQ (Seashore, Wesman, and Doppelt; 1950). Also established is the fact that on the average, blacks attain an IQ of about 80 to 85 compared to the average of 100 for whites (Kennedy, van de Riet, and White, 1963; Shuey, 1966). In evaluating the latter finding it is necessary to consider that blacks are disproportionately represented in the low SES, thereby confounding SES and racial variables in much of the research.

Group differences such as those just cited have resulted in serious criticism of intelligence testing, especially since the 1950s (Cronbach, 1975; Kamin, 1974). Relevant to this concern is the issue of standardization of the tests. Adequate test construction always begins with selection of possible test items and administration of the items to a group of individuals who represent the population for whom the test will be used. The standardization sample must always be carefully chosen to represent future examinees. Unfortunately, this procedure was not always followed in early test construction. The poor child of certain ethnic/racial background was often not properly represented in the normative data to which he or she was compared. The situation has been improved for the recent, better-constructed tests.

But the issue of bias goes beyond inadequate standardization. It is correctly argued that tests are always culturally biased in that they contain a predominant number of items more relevant to the experience of the white middle and upper classes than to other groups. Eells (1953) likened the situation to that of an American citizen being asked during a visit to Australia about mutton, kangaroos, and local information in strangely connoted words—and then, on the basis of the answers, being judged on some inherent quality called "intelligence." To rectify cultural bias, tests have been constructed that attempt to eliminate aspects most related to SES differences, such as specific content, emphasis on language, and the effects of speed (Anastasi, 1968). Raven's Progressive Matrices (which requires the examinee to match drawn figures) and the Goodenough-Harris Drawing Test (which requires the drawing of a man, woman, and child) are examples of tests that are considered less culturally bound than others. However, it is probably not possible to design instruments that are completely devoid of cultural content, a fact that must be considered in assessing the economically poor child and the child from a minority background.

ADAPTIVE BEHAVIOR

With the advent of intelligence tests, IQ scores became the central and sometimes single criterion for judging mental retardation. Although

The ability to perform everyday adaptive behaviors has become an important criterion in evaluating mental retardation.

the precison of intelligence tests was of obvious advantage, many persons considered IQ too limited. Growing discontent culminated in AAMD extending its criteria to include adaptive functioning. Such behavior centers on the domain of everyday life—on current ability to cope with environmental demands. Adaptive behavior is difficult to measure because it requires information on what a person actually does in the environment (Grossman, 1977). Ideally, many different kinds of behavior are observed in many settings. AAMD recommends a combination of tests, clinical observations, and all available sources of information on the person's everyday behavior. Part of the evaluation may involve the use of adaptive behavior scales.

The construction of instruments to measure adaptive functioning is currently moving forward with vigor; one review reports that well over a hundred are in existence (Myers, Nihira, and Zetlin, 1979). Most depend heavily on interviews with parents and other care-

takers. The scales are nowhere near as developed as intelligence tests; many are unpublished, inadequately standardized, and lacking in research to establish validity and reliability. Despite their shortcomings, however, they do aid in the assessment of self-sufficiency, responsibility, and—in some cases—social maladaptation.

Vineland Social Maturity Scale

Edgar Doll played a critical role in strengthening the concept of adaptive behavior in the United States. Working for many years at the Vineland Training School in New Jersey, Doll (1941) emphasized the importance of social adequacy and the ability of the retarded to manage their lives. In 1935 he published a scale to measure social competency, which he assumed grew with chronological age (Myers et al., 1979). Doll also believed that social competency could be quantified by summing performance on different age-related items. The 117 items that comprise the scale are grouped into self-help general, self-help eating, self-help dressing, self-direction, occupation, communication, locomotion, and socialization (Doll, 1965). Ratings are made primarily from reports of caretakers. A social age (SA) and a social quotient (SQ), analogous to MA and IQ, are calculated. These scores reflect the examinee's standing as compared to nonhandicapped individuals.

AAMD's Adaptive Behavior Scale

The ABS (and the ABS-Public School Version) are based on the performance of mentally retarded, emotionally disturbed, learning disabled, and normal children (Myers et al., 1979). They include a wide range of behaviors and are used both for diagnosis and for evaluation of treatment programs. As shown in Table 9–3, Part I of the ABS consists of ten areas of self-care and socialization. Part II rates fourteen areas of maladaptive behaviors. The latter are included because they are considered in judgments about school, occupational, and residential placements.

LEVELS OF RETARDATION

Historically mental retardation has been categorized according to severity. AAMD sets levels in terms of both tested intelligence and adaptive behavior. As we have already seen, subaverage intellectual functioning is identified by AAMD as an IQ that falls more than two standard deviations below the mean on a test of general intelligence. For children evaluated with the Stanford-Binet, an IQ of 67 or below meets this criterion. Due to minor differences in test construction, the equivalent IQ on the Wechsler scales is 69 or below. Table 9–4 indicates the ranges of IQ scores on standard intelligence tests that are associated with four levels of functioning; mild, moderate, severe, and profound.

As with tested intelligence, adaptive behav-

Table 9-3   Areas of Competence and Maladaptive Behavior Assessed by AAMD's Adaptive Behavior Scale

Part I	Part II
Competence	*Maladaptive Behavior*
Independent functioning	Violent and destructive behavior
Physical development	Antisocial behavior
Economic activity	Rebellious behavior
Language development	Untrustworthy
Numbers and time concepts	Withdrawal
Domestic activity	Stereotyped behavior, odd mannerisms
Vocational ability	Inappropriate interpersonal manners
Self-direction	Unacceptable vocal habits
Responsibility	Unacceptable or eccentric habits
Socialization	Self-abusive behavior
	Hyperactive tendencies
	Sexually aberrant behavior
	Psychological disturbances
	Use of medication

From Nihira, Foster, Shellhaus, and Leland, 1974.

Table 9-4 Levels of Retardation According to Performance on Intelligence Tests

Level	IQ Range for Level
Mild	50–55 to approximately 70
Moderate	35–40 to 50–55
Severe	20–25 to 35–40
Profound	Below 20 or 25

From Grossman, 1983.

ior is categorized by AAMD according to degree of impairment, from mild to profound. However, due to the imprecision of the adaptive behavior scales, levels are assigned by comparisons to general patterns of skills and do not appear to be used as much as IQ levels. Table 9–5 illustrates two of the standard descriptions and levels provided by AAMD (Grossman,

1983). Assignment of levels requires that the behavior of the individual first be matched as well as possible to a description of that person's highest level of functioning. Next, using the left-hand column, age is matched and the level is assigned. Since all ages are not included, it is necessary to estimate levels for some ages.

Levels of retardation set by educators correspond closely to those set by AAMD and are judgments of the learning ability of the retarded person. The three categories are *educable, trainable,* and *custodial.* Educable persons are viewed as being able to learn some academic skills, while the trainable retarded probably will not progress much beyond basic self-help and simple vocational skills. Children labeled custodial require considerable help, even with self-help tasks; they frequently are institutionalized. Table 9–6 shows the general parallel between categories set by educators and by AAMD according to IQ scores. It is noteworthy that the

Table 9-5 Illustrations of Adaptive Behavior Levels According to AAMD

Age and Level	Highest Level of Adaptive Behavior Functioning
Age 3 years: SEVERE Age 6 years and above: PROFOUND	**Independent Functioning:** Feed self finger food; "cooperates" with dressing, bathing, and with toilet training; may remove clothing (e.g., socks) but not necessarily as act of undressing as for bath or bed. **Physical:** Stands alone or may walk unsteadily or with help; coordinates eye-hand movements. **Communication:** One or two words (e.g., Mama, ball) but predominantly communicates through vocalization or simple gestures. **Social:** May respond to others in predictable fashion; communicates by gestures and noises or pointing; plays "patty-cake" or plays imitatively with little interaction; or occupies self alone with "toys" few minutes.
Age 3 years: MODERATE Age 6 years: SEVERE Age 9 years and above: PROFOUND	**Independent Functioning:** Tries to feed self with spoon; considerable spilling; removes socks, pants; "cooperates" in bathing; may indicate wet pants; "cooperates" at toilet. **Physical:** Walks alone steadily; can pass ball or objects to others; may run and climb steps with help. **Communication:** May use four to six words; may communicate many needs with gestures (e.g., pointing). **Social:** Plays with others for short periods, often as parallel play or under direction; recognizes others and may show preference for some persons over others.

From Grossman, 1983.

Table 9-6 Parallel Between Levels of Retardation Set by Educators and AAMD According to IQ Scores

	IQ																			
SYSTEM	100	95	90	85	80	75	70	65	60	55	50	45	40	35	30	25	20	15	10	5	0
AMERICAN ASSOCIATION ON MENTAL DEFICIENCY							Mild			Moderate		Severe			Profound					
AMERICAN EDUCATORS						Educable				Trainable				Custodial						

From Hallahan and Kauffman, 1978.

range of IQ for the educable category includes IQ scores on the high end that are not presently included in AAMD's definition of retardation.

EPIDEMIOLOGY

Mental retardation is often estimated at about 3 percent of the population, but the figure actually has varied since 1894 from .05 to 13 percent (Windle, 1958). This is not surprising, if for no other reason than that the definition of mental retardation has fluctuated.

Let us look at the problem of estimating prevalence with regard to IQ scores, the most common way prevalence is estimated. Intelligence tests are constructed on the assumption that intelligence is a variable that is normally distributed in the population. Figure 9-1 depicts the theoretical normal curve of intelligence, showing that an IQ of 100 is the mean. Standard deviations are statistical units that provide information about the variability among scores. Standard deviations are related to the percentage of scores under the curve. As shown in the figure, about 16 percent of all scores are below the mean by more than one standard deviation, and 2.27 percent are below by more than two standard deviations. Thus, when the IQ criterion for mental retardation is two or more standard deviations below the mean on tests of intelligence, about 2.27 per-

cent of the population is necessarily defined as retarded. Not long ago AAMD itself had taken one, instead of two, standard deviations below the mean as the cut-off point for retardation. This meant that almost 16 percent of the population theoretically fulfilled the IQ criterion! Those whose IQ fell between one and two deviations below the mean were categorized as borderline retarded, attaining IQs of about 70 to 84. Many of the children who fell into this category were of low socioeconomic class or minority ethnic/racial background. Concern about group bias and the labeling of such a large percentage of the population as retarded influenced AAMD to take two standard deviations below the mean as its IQ criterion.

So far we have omitted from discussion any

Figure 9-1 Theoretical normal distribution of IQ scores.

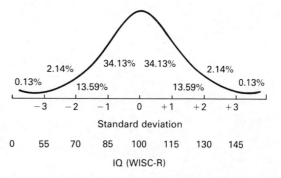

consideration of prevalence in terms of adaptive behavior. In fact, because measurement is imprecise, this factor is rarely taken into account (Hallahan and Kauffman, 1978). Some investigators suggest that were adaptive behavior considered, prevalence of retardation would be approximately 1 percent.

The epidemiological landscape is considerably refined when specific variables are examined. In addition to social class, age is of interest. Preschool youngsters are rarely identified as retarded; perhaps 1 percent are so classified (Cytryn and Lourie, 1980), and these are undoubtedly the more severe cases. As shown in Figure 9–2, prevalence is at its peak with school-age children, who are expected to perform intellectually and are readily called to attention. Adults are not as likely to be labeled, perhaps because less emphasis is placed on academic functioning, they are less available for assessment, and they are more integrated into the community in a range of occupations and living circumstances. Finally, it appears that mental retardation is more prevalent among boys than among girls (Robinson and Robinson, 1976; Work, 1979), probably due both to greater biological risk in the male and to differential social expectations.

ETIOLOGY

There are many known and suspected causes of mental retardation. AAMD recognizes a ''medical'' classification based on etiology that includes a wide array of variables: infection, trauma, metabolic and nutritional disorders, gross brain disease, conditions associated with perinatal influences, chromosome abnormality, and gestational disorders (Grossman, 1983).

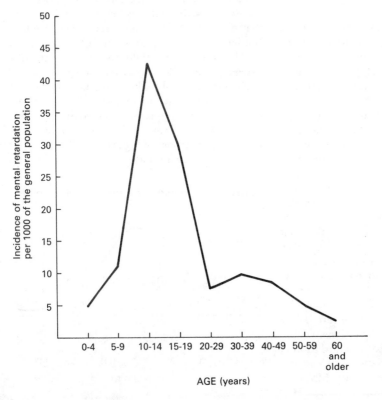

Figure 9–2 Incidence of mental retardation according to age. *From O'Connor and Tizard, 1956. Reprinted by permission of Pergamon Press.*

These variables implicate both biological and environmental processes. They are generally viewed as agents or conditions that detrimentally alter normal development. Moreover, while they may be associated with all levels of retardation, they are particularly associated with the more severe levels. In contrast, mild retardation is frequently seen as being within the range of the normal distribution of intelligence in the population, albeit at the low end. Here, psychosocial factors are thought to play a relatively strong role in etiology.

Chromosome Aberrations

Aberrations in the number and structure of the chromosomes are associated with specific syndromes of mental retardation. The following discussion describes a few of these abnormalities.

Down's Syndrome. Down's syndrome was described in 1866 by Langdon Down, a British physician. For several years it was noted that older mothers in particular had babies with the syndrome and that concordance in monozy-

gotic twins approached 100 percent (Rainer, 1980). The latter fact, especially, made genetic causation suspect. In 1959, only three years after human chromosomes were fully described, Lejeune and others discovered trisomy 21 in persons with Down's syndrome. As shown, the #21 chromosome appears in a triplet instead of a pair. As many as 95 percent of all cases are attributed to this aberration (Holmes, 1978). [The remainder are attributed to mosaicism or translocations. In mosaicism the anomaly occurs early in cell division and the child ends up with some normal and some trisomy cells. In translocations material is interchanged among the chromosomes; this condition may be inherited from either parent.]

The incidence of Down's syndrome increases with maternal age, but the exact figures vary from report to report. Miller and Erbe (1978) cite the incidence of 1 per 2000 live births at maternal age 20, 1 per 330 live births at maternal age 35, and 1 per 20 live births at maternal age over 42. Trisomy 21 is responsible for this pattern, with the aging ova probably playing a critical role. It is believed that non-

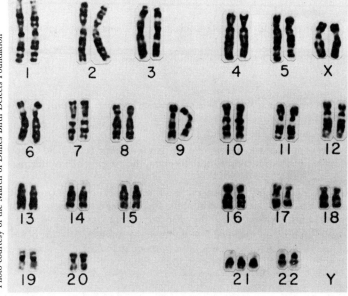

The chromosome complement of a female with #21 trisomy.

disjunction (failure to divide) in meiosis of the chromosome pair occurs with advanced age of the ova. This is one reason why amniocentesis is frequently recommended to older pregnant women.

Down's syndrome children are born with a variety of physical abnormalities that make them look strikingly alike. Most characteristic is the epicanthal folds at the corners of the eyes and the upward slant of the eyes, which gave rise to the now-outdated name "mongolism." Other frequently seen attributes are listed in Table 9–7. Of serious consequence are poor brain development, a heart defect that is present in perhaps 40 percent of the cases, blockage and malfunctioning of the intestines, and a 1 percent risk of developing leukemia (Robinson and Robinson, 1976).

Aside from the recognizable physical characteristics and early motor "floppiness," Down's syndrome babies may not initially appear deficient in mental development. However, they typically show deficits during the first two years of life, and thereafter decline at slower rates. Tested intelligence ranges from mild to profound levels. As Figure 9–3 shows, development in many areas lags behind that of the average child and may continue over a much longer period of time. Less complex learning (for example, rote learning, concrete language) is not as strongly influenced as skills in abstraction, concept formation, and expressive language. Down's syndrome children have a reputation for being content, friendly, affectionate, and lovable; however, considerable heterogeneity exists (Gunn, Berry, and An-

Table 9–7   Common Physical Attributes of Down's Syndrome Children

Poor *muscle tone* makes the babies "floppy," with prominent abdomens. Tone improves with age.

Head is small and back of head is flat. Fontanels (soft spots) may be large and close late.

Face appears flat, with flat nose. Eyes slant upward and have folds in the corners that become less noticeable with age; iris may have light-color spots ("Brushfield spots"); opaque lens and crossed eyes are common. Small ears. Small mouth with short roof may make the tongue protrude; furrowed tongue may develop. Teeth eruption is delayed, and teeth may be small and missing.

Neck is short and broad with loose skin at sides and back.

Hands are often small and square with short fingers. Fifth finger is especially short. Lines in hands and fingerprints are atypical.

Feet have wide space between first and second toes with crease between them on the sole.

Skin may be mottled, dry, and chap easily.

Hair may be sparse, fine, and straight.

Height lags behind, especially after age 4. Average final height for men is about five feet; for women, about four feet seven. Build tends to be stocky.

Weight begins in normal range, but mild to moderate obesity tends to develop.

General health is affected, and 20 to 30 percent of babies do not survive the first few years. If the child escapes serious heart or intestinal complications and the risk of leukemia and infection, the prospect of reaching middle age is quite good.

Sexual development may be delayed or incomplete. Sex organs and secondary characteristics are underdeveloped. Sex drive is probably diminished. Males appear infertile. Females menstruate in usual pattern and time, but only a few have reproduced, with about half the offspring having Down's Syndrome.

Aging tends to occur early, and brain aging has been documented in autopsy of persons over 35 years of age. Mortality is high after age 40, from causes similar to those in normal aging population.

Taken from Robinson, N. M. and Robinson, H. B., 1976. Used with permission.

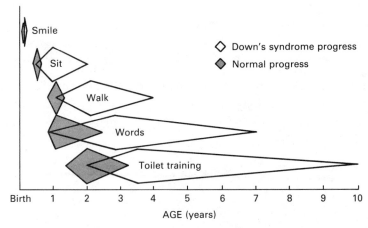

Smile

◇ Down's syndrome progress

◆ Normal progress

Sit

Walk

Words

Toilet training

Birth 1 2 3 4 5 6 7 8 9 10

AGE (years)

Figure 9–3 Development in the average and Down's syndrome child reared at home. The widest point of each diamond shows the average age of development. The length of the diamonds shows the age range at which development occurs. *From Smith and Wilson, 1973.*

drews, 1981). Many of these children are reared at home, but they account for 10 to 15 percent of the institutionalized retarded population.

Sex Chromosome Aberrations. Klinefelter's and Turner's syndromes, both named after the people who described them, are among the most widely recognized disorders due to aberrations of the sex chromosomes.

Klinefelter's syndrome occurs in phenotypic males, who usually have an extra X chromosome (47,XXY) but can have several additional X's. The disorder is seen in 1 out of every 450 male births. As in Down's syndrome, the mothers tend to be older than those in the general population, and an error in meiosis is suspected. The sex organs are underdeveloped and sperm may be lacking. There is also evidence of social immaturity and antisocial behavior, although these may be secondary manifestations. Most relevant for our purposes, 25 to 50 percent of these males show mental retardation, although it is not severe (Robinson and Robinson, 1976). Testosterone therapy can be beneficial to varying degrees, promoting a deeper voice, hair growth, and penis enlargement.

Turner's syndrome is found in phenotypic females who have only one X chromosome (45,XO). Many of the fetuses apparently die, but the frequency of the disorder is still 1 in 2,500 female births. Either parent may be responsible for the missing X chromosome, but the father is implicated more than the mother (Robinson and Robinson, 1976). The syndrome occurs disproportionately among monozygotic twins (Rosenthal, 1970), and some association with maternal age has been reported (Reed, 1975). Turner's syndrome girls lack ovarian tissue and fail to develop secondary sexual characteristics. They may also display short stature, a webbed neck, prominent earlobes, and abnormalities of the elbows, knees, kidneys, and aorta. Mental retardation is uncommon, although mild levels are reported. More typical is a specific cognitive defect in space-form perception (Rovet and Netley, 1982). These children find map reading and maneuvering in complex spatial environments difficult. Treatment with female sex hormones can bring on secondary sex characteristics, and adjustment may be relatively good.

Mendelian Inheritance

A number of specific syndromes associated with mental retardation are known to be inherited in Mendelian patterns. Many involve defects of metabolism, with recessive genes being implicated. Although all the known hereditary defects of metabolism account for a

Box 9–1 The "Fragile X" Chromosome and Mental Retardation

Relatively recent discovery of a "fragile X" chromosome may provide clues about the cause of many cases of mental retardation. The chromosome is termed "fragile" because of its propensity to break. According to W. T. Brown and his colleagues, the frequency of the chromosome in the general male population is about 1 in 1,100, and in females about 1 in 600 (Brown, Mezzacappa, and Jenkins, 1981). The disorder may be the second most common cause of mental retardation, and as many as 10 to 20 percent of retarded males may have an undiagnosed fragile X chromosome. All levels of deficiency appear to be associated with the condition.

The fragile X chromosome is transmitted in a sex-linked pattern. It is generally found that females with the chromosome are less deficient than males with the chromosome. This pattern is readily explained on the basis of inheritance. Since females have two X chromosomes, the normal X tends to overcome or limit the influ-ence of the defective chromosome. Males, however, suffer the full consequences of the fragile X that they inherit from their mothers, since they lack a second X chromosome.

Males with the condition tend to have long faces, large ears, and oversized testicles. No explanation is available for these attributes. Nor is it yet understood precisely how the fragile X operates to cause mental retardation. However, measurement of testicular size in retarded males could be a valuable screening procedure. Moreover, the defective chromosome can be identified from a chromosome analysis. For example, Jenkins and his co-workers (1981) described the case of a pregnant woman who sought genetic counseling due to a family history of mental retardation. She terminated the pregnancy when it was determined that the fetus was a male, with a 50 percent risk for the fragile chromosome. Subsequent analysis confirmed the presence of the defective chromosome.

---

small proportion of mental deficiency, further biochemical research may establish that metabolic errors account for at least 10 percent of the cases (Cytryn and Lourie, 1980). Such research is exciting because it presents the possibility of identifying a pathological process that may be treated specifically or prevented altogether. Treatment often involves dietary control to reduce the biochemical substance that is not appropriately metabolized or to add a missing biochemical. Table 9–8 lists some of the metabolic defects known to be associated with mental retardation. (See also Box 2.1 for a review of PKU.)

Prenatal, Perinatal, and Postnatal Variables

The wide array of pregnancy, birth, and postnatal variables implicated in mental retardation have been discussed previously (see pp. 52–54). Prenatal exposure to disease, chemicals, drugs, radiation, poor nutrition, and Rh incompatibility may jeopardize the intellectual development of the child. Birth injury and anoxia, too, may take their toll. Low birth weight and prematurity, which are linked to socioeconomic status, are associated with neurological and intellectual deficits. Mental retardation may also be caused by postnatal disease, head injury, seizures, and malnutrition. It is believed that all these factors interfere with nervous system development and functioning.

Family and Sociocultural Factors

Although biological syndromes in the etiology of mental retardation may be clearly identified, the cause of the overwhelming number of cases is controversial. Clinically these children usually appear physically normal and possess relatively good adaptive skills. They are

Table 9-8   Some Inherited Metabolic Disorders Associated with Mental Retardation

Disorder and Mechanism	Metabolic Disturbance	Manifestation	Treatment
Maple Syrup Urine Disease (named after characteristic odor of urine) recessive inheritance	Abnormal metabolism of amino acids—leucine, isoleucine, valine	Infants develop rigidity, seizures, respiratory irregularities, hypoglycemia. Most die in few months if untreated or are severely retarded.	Diet low in leucine, isoleucine, valine
Hartup Disease (named after family in which it was detected) recessive inheritance	Defective transport of amino acid, tryptophan	Symptoms vary. Mental deficiency; photosensitive skin rash; coordination problems. Personality change and psychoses may be only symptoms. Mild cases not detected until late childhood or adolescence.	Nicotinic acid and antibodies may relieve rash, but retardation is not relieved
Niemann-Pick Disease recessive inheritance	Abnormal metabolism and storage of fats in neurons, liver, spleen	Early mental regression and developmental arrest. Abdominal enlargement; anemia; emaciation; occasionally a red spot in retina.	No known treatment; death usually occurs before age 4
Schilder's Disease sex-linked inheritance	Decrease in fats in CNS resulting in demyelination of cerebral white matter	Onset more common in older children and adults. Personality and behavioral changes. Paresis, cortical blindness and deafness; convulsions; dementia.	No established treatment; may respond to steroids
Galactosemia recessive inheritance	Inability to convert galactose (carbohydrate) to glucose	After few days of milk intake, jaundice; vomiting; diarrhea; failure to thrive. Leads to rapid death or mental retardation; cataracts; liver insufficiency; occasional hypoglycemia convulsions.	Early galactose-free diet permits normality
Wilson's Disease (juvenile form) recessive inheritance	Disorder of copper metabolism	Onset at 7–15 years Personality, behavioral, mental deterioration. Palsy; spasticity; green-brown ring in iris; wing-flapping movement; fatuous facial expression.	Usually unresponsive to treatment

From Cytryn and Lourie, 1980.

identified as mentally retarded largely on the basis of IQ performance when they enter the highly organized learning situation of the school (Work, 1979). Their IQs are in the range of 50 to 70 (mild retardation), and upon reaching maturity they blend into the larger population because they are capable of occupational and social adaptation.

Retardation in the 50 to 70 IQ range is often conceptualized as representing those individuals who fall into the lower end of the normal distribution of intelligence in the population.

Various labels have been applied to these children, including garden variety, undifferentiated, familial, subcultural, and cultural-familial. Many of these labels reflect the importance given to family and social variables. Still, etiology has been a multifaceted issue, involving controversy over inheritance and environmental effects (see Box 9–2).

It is noteworthy that lower SES children are more heavily represented in the 50 to 70 IQ range than in the lower ranges for which clear biological syndromes are more easily recognized. The effects of poverty need only be briefly mentioned here, since they have been discussed previously (p. 30). It is likely that economically disadvantaged youngsters are at risk for inherited and other biologically related etiologies. Prenatal risk and prematurity are relatively high, as are postnatal malnutrition, disease, and lack of medical attention. Large family size, often found among the poor, may be inversely correlated with children's IQ (e.g., Belmont and Marolla, 1973). Modes of parent-child interaction may also be related to SES and intellectual development (e.g., Hess and Shipman, 1968; Kohn, 1963). For example, maternal involvement with the child and provision of play material have been found to be related to increases in functioning for children from 6 to 36 months of age (Caldwell, Bradley, and Elardo, 1975). On the other hand, inadequate organization of the physical and temporal environment in the home has been associated with decreases in functioning. Verbal processing may be especially affected by parent-child interaction. Finally, low expectations and motivations for certain kinds of achievement must be taken into account. The possible influence of some of these factors can be seen in the following example of Johnny, a 6½-year-old child who was in his second year of kindergarten in a predominantly middle-class school:

He was fifth of eight children of a rather pleasant, quiet mother who had seemed not at all upset when the teacher informed her that Johnny would not be promoted. His father, a cloth man in a textile mill, provided the family living by loading finished bolts of material from weaving machines onto carts to be taken elsewhere in the mill. Johnny's mother occasionally worked in the mill while the grandmother took care of the younger children. Three of Johnny's four older brothers and sisters were in the slowest groups in their schoolrooms.

Johnny was not able to master the reading-readiness materials of the kindergarten. He had difficulty in wielding a pencil, folding paper, coloring within lines, and differentiating one symbol from another. He usually had a pleasant smile and often seemed to be listening carefully to what the teacher told him, but half the time he was unable to repeat her instructions. His attention span was considerably shorter than that of his classmates. Johnny liked the other children, but they paid him little attention and usually left him out of their play at recess. At best, he was allowed to be one of the firemen who held the ladder while the others put out the fire.

The school psychologist administered a Stanford-Binet to Johnny, who gave a rather even, cooperative performance and attained an IQ of 67 (a mental age of 4 years, 9 months.) On the Goodenough Draw-a-Man Test, his drawing, a large head with arms and legs extending from it, earned an IQ of 73.

Johnny's parents, their children, and the maternal grandmother lived in a four-room house situated on the edge of town, near a middle-class apartment development. The family kept a cow and several chickens. Johnny shared a bed with three older brothers; three sisters were in another bed. The house was untidy and run-down. Meals were cooked somewhat erratically, and the children often ate their meals cold while walking about the house.

His mother reported that Johnny was a very good child who played outdoors much of the day and seldom cried. His health was mediocre; he usually had a runny nose and cough throughout the winter. She was somewhat surprised by the teacher's interest in Johnny's "special" problem, since he seemed so much like her other children and had never given her any trouble. (Robinson and Robinson, 1976, pp. 167–168)

Box 9–2 Nature versus Nurture: Continuing Debate about Intelligence

It has long been noted that intellectual performance tends to run in families. Sir Francis Galton (1869), a half cousin to Darwin, demonstrated the phenomenon by establishing the family patterns of eminent men of law, science, and the arts. On the other end of the spectrum, deficits, too, run in families. In his fascinating and historically important study of the Kallikak family, Goddard (1912) traced the quite distinct genealogical lines of Martin Kallikak. One of them originated from Kallikak's liason with a barmaid; the second had its basis in his later marriage to a woman of ''better stock.'' From information on several hundred of Kallikak's descendants, Goddard found a pronounced difference in the two families; namely, that the first liason had resulted in more mental deficiency, criminality, alcoholism, and immorality. Obvious weaknesses existed in this study—most notably, the questionable accuracy of reports gathered from different people removed in time from the subjects. Moreover, the results were taken as evidence that feeblemindedness was inherited (McClearn, 1963), although family environment could just as well have been causative.

The idea that family likeness in intelligence is due to inheritance persists today. IQ scores for unrelated individuals show small correlations, but as the degree of relationship increases, so do the correlations. More important for the hypothesis of inheritance, monozygotic twins are more alike on IQ scores than are dizygotic twins. Also, research with foster and adoptive families indicates higher correlations between adoptees and their biological families than between adoptees and their adoptive families (DeFries and Plomin, 1978; Munsinger, 1975; Plomin and DeFries, 1980; Scarr and Weinberg, 1976). The following table specifies this general pattern as summarized by Plomin and DeFries (1980), using older and newer data (which is considered more reliable) from many investigations. These findings do indicate some influence of hereditary factors.

Correlation Coefficients for Older and Newer Data As Summarized by Plomin and Defries (1980)

	Older Data	Newer Data
Genetically identical		
Identical twins reared together	.87	.86
Identical twins reared apart	.75	—
Genetically related (first-degree)		
Fraternal twins reared together		
(Same sex or opposite sex)	.53	.62
Nontwin siblings reared together	.49	.34
Nontwin siblings reared apart	.40	—
Parent-child living together	.50	.35
Parent-child separated by adoption	.45	.31
Genetically unrelated		
Unrelated children reared together	.23	.25
Adoptive parent-adopted child	.20	.15
Unrelated persons reared apart	−.01	—

It should be noted that some of the early studies of the inheritance of intelligence have been severely criticized on several grounds. It was Jensen's publication in 1969 of an article in the *Harvard Educational Review* that set off the most recent controversy. Jensen presented family, twin, and adoption study data that he interpreted as supporting a genetic explanation for

IQ differences among individuals and racial and socioeconomic groups. Many lay and professional people were outraged, and various arguments were put forth to combat Jensen's position. For example, Kamin (1974) pointed out that twins who reportedly were reared apart actually had contact with each other that could have inflated the correlations. Kamin also questioned the contributions of Cyril Burt that had been among the most supportive of the genetic hypotheses. Indeed, Burt's data have been challenged by others as well (for this controversy see Dorfman, 1978; Jensen, 1978; McAskie, 1978). Some of the past abuses of the use of intelligence tests with minority groups were also discussed by Kamin; these include administration of tests to people who lacked skill in the English language and the issue of cultural bias.

The many valid arguments against Jensen's hypothesis require continued evaluation of the use and interpretations of intelligence tests. Ongoing research is methodologically sounder than past investigations, and the findings are generally accepted as indicating some influence of hereditary factors. The data also indicate environmental effects in that related individuals living together show higher correlations in IQ than their counterparts living apart. It is obvious that the issues are extremely complex, but intelligence certainly is the result of the transaction between organismic and experiential factors.

COGNITION AND LEARNING

Efforts to understand mental retardation include the search for cognitive processes that underlie deficient intellect. The field is currently rich in hypotheses but lacking in both integration and a comprehensive theory. Some investigation is being conducted within the Piagetian framework. However, most of the research has its basis in experimental studies of learning and information processing.

Piagetian Theory

Piaget himself wrote little on mental deficiency and deemphasized individual differences. Extension of his theory has been undertaken by his colleagues and followers and is proceeding slowly. The potential strength of the use of Piaget's work lies in its developmental approach (Robinson and Robinson, 1976). Within this perspective the mind of the child is viewed as changing qualitatively as the organism adapts to its environment by assimilation and accommodation (see p. 26). The theory details growth in the capacity of the intellect to integrate information, as can be demonstrated by the child's ability to solve increasingly complex tasks. Such a developmental framework could offer insight into the ways in which functioning of the mental apparatus might go awry.

Piagetians have proposed that the mentally retarded child would be expected to progress in the universal sequence of stages; that is, sensorimotor, preoperational, concrete operations, and formal operations. However, progress would be slower than for the average child and would not advance beyond a certain level. Inhelder, Piaget's colleague, was the first to study mental retardation from this perspective (Woodward, 1979). She suggested and found evidence that the profoundly retarded advance no further than the sensorimotor stage; the severely retarded no further than the beginning of preoperations; the moderately retarded no further than preoperations; and the mildly retarded no further than concrete operations (1968/1943). Formal operations are regarded as beyond the reach of the mentally deficient. Other studies have tended to corroborate these findings (Robinson and Robinson, 1976).

One of the applications of Piaget's work is the attempt to construct intelligence tests on the basis of how the intellect is assumed to operate. Standard IQ tests are empirically derived: The items are ordered according to level of difficulty revealed by children's actual performance. Piagetian tasks, on the other hand, can be arranged on the basis of theoretical assumptions about cognitive growth. Several teams of researchers are at work standardizing scales composed of Piagetian tasks (Robinson and Robinson, 1976). The most elaborate is the ten-hour battery being standardized by Pinard and Laurendeau on French-speaking Canadian children. It consists of sixty-two tasks aimed at evaluating the concepts of time, space, movement, speed, number, causality, chance, deduction, and the like. The examiner encourages the child to reach her or his highest limits of reasoning. Uzgiris and Hunt's test (1975; Uzgiris, 1976) emphasizes early cognitive developmental tasks (for example, object constancy, vocal imitation, gestural imitation); it has been useful with retarded children in the age range of 4 to 10 years. These and other Piagetian tests hold promise for the evaluation, understanding, and remediation of mental retardation.

Developmental versus Difference Controversy. Piaget's theory has been intricately tied to an ongoing debate about the nature of mental retardation known as the developmental versus difference (or defect) controversy. The developmental position, advanced by Zigler (1969) and others, holds that mentally deficient individuals display a quantitative but not a qualitative difference as compared to the nonretarded. That is, they may indeed grow more slowly in cognitive capacity and reach lower ceilings, but they do not reason in ways that are different than those employed by nonretarded persons. Strictly taken, this hypothesis applies only to retardation in which clear organic factors are absent. In contrast to this position, those who espouse the difference hypothesis argue that even when retarded and nonretarded individuals are matched on intellectual level (that is, matched on mental age, not chronological age), they exhibit different cognitive processes (Weisz and Yeates, 1981). While this issue is not limited to a Piagetian framework, it was stimulated by Piaget's work and has been evaluated by research employing Piagetian stages and cognitive tasks.

The developmental versus difference controversy actually encompasses two related hypotheses (Weisz and Yeates, 1981; Weisz and

Zigler, 1979). One is that both the retarded and nonretarded pass through the identical sequence of cognitive development. In their review of relevant research, Weisz and Zigler (1979) found substantial support for the stages postulated by Piaget. The second hypothesis is that the retarded and nonretarded are alike with regard to their reasoning processes. Weisz and Yeates (1981) evaluated this by reviewing thirty studies that involved 104 comparisons between the retarded and nonretarded, matched on mental age. The comparisons supported the developmental hypothesis. The reviewers thus suggest that nonorganically impaired retarded persons are best described as manifesting a developmental lag. However, they cautiously note some of the weaknesses in the research, such as imprecise MA matching and lack of control of motivational factors known to affect performance of the retarded. They also point out that if the organically impaired are not systematically excluded, the difference hypothesis is supported. Finally, it is noted, the controversy addresses processes of learning and reasoning that are outside the range of Piagetian theory, but these have yet to be adequately evaluated.

Learning and Information Processing

Investigations into the learning processes of the retarded have proliferated since the mid-1950s, producing a considerable wealth of information. Early studies tried to show that retarded people do not learn as easily as the nonretarded but that learning is indeed possible (Haywood, Meyers, and Switsky, 1982). Classical and operant conditioning and imitation were demonstrated in even severely and profoundly deficient individuals. Later research, especially with the mildly and moderately retarded, has tended to focus on more complex processes of learning and information processing. The analyses have become detailed, taking into account age, IQ, sex, and school or other settings. General patterns have begun to emerge from the mass of data.

Attention in Discrimination Learning. The study of discrimination learning has contributed to our understanding of the role of attention in learning in the retarded. In the typical discrimination task the individual is required to select the correct stimulus on the basis of feedback from previous trials. In the simplest case, for example, two stimuli may be presented, each of which varies on two values of two dimensions. That is, each may be pink or gray (two values of the color dimension) and small or large (two values of the size dimension). One value is predetermined to be "correct." The person selects one stimulus, is told whether or not the choice is correct, and is given another trial with two stimuli that vary on the same values as the first pair. The usual learning pattern is for the person to begin with certain selections, at some point "suddenly" find the solution on the basis of feedback, and from then on perform correctly.

Zeaman and House (1963, 1979) extensively studied discrimination learning in normal and retarded populations. They found that retarded children, at least in some IQ ranges, performed more poorly than average children and that higher IQ in retarded children was related to better performance. Furthermore, these investigators demonstrated that individual differences in performance largely depend on the person's *attention* to the attributes of the stimuli. Individuals must first attend to the relevant dimension (for instance, color) and then attend to the relevant value of the dimension (for instance, pink). Zeaman and House found that retarded children have a low probability of attending to the relevant dimension. Once they do so, however, they rapidly select the correct value and solve the problem.

Mediation in Paired-Associate Learning. Mediation is a process whereby something is interposed between objects or processes to connect or reconcile them. In learning, a mediator may be a mental image or verbal cue that is employed for the purpose of connecting stimuli or stimuli and responses. Mediational processes are extremely important in all but the simplest of learning tasks. They have been studied in various situations, including paired-associate learning.

In this task pairs of stimuli (usually words or pictures) are initially presented, and the subject is then given one stimulus of each pair and asked to recall or reproduce the other stimulus of each pair. By age 5 or 6 most children are able to produce and employ mediators that help them associate the stimuli of the pairs. They may, for instance, connect the stimuli "snow" and "ice cream" by thinking the word *cold* or imagining huge mounds of a white substance. Both the production and use of mediators improves throughout childhood (Flavell, Beach, and Chinsky, 1966).

Research with the retarded has shown that they have difficulty mediating in paired-associate learning. Specifically, like very young normal children, they do not seem to generate and use mediators. However, in studies in which they are provided mediators by the experimenter or are actually instructed to use mediating techniques, the retarded often are able to do so, thus improving their performance (Borkowski and Cavanaugh, 1979; Jensen and Rohwer, 1963). They are said to show a production deficiency that can, at least in part, be overcome by instruction and training.

Problem Solving. An important aspect of learning is problem solving that requires the individual to attend, abstract, plan, and think logically. Retarded persons have been shown to be deficient on several problem-solving tasks. Studies involving both verbal and game-playing tasks have, in fact, revealed some of the most striking differences between the retarded and nonretarded (Spitz, 1976).

To demonstrate this let us look at the work of Spitz and Winters in which they used a tic-tac-toe game. Subjects were presented with incompleted tic-tac-toe configurations and were requested to make one response that would assure a win (Figure 9–4). Pretraining and checking procedures guaranteed that they knew how to play the game. Nevertheless, retarded individuals performed about 1½ years below expectations based on the performance of nonretarded children of equal mental age. The investigators noted that this game requires an

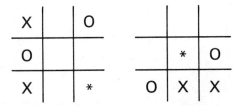

Figure 9–4 Examples of the incomplete tic-tac-toe games used by Spitz and Winters. The asterisk indicates the X response that assures a win. *From Spitz, 1976.*

"if-then" analysis in which the player must plan ahead by visualizing how a response will change the game situation (Spitz, 1976).

Memory. Unlike the learning tasks just discussed, research on memory grows out of the information-processing approach, which can be viewed as part of cognitive psychology. This branch of the discipline, in turn, can be seen as a grand attempt to understand all thinking and reasoning. (See, for example, Hunt's discussion, "How the mind works," which appeared in the *New York Times Magazine,* January 24, 1982.) Having roots in verbal learning, human engineering, computer science, and linguistics (Merluzzi, Rudy, and Glass, 1981), cognitive psychology is a reaction to the perceived shortcomings of strict behavioristic analyses that examined S-R connections while ignoring mental processes that intervene to guide stimuli and responses. Most of today's experimental learning theorists do not, in fact, ignore mental processes, as we have just seen. Thus, the findings of experimental learning research overlap considerably with research in information processing, much of which focuses on memory as the very essence of learning (Haywood, Meyers, and Switsky, 1982).

Atkinson and Shiffrin's (1968) widely recognized analysis of memory serves as a framework with which to examine memory in the retarded. These investigators view memory as consisting of three structural features: the sensory register, the short-term store, and the long-term store (Figure 9–5). The sensory register receives environmental information through the senses; it has a relatively large capacity but holds impressions only fleetingly. Some of the information is lost, and the remainder is passed into the short-term store. Attentional processes probably have a role in determining what is passed on. Short-term store has quite limited capacity and is considered temporary working memory, holding information perhaps thirty seconds. Once again, information can be lost or forwarded, this time to long-term store. The latter is viewed as having a large capacity and as more or less permanently holding information that can be retrieved with varying degrees of ease. These structural features of memory are likened to the hardware of computer analysis; that is, to the computer itself, which cannot be modified. Atkinson and Shiffrin also identify control processes—the software, or program, of the system. These are under the volition of the individual and can be modified. They consist of techniques that are known to facilitate memory, such as mediation, rehearsal, clustering or categorizing material, and the like. Control processes are considered particularly crucial in the workings of the short-term store because they increase the chance that information will be held longer and will fit with material already in long-term store, conditions that expedite long-term store.

Applying this model to the retarded, it is reasonable to postulate that memory may go awry at any point in the system, involving either or both structural or control features. As Robinson and Robinson (1976) have noted, unmodifiable structural deficits could be hypothesized, particularly when specific organic syndromes are evident. Research has overwhelmingly focused on control processes (Glidden, 1979), however, perhaps because they are seen as subject-controlled and modifiable. Indeed, even prior to the construction of memory models, such strategies had been investigated—as we saw, for example, in the study of mediation in paired-associate learning.

Overall, the retarded show clear deficits in the use of control processes or strategies (Bor-

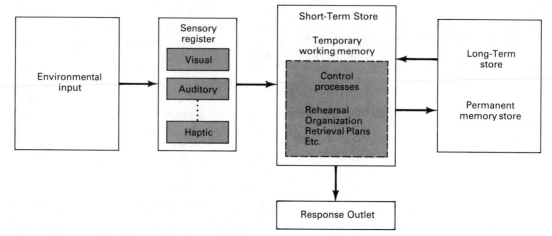

Figure 9-5 A model of the memory system, as proposed by Atkinson and Shiffrin, 1968.

kowski and Cavanaugh, 1979; Brown, 1974; Butterfield and Belmont, 1977; Butterfield and Dickerson, 1976; Campione and Brown, 1977; Glidden, 1979; Spitz, 1976). Individuals who succeed in memory tasks spontaneously use mediation, rehearse material, reorganize material by clustering it in some way, transform material so that it fits with what is already stored, and the like. The retarded frequently fail to employ these strategies, or use them ineffectively. However, their performance can improve when they are taught strategies and/or are instructed to employ them. Strategy maintenance—that is, the continued use of acquired strategies later on with the identical task—has also been demonstrated. On the other hand, intensive intervention is often required, individual differences are quite striking, and maintenance cannot be taken for granted. Future research must address the causes of success and failure in strategy training (Glidden, 1979). Moreover, it is common to see failure of generalization—that is, failure to adapt acquired strategies to new tasks.

Much has been made of the failure of generalization. What can be done about it? Borkowski and Cavanaugh (1979) suggest that too often the child is blamed rather than the inadequacy of the training procedures. Generali-

zation cannot be expected unless it is specifically targeted in training. Some researchers have focused on the role of the executive function and metamemory in generalization. As discussed by Butterfield and Belmont (1977), the executive function refers to the ability to select, monitor, evaluate, and revise strategies, depending on the situation. These researchers maintain that training for specific tasks would be an endless endeavor and that, even then, retarded persons might still be unable to select the appropriate strategy. Thus, they recommend training executive functions. Metamemory refers to understanding or awareness of one's memory and strategic functioning (Brown and Barclay, 1976; Flavell and Wellman, 1977). It includes understanding the demands of the task, one's own capacity, and how these aspects might interact. Executive functioning is closely related to metamemory and can be considered to overlap with it. Retarded individuals are deficient in their ability to select, monitor, and change strategies. They also show deficits in metamemory functions such as estimation of their memory span and evaluation of their readiness for recall (Glidden, 1979; Haywood, Meyers, and Switsky, 1982). Although there is some evidence that executive functioning and metamemory can be trained, the degree to which strategy maintenance and generalization can be improved remains to be seen.

PERSONALITY AND MOTIVATIONAL VARIABLES

A large amount of research has been conducted on personality or motivational variables in mental retardation. This work attempts to examine behavioral tendencies that might be especially dominant in retarded individuals. For the most part, it has accented the moderately and mildly retarded, for whom specified organic impairment is not an overriding factor. Comparisons have been made with nonretarded children matched on mental age (same intellectual level) and chronological age. Hypotheses have been proposed to explain revealed differences in terms of the social experiences of the retarded.

The research is not without serious flaws. Procedural details of studies have often gone unreported, and perhaps most serious, generalizations of results have too readily been made (Siegel, 1979). Nevertheless, this area of investigation is too important to dismiss, carrying practical as well as theoretical implications. Thus, we have elected to highlight a number of the variables that have been given consideration while acknowledging that much is yet to be established. In doing so, we draw heavily on the work of Zigler and his colleagues and specifically on reviews by Balla and Zigler (1979) and also by Siegel (1979).

Effects of Social Deprivation

One of the most important of Balla and Zigler's propositions is that the retarded are influenced strongly by past or present social deprivation. The results of deprivation, they claim, can be seen in a sensitivity to authority figures that at first glance appears contradictory. On the one hand, the retarded seem highly motivated to interact with a supportive adult; on the other hand, they seem reluctant and wary of adult interaction.

According to Balla and Zigler, active seeking of attention and affection is often seen in the retarded. The measure used to assess such dependency on others is the extent to which the individual persists at a boring activity that periodically results in social reinforcement. Zigler and his co-workers found that retarded children, with MAs from about 7 to 12, were indeed more motivated for social reinforcement than MA-matched normal children. Social deprivation, either in the past or the present, was associated with this dependency. In institutionalized retardates social deprivation prior to institutionalization was related to persistence in working for social reinforcement. Moreover, the institutionalized were more dependent than the noninstitutionalized, a finding consistent with the assumption that social deprivation is greater in institutions.

In contrast to these findings, the researchers also demonstrated a "negative reaction tendency." For example, in one study (Shallenberger and Zigler, 1961) intellectually average and institutionalized retarded individuals were exposed to either positive interaction with an adult (success and praise) or negative interaction (failure and disapproval). They were then administered an experimental task that permitted a measure of wariness. Both groups showed more wariness following negative interaction than following positive interaction. But the retarded were more strongly influenced by negative interaction than were the nonretarded. Wariness, like responsiveness to social reinforcement, was also found to vary with previous social deprivation and was by no means inevitable.

Effectiveness of Reinforcers

Another widely studied proposition is that mentally retarded children may respond differently than intellectually average children to certain kinds of reinforcement.

One specific hypothesis is that the retarded are less responsive to nontangible reinforcers than are average children. Zigler and deLabry

(1962) tested the impact of reinforcers on MA-matched retarded, middle-SES, and lower-SES children on a concept-switching task. In the nontangible-reinforcers condition the children were informed that they were correct. In the tangible-reinforcer condition they were rewarded with a toy of their choice. Under nontangible reinforcement both retarded and lower-SES groups did less well on the task than did middle-SES children. In the toy condition, however, they performed as well as the middle-SES group. As a result of these findings, Zigler and his co-workers, while recognizing the difficulty of making generalizations about reinforcement, argue that group differences on intellectual tasks may be due in part to *incentive* rather than to intellectual differences.

This proposition was also evaluated with regard to White's (1959) formulation about mastery, which suggests that mastery in itself is a powerful motivator of human behavior. Harter and Zigler (1974) constructed measures of components of mastery motivation: curiosity, variation seeking, competence seeking, and preference for challenges. They then compared groups of children. On all the components intellectually average children showed greater mastery motivation than noninstitutionalized and institutionalized retarded children. Those living out of institutions also displayed more curiosity than the institutionalized. Haywood and Weaver's work on intrinsic-extrinsic motivation dovetails with the above studies (Haywood, 1968; Haywood and Weaver, 1967). These researchers distinguished subjects who were motivated by need for achievement, responsibility, and the like (intrinsic motivation) from those who were motivated by extrinsic factors such as ease, comfort, and safety. They found that intrinsic motivation tended to increase with IQ. Moreover, overachievers (those who performed highest on reading, spelling, and arithmetic tests relative to their IQ group) were more highly motivated by intrinsic factors. All these findings point to the importance of understanding the role of incentive in the performance of the retarded.

Expectations for Failure and Success

It has been widely hypothesized that retarded individuals have low expectancy for success and high expectancy for failure. These expectations, presumably due to repeated experience with tasks that are beyond their abilities, result in the retarded responding in ways that may not be constructive. This hypothesis has been tested by many investigators using various experimental situations.

One line of research has involved documenting the effects of expectancies on problem-solving behavior. Zeaman and House (1963) suggested that their retarded subjects were so disabled by a series of failures that they were no longer able to solve problems that they had previously mastered. Another interesting finding concerns the way in which expectancy of failure influences behavior on insolvable tasks. Typically subjects are given a task that they do not know is insolvable and for which they are provided partial reinforcement for certain choices. Intellectually average children often do not use the strategy that will maximize partial reinforcement; instead, they try to find a solution. Retarded children, however, tend to persist on the maximizing strategy. This behavior is interpreted to mean that they are so familiar with failure that they easily settle for less. Indeed, it has been found that children with low expectancies for success use maximizing strategies more than those with high expectancies for success (Balla and Zigler, 1979).

Another approach has been to document feelings of failure in the retarded (e.g., Cromwell, 1963; MacMillan, 1969; MacMillan and Keogh, 1971). MacMillan and co-workers prevented children from completing a task and then asked why the tasks went unfinished. In one manipulation (MacMillan and Keogh, 1971), for example, educable retarded and average children were also given different experiences: They were either given no explanations for the interruption, or they were told that the interruption was due to their doing poorly (failure) or due to their doing well (success). The aver-

Special Olympics is one example of community programs that attempt to normalize the lives of retarded persons and to provide them with success experiences and a sense of self-worth.

age children overwhelmingly blamed themselves, but only when they had experienced failure. In contrast, the retarded children blamed themselves following all three experiences.

FAMILY ADJUSTMENT

The birth of a handicapped child can be a devastating experience to a family. Hagamen (1978, 1980b) has discussed some of the issues concerning reactions and adaptation to a mentally retarded child. Initial reactions of the parents are, of course, related to the expectations held for the anticipated offspring. Most parents expect that their children will be attractive,

smart, athletic, graceful, and loving. Parents of a handicapped child not only mourn the loss of unfulfilled expectations but often face enormous strain on their psychological and economic resources.

Families vary greatly in their capacity to adapt to and accommodate the retarded child. A number of factors determine adjustment. Perhaps the most influential is the range of limitation involved in the retardation. Moderate and severe levels require planning for a lifetime of extensive care and supervision; with mildly retarded children parents often experience long, dreadful periods of uncertainty about the existence of deficits. Family adaptation is also influenced by the availability and quality of professional services. Most retarded children eventually come into contact with many diverse professionals, and professional attitudes and competencies continuously affect parental comprehension, decisions, and acceptance of the child. Other salient factors include marital interaction, religious beliefs, educational levels and intellectual functioning of the parents, family size and structure, and socioeconomic status. A high level of intelligence and education do not guarantee good adjustment, but it is generally believed that the capacity to clearly understand what is wrong and what resources exist facilitates treatment planning. If the retarded child is a firstborn, adjustment may be more difficult, because firstborns are often given a special place in the family. Large families may be better able to accommodate the retarded child because siblings may serve as additional caretakers. Ability to incorporate the handicapped child into the family has been demonstrated at all socioeconomic levels, but affluent parents are less likely to comfortably maintain the child in the home, especially if the mother is career oriented.

Hagamen (1980b) suggests, bearing in mind the above variables, that a few generalizations may be offered with regard to parents' reactions to being informed that their newborn is mentally retarded. The reality of the situation is only partly perceived at first, and awareness and understanding develop over the weeks and years. Hagamen draws on a hypothetical model of parental reactions to congenital malformations to outline the possible emotional reactions to mental retardation. As Figure 9–6 indicates, the initial reactions are shock and then denial. When the diagnosis is confirmed by other professionals and further information is gathered, realization of the child's special needs occurs. Anger, guilt, and chronic sorrow are commonly observed, but equilibrium and reorganization eventually appear. When there is no visible malformation, families are more apt to deny the diagnosis for longer periods of time. The child who is diagnosed late is frequently a source of conflict among family members who have different perceptions of the deficits. Reorganization, in this case, may take months or

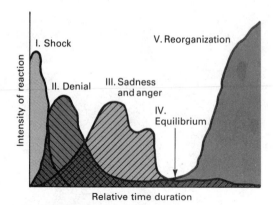

Figure 9–6 Hypothetical model of the reactions of parents to the birth of a handicapped child. *From Drotar, Baskiewicz, Irvin, Kennell, and Klaus.*

years; but in other instances, too, it requires much time and perhaps never reaches a constructive level.

Family reaction and adaptation is critical in determining how the child is to develop and be cared for. Adequate intervention requires not only that parents be knowledgeable but also that they be willing to work with their child to provide stimulation and behavioral management. Fortunately, greater recognition is being given to the need for support, counseling, and training of the family.

ISSUES IN TREATMENT AND EDUCATION

Although mental retardation can be viewed as a psychological, medical, or educational problem, in the final analysis it is a social problem (Cytryn and Lourie, 1980). Attitudes toward the mentally retarded have reflected more general feelings of the times. In modern history three distinct periods of high interest and creative thinking about the retarded are associated with social upheaval and liberal, democratic attitudes toward the less fortunate members of society. The first coincided with the French and American revolutions of the eighteenth century; this was the time of Itard and Pinel. The second period followed the rash of revolutions in Europe in 1848 and was characterized by a favorable climate toward special educational opportunities. Itard's student, Sequin, was a leader in this movement, which spread rapidly to the United States. The third and present period began after World War II, bringing with it some rather remarkable change. The following discussion highlights a few developments that are currently receiving much attention.

The Right to Education and the Least Restrictive Environment

If Itard's endeavor to train the Wild Boy of Aveyron marked the beginning of modern efforts to educate the retarded, it was not until this century that wide-scale and improved methods of assessment and individualized education came into their own. Compulsory education began around 1850 in the United States, and soon after the turn of the century, a population of children was recognized as having special educational needs (Lilly, 1979d). From around 1925 until 1960 there was a dramatic expansion of special education for the mildly retarded, who now became the "educable mentally retarded" (EMR). In the decade 1950–1960 expansion was at its greatest. Universities were funded to train special-education teachers and to conduct research, although these activities could hardly keep pace with the rate of growth in services. The picture was quite different with regard to the moderately and severely retarded. The public schools were not compelled to admit these children, nor were parents provided public assistance in educating them. Special day schools run by private agencies, such as the National Association for Retarded Children, largely took over this task. Only in the late 1950s did the lack of public education for the moderately retarded come under scrutiny, sometimes in the form of legal battles. A considerable amount of litigation has characterized the last few decades and has resulted in laws that reflect a changing philosophy about education for the retarded (Katz-Garris,

1978). A growing commitment to the idea that all handicapped children have a right to appropriate education culminated in Public Law 94–142, known as the *Education for all Handicapped Children Act of 1975*. Its stated purpose is to assure that all handicapped children obtain a free public education designed to meet their unique needs; to assure the rights of the handicapped and their parents and guardians; to assist states and localities in providing education; and to assess and assure the effectiveness of efforts toward education. P.L. 94–142 specifies (Lilly, 1979c):

1. An individualized education program for all handicapped persons between the ages of three and 21 years.

2. That an individualized educational program (IEP) be constructed for each child, including present level of functioning, goals, educational services to be provided, date and anticipated length of services, and procedures for evaluating educational progress.

3. That handicapped children to the maximum extent appropriate be educated with children who are not handicapped. This stipulation for the least restrictive environment requires that children be removed from the regular classroom setting only when the handicap demands it.

4. That procedures be established that assure parents and guardians a role in the placement process and legal rights to dispute the educational plan.

5. That diagnostic and assessment procedures be established that are considered free of cultural and racial bias.

P.L. 94–142 has brought about many changes. In particular, it has strengthened individualized programming, increased parent participation in decision making, and encouraged maintenance of the retarded in the community and in regular classrooms. Let us look more closely at this last issue.

Least Restrictive Environments. Historically special education for the educable retarded has meant assigning them to special
classes or special community schools, thus removing them from most other children. The
least restrictive environment clause of P.L. 94–
142 requires that such isolation be minimized
by mainstreaming retarded children in regular
school settings whenever feasible. At least three
events in the field of education are responsible
for the idea that general and special education
should be amalgamated (Corman and Gottlieb,
1978; Dunn, 1968).

First, many professional and minority groups
began to argue that minority group children
were labeled retarded and were overrepre-
sented in special education on the basis of biased
IQ tests. Legal decisions supported this contention. In this process special education was
looked upon in an unfavorable light. Secondly,
it was contended that special education did not
seem to help many EMR children learn basic
reading, arithmetic, social competence, and occupational skills (Dunn, 1968). Perhaps this
factor more than any other supported the move
away from special education classes. Finally, it
was argued, substantial progress had been made
in individualizing instruction in regular classes
through team teaching, flexible grouping,
audio-visual material, ancillary personnel, and
the like. Why, then, shouldn't the mentally retarded be assigned to the regular classroom,
which presumably reduces the child's isolation
and sense of deficiency?

Endorsing the above position, P.L. 94–142
reverses the seventy-five-year-old trend of placing handicapped children in self-contained special settings (Corman and Gottlieb, 1978). Since
special students make up as much as 10 percent
of the student body in many urban schools, impact on all students can be anticipated. At the
present time, despite considerable research efforts, the effects of mainstreaming are not well
established. It appears that academic performance is hardly affected by type of classes but
may be slightly benefited by integrated classes
(Corman and Gottlieb, 1978; Haywood, Meyers, and Switzky, 1982). On the other hand,

Programs like "The Kids on the Block" attempt
to teach nondisabled children about various
disabilities. Puppets like Ellen Jane Peterson, a
veterinarian's assistant who is mentally retarded,
interact with the students and help them to
understand and accept children with special
needs.

By permission of the New York State Department of Mental Retardation and Developmental Disabilities.

segregated classes appear to benefit social acceptance of the retarded. This area warrants
better-controlled research and analysis of the effects of *specific* ways in which students are handled, since both regular and special classes vary
a good deal.

Deinstitutionalization

The issue of deinstitutionalization of the retarded is intricately related to the concept of
mainstreaming. Its thrust is to keep retarded
persons out of institutions and to find alterna-

tives for those already institutionalized. It is reflected in the fact that in 1970 approximately 187,000 mentally retarded persons were in public institutions, but by 1977 this figure had decreased by 20 percent to approximately 151,000 (Bruininks, Thurlow, Thurman, and Fiorelle, 1980).

Many observers have convincingly put forth arguments against institutionalization. State-supported residences are often large, with limited staff. In fact, an inverse relationship exists between number of residents and number of professional staff: In an institution with 600 residents, the ratio of residents to psychologists may be 100:1, while in an institution with 3,000 residents it may be 500:1 (Leland, 1978). Thus, residents do not receive the individualized modern-day training and medical treatment, much less the normal human interaction, that is needed. They may actually learn behavioral patterns that are generally not beneficial: excessive dependency, servility, lack of curiosity, poor self-concept. It is not surprising, therefore, that writers such as Braginsky and Braginsky (1971) view institutionalization as a mechanism by which surplus, unwanted, and often poor persons can be discarded.

In describing the service model that has been operating during most of this century, Leland (1978) has noted that first consideration is given to residential state-supported hospitals or schools. Only when institutionalization cannot be accomplished, due often to lack of space, is consideration given to community resources such as day care, sheltered workshops, and community mental health centers. Leland argues that selection of services should flow in the reverse order. A special-education model proposed by Deno (1970) is consistent with this view. As shown in Figure 9-7, children would first be assigned to outpatient programs, with the largest number being mainstreamed. As the child needs special treatments, these would be made available. Both Deno and Leland recognize the need for institutionalization when all else fails; that is, when the handicaps are so poorly understood that they cannot be effectively treated in the community. In that case

Leland envisions institutions as small, *specialized teaching-research* settings designed to study and help its residents.

The solution to the problems of large institutions is not simply to return the handicapped to the family without support systems. Family members need some freedom to pursue their interests and social activities without the burden of supervising the retarded child (Hagamen, 1978, 1980b). They also require relief in times of increased stress. Requests for residential care for a child are rarely due to a change in the child's behavior but, instead, result from family illness, marital discord, or exhaustion of the caretaker. Home support programs might take many forms: provision of part-time child care by trained personnel; temporary foster care; family visits; partial institutionalization. An example of an alternative program is the "five-two" plan implemented at Sagamore Children's Center for psychotic children. In this program the handicapped child lives at home for a minimum of five days and spends the weekends in the hospital, giving the family respite from care (Drabman, Spitalnik, Hagamen, and Van Witsen, 1973). There will, however, always be situations in which the mentally retarded child cannot live with the family. Moreover, there is a pressing need for alternatives for retarded adults, such as foster care, supervised apartment living, personal care homes, and similar semi-independent arrangements (Bruininks et al., 1980).

Behavior Modification

Comprehensive treatment of the mentally retarded may include medical procedures (for example, diets, medication) and individual and family therapy, but the single most important innovation has been the application of behavioral techniques. Fuller's 1949 study, in which a profoundly retarded 18-year-old male was operantly conditioned to raise his hand, is a landmark in the use of behavior modification. Widespread application in institutions took another decade or so (Birnbrauer, 1976) but became a major catalyst in transforming custodial

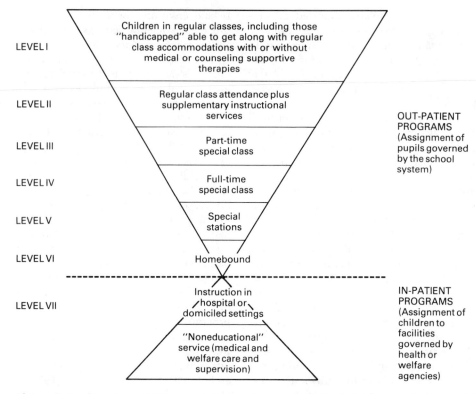

LEVEL I — Children in regular classes, including those "handicapped" able to get along with regular class accommodations with or without medical or counseling supportive therapies

LEVEL II — Regular class attendance plus supplementary instructional services

LEVEL III — Part-time special class

LEVEL IV — Full-time special class

LEVEL V — Special stations

LEVEL VI — Homebound

LEVEL VII — Instruction in hospital or domiciled settings

"Noneducational" service (medical and welfare care and supervision)

OUT-PATIENT PROGRAMS (Assignment of pupils governed by the school system)

IN-PATIENT PROGRAMS (Assignment of children to facilities governed by health or welfare agencies)

Figure 9–7 Deno's model for special education services that incorporates the philosophy of the least restrictive environment. The tapering indicates the differences in number of children at different levels. *From Deno, 1970.*

care into active treatment. Learning principles, especially operant procedures, currently are used to train self-help, imitation and attention, academic and work skills, social skills, and language, and to reduce inappropriate behaviors such as aggression, self-stimulation, self-injury, tantrums, and pica (Whitman and Scibak, 1979). Such training is of considerable benefit.

For example, the ability to dress, feed, bathe, and otherwise care for one's basic physical needs is extremely important in facilitating integration of the retarded with others. Children who cannot feed and dress themselves not only require much from caretakers but also are hindered in participating in social or educational activities. Self-help programs have targeted the use of utensils in eating, inhibition of sloppy

eating and food stealing, dressing and undressing, washing and combing the hair, and toothbrushing (Azrin and Armstrong, 1973; Azrin, Schaeffer, and Wesolowski, 1976; Barton, Guess, Garcia, and Baer, 1970; Whitman and Scibak, 1979).

An excellent example of a program to teach academic skills is the work of Bijou, Birnbrauer, Kidder, and Tague (1966), in which severely retarded children were trained in arithmetic, reading, and writing. Motivation for success came in the form of tokens for correct answers, which could be traded for trinkets, money, and candy or could even be accumulated for trips. The academic material was carefully presented in small steps that could be mastered. Previous to this, however, it was necessary to shape by reinforcement appropriate behaviors such as sitting still and paying attention. A time-out room was available as a consequence for disruptive behavior but rarely had to be used. In fact, the overall success of the program led the researchers to suggest that the academic potential of many retarded children is greater than stereotypes would have us believe, provided that the environment is set up to facilitate learning.

Such an optimistic tone, adopted by many behavior modifiers, has probably well served the retarded child, who has so often in the past been considered virtually unable to learn. This is not to say that the application of behavioral techniques is simple, accomplished without great effort, or effective in every instance. Enormous gains have been made, but much is yet to be achieved. In reviewing the research on behavior modification, Birnbrauer (1976) has well summarized the present state of affairs with these words: ". . . in that retarded persons treated with behavior modification techniques are still retarded, the results are disappointing. In that strides have been made in developing ways of working with the retarded and an unprecedented amount of information has been accumulated, the results are encouraging indeed" (pp. 396–397).

SUMMARY

Mental retardation is defined in terms of subaverage general intellectual functioning and deficits in adaptive behavior that become manifest between birth and 18 years of age.

General intellectual functioning is evaluated by performance on a standard test of intelligence, such as the Stanford-Binet and the Wechsler scales. These tests consist of various tasks of increasing difficulty. They are reasonably valid measures of intelligence, as intelligence was first perceived by Binet when he tested schoolchildren in France. Scores on the S-B and Wechsler tests correlate with school performance and teachers assessments. These IQ tests are also fairly reliable (consistent).

However, some cultural bias exists in most intelligence tests that benefits those who have middle-class experiences. Issues regarding validity, reliability, standardization, and bias are critical to interpreting and appropriately using intelligence tests to diagnose mental retardation.

Such diagnosis also should take into account how the individual copes with the everyday environment. Assessment of adaptive behavior may include observations or reports of the individual's behavior in many settings. Adaptive behavior scales, such as the Vineland Social Maturity Scale and AAMD's Adaptive Behavior Scale, aid in evaluating self-sufficiency, responsibility, and—in some cases—maladaptation. However, the development of these scales lags behind that of IQ tests.

Subaverage intelligence is identified by AAMD as an IQ score that falls more than two standard deviations below the mean on a test of intelligence. This category includes less than 3 percent of the population. Four levels of retardation are usually recognized: mild, moderate, severe, and profound. Educators typically recognize the categories of educable, trainable, and custodial retardation, depending upon judgments of learning capacity. It is also possible to set levels of retardation according to adaptive functioning, although this is not common practice.

There are many known or suspected causes of mental retardation: chromosome aberrations, Mendelian inheritance, pregnancy and birth complications, and family and sociocultural influences. The etiology of most cases of mental retardation cannot be definitively traced, however. These cases involve children who appear physically normal and are only mildly retarded. A disproportionately large number come from the lower social classes. It is likely that sociocultural effects are important to our understanding of these children. Nevertheless, the nature versus nurture argument looms over any discussion of the etiology of mild retardation.

Efforts to understand mental retardation include research into underlying cognitive processes. Piagetian theory can serve as a general developmental guide. It has been central in the ongoing developmental versus difference controversy regarding the nature of mental retardation. Investigations into learning processes have revealed deficits in attention, mediation, problem solving, memory, and generalization of learning.

Research has also focused on the possible effects of motivational variables. The social experiences of retarded persons may cause them to be somewhat different from the nonretarded with respect to authority figures, responsiveness to reinforcers, and expectations for failure and success. Experiences in the family are of obvious importance to the growth of the mentally retarded child. Families must adapt to having and caring for the handicapped child, and probably do so in a series of phases.

Attitudes toward treatment of the mentally retarded have reflected the general feelings of the times. Presently we are witnessing high interest and a thrust toward appropriate education for all. P.L. 94–142 serves the mentally retarded by compelling appropriate services within the least restrictive environment. However, the mainstreaming of retarded children in regular classes argues for continued research into the effects of such placement. The philosophy of P.L. 94–142 is consistent with current attempts to deinstitutionalize the retarded whenever possible. Although few would oppose this philosophy, there is great need for alternative placements and treatment techniques. Comprehensive treatment of mental retardation includes medical procedures, therapy, and the innovations of behavior modification.

10

HYPERACTIVITY AND LEARNING DISABILITIES

MINIMAL BRAIN DYSFUNCTION

HYPERACTIVITY

What Is Hyperactivity?
Etiology
Identifying the Hyperactive Child
Treatment
The Changing Face of Hyperactivity

LEARNING DISABILITIES

Definition and Clinical Description
What Causes Learning Disabilities?
Specific Learning Disabilities
Treatment and Assessment

SUMMARY

He never sits still; he's always into something, no matter where he is.

She won't pay attention for one minute.

In school, he's up and out of his seat in a flash.

She just doesn't get along very well with other children.

She seems smart enough in many ways, but she just can't seem to learn to read.

The teacher says he's still mixing up "b" and "d."

He's never done well in school, and now he's two grades behind his age peers.

These kinds of complaints, commonly voiced by parents and teachers, are the primary presenting problems for children who are said to suffer from *hyperactivity* and *learning disabilities*. The two diagnoses are not necessarily related, but overlap in presenting complaints is frequent. Furthermore, hyperactivity and learning disabilities have been linked historically by the concept of minimal brain dysfunction.

MINIMAL BRAIN DYSFUNCTION

The concept of minimal brain dysfunction (MBD) has its antecedents in the relationship between known brain damage and its demonstrated or hypothesized consequences. This relationship was established by investigators of diverse interests. Broca, for example, studied two men who had lost the ability to speak in midlife. Upon their deaths he was able to show by autopsy that both had suffered atrophy of a specific site on the left frontal hemisphere of the brain (Bryan and Bryan, 1975). In studying brain-injured World War I soldiers, Goldstein hypothesized that they suffered perceptual handicaps as well as behavioral rigidity, loss of initiative, and disorganization. Much research was also conducted on children who had suffered from an epidemic of encephalitis after World War I. They were described as emotionally unstable, irritable, obstinate, memory

impaired, inattentive, hyperactive, depressed, motorically impaired, and antisocial (Kessler, 1980).

All of this work started with *known* brain damage and examined its apparent consequences. But a second approach soon became widespread: the reconstruction of etiology in the absence of known history (Kessler, 1980). That is, investigators identified behavioral disturbances that previously had been associated with brain damage and attributed them to brain dysfunction without independent evidence that brain damage actually existed. For instance, Kahn and Cohen (1934) described school behavior problems (hyperactivity, distractibility, impulsivity, poor attention) and attributed them to brain stem lesions (Satz and Fletcher, 1980). At the Emma Pendleton Bradley Home in Providence, Rhode Island, which had been established as a memorial to a postencephalitic child, Laufer and Denhoff defined the hyperkinetic impulse disorder, which included learning problems, and associated it with presumed brain dysfunction (Kessler, 1980; Laufer, Denhoff, and Solomons, 1957; Laufer and Denhoff, 1957). Meanwhile Strauss and Werner had begun studies of the mentally deficient to determine if manifestations of brain injury in adults, as outlined by Goldstein, could be found in children. This work established a long line of research, primarily centered on educational remediation, that identified children of more or less average intelligence who displayed learning, motor, perceptual, language, and behavioral deficits (Strauss and Kephart, 1955; Strauss and Lehtinen, 1947). It was argued that these children suffered from brain damage.

It soon became apparent, however, that brain damage could not be demonstrated in most children who showed these problems. The term *minimal brain damage* thus came into existence, implying that the brain was damaged only to a degree that could not be detected by usual clinical methods (Cantwell, 1981). This term was further changed to *minimal brain dysfunction* (MBD), indicating that although damage itself might not exist, central nervous system dysfunction was presumed to be present.

In 1966 a task force cosponsored by the National Society for Crippled Children and Adults and the National Institutes of Neurological Diseases and Blindness set forth an important definition:

> The term "minimal brain dysfunction syndrome" refers . . . to children of near average, average, or above average general intelligence with certain learning or behavioral disabilities ranging from mild to severe, which are associated with deviations of function of the central nervous system. These deviations may manifest themselves by various combinations of impairment in perception, conceptualization, language, memory, and control of attention, impulse, or motor function. (Clements, 1966, pp. 9–10)

As leader of the task force, Clements attempted to further delineate the minimal brain dysfunction syndrome by citing, in order of frequency, the ten most mentioned symptoms, as shown in Table 10-1. Today the syndrome is noted or implied by numerous terms: minimal cerebral dysfunction, minimal brain damage, hyperactivity, developmental hyperactivity, hyperkinesis, learning disability, specific learning dis-

Table 10-1   The Ten Symptoms Most Frequently Associated with the Term *Minimal Brain Dysfunction*

Hyperactivity
Perceptual-motor impairments
Emotional lability
Coordination deficits
Disorders of attention
Impulsivity
Memory and thinking disorders
Specific learning disabilities
Disorders of speech and language
Equivocal neurological signs and EEG irregularities

ability, psychoneurological learning disability, perceptual handicap, and educational handicap.

The concept of minimal brain dysfunction is not without criticism, however. Gardner (1980), who views it as viable, recognizes "holdouts" who "deny the existence of the disorder . . . and consider the dysfunction to be more in the heads of those who make the diagnosis than in the brains of the children being so labeled" (p. 269). After describing his failed efforts to clarify the criteria of MBD, Routh (1980) ended by saying, "Before I will seriously wish to use the concept of MBD again, I will wait to be *shown* that such a syndrome exists" (p. 62). Others have referred to minimal brain dysfunction as a sophisticated term of ignorance or as an empty term that saves us the trouble of thinking clearly (Satz and Fletcher, 1980).

Perhaps the most obvious criticism is directed to the circular reasoning that is seen all too often: Brain dysfunction, it is said, can lead to certain signs—so the presence of the signs means the existence of brain dysfunction. But these same signs may be manifestations of environmental variables and so are not definitive indicators of CNS etiology. Moreover, the majority of children said to have MBD give no consistent evidence of soft neurological signs, EEG irregularities, or perinatal complications, while many obviously brain-damaged children give no evidence of hyperactivity and academic failure (Safer and Allen, 1976; Satz and Fletcher, 1980). Thus, it seems reasonable to discard the concept of minimal brain dysfunction as a presumed etiological umbrella that too frequently ends up as a diagnostic term. This is not to say that brain dysfunction is untenable as an etiological *hypothesis*. The most useful strategy, though, is to start with observable behavior and bring scientific methods to bear on the questions of diagnosis, etiology, and treatment. Recent efforts with children described in this chapter have led to recognition of two overlapping areas: One centers on behavioral problems and is labeled hyperactivity; the other focuses on academic failure and is labeled learning disabilities or specific learning disabilities. We will look at each of these in turn, first examining hyperactivity.

HYPERACTIVITY

Few disorders of childhood garner as much interest and controversy today as hyperactivity. First described in 1845 by the German physician Henrich Hoffman (Cantwell, 1975), it was not widely studied until the late 1950s. At that time concern was increasing for children with learning and behavior problems (Safer and Allen, 1976). The introduction of pharmacological treatment for hyperactivity in the late 1960s brought with it additional interest and controversy.

The prevalence of hyperactivity is frequently estimated at about 5 to 10 percent of the school-age population (Lambert and Sandoval, 1980; O'Leary, 1980; Ross and Pelham, 1981; Safer and Allen, 1976). However, prevalence data show a good deal of variability, reaching as high as 20 percent (Trites, Dugas, Lynch, and Ferguson, 1979). This variability can be largely attributed to the use of different instruments for rating hyperactivity, differing cut-off points on any one instrument, and differences in the raters. Some quite consistent patterns have been found, nevertheless. Perhaps most clear is that boys are rated hyperactive more often than girls, with the ratio ranging from 3:1 to 10:1 (American Psychiatric Association, 1980; Safer and Allen, 1976). There is also some evidence that hyperactivity is associated with lower SES (Schachar, Rutter, and Smith, 1981).

What Is Hyperactivity?

Our understanding of hyperactivity has advanced considerably in recent years, with the focus shifting from a disturbance in activity level, to attentional deficits, to broader issues in social development (Barkley, 1981a). There has been a strong inclination to view hyperactivity not simply as overactivity but as a syndrome, most often referred to as the hyper-kinetic syndrome, hyperkinetic impulse disorder, or hyperkinesis. Because of its strong historical association with minimal brain dysfunction, it is common to see the term *MBD-hyperactivity*. In all these instances the hyperactive child has been viewed as exhibiting a cluster of maladaptive behaviors.

Hyperactive children are *overactive* beyond what is considered age-appropriate. Parents and teachers who can no longer keep up with them report that they fidget, cannot sit still, and are restless and always on the run. The quality of the motion also stands out from ordinary activity by its haphazardness, poor organization, and lack of goals. This overactivity, which probably began early in childhood, is almost always a problem when the child begins school. One investigation showed, for example, that nonhyperactive youngsters appeared much less active in relatively restricted regular classrooms than in open-structured classrooms but that hyperactive children behaved in a similar manner regardless of the room structure (Jacob, O'Leary, and Rosenblad, 1978).

Another behavior seen in hyperactive children is short attention span. At home, unlike most of their peers, they rarely sit through a television program but instead move rapidly from one activity to another. In school there are complaints of lack of attention to directions for the task at hand and perhaps poor concentration. There is growing consensus that *attentional deficits* are central in hyperactivity, but as Douglas (1980a,b) has pointed out, lack of agreement exists over the nature of the deficits. Some researchers believe that distractibility is the problem; that is, the child cannot ignore disruptive environmental influences. It is suggested that a defective filtering mechanism causes hyperactive children to take in a great amount of information that is irrelevant to the situation. Douglas herself favors the hypothesis that external distraction is not the primary difficulty but that the child is unable to *sustain* attention or concentration. Although further research is needed to elucidate mechanisms of attention in hyperactivity, their role is presently considered of utmost importance (e.g., Levy

Many children are highly active. It is only when children are overactive beyond what is considered age-appropriate and when they are always restless and fidgety that they are considered hyperactive.

and Hobbes, 1981). This is reflected in the fact that DSM-III has discarded the diagnostic term *hyperkinetic reaction* in favor of *Attention Deficit Disorder with Hyperactivity*. Table 10–2 presents the criteria for this disorder, including inattention and overactivity, which we have already mentioned, and impulsivity.

The essence of *impulsivity* is acting without thinking. The child may jump into the swimming pool without being able to swim or run out into a busy street in front of automobiles (Cantwell, 1975). In the classroom impulsivity may be displayed by interrupting others, calling out, and clowning (Routh, 1980). In the laboratory the tendency to act impulsively can

be assessed by having the child select from a set of slightly varying pictures the one that matches a standard picture. Relatively fast selection and a large number of errors on the Matching Familiar Figures Test (MFFT) are taken as indicators of impulsivity. They have been shown to discriminate hyperactive from normal children (Messer, 1976; Routh, 1980).

Secondary Manifestations. The behaviors we have just discussed are considered central in hyperactivity, but two other manifestations or correlates are also widely recognized. These are conduct problems and academic deficits.

Misconduct is notable in over 80 percent of

Table 10–2   DSM-III Criteria for Attention Deficit Disorder with Hyperactivity

---

*A. **Inattention.** At least three of the following:*
  1) Often fails to finish things he or she starts
  2) Often doesn't seem to listen
  3) Easily distracted
  4) Has difficulty concentrating on schoolwork or other tasks requiring sustained attention
  5) Has difficulty sticking to a play activity

*B. **Impulsivity.** At least three of the following:*
  1) Often acts before thinking
  2) Shifts excessively from one activity to another
  3) Has difficulty organizing work (this not being due to cognitive impairment)
  4) Needs a lot of supervision
  5) Frequently calls out in class
  6) Has difficulty awaiting turn in games or group situations

*C. **Hyperactivity.** At least two of the following:*
  1) Excessively runs about or climbs on things
  2) Has difficulty sitting still or fidgets excessively
  3) Has difficulty staying seated
  4) Moves about excessively during sleep
  5) Is always "on the go" or acts as if "driven by a motor"

*D. **Onset before the age of seven.***

*E. **Duration of at least six months.***

*F. **Not due to schizophrenia, affective disorder, or severe or profound mental retardation.***

American Psychiatric Association, 1980.

hyperactive children (Safer and Allen, 1976). Parents and teachers complain of fighting, quarreling, disobedience, and belligerence. Research on peer interaction shows that the hyperactive child is aggressive and is perceived negatively (King and Young, 1981). As associated features of hyperactivity, DSM-III includes obstinacy, negativism, bossiness, bullying, temper tantrums, low frustration tolerance, and poor response to discipline. Such troublesome conduct, more than the primary manifestations of hyperactivity, may lead parents to seek professional help.

Academic difficulties frequently have been associated with the syndrome (Cantwell, 1975; Cantwell and Satterfield, 1978; Safer and Allen, 1976; Silver, 1981). Palkes and Stewart (1972) reported that hyperactive children had lower achievement than nonhyperactives in reading, spelling, and arithmetic, although the differences disappeared when adjustment was made for the lower IQ scores of the hyperac-

tives. Minde and colleagues (1971) found hyperactive children to be rated lower than classmates on ten academic subjects. Furthermore, this difference could not be accounted for by lower IQ scores. By the time hyperactive children reach adolescence, 50 to 60 percent have repeated more than one grade, and some have repeated two or more (Milich and Loney, 1979). The association between hyperactivity and academic difficulties is so pervasive that one can easily be led into assuming that it is universal. However, it is quite possible that hyperactivity unaccompanied by academic problems goes unidentified—or is labeled mischievous or even creative (Keogh and Barkett, 1980).

Explanations for the relationship between hyperactivity and poor school performance have not been firmly established (Cantwell, 1975). Keogh (1971) suggested three possibilities: that some type of neurological impairment causes both behavioral and learning deficits, that hyperactivity interferes with attention and thus learning, and that impulsivity interferes with learning. It is reasonable, too, to suspect that the child may get caught in an interacting web of learning problems, behavioral patterns that generate negative consequences from others, and poor self-concept.

Is Hyperactivity A Syndrome? The presumption that hyperactivity is a syndrome has sparked much controversy. In the United States the concept of the syndrome rests on the belief that overactivity, inattention, and impulsivity frequently appear together. Many professionals appear comfortable with the assumption that these behaviors cluster, but others do not. In fact, in several studies these primary manifestations of the syndrome were not significantly related to each other in either hyperactive or normal populations (Barkley, 1981a; Kenny, 1980; Langhorne, Loney, Paternite, and Bechtholdt, 1976; Routh and Roberts, 1972). This finding gives credence to the idea that children labeled hyperactive are a heterogeneous group—some overactive, some inattentive, some impulsive, and some a combination of these behaviors (Barkley, 1981a).

Another finding that weakens belief in a hyperkinetic syndrome is the lack of specific etiological influences for overactivity, inattentiveness, and impulsivity (Shaffer and Greenhill, 1979). As already noted, it was thought that these behaviors originated from minimal brain dysfunction, and the terms *hyperactivity* and *MBD* are still sometimes used interchangeably. Nevertheless, several etiological influences appear to be operating.

Finally, the manifestations of hyperactivity are reported to occur in large numbers of children who receive other diagnoses (Shaffer and Greenhill, 1979). The problem of overlap between diagnostic categories is especially relevant to conduct disorders. For example, many children who are labeled hyperactive in the United States apparently are diagnosed as conduct disordered in England (Schachar, Rutter, and Smith, 1981; Stewart, Cummings, Singer, and DeBlois, 1981). In the United States itself

some researchers argue that hyperactivity is simply a form of conduct disorder (e.g., Lahey, Green, and Forehand, 1980), but others have provided evidence that it is a separate clinical entity (Loney, Langhorne, and Paternite, 1978; Milich, Loney, and Landau, 1982; O'Leary and Steen, 1982; Prinz, Connor, and Wilson, 1981). It seems likely that hyperactivity will continue to be viewed as a specific syndrome, with attentional deficits being central. It is increasingly being recognized, though, that there may exist subgroups of children who are designated hyperactive; for example, those with and without aggression.

Etiology

The search for causes of hyperactivity has implicated many variables. Here we briefly review some of the most pertinent findings.

Genetics. Not infrequently parents with high-activity children come into clinics with the belief that such disturbing behavior runs in the family. For example, one of the authors recently talked to a mother who claimed that many of the cousins of her young hyperactive son behaved in a similar way. This mother suspected hereditary causation. Although her observation may indeed have been accurate, only controlled research can help determine the role played by heredity and familial environmental factors.

There is tentative evidence that inheritance may play some role in hyperactivity (e.g., Cantwell, 1975; Eisenberg, 1979; Laufer and Shetty, 1980; Ross and Pelham, 1981). To begin with, activity level itself is likely to be constitutional within the general child population (Buss and Plomin, 1975; Chess and Thomas, 1977). Willerman (1973) found that mothers of monozygotic twins rated them more alike on the Werry-Weiss-Peters Activity Scale than did mothers of dizygotic twins. This suggests that overactivity may be influenced genetically. In another study all four of the monozygotic twin pairs examined were concordant for the hyperactivity syndrome, while the same was true for only one out of six pairs of dizygotic twins (Lopez, 1965). Evidence from adoption studies appears consistent with the genetic hypothesis, although these studies are not strong methodologically (Cantwell, 1975; Ross and Ross, 1976). Further research is needed in this area before any definite statement can be made about a hereditary component in the etiology of hyperactivity. It is worth noting that limited research so far has not revealed the presence of chromosome aberrations (Eisenberg, 1979; Cantwell, 1975).

Perinatal Factors. Perinatal complications have been examined in several studies. Ross and Pelham (1981), who provide a succinct review of investigations of large populations, concluded that differences in perinatal factors between hyperactive and control children are suggested by the literature. However, the differences are small and limited in predicting behavior problems. For example, the Collaborative Project of the National Institute of Neurologic Disease and Stroke followed several thousand pregnancies until the children were 7 years of age. Some weak relationships were found between perinatal factors and hyperactivity assessed on clinic ratings and judgments. None of the perinatal factors, however, increased the chance of hyperactivity at age 7 by more than 5 percent (Nichols, 1976, as cited by Ross and Pelham, 1981). In Werner's (1971) longitudinal research with a thousand children from Kauai, no relationship was revealed between sixty prenatal, perinatal, and neonatal events and teacher ratings of behaviors associated with hyperactivity. The conclusions drawn by Ross and Pelham (1981) have been reached by others as well (e.g., O'Leary, 1978; Rapoport, Quinn, Burg, and Bartley, 1979).

Dysfunctioning Nervous System. For several decades researchers have hypothesized disordered nervous system functioning to explain hyperactivity (Ferguson and Pappas, 1979). Most proposals, regardless of the specific mechanisms discussed, assume some abnormality of the arousal functions of the CNS. Intuitively it seems that CNS arousal might go hand in hand with excessive motor activity and attentional deficits. Furthermore, stimulant drugs, which are beneficial to some hyperactive children, affect certain neurotransmitters that, in turn, appear related to arousal level. Interestingly, both overarousal and underarousal have been suggested (e.g., Laufer, Denhoff, and Solomons, 1957; Satterfield, 1975; Wender, 1971).

Responses of both the autonomic and central nervous system have been examined. Psychophysiological measures of the autonomic system, such as skin conductance and heart rate, have shown conflicting results, although it may tentatively be concluded that hyperactive children are autonomically less responsive than comparison children (Ross and Pelham, 1981). Central nervous system arousal has been studied by comparing brain wave activity in hyperactive and normal children. Overall, no differences exist in background EEG, but a minority of hyperactive children do exhibit excessive slow-wave activity (Hastings and Barkley, 1978). Since 10 percent or more of normal children also show this pattern, the significance of the finding is debatable. Brain responses to auditory and visual stimuli appear conflicting and difficult to interpret. While these lines of research may yet prove helpful, little can be drawn from them at present. Most investigations have not determined that the hyperactive child is different from the normal child; a few report evidence for overarousal, and a larger number support the proposal of underarousal.

As with other behavior disorders, neurochemical dysfunctioning has also been examined. The main hypotheses cite a deficiency of the neurotransmitters serotonin, norepinephrine, and dopamine (Ferguson and Pappas, 1979). At the present time there is little support for these proposals.

Diet. In 1975, Feingold, a physician-researcher interested in allergies, published a book, *Why Your Child is Hyperactive,* that inspired both controversy and a wave of investigations into the effects of diet on hyperactivity. Feingold asserted that ingestion of food con-

taining artificial dyes and flavors, certain pre-
servatives, and naturally occurring salicylates
(for example, in apricots, prunes, tomatoes,
cucumbers) is related to hyperactivity. He
claimed that 25 to 50 percent of hyperactive-
learning disabled children responded favorably
to diets that eliminated these substances (Harley and Matthews, 1980; Tryphonas, 1979). On
the other hand, it was stated that when children
on the recommended Kaiser-Permanente diet
ingested a prohibited food, hyperactivity dramatically occurred and persisted for forty-eight
to seventy-two hours. Feingold's position received pervasive media coverage and was rapidly espoused by many parents, who reported
impressive anecdotes about behavioral improvement in their children on Feingold's diet.
Some of this fanfare undoubtedly can be attributed to the fact that Feingold advocated his diet
as treatment for mental retardation, delinquency, learning disabilities, and autism, as
well as for hyperactivity. Early evaluation by
skeptical interdisciplinary committees called for
well-designed research to settle the question of
the efficacy of the Feingold diet.

Since that time a number of studies have
been conducted on hyperactivity, primarily focusing on the influence of food dyes. Conners
and his colleagues were among the first to examine hyperactive children while they were on
a diet restricting food dyes and salicylates and
while they were on a control diet. Teachers, but
not parents, found the restrictive diet to be more
effective, as measured by the Conners rating
scale. Subsequently three "challenge" studies
were run in which children who were placed on
the Feingold diet and showed improvement
were "challenged" by either a cookie containing a blend of food dyes or a cookie with no
dyes. The results of these investigations were
equivocal but for the most part did not support
Feingold's claims (Conners, 1980). Other similarly designed research has followed this pattern (Harley and Matthews, 1980; Levy,
Drumbrell, Hobbes, Ryan, Wilton, and Woodhill, 1978). One well-designed challenge study
by Swanson and Kinsbourne (1980) stands out

as evidence that artificial food color may affect
children's cognitive functioning. In this research much larger doses of food color were
given and children's performance was measured on a paired-associate learning task. There
is some question as to the reasonableness of the
dosage and the meaningfulness of the dependent measure, but replication and extension
seem worthwhile.

It should be noted that it is extremely difficult to conduct well-controlled diet studies of
hyperactivity. Food ingestion is not easy to
manage, measures of hyperactivity are controversial, and it may well be that the Feingold
diet makes other, unknown nutritional changes
in addition to the ones intended (Prinz, Roberts, and Hantman, 1980; Swanson and Kinsbourne, 1980). Nevertheless, Swanson and
Kinsbourne (1980) note that in general the
more controlled and objective the investigation,
the less supported are Feingold's claims. At
best, it appears that perhaps some hyperactive
children, particularly of preschool age, benefit
from the diet (Barkley, 1981b; Weiss, 1982).
This is not a strong base from which to adopt
policies and programs advocated by Feingold
and his followers, such as diet-restricted school
lunches and routine dietary treatment of the
hyperactive child (Harley and Matthews, 1980).
However, the findings appear interesting
enough to warrant further investigation.

Ecological Variables: Lead and Lighting.
Ecological variables have been examined as
possible contributors to the etiology of hyperactivity. One of these is the amount of lead that
has been introduced into the body (Eisenberg,
1979; Henker and Whalen, 1980; Laufer and
Shetty, 1980). That lead exposure can lead to
coma, seizure, mental retardation, and death is
not in dispute (Hansen, Belmont, and Stein,
1980). Animals experimentally exposed to lead,
and children exposed to undue levels of lead
during early development, also have been shown
to exhibit atypical motor activity, irritability,
learning difficulties and the like (Henker and
Whalen, 1980). The question presently at hand

is whether low levels of exposure over long periods of time may also adversely affect children. For obvious reasons the variable of interest cannot be manipulated, and so indirect verification must be sought.

In several studies children who were presumed to reside in a lead-polluted environment or who showed a somewhat raised level of lead in their blood were compared with a matched group that had neither of these attributes. Psychological, neurological, and clinical assessment did not, on the whole, find much evidence for the effect of lead exposure (Hansen, Belmont, and Stein, 1980). However, there were some reports of overactivity and fine motor disturbance. David and his co-workers (1976) were able to show improvement in the behavior of some hyperactive children subsequent to treatment with an agent thought to reduce the amount of lead in the body.

It is difficult to draw conclusions about the research in this area because unresolved issues could account for the results (Hansen, Belmont, and Stein, 1980). For example, age of exposure might be important but is unknown in some studies. Investigations have varied, too, in the lead level considered damaging. Nevertheless, Needleman and colleagues (1979) have conducted an impressive study in which they measured lead levels in the dentine of teeth. Children 5 to 7 years of age attending regular schools donated their first set of teeth as they were lost. The youngsters were categorized as high or low exposure subjects, based on lead level. They were then examined extensively through social histories, neurophysiological and medical examinations, parental reports, and teacher ratings. Children who had higher levels of dentine lead, as compared to those with lower levels, performed less well on tests of intelligence, language, and attention. Moreover, they were judged to have more problems when rated by teachers for distractibility, impulsivity, and not following a sequence of directions. It thus appears that further research in this area is needed. Even with restriction of lead paints, a high technology society may produce damaging

amounts of lead from factories, autos, paint from old buildings, and the like.

A second, albeit less serious, ecological variable implicated in the etiology of hyperactivity is fluorescent lighting. Based on the finding that x-ray exposure led to hyperactivity in rats, a photobiologist, Ott, hypothesized that fluorescent lighting, which emanates some x-rays, might similarly affect children (O'Leary, 1978). To test this idea he exposed two classrooms of children to fluorescent lighting and two classrooms to full spectrum light (Mayron, Ott, Nations, and Mayron, 1974). The latter group reportedly were less hyperactive than the former. O'Leary, Rosenbaum, and Hughes (1978) attempted to replicate this work by alternating lighting conditions in a classroom of seven first-grade children labeled conduct disordered and/or hyperactive. No effects were found for hyperactivity as assessed by ratings of task orientation and activity level. At this time no convincing support exists for an etiological role for this variable.

Psychosocial Factors. There is some evidence that children of lower SES are at high risk for hyperactivity (Barkley, 1981b; Schachar, Rutter, and Smith, 1981). This may be related to the greater risk of biological damage in the poor, or perhaps to disorganization and disruption in the home. It is quite reasonable to assume that a burdened or chaotic home, regardless of socioeconomic status, may lack stimulus situations that foster the development of attention and reflective behavior. Organized and regular mealtime, being read to, sedentary games, exposure to rules under adult supervision, and so forth may indeed be important (Eisenberg, 1979). Learning theorists have not specifically proposed that the hyperactivity syndrome is learned, but it is obvious that relevant behaviors are shaped or maintained by environmental conditions (O'Leary, 1978). For example, children's impulsivity-reflectivity can be modified by exposure to film-mediated models or the actual style of their teachers (Yando and Kagan, 1968; Ridberg, Parke, and Hetherington, 1971). Remaining in one's seat, attending to a task, and other relevant classroom behaviors have been modified with various behavioral techniques (e.g., Ayllon and Rosenbaum, 1977; O'Leary, Pelham, Rosenbaum, and Price, 1976).

Henker and Whalen (1980) have contributed to our understanding that hyperactive behaviors vary with the external setting. In one investigation they exposed boys to four study situations that varied both in difficulty of material and in whether or not the child had to pace himself to external cues. Nonmedicated hyperactive boys attended to the task just as did medicated hyperactives and normals when the situation was least challenging. However, they attended less than the other children when the situation was most challenging. Demonstrations that specific settings influence hyperactivity do not, of course, prove that attributes of the environment cause disturbed behavior in the sense of originating it. They do suggest, though, the power of the environment to elicit and maintain such behavior. Perhaps some hyperactivity can be accounted for by a predisposition toward high activity or responsivity in conjunction with environmental circumstances that exacerbate this tendency.

Identifying the Hyperactive Child

Due to the long association of hyperactivity with MBD, an extensive number of reports concerning assessment include methods to reveal MBD, particularly the neurological examination and the EEG. Some children referred for hyperactivity-MBD show soft signs (Kenny, 1980). Nevertheless, soft signs and EEG abnormalities have limited value in differentiating hyperactives from normals or from children with other disturbances, much less in treatment planning (Dubey, 1976; Kenny, 1980). The same may be said for medical history and psychological assessment aimed at establishing MBD. It could be argued that these methods should be retained when biological factors are highly suspect, particularly since a subgroup of

hyperactive children may suffer MBD. In all cases, however, procedures to assess specific behaviors and interactions of the child are of utmost importance.

Barkley's (1981a) recommendation for the assessment of hyperactivity can serve as a model for this approach. Interviews with the child, parents, and teachers—along with rating scales and direct observation—are the components of this method. The child's interview, which includes informal observations of behavior, focuses on interactions with others, both parents and peers. Barkley has reservations about the usefulness of information obtained from the child, who may have little insight into the problem and want to present a socially acceptable picture. Nevertheless, he believes that establishing rapport and detailing physical, cognitive, and behavioral characteristics are beneficial.

The parent and teacher interviews are alike in their emphasis on social interaction. In working with parents Barkley finds it useful to ask nine questions about several situations, as shown in Table 10-3. An illustration of the question format in an interview with a parent is presented in Table 10-4. The situation being explored is how the child acts when visitors are in the home. Note that noncompliance is quite evident and that the chain of interaction is increasingly aversive. This seems to be a common pattern in hyperactive child-parent exchanges.

Somewhere in the process of speaking with parents and adults, it might be quite useful to request the completion of a behavior-rating scale. These scales are widely employed in the clinic and in research, although they would profit from efforts to improve their reliability, validity, and standardization (e.g., Glow, Glow, and Rump, 1982; Wallander and Conger, 1981). The scales can help determine whether the child's behaviors are deviant from the norm and can also help monitor treatment change. The Werry-Weiss-Peters Activity Rating Scale (Werry, 1968) consists of thirty-one items rated by parents across seven situations: mealtime, television, homework, play, sleep, public places, school. The scale correlates posi-

Table 10-3   Interview Format Suggested by Barkley

Questions	Situations
1. Is this a problem area?	Overall interactions
2. What does the child do in this situation?	Play alone
3. What is your response?	Play with others
4. What will the child do next?	Mealtimes
5. If the problem continues, what will you do next?	Dressing in morning
6. What is usually the outcome of this interaction?	Washing and bathing
7. How often do these problems occur in this situation?	Parent on telephone
8. How do you feel about these problems?	During television
9. On a scale of 0 to 10 (0 = no problem, 10 = severe problem), how severe is this problem to you?	Visitors at home
	Visiting others' homes
	In public places
	While mother is occupied
	Father at home
	Chores
	Bedtime
	Other situations

Copyright by Guilford Press, 1981. Reprinted with permission from R. Barkley, Hyperactivity. In E. Mash & L. Terdal (eds.) *Behavioral Assessment of Childhood Disorders.* New York: Guilford Press, 1981.

tively with scales developed by Conners, which are perhaps the most widely employed. The Conners Parent Rating Scale yields scores on the factors of impulsivity-hyperactivity, conduct problems, learning problems (attention), psychosomatic problems, and anxiety (Goyette, Conners, and Ulrich, 1978). The Conners Teachers Rating Scale (Conners, 1969) has thirty-nine items reflecting the same factors (see Table 10-5). An Abbreviated Teacher Rating Scale consists of ten overlapping parent and teacher items (Conners, 1973). As with the other Conners scales, the rater reports the degree to which the child exhibits each behavior from not at all (0) to just a little (1) to pretty much (2) to very much (3).

The final procedure suggested by Barkley is direct observation. In the home compliance and stimulus-consequence patterns are important. In the school social interaction is equally important, along with behaviors such as "out of seat," aggression, disruption, attention, and

vocalization. Several coding systems exist as aids in direct assessment, but a certain degree of training in their use is required.

Treatment

Pharmacologic.   The use of medication for the hyperactive child is usually traced to Bradley's use, in 1937, of amphetamines (benzedrine) for behavior disorders. He noted that distractible and overactive children responded to these stimulants "paradoxically," by becoming more attentive, quieter, and better able to learn (Eisenberg, 1979). Drug treatment is ubiquitous today, with the amphetamines, methylphenidate, pemoline, and imipramine being the medications of choice (Laufer and Shetty, 1980; Winsberg, Yepes, and Bialer, 1976). Table 10-6 provides additional information about these agents.

The effects of stimulant medication on hyperactivity have been examined in a wealth of

Table 10-4 Illustration of Interview Format Suggested by Barkley

Examiner: How does your child generally behave when there are visitors at your home?

Mother: Terrible! He embarrasses me tremendously.

E : Can you give me some idea of what he does specifically that is bothersome in this situation?

M: Well, he won't let me talk with the visitors without interrupting our conversation, tugging on me for attention, or annoying the guests by running back and forth in front of us as we talk.

E : Yes? And what else is he likely to do?

M: Many times, he will fight with his sister or get into something he shouldn't in the kitchen.

E : How will you usually respond to him when these things happen?

M: At first I usually try to ignore him. When this doesn't work, I try to reason with him, promise I'll spend time with him after the visitors leave, or try to distract him with something he usually likes to do just to calm him down so I can talk to my guests.

E : How successfully does that work for you?

M: Not very well. He may slow down for a few moments, but then he's right back pestering us or his sister, or getting into mischief in the kitchen. I get so frustrated with him by this time. I know what my visitors must be thinking of me not being able to handle my own child.

E : Yes, I can imagine it's quite distressing. What will you do at this point to handle the situation?

M: I usually find myself telling him over and over again to stop what he is doing, until I get very angry with him and threaten him with punishment. By now, my visitors are making excuses to leave and I'm trying to talk with them while yelling at my son.

E : And then what happens?

M: Well, I know I shouldn't, but I'll usually grab him and hold him just to slow him down. More often, though, I may threaten to spank him or send him to his room. He usually doesn't listen to me though until I make a move to grab him.

E : How often does this usually happen when visitors are at your home?

M: Practically every time; it's frustrating.

E : I see. How do you feel about your child creating such problems in front of visitors?

M: I find myself really hating him at times (*cries*); I know I'm his mother and I shouldn't feel that way, but I'm so angry with him, and nothing seems to work for me. Many of our friends have stopped coming to visit us, and we can't find a babysitter who will stay with him so we can go out. I resent having to sacrifice what little social life we have. I'm likely to be angry with him the rest of the day.

Copyright by Guilford Press, 1981. Reprinted with permission from R. Barkley, Hyperactivity. In E. Mash & L. Terdal (eds.) *Behavioral Assessment of Childhood Disorders.* New York: Guilford Press, 1981.

relatively well-designed and well-controlled research. In fact, no other group of psychoactive drugs used with children has been as well investigated (Barkley, 1981b). There is no doubt that immediate and short-term benefits accrue (Cantwell, 1975; O'Leary, 1980; Ross and Pelham, 1981; Ross and Ross, 1976; Sroufe, 1975). Weiss (1979) notes that the following improvements have been discerned: reduced aggression, more goal-directed activity; more sustained attention, decreased impulsiveness, improved short-term memory, better performance on rote-learning and fine motor tasks. Overall, it is believed that stimulants increase attention and decrease impulsivity, which in turn may improve perception, motor ability, and learning. Nevertheless, academic achievement does not appear to be influenced very much. The specific way in which these drugs act is still disputed, but their relationship to the neurotransmitters, dopamine and norepinephrine, is being intensively studied (Shetty, 1979;

Table 10-5   A Few of the Items on the Conners Teacher Rating Scale

Restless or overactive
Excitable
Sits fiddling with small objects
Difficulty in concentrating
Inattentive
Oversensitive
Temper outbursts
Disturbs other children
Destructive
Appears to be unaccepted by group

From Conners, 1969.

actives (Rapoport et al., 1978; Weingartner et al., 1980).

When the short-term ameliorative effects of medications were first noted, it was assumed that continued pharmacological treatment would result in trouble-free adolescents or young adults (Weiss, 1979). However, physicians began to report that many children who they had treated for several years still had serious difficulties. In particular, these patients continued to display academic deficits and antisocial behavior, and were socially rejected. Subsequent follow-up research tends to show that hyperactive children improve over time but still have academic and social problems (Charles and Schain, 1981; Hoy, Weiss, Minde, and Cohen, 1978; Keogh and Barkett, 1980; Milich and Loney, 1979; O'Leary and O'Leary, 1980). Furthermore, long-term medication appears to be of no greater value than short-term treatment (Charles and Schain, 1981).

Soyka, 1979). On the surface, these stimulants seem to sedate, because the overactive child calms down. This paradoxical effect occurs, it is proposed, because hyperactivity involves an underaroused CNS that causes a quest for stimulation. The medication normalizes the CNS, thereby eliminating the restless seeking of stimulation. Whether this speculation will hold remains to be seen. It is challenged, however, by demonstrations that normal children respond to the medications in a manner similar to hyper-

Other weaknesses and criticisms of drug efficacy have come to the fore, sometimes with strong condemnation. In *The Myth of the Hyperactive Child* journalists Peter Schrag and Diane Divoky take the position that hyperactivity (along with learning disability and minimal brain dysfunction) is a societal invention designed to control children's behavior by medication and other procedures. Although this book

Table 10-6   Medications Used in Treatment of Hyperactivity

Generic Name	Proprietary Name	Action	Possible Short-Term Side Effects
Racemic Amphetamine	Benzedrine	CNS Stimulant	Anorexia; insomnia; headache; dryness of mouth
Dextroamphetamine	Dexedrine	CNS Stimulant	Anorexia; nausea; insomnia; stomach aches; headaches; leg pains; dryness of mouth
Methylphenidate	Ritalin	CNS Stimulant	Anorexia; nausea; tension; tachycardia
Pemoline	Cylert	CNS Stimulant	Anorexia; insomnia; nausea; gastrointestinal symptoms; irritability; depression; headache; hallucinations; dyskinesia; skin rash
Imipramine	Tofranil	Tricyclic Antidepressant	Hyperirritability; urinary retention; excessive sedation; insomnia; nausea; skin rash

is informative, its highly charged emotional appeal leads one to suspect an overzealous presentation, at the least (O'Leary, 1980). Nevertheless, overdiagnosis of hyperactivity is of concern. Moreover, less emotional reports of drug treatment have frequently raised the following valid issues (O'Leary and O'Leary, 1980):

1. As many as 30 percent of the children treated may not respond to medication.
2. Failure of drugs to change problem behaviors in the home frequently has been reported. Perhaps this is related to the fact that drugs are usually administered early in the day, and their effects wear off by late afternoon or evening.
3. Negative side effects occur. Although these may be transitory and can sometimes be moderated by change in drug or dosage, they are of concern. Besides the short-term effects listed in Table 10–6, growth retardation, increased heart rate and blood pressure, nervous tics, and drug abuse later in life have been raised as possibilities (e.g., Barkley, 1981b; Winsberg, Yepes, and Bialer, 1976). Further research is needed in this area.
4. It may be disadvantageous to children to be taught to rely on fast-and-easy, external control of their behavior (Whalen and Henker, 1976) rather than to learn other methods. The same can be applied to parental over-reliance on drugs in the treatment of their children.
5. On the other hand, some parents are so resistant to drug use that the approach is virtually precluded. (See Box 10–1).

All these concerns have worked toward the general view that while medications are useful, they are not a panacea and have serious drawbacks. Thus, other treatments vie for a place in the management of the hyperactive child.

Behavioral Intervention. Behavior therapy is probably the second most popular treatment approach. Studies of the efficacy of behavioral methods have varied in design and completeness of control. As an example of this work, we

have chosen one of the earlier studies conducted by O'Leary, Pelham, Rosenbaum, and Price (1976).

These investigators selected children on the basis of the Conners Abbreviated Teacher Rating Scale. Averaging 10 years of age, the youngsters had been referred by their teachers in a lower-middle-class community. Evaluation showed them to be of average intelligence, lagging academically, and overactive as rated by parents on the Werry-Weiss-Peters Activity Scale. They were randomly assigned to a treatment or no-treatment control group. Treatment consisted of ten weeks of home-based reinforcement for meeting academic and social goals in the classroom. The goals were set individually for each child, as were the reinforcers. Teachers completed a daily checklist, which the child carried home. Reinforcers could be earned each day as well as at the end of the week. They consisted of an array of enticing items: special dessert, time playing with parents, dinner at a fast-food restaurant, and the like. There were two dependent measures in this experiment, neither of which showed any initial difference between the groups. The Problem Behavior Rating Scale was an individualized list of four or five problems rated according to severity. At the end of the treatment period, the experimental group had decreased in ratings and was significantly different from the control group. The second dependent measure was ratings on the Conners Teacher Rating Scale. Here both groups showed decline, but only the change in the treatment group was significant. Thus, the investigation by O'Leary et al. documented that short-term salutary effects could occur in the classroom without medication. The researchers made their view clear with this statement:

It is curious that, although stimulant drugs such as ritalin are recommended 'as adjunctive therapy to other remedial measures' . . . an all-too-common practice seems to be that of medicating these children to the exclusion of other remedial measures. . . . On the basis of other controlled case studies and our own observa-

---

Box 10-1. Attitudes That Affect Pharmacological Treatment of Children

C. Keith Conners (1978) has noted that whether or not a pharmacological agent will be used in treating a child and whether it will be effective depends partly on the attitudes of physicians, the family, and the child involved.

Physicians and other mental health workers have quite diverse dispositions toward drug use. For example, many child psychiatrists, who are often psychodynamically oriented, eschew medication; pediatricians, however, are more organically inclined. Physicians who use drugs halfheartedly achieve poor results, perhaps partly because they do not monitor dosage adequately. Solomons (1973, as cited by Barkley, 1981b) indicated the seriousness of this situation in a study at the University of Iowa Hospitals that revealed that only 55 percent of the hyperactive children on stimulants were adequately monitored. Adequacy was defined as two telephone contacts between the physician and family during a six-month period.

With regard to family attitudes, some families appear to be medication accepting while others are medication rejecting. Parental doubts about drugs can easily undermine any treatment plan. Doubts may arise from a number of sources, such as sensationalistic newspaper articles or previous experience with a child who abused drugs. On the other hand, families may want to rely too heavily on pharmacological agents. This reduces the burden of child management and may even help alleviate guilt about being the cause of the behavioral pathology. Ideally, medication improves the child's behavior to the extent that it is more manageable by parental techniques. Barkley (1981b; 1976) found that the better the parent-child relationship, the more effective was the response of hyperactive children to stimulants. He speculated that mothers who are more appreciative and reinforcing of the initial improvement in their children from drug treatment produce further positive changes.

Finally, the child's attitude is also important. Children usually cooperate in medication use if they have adult support and believe they will be helped. Conners (1978) advocates, however, that they be provided with a suitable explanation so that they do not make idiosyncratic attributions about medication effects. Little would be gained by a child believing that a pill is a "smart pill." It is better to inform the child, "These medicines may help you to be more in charge of yourself" or "They won't take away your school problems, but if you want to do better in school, you may be able to do so" (p. 88).

---

tions, behavior therapy appears to be an effective adjunct (pp. 513–514).

Conclusions drawn from other research, including both group and single-subject designs used in school and home settings, indicate that behavior therapy is the current nonmedical choice for hyperactive children (Mash and Dalby, 1979; Ross and Ross, 1976). This approach assumes that hyperactivity, regardless of etiology, results in conflicts with the social environment that can be treated by focusing on environmental events. Diverse interventions have been applied, but positive reinforcement by teachers and parents is predominant. Family intervention focusing on noncompliance, irritability, and aggression in the home has included training in behavioral observation and contingency management (Dubey, Kaufman, and O'Leary, 1977; O'Leary and Pelham, 1978). A more recent approach centers on cognitive interventions in which the child becomes the locus of his or her own change.

Cognitive behavior modification emphasizes self-regulation in the form of self-observation, self-instruction, and self-reinforcement (Meichenbaum 1977; O'Leary and Dubey, 1979). Self-regulation specifically targets what is considered the heart of the problem of hyperactivity: impulsivity, attentional deficits, and lack of a deliberate approach (Mash and Dalby, 1979). It is assumed that once these primary deficits are overcome, the secondary problems of academic failure and social failure will decrease. Moreover, if the child's behavior is under internal control, generalization to other situations may increase, since it does not depend on the external cues and contingencies in the new situations. Some success has been achieved with cognitive interventions (Barkley, 1981b; Bornstein and Quevillon, 1976; Kauffman and Hallahan, 1979). For example, on-task behavior in the classroom was shown to improve in six hyperactive children when they were trained to follow a set of guidelines and award themselves points for appropriate behavior (Barkley, Copeland, and Sivage, 1980). Nevertheless, continued research is required to validate the assumptions of this approach and pinpoint the situations in which it might be most effective. To date, the procedures seem difficult to implement, and generalization across time and tasks has been weak (Lahey, Delamater, and Kupfer, 1981).

Medication versus Behavior Modification. Since both pharmacological and behavioral interventions are somewhat successful in treating hyperactivity, the question has been posed as to their relative effectiveness. Several studies have directly compared the two approaches. An investigation by Gittelman and her colleagues is widely cited as well designed and well controlled. These researchers randomly assigned hyperactive children to Ritalin, behavior modification with placebo, or Ritalin and behavior modification (Gittelman, Abikoff, Pollack, Klein, Katz, and Mattes, 1980). Behavior modification involved extensive discussion with both teachers and parents, culminating in the stipulation of positive and negative behaviors. Positive reinforcers and punishment (loss of privileges and time out) were controlled by the parents. There was much contact with parents during the eight-week treatment. The dependent measures in this study were ratings and classroom observations involving teachers, parents, psychiatrists, and trained raters. The consistent pattern that emerged was that all treatments were effective but that the combination of Ritalin and behavior modification was the best treatment. Ritalin alone was next best and was not significantly different than the combination treatment except for one instance. Behavior modification with placebo was the least effective, and it was significantly less effective than Ritalin on several measures.

In the study by Gittelman et al., medication dosage reached high levels and a no-treatment control was lacking. These facts do not invalidate the findings, but continued research is warranted. The most useful question is, Under what conditions are what treatments optimal? The specific targeted problems, the child's response to medication, and family and teacher cooperation are of obvious relevance. Use of medication does not appear salutary to poor academic achievement, and continued drug treatment does not improve long-term outcome (Charles and Schain, 1981). It is thus not surprising that behavior modification continues to be highly regarded along with stimulant medication.

The Changing Face of Hyperactivity

In the preceding discussion hyperactivity has been discussed as a behavior problem and diagnosis that is in transition. Many old beliefs about hyperactivity are giving way to new ideas. Perhaps the most central change is a shift of focus from overactivity to attentional deficits. Table 10–7 summarizes other issues discussed by Henker and Whalen (1980) concerning "the changing faces of hyperactivity." It is likely that the next decade will bring new understanding of many of these issues.

LEARNING DISABILITIES

In 1963 representatives from several organizations met at a symposium sponsored by the Fund for Perceptually Handicapped Children. In his address to the conferees, Samuel Kirk (1963) noted that their object of concern was

Table 10-7   The Changing Face of Hyperactivity

Disappearing Myth	New Face
Hyperactivity Resides in the Child	Children are not simply affected by the "Hyperactive Child Syndrome." They vary a great deal and are labeled by different social systems. Understanding is best accomplished by examining person-by-situation interactions.
Hyperactivity is in the Eyes of the Beholder	Objective documentation shows that many hyperactive children do display learning and performance deficits.
Hyperactivity Vanishes with Adolescence	Social and academic difficulties, in particular, tend to continue.
Medication Treatment is Becoming Epidemic	The popular outcry against medication use was based on faulty assumptions that perhaps 10 percent of children were so treated. The figure is more like 1–2 percent and is not increasing.
There is an Optimal Response to Medication	Improvement may come in attention, activity level, social relationships, depending upon the child, situation and dosage.
Hyperactive Children Respond Paradoxically to Stimulant Medication	Evidence that normal children respond similarly to hyperactives questions this assumption.
Stimulant Medication is Necessary and Sufficient for Treatment	Immediate effects are gratifying, but medication use has disadvantages. Behavioral and cognitive behavioral modifications can be adjuncts or even alternatives. Research is needed.

From Henker and Whalen, 1980.

children usually labeled according to either etiology (for example, cerebral dysfunction, MBD, psychoneurological disorder) or behavioral manifestations (for example, perceptual disorders, hyperkinesis, dyslexia). Kirk suggested that the term *learning disability* would encompass all of the target population, avoid the dilemma of establishing brain dysfunction, and point the way to proper assessment and educational remediation.

The term *learning disability* gradually became widely accepted by various professional groups and parents and a field of study grew up around it. Parents whose children might otherwise be labeled mentally retarded were given hope that the problem was limited and could be treated. Teachers were relieved of the suspicion that they were to blame for the failure of certain stu-

dents. School administrators and other concerned professionals were provided with a label that could make children eligible for special services. Thus, the number of youngsters identified as learning disabled grew enormously. Estimates of prevalence vary markedly, however, from 1 to 40 percent, depending upon definition and method (Gottlieb, 1979; Hallahan and Kauffman, 1978; Schapiro, 1979; Zinkus, 1979). It is agreed that boys exhibit learning disabilities more than girls, but estimates of sex ratios are likely to be misleading.

Definition and Clinical Description

Over sixty definitions of learning disabilities exist (Sabatino, 1979). The one proposed by the National Advisory Committee on Handicapped

Children (1968) is now widely employed and accepted as a guideline by the federal government. It states:

Children with special learning disabilities exhibit a disorder in one or more of the basic psychological processes involved in understanding or using spoken or written language. These may be manifested in disorders of listening, thinking, talking, reading, writing, spelling, or arithmetic. They include conditions which have been referred to as perceptual handicaps, brain injury, minimal brain dysfunction, dyslexia, developmental aphasia, etc. They do not include learning problems which are due primarily to visual, hearing, or motor handicaps, to mental retardation, emotional disturbance, or to environmental disadvantage. (p. 34)

DSM-III recognizes learning disabilities as *Specific Developmental Disorders* that are not due to another disorder, for example, to autism or mental retardation. The major subcategories are reading, arithmetic, language, and articulation disorders. Within these the child may function at a level that is normal for younger children; however, it is not assumed that the learning disabled child will simply catch up. Nor is functioning viewed as representing the lower end of a normal continuum.

Several themes are common to the many conceptualizations of learning disabilities (Bryan and Bryan, 1975; Hallahan and Kauffman, 1978; Lilly, 1979b):

1. Most definitions refer to a failure to learn in spite of average or near-average intelligence. A discrepancy is noted between the child's potential to learn and what is being learned. Potential is measured primarily by performance on a general test of intelligence. However, several studies indicate that the learning disabled child tends to have somewhat lower I.Q. (Bryan and Bryan, 1980; Coles, 1978). Since intelligence tests tap the very skills that are posited to be lacking, this finding is not surprising.

2. An uneven pattern of skills is often evident. The child may, for instance, do quite well on tests of writing but not reading, or on receptive but not expressive tasks.

3. By definition learning disabilities are usually viewed as causally independent of emotional disturbance and environmental disadvantage. This is not to say that every learning disabled child is free of emotional problems or the negative effects of low socioeconomic status, but these factors are not considered primary in the disorders.

4. Similarly, physical deficiencies in sensation and motor ability are often excluded. More subtle cognitive deficits are assumed to be operating, and these may involve perception.

5. Academic failure *per se* is not synonymous with learning disabilities, since school performance is the result of many factors. Failure in the educational system may be anticipated, however. Moreover, it is often used to identify the learning disabled child.

6. Finally, dysfunction of the CNS is still commonly assumed. It is at least implied in the definition of the National Advisory Committee on Handicapped Children. Some workers suggest the existence of a maturational lag; that is, that brain development is slower than average and that some parts lag behind others, producing the unevenness of skills.

A number of factor analyses of children's problems have extracted clusters of attributes that are labeled learning disabilities (Lahey, Vosk, and Habif, 1981). The items include difficulties in reading, language and speech, memory, telling time, as well as general disorganization in school performance. However, children receiving the diagnosis show considerable individual differences. Some have difficulties in one academic area and not another, while others show deficits across the board. Antisocial behavior has, for over half a century, been observed to correlate with reading deficits (Berman, 1981; Sturge, 1982), but no one would claim that all learning disabled young-sters are antisocial. Hyperactivity is com-monly—but not always—observed. Thus, there is a need to refine what is meant by learning disabilities and to examine its relationship to other variables. An example of this approach is the study by Delamater, Lahey, and Drake (1981), which provides some support for dif-ferentiating learning disabled children who are hyperactive from those who do not display hyperactivity. These investigators found that the children with hyperactivity scored lower on IQ tests, were more likely to be firstborns, and were more likely to come from families that ex-perienced severe psychosocial stress. There were no differences on physiological measures, perinatal complications, sex, age, and social-class indicators.

What Causes Learning Disabilities?

The simplest and most accurate answer to this question is, "We don't know." Since learn-ing disabilities has so frequently been associ-ated with hyperactivity and minimal brain damage, proposed etiologies and the relevant findings are often similar to or identical with these conditions.

That learning disabilities tend to run in fam-ilies is generally accepted (Benton, 1978; Jan-sky, 1980). For example, reading difficulties have been revealed in 37 to 90 percent of rel-atives of dyslexic children, depending upon the criteria for the disorder. Prevalence in the pop-ulation at large is estimated at 10 percent. In the few twin studies that have been conducted, monozygotic twins were concordant in every instance, while dizygotic twins showed about 33 percent concordance (Benton, 1978). To date, it is suspected that genetic factors play some role, but further research is needed to establish the strength of inheritance and distinguish it from environmental family variables.

It is a truism that brain function is involved in learning. We know, too, that particular areas of the brain are primary sites for specific func-tions; for example, the left frontal hemisphere is primary for language skills. But it has so far

not been possible to conclusively pinpoint an-omalies in the brain or nervous system with most specific learning disorders. Research goes forward in neurological, neurophysiological, and neurochemical analyses (Coles, 1978; Feuerstein, Ward, and LeBaron, 1979).

As with hyperactivity, ecological variables such as exposure to lead and dietary compo-nents have been implicated in etiology; their role, if any, remains unclear. By most defini-tions of learning disabilities, the effects of en-vironmental deprivations are automatically excluded. However, this is unsatisfactory to some workers in the field, who, like Sabatino (1979), argue that problems in learning must be viewed within the context of motivational and social factors. Environmentally disadvantaged youngsters are at risk for learning disorders, and we might suspect that an array of social ex-periences could underlie their functioning. This view seems more popular among those who adopt a broad, less precise definition of learning disabilities that comes close to general academic failure.

At the psychological level it is speculated that deficits in information processing underlie learning deficits. Much of the relevant research has focused on attention and perception in chil-dren who are considered hyperactive or brain damaged, or who display reading problems. Bryan and Bryan (1980) have reviewed some of the evidence pertaining to the widely held prop-osition that attentional deficits are central. At least some learning disabled children appear distracted by irrelevant stimuli and unable to maintain attention to appropriate stimuli (e.g., Anderson, Halcomb, and Doyle, 1973; Keogh and Margolis, 1976). A number of investiga-tors have implicated impulsivity, in that im-pulsive children attend less to the distinctive features of stimuli than reflective children (Ka-gan, 1965; Keogh and Margolis, 1976). Im-pulsivity also has been found to be related to academic failure.

Various perceptual deficits have been pro-posed as explanations for learning disabilities. There is some evidence that brain-damaged children have deficits in discriminating tones and that learning disabled youngsters have difficulty in synthesizing sounds (Conners, Kramer, and Guerra, 1969; Dykman, Ackerman, Clements, and Peters, 1971). Brain-damaged subjects also have been shown to be deficient in reproducing sequences of flashing lights (Poppen, Stark, Eisenson, Forrest, and Wertheim, 1969) and in responding quickly and accurately to visual stimuli (Czudner and Rourke, 1970; Dykman et al., 1971). Poor readers respond slowly to visual input and have difficulty in perceiving critical details of geometric lines and letters of the alphabet (Goyen and Lyle, 1971; Lyle and Goyen, 1968). Bryan and Bryan (1980) caution that many factors, including age, complexity of the tasks, and type of task, influence performance on perceptual tasks. Moreover, verbal skill may be involved in, for example, sound discrimination and perceptual memory tasks. Given the enormous current interest in cognition, we might anticipate that our knowledge of the psychological correlates of learning disabilities will increase rapidly.

Specific Learning Disabilities

Children who are labeled learning disordered may display one or more specific disorders.

Language. Developmental language disorder involves difficulty in comprehending oral language or in expressing verbal language. Its prevalence is estimated from 1 to 8 per 1,000 children in the general population (American Psychiatric Association, 1980; Baker and Cantwell, 1980; Weiner, 1980). Developmental language disorders are more common in boys than in girls, and the receptive type, which is considered more serious, is less prevalent than the expressive type. Other terms for the disorders are *aphasia* or *developmental aphasia*. Although not accurate (since *aphasia* means loss of language that was already acquired), these terms remain popular. However, *dysphasia* is also being used in their place. Language retardation is often apparent by 18 months of age or earlier. Even simple words such as *mama* and *dada* may be absent, and gestures are employed to gain whatever is desired. Dysphasic children seem to want to communicate, however: They maintain eye contact, enjoy games such as pat-a-cake, and relate to others (Baker and Cantwell, 1980).

Receptive language disorders involve failure to develop comprehension—to decode language—as well as failure to develop vocal expression—to encode language. The child may appear deaf at times, and he or she does not respond to speech and may show little interest in television. When language production begins, it is marked by poor articulation, limited vocabulary, and jargon. Echolalia may be present, and frustration on the part of the child is evident. Language acquisition occurs only gradually. In the expressive type of dysphasia the essential feature is a failure to develop vocal expression despite comprehension of language. The child seems to have 'inner language'; that is, to know age-appropriate concepts and to understand. Thus, he or she obeys simple commands, uses objects correctly, and points to objects when they are named.

Since language is intricately tied to virtually all intellectual and social endeavors, children with language difficulties may be broadly affected. Language is part of the "basics" of reading, writing, and arithmetic, as well as of cognitive strategies such as rehearsal, mediation, and concept formation. With regard to social relationships, little systematic research has been conducted, and both poor and good adjustment have been reported (Bryan and Bryan, 1975; Weiner, 1980). Socioemotional problems may be anticipated in cases in which rejection and isolation from others has occurred. Social relationships may also be disturbed in subtle ways because the language disordered child is delayed in becoming a competent communicator.

Articulation. Although articulation is part of language skill, it is usually placed under the rubric of speech rather than language. Baker and Cantwell (1980) have summarized what is known about this disorder.

Articulation disorder occurs in the presence of language development that is in the normal range. Its essential feature is failure to develop consistent articulations of the later-acquired speech sounds, such as *r, sh, th, f, z, l,* or *ch.* The condition cannot be accounted for by structural, physiological, or neurological anomalies. Prevalence figures are not available, but articulation problems are common and occur with greater frequency in boys than in girls.

Children with articulation disorder may distort, substitute, or even omit the phonemes (speech sounds) they are unable to articulate. In distortion the phoneme is approximated but said incorrectly. Substitutions involve the use of incorrect phonemes for the more difficult ones—for example, in *wabbit* for *rabbit* and *fum* for *thumb.* In omissions, the most severe misarticulation, difficult phonemes are entirely missing, as in *bu* for *blue* and *wha a* for *what's that.* There is a good deal of inconsistency, however. A phoneme may be produced correctly in one sentence and incorrectly in the next. Articulation in a single word may be better than the articulation that occurs when a long phrase is used. Speaking rapidly usually results in more faulty pronunciation.

The cause of articulation disorder is unknown, but constitutional factors seem of major importance. Maturational delay is believed to be involved, and a high proportion of children with the disorder have relatives with a similar disorder. However, second-born children, twins, and children of low SES are disproportionately identified, and it is now thought that inadequate speech stimulation and reinforcement put the child at risk.

In mild cases spontaneous recovery is common. After the fourth grade treatment is usually indicated to remediate any remaining difficulties. Severe cases are seen, however, in which speech is virtually unintelligible. Immediate treatment, the earlier the better, is then warranted, particularly because these children are the victims of much teasing and frustration. Shyness, enuresis, and stuttering may result, and older children may have school problems, especially with reading.

Reading. The inability to read probably has greater consequences at this time than ever before in history. In agrarian societies of the past, the skill of reading enhanced one's social and economic status. In today's technical societies it is a prerequisite for virtually all areas—work, leisure, consumerism, politics—in short, all day-to-day activities.

As early as 1877 attention was called to "word blindness," a disorder in which individuals were unable to read in spite of normal vision, intelligence, and speech (Goldberg and Schiffman, 1972). The condition was once labeled *alexia,* which technically means the loss of a previous ability to read. Orton suggested the term *strephosymbolia,*—twisted symbol—to denote the frequency of letter reversals. *Dyslexia,* more technically correct, is commonly used today, along with *developmental dyslexia.*

The essential features of developmental reading disorder is impairment in reading skills not accounted for by intelligence level or inadequate schooling. Children who display problems in reading may also show subtle language deficits, such as impaired sound discrimination and difficulties in sequencing. Their spelling may be characterized by bizarre errors. Behavioral problems may include overactivity, inattention, and impulsivity. A proportion of the children, especially the younger ones, may also show soft neurological signs.

The prevalence of developmental reading disorder in the general population of children is estimated at between 3 and 15 percent (Jansky, 1980). It is higher in boys than in girls and

Figure 10–1. The writing of some children with learning disabilities shows mirror images and reversal of letters.

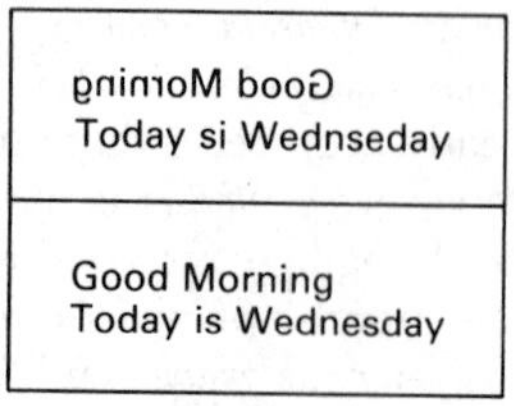

higher than average in juvenile offenders and among the socioeconomically disadvantaged.

Many researchers have suggested that specific impairment in brain function underlies reading problems. Orton (1937), for whom the well-known Orton Society is named, proposed that a lack of cerebral dominance is responsible for the reversals and mirror images often displayed in the writing of reading disabled children. This led to the idea that left-handedness, left-eyedness, or mixed laterality (that is, where the person is right-handed and left-eyed, or vice versa) are related to reading problems. However, this does not appear to be the case, although confusion between right and left is associated with reading problems (Jansky, 1980; Ross, 1976; Rourke, 1978; Rutter, 1978d). Some support for biological factors has been found in reports of higher incidence of prenatal/perinatal problems, neurological signs, and EEG abnormalities (Jansky, 1980; Rutter and Yule, 1975). The view is growing, though, that reading disorder is determined by a multitude of factors—failure in the maturation of certain cerebral functions, neurological damage, lack of environmental stimulation, family and school circumstances—or some combination of these (Yule and Rutter, 1976).

Much of the speculation and research about reading has concerned psychological operations. Reading is a complex process (Rutter, 1978d). It involves perceptual discriminations such as closure (for example, between O and C), line-to-curve transformations (for example, between V and U), and rotational transformations (for example, between b and d or M and W). Sequencing ability is needed to distinguish *dog* from *god* and to know that *Ann loves Rob* does not mean the same as *Rob loves Ann*. Transferring information from one sensory system to another is required in reading-related tasks such as taking dictation. Linguistic skill is necessary to derive meaning from the written symbols; the child who reads mechanically without understanding is hardly reading at all. Thus, attention, perception, and higher thinking processes are all involved in reading.

Theories of reading disorders fall into three types: perceptual deficit, inadequate sensory integration, and verbal-processing deficit (Bryan and Bryan, 1975). The *perceptual deficit* hypothesis, which probably has been the most popular explanation, argues that abnormalities in visual perception underlie reading problems. Investigators have sought to understand the perceptual operations involved, for example, in errors such as confusing p and q and reading from right to left. Theories that posit inadequate *sensory integration* suggest that at least some poor readers have difficulty in integrating information received from the senses, particularly auditory and visual information (Belmont and Birch, 1965). The *verbal deficit* hypothesis argues that poor readers are deficient in one or more areas of verbal processing: vocabulary, ability to name objects, ability to categorize verbal concepts, syntax, phonetics, and the like (Vellutino, 1979). Although the importance of language to reading is widely acknowledged, these three explanations still vie with one another. The perceptual deficit and sensory integration hypotheses have been severely criticized by Vellutino (1979), who stresses the critical importance of linguistic knowledge.

In fact, no clear picture exists concerning the relative importance of particular skills in reading. A few investigations have distinguished groups of dyslexic children on the basis of types of deficiencies. Mattis, French, and Rapin (1975) identified three deficits that accounted for 90 percent of their dyslexic population: language, dysarticulation-motor coordination, and visual perception. Two other studies revealed similar groupings and also found evidence for a group of children whose main difficulty was sequencing (Mattis, 1978). Interestingly, language disorder was far more prevalent than the other deficits. Drawing on other kinds of evidence, Rutter (1978d) has reported on the importance of language and speech. In one study one-third of the speech-retarded but only one-twentieth of the control children were behind in reading and spelling two years after starting school. In contrast, visual perception appeared less important. How can this be explained when visual discrimination is so obviously a part of reading (Kavale, 1982)? Rutter suggests that older children, even with perceptual deficits, may still reach the level of performance required for reading. In this case impairments in visual perception may be more important in the etiology of reading disorders in younger children. There is, in fact, some evidence for this (Bryan and Bryan, 1975). For the present, the presumption that several independent causal deficits underlie dyslexia is a tenable hypothesis (Mattis, 1978).

Arithmetic. Developmental arithmetic disorder, or *dyscalculia,* is diagnosed on the basis of the child's performance on arithmetic tasks, which must be significantly below other school subjects, other achievement test scores, and full-scale IQ. Its prevalence is unknown (Cantwell, 1980b). Researchers differ in their estimates of how widespread problems in mathematical ability are, because there are varying diagnostic criteria and assessment procedures. Also, there has been a dearth of research regarding arithmetic deficits in comparison to language and reading difficulties. One possible explanation for the vast difference is that there seems to be less of a social stigma associated with poor mathematics skill. It is quite possible that children with marked difficulties in arithmetic are not identified early unless they show problems in language, reading, and the like (Rourke and Strang, 1978). It is recognized that spatial ability, verbal ability, and problem-solving ability all play a role in learning mathematics (Bryan and Bryan, 1980).

Neurological deficits have been proposed as interfering with mathematics operations. The connection between brain dysfunction and dyscalculia stems from early clinical studies with adults who suffered brain damage (Cantwell, 1980b; Bryan and Bryan, 1975). Monozygotic twin studies that show high correlations between twins' performance on mathematical tasks suggest a genetic predetermination to developmental arithmetic disorder. However,

Bartel (1975, cited by Johnson, 1979) identifies ineffective instruction as a causal factor. Cantwell (1980b) notes that developmental arithmetic disorder is probably multiply determined through the interaction of various social, emotional, cognitive, genetic, and situational variables.

Treatment and Assessment

Although learning disabilities have primarily been viewed as an educational problem (Strichart and Gottlieb, 1981), they have been addressed by several disciplines. Overall, treatment and assessment have strongly emphasized presumed underlying processes. Many efforts clearly draw on the assumption of MBD and thus attempt to measure and remediate the hypothesized correlates of such biological dysfunction (Lahey, Vosk, and Habif, 1981; Lahey, Delamater, and Kupfer, 1981). Methods oriented toward motor and perceptual deficits that are presumed to interfere with learning were among the earliest to capture the imagination of some of the best educational specialists. More recently a shift has occurred toward inferred underlying cognitive processes, such as communication and attentional mechanisms. However, many professionals are now disputing the usefulness of focusing on *any* underlying general psychological processes; they argue instead for behavioral analysis of each child's performance on specific academic tasks.

Perceptual-Motor Approaches. The hypothesis that motor and perceptual-motor development is intricately tied to learning disabilities had early roots. Kephart (1971), Cruikshank (1977), Frostig (1972), and Barsch (1967) are among those who espoused this proposition and constructed treatment programs aimed at perceptual-motor training.

An example of this approach is the work of Kephart (1960; 1971), who posited that children develop through a hierarchy of six stages—from the motor, through the perceptual, to the conceptual-perceptual. In some learning disabled children this progression is assumed to

Visual-motor activities like working with blocks, puzzles, and pegboards are considered critical by some theorists in the treatment of some learning-disabled children.

have broken down, and treatment requires special experiences to produce normal developmental outcomes. Kephart advocated individual assessment and emphasized deficits in early motor-perceptual abilities. Various activities were suggested to train the child to integrate and manipulate information received from the environment (Kirk, 1972). The activities included (1) the use of walking boards, trampolines, and games to teach movement, (2) chalkboard exercises to develop the matching of movement and visual perception, and (3) form perception exercises such as peg boards and puzzles. All activities were designed to establish a "perceptual-motor match" in which children receive information from their own movements that allows them to monitor the correctness of their perceptions and motor actions.

Another method that has enjoyed considerable success is Frostig's visual-perception method. Frostig and Horne (1964) delineated five areas of visual perception that they considered critical to learning:

Eye-hand coordination, which involves, for example, the child being able to draw a line accurately between two other lines.

Figure-ground discrimination; that is, the perception of a figure as separate from the background of the stimulus.

Shape constancy, which involves recognition of shape regardless of size, position, and context.

Position in space, in which reversals and rotations of figures are discriminated.

Spatial relationships of forms and patterns.

The Frostig method of treating the learning disabled child consists of evaluation of these areas and a specific program of practice in the form of worksheets. The evaluative instrument, the Developmental Test of Visual Perception, has been used in assessing learning disabilities. It should be noted, however, that Frostig herself employs many diagnostic tests and eclectic remediation (Kirk, 1972).

Behavioral Approaches.

Behavioral approaches to learning disabilities are based on the belief that certain children have not learned to act appropriately in the learning situation, for whatever reason. In addition to its theoretical assumption, the behavioral approach grew from criticisms of earlier treatment methods, particularly those that stressed perceptual processes and training. Some of these criticisms were described by Strichart and Gottlieb (1981). For example, Hammill and Larsen (1974) concluded that the hypothesized relationship between perceptual skills and academic performance is untenable; Vellutino (1979) criticized the visual-perceptual hypothesis of reading; Ross (1976) allowed that "nobody ever learned to read by balancing on a walking beam" (p. 168). Arter and Jenkins (1977) failed to find improvement from modality preference instruction, a widely employed approach that addresses the perceptual modality of strength (for example, teaching reading by the sight method rather than by phonics to children with visual but not auditory strengths). These authors also seriously questioned the diagnostic-prescriptive teaching technique that is dominant in special education. This technique consists of matching instruction to the individual needs of the child, based on diagnosis of abilities such as visual or auditory skills. On the surface, such a tactic may seem quite reasonable. However, Arter and Jenkins (1979) found no support for the hypothesis that remediation of weak "underlying" abilities improves academic performance.

For the most part, behavioral intervention emphasizes the application of contingencies, primarily positive reinforcement for desired behaviors. Since learning disabled children often display impulsive, disruptive, restless, nonattentive, or overactive behavior, these have been successfully targeted for change. Nevertheless, reduction of behavior viewed as interfering with learning frequently has not resulted in academic improvement (Kauffman and Hallahan, 1979; Lahey, Delamater, and Kupfer, 1981). Thus, some researchers argue that attention deficits, impulsivity, and overactivity should not automatically be the aim of intervention (Lahey, Vosk, and Habif, 1981). Instead, *specific academic deficits* must be pinpointed and changed. Children who reverse letters can be reinforced for nonreversals; those who lack adequate vocabulary can be rewarded for recognizing and using new words. Systematic efforts to improve academic deficiencies have been shown to be effective, although identifying the most appropriate ways to teach academic skills to the learning disabled is still a major area of inquiry (Strichart and Gottlieb, 1981). It is of considerable interest that targeting school performance itself may also change behaviors that interfere with learning. For example, Ayllon, Layman, and Kandel (1975) worked with three hyperactive children in a learning disabilities class. When the Ritalin these children had been taking was discontinued, inappropriate behavior initially increased. However, a token program that rewarded math and reading performance resulted not only in large academic improvement but also in control of hyperactivity (Figure 10-2). Such a finding argues for direct targeting of learning deficiencies rather than presumed underlying deficits.

Nevertheless, it would be a mistake to imply that each learning disabled child can be treated in an identical manner. In the study by Ayllon et al. it was not necessary to train academic skills; merely reinforcing them was sufficient. Apparently, the children involved already had the requisite skills. Other children might have

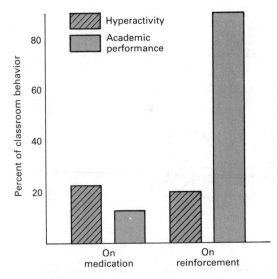

Figure 10-2. Average percentage of hyperactivity and academic performance for three children when they were on medication and off medication with reinforcement for academic tasks. *From Ayllon, Layman, and Kandel, 1975.*

required instruction. As always, individual assessment paves the way for proper treatment.

SUMMARY

Hyperactivity and learning disabilities have long been associated with each other and with the concept of minimal brain dysfunction. Nevertheless, these disorders do not necessarily occur together, nor can MBD be assumed.

Most estimates of hyperactivity put its prevalence at about 5 to 10 percent in school-age children, with higher prevalence in boys than in girls. Hyperactivity is usually diagnosed on the basis of overactivity, poor attention, and impulsivity. Recent emphasis on attentional deficits has resulted in a new diagnostic term: *attention deficit with hyperactivity.* Conduct disorder and academic deficit are very often secondary manifestations. Whether or not hyperactivity should be considered a syndrome is not agreed upon.

Many variables have been implicated in the etiology of hyperactivity, including genetics, perinatal factors, nervous system dysfunction, diet, lead, lighting, and psychosocial circumstances. The latter is viewed as eliciting or maintaining the disordered behavior rather than originating it.

The best approach to identifying hyperactivity is to evaluate the child's behavior in specific situations by interviews, rating scales, and direct observation. Pharmacologic treatment, largely with stimulants, is effective in perhaps 70 percent of children—at least in improving many behaviors. However, medication fails to help some children, has side effects, can involve either over- or underreliance on drugs, and does not eliminate later academic and social problems. Behavioral treatment is widely accepted as appropriate, with or without medication.

The term *learning disabilities* refers to children who are at normal or near-normal intelligence but nevertheless fail to learn. Such failure is not attributed to emotional disturbance, socioeconomic disadvantage, or sensorimotor defects. Subtle cognitive deficits (for example, attention, perception) are usually assumed, as is CNS dysfunction.

As with hyperactivity, the full range of causes has been suggested. Genetic mechanisms may be operating in some cases, but clear conclusions about etiology cannot be drawn. The learning disabled child may exhibit one or more specific deficits—in language, articulation, reading, or arithmetic. Much research has been conducted on language and reading, but knowledge of arithmetic disorder lags behind.

At one time it was common to treat the learning disabled child by identifying and training assumed motor-perceptual deficiencies. However, this approach has been severely criticized. Efforts to remediate underlying attention deficits, impulsivity, and overactivity are also of questionable efficacy. The more recent thrust—training specific academic deficits—holds promise but requires more research.

11

CONDUCT DISORDERS

WHAT ARE CONDUCT DISORDERS?

The DSM-III Definition
Empirically Derived Syndromes
Prevalence
The Stability of Conduct Disorders

CAUSES AND CORRELATES
OF CONDUCT DISORDERS

Family Influences
Moral Development
Underarousal and Conduct Disorders
Biological Influences on Conduct
  Disorders

CONDUCT DISORDERED
BEHAVIORS

Aggression
Oppositional-Noncompliant Behavior
Juvenile Delinquency

SUMMARY

Andrew was referred at age thirteen years with a long history of delinquent behavior. Playing truant started when he was six and became more frequent as he got older. When he was nine Andrew was taken to Court for this offence. His behavior at school was disturbed and difficult and he was placed at a day school for maladjusted children. A year later he was suspended from this school for breaking things and was placed at another special school. At eleven he was first taken to Court for theft—on that occasion stealing from an empty shop. Stealing with other boys from shops and yards continued from then on. He lied freely and had a rather belligerent anti-authority attitude. Andrew was a generally friendly and amusing lad who had plenty of friends, most of whom were also delinquent, and also several girlfriends. He was keen on sport and was an outstanding athlete. However, he was quick-tempered, selfish and aggressive to boys outside his circle of friends.

His early development was normal and he gained bladder control by eighteen months of age. Then at age five he started wetting again after a frightening attack in which he was mauled by an Alsatian. His father, who died in a road accident just before Andrew was born, had been an aggressive man who drank and gambled heavily and was usually out of work. His mother was a rather immature woman who had been orphaned in middle childhood and married immediately after she left school. She remarried when Andrew was two. The stepfather was a rather intolerant, selfish man. He had a small business of his own. Andrew had two older brothers both of whom had a long history of delinquent behavior involving theft, breaking and entering and damage to public property. The oldest brother was also a heavy gambler and both had severe difficulties in reading. The three younger sisters posed less of a problem but they were all quick-tempered and one had great difficulties in reading. Andrew was found to be of normal intelligence, but even at fourteen his reading and arithmetic were only

at the standard normally expected of a seven year old. (Rutter, 1975, pp. 244–245)

Andrew's case description illustrates many of the features that characterize children who exhibit aggressive and antisocial behavior. This chapter deals with those children to whom the labels of Conduct Disorder or Juvenile Delinquency are often applied.

WHAT ARE CONDUCT DISORDERS?

The DSM-III Definition

According to DSM-III, the essential feature of the diagnosis of Conduct Disorder is "a repetitive and persistent pattern of conduct in which either the basic rights of others or major age-appropriate societal norms or rules are violated" (DSM-III, p. 45). Four subtypes are distinguished by the presence or absence of social attachments and the presence or absence of aggressive behavior: Undersocialized, Aggressive; Undersocialized, Nonaggressive; Socialized, Aggressive; and Socialized, Nonaggressive. A youth diagnosed as "socialized" Conduct Disorder is likely to have one or more peer-group friendships and to show concern or extend himself or herself for these friends. The term unsocialized refers to an absence of such bonds. Physical violence against a person or property are considered as aggressive behaviors, whereas behavior such as truancy, running away, and persistent lying are considered nonaggressive. The developers of DSM-III acknowledge that the validity of these subtypes is controversial. Other features are also associated with all four subtypes. Difficulties at home and in the community, precocious sexual activity, early abuse of substances such as alcohol, irritability, temper outbursts, recklessness, and poor academic achievement are commonly described. In addition, reports of low self-esteem—often accompanied by an image of toughness, mistrust, and blaming of others—are frequent.

A separate diagnostic category of Oppositional Disorder is also provided by DSM-III. This category has many features in common with conduct disorder (for example, opposition to authority); however, there is an absence of violations of the rights of others and of age-appropriate societal norms. It is unclear from empirical attempts at classification that this distinction is valid, and the behaviors associated with both diagnoses are considered together by many workers (cf. Atkeson and Forehand, 1981).

Empirically Derived Syndromes

Empirically derived syndromes involving aggressive, oppositional, destructive, and antisocial behavior have been identified in a wide variety of studies (cf. Achenbach and Edelbrock, 1978; Quay, 1979). Various authors have named these syndromes Undercontrolled, Externalizing, or Conduct Disorder. The characteristic behaviors associated with these syndromes are listed in Table 11-1. Edelbrock and Achenbach (1980) have also suggested that profile subtypes can be identified. Their findings suggest that conduct disorders, though a stable syndrome over time, are manifested by different patterns of behavior in different age-gender groups and are somewhat different than those suggested by DSM-III.

Prevalence

The exact prevalence of conduct disorders is difficult to establish. Differences in definition and socioeconomic and familial factors clearly influence the number and kinds of problems reported. Nonetheless, aggression—as well as antisocial, oppositional, and similar behaviors—certainly are among the most common childhood problems. Surveys suggest that they account for one-third to one-half of the referrals to mental health centers from parents and teachers (Atkeson and Forehand, 1981). Disobedience, tantrums, demanding, and whining also were among the most common concerns expressed by parents in a private pediatric setting (Mesibov, Schroeder, and Wesson, 1977;

Table 11-1   Characteristics Associated with the Undercontrolled, Externalizing, or Conduct Disorder Syndrome

Fighting, hitting, assaultive

Temper tantrums

Disobedient, defiant

Destructiveness of own or other's property

Impertinent, "smart," impudent

Uncooperative, resistive, inconsiderate

Disruptive, interrupts, disturbs

Negative, refuses direction

Restless

Boisterous, noisy

Irritability, "blows-up" easily

Attention-seeking, "show-off"

Dominates others, bullies, threatens

Hyperactivity

Untrustworthy, dishonest, lies

Profanity, abusive language

Jealousy

Quarrelsome, argues

Irresponsible, undependable

Inattentive

Steals

Distractibility

Teases

Denies mistakes, blames others

Pouts and sulks

Selfish

Adapted from Quay, 1979.

Schroeder, 1979). Many of these behaviors are also reported by parents of children not referred for problems (Achenbach and Edelbrock, 1981). Boys show more of the behaviors associated with conduct disorders than do girls. In most cases the reported ratio is at least 3:1 (Graham, 1979), although DSM-III suggests that the ratios are as great as 4:1 to 12:1. The relationship of conduct disordered behaviors to socioeconomic status is somewhat ambiguous. Most studies indicate little if any relationship between father's occupation and the diagnosis of

Conduct Disorder in the child. This is in contrast to the broad agreement that low income, poor housing, and large families are strongly associated with delinquency and recidivism. As Graham (1979) suggests, social adequacy and material possessions, both of which may be central in the genesis of antisocial behavior, may vary widely among families of fathers in the same occupation.

The Stability of Conduct Disorders

Perhaps the most disturbing aspect of conduct problems is their reported stability over time (e.g., Macfarlane, Allen, and Honzik, 1954; Rutter, Tizard, Yule, Graham, and Whitmore, 1976; Thomas and Chess, 1976). One particular study investigated the stability and change of various dimensions of disturbance in a sample of children aged 6 to 18 years from a representative cross-section of Manhattan, New York, households (Gersten, Langner, Eisenberg, Simcha-Fagan, and McCarthy, 1976). Mothers from 1,034 households were interviewed, responding to a structured questionnaire. On the basis of this information, two psychiatrists also rated each child as to degree of impairment—a rating of 1 indicating minimal impairment, and 5 indicating severe impairment. The 654 items were then factor analyzed to yield dimensions of child behavior. A total of 732 of the original families were available for an interview approximately five years later. This sample did not differ from that portion of the original sample that was not available. The patterns of behavior associated with conduct disorders appear to have remained stable or to have increased over time. Six dimensions exhibited higher than average correlation with psychiatrists' ratings of total impairment. Of these, the three that reflected aggressive or antisocial behaviors (conflicts with parents, delinquency, and fighting) either increased or remained constant. In contrast, the three that tapped nonaggressive behavior (mentation problems—thinking and language, regressive anxiety, and isolation) declined over time.

It is also possible, with reference to the data

compiled by Gersten et al., to examine changes in behavior in a five-year period for specific age groups (Figure 11-1). The authors divided the children into six age cohorts based on their age at the first and second evaluation: (1) 6.7–11.5; (2) 8.4–13.4; (3) 10.6–15.4; (4) 12.6–17.5; (5) 14.4–19.6; and (6) 16.4–21.5. Looking again at the three dimensions reflecting aggression or antisocial behavior, some interesting patterns are evident. Conflicts with parents remained at the same level for younger cohorts but changed more for age groups ranging from later adolescence to adulthood. Fighting (aggression against one's peers) changed the most during middle age periods, while delinquency (antisocial behaviors) showed increased correlations between the two evaluations as age of initial assessment increased.

The effect of aggressive and antisocial behavior also appears to persist beyond childhood. Robins found that for both black and white boys, juvenile antisocial behavior was the single best predictor of adult psychiatric status (Robins, 1966; Robins, Murphy, Woodruff, and King, 1971). Also, follow-up of disturbed adolescents into adulthood revealed that males and females classified as externalizers exhibited

Figure 11-1 Correlations between the first and second evaluations for different age cohorts. *From Gersten, et al., 1976.*

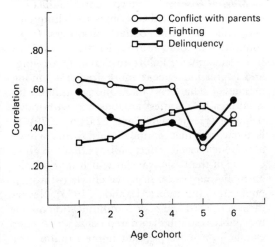

poorer adjustment (as indicated by a variety of academic, employment, socioeconomic, marital, and mental health measures) than did youths classified as internalizers (Hafner, Quast, and Shea, 1975).

CAUSES AND CORRELATES OF CONDUCT DISORDERS

Family Influences

There is widespread agreement that family influences play an important role in the genesis of conduct disordered behavior. A high incidence of deviant or criminal behavior has been reported in families of delinquents and young children with conduct problems (Becker, Peterson, Hellmer, Shoemaker, and Quay, 1959; Glueck and Glueck, 1950; Johnson and Lobitz, 1974a; McCord and McCord, 1958). Furthermore, programs emphasizing improved parenting practices or effective family problem-solving and coping techniques report decreases in antisocial behavior and recidivism rates in untreated siblings. It seems, then, that conduct disordered children are part of a deviant family system. A number of family variables have been implicated in the genesis of aggressive and antisocial behavior (Hetherington and Martin, 1979).

Marital Discord.   Interparental conflict has frequently been cited in homes of delinquents and children with conduct disorders (e.g., Johnson and Lobitz, 1974a; Rutter, 1974b). In fact, detachment, failure to agree, quarreling, and aggression appear more frequent among families of delinquents than among families with children who manifest anxious and withdrawn behavior (Hetherington and Martin, 1979). It is noteworthy that marital discord seems to have a more deleterious effect on boys than on girls.

One of the basic ways in which marital disharmony may cause negative effects is through poor communication (Alexander, 1973). Nevertheless, discord and poor communication do not inevitably result in disordered behavior. A later change to a more pleasant home situation, or the presence of one warm parent, can reduce negative outcomes (Rutter, 1971, 1974b). Hetherington and Frankie (1965), for example, assessed parental conflict, dominance, and warmth in family interactions. In a separate session children imitated the hostile dominant parent if they came from homes high in conflict and with two parents low in warmth. Imitation of an aggressive parent was lower if conflict was low or the other parent was warm.

The high divorce rate has produced increased concern over the finding that children with conduct difficulties often come from broken homes. The relationship is clearly complex and one that we are just beginning to understand (see Box 11-1). The basis for separation; the child's age; the length of separation; characteristics of the child, such as gender; and the level of adjustment of the entire family may all affect the impact of a broken home on the child's development (Ahrons, 1981; Emery, 1982; Kurdek, 1981).

Parent-child Interactions.   The manner in which parents interact with their children also contributes to the genesis of conduct disordered behavior. Although a majority of studies has investigated the impact of a single variable, it has become increasingly clear that a number of different configurations of parenting variables can contribute to the appearance of a conduct problem. As indicated earlier (p. 33), either extreme of the parental control dimension of permissiveness-restrictiveness may lead to aggressive or antisocial behavior, depending, in part, on parental warmth (Martin, 1975). For example, parents who are hostile and restrictive or warm and permissive may both produce children who are aggressive and disobedient, and exhibit poor self-control. The sex of the child, the particular type of conduct disorder, and intra- and interparental consistency of discipline also contribute to making this a complex relationship (Hetherington and Martin, 1979).

Moral Development

Since many of the behaviors characteristic of conduct disorders violate societal rules or

Box 11–1   The Broken Family and Behavior Disorders

National alarm about the effects of broken families on children was well demonstrated in the popularity of the Academy Award–winning film *Kramer vs. Kramer*. Concern is legitimate: According to census bureau figures, a 79 percent increase in the number of single-parent families occurred between 1970 and 1980 (Emery, 1982). Much of this increase is due to the heightened divorce rate. Moreover, divorce has been associated with problems in children, particularly with undercontrol and particularly in boys.

In the vast majority of divorce cases, custody has been awarded to the mother. Thus, despite recent increases in paternal or joint custody (e.g., Clingempeel and Reppucci, 1982), research has concentrated on the impact of father absence. Boys from mother-headed families have been found to be more antisocial, impulsive, and likely to be a member of delinquent groups than boys from families that remain intact. They also exhibit less self-control, delay of gratification, and internalized standards of moral judgment (Hetherington and Martin, 1979).

Why are boys affected more than girls by divorce? The greater aggression of the culturally proscribed male role may result in the necessity for firmer and more consistent discipline of boys. The absence of a male model for related prosocial behavior probably has a greater immediate impact on boys as well. It also appears that boys may actually be exposed to greater stress and have fewer supports following divorce (Hetherington, 1979; Kurdek, 1981).

Although separation from the father clearly may have negative effects (Emery, 1982), it is also reasonable to question the role of the disruption and stress that precede and follow divorce. The single mother may well be faced with excessive responsibilities, financial pressure, little relief or respite, and lack of social and emotional supports. The existence of only a single and female adult model adds additional challenges. In fact, single parenting *itself* does not seem to account completely for the higher incidence of conduct disordered behavior. Girls from single-parent and nuclear families exhibit equivalent and low rates of such problems. Also, children whose fathers died do not usually exhibit these difficulties (cf. Felner, Stolberg, and Cowen, 1975; Hetherington, 1979).

Divorce and death of the father both present the single-parent family with many of the same stresses. However, there are probably also key differences. Social reaction to the two circumstances is likely to differ and produce differences in available support. The mother's reaction to divorce may also provide an example of anger and hostility as a coping technique, while depression and withdrawal are more likely to be modeled following death (Felner, Stolberg, and Cowen, 1975). Clearly, not all children from broken homes exhibit difficulties, and children from well-functioning single-parent homes are probably less prone to adjustment difficulties than children from nuclear families in which conflict is high (Nye, 1957; Porter and O'Leary, 1980; Rutter, 1971).

norms, some workers have related the process of moral development in children to conduct problems. The psychodynamic and behavioral-social learning perspectives emphasize interaction with others as the mechanism by which societal standards become internalized. Both agree that parents play a primary role in this process through resolution of psychosexual conflicts (primarily Oedipal) and through modeling and parenting practices, respectively. Important influences other than parents—peers

and the mass media—also receive significant attention from a behavioral-social learning perspective. Research over the last several decades has documented the role of parents, peers, sex-role socialization, television, guilt, the development of empathy, and cognitive development on moral thought, feeling, and behavior (Ellis, 1982; Hoffman, 1979).

An interesting approach to the question of the moral development of juvenile delinquents has evolved from Piagetian theory (1932/1965).

Kohlberg (1964, 1976) has extended and revised Piaget's original account of how the child's understanding of moral rules undergoes transformations. His stage theory, like Piaget's, is based on the assumption that each stage represents hierarchically more complex and abstract levels of reasoning (Table 11-2). Children are assumed to pass through the stages— (1) punishment and obedience, (2) instrumental relativism, (3) interpersonal concordance, (4) law and order, (5) social contract, and (6) universal ethical principles—in a fixed order. Movement to the next stage occurs only after the reasoning of the earlier stage is mastered. It is also assumed that an individual's level of moral development may stop at any point and

thus be below the level characteristic of most same-age individuals.

An individual child's level of moral reasoning is assessed through administration of hypothetical dilemmas such as the following:

Bill saved up $10 for a catcher's mitt. When he arrives at the store, he sees the sales clerk going down the stairs to the cellar. The clerk doesn't see Bill. Bill looks at the gloves, and just as he sees one he likes, he reaches for his money. It's gone, he realizes he has lost it. He feels awful. It occurs to Bill that the mitt would just fit under his jacket. He hides the mitt and walks out of the store. Now you finish the story. (Kohlberg, 1964, p. 410)

Table 11-2   Levels and Stages of Moral Judgment in Kohlberg's Theory

---

Level I

Preconventional or premoral: Moral and self-serving values are not differentiated.

Stage 1—Punishment and obedience: Goodness or badness of an act is judged in terms of its physical consequences. Avoidance of trouble and deference to superior power are emphasized.

Stage 2—Instrumental relativism: Moral value resides in the instrumental gratification of one's needs and is directed by concrete exchange of favors.

Level II

Conventional: Moral value is defined in terms of social conformity, mutual interpersonal expectations, and interdependent relationships.

Stage 3—Interpersonal concordance: Moral reasoning is guided by stereotyped images of "nice" or "natural" behavior with emphasis on gaining approval and meeting expectations of others.

Stage 4—Law and order: Moral judgment is structured in terms of maintaining the given social order for its own sake and doing one's duty and showing respect for authority.

Level III

Postconventional or principled: The rules and conventions of a particular social system are differentiated from shared or shareable standards and ubiquitous moral principles.

Stage 5—Social contract: Emphasis is placed on individual rights and rational considerations of social utility and welfare guided by democratic processes.

Stage 6—Universal ethical principles: Moral judgment is determined by mutual respect, trust, justice, and equality embodied in principles that appeal to logical universality, comprehensiveness, and consistency. (It should be noted that Kohlberg's longitudinal studies have failed to confirm the sixth stage as a valid developmental construct. It is now seen as an elaboration of the fifth stage.)

Adapted from Jurkovic, 1980. Reprinted by permission of the author.

The child's verbal response to this and other dilemmas are scored to provide an index of moral stage and moral maturity.

Jurkovic (1980), in his review "The Juvenile Delinquent as a Moral Philosopher: A Structural-Developmental Perspective," suggests that while there is support for the notion that immature levels of moral reasoning may contribute to delinquency, the issue is a complex one. A number of researchers have compared the verbal responses of delinquents and nondelinquents to moral reasoning dilemmas and found that delinquents reasoned at preconventional levels (Stages 1 and 2), while nondelinquents functioned primarily at conventional levels (Stages 3 and 4) (e.g., Campagna and Harter, 1975; Hudgins and Prentice, 1973). However, findings of no differences have also been reported (e.g., Fodor, 1972; Jurkovic and Prentice, 1974). At least part of the variability of findings may be due to considering all delinquents as a homogeneous group (Fodor, 1973; Jurkovic and Prentice, 1977).

While available studies may suggest deficiencies in moral reasoning among delinquents, Scharf (1971, cited by Jurkovic, 1980) suggests that contextual influences may affect the level of moral reasoning exhibited. To demonstrate this possibility youthful offenders at a state reformatory were presented with Kohlberg's standard dilemmas as well as with moral dilemmas that represented actual situations that might occur in prison life. One example of the latter raised the question of whether an inmate should act on behalf of a boy from his home town who was being shaken down for cigarettes by older inmates. As Scharf suspected, the average moral maturity score was lower for the prison stories than for the standard dilemmas. Youths who scored at Stage 3 or 4 on the Kohlberg dilemmas tended to regress on their prison stories, while those who scored at Stage 2 on the standard dilemmas maintained this level on the prison stories. Individual scores on the prison story never exceeded the scores on the standard dilemmas. It thus appears that some of the boys adjusted the level of moral reasoning they were capable of exercising to fit the prison situation. McCaan and Prentice (1973) also demonstrated that the delinquents who scored low on a measure of moral development significantly increased their level of moral reasoning when they were given a monetary reward if they could match the teacher's answer.

Jurkovic (1980) suggests that while low levels of moral reasoning appear to place a child at risk for delinquency, even children at normal levels may be at similar risk. A variety of social, behavioral, and emotional variables may affect the level of moral reasoning a child achieves or exhibits; and the relationship between level of competence, moral reasoning employed, and moral behavior is likely to be a complex one. It is also wise to remember that the social context has a profound effect on how the child develops and that level of development need not reflect some inherent deficit. As Brown and Herrnstein (1975) suggest:

Is the thinking of delinquents and criminals largely preconventional because their moral notions have turned them into delinquents or criminals? Or has the preconventional world many of them grew up in caused them to form the only intelligently realistic theories about the way the world works? (p. 325)

Underarousal and Conduct Disorders

Antisocial Personality Disorder (also referred to as psychopathy or sociopathy) is the DSM-III adult diagnosis corresponding to Conduct Disorder in children. It has been suggested that antisocial or psychopathic behavior is, in part, accounted for by a need for stimulation. On the basis of the hypothesis that there is an optimal level of arousal for all human beings, it is reasoned that a person will seek to adjust his or her arousal level when it is either too high or too low. The psychopath is viewed as an individual with chronic underarousal, more rapid adaptation to sensory inputs, and less responsiveness to stimulation than that shown by most people. The psychopath is thus motivated to provide additional arousal. Impulsivity, thrill seeking, and adventurous behavior fulfill the need to avoid boredom and routine. (Quay, 1965, 1977).

The autonomic nervous system plays a central role in emotional states and arousal. If psychopaths have arousal deficits, it might be expected that their autonomic nervous systems would respond atypically. In summarizing the available evidence, Hare (1970) found that psychopathic subjects in a resting state do appear to be less active than normal on a number of autonomic measures. It is not as clear whether psychopaths differ in their autonomic responsiveness to stimulation, but some evidence exists for both lower reactivity and quicker adaptation to stimulation (Borkovec, 1970; Hare, 1970; Quay, 1977).

The underarousal of the psychopath is thought to create a state of sensory deprivation and a resulting need to seek stimulation. In support of this notion, Orris (1969) found that delinquents who had high scores on the conduct disorder dimension, rather than on anxiety-withdrawal or socialized-aggression measures, performed more poorly on a vigilance task that provided little stimulation but required continuous attention. These boys also engaged in more boredom-relieving activities such as singing and talking to themselves. Skrzypek (1969) compared the preferences for novelty and complexity of conduct disorder and anxiety-withdrawal delinquents.

On a pretest the conduct disorder group had higher novelty and complexity scores and a lower anxiety score. The two groups then experienced one of three experimental conditions: perceptual isolation, arousal, or a control condition. After isolation both groups increased their preference for complexity, but the conduct disorder group did so to a greater degree. Only the conduct disorder group increased its preference for novelty. Arousal increased anxiety and decreased preference for complexity for the anxiety-withdrawal group but left the conduct disorder group unchanged. These results seem to support the hypothesis that conduct disorder delinquents may enjoy stimulation seeking. This need for novelty also seems to be present in younger conduct disorder children (DeMyer-

It is hypothesized that thrill seeking may function to relieve underarousal.

Gapin and Scott, 1977; Whitehill, DeMyer-Gapin, and Scott, 1976.).

Biological Influences on Conduct Disorders

Perhaps the most dominant theme involving biological influences concerns the inheritance of aggression or criminality. As early as the late nineteenth century, the Italian physician Lombroso wrote of the "stigmata of degeneration." Law violators were described as a distinct physical type at birth with distinct physical features such as long ear lobes, fleshy and protruding lips, and abundant wrinkles. Females were said to commit fewer crimes because their lesser intelligence and sexual coldness overcame their naturally jealous and vengeful nature (cited in Empey, 1978). This conceptualization had extensive impact on criminology and social policy for over a third of a century, but current-day scientists have accumulated sufficient evidence to reject it. Versions of genetic contributions to antisocial behavior still exist, however. More recent ones generally appreciate that the interactions between biological and environmental factors are so complex that linkages between biology and the various expressions of conduct disorders or criminality will be nowhere as direct as implied in earlier theories.

A sex-chromosome aberration, XYY in males, has received much attention as a basis for criminality. Early reports indicated an association with mental retardation and aggressive behavior (Jacobs, Brunton, and Melville, 1965). The disorder was reported to occur at a high rate among institutionalized criminals. Subsequently, much was made of this disorder as a genetic (although not hereditary) basis for violence. Later research argues against such an interpretation. Witkin, Mednick, and their colleagues (1976) studied over 4,000 men in Denmark and substantiated the earlier reports of atypical height, low intelligence scores, and high incidence of XYY men in penal institutions. These criminal males had not, however, been involved for the most part in violent acts. The investigators considered low intelligence rather than high aggression to be the basis for the criminal behavior. Interestingly, these researchers have offered evidence for low responsiveness and slow recovery of autonomic nervous system reactivity among XYY men (Mednick and Hutchings, 1978).

The relationship between gender and antisocial behavior is another common basis for examining biological influences. Greater aggressiveness among males is probably the most agreed-upon sex difference in the literature (e.g., Hoffman, 1977; Maccoby and Jacklin, 1974). Differential socialization practices are widely viewed as the basis for this finding. However, it is argued by some that differential socialization cannot completely explain sex differences and that the male's greater aggression has a biological component. Several kinds of evidence are noted. Greater mesomorphy (that is, wide shoulders, muscular development)

among males may be a manifestation of some underlying biological structure, or it may merely make it more likely that aggressiveness will be reinforced. Animal research also indicates that although the male exhibits more aggressive behavior, administration of the male hormone either pre- or postnatally makes the female equally aggressive. Finally, males have been shown to have higher activity levels than females—and activity may be a precursor to high levels of aggression (Eme, 1979; Maccoby and Jacklin, 1974).

Rosenthal's (1975) review of the literature leads him to conclude that a connection between heredity and criminality is indicated by adoption and twin studies. He hypothesizes that what is inherited are certain characteristics (for example, body build, EEG abnormalities, sensitivity to alcohol) that make an individual prone to criminal behavior in response to environmental pressures. Thus it appears that, as suggested by Rosenthal, biological influences do contribute to antisocial and criminal behavior, but that environmental influences such as social conditions, family variables, and certain social learning experiences are major factors in determining etiology.

CONDUCT DISORDERED BEHAVIORS

Aggression

Despite a recent trend toward greater interest in its prosocial alternatives (Masters, 1981), the genesis of aggression has been the focus of appreciable research and theorizing.

Freud's Theory. Freud presented two views of aggression. His initial belief was that aggression results from the frustration experienced when id impulses are blocked. Later he revised his theory and viewed aggression, along with libido or the sex drive, as one of two basic instincts. While deviating in some ways from Freud's (1930, 1961) original conceptualization, many analysts still regard aggression as a basic instinct. Emphasis is placed on the anal stage as the period during which the aggressive drive reaches its peak. This means that during this period wishes to harm or destroy are equally as important as the anal interests (for example, elimination and toileting) themselves. The stage therefore involves resolution of themes related to both aggression and toileting. Indeed, it is referred to by some as the anal-sadistic phase (Kessler, 1966).

The Frustration-aggression Hypothesis. The concept of aggression as a response to frustration led to one of the first systematic attempts to study aggressive behavior. John Dollard and his co-workers hypothesized that frustration is always followed by aggression and that aggression is produced only by frustration (Dollard, Doob, Miller, Mowrer, and Sears, 1939). Like Freud, they viewed aggression as a catharsis. Expression of the emotions of frustration are necessary to reduce aggressive impulses. This frustration-aggression hypothesis appears to be too strong a position. Although some aggres-

sion may be a response to frustration, other factors can affect whether or not a child is aggressive. In addition, frustration or other emotional arousal does not always lead to aggression. The cathartic effect of aggressive behavior has been challenged as well (e.g., Mallick and McCandless, 1966). Indeed, aggression has been shown to increase, rather than reduce, the likelihood of subsequent aggressive acts (cf. Patterson, 1976; Slaby, 1975).

Aggression as a Learned Behavior. Although certain antecedents may elicit aggression, greater attention has been paid to how aggression is learned. The majority of this research has been conducted from a social learning perspective. Children clearly may learn to be aggressive by being rewarded for such behavior (Walters and Brown, 1963; Patterson, 1976). For example, Patterson, Littman, and Bricker (1967) found—as predicted—that among nursery school children aggressive acts that were followed by "positive" consequences

Considerable concern has been expressed about children's exposure to aggressive behavior on television and in other media.

(for example, passivity or crying by the victim) were likely to be repeated, while "negative" responses (for example, retaliation or telling the teacher) resulted in the aggressor switching either behaviors or victims. Another interesting finding emerged from this study. Children who were initially passive and unassertive were frequently victimized. They, however, eventually exhibited aggressive behaviors, were reinforced by positive consequences, and increased their frequency of such behavior. While illustrating the importance of reinforcement for aggression, this study also suggests another source of learning—imitation of aggressive models.

A great deal of attention has been focused on how children learn through imitation of aggressive models. Such studies also illuminate the conditions that facilitate the occurrence of imitation. Bandura's (1965) study with nursery school children, described earlier (p. 62), demonstrated that children imitated an aggressive, filmed model and that the consequences experienced by the model affected the performance, but not the acquisition, of imitative aggression. It has also been demonstrated that children may not only learn new and novel responses following observation of an aggressive model, but that aggressive responses that were previously in the child's repertoire are more likely to occur—disinhibition of aggression.

Children certainly have ample opportunity to observe aggressive models. Parents who physically punish their children serve as models for aggressive behavior. In fact, children referred for professional help due to aggressive or antisocial behaviors are likely to have fathers and siblings with records of aggressive and criminal behavior (Hetherington and Martin, 1979) and to have observed especially high rates of aggressive behavior in their homes (Arnold, Levine, and Patterson, 1975; Patterson, 1976). But coercive behaviors also occur at high rates in homes of normal families (Jones, Reid, and Patterson, 1975) and in the classroom (Patterson et al., 1967). Exposure to aggression is also ubiquitous on television and in other media (see Box 11–2).

Box 11–2   Does Watching Televised Aggression Cause Aggressive Behavior?

Soon after television gained popular appeal, critics and parents alike began to express concern about its influence on children. They had good reason: The young seemed especially attracted to the new medium and sat "glued" in front of the TV set for an average of two to three hours daily (Liebert and Poulos, 1976). Concern heightened as aggression and violence became the dominant theme of television entertainment in the 1960s and 1970s. Amid much controversy researchers took to the laboratory and the field to determine whether the young were adversely affected by their new "baby sitter." On the surface the task appeared simple enough. In fact, it was not. Since children are exposed to so many influences, how could the effects of one be isolated? Several years of investigation, employing different methods, were required before the evidence was in.

Experimental laboratory research was conducted in which children's aggression was measured subsequent to their viewing either aggressive or nonaggressive models on television. Overall, compared to control children, those who saw the aggressive examples later displayed similar behaviors (Liebert, Sprafkin, and Davison, 1982; Stein and Friedrich, 1975). This finding held across the age span from early childhood to late adolescence. The studies were compelling because they were experimental in design and well controlled. They thus established that viewing televised aggression could cause aggression in children under certain conditions. At the same time, however, the laboratory setting raised doubts that the findings would generalize to the "real" world. Researchers attacked this problem with experimental field studies and correlational research.

An example of experimental field research is the work of Stein and Friedrich (1972), which examined the cumulative effects of different TV content on nursery school children. During an initial measurement period the free play of the children, ages 3½ to 5½, was observed and rated. The youngsters were then systematically exposed for a four-week period to either aggressive cartoons (such as Batman and Superman), prosocial programs from Mister Rogers' Neighborhood, or neutral programming. During this time and during a two-week postviewing period, the children's free-play behavior continued to be observed. Children who were initially in the upper half of the sample in terms of interpersonal aggression exhibited greater aggression when playing if they had been exposed to aggressive programming rather than prosocial or neutral programming. These results were especially important because the effects occurred in a naturalistic setting rather than in a laboratory and because a cause-and-effect relationship could be drawn from the experimental design. Stein and Friedrich found that despite the fact that the children watched less than six hours of television over a four-week period, aggressive behavior, removed in time and setting from the viewing experience, was affected.

Moving even closer to the "real" world has been correlational research, designed to determine the association between aggression in the natural environment and the viewing of television violence. The most extensive work in this area is that of Eron and his colleagues. In the *Rip Van Winkle Study* Eron, Huesmann, Lefkowitz, and Walder (1972) studied a sample of 875 children who constituted the entire third-grade population of a semirural county in New York. The researchers found a relationship between the amount of television violence subjects watched when they were 8 or 9 years old and how aggressive they were at the time. Even more interesting was the finding of a relationship between the early television viewing and aggressiveness at age 19. Among the 475 subjects who could be located ten years later, it was found that, for boys, preference for violent television programs during the third grade was significantly related to both peer- and self-rated

measures of aggression at age 19. In fact, amount of early viewing of violent television predicted later aggression better than any of the other variables measured, such as IQ, social status, religious practice, ethnicity, and parental disharmony. Another follow-up of these males is in progress. Meanwhile, Eron and his colleagues have turned to a new population of youngsters.

The *Chicago Circle Study* followed approximately 750 children, ages 6 to 10 years, for three years. Viewing of TV violence was positively associated with aggressive behavior, but this time for both boys and girls. This same finding is showing up in replications of the study in Finland, Poland, and Australia (Eron, 1982). The *Chicago Circle Study* was also designed to further examine some of the variables and processes implicated in the *Rip Van Winkle Study*. An interesting picture is emerging of the aggressive child who watches violent television. Observation of aggressive models does cause aggression, but aggressive children also prefer to watch more and more violent TV. It is likely that since aggressive youngsters are unpopular, they spend more time in front of the television set. TV violence may assure them that their own behavior is appropriate and teach them new coercive techniques. When coercion is used with peers, the youngsters become increasingly unpopular and are driven back to television watching. In addition, aggressive children appear to be low achievers, and they may have fewer resources to deal with the world. They tend to identify strongly with TV characters and thus more readily adopt the violent lessons of the medium. Peer isolation and excessive TV watching may also increase school failure. Thus, a circular process may be operating that involves adoption of aggressive behavior, unpopularity, low achievement, and excessive television watching.

The Work of Patterson and His Colleagues. Gerald Patterson and his colleagues, operating from a social learning perspective, have developed an intervention program for families with aggressive children (Patterson, Reid, Jones, and Conger, 1975). Patterson has

developed what he refers to as coercion theory to explain how a problematic pattern of behavior develops in children labeled aggressive. Observations of referred families suggest that acts of physical aggression are not isolated behaviors. On the contrary, they tend to occur along with a wide range of noxious behaviors which are used to control family members in a process labeled coercion. How and why does this process of coercion develop?

Normal child rearing presents mothers with high rates of aversive events, many of which originate from the young child. Although individual constitutional differences in children may account for differences in early rates of such behaviors, it is expected that by the age of about 3 or 4 years, the child has learned an array of nonaversive verbal and motor skills for gaining parent interaction, play, or attention. What, then, goes awry in some families that re-

sults in the child continuing to emit high rates of noxious behaviors?

According to Patterson (1976, 1980), parental deficits in child management lead to an increasingly coercive interaction within the family. The key elements of this process are presented in Figure 11-2. Central to this viewpoint are the notions of negative reinforcement and the "reinforcement trap." For example, a mother asks a child to stop playing with a valuable vase; the child begins to hit the mother; eventually the mother gives in and stops asking the child not to touch the vase. The short-term consequence is that things are more pleasant for

By using physical punishment parents may be inadvertently modeling the aggressive behavior they are trying to discourage.

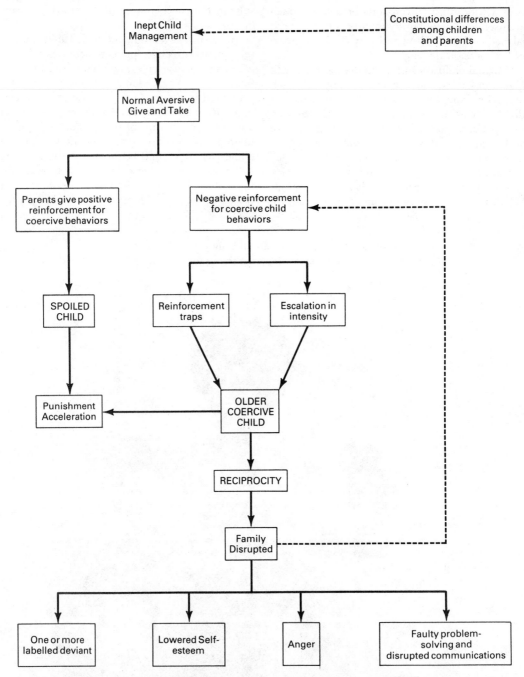

Figure 11–2 A diagram of Patterson's model illustrating how a coercive family system operates. *From Patterson, 1980.*

both parties. The child has used an aversive event (hit) to maintain the status quo (continued play), and the mother's giving in has terminated an aversive event (hit) for her. These short-term gains, however, are paid for in long-term consequences. The mother, though receiving some immediate relief, has increased the probability that her child will employ hitting in the future. She has also been provided with negative reinforcement that increases the likelihood that she will give in to future hitting. In addition to this negative reinforcement trap, coercive behavior may also be increased by direct positive reinforcement. Aggressive behavior, especially in boys, may meet with social approval. Indeed, Patterson and his co-workers have found that parents of aggressive boys provide higher than usual rates of positive consequences for coercive behavior (Patterson, 1976).

The concept of reciprocity also suggests how aggression may be learned and sustained. Children as young as nursery school age can learn in a short time that attacking another in response to some intrusion can terminate that intrusion. In addition, the victim of the attack learns from the experience and is more likely to initiate attacks in the future (Devine, 1971; Patterson, Littman, and Bricker, 1967). Siblings may enter into such interactions as well. The eventual victim of escalating coercion also provides a negative reinforcer by giving in. This also increases the likelihood that the "winner" will start future coercions at higher levels of intensity and thereby get the victim to give in more quickly.

This process is exacerbated by the ineffectiveness of punishment. The finding that in problem families punishment does not suppress coercive behavior but may serve to increase it has been referred to as "punishment acceleration." The ineffectiveness of punishment may be due to a strong reinforcement history for coercive behavior and to inconsistent use of punishment in these families (Patterson, 1976).

Patterson's formulation has led to the development of a treatment program that addresses the entire family and focuses on improved parenting skills (Patterson et al.,

1975). The program developed at Oregon Research Institute teaches parents to pinpoint problems, to observe and record behavior, to more effectively use social and nonsocial reinforcers for appropriate or prosocial behavior, and to more effectively withdraw reinforcers for undesirable behavior. Families are introduced to these procedures by studying a programmed text (Patterson, 1975; Patterson and Gullion, 1968). Each family also attends clinic and home sessions and has regular phone contact with a therapist who helps develop interventions for particular targeted behaviors and who models desired parenting skills. Problematic behaviors in the school setting are also targeted, and interventions involve both the parents and school personnel. Active treatment is terminated when both the therapist and family believe that a sufficient number of problematic behaviors have ceased, appropriate behavior has stabilized, overall family functioning has become more positive, and the parents have become able to handle additional problems with little, if any, assistance.

Patterson (1974) reported on the use of this program for twenty-seven boys with conduct problems. Behavioral and attitudinal measures indicated that treatment was successful in most of the families. In response to questions raised by other investigators concerning the analysis and replicability of the home portion of Patterson's work (Eyberg and Johnson, 1974; Ferber, Keeley, and Shemberg, 1974; Johnson and Christensen, 1975; Kent, 1976), Fleischman (1981) conducted a replication of Patterson's intervention program.

Thirty-five families whose presenting problem centered on the child's aggressive or antisocial behavior participated in the treatment program which, with minor modifications, replicated the program described above. Twenty of the thirty-five families completed the program. Observations by trained observers indicated significant reductions in total aversive behavior for the samples. These behaviors did not increase during the one-year period following termination, suggesting that treatment gains had been maintained. Furthermore, though baseline levels of aversive behavior were greater than in a sample of normal children, the treatment sample was not more deviant than the normal group by the end of follow-up. Decreases in problem behavior were also obtained for the parents' direct observations and their reports of symptom occurrence. Parents' opinions regarding the target child improved; and, encouragingly, for the two attitudes most centrally related to treatment objectives (opinions of whether less aggression and fewer conduct problems existed), positive changes were maintained a year later according to both parents.

It would appear that a social-learning-based program such as that developed by Patterson and his co-workers can be successful in reducing the problem behaviors of boys labeled as aggressive and that modification of problematic parenting skills can serve as the primary mechanism for decreasing the disruptions in these families.

Oppositional-Noncompliant Behavior

DSM-III describes the essential feature of Oppositional Disorder as disobedience, negativism, and provocative opposition to authority figures, particularly the parents. There is a repeated pattern of the child failing to comply with the parents' requests or commands. Indeed, the child is likely to become argumentative or blatantly behave in a manner which is in opposition to the request. Many workers view oppositional and noncompliant behavior as a common feature of a variety of childhood problems, particularly aggressive and antisocial behavior (Forehand, 1977; Patterson, 1976). Children with learning disabilities and young developmentally delayed children have also been reported to exhibit high rates of noncompliance (Doleys, Cartelli, and Doster, 1976; Terdal, Jackson, and Garner, 1976).

Noncompliance is clearly a common problem. It is one of the most frequently reported problems of children referred to clinics (Christophersen, Barnard, Ford, and Wolf, 1976; Patterson, 1976). Reports from a number of

sources indicate that referred children are more noncompliant than nonclinic children (Delfini, Bernal, and Rosen, 1976; Forehand, King, Peed, and Yoder, 1975; Patterson, 1976). However, noncompliance is also prevalent among nonclinic children (Johnson, Wahl, Martin, and Johansson, 1973). "Normal" children comply with about 60 to 80 percent of parental requests. Compliance does seem to increase with age, but there seems to be no difference between the compliance rates of boys and girls (Landauer, Carlsmith, and Lepper, 1970; Terdal et al., 1976).

Given that noncompliance occurs in both clinic and nonclinic samples, what factors might account for the greater rate of noncompliance in some families? Available evidence suggests that parents of clinic and nonclinic children differ in both the number and types of commands they give. Parents of clinic-referred children issue more commands, questions, and criticisms and also issue commands that are more negative—presented in an angry, humiliating, or nagging manner (Delfini et al., 1976; Forehand et al., 1975; Lobitz and Johnson, 1975). Such parental behavior has been associated with deviant child behavior (Johnson and Lobitz, 1974b). In a laboratory analogue study, Forehand and Scarboro (1975) had mothers issue twelve standard commands. Children exhibited a slower initiation of compliance to the second six commands than to the first six. Thus, one consequence of issuing numerous commands may be that the parent is less likely to receive rapid compliance.

Two types of commands have also been distinguished. Alpha commands are those to which a motoric response is appropriate and feasible. Beta commands are vague, interrupted, or carried out by the parent, and thus the child has no opportunity to demonstrate compliance (cf. Peed, Roberts, and Forehand, 1977). Consequences that parents deliver also affect the child's noncompliant behavior (Forehand, 1977; Wahler, 1976). A combination of negative consequences (ignoring and verbal reprimands) for noncompliant behavior and rewards and attention for appropriate behavior seems to be related to increased levels of compliance (Forehand, 1977).

On the basis of these findings and an earlier program described by Hanf (1972, cited by Forehand, 1977), Forehand and his colleagues have developed a treatment program for non-compliant children (4 to 7 years old) and their families. During Phase I the parent is instructed to engage in any activity the child chooses (Child game), to attend to the child's behavior, and to eliminate all commands, questions, and criticisms. During the second segment of Phase I, the parent is trained to use contingent rewards, to structure daily ten-minute Child games at home, and to develop programs outside the clinic setting. In Phase II the parent is instructed to engage the child in activities determined by the parent (Parent's game) and is taught to give direct, concise commands, allow the child sufficient time to comply, and to reward compliance with contingent attention. If compliance is not initiated, the parent is instructed in the use of a time-out procedure. First, a warning is given that spells out the time-out procedure. If compliance still does not occur, the child is placed in a chair in the corner of the room. If the child leaves the chair, a warning of a spanking is given. Should the child leave the chair again, two quick spanks are delivered to the child's rear and the child is returned to the chair. The procedure is repeated until the child remains quietly in the chair for two minutes. Following the time-out procedure the child returns to the uncompleted task, and the parent repeats the initial command. Once compliance occurs, it is followed by contingent attention from the parent (Wells, Forehand, and Griest, 1980).

The effectiveness of this program has been investigated in a number of studies. Peed, Roberts, and Forehand (1977) randomly assigned mother-child pairs to either a treatment or no-treatment (waiting-list) control condition. Significant increases in child compliance and parental use of positive statements and contingent verbal rewards occurred for treatment families in both the home and clinic settings. Decreases in Beta commands also occurred in both set-

tings. In contrast, there was no change in the behavior of any of the control families during the waiting period. Positive changes were displayed, however, in the attitudes of both groups of parents. As the authors point out, this suggests that changes in the parents' attitudes may occur despite the absence of change in parent or child behaviors.

Forehand and his colleagues have also demonstrated successful generalization of certain aspects of their treatment program. For example, successful treatment of noncompliance also seems to result in significant reductions in deviant behaviors such as tantrums, aggression, and crying. Untreated siblings also increase their compliance, and it seems likely that this is due, at least in part, to the mother's use of her improved skills with the untreated child (Humphreys, Forehand, McMahon, and Roberts, 1978).

One final measure of the success of this treatment program is provided by a comparison of fifteen clinic-referred children and their mothers to an equal number of nonclinic child-mother pairs (Forehand, Wells, and Griest, 1980). The results of this study are presented in Table 11–3. Of particular interest is the finding that prior to treatment clinic children were more noncompliant and deviant and were rated by their parents as less well adjusted. By the end of treatment and at a two-month follow-up, the behavior of the clinic and control children did not differ. Although the parents of clinic children initially perceived their offspring as less well adjusted than did parents of non-clinic children, this was not true at two-month follow-up. These findings indicate that the success achieved is not only statistically significant but clinically and socially relevant as well.

It should be stated that there are ethical issues involved in reducing noncompliance in children (Forehand, 1977). Compliance is not always a positive trait, and the ability to say "no" to certain requests is something that seems desirable to either train or retain. In this regard it is also important to assure that parents do not expect 100 percent compliance. This is neither the norm nor desirable in our society.

Table 11-3 Behavior Observation and Parent Perception Data for Clinic and Nonclinic Groups

Measures	Clinic			Nonclinic		
	Pre	Post	Follow-up	Pre	Post	Follow-up
Behavior Observation						
Parent						
Attends & rewards[a]	.46	1.45	1.37	.37	.36	.48
Beta commands[a]	.91	.67	.65	.79	.82	.75
Contingent attention[b]	6.00	33.00	25.80	7.00	8.00	7.80
Child						
Compliance[b]	27.0	36.0	36.8	33.0	33.0	38.6
Deviant behavior[b]	9.3	6.6	8.6	5.6	6.0	5.7
Parent Perception of Child Adjustment[c]						
Home attitude	14.8	8.3	9.4	5.1	5.8	6.1
Behavior rating	26.7	18.7	20.2	12.7	12.6	13.9

[a] Rate per minute
[b] Percent
[c] Lower scores indicate more positive perception

Adapted from Forehand, Wells, and Griest, 1980. Copyright by the Association for Advancement of Behavior Therapy. Reprinted by permission of the publisher and the author.

As indicated above, certain commands should be refused: A quiet, docile child should not be the treatment goal.

Juvenile Delinquency

The term *delinquency* is a legal rather than a psychological one. It refers to a juvenile (usually under 18) who has committed an act that would be illegal for adults as well (theft, aggravated assault, rape, or murder) or an act that is illegal only for juveniles (for example, truancy, association with "immoral" persons, violation of curfews, or incorrigibility). There is little doubt that juvenile crime is a serious problem. The frightening picture presented in the media is supported by official statistics.

The proportion of juveniles seen in juvenile court showed a dramatic and fairly steady increase between 1957 and 1975, approximately doubling over that time period (Empey, 1978). This is more alarming when it is realized that approximately half of the juveniles who might become court cases are actually handled entirely by the police and then released. Arrest rates present an even gloomier picture. Juveniles under 18 represented 29 percent of the population but accounted for 40.5 percent of the arrests for the eight serious felonies that comprise the FBI's Crime Index Offenses (FBI, 1979). Significant increases have occurred in most index crimes among juveniles, but the increase is most alarming for violent crimes—manslaughter, forcible rape, aggravated assault, and robbery. While males still account for a greater number of arrests than do females, increases in index crimes present a different picture. During the period from 1970 through 1979, the total of index crimes increased 13.9 percent for boys and a striking 32.5 percent for girls. The statistics are even more alarming for violent crimes. Boys showed an increase of 39 percent in arrests for violent crimes, while the increase was a dramatic 65.3 percent for girls (FBI, 1980). It is difficult to determine what accounts for this trend. Of obvious interest is the question of the possible influence of shifting roles and expectations for women.

The Problem of Definition. Although the scope and seriousness of the problem seems clear, it is widely agreed among workers in the field that the study of delinquency is faced with a problem of definition. Whether an act by a juvenile gets classified as delinquency may depend as much on the actions of others as it does on the youth's behavior. The norm violation must, of course, be noticed by someone and be reported to a law-enforcement official. A police officer can then arrest the youth or merely issue a warning. If the youth is arrested, he or she may or may not be brought to court. Once in juvenile court, only some individuals receive the legal designation of delinquent; others may be warned or released in the custody of their parents. Various definitions of delinquency can be used anywhere in this process, and in examining research, one must be aware of the definition employed. Furthermore, estimates of the prevalence of the behaviors that lead a child to be labeled as a juvenile delinquent may be underestimated. What of the individuals who commit similar behaviors but don't get caught? Anonymous questionnaires completed by "normal" adolescents suggest that 75 percent of them may engage in behaviors that could be labeled as delinquent if they were caught (Offer, Sabshin, and Marcus, 1965).

The picture becomes even more complicated if we attempt to examine correlates of delinquent behavior; for example, socioeconomic status, race, or gender. These variables may themselves influence whether an act is noticed and judged in violation of some norm. For example, many sexual behaviors may more likely be judged deviant in a girl than in a boy. Information on official delinquency suggests that the rate of delinquency is significantly higher among lower-class children. However, as Empey (1978) points out, studies employing self-reports of law violation—undetected delinquency—have repeatedly found that its relation to social class is either small or nonexistent.

Subtypes of Delinquency. Beyond the question of definition and the difficulties this may introduce into the study of delinquency, is it valid to assume that all youths who engage in law-violating behavior or who are delinquent are alike? The answer seems to be "no." On the basis of a factor analysis of the case history data of 115 institutionalized male delinquents, Quay (1964) identified and labeled four dimensions of delinquent behavior: socialized-subcultural delinquency, unsocialized-psychopathic delinquency, disturbed-neurotic delinquency, and inadequate-immature delinquency. The first three have been identified with considerable consistency in subsequent studies (Quay, 1979).

The *socialized-subcultural* dimension, defined by characteristics such as (1) has bad companions, (2) steals in company with others, (3) belongs to a gang, or (4) stays away from home and school, has probably received the most attention. This group of children does not seem to experience distress or appreciable psychopathology nor to have difficulty relating to peers. The definition of this group of delinquents seems, therefore, to be based on an acceptance of the values of and association with a delinquent subgroup.

Lower socioeconomic status is frequently described as contributing to this form of delinquency. It is presumed that atypical values and norms are supported among lower-class youth. In addition to peer support for antisocial behavior, the real economic, social, and educational problems associated with poor neighborhoods are presumed to encourage antisocial behavior. Yet not all youths from high delinquency areas become delinquent. Subcultural factors, therefore, cannot provide a complete explanation. Glueck and Glueck (1970) conducted a series of studies in which they compared delinquent and nondelinquent boys from high-crime neighborhoods. A number of factors were more common among the delinquent boys: muscular (mesomorphic) body build, lower verbal IQs than performance IQs, unstable and disorganized homes, and parents with psychological and physical problems.

Other studies support the notion that these youths are disadvantaged in a number of ways. Recent longitudinal studies of Danish boys by Mednick and his colleagues suggest that the relationship between SES and later delinquent and criminal behavior is mediated by poor educational performance (McGarvey, Gabrielli, Bentler, and Mednick, 1981; Moffitt, Gabrielli, Mednick, and Schulsinger, 1981). That is, SES predicts verbal ability and educational performance, and poor language skills and educational performance in turn lead to criminal activity. This explanation is consistent with a frequently cited association between specific reading difficulties and antisocial behavior (e.g., Rutter, 1975).

The second subtype, the *unsocialized-psychopathic* dimension, corresponds to the conduct disorders-externalizing-undercontrolled dimension previously described (pp. 96, 258). Delinquents scoring high on this dimension do not seem to be part of a delinquent subgroup. *Disturbed-neurotic* delinquency is related to the anxiety-withdrawal, internalizing, overcontrolled dimension (pp. 96, 139). The dimension is associated with shyness, guilt, anxiety, depression, and low self-esteem, which are assumed to underlie the delinquent behavior. It has also been suggested that a separate syndrome of drug abuse exists among delinquents (e.g., Stein, Sarbin, and Kulik, 1971).

Much of the difficulty in establishing a coherent picture of the delinquent youth and in evaluating the effectiveness of interventions probably results from a failure to differentiate among subtypes. Despite the urging by some workers (e.g., Warren, 1969) that some systematic approach to classification be employed for both research and treatment, it is only relatively recently that investigators have begun to utilize the dimensions that have emerged from factor-analytic studies. The validity of the subtypes described above does seem to be supported; groups of delinquents differing on these dimensions also seem to differ on some cognitive, motivational, learning, and physiological variables (Quay, 1979). In addition, it appears that different patterns of family interaction are found among the subtypes (Hetherington, Stouwie, and Ridberg, 1971).

Treatment of Delinquency. Institutionalization is a traditional and perhaps obvious approach to intervention with delinquents. Reform schools, training schools, and detention centers may include some therapeutic, educational, or rehabilitative programming or may only provide custodial care. The evidence for incarceration as a means of reducing recidivism is not encouraging, even when a variety of programs are employed (cf. Martinson, 1974). Only 20 to 30 percent of boys released from such institutions are not rearrested within the next few years (Cohen and Filipczak, 1971; Gibbons, 1976). Placing youths in such institutions may expose them to a pervasive and sophisticated delinquent subculture in which deviant behaviors may be learned and reinforced. This and other concerns with the juvenile justice system have led to attempts to deal with delinquency outside of institutionally based programs.

One approach to this problem has been labeled diversion (Lemert, 1971). The goal of such programs is to divert youthful offenders from the juvenile justice system and to provide services for them through a variety of different agencies (for example, educational, job training). It was hoped that by providing adequate skills and avoiding stigmatization and labeling, recidivism would be reduced. Some investigators do report success with diversion projects, especially for children referred before any contact with the court system has occurred (e.g., Quay and Love, 1977). However, these projects seem to have exploded in popularity without adequate evidence of their effectiveness. Furthermore, some have argued that the original intent of these programs has not been fulfilled and that many of them have been preempted or co-opted by law enforcement agencies (Lemert, 1981).

COMMUNITY ALTERNATIVES TO INCARCERATION. Small residential treatment centers and community-based nonresidential treatment

Box 11–3 The Use of Drugs and Alcohol

From the inner city ghetto to the affluent suburb, adults have become increasingly alarmed over the use of drugs and alcohol by teenagers. Is this concern justified? The answer, based upon statistics from the U.S. Department of Justice (1980) and the FBI (1980), would seem to be "yes."

Questioned about the availability of certain substances, 90 percent of a sample of high school seniors replied that marijuana was very easy or fairly easy to get. Even more alarming, 59.9 percent gave the same answer about amphetamines and 49.8 percent about barbiturates. Not only are drugs available, but they seem to be widely used. Although the director of the National Institute on Drug Abuse was able to tell a Senate subcommittee that use of some drugs had declined in recent years, he warned that American youths still had the highest use rate in the industrialized world and that use of amphetamines and other stimulants was on the rise.

Optimism is also dampened by what appears to be an increasing rate of alcohol abuse. Eighty-eight percent of high school seniors report using alcohol in the last twelve months, and 71.8 percent in the previous thirty days, suggesting that drinking is a frequent occurrence. Alarmingly, in 1972, 24 percent of children between the ages of 12 and 17 reported drinking in the last thirty days, but by 1979 this figure had become 37.2 percent.

How and why do young people come to use drugs and alcohol? Recent longitudinal studies seem to confirm a developmental sequence in usage patterns (Kandel, 1982). The use of legal drugs such as alcohol and tobacco precede the use of illicit drugs. It is virtually never the case that a nonuser goes directly to the use of illegal drugs. At least four distinct developmental stages in adolescent drug use have been identified: (1) beer or wine, (2) cigarettes or hard liquor, (3) marijuana, and (4) other illicit drugs. It has recently been suggested that problem drinking may be a fifth stage that occurs between marijuana and other illicit drugs.

Participation in one stage does not necessarily mean that the young person will progress to the next stage. Only a subgroup at each stage progresses to the next level of use. However, it does appear to be the case that the earlier the youngster begins one stage of drug use, the greater is the likelihood of other drug use. Thus, the earlier legal drugs are used, the greater the likelihood of illicit drug use. Also, heavier use at any stage seems to be associated with "progress" to the next stage.

Why do youngsters initiate drug use? Most experts agree that there are multiple determinants of drug use and that adolescent drug users are not a homogeneous group. Thus, for any one individual there is probably no single cause, and different youngsters may begin and continue to use drugs for differing combinations of reasons. Certainly, exposure to parents and peers who drink and use drugs is a major factor. Numerous authors have also suggested that drug use is one expression of a rebellion that is characteristic of adolescence. An atmosphere in which drug use is supported by peers and not strongly opposed by parental attitudes and values is likely to be supportive of this particular expression of independence and rebellion. Current social fads in drug use and availability are also important influences.

Drug use may also be part of a general pattern of deviant and rebellious activity. Boys rated as aggressive when they were quite young are more likely to become involved in drug use (Kellam, Brown, and Fleming, 1982), and the association between drug use and delinquency has frequently been reported (Jessor and Jessor, 1977; Stein et al., 1971). Drug use among adolescents also seems to be associated with greater sexual involvement, school misbehavior, and poor school performance (Hundleby, Carpenter, Ross, and Mercer, 1982).

Only a small proportion of youngsters who start to use alcohol and drugs ever progress to the use of illicit drugs other than marijuana or to serious alcohol abuse. However, a small percentage is still an appreciable number of youths. The serious personal and societal consequences of such abuse and the general alarm over drug use have led to a search for methods of prevention and treatment. Drug abuse has, however, proven to be a particularly difficult problem to treat, and no current approach can be termed a proven success. Unfortunately, educational and legal attempts to prevent drug abuse have, to date, met a similar fate.

programs were conceived of as another alternative to incarceration. The Community Treatment Program of the California Youth Authority, directed by Margarite Q. Warren and begun in the 1960s, is one example of such efforts. Youths randomly assigned to the experimental condition were first evaluated and placed into one of several theoretically derived maturity subtypes. Classifications were based upon the individual's view of himself or herself and typical way of interacting with others (Warren, 1969). Following this, youths were assigned to a parole agent who was trained to treat the needs of that delinquent. Control youths were assigned to one of the state institutions for confinement and released on regular parole. The results suggest that matching of delinquent subtypes with workers reduced recidivism and that differential success among subtypes was obtained. After two years 58 percent of the experimental boys and 66 percent of the girls had not had their parole revoked, as compared to 46 and 52 percent, respectively, of control boys and girls. However, it appears that this may have as much to do with differences in the tolerance and attitudes of regular parole agents and program staff as it did with the youths' behavior. One indication of this is that the average number of new offenses among experimental boys was 2.8 versus only 1.6 for controls (Empey, 1978; Warren and Palmer, 1966).

BEHAVIORAL APPROACHES. A large number of behaviorally based programs have been designed to deal with the problems of juvenile delinquents. The general assumption of all these programs is that the problem youth has deficiencies in socially appropriate behavior as well as some socially unacceptable behaviors. Most applications have been based on operant principles (see Braukmann and Fixsen, 1975; Burchard and Harig, 1976; and Davidson and Seidman, 1974, for reviews). One of the first such programs was the CASE II project (Contingencies Applicable for Special Education), begun in 1965 at the former National Training School for Boys in Washington, D.C. (Cohen

and Filipczak, 1971). The program stressed training in academic, vocational, social, and self-help skills. A token economy system was set up in which the boys earned points for accurate completion of programmed instructional material and for improvement in skills. These points could be exchanged for backup reinforcers such as store items, better food, use of a lounge, a private room, and other privileges. CASE II was effective in increasing the academic and social skills of participants and in reducing recidivism over a three-year period.

Achievement Place, a home-style residential treatment program begun in 1967 by the faculty and students of the Department of Human Development at the University of Kansas (Fixsen, Wolf, and Phillips, 1973; Phillips, 1968), is one of the most outstanding examples of the application of behavioral principles to problem behaviors. Adolescents who have legally been declared delinquent or dependent-neglect cases live in a house with two trained teaching-parents. The youths attend school during the day and also have regular work responsibilities. The academic problems, aggression, and other norm-violating behaviors exhibited by these adolescents are viewed as an expression of failures of past environments to teach appropriate behaviors. Accordingly, these deficits are corrected through modeling, practice, instruction, and feedback. The program centers on a token economy in which points and praise are gained for appropriate behaviors and lost for inappropriate behaviors. Points can be used to purchase a variety of privileges that are otherwise unavailable. If a resident meets a certain level of performance, the right to go on a merit system and thus avoid the point system may be purchased. This is seen as providing a transition to usual sources of natural reinforcement and feedback, such as praise, status, and satisfaction. A youngster who is able to perform adequately on merit is gradually transferred to his or her natural home. Teaching-parents help the natural parents or guardians structure a program to maintain gains made at Achievement Place. Recidivism rates for youths released for at least one year were 19 percent for

By permission of the New York State Division for Youth

Home-style residential facilities provide a setting for a variety of youths requiring special placement.

boys from Achievement Place, 53 percent for youths from Kansas Boys School, and 54 percent for boys placed on probation. School grades also revealed the greater success of Achievement Place boys (Phillips, Phillips, Fixsen, and Wolf, 1973).

One of the outstanding features of the Achievement Place program is the large quantity of research the program has produced. Numerous single-subject design experiments have continually evaluated the components of the program, thereby suggesting cause-and-effect relationships. Although the findings of the research program are too numerous to mention, several developments are worthy of note. Through the years of operation Achievement Place has shifted to a greater use of self-government, due to empirical demonstrations of greater effectiveness for such systems. In addition, social reinforcement, along with social interaction with and modeling by the house parents, has been determined as central to the program's success (cf. Fixsen, Phillips, and Wolf, 1973; Fixsen, Wolf, and Phillips, 1973; Phillips, Phillips, Wolf, and Fixsen, 1973; Solnick, Braukmann, Bedlington, Kirigin, and Wolf, 1981). A tribute to the impact of Achievement Place is the number of group homes that have subsequently imitated its goal and procedures.

A treatment program for delinquents and their families that seems to integrate behavioral-social learning, cognitive-behavioral, and family systems perspectives has been developed by Alexander, Parsons, and their colleagues (Alexander and Parsons, 1973; Parsons and Alexander, 1973). The treatment program focuses on the interpersonal processes of the family system. The goals of therapy are to improve the communication skills of families; to modify cognitive sets, expectations, attitudes, and affective reactions; and to establish new interpretations and meanings of behavior (Alexander, Haas, Klein, Warburton, 1980). Therapists employ a variety of techniques: modeling, prompting, shaping and rehearsing effective communication skills, and feedback and reinforcement for positive changes. In addition, contracting is used to establish reciprocal patterns of positive reinforcement that may have broken down or that rarely existed in these families. For example, a contract regarding a privilege for a certain family member also specifies that person's responsibilities for securing those privileges and provides bonuses for all parties for compliance with the contract.

The program has been demonstrated to significantly improve the interactions of families of what is termed a "soft" delinquent population—arrests for running away or possession of alcohol. Significantly low rates of recidivism were also obtained six to eighteen months following treatment (Alexander and Parsons, 1973; Parsons and Alexander, 1973). Klein, Alexander, and Parsons (1977) also demonstrated preventive impact for the treatment program. Examination of juvenile court records for siblings of initially referred delinquents indicated that after 2½ to 3½ years siblings from this behavioral-family systems treatment had significantly lower rates of court referrals than siblings from other treatment groups, or nontreated controls.

These results, along with the work of Patterson and his colleagues with aggressive children and Forehand's work with noncompliant children, suggest the potential success of treatments aimed at modifying parent-child and family interactions (Griest and Wells, 1983). However, although some families respond well to behavioral programs designed to change coercive interactions and reduce conduct disordered behaviors, others do not. The families that do not respond to treatment are often beset by poverty and its related problems (Wahler, Berland, Coe, and Leske, 1977). Thus, Wahler and others (Lutzker, 1980; Wahler and Graves, 1983) have called for a broader analysis when dealing with deviant family systems. It has been suggested that changes in communitywide systems will be more effective in dealing with these difficulties and will also avoid "blaming" the individual child or family victim (cf. Rappaport, 1977). The successful treatment of conduct disordered and delinquent youths is a difficult task, and any approach that ignores changing the environments in which these youths reside seems destined to fail.

SUMMARY

There is fairly broad agreement among clinicians, and support from empirical efforts as well, that some children exhibit a cluster of behaviors that are frequently characterized as aggressive, destructive, oppositional, and antisocial. This syndrome is commonly referred to as conduct disorder. DSM-III distinguishes four subtypes of its diagnostic category of Conduct Disorder—Undersocialized, Aggressive; Undersocialized-Nonaggressive; Socialized-Aggressive; and Socialized-Nonaggressive. A separate diagnostic category of Oppositional Disorder is also provided. It is questionable whether these separate diagnostic categories are justifiable, although differences among subtypes of delinquents have been cited. It is more likely that a general syndrome exists, the characteristics of which shift with the age of the child and with situational variables.

Considerable concern is expressed over the seeming stability of conduct disordered behavior, however. Thus, although the form it takes may change, it is a common finding that the general behavioral pattern is a stable one. Success in working with younger children who exhibit noncompliant and aggressive behavior has been reported. The success of these efforts and the difficulty in working with delinquent adolescents and antisocial adults argues for the importance of early intervention.

Biological influences and differences in arousal levels have been suggested as the basis for conduct problems. The contribution of biological factors is probably not as direct as was once thought, and currently social-environmental influences appear to be of primary importance. Numerous authors emphasize the impact of family variables. Different family and child-rearing styles have been implicated. Recent concern has developed around the finding that conduct disordered behavior is more common among boys from broken homes. The high divorce rate has made this observation especially important. Available research suggests that the relationship between marital discord-divorce and these problems is a complex one that we are just beginning to understand. The age of the child at the time of separation, the availability of alternative sources of support, and other influences make conduct problems far from an inevitable outcome of discord or divorce.

Much current research suggests that aggression is a learned behavior. The role of aggressive models has received considerable attention. The effect of televised violence is an important example of current research. Recent evidence implicates a circular process involving adoption of aggressive behavior, unpopularity, low achievement, and television watching.

The consequences of aggressive behavior also seem to contribute to the development of conduct problems. The work of Patterson and others demonstrates that aggression and coercion frequently result in positive outcomes for the aggressor. In addition to positively reinforcing such behavior, "victims" often create a negative reinforcement trap. For example, demands are often removed following repeated or high levels of coercive behavior by the child. The child's problem behavior is reinforced by the termination of the demands, and the victim is reinforced in the short run, since the child's aversive behavior stops temporarily. However, the child has learned that coercive behavior will succeed, and the victim has learned that submission will terminate an unpleasant situation. Training parents in appropriate child management skills seems to be a useful approach to reducing noncompliant, aggressive, and coercive behavior and to improving the general family climate.

Although the definition of juvenile delinquency is somewhat unclear, it is certain that the implications of such criminal behavior are serious. The treatment of youthful offenders is difficult. A variety of interventions—ranging from institutionalization, to diversion and community-based programs—have been attempted. While some success is reported, rates of recidivism are still quite high.

12

PSYCHOLOGICAL FACTORS AFFECTING PHYSICAL CONDITIONS

ASTHMA

Prevalence and Prognosis
Causes
Psychological Aspects of Asthma

ULCERATIVE COLITIS

Description and Incidence
Etiology
Treatment

PSYCHOLOGICAL CONSEQUENCES
OF CHRONIC ILLNESS

A Description of Juvenile Diabetes
  Mellitus
Management of the Diabetic Condition
Reactions to the Illness

PSYCHOLOGICAL MODIFICATION
OF PHYSICAL FUNCTIONS

FACILITATING MEDICAL
TREATMENT

Fear Reduction in Dental Treatment
Compliance with Medical Regimens
Hospitalization

THE DYING CHILD

SUMMARY

The disorders discussed in this chapter have usually been called psychosomatic disorders. They are actual physical conditions such as asthma, headaches, ulcers, and nausea, which are known or presumed to be affected by psychological factors. The terminology for describing these disorders has undergone a number of changes in the last few decades. The term *Psychosomatic Disorders* was replaced in DSM-II by *Psychophysiological Disorders,* and DSM-III has substituted *Psychological Factors Affecting Physical Conditions.*

The uncertainty over terminology reflects a longstanding controversy over the nature of the relationship between mind and body, the psyche and the soma. One of the most influential statements concerning the mind-body problem is found in the writing of Rene Descartes, the early seventeenth-century French philosopher. Descartes, influenced by strong religious beliefs, viewed human beings as part divine and as possessing a soul (mind) that somehow must affect the mechanics of the body. The point of contact between the two systems was presumed to be the pineal gland, located in the midbrain. This version of mind-body dualism was part of a long history of shifting opinion about whether or how spiritual or psychological factors affected bodily conditions.

During the twentieth century interest in the impact of psychological processes on the body resulted in development of the field of psychosomatic medicine. Early workers began to accumulate evidence and develop theories of how psychological factors played a causative role in specific physical disorders (e.g., Alexander, 1950; Grace and Graham, 1952; Selye, 1956). As this field developed, several trends emerged. An increasing number of physical disorders were seen to be related to psychological factors. Even the common cold was thought to be affected by emotional factors. The question therefore arose as to whether it was fruitful to identify a specific group of psychosomatic disorders or whether psychological factors were operating in all physical conditions. In addition, the focus began to shift from psychogen-

esis, that is psychological cause, to multi-causality, the idea that social and psychological (as well as biological) factors all contribute to both health and illness at multiple points. The latter view is holistic, assuming a continuous transaction among influences.

With this shift in thinking, the field began to expand considerably. The ongoing role of psychological factors in physical conditions, the psychological and developmental consequences of physical conditions, the role of psychological treatments for physical disorders, psychological aspects of medical treatments, and the role of psychological variables in prevention and health maintenance all began to receive increased attention (cf. Drotar, 1981; Routh, et al., 1983). Indeed, the concept of psychosomatic disorders as physical conditions caused by emotional factors became inadequate to encompass this expanded perspective. Some writers suggested other definitions (Wright, 1977), and various other terms came into existence, such as *behavioral medicine, pediatric psychology,* and *health psychology.*

The present chapter is in keeping with changes in the field. It first examines disorders, such as asthma and ulcerative colitis, which occur in children and have been considered psychosomatic—that is, caused by or affected by psychological factors. Contributions from the expanded perspective on the relationship between psychological factors and physical conditions are then described.

ASTHMA

Asthma is a disorder of the respiratory system. Hyperresponsiveness of the trachea, bronchi, and bronchioles to various stimuli occur with the result that the air passages are narrowed and air exchange is impaired, particularly during expiration. For the child this produces intermittent episodes of wheezing and shortness of breath (dyspnea). Severe attacks, known as status asthmaticus, are life threatening and require emergency medical treatment. The fear

Box 12-1   Life Stress and Illness

Many early workers in the field of psychoso-matic medicine tried to find a relationship be-tween a certain type of psychological stress and a particular physical illness. For example, it was hypothesized that stress created by unsatisfied dependency needs led to peptic ulcers. More recently the specific stress–specific illness model has been abandoned. Instead, it is thought that repeated stressful life events summate and lead to a general increase in susceptibility to illness. Individual constitutional differences are pre-sumed to determine which organ system is most vulnerable.

Much of the research in this area has been con-ducted with adults. Rating scales have been de-veloped to measure stressful life events. Total life stress, as measured by these instruments, has been found to be related to disorders such as heart disease as well as to general health status (cf. Rabkin and Streuning, 1976).

It seems reasonable to assume that children's health is also affected by the amount of life stress experienced. What life events are stressful to children? It had long been assumed that certain stresses (for example, maternal deprivation)

could lead to changes in the child's physical sta-tus. No systematic method for measuring the variety of stresses experienced by the child was available, however. Coddington (1972) began to develop such an instrument. He obtained ratings from a large number of teachers, pedia-tricians, and mental health workers of how stressful they felt a variety of life events would be to children.

Yamamoto (1979) then asked children them-selves about their lives. Close to 400 fourth, fifth, and sixth graders rated twenty life events on a scale from the most upsetting (7) to the least upsetting (1). The children also reported whether they had personally experienced each event. Although there were some similarities between how stressful children and adults per-ceived events to be (for example, loss of a par-ent), discrepancies also existed. Children rated parents' fights as more stressful and birth of a sibling as less stressful than did professionals. Below are the scale values obtained from the children and also the percentage who reported that they actually experienced the events.

Life Events	Scale Value	% Experiencing
New baby sibling	1.27	25.6
Giving class report	2.58	68.1
Going to dentist	2.73	77.7
Losing in game	3.16	81.2
Picked last on team	3.30	49.6
Not making 100	3.75	83.1
Scary dream	4.08	76.6
Moved to new school	4.60	42.8
Ridiculed in class	5.28	46.9
Getting lost	5.49	56.1
Having an operation	5.51	30.5
Sent to principal	5.75	42.0
A poor report card	6.23	46.0
Suspected of lying	6.53	82.3
Caught in theft	6.63	12.3
Parental fights	6.71	64.0
Wetting in class	6.74	6.0
Academic retainment	6.82	10.9
Going blind	6.86	4.1
Losing parent	6.90	20.2

Once we can measure how stressful certain life events are to children, information on the events experienced by particular children during a certain period can be obtained. From this a measure of the total social-psychological stress experienced by that child can be derived. Is this total life stress related to illness in children? Clinical impressions and the results of a few empirical studies suggest that it is.

Gad and Johnson (1980) measured the stressful life events experienced by 167 adolescents ranging in age from 12 to 14. They found that lower-SES adolescents experienced more negative life events than did middle- and upper-SES youths. This difference did not exist for positive life events. At all SES levels significant correlations existed between negative life events and measures of general physical health. High negative life event scores were related to more frequent visits to the doctor and higher rates of diagnosed illness during the preceding year, as well as to the existence of current physical health problems.

Other research supports the relationship between stressful life events and particular physical illness. For example, the stress engendered by preparing to leave home alone for the first time seems to produce changes in the hemostatic defense mechanisms of young hemophiliacs (Buxton, Arkel, Lagos, Desposito, Lowenthal, and Simring, 1981). Five male hemophiliacs between the ages of 8 and 10 exhibited diminished blood platelet aggregation (a process thought to be related to spontaneous bleeding in hemophiliacs) in response to this stress. Life stress has also been related to respiratory tract illness and the frequency of accidents in children (Boyce, Jensen, Cassel, Collier, Smith, and Raimey, 1977; Padilla, Rohsenow, and Bergman, 1976).

Individual differences in response to stress may also exist. Lawler and Allen (1981) report that children with high, but not low, resting blood pressure responded physiologically to laboratory-induced stress in a manner similar to hypertensive adults.

This new area of research is promising. Relating stressful life events to serious health conditions or even to the common cold can improve our understanding of the role of psychological factors in physical health. The ultimate goal is to help treat or even prevent physical illness in children.

---

of not being able to breathe and the danger of severe attacks are likely to create appreciable anxiety in the child and other family members.

Prevalence and Prognosis

It is estimated that 2 to 4% of the population has asthma, with onset usually between 3 and 8 years of age. Asthma occurs in boys twice as often as in girls. The impact on the asthmatic child is considerable. In addition to the psychological difficulties experienced by many children, asthma has been estimated to account for 25 percent of school days lost due to all chronic diseases combined (Purcell, 1975).

Clearly, the greatest threat is loss of life, and all measures used to treat the physical symptoms of asthma—daily medication to prevent wheezing, environmental control of potential irritants, desensitization to allergens, avoidance of infection, and emergency treatment to stop wheezing—are geared to prevent death. Fortunately, with appropriate treatment asthma tends to get better with age. Approximately 70 percent of asthmatics are reported to be considerably improved or free of attacks twenty years after the onset of symptoms, and the fatality rate appears to be less than 1 percent (Bronheim, 1978; Purcell, 1975).

Causes

The causes of asthma are complex, and there is a considerable history of controversy concerning etiology. To help clarify the problem of etiology, Figure 12-1 presents a schematic description of the asthmatic process. Some cause or variety of causes produces a hypersensitivity

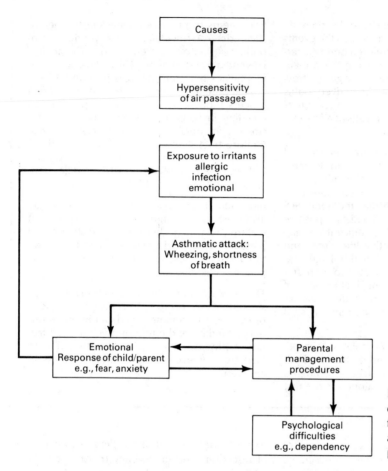

Figure 12–1 Schematic diagram of a general model for the development of asthma and its concomitant psychosocial effects.

of the air passages. Once established, this hypersensitivity results in the child responding to a variety of irritants more easily than would a nonasthmatic individual. The resulting wheezing and shortness of breath may have additional psychological consequences. Anxiety and fear may occur in anticipation of attacks or during them. This in itself may be a contributing irritant that increases the probability or intensity of attacks. A second class of possible psychological consequences is dependency, isolation from peers, and other behavior problems that may result from the management of the asthmatic child's physical symptoms.

Both medical and psychological explanations of asthma often fail to distinguish between the

causes of greater sensitivity and reactivity of the bronchia and factors which precipitate attacks in individuals with such hypersensitivity. Some workers suggest that available evidence points to hereditary factors as the cause of hypersensitive air passages, although the exact biological mechanism by which this occurs is not well established (e.g., Bronheim, 1978). Others, such as Alexander (1980), suggest that hereditary factors may be less important than is often assumed. Concordance rates of only 19 percent in monozygotic twins and lack of a strong relationship between the existence of allergies in parents and children are cited in support of this position.

Whatever its etiology, individuals with

highly sensitive and labile respiratory tracts are potentially exposed to a second set of factors that influence whether or not asthmatic attacks occur. This second set of influences has come to be thought of as trigger mechanisms or irritants rather than as causes of asthma. It is widely held that a variety of agents can trigger wheezing in different individuals or on different occasions for the same individual. Only a small percentage of cases can be traced to only one agent (Alexander and Solanch, 1981). Respiratory infection and allergies can set off an attack; indeed, asthma is often preceded by repeated respiratory infections or chronic allergic rhinitis (runny nose) during infancy. Allergies may exist to inhaled substances such as dust, the dander of a pet, or pollen, or to ingested substances such as milk, wheat, or chocolate. Physical factors such as cold temperatures, tobacco smoke, pungent odors, and exercise and rapid breathing may also contribute to wheezing. Further, psychological stimuli and emotional upset are often considered important triggers of asthma attacks, although their exact role is controversial.

Psychological Aspects of Asthma

Before discussing the involvement of psychological factors in asthma, it might be helpful to consider Alexander's brief description of the young asthmatic patient:

The early-onset asthma patient and his or her family face some very severe hardships. These youngsters tend to grow up watching the other children play from the livingroom side of the front window. Most have poor self-concepts. Often both academic and social development suffer greatly because of the amount of time lost from school and the restricted and specialized contacts with agemates. They face both peers and adults who are variously overindulgent, or lacking in understanding of their difficulties. Often these children react with shame and embarrassment, and/or demandingness to the extreme. At home their asthma may become the sole focus around which all family activities and concerns come to revolve. Their parents may

feel responsible, guilty, and helpless; and at other times resentful and angry. Certainly, an asthma sufferer can learn to manipulate others with the disorder, or use it to avoid unpleasant activities or situations. It is also often difficult for the patient to sort out clearly what he or she can really do, from what is accomplished in the face of asthma. Many maladaptive and inappropriate behavior patterns can develop, as patient and family struggle with the ravages of this disorder. Such patterns can severely cripple family life and retard the social and psychological development of the child. Often, the undesirable behavior patterns affect the course of the disorder substantially. Asthma is, of course, potentially life-threatening, and many patients have experienced bouts of status asthmaticus, which on occasion may have brought them close to death. Such experiences often generate enduring anxiety responses which can manifest themselves in fears of death, hospitals, and treatment. Some patients develop conditioned fear responses, which can begin at even the first signs of wheezing. The frantic, worried behavior of parents and those treating the patient can exacerbate the young patient's fear. Moods, too, vary with the severity of symptoms and also in relation to medication taken, . . . (Alexander, 1980, p. 274)

Psychological Causes. In much of the early literature asthma was viewed as a disease with psychological causes. This traditional psychosomatic approach appeared reasonable: For many years those working with asthmatic children had observed problematic psychological and emotional phenomena even as they lacked adequate physiological models. Professionals also had noted a reduction or remission of symptoms when, for one reason or another, children were separated from their families. Indeed, in the 1950s ''parentectomy'' was suggested as the treatment of choice for some children (Peshkin, 1959).

A presumed psychogenesis for asthma led many investigators to postulate that asthmatics would show higher levels of psychopathology and exhibit a characteristic personality type.

By permission of U.S. Department of Health & Human Services-Public Health Service (ADM; 77-497)

Parental concern over precipitating a symptomatic attack often leads children with chronic physical illnesses, such as asthma, to spend appreciable time isolated from their peers.

The asthmatic personality was given various descriptions but usually garnered a number of negative labels such as overdependent, depressed, impulsive, overly aggressive, and overly passive. However, many of the studies of personality had appreciable methodological difficulties, and it is difficult to determine if the psychopathology measured was a cause or result of asthma (Greer, 1978). Neuhaus (1958) compared eighty-four asthmatic children and their siblings, eighty-four chronic cardiac patients and their siblings, and a group of normal controls matched for IQ and demographic characteristics. A personality inventory and projective tests indicated that the asthmatic children did differ from the normal controls. Interestingly, however, they did not differ from the cardiac patients or from their own siblings. Williams and McNicol (1975) conducted a controlled study of a representative sample of 400 asthmatic and 100 control children from a population of 23,000 schoolchildren. These children were evaluated at 7, 10, and 14 years of age. Overall, behavioral disturbances were not common among asthmatic patients, and these children did not differ from normal controls. Only in a small group of children with the most severe and prolonged asthma was there evidence of behavioral disturbance. These children were less socially mature, more demanding, more aggressive toward their mothers, and more anxious. It thus appears that if psychological disturbance is associated with asthma, it is likely the result of serious illness rather than a cause. This does not mean, however, that some psychological mechanism does not play a role in etiology.

Probably the earliest and most widely known psychosomatic explanation of asthma was the psychoanalytic explanation originally offered by French and Alexander (1941). Asthma was hypothesized to arise from an excessive, unresolved dependence on the mother and a resultant fear of separation. The symptoms of wheezing and shortness of breath were viewed as ''a suppressed cry for the mother,'' brought on because crying, and the desire for the mother it represents, become intolerable to the parent. Much of the support for this theory came from individual case studies or reports of groups of case studies. Research studies designed to evaluate the hypothesis often suffered from serious methodological flaws (Freeman, Feingold, Schlesinger, and Gorman, 1964) or failed to demonstrate a relationship between mother-child interactions and the severity of asthma (e.g., McLean and Ching, 1973). Moreover, Purcell and his co-workers found that among chronic asthmatic children, the awareness that separation from their parents was about to occur did not increase asthmatic symptoms (Purcell, Brady, Chai, Muser, Molk, Gordon, and Means, 1969).

Explanations based upon learning theory have also been offered. As early as 1886 Sir James McKenzie described a woman who was reported to develop wheezing from the sight of a paper rose under glass (cited by Alexander, 1980). More recent versions of this position suggest that asthmatic symptoms are classically conditioned. The respiratory symptoms might, for example, initially occur because of an allergic response (unconditioned response) to pollen (unconditioned stimulus). Later, wheezing may occur to just the sight of flowers and weeds or other stimuli that were accidentally associated with the pollen. Although this hypothesis seems reasonable on the surface, there have been no laboratory demonstrations of conditioned asthma in humans. Alexander (1980) also points to the finding that conditioned responses extinguish quickly in the absence of repeated pairings of conditioned and unconditioned stimuli. This is not consistent with the persistence of asthmatic symptoms.

Operant explanations of asthma suggest that initial obstructions of the respiratory passages result in consequences that increase the possibility of the same or similar response occurring in the future. Wheezing or shortness of breath caused by allergy or infection might, for example, bring the child attention from parents or enable the child to avoid some unpleasant task. Recent demonstrations of operant control of respiratory functioning in asthmatics offer some support for this position (Feldman, 1976; Vachon and Rich, 1976). However, the conditioned changes have been small, and additional controlled studies need to be conducted. It should also be remembered that operant control of respiratory function in asthmatics does not necessarily mean that asthmatic symptoms originally developed due to the consequences they incurred.

All in all, there is little, if any, convincing evidence that psychological factors play a significant role in the genesis of the reduced respiratory capacity found in asthma. However, there is evidence that psychological factors may play an important role in *precipitating* asthmatic attacks. Family variables are among those that seem central.

Psychological Irritants. Like many investigators, Purcell and his colleagues—working at the Children's Asthma Research Institute and Hospital in Denver—observed that some children became symptom free fairly soon after being sent away from their parents for treatment. Were these effects due to changes in the emotional environment or physical environment? What other variables accounted for this reaction?

An interesting study on separation provides some of the answers to these questions (Purcell, Brady, Chai, Muser, Molk, Gordon, and

Means, 1969). Prior to the beginning of the study, parents of asthmatic children were interviewed and asked about the degree to which emotions precipitated asthmatic attacks. Children for whom emotions were important precipitants were expected to respond positively to separation from their parents (predicted positive), while children for whom emotions played less of a role were not expected to show improvement. Twenty-five asthmatic children participated in four two-week periods labeled (1) qualification, (2) preseparation, (3) separation, and (4) reunion. During the qualification period the families were aware that the project involved a careful evaluation of asthma in children but were unaware of possible separation. During the second phase, preseparation, the idea of separation was introduced. The third phase was a two-week period during which the children had no contact with their families

but continued their normal daily routines at home under the care of substitute parents. In the fourth phase the children were reunited with their families. A postreunion evaluation was also conducted.

For the predicted positive group all measures of asthma—including peak expiratory flow rate, amount of medication required, daily history of asthma, and daily clincial examination—improved during the separation period. Figure 12–2 illustrates this finding for the peak expiratory flow rate (PEFR) measure. This measure of the maximum expiration of air possible is the most frequently employed reliable measure of air passage obstruction. The children who were not predicted to respond to separation exhibited no differences across phases on any measure.

Other evidence also points to the contribution of psychological factors. Tal and Miklich

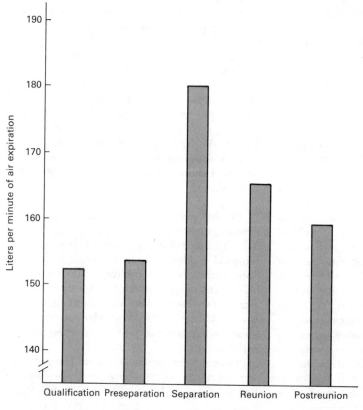

Figure 12–2 Mean daily peak expiratory flow rate for predicted positive group during each period of study. *From Purcell, et al., 1969. Reprinted by permission of the publisher.*

(1976) found that 38 percent of the asthmatic children instructed to revisualize the most frightening and most angry experience in their life had significant reductions in air respiratory flow. Asthmatic children have also been found to react to experimentally induced stress with lowered airway conductance (Mathé and Knapp, 1971). A compelling argument for psychological influences is provided by the findings of Luparello, Lyons, Bleecker, and McFadden (1968). These investigators found that when asthmatic patients were told that the aerosolized saline solution they were inhaling was an allergen or irritant, they exhibited increased respiratory resistance. This effect could be reversed by the patients inhaling another saline placebo that was described as a standard broncho-dilator. Thus, there seems little doubt that psychological factors play a role in the occurrence and exacerbation of asthma. The anxiety created in the child and the family can affect not only the actual asthmatic attack but the entire lifestyle of the family. Behavioral problems that result from the asthma can interfere with successful medical management. Also, the creation of problematic parent-child interactions and the family's handling of the physical disorder can threaten all aspects of the child's social and emotional development. It is therefore not surprising that psychological interventions in childhood asthma have focused on these precipitants and consequences.

Psychological Intervention in Childhood Asthma.   Many of the treatments employed to help the asthmatic child reflect the changing view of the role of psychological variables. Emphasis is placed on increasing coping skills rather than on any presumption of psychopathology. The use of relaxation therapy, one of the best-investigated procedures, illustrates this approach. Relaxation has been employed by itself or as part of systematic desensitization. Systematic desensitization, which involves having the person imagine scenes of increasing anxiety-evoking potential and pairing these visualizations with relaxation, was probably the earliest application of behavior therapy to

asthma (Walton, 1960; Cooper, 1964). It is assumed that the scenes will evoke less anxiety—and thus less asthma—after desensitization. Miklich and his colleagues conducted an outcome investigation of systematic desensitization for asthmatic symptoms (Miklich, Renne, Creer, Alexander, Chai, Davis, Hoffman, and Danker-Brown, 1977). Twenty-six severely asthmatic children with a mean age of 11 years, in residence at the National Asthma Center in Denver, were assigned to either a systematic desensitization therapy or a nontreatment control condition. All children received the same management and care throughout the study, except that only treatment subjects received systematic desensitization. Of several measures taken, only morning pulmonary function was significantly different for the groups, and this was due to a decline in the control group's functioning. Thus, results of this study do not support the use of systematic desensitization to improve lung function. It is still possible, however, that systematic desensitization may be helpful in alleviating the anxiety that surrounds the asthmatic child and family. Reduction of anxiety may have beneficial effects on the management of the asthmatic child and may help minimize the disruptive consequences of the disorder.

Despite this discouraging finding regarding systematic desensitization, the results of the study by Miklich et al. (1977) did suggest that relaxation by itself might be useful. PEFR often improved during the twenty to thirty minutes of relaxation training preceding systematic desensitization, and improvement did not seem due to rest alone. On the basis of this observation, Alexander and his coworkers began a series of studies to investigate the possible beneficial effects of relaxation training. Their results indicated that relaxation did result in improved respiratory functioning and that prepost changes in PEFR improved with training. However, improved functioning was not related to the amount of anxiety reduction achieved by relaxation (Alexander, 1972).

Alexander, Cropp, and Chai (1979) attempted a more rigorous test of relaxation.

Fourteen asthmatic children experienced a series of laboratory sessions, each consisting of three phases: resting, relaxation training, and use of relaxation as previously trained. Evaluations of pulmonary functioning were done immediately prior to (pretest) and following rest or relaxation (test point 1). In addition, three additional assessments were conducted at succeeding half-hour intervals (test points 2, 3, and 4). In order to evaluate the impact of relaxation on clinically significant symptoms, sessions were conducted just prior to the next scheduled medication, the time at which the broncho-dilator given six hours earlier was having its minimum effect. Figure 12–3 illustrates that the influences of relaxation persisted up to two hours following relaxation but that the effects of rest dissipated quickly over time.

Other behavioral procedures have also been employed in the treatment of asthmatic children. Biofeedback refers to a procedure in which some device provides immediate feedback to the person about a particular biological function. Feedback is usually provided by a signal such as a light or tone or by some graphic display. Biofeedback, provided by a signal that comes on when the child's breathing into a machine indicates better respiratory flow, has been reported to improve pulmonary functioning (Feldman, 1976; Vachon and Rich, 1976). However, this and other procedures (cf. Kotses, Glaus, Crawford, Edwards, and Scherr, 1976) have not been subjected to sufficiently controlled studies that can safely attribute changes to the biofeedback procedures (Alexander and Solanch, 1981).

Total treatment of the asthmatic child requires addressing factors other than airways functioning (Creer, 1982). Behavioral procedures have, for example, been employed to reduce the anxiety associated with attacks (Alexander, 1977), to shape proper use of inhalation therapy equipment (Renne and Creer, 1976), to reduce inappropriate requests for hospitalization (Creer, Weinberg, and Molk, 1974), and to increase school attendance and performance (Creer and Yoches, 1971). It is acknowledged that working with the child alone

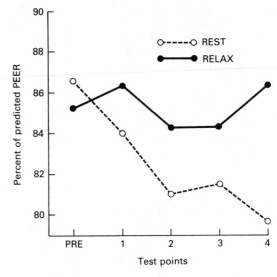

Figure 12–3   Group mean percent of predicted peak expiratory flow rate (PEFR) during resting and relaxing for pretest and the four posttesting assessment points. *From Alexander, Cropp, & Chai, 1979.*

may not be sufficient. Behavioral interventions involving the responses of the family to the child's attacks and the asthmatic's attempts to control the family may be an important adjunct to other treatments (cf. Bronheim, 1978).

Minuchin and his colleagues have described a family systems model and treatment procedure similar to that described for anorexia (p. 125; Minuchin et al., 1975). It is hypothesized that the child's asthmatic symptoms have become enmeshed in patterns of family conflict. Although these workers report success in treating asthmatic families using structural family therapy, controlled research is lacking.

ULCERATIVE COLITIS

Description and Incidence

Ulcerative colitis is a serious disorder of the gastrointestinal system, which is characterized by inflammation and ulceration of the colon and rectum. Diarrhea, blood and mucus in the stool, loss of appetite, weight loss, and anemia usually accompany the disorder. If the condition persists, growth may be affected. A gradual onset with periodic attacks separated by intervals of relative quiescence is the most common form. About 10 percent of children with ulcerative colitis, however, experience an acute onset of symptoms (Werry, 1979c). Mortality rates from 15 to 20% and a strong predisposition to cancer have been reported (Wright, 1979).

Children and young adolescents account for about 10 percent of all ulcerative colitis cases and about 1 out of every 1,000 admissions to children's hospitals. Although reports vary, the sexes would appear to be equally represented, as are all socioeconomic groups. However, the disorder seems to be more common among Caucasians (Werry, 1979c; Wright, 1979).

Etiology

Historically a split has existed in the medical community between those who favor physical theories of etiology and those who espouse psychogenesis. A variety of physical theories have been suggested, but the view that ulcerative colitis is an auto-immune disorder is currently the most popular (Finch, 1980; Werry, 1979c). The blood of the patient is considered to contain some as-yet-unidentified substance that is toxic to the cells of the colon.

Ulcers in general, and ulcerative colitis in particular, were among the first disorders to be considered classically psychosomatic. That is, psychological factors were presumed to cause the disorder. Explanations have focused upon both the characteristics of the children themselves and the children's families. The conclusions drawn from these largely descriptive studies must, however, be viewed with caution, since they are mostly retrospective, employed highly selected and small samples, lacked control groups of normal children or those displaying other physical problems, and used unproven or poor methods of evaluation (Feldman, Cantor, Soll, and Bachrach, 1967; Werry, 1979c).

The few better-controlled studies that do ex-

ist have failed to confirm the role of psychological factors. For example, Feldman et al. (1967) failed to find any differences between thirty-four ulcerative colitis patients (25 percent of whom were under 20), patients with other gastrointestinal disease, and normal controls. These authors found no evidence for psychological precipitation or aggravation of symptoms. West (1970) found adolescent ulcerative colitis patients to be better adjusted on the eight MMPI scales on which they differed from patients having other disorders considered to be psychosomatic.

Beyond a failure to find psychological causes for the disorder or psychological disturbance in children with ulcers, some workers suggest that it is even unclear whether emotional factors play a role in aggravation of symptoms (Werry, 1979c). Others, however, consider the disorder to be an organic one, the course of which is affected by stress and psychological characteristics of the child (Vandersall, 1978). Finally, there are those who, though acknowledging the primary etiological contribution of constitutional factors, continue to discuss the disorder as if it were a "classic" example of a psychosomatic disorder—that is, caused by psychological factors (Finch, 1980; Josselyn et al., 1966).

Treatment

Treatment for ulcerative colitis in children is largely medical in nature. Surgery has become increasingly popular (over 40 percent of cases) and is done earlier in the course of the disorder. Removal of the colon often results in a growth spurt in children whose growth had been arrested and also reduces the threat of cancer. In some cases management of the disorder can be achieved by the use of corticosteroids and other drugs (Werry, 1979c; Wright, 1979).

There are no controlled studies of the effectiveness of psychotherapy with children suffering from ulcerative colitis. Furthermore, available data suggest that there is no relationship between psychological and physical improvements (McDermott and Finch, 1967). This tends to cast further doubt on the role of psychological factors in the etiology or course of the illness. The primary role for psychological treatment seems to be in facilitating child and family adjustment to the condition and its treatment.

Ulcerative colitis, even more than asthma, illustrates the transition in thinking concerning psychosomatic disorders in children. There has been a general failure to establish the importance or exact role of psychological factors in its etiology. There is still some belief that psychological factors play a role in the course of the disorder, but what these influences are and how they operate is still largely speculative. The consequences of having a chronic illness may be the major psychological factor in this and other disorders previously viewed as psychosomatic.

PSYCHOLOGICAL CONSEQUENCES OF CHRONIC ILLNESS

The effects of any life-threatening illness on both the child and family are likely to be pervasive. Stress and anxiety experienced by the child may be substantial, and limitations due to illness often place obstacles in the way of normal developmental processes. For example, contact with peers may be limited, adversely affecting socialization experiences and social skill development. The entire family may experience considerable anxiety and have appreciable stress placed on its daily routines. This affects the family's behavior and its interactions with the ill child. Dependency and manipulativeness may be consequences of parental styles of coping. It is also important to remember that families with an ill child are not immune to the other considerable stresses experienced by all families. Kalnins, Churchill, and Terry (1980) followed forty-five families of children with leukemia over a twenty-month period following diagnosis. In addition to the stress of caring for the leukemic child, the vast majority of these families also had to cope with a variety of other problems (Table 12-1). The impact of chronic physical illness in children has begun to receive the attention of psychologists and other professionals. Although specific factors may vary somewhat from disorder to disorder, available information concerning diabetes illustrates the possible ramifications.

A Description of Juvenile Diabetes Mellitus

Juvenile diabetes is the most common endocrine disorder in children. It is a chronic, lifelong disorder of energy utilization that results from the pancreas producing insufficient

Table 12-1   Concurrent Problems Experienced by Families of Leukemic Children

Categories of Events	Frequency of Occurrence	Percentage of Families Who Experienced Event
Major complications related to the child's leukemia	12	27
Death of another leukemic child	17	35
Death of a family member or friend	9	13
Concurrent illness in a family member requiring hospitalization, surgery, or regular medical care	35	44
Occupational changes	12	22
Financial problems	6	13
Miscellaneous events: moving, purchase or sale of home, postponement of major trip or a marriage, automobile accidents	25	40

Adapted from Kalnins, Churchill, and Terry, 1980.

insulin. Diabetes is characterized by free fatty acids (ketones) in the blood and increased sugar in the blood (hyperglycemia) and urine (glycosuria). Overt symptoms include excessive thirst, increased urination, weight loss, and fatigue. If the disorder is not controlled, the child lapses into a coma. A genetic basis is undoubtedly involved, but the mechanism of inheritance remains unclear (Wright et al., 1979).

Juvenile diabetes, also referred to as "brittle" or "insulin-dependent," is one of two forms of diabetes. The other form, adult-onset, is more common. Although there is some disagreement about prevalence, juvenile diabetes accounts for about 30 percent of all diabetes cases, and approximately 1 child in every 2,500 under the age of 15 suffers from the condition. Onset most frequently occurs between the ages of 10 and 16, although it may occur earlier (Garner and Thompson, 1978). While adult-onset diabetes can often be controlled through diet or weight reduction, the child with juvenile diabetes is dependent upon daily injections of insulin. The treatment regimen usually includes two injections per day, testing of urine two to four times a day, weekly twenty-four hour collections of urine, and dietary restrictions. On the basis of the daily tests for level of sugar in the urine and consideration of factors such as diet, exercise, physical health, and emotional state, the daily dosages of insulin must be adjusted. This is a complex therapeutic regimen, and under the best of circumstances "insulin reactions" occur often. These reactions involve irritability, headache, shaking, and—if not detected early enough—unconsciousness and seizures. Thus, parents and child are faced with a difficult, often unpredictable, and emotion-laden therapeutic program. Management of the regimen and its integration into daily life presents a considerable challenge (Fisher, Delamater, Bertelson, and Kirkley, 1982).

Management of the Diabetic Condition

The victim and loved ones understandably experience a variety of fears, anxieties, and depressive thoughts in their initial reaction to the diagnosis. The first task in treatment is for the team of professionals to gain and maintain control of the diabetic condition. As this is achieved, insulin requirements often decrease and the initial psychological reactions usually abate (Koski, 1969). This "honeymoon period" often causes undue optimism, since the period of partial remission will terminate gradually. Interestingly, overoptimism in both children and parents seems to occur even later on (Thompson, Garner, and Partridge, 1969). The danger in this attitude is that it may result in less attention to the necessary therapeutic regimen. The problem seems most serious during adolescence, when usual attempts at independence and rebellion may be adversely expressed in various aspects of the therapeutic program.

Once initial clinical control is achieved, responsibility must be shifted from the professionals to the parents—and ultimately, to the child. The first step is to educate the family about the disorder and its management. The importance of including the child in this educational process is made clear by the example of the young girl who during an initial hospitalization perceived a remark concerning her diabetes as "die-abetes," leading her to think that she was about to die "of betes" (Garner and Thompson, 1978).

Very often, because of the complexity of the disorder and its treatment, formal classes are conducted, and instruments have been developed to assess the parents' and child's knowledge (Collier and Etzwiler, 1971). Available data suggest that the child's understanding of diabetes increases with age and that by around age 12 is sophisticated enough for the child to assume responsibility for self-care (Etzwiler, 1962; Partridge, Garner, Thompson, and Cherry, 1972). A similar estimate of age of transfer to self-care emerges from reports of patients themselves (Garner and Thompson, 1974). Nevertheless, despite educational efforts, teenage patients and their parents often have misconceptions and insufficient knowledge of the disorder (Collier and Etzwiler, 1971; Frankel, 1975; Garner and Thompson, 1974).

Clearly, psychologists and educators can

make a valuable contribution to the task of family education. One such effort by Etzwiler and Robb (1972) utilized a programmed-instruction format to teach young diabetics and their families. Knowledge significantly increased, but no significant improvement in diabetic control occurred. This is consistent with other data that show that knowledge of the disease is not always associated with compliance with treatment regimens (e.g., Garner and Thompson, 1974).

Lowe and Lutzker (1979) conducted a single-subject experiment on the use of written instructions ("memo") and a point system to increase compliance with medical regimen by Amy, a 9-year-old diabetic girl. Observations were made of three behaviors: dieting, urine

Figure 12–4   Percentage compliance to foot care, urine testing, and diet. *From Lowe and Lutzker, 1979. Reprinted by permission of the publisher and the author.*

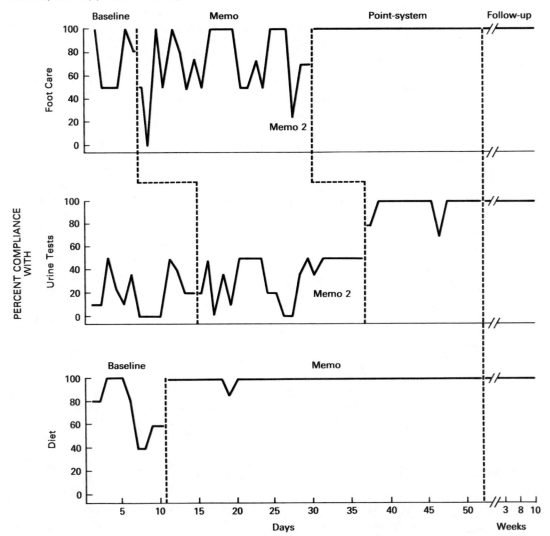

testing, and foot care required to detect sores and prevent gangrene. Following a baseline period memos regarding foot care were given to Amy and posted in the home. In order to demonstrate that changes were the result of planned interventions, memos were introduced at different points in time for the other two behaviors. A point system was introduced next, also at different points in time for the different behaviors. Points earned for following the regimen could be exchanged for daily and weekly reinforcers. Compliance with diet regimen increased to a consistently high level using the memo alone. The point system achieved similar success for foot care and urine testing (see Figure 12–4). Improvements were maintained at a ten-week follow-up. These results suggest cautious optimism regarding the use of behavior management procedures to improve compliance with medical regimen in diabetics and children with other chronic disorders.

Reactions to the Illness

The importance of achieving relatively stable control of diabetic symptoms is suggested by the association between poor control and poor school performance, psychological difficulties, and more frequent physical complications (Melamed and Johnson, 1981). There is also some indication that psychological stress can affect the course of diabetes. Hinkle and Wolf (1952) were successful in correlating increases in blood ketones and urine output with laboratory-induced stress, and similar findings have been obtained by other investigators (Melamed and Johnson, 1981). With regard to naturally occurring stressors, it has been found that following their initial reactions families appear to develop different methods of coping and to achieve different levels of comfort in handling their situations (Garner and Thompson, 1974; Koski, 1969). The two cases presented in Table 12–2

Table 12–2   Illustrative Cases of the Reactions of Two Families to Juvenile Diabetes

Case 1   A nine-year-old boy, in preliminary interview, agreed reluctantly to participate with his family in the study but seemed frightened. His first comment to the experimenter was, "Well, anyhow, I have lots of friends." During his half-day visit with the research team, he declined to remove his heavy jacket although the laboratory rooms (in a hospital setting) were hot. His parents seemed tense, uneasy, and hasty in their responses to questions, frequently interrupting the interviewer. Insulin injections were handled exclusively by the mother, because the father reported he had a "phobia of blood" and so could not help, although no blood is involved in the injections. The parents described the child as "not spoiled," but they felt he got more attention than the other children in the family. After considering the history of their marriage and of their family, the parents agreed that the son's diabetes was "the worst thing that ever happened to us." The mother volunteered that she was already worried over what might happen to the boy's diabetic regimen when he reached adolescence and "rebelled." She also voiced the hope that she would never have any grandchildren lest they be afflicted with the diabetic condition. A variety of measures agreed in characterizing this family as "least comfortable" of all the families studied.

Case 2   Another little boy raced through the half-day of experimental procedures with a grin on his face. He was active in the local 4-H program, spent each summer in a regular camp, played trumpet in the school band, and was generally successful in a variety of school activities. Because of his special knowledge, he was greatly sought after in the school to give special talks on human physiology and on diabetes in particular; he always obliged willingly. The parents reported that they took turns administering the insulin but that the boy handled much of it himself, measuring the insulin and performing the injections efficiently. During the summer before the study, the entire family had gone on a camping trip through Mexico. They reported that they had been able to cope with urine testing, injections, and special diets with no difficulty. In fact, the parents reported they did not consider diabetes a particularly bad thing and that it had not, in their view, affected the family adversely. At the close of the interview, the mother volunteered, "I know what you mean; there are some families with diabetes that go into a tizzy over it. We aren't like that." A variety of measures agreed in characterizing this family as "most comfortable" of all the families studied.

From Garner and Thompson, 1978.

illustrate two extremes of family "comfort" with a diabetic child.

The work of Minuchin and Baker and their colleagues suggests that some family patterns may directly influence the course of the disorder (Minuchin, Rosman, and Baker, 1978). Physiological responses of young diabetics were monitored during a stressful family interview. Arousal and free fatty acid production increased and did not "turn off" once the interview was terminated. Other evidence also suggests that family influences are related to diabetic condition (cf. Koski and Kumento, 1977). Minuchin and his colleagues have also reported that children with unstable diabetes improve with family therapy, but no control group comparisons have been conducted (Min-

uchin, Baker, Rosman, Liebman, Milman, and Todd, 1975).

Given the difficulty and strain involved in managing juvenile diabetes or other chronic disease, it seems likely that at least some families would benefit from family therapy or some other form of psychological intervention. The reduction of stress and achieving "comfort" with the disorder may be facilitated by such assistance. It is necessary for each family to achieve some balance between the extremes of ignoring a chronic disorder and making it the center of the family's and child's entire life. The reactions of one child and family to pediatric cancer illustrate some of the difficulties and adjustments involved (Box 12–2).

Box 12–2   Surviving Pediatric Cancer

Cancer is the disease that causes the greatest number of deaths among children between the ages of 3 and 14. It is the second leading cause of childhood death, after accidents. For at least one form of cancer, acute lymphoplastic leukemia, the picture is becoming brighter. With proper treatment many children are beginning to survive who would not have stood a chance only a short time age. While it is too early to judge long-term survival, there is reason for optimism. The focus in working with children who have cancer thus involves maintenance of the quality of life as well as preparation for death.

As with any life-threatening illness, cancer has far-reaching effects on the child and the entire family system. During what is a highly emotional time, family routines must be altered, the child's activities and contact with peers shift dramatically, and expectations and plans for the future are challenged. The impact on the child and family is complex, and we still have much to learn.

The following excerpts from an interview conducted by JBW with "D," a 14-year-old boy who had been diagnosed as having leukemia at age 6 and had entered remission at age 7, gives some idea of the experience from the child's perspective.

J: What did they tell you about leukemia?
D: They didn't really say anything. They didn't explain it too much. My mother did, once we got to Baltimore, because I didn't want to have any treatment. I didn't want to get bone marrows or any of that stuff. Then my mother finally told me how serious it was, and told me about it.
J: What was the hardest thing about the beginning time when you were sick?
D: Just that I always had all kinds of pains. Either I was in the hospital having a lot of pain or I was in the hotel having a lot of pain. In fact, my father once took me to a toy store and said I could have anything I wanted in the toy store, and I said that I wanted to go home, I wanted to go back to the hotel (which I called home since I'd stayed there so long) and go back to bed.
J: Do you think it was helpful that your family could stay at the hotel nearby the hospital so that you could be together?
D: Yeah, that helped. But when I was in the hospital I missed them sometimes at night. And I know my brother missed me cause he always used to call me in the morning.
J: What were you most afraid of when you were sick?
D: The bone marrows, getting the needles, 'cause they hurt.

J: They hurt?

D: The first time I got it they didn't use any numbing medicine. When I finally got to Baltimore they had to stick me five times.

J: How do you think it changed you, having the illness?

D: It probably made me grow up more quickly, 'cause that was like an adult experience. I was the one who was responsible for myself. So it probably made me more responsible . . . my mother couldn't help me with the needles going in my arm and stuff like that.

J: How about you and your brother? Did things change between you when you were sick?

D: I think it probably made us closer together. When we were home, we'd usually fight a lot. But when I got sick, he seemed to care for me more . . . he knew I might die.

The feeling of having control was important to "D" and seems to be an important factor in the adjustment of pediatric cancer patients and their families (Nannis, et al., 1982). Also of importance is the child's desire for information about his or her illness and about medical procedures. It may be helpful for a sick child to have the opportunity to talk with another child who has been ill with the same disease.

J: Were you ever afraid that the treatment wouldn't work?

D: I was too young to really know about it. I didn't really know what it was for. I knew that it was to fight against it (the leukemia) but I didn't really keep up with it until I got a little older.

J: Do you remember if you liked it when people told you information about it (leukemia)?

D: Nobody really did . . . my mother did, but I don't really remember.

J: Do you wish you'd been told more about it all the way through?

D: It probably would have helped, because then I would have taken stuff a lot more seriously.

J: How about the effects of the chemotherapy. Did they warn you that there'd be changes in your weight and that your hair would get thinner?

D: They told me that my hair was gonna come out. I was usually around all the times with my mother, and the doctor would come and talk to her about it. So I'd be listening and I'd hear it. My mother had told me about it. She had told me I was gonna die unless I'd take the treatment and all that.

J: Do you think it's important for kids who have leukemia to be able to talk about it?

D: Yeah, you want to talk about it, because you want other people to know that you have it and you want them to care for you . . . not to feel sorry for you but to help you.

J: Let's say you were going to be a counselor and you were going to talk to a family in which one of the kids had leukemia. What would you do to help that family?

D: I would just tell them what I went through. That's what we're doing right now. There's a lady on my paper route who my mother knows, and her kid just got leukemia. And so I just went to see him this afternoon. I gave him my phone number, in case he wants to talk to me about it or whatever. I would have liked to have someone to talk to about it, who's already had it.

J: He'll probably really appreciate it, that he has someone to talk to about it.

D: Yeah, he asked me a lot of questions this afternoon and I'm sure he'll end up calling me a few times.

Many factors contribute to a child's experience of recovery from a life-threatening illness. "D"'s sense of control, hope, and reentry into his previous lifestyle were facilitated by support of family and peers.

D: . . . Once we got the right medicine, it made me feel a lot better. I did more things; I didn't just lay in bed all the time . . . it made me almost back to normal. I'd had so many bad cells and all that, then I knew I was almost back to a normal person.

J: You say you went back to normal. Did you feel like you weren't normal?

D: I'm talking about a normal person . . . like a six-year-old who's in school. He doesn't have pains all the time, and he's out playing baseball and running around. What I was doing was just sitting in a motel room or laying in a hospital.

J: How about school? Did you fall behind a lot in school?

D: No. My father would come (to Baltimore) over the weekends. He'd meet my teacher before, and just get the important stuff. And he'd go over it with me on the weekends, and I'd get it done. And then he'd take it back to the teacher. I was in first grade, and I passed it easily.

J: What do you think helped you have such an easy time with it?

D: Well, probably because my parents were teaching it to me. It's a little different than when a teacher does it. Plus I knew that I wanted to get through that schoolwork, 'cause I didn't want to have to fail.

J: How were the kids at school when they heard about it?

D: Well, when I had first gotten sick, I must have gotten a card from every person. My mother went and got the cards. I had gotten pictures, and all kinds of stuff. I've still got them. And then when I got back, they were surprised to see that I didn't have any hair . . . They got used to it.

J: You didn't get teased or anything?

D: A few times, but I wasn't worried about it.

The experience of life-threatening illness on a child may have bearing on later behavioral patterns or goals. The influence is not necessarily negative.

J: Do you think that when you get little illnesses now, like colds or flu, you get more scared?

D: No, because right now I'm in real good shape. I'm nowhere near a relapse. I've got good counts so that'll fight back the colds. If my counts were low, yeah I'd be scared, but they're not low.

J: What are your plans like for the future? Do you ever think about what you want to be?

D: I want to be probably either a doctor or a dentist. A doctor—you know I know quite a bit, so that would help . . . of course I'd have to go to med school and all that. But that, right now, is what I'd like to be.

J: Do you think that because you were ill and you became more aware about medicine, about health, and about doctors, that had an influence?

D: Yeah, a big influence . . . I already know about some of those things.

J: How about when you meet new friends. Do you tell them that you had leukemia?

D: I've really had about the same friends, and if I do meet someone, I usually don't tell them because I don't think about it. I don't think about having it. It wouldn't influence anything. If told my friends I had it they wouldn't think anything different, 'cause I've had the same friends since first grade, and I've still got them as friends. It don't bother me.

J: How often do you think about it (the leukemia)?

D: Sometimes at night I'll think about it, what I had been through. I think about it every now and then, but not really that often.

PSYCHOLOGICAL MODIFICATION OF PHYSICAL FUNCTIONS

The Eastern mystic who walks on hot coals, voluntarily slows the heart, and by the power of the mind closes a wound has always fascinated inhabitants of the Western world. Fascinating too are the primitive shaman's cures by removal of evil spirits; the miracles of faith healers; and cures of medical ailments by inert placebos (cf. Ullmann and Krasner, 1975). These phenomena highlight in a dramatic fashion the possible role of psychological interventions in the treatment of medical disorders. Each of these suggest that psychological procedures can directly affect physical functioning. The *systematic* and *scientific* study of how psychology can be used to treat physical symptoms directly is part of the shifting emphasis in understanding mind-body relationships.

Experimental research has demonstrated that responses of the autonomic nervous system can be modified by classical and operant conditioning (Blanchard and Young, 1974; Miller, 1969). Heart rate (e.g., Bleeker and Engle, 1973), blood pressure (e.g., Shapiro, Schwartz, and Tursky, 1972), and pulmonary resistance (Kotses, Glaus, Crawford, Edwards, and Scherr, 1976), as well as other functions, have been altered. This suggests that procedures such as relaxation and biofeedback can be employed to train a person to control systems that are overreactive in a particular physical ("psychosomatic") disorder. However, current knowledge warrants cautious optimism, at best.

One successful application of nonpharmacological interventions for physical disorders has been the use of relaxation and biofeedback to treat headache. The vast majority of this work has concentrated on adults, but some workers have recently turned their attention to the problem of headaches in children.

Research with adults suggests that among psychological treatments, temperature biofeedback alone, relaxation training alone, or temperature biofeedback combined with autogenic training (the person recites phrases such as "I feel quiet . . . my hands are warm") are equally effective and superior to a placebo in treating migraine headaches. The rationale for using temperature biofeedback is based on the role of the vascular system in these headaches. Sym-

pathetic nervous system overactivity is thought to cause the vascular responses that lead to migraine. The person is taught to control hand temperature, and this temperature control is assumed to turn off sympathetic nervous system overactivity. The treatment of childhood headache has relied almost entirely on medication especially for migraine (Diamond and Dalessio, 1978; Rothner, 1979). The possible consequences of prolonged use of medication (for example, serious side effects, potential for abuse) suggest extension of successful nonpharmocological treatments to children.

Andrasik, Blanchard, Edlund, and Rosenblum (1982) conducted an investigation of the effectiveness of combined temperature biofeedback and autogenic training in the treatment of childhood vascular headache. The treatment procedure was applied to two girls aged 12 and 14. To achieve experimental control baseline procedures were continued for the second girl while treatment was being introduced for the

In biofeedback some physiological function such as finger temperature or muscle tension is monitored. The child is then taught to control this function through feedback provided by a display, as pictured above, or some other signal.

first. The same treatment was then begun for the second girl. Temperature was measured from the index finger, and feedback was available visually and aurally. Subjects were taught to increase finger temperature by saying autogenic phrases, and the notion of passive striving (nonactive techniques such as picturing a pleasant scene) to reduce sympathetic nervous system overactivity was emphasized. Daily ratings of headache intensity, frequency, and headache-free days indicated a significant improvement on all three measures and maintenance of these gains four to five months following treatment (Figure 12–5).

Psychological procedures have begun to be applied to a variety of children's disorders, such as asthma (Alexander et al., 1979; Kotses et al., 1976), seizures, and hyperkinesis (Lubar and Shouse, 1977; Mostofsky and Balaschak, 1977). Initial reports suggest the usefulness of treatments such as biofeedback and relaxation. However, it is too early to confidently attribute obtained improvements to these procedures. Other social-psychological influences that are present in the biofeedback context (for example, psychological placebo) may contribute considerably to these results (Andrasik and Holroyd, 1980; Plotkin and Rice, 1981).

Figure 12–5 Number of headache-free days per week for two children during baseline, biofeedback treatment, and follow-up. *From Andrasik, et al., 1982.*

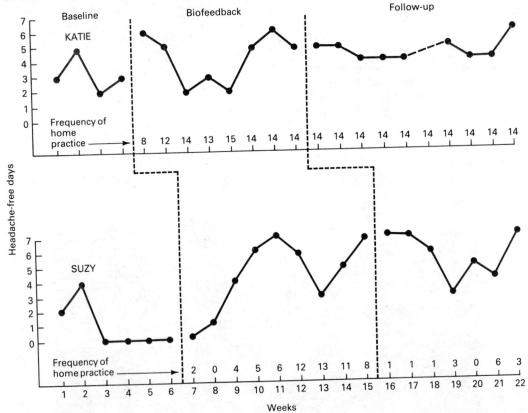

FACILITATING MEDICAL TREATMENT

Psychological factors also influence the effective delivery of medical treatments for physical disorders. Understanding the contribution of psychological influences and developing psychologically based procedures for enhancing the effectiveness of medical treatment is another important and growing area of interest. Procedures for reducing fear of dental treatment, for increasing compliance with medical regimens, and for dealing with hospitalization illustrate this potentially important contribution.

Fear Reduction in Dental Treatment

Fear, and the disruptive behaviors that often accompany it, frequently interferes with providing good medical treatment. Procedures that reduce fearful behavior can thus be quite valuable. The reduction of dental fears and disruptive behaviors during dental care is one example of such efforts (e.g. Nocella and Kaplan, 1982). Viewing a film showing a cooperative peer model undergoing dental treatment has been shown to reduce disruptive behavior and to lower ratings of anxiety in children with no previous dental treatment experience (Melamed, 1979). As might be expected, the child's age and previous experience seem to be important factors in determining the best preparation procedures.

Melamed and her colleagues assigned children between the ages of 4 and 11 to one of five film conditions (Melamed, Yurcheson, Fleece, Hutcherson, and Hawes, 1978). Children in the "long model" condition observed a ten-minute film of a child undergoing examination, anesthetic injection, cavity preparation, and placement of the restoration. The model remained cooperative and fearless throughout these procedures. The "long demonstration" condition involved a film in which the dentist and assistant went through the same procedures without a child model in the chair. "Short model" and "short demonstration" conditions paralleled

the first two conditions, except that the examination and injection were the only procedures viewed. Children in the control condition viewed a film of a child enjoying unrelated activities. A variety of measures were employed to evaluate the child's subjective, behavioral, and physiological anxiety. Cooperation during an initial dental clinic visit and during a second visit that was preceded by one of the films described above was also assessed. Children who viewed a model exhibited less disruption and apprehension than those who viewed a demonstration. The effect was strongest for children who were most similar in age to the model. Although the length of the presentation did not have any effect on older children, younger children (4 to 6) benefited more from the longer presentation, as measured by heart rate and self-reports of fear. Interestingly, children with previous treatment experience benefited most from observing the model undergoing the entire treatment or from the short demonstration without a peer model. Children with no prior experience, however, were sensitized (more disruptive) after viewing this short demonstration.

Compliance with Medical Regimens

Failure to comply with a prescribed medical regimen (for example, taking medication or adhering to a diet) is one of the best documented but least understood problems in providing adequate medical care. Patient noncompliance may have a number of adverse effects—reduced efficacy of medical therapy, complication or exacerbation of the disorder, and bias in interpretation of clinical therapeutic research trials. The accumulation of unused medicines in the home also increases the risk of accidental poisonings.

Under certain circumstances as many as 80 to 90 percent of patients do not follow, or err in following, prescribed medical regimens (Davis, 1966; Dunbar and Agras, 1980). Accurate compliance appears to vary with characteristics of the regimen itself, comprehension of the regimen, characteristics of the prescrib-

Courtesy of New York State Department of Health

Fears of medical procedures are common among children. Particularly for children who must undergo frequent treatment, techniques that reduce fearful behavior can facilitate good medical care.

ing clinician, and characteristics of the treatment setting. Social support is also associated with compliance—and might be particularly important for children. Each of these factors is modifiable. Although this is a relatively new research area, in which studies often lack adequate experimental control, available evidence suggests that interventions are likely to contribute to increased adherence (Dunbar and Agras, 1980).

A number of controlled experiments have been conducted with children. As we saw earlier in this chapter, Lowe and Lutzker (1979) demonstrated that posting written reminders and rewards for compliance increased adherence to diet, foot care, and urine testing by a diabetic girl. Central to diabetes treatment is accurate testing of urine glucose levels by the patient. Errors in testing are quite common, with inaccurate estimates probably occurring as much as 55 percent of the time (e.g., Epstein, Coburn, Becker, Drash, and Siminerio, 1980). Epstein and his colleagues have shown that at least short-term improvements can be achieved with diabetic youngsters (Epstein, Figueroa, Farkas, and Beck, 1981). After being screened for accuracy with a series of ten prepared samples varying in glucose level, youngsters who were at least 50 percent inaccurate were as-

signed to one of two conditions. Children in the extended practice condition tested twenty additional prepared samples under conditions similar to screening. Youngsters in the feedback condition also tested twenty more samples but were informed of the correct concentration following each trial. All children were then retested approximately twenty minutes later. The children experiencing feedback improved their accuracy from screening to posttraining, while those who had only extended practice became slightly less accurate (Figure 12–6).

Hospitalization

Children suffering from chronic illnesses often require periodic hospitalization to stabilize their functioning. Normal children, too, often need to enter the hospital for minor surgery, such as tonsillectomy. In the mid-1950s the importance of the child's psychological reaction to early hospitalization and surgery began to be recognized. Researchers noted that a majority of children experienced mild to extreme stress reactions during and following hospitalization and that many demonstrated behavioral problems following surgery (e.g., Prugh, Staub, Sands, Kirschbaum, and Lenihan, 1953). Psychological upset seemed to be

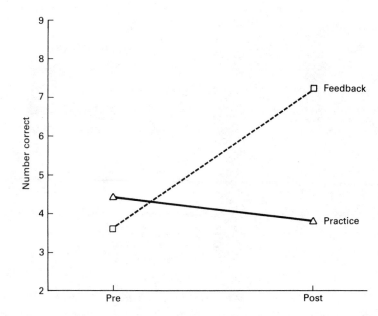

Figure 12–6 The number of correct estimates of glucose level for diabetic children in practice and feedback conditions. *From Epstein, et al., 1981.*

determined most frequently by separation from parents and unfamiliarity with the hospital and medical procedures. Children between the ages of 6 months and 4 years appeared to be at highest risk (Vernon, Foley, Sipowicz, and Schulman, 1965). Much of the early work was methodologically flawed; improved methodology (e.g., Vernon, Schulman, and Foley, 1966) suggested that many children show no adverse effects, or only short-term difficulties. Subsequent research has supported these findings (Peterson and Shigetomi, 1982). The more recent findings may be partly due to changes in hospital procedures inspired by the early findings: preoperative information to the parents and child, full visitation privileges for parents, "rooming-in" of the mother with the child. Nonetheless, the fact that large numbers of children will undergo hospitalization, that many will find the experience stressful, and that a few may experience long-term consequences argues for the importance of identifying the most vulnerable and providing assistance in reducing stress.

Douglas (1975) examined the long-term effects of early hospitalization. Follow-ups were conducted on a sample consisting of one out of every four children born in Great Britain during a particular week. Approximately 20 percent of the children who were later hospitalized seemed to experience some immediate adverse effect. Unrestricted visiting and no surgery seemed to reduce upset. Adolescent conduct disorders and reading difficulties seemed to occur more frequently among some small proportion of those children who had experienced early hospitalization. A secure child, a stay of less than one week, an age less than 6 months and more than 3 years, a single admission, and a working mother were negatively correlated with difficulty in adolescence.

Burstein and Meichenbaum (1979) found that children differed in their disposition to engage in the constructive "work of worrying" prior to hospitalization. Twenty children, ranging in age from 4.8 years to 8.6 years, who were scheduled for minor surgery were tested on three occasions: at home a week before surgery, in the hospital the night before surgery, and at home one week after surgery. At the first testing a questionnaire evaluating the tendency to deny common weaknesses (defensiveness) and

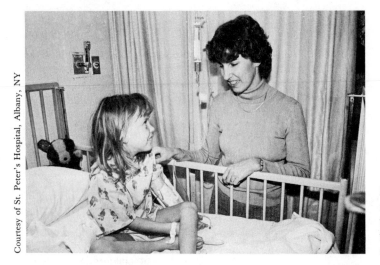

Courtesy of St. Peter's Hospital, Albany, NY

Preparation beforehand, rooming-in of the mother, and familiar toys can help reduce the potential negative impact of hospitalization for the child.

a scale measuring situational anxiety were administered to all children. In addition, observations were made of the child's play with stress-related toys (doctor kit or a game called "Operation") or nonrelated toys matched for attractiveness. Anxiety and play measures were also administered on the other two occasions. The play choices of nonhospitalized control subjects were made on three occasions one week apart.

Control children played equally with both types of toys, and this pattern did not change over time. For the other children increased scores on the anxiety scale and disruption of play during hospitalization indicated that hospitalization was anxiety arousing. However, there seemed to be two types of children. One group, which was low on defensiveness and played with stress-related toys prior to hospitalization, experienced minimal distress and anxiety following surgery. In contrast, children who initially had been more defensive and avoided playing with stress-related toys reported the most anxiety following surgery. The researchers suggested that children differ in the disposition to engage in preparing themselves for hospitalization and that engaging in the constructive "work of worrying" serves an

adaptive function. A seven-month follow-up revealed that children disposed to engage in this "work" remembered more specific parental preparations prior to surgery and had developed a better-articulated and specific conception of the experience and how to cope with it.

The majority of nonchronic-care pediatric hospitals now offer prehospital preparation for both the child and parents (Peterson and Ridley-Johnson, 1980). One method of preparation involves the use of models who, although apprehensive, cope with the hospitalization stresses. Melamed and Siegel (1975) showed a film to children, between 4 and 12 years old, before they were admitted for nonemergency surgery. The film showed a 7-year-old boy prior to, during, and after surgery. A similar group of children matched for age, sex, race, and type of operation served as controls and viewed a film of a boy on a nature trip. Measurements were taken before and after viewing the film, the night before surgery, and at a one-month postsurgery follow-up. Children who had seen the coping-model film had lower sweat-gland activity, reported fewer medical fears, and exhibited less anxiety-related behavior. These differences were exhibited both before surgery and at the one-month follow-up. Interestingly, only control group parents reported increases in behavioral problems among their children following hospitalization.

THE DYING CHILD

Clearly, one of the most distressing aspects of working with some ill children is the prospect of death. This is a multifaceted problem, with many complex questions. What is the child's understanding of death? How can we best prepare the child? The family? How do we balance preparation for death with a need to sustain the motivation for adherence to life-prolonging treatment regimens? Can we help the family begin to accept the child's impending death but yet prevent it from premature distancing from the child? What do we do after the child dies? How is the helper affected by working with the dying child? These difficult questions have only recently begun to be addressed.

Not much is known about children's reaction to impending death. It does appear that children's conceptions of death are influenced by their parents' views and change during development. Young children may think of death as being less alive and assume it to be reversible. At about 5 years of age, an appreciation of the finality of death may be present, but death is still not inevitable. An understanding of death as final and inevitable and of personal mortality emerges at about age 9 or 10. Cognitive development plays a role in the evolving conceptualization of death. Koocher (1973), employing a Piagetian framework, evaluated seventy-five healthy children ranging in age from 6 to 15 years to determine their primary level of cognitive functioning. In addition, they were asked four questions: "What makes things die? How can you make dead things come back to life? When will you die? What will happen then?" The children's understanding became more realistic and reflected higher levels of cognitive organization as their levels of cognitive functioning progressed from preoperational, to concrete-operational, to formal operational. While developmental differences in cognitive understanding may exist, it must also be appreciated that children may be aware of death and worried about their fatal illness even if they do not have a fully developed concept of death.

Spinetta (1974) found that although there has been substantial concern about this issue, little controlled research has been conducted. Disagreement exists as to the child's awareness of the seriousness of the illness, the experience of death anxiety, and the age at which awareness and reactions to possible death occur. Research suggests and practitioners increasingly agree, however, that fatally ill children as young as 6 are aware and concerned. Although the expression of this concern may not always be direct, the fatally ill child reacts with greater anxiety to his or her illness than the chronically but not fatally ill child (Spinetta, 1974).

What of family members? Certainly, they too must be made aware of the seriousness of the child's illness. However, what is the appropriate balance between acceptance and hope? It is a genuine challenge to prepare the parents for the death of the child yet enable them to help emotionally and assist with the treatment regimen. It requires mental health staff who are knowledgeable and sensitive. As our ability to lengthen survival—and perhaps raise hopes of some future cure—increases, the problem will become even more difficult. Integration of support services into the total treatment program and immediate availability and access will probably facilitate delivering needed help. Also, the family should not be abandoned after the child's death (Rando, 1983). Provisions for continued assistance and support should be conceptualized as part of the total treatment.

Caregivers, too, are not immune to the effects of observing a child dying. Koocher (1980) suggests that efforts must be made to reduce the high cost of helping: the inevitable stress and feelings of helplessness and the likelihood of burnout. This is not a trivial matter. The helpers' adjustment and efficiency are not the only concern. The potential impact of their behavior on the family and child is also significant. In

"Who's Afraid of Death on a Leukemia Ward?" Vernick and Karon (1965) offer poignant anecdotes to this effect. One such anecdote describes the impact of helpers' behavior on a 9-year-old patient who, after taking a turn for the worse, received some medical treatment and began to show improvement.

One day while she was having breakfast I commented that she seemed to have gotten her old appetite back. She smiled and agreed. . . . I mentioned that it looked as if she had been through the worst of this particular siege. She nodded in agreement. I went on to say that it must have been very discouraging to feel so sick that all she could do was worry—worry about dying. She nodded affirmatively. I recognized that the whole episode must have been very frightening and that I knew it was a load off her mind to be feeling better. She let out a loud, "Whew", and went on to say that except for me, nobody really talked with her. "It was like they were getting ready for me to die." (p. 395)

Certainly, one of the most difficult decisions is what to tell the dying child. The approach that Koocher and Sallan (1978) label "protective" or "benign lying" was advocated in the 1950s and 1960s. The child was not to be burdened, and a sense of normalcy and optimism was to be maintained. Many workers now feel that this approach is not helpful and probably is doomed to failure anyway. The stress on the family of maintaining this deception is great, and the likelihood that the child will believe the deception is questionable. Some individual, yet difficult, balance must be struck. Koocher and Sallan (1978) explain this balance in the following excerpt:

A child with a life-threatening illness should be told the name of the condition, given an accurate explanation of the nature of the illness (up to the limit of his ability to comprehend), and told that it is a serious illness of which people sometimes die. At the same time, however, the child and family can be told about treatment options and enlisted as allies to fight the disease. An atmosphere must be established in which all concerned have the opportunity to ask questions, relate fantasies, and express concerns, no matter how scary or far fetched they may seem.

When the patient is feeling sick, weak, and dying, there is no need to remind him of the prognosis. If a family and patient know a prognosis is poor but persist in clinging to hope, one has no right to wrest that from them. The truth, humanely tempered, is important, but we must be mindful of the patient and how his needs are served. To tell the "whole truth" or a "white lie" for the benefit of the teller serves no one in the end. (p. 300)

SUMMARY

Attempting to determine the role of psychological factors in physical disorders is part of a long tradition of trying to understand the relationship between mind and body. The DSM-III diagnostic category of Psychological Factors Affecting Physical Conditions reflects the current view that psychological factors are relevant to physical disorders in a number of different ways. This represents a shift from the earlier psychosomatic disease conceptualization—physical diseases caused by emotional factors.

Current studies address three different aspects of the interface between psychology and medicine: the role of psychological factors in the etiology and maintenance of physical conditions, the role of psychology in treatment, and the psychological consequences of physical disorders.

Current conceptualizations of the role of psychological factors in asthma illustrate many of the changes that have occurred regarding causation. For example, a distinction is made between the causes of the asthmatic disorder and the mechanisms which trigger an asthmatic attack. Psychological influences are one of a variety of possible trigger mechanisms that can bring on an asthmatic episode. There is, however, little support for the idea that psychological factors play a role in causing reduced respiratory capacity. For asthma, as well as for other disorders such as ulcerative colitis, there has been a shift from exploring the role of emotional factors in the genesis of physical conditions to examining the multiple ways that psychological factors affect children with these conditions.

The appreciable social and emotional consequences of chronic illness have received increasing attention. For juvenile diabetes and other chronic illnesses, there is likely to be considerable individual variability in how children and families cope. The first task for the professional is to achieve and maintain control of the diabetic condition. The child and family's acceptance of the disorder and attitude toward its control are crucial in successful treatment. Shifting of responsibility from the professional to the family, and ultimately to the child, is required if control of the condition is to be maintained. At the same time, the impact on the child's overall development and the family's functioning is likely to be substantial, and this needs to be incorporated into any comprehensive treatment program.

Psychology can contribute to effective treatment of medical conditions in a number of ways. Beyond its obvious role in dealing with the psychological consequences of illness, psychological treatments (for example, relaxation and biofeedback) may be able to modify physical functioning directly. Initial successes with disorders such as asthma and migraine headache suggest an appreciable potential. Psychology may also facilitate the delivery of medical interventions. By reducing the anxiety felt by children undergoing medical procedures, not only do psychologists make the child more comfortable, but they also make the role of medical personnel easier. Also, medical treatment is often rendered ineffective due to failure of the patient and family to adhere to the prescribed treatment regimens. A number of researchers have demonstrated how behavioral interventions can increase adherence.

The prospect of death is one of the most distressing aspects of working with physically ill children. Psychological contributions to understanding the child's conception of death and the mechanisms of coping with this possibility can aid effective and caring treatment. The impact of death on the professional working with these children is important for that person as well as for the influence it will have on the ability to help.

13

EVOLVING CONCERNS FOR THE CHILD

PREVENTION OF BEHAVIOR
DISORDERS

Rochester Primary Mental Health
   Project
Head Start and Early Intervention
Child Abuse and Its Prevention
Crisis Intervention: Sudden Infant
   Death Syndrome
Prevention of Schizophrenia
Issues in Prevention

THE CHILD AS A COMPETENT
HUMAN

Building Competencies in Children

THE RIGHTS OF CHILDREN

The Problem of Child Placement
What Children Think about Their Rights
Progress in Children's Rights

THE CHALLENGE OF THE FUTURE:
WHO IS FOR CHILDREN?

SUMMARY

Every society depends on its children for its future. Despite this obvious fact, attitudes toward the welfare of the young change with social, political, and economic conditions. Today we are witnessing some of the positive reverberations from the chaotic and stimulating 1960s. Central to this decade was a concern for the care and rights of groups of individuals deemed disadvantaged and powerless in society. Children fell under this rubric for a variety of reasons—some because they were poor or physically and mentally handicapped, others due to negligence and abuse, and still others because the young were considered lacking in political and legal clout. In addition to this broad social thrust, progress in understanding the development and health of children has stimulated efforts toward optimizing the potential of the young. In this final chapter we turn to some of the evolving concerns for children and the ways in which they are manifested in societal programs and policies.

PREVENTION OF BEHAVIOR DISORDERS

Few would dispute the proposition that prevention of behavior disorders, at least in the abstract, is superior to alleviation of problems that already exist. Current interest in prevention was spurred by the observation that treatment had scarcely—if at all—kept up with the need for intervention. Other factors also were influential. Professionals had become acutely aware of the difficulty of undoing some kinds of damage once it had set in. Also, widespread dissatisfaction existed with traditional approaches to treatment that are costly, lengthy, and largely unavailable to or ineffective with diverse groups of needy people.

Some conditions are clearly preventable, or preventable in large measure. Knowledge of etiology, especially if a single etiological agent is central, helps tremendously. The American Public Health Association considers six categories of mental disorders preventable: those caused by poisoning, infectious agents, genetic processes, nutritional deficits, injuries, and systemic anomalies (Bloom, 1981). Most of these disorders result in chronic brain syndromes. It is also possible, however, to prevent disorders in the absence of known etiology. The general model calls for the epidemiological study of people identified as having the disorder so that hypotheses can be constructed concerning its path of development. Interventions can then be mounted and evaluated. For example, the discovery that a particular disease is high among people using a specific water supply could reasonably lead to treatment of the water on a trial basis. As it turns out, however, this model, too, seems most effective when a necessary biological precondition is operating (for example, infectious agents, vitamin deficiency). For most mental disorders a necessary biological precondition has not been determined. How, then, can preventive interventions for psychological problems be mounted?

Much of our current thinking about this question has evolved from Caplan's work *Principles of Preventive Psychiatry,* published in 1964. This public health approach seeks to reduce the prevalence of mental disorders in the population by prevention rather than treatment. Caplan suggested a three-prong attack consisting of tertiary, secondary, and primary prevention.

Primary prevention attempts to reduce the rate of new cases—that is, to stave off disorders in the first place. It can be accomplished by provision of the physical, psychosocial, and cultural factors considered necessary for healthy development and by special support during developmental and accidental crises. *Secondary prevention* is usually defined as the effort to shorten the duration of existing cases through early referral and diagnosis and through rapid treatment. It often, but not always, focuses on populations at high risk for disorders. *Tertiary prevention* aims to reduce defective functioning that is residual to disorders. Thus, it might seek to minimize the impact of hospitalization or of negative stereotypes of mental illness. Although tertiary efforts certainly may reduce the prevalence of malfunctioning in the population, secondary and primary programs are what commonly come to mind when the term *prevention* is used.

Preventive programs vary tremendously in focus and setting. They include, for example, *genetic screening,* which aims to decrease the proportion of infants born with hereditary disorders. The purpose of *high-risk infant programs* is to provide specific early inputs that might overcome influences associated with less-than-optimal growth. For example, parents are taught how to optimally interact with children who suffer cerebral palsy, who were born prematurely or at low weight, or who display certain temperamental styles (Brown, 1981). *Early screening* of general intelligence, reading retardation, hyperactivity, school maladjustment, and other problems is often considered crucial for preventive programming. Still another approach is to focus on the *alleviation of potential crises,* such as the child's entrance to school or the need for hospitalization. Finally, some practitioners expressly aim to *develop competence,* on the assumption that good mental health can be built to ward off breakdown. Let us take a closer look at some of these efforts, sampling their great variety as well as focusing on areas that are presently of great concern.

Rochester Primary Mental Health Project (PMHP)

The Rochester Primary Mental Health Project, initiated well over twenty years ago by Cowen, Zax, and their colleagues, took the school as its focus for preventive efforts (Cowen et al., 1975; Zax and Cowen, 1967). The school was selected not only because it is the setting for much socialization and learning but also because three out of every ten American children experience school maladjustment. Moreover, schools can provide an easily reached, large population of children. Although PMHP has evolved over the years, its continuing thrust has been early identification and treatment of children's maladjustment to school. Thus, the project's focus is secondary prevention.

One of the innovative aspects of PMHP is mass screening of youngsters soon after they begin first grade. Screening methods have consisted of parental interviews, psychological testing, teacher reports, and direct observations. Diverse kinds of data are collected concerning developmental and health history; adjustment to community playmates; adaptation to family training; parental education, employment history, attitudes, and aspirations; manifestations of school adjustment problems; estimates of intellectual functioning; and measures of positive skills. Of special interest is the development of AML and CARS, both of which are objective teacher rating scales of problem behaviors (Cowen, Gersten, and Wilson, 1979; Lorion and Cowen, 1978). Three dimensions of behavior are tapped by these scales: aggressive-acting out, moody-anxious, and learning disability. A considerable amount of research has been conducted that demonstrates reliability and validity (e.g., Carberry and Handal, 1980; Durlak, Stein, and Mannarino, 1980).

Children identified in PMHP as already manifesting maladjustment or as likely to do so in the future become the recipients of special treatment by nonprofessional child-aides. The activities of the aides depend on the needs of the individual child and the propensities and interaction of the teachers and aides. During the early stages of the project, the aides spent much time in the classroom, talking to individual children or to groups, telling stories, playing games, or helping with remedial work. This arrangement resulted in the teachers feeling that they had been forced into the role of disciplinarian ogres while the aides had assumed the role of mother or friend who neither defined nor set limits. The program was restructured to eliminate this weakness. The aides were moved out of the classroom and met with individual students who were referred by the teachers. In addition, a team approach was fostered by having the teacher and the aide meet together with the "mental health team" (that is, the project social worker, psychologist, and perhaps consultant) to discuss a specific child and work out a concrete treatment plan.

The utilization of minimally paid nonprofessionals as "therapists" is a noteworthy dimension of the Primary Mental Health Project. Many of the child-aides are mothers with relatively modest formal education. They receive some training at the project, but personal qualities are also considered a potent treatment resource.

Cowen and his colleagues have conducted considerable research on PMHP, designed to improve the program and to demonstrate possible benefit. With regard to early detection of childhood problems, it was found that many children labeled at high risk by the screening procedures performed poorly in school in subsequent years. Without treatment, many of them eventually required mental health services. In contrast, children who were given the opportunity to work with the nonprofessional aides were later judged as improved by teachers, aides, parents, and mental health workers. An extensive evaluation of several hundred

Many programs for children rely on the use of nonprofessional as well as professional workers.

children who participated in PMHP at some time during 1974–1981 suggests reductions in acting-out, shyness, and learning problems, as well as gains in sociability, assertiveness, and tolerance of frustration (Weissberg, Cowen, Lotyczewski, and Gesten, 1983). However, the raters knew that the children were PMHP participants, and the study had no control group. Not all the findings over the years have been positive either; some data indicate that those most helped were the shy-anxious children, the younger children, and those of higher SES (Rappaport, 1977). This kind of information has been helpful to the project; for example, greater efforts were instituted to facilitate the aides' effectiveness with acting-out and learning disabled youngsters (Cowen, Gersten, and Wilson, 1979). PMHP began as a single demonstration project, but in 1983 twenty PMHP projects were operating in the Rochester, New York, area. Furthermore, through a national dissemination effort 80 school districts and 300 schools around the country had initiated conceptually related programs.

Head Start and Early Intervention

The War on Poverty was formally initiated in 1964 by the Economic Opportunity Act. The Head Start program was earmarked by this legislation and began in the summer of 1965. Its underlying assumption is that poor youngsters are at risk for low academic achievement, which, in turn, works against their attaining decent jobs and a healthy, fulfilling life. Since the early years of life appear extremely important for later learning, children from age 3 to school-entry age are enrolled in "compensatory" education. However, from the beginning Head Start encompassed more than school experience per se. It is a comprehensive developmental program with four major components (U.S. Department of Health and Human Services, 1980) which aim at secondary or primary prevention.

1. Education. The educational component places children into classes that have a high teacher-student ratio and that try to meet each child's needs. The ethnic and cultural characteristics of the community are considered in structuring the educational experience. For example, at least one teacher or teacher aide must speak the native language when a majority of children are bilingual.

2. Health. Physical and mental health are emphasized. The children are served meals that meet at least one-third of their daily minimal nutritional needs. Parents are offered education in nutrition. Medical examinations are conducted that include hearing, vision, and dental check-ups; follow-up medical treatment is provided when appropriate. A mental health professional is available to evaluate special needs and to provide training in child development for staff and parents.

3. Parent Involvement. Community involvement is fundamental to Head Start. Parents participate in decision making concerning program planning, operating activities, and management. Many serve as volunteers or employees. They join workshops on various topics related to the welfare of their children or the family.

4. Social Services. Head Start families often have needs for other services; it is the task of the Head Start social service coordinator to help obtain these services. The object is to strengthen the family unit so that it may do the best job possible in rearing children and supporting its adult members.

In addition to the typical Head Start programs described above, Head Start has several special projects designed to evaluate new ways of helping children and families. *Home Start,* for example, began as a three-year demonstration project that brought health and educational services directly to the home. It was predicated partly on the belief that the mother-child relationship is critical and should not be disturbed by removing the child from the home. In addition, training a mother to work with her child may be highly efficient because she may generalize the experience to her other youngsters (e.g., Bronfenbrenner, 1974; Levenstein, 1974).

Although it appears that out-of-home programs may certainly be effective (Palmer and Semlear, 1977; Zigler, 1978), home-based projects fulfill the needs of certain situations.

Another demonstration project is *The Child and Family Mental Health Project,* launched in 1979 to examine ways in which to deliver mental health services to Head Start families for prevention of later problems. The goal of the fourteen demonstration programs is to increase competence, coping skills, and positive self-concepts so that children will be less vulnerable to challenges and stress (Stone et al., 1982). Services are offered to all families, not just those with identified problems. Mental health professionals in the community either directly or through a special Head Start paraprofessional assist parents, teachers, and other staff in their educational and caregiving roles. They provide training, consultation, and crisis intervention counseling.

Evaluation. Unquestionably, Head Start is responsible for better health services to poor families. However, most evaluations of the program have focused on the educational component. Indeed, Head Start barely got off the ground when several researchers concluded that the program, or similar preschool interventions, did not result in intellectual advancement for preschoolers (e.g., Jensen, 1969; Cronbach, 1975). Others disagreed (e.g., Bereiter, 1972; Levenstein, 1974; Palmer and Semlear, 1977; Zigler, 1978; Zigler and Trickett, 1978). The test of time appears to favor the conclusion that preschool programs can be beneficial (U.S. Department of Health and Human Services, 1979). For example, a major reanalysis of the data from twelve independent preschool interventions revealed that preschool participants were doing better academically several years later than were control children. They were less likely to have been retained in grade and less likely to have been assigned to special education classes (Figure 13–1). Treatment children also performed better on standard IQ tests for at least three years after the program, but this difference tended to disappear over time.

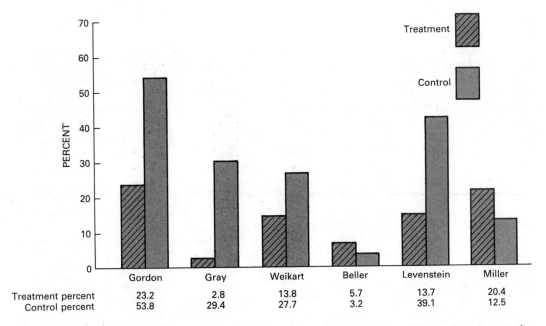

Figure 13-1 Data from six independent studies of preschool programs, showing the percent of treatment and control children assigned later to special education. *From U.S. Department of Health and Human Services, 1979.*

It thus appears that preschool interventions that are carefully designed and conducted can be of academic benefit to poor children, but it is less clear why this is so (e.g., Zigler, Abelson, Trickett, and Seitz, 1982). Perhaps children's motivation, values, aspirations, and coping are increased; perhaps their classroom behavior is affected; perhaps family perceptions are positively changed in some way. Indeed, Head Start parents have overwhelmingly reported the program a success (e.g., Zigler, 1978). Among other things they have noted improved understanding of children, increased opportunity for education and employment, increased aspirations, and increased commitment to the community. In the words of two mothers:

. . . Parents are invited to be in the classroom as volunteers. I feel this is good for us because a lot of times we can see a more positive way to handle our children . . . we can see things to do at home to increase our child's awareness, emotional stability, and sociability.

. . . the best has come out of the changes in myself. I started out as 'just a depressed housewife,' but my experience made me feel that I was not stupid and my confidence began to grow. For me, the most important change is in the way I can work with the system—the public schools, hospitals, and other agencies. (O'Keefe, 1979, pp. 22, 24).

These kinds of reports as well as other data serve to remind us of the importance of family involvement in programs for disadvantaged children—a view that is consonant with the overall goals and approach of Head Start.

Child Abuse and Its Prevention

Abuse of children has always existed. In the United States concern about maltreatment of the young resulted, in 1874, in the establishment of the Society for the Prevention of Cruelty to Children. In the 1940s unexplained medical reports of injuries to children—especially multiple bone fractures and skull swelling and bleeding—awakened new suspicions about abuse (Gil, 1970). Two decades later the term *battered child* was used by Kempe to refer to children who were intentionally physically injured by their caretakers (Kempe, Silverman, Steele, Droegemueller, and Silver, 1962). The problem became so widely recognized that in the early 1960s legislation was enacted in all fifty states that required the reporting of all suspected physical abuse (Green, 1978). Currently the phenomenon is being attacked from several vantage points: active monitoring of families that have been reported for possible abuse, legal action, preventive programs, and research into the demography and causes of maltreatment. Moreover, attention is being given not only to physical abuse (including sexual acts) but also to neglect and emotional abuse. Neglect is viewed as a chronic pattern involving little interaction between parent and child and the failure to provide the basic needs of food, clothes, cleanliness, and medical care (Friedman, Sandler, Hernandez, and Wolfe, 1981). It is an act of omission that may or may not be associated with the commission of physical abuse. Emotional abuse is extremely difficult to define and identify (Kavanaugh, 1982) and perhaps for this reason often escapes direct examination.

How pervasive is physical abuse of children? Accurate statistics are difficult to come by because abusive adults and their victims are ashamed or afraid to admit such deeds. In addition, conflict frequently occurs in the privacy of the home and children, especially the very young, are unable to describe events. Then, too, bruises, cuts, and even more serious damage can occur accidentally, so that parental explanations of "accidents" cannot easily be refuted. It is thus probable that maltreatment is underreported. Even so, conservative estimates place the annual incidence at between 200,000 and 300,000 cases (Broadhurst, Ed-

munds, and MacDicken, 1979; Green, 1978). On the basis of a survey of parents about their own practices, Gelles (1979) has extrapolated that between 3.1 and 4 million children have been kicked, beaten, or punched at some time in their lives, between 1.4 and 2.3 million have been beaten up, and 900,000 to 1.8 million have been attacked with a gun or a knife. All these children may not have sustained injury, but the data certainly indicate the pervasive use of physical force. In the extreme such violence is the cause of death, which occurs more frequently in infants than in older children (Greenland, 1980). Box 13–1 describes two such tragedies.

What kind of adults are involved in child abuse? Females are perhaps more likely to be abusers (Blumberg, 1974; Gelles, 1979), because they bear heavier burdens of rearing children and spend more time with them. Gladston (1965) has suggested that abusive parents distort how the child should be perceived. The parents may reverse roles and refer to the child as if the child were an adult—and a hostile, persecutory, and dominant one at that. An example of this is provided by the military police sergeant who split open the head of his 9-year old son and said, "He thinks he's boss—all the time trying to run things—but I showed him who is in charge around here" (p. 442). Such a parent might be quite disturbed, but most abusers are not blatantly disturbed. Nor does a specific "abusive" personality seem to exist (Green, 1978; Parke and Collmer, 1975). However, some proportion of abusive parents were themselves abused, rejected, and deprived as children. Perhaps they had learned to imitate aggression, or perhaps the lack of mothering and care somehow operated to repeat itself (Steele and Pollack, 1968).

It has long been noted that one particular child in a family is often the target of abuse. When researchers set about to examine this phenomenon, they discovered interesting facts. Premature and low-birth-weight babies, along with children who display general developmental deviations (for example, mental retardation, language pathology) are at greater risk

---

Box 13–1   Child Abuse: The Deaths of Maria and Rubin

Maria Colwell

Maria was born in Hove, England, on March 25, 1965. She was the youngest of five children. The parents separated within a few weeks of Maria's birth. Her father died a few weeks later. At the age of four months Maria was given to her aunt and uncle, Mr. and Mrs. Cooper, to be cared for. The other four children, who were found to be neglected, were taken into care. The mother, Mrs. Colwell, having established a relationship with a Mr. William Kepple, insisted on resuming the care of Maria. Maria was formally returned to the care of her mother and stepfather on November 17, 1971. She was then almost seven. Numerous reports of abuse and neglect were made to the social services. More than 56 official visits were made to the Kepple household in the 14 months before Maria died. On January 6, 1973, she was beaten to death by her stepfather, who was sentenced to eight years' imprisonment.

Rubin A. Almeyda

Rubin was born in Bellevue Hospital, New York, on March 11, 1977. He was dead on arrival when admitted to the Columbia Presbyterian Medical Center on June 24, 1977. He was 105 days old. The cause of death was "battered child—homicidal." "Every rib in his body had been broken two or more times." "Body badly burned." "Fractured skull and subdural haematoma." The father, Ralph Almeyda, age 20, was indicted for murder. The mother, Lourdes Delgado, also age 20, who was crippled by polio and confined to a wheelchair, was not charged.

From Greenland, 1980.

(Friedman et al., 1981). We may speculate that children who require greater care and effort in rearing, who are physically unattractive, or who are particularly annoying elicit loss of control in the parent, a deliberate desire to punish the child, or an attempt to end aversive stimulation. There is some evidence, too, that abused children display more behavior problems as well as undesirable behaviors such as stubbornness, negativism, apathy, and fearfulness (Green, 1978; Trickett and Susman, 1982). We cannot safely conclude, however, that these behavioral characteristics cause the abuse, for they may result from maltreatment or other factors.

Comprehensive accounts of child abuse must also take into consideration broad social variables such as family stress and interaction as well as societal conditions and attitudes. From one of the first large-scale studies of abusing families, Gil (1970, 1979) concluded that the stress of poverty is related to abuse. Large family size, low income, low educational levels, unemployment, and poor housing are associated with maltreatment of children. Nevertheless, child abuse is not found in all poor families and does occur in families not suffering from poverty (Parke and Collmer, 1975). Social isolation of the family, especially in time of stress, is frequently found (Friedman et al., 1981). So too is marital conflict (Belsky, 1980). An important factor in the United States is the acceptance of physical force in child-rearing practices. Gil (1970, 1979) and others suggest that this attitude is embedded in society's broad sanctioning of violence as a way of resolving conflict. The age-old belief that children are the property of the family, to be treated according to parental wish, also contributes to abuse of the young (Belsky, 1980).

Considerable progress has been made in understanding the variables operating in child abuse. It is generally regarded as the result of a complex of interacting factors, but exactly how these variables interface remains to be studied. Several major investigations, many funded by the federal government through the National Center on Child Abuse and Neglect, are in the process of studying these issues. Treatment and prevention programs have also been initiated.

Primary prevention of child abuse is inher-

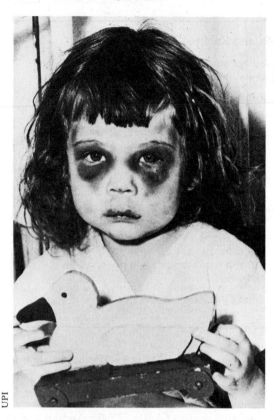

UPI

A 3-year-old victim of suspected child abuse.

ent in various educational and parent training programs, for example, Head Start. These are not aimed exclusively at maltreatment of the young, but it is assumed that knowledge of child development and skills in handling conflict reduce the chance of abuse. Similarly, the alleviation of stress would be expected to improve the management of children. The same can be said for self-help groups, such as Parents Anonymous, which provide opportunities and support to parents so that they can discuss their problems and learn alternative parenting styles. Families at high risk for child abuse and those in which abuse has already begun are the focus of secondary prevention programs. With recent advances in theoretical understanding of the phenomenon, some high-risk parents, vulnerable children, and stressful environments can

be identified by professionals. However, the nature of the problem and its legal ramifications complicate preventive efforts. Since children can be legally removed from the family due to child abuse, adults may be afraid to come forth for help or even to subtly hint that their children are endangered. The prevention program described below directly confronts this situation.

The Voluntary Intervention and Treatment Program (VITP). Funded by the National Center on Child Abuse and Neglect, VITP operates within the Child Protective Services Unit of Children's Services of Erie County, Pennsylvania. VITP seeks to encourage families to *request* assistance with child abuse problems and then provides services to meet the individual needs of each participant family (DePanfilis, 1982). The main objectives are to prevent abuse and neglect, prevent placement of children outside the home because of abuse, and prevent court involvement.

As a strategy to encourage self-referrals, the project launched a public awareness campaign called, "It's Not Easy to Be a Parent." Pamphlets and posters were developed and distributed among other professionals who were likely to come into contact with families "at risk." The pamphlets were also left in the waiting rooms of facilities likely to be frequented by parents. Information regarding VITP services were provided to community and professional organizations. With increased community awareness, self-referrals grew dramatically.

Once parents refer themselves to VITP, they become involved in an intensive assessment period. Individual interviews and questionnaires are administered to identify all stressors that could be contributing to the abuse or neglect pattern of the family. An individual treatment plan is then designed in which families identify goals and contract for services. The treatment plan contract is usually in effect for a six-month period and can be terminated by the parents or renegotiated if goals have not been achieved.

Services offered to the families include individual counseling, emergency financial assistance, day care, and homemaker assistance. The services of a parent aide—for transportation, baby sitting, and other support—is given to socially isolated families. In addition, peer support is provided through monthly social gatherings. A parent education and training group meets weekly. Finally, project workers provide information about services from other social agencies.

DePanfilis (1982) has described the success of VITP. She notes that parents were from all socioeconomic backgrounds, with 45 percent of the sample receiving some kind of public assistance. Over 33 percent of the parents who referred themselves for treatment admitted that actual physical abuse had occurred. Physical abuse was recorded if the parents reported "losing control" while administering punishment, or if they had injured or physically assaulted the child. Over 46 percent admitted actual physical abuse and/or neglect. Nevertheless, 75 percent of the families were not receiving services from Child Protective Services at the time of referral, and 48 percent had no history of contact with Children's Services.

The project was successful in meeting its objectives. There was only one known incident of abuse during treatment. No child was placed outside the home for long-term care. Further, there were no referrals to the court system or to Child Protective Services regarding a VITP participant during treatment. Finally, the average length of completed treatment for families in the project was much less than the average length of contact that comparable families had with Children's Services. The initial results of the project thus suggest that it has been successful in encouraging parents to refer themselves for treatment and in providing effective and efficient intervention.

Crisis Intervention: Sudden Infant Death Syndrome

Crisis intervention is considered by many to be an important part of preventive efforts. Caplan (1964) recognized two categories of crisis: developmental and accidental. Developmental

crises can occur at the transitions that mark the usual course of growth, for example, at entry into school and at adolescence. Accidental crises are precipitated by life's hazards—natural disasters, the loss of a loved one, and the like. In both developmental and accidental crises, the individual experiences an imbalance between a difficulty and the resources available to cope with it. "Upset" is characterized by emotional states such as anxiety, guilt, or shame, depending on the situation. The person in crisis often feels helpless and ineffective and may function in a disorganized manner. Nevertheless, crisis also can stimulate the formation of new coping patterns. Since individuals in crisis may be particularly open to influence from others, crisis intervention is considered an opportunity both to give aid and to positively affect future mental health.

An example of an area in which such intervention may be appropriate is the reaction of a family to the loss of an infant by the Sudden Infant Death Syndrome (SIDS). "Crib death," as it is widely called, occurs completely unexpectedly in infants up to a year old, most commonly at 3 to 4 months. Typically the apparently healthy child is put to bed for the night or for a nap and is discovered dead by parents or siblings. The frequency of sudden infant death is 2 to 3 per 1,000 live births, a figure that is quite constant across different countries (Lowman, 1979).

Despite a surge of research into the etiology of SIDS, its cause is yet to be understood. No warning from the child is given, and as of yet no way exists to identify potential crib deaths. Genetic transmission, congenital abnormalities, infection, and suffocation have largely been ruled out. The possibility of a sleep disorder involving the temporary cessation of breathing (sleep apnea) is under intensive investigation.

The reaction of families to sudden infant death has not been studied as much as we might like, but the grief process appears similar to other crisis reactions. Parents report psychological shock and numbness as well as disruption in eating, sleeping, thinking, and working, all of which usually dissipate over time (Lowman,

1979). But the SIDS crisis may have special effects as well. Finding their infant dead is particularly stressful to parents, and denial of death may persist longer than is typical for other kinds of loss. Most striking is the extreme feeling of responsibility and guilt, which is exacerbated by lack of knowledge about SIDS and its etiology. Parents also appear to have special difficulty in dealing with the situation vis-á-vis their surviving children (Goldston, 1977). To date, little is known about children's reactions to the sudden death of a sibling, much less to SIDS. However, many professionals believe that parents and siblings in these crisis-torn families can be aided in ways that will facilitate coping and ward off potential maladjustment and psychopathology. Lack of funding has limited preventive programs, but some counseling and support have been offered by federally funded projects.

A statewide program in North Carolina provides an example of how crisis services might be offered. This program focused on grief intervention, education about SIDS for professionals and community workers, and the collection of epidemiological data to help shed light on etiology (Lowman, 1979). Five mature and experienced nurses were hired to contact SIDS families throughout the state. Three home visits were planned to each family, at three to five weeks, seven to nine weeks, and four to six months after the infant death. The visits occurred when the fathers and siblings could be present, and effort was made to minimize professional barriers. The nurses wore regular street clothes, accepted offers of refreshment, and communicated their feelings of sympathy and concern. During the first visit data were collected about the family and the death for research purposes. An extremely important part of the visit was dissemination of information concerning SIDS. Three psychological goals were set: to reduce guilt and blame by countering any inaccurate explanations of the tragedy, to encourage the expression of emotions and assure families that their reactions were normal and would lessen over time, and to provide support for coping and for economic and other practical problems. The effectiveness of

this project was not systematically evaluated, but anecdotal impressions suggest that the families found participation helpful. For example, they expressed gratitude for the information that they were not directly responsible for their infants' deaths. Indeed, in this project the major therapeutic and preventive aspect may have been such assurance to the families. Nevertheless, systematic investigation is required to assess the efficacy of this and other crisis intervention projects.

Prevention of Schizophrenia

We turn now to work that has a quite different focus and method. It stems largely from interest in schizophrenia. Individuals labeled schizophrenic suffer severe and often chronic debilitating behavior: thought, attention, and perception disorders; motor symptoms; and affective abnormalities that result in an inability to handle everyday life (Davison and Neale, 1982). Varied treatments have been tried but so far have enjoyed little success. Since etiology remains unknown, few clues exist for new treatment approaches or preventive efforts. One attempt to overcome this discouraging situation aims at (1) detecting individuals who have potential for schizophrenia and (2) exploring possibilities for preventive interventions (Mednick and Witkin-Lanoil, 1977). To date, emphasis has been on detection, and the work is highly research oriented. As a demonstration we describe the first extensive study of its kind, conducted by Mednick and Schulsinger and their colleagues in Denmark (Mednick, 1970; Mednick and Schulsinger, 1968; Schulsinger, 1976).

These researchers employ the longitudinal method to study people who are at high risk for schizophrenia; that is, who have a parent who has been diagnosed as schizophrenic. Such individuals are about fifteen times more likely to develop the disorder than are individuals in the general population. Mednick and Schulsinger initially selected 207 high-risk adolescents who were functioning normally and matched them with low-risk individuals on age, sex, residence, and the like. Midwives provided information about the births of all the subjects, and teachers reported on academic and social performance. In addition, each adolescent was given psychological tests, such as an intelligence test and a word association test. Finally, each completed a classical conditioning task in which a neutral tone (CS) was paired with an aversive noise (UCS), and generalization of the conditioning to other neutral tones was evaluated. During this procedure heart rate and galvanic skin responses (GSR) were recorded to evaluate the reactivity of the autonomic nervous system. Compared to the low-risk controls, the high-risk adolescents had longer and more difficult births, greater conflict in the home, somewhat lower intelligence scores, deviant school behavior, poorer responses on the word association test, and more reactive autonomic responses.

Follow-up within a few years established that twenty of the high-risk individuals had displayed some behavioral problems, twelve having been hospitalized for psychiatric disorders and eight having been diagnosed as schizoid, alcoholic, or delinquent. When these disturbed subjects were subsequently compared to high-risk subjects who had remained well, the following characteristics were found:

1. Early loss of mothers to institutions, indicating more severe disturbance, more stress in the home, or both. More fathers of the disturbed subjects also showed psychopathology as compared to fathers of the non-disturbed subjects.

2. Disordered associations in thinking, indicated by the disturbed subjects doing more poorly on the word association task.

3. Hyperactivity of the autonomic nervous system, shown by stronger GSRs to noise, greater classical conditioning, greater generalization of the conditioned response, and slower extinction of the conditioned response.

4. Pregnancy or birth complications among the disturbed subjects.

When they began their study, Mednick (1958) and his colleagues had hypothesized that schizophrenia is a learned disorder that is predisposed by high reactivity of the autonomic nervous system. Their findings do show some support for this hypothesis and also implicate pregnancy and birth complications. Nevertheless, the picture is far from clear. At the latest follow-up of the original sample, seventeen of the high-risk subjects (and only one of the low-risk subjects) had been diagnosed as schizophrenic. Most of these seventeen, however, had not been among those considered disturbed at the first follow-up. Examination of these individuals is presently underway in an effort to determine if and how they are distinguishable from low-risk controls and from high-risk subjects who have not developed schizophrenia.

The Mednick and Schulsinger project is the only high-risk research study that has been operating for a sufficient number of years to provide longitudinal data. However, several other investigations have provided cross-sectional data from comparisons between high-risk and control groups. Neale and Oltmanns's (1980) review of the findings indicates that although the data are not always consistent from project to project, some differences between high risk and control children have been found in several areas of functioning. Obtained differences are often small, but this would be expected, because the majority of the high-risk children will not, in fact, develop later pathology. Interestingly, there is a parallel between the high-risk children and the behavior of adult schizophrenics. For example, both groups show some neurological impairment, disturbances in association and attention, and social dysfunction. As Neale and Oltmanns point out, it remains to be seen whether these variables will be predictive of later schizophrenia or other problems. It is hoped, of course, that identification of predictors will give clues to both etiology and prevention. In the meantime Mednick and his colleagues have begun a project which already includes preventive efforts.

This longitudinal investigation is being conducted on the Island of Mauritius, which has a population of Hindus, Tamils, Moslems, Creoles, and Chinese (Mednick and Witkin-

Lanoil, 1977). From a pool of 1,800 3-year-old children, a group has been selected that is considered high-risk on the basis of psychophysiological screening. Intervention consists of a special nursery school experience. Early reports indicate that definite behavioral change is occuring in this high-risk group. Having originally displayed fright and aggressiveness in school, the children now play spontaneously and greet strangers with liveliness and interest. So far these changes have not been related to psychophysiological functioning, however. Nor is it yet known what aspects of the nursery school are associated with change; for example, the protein-rich diet, warm teachers, separation from the home environment, or placement with other frightened children. Finally, it remains to be seen whether changes in the children's behavior will be associated with the incidence of later psychopathology.

Issues in Prevention

Although in principle the benefits of prevention seem indisputable, preventive efforts have been resisted and criticized on a number of grounds. To begin with, society's commitment to the treatment mode has a long history and remains strong. Professionals are trained for treatment and are financially rewarded for treatment. Since adequate resources are lacking to meet the needs of those already displaying problems, there is a reluctance to divert funds into the prevention mode (Bloom, 1981). At the national level no one agency is in charge of prevention or health maintenance, so that efforts are fragmented. Also, serious questions have been raised about the efficacy and potential efficacy of prevention, especially primary prevention.

Lamb and Susman (1981), for example, claim that the techniques necessary for primary prevention have not yet been developed, except in a few limited areas (for instance, genetic counseling, prenatal care, control of environmental toxins). They suggest that shrinking resources demand that prevention be limited to "diagnosable mental illness." They reject the idea that prevention can reasonably deal with the many individuals who have no recognizable psychiatric illness but who want help with everyday living and interpersonal problems. Lamb and Susman further argue that mental health services should not be concerned with improving the quality of life for everyone or with resolving basic social problems. Not only do these psychiatrists consider such efforts cost inefficient, but they also question the cause-and-effect relationship between social conditions and "mental illness." Programs that are geared toward the development of competence are similarly eschewed on the grounds that no evidence exists that competence building prevents "mental illness." Lamb and Susman nevertheless allow that high-quality programs, such as the Rochester Primary Mental Health Program, are worthy of longitudinal follow-up to ascertain possible benefits.

Opposing viewpoints have been set forth by writers such as Cowen and Albee, who are strong proponents of broad preventive programs. Cowen (1980) wholeheartedly accepts the goal of "psychological adjustment, effectiveness, happiness, and coping skills of large numbers of individuals" (p. 264). He views primary prevention as intentional mental health building or harm avoiding that can be attained through education, analysis and modification of social systems, competence training, stress reduction and coping, and support networks. Albee (1982) adamantly argues that reduction of emotional distress and of problems such as shyness and reading deficits—whether one calls them "mental illness" or problems in living—are legitimate focuses of prevention. For Albee the causal connection between emotional disturbance and poverty, sexism, and racism is clear. He thus argues for broad social change and competence building, noting that his position is threatening to those who hold that certain groups (for example, women, blacks, Southern Europeans) are defective due to organic factors.

The professional/political issues raised by Albee have brought us to the problem of ethics in prevention. Ethical questions always exist when human behavior is examined or modified. They become even more compelling in the wake of efforts to operate on large segments of the population—which is precisely the stated intent of the preventive ideology. Of major concern is the locus of power in the selection of values and alternatives. To illustrate, let us look again at early intervention efforts with children of low SES.

The components and goals of Head Start and related programs have already been reviewed. They appear simple enough: to provide better health care, educational inputs to the young, and community support to poor families. It is interesting that these programs have been referred to as "compensatory"—and herein lies an ethical difficulty. Although the term *compensatory* need not imply the existence of an error or defect, more often than not such an implication has been carried in assumptions about the poor—particularly black, poor individuals (Baratz and Baratz, 1970; Ginsburg, 1982; Rappaport, 1977). Early intervention, it can be argued, has thus been based on the *deficit model* that suggests that poor (black) children are disadvantaged by genetic endowment, inferior subculture, or both. Intervention therefore requires the injection of middle-class culture, the earlier the better. However, advocates of the *difference model* argue strenuously that poor children are not deficient. They learn, think, and operate successfully in their environments, although they may learn somewhat different content, as reflected on intelligence and achievement tests. Nevertheless, the schools ignore such learning and relegate poor children to an inferior status. Professionals who endorse the difference model want to build on what children already possess, recognizing the richness of the environments of the poor and culturally different. Such a tactic may involve the use of nonstandard language, with the gradual addition of middle-class language and customs. Only in this way, it is argued, can the young develop intellectually and emotionally with self-respect and motivation.

Ethical concerns, exemplified by differences in social values, combined with the questions about the efficacy and know-how of prevention, continue to cast a shadow over all preventive efforts. Reduced economic resources also work against a commitment to prevention, although this may result in a "penny-wise, pound-foolish" strategy.

THE CHILD AS A COMPETENT HUMAN

As already noted, the concept of competence is interwoven with the ideology of primary prevention. The goal of promoting competence in groups and systems rather than alleviating individual problems is the essence of this approach. That competence may be related to adjustment was demonstrated by the early work of Zigler and his colleagues (e.g., Phillips, Broverman, and Zigler, 1966; Zigler and Phillips, 1961). In a series of studies they found that the social maturity (social competence) an individual brings to problem solving at various life stages is associated with the kinds of psychological difficulties the individual develops—as well as with prognosis and response to treatment. For example, patients with higher social maturity scores are hospitalized for shorter durations and are less likely to be hospitalized.

As interest in competence increased, definitional problems became more obvious. In a now-classic paper, White (1959) had defined competence as fitness, ability, capacity, efficiency, and skill. He applied the term to activities such as grasping, exploring, walking, attention, perception, language, thinking, and manipulating the surroundings—all of which promote effective interaction with the environment. White also wisely noted that a behavior is competent only relative to a specific context: A response that is successful in attaining its objective is competent. So, for example, if a baby's cry is sufficient to elicit attention from the caretaker, it is competent. However, the baby's competence is partly a function of the mother's responsiveness (Ainsworth and Bell, 1974). Thus, competence lies in a transaction between the individual's behavior and the environment, not in qualities of either.

More recently the task of definition was faced by a panel formed by the Office of Child Development of HEW (Anderson and Messick, 1974). The panel employed a variety of approaches to describe areas that needed attention, but complications attended each of these approaches and value judgments were present at every decision point. A given behavior, for example, may have different meanings in different subcultures (Ogbu, 1981) and at different developmental periods. Maternal concerns about friendly behavior in ghetto children (Strodtbeck, 1965) is an example of the former. The latter is illustrated by behavior that is considered active exploration by a 2-year-old but is viewed as poor impulse control in an older child. Despite these complexities, the panel was able to arrive at a list of eight categories believed to comprise the domain of competence. (See Table 13–1.) Translating such categories into specific developmental goals presents an appreciable challenge, however. Moreover, even when competence is defined in some specific manner, creating programs to produce it requires considerable effort.

Building Competencies in Children

Competency building in children can be implemented in a number of ways. The child's

stage of development is always relevant to the planning of interventions. Competence in infancy, for example, may be largely determined by the mother's ability to provide a suitable environment for growth and exploration. McNeill (1974) has suggested that the competent mother answers her baby's questions, elaborates interesting events, and generally facilitates the growth of early competencies. The incompetent mother, by contrast, may—due to her own sense of powerlessness—be frustrated by the demands of mothering. She may fail to aid the baby in the regulation of his or her experience. This may then contribute to social disability in the child (Vance, 1973). Parent training is thus clearly suggested as a mode of intervention for training competencies in infants and young children.

Jason (1977) incorporated parent training into an intervention program for 1- to 2-year-olds who had been described by health care professionals as developmentally immature. The program provided a stimulating environment for the children, who attended three weekly sessions of play and instruction. During clinic and home sessions parents were exposed to modeling and guided participation for facilitating parent-child interactions. Later academic measures indicated that gains were maintained by those children whose parents expressed satisfaction with the program. Jason attributes this maintenance to the parents' motivation to con-

Table 13–1 Categories of Competence Proposed by the Office of Child Development

A. Personality (self-esteem, level of aspiration, sense of power)

B. Sensitivity and social perception

C. Morality, self-control, prosocial behavior

D. Perceptual-motor skills

E. Attention

F. Cognitive and language ability (creativity, problem solving, number and conservation skills)

G. Motivation, curiosity

H. Ability to play, humor

Adapted from Anderson and Messick, 1974

tinue to work with their children following the termination of the program.

While parent training is a competence-building strategy that clearly can benefit children, perhaps the most interesting programs are those that directly train the child. As the child begins and then progresses through school, direct training can be incorporated into curricula. During this period peer interactions play an increasing role in the child's development. Effective competence building during the school years necessarily must address growing social relations.

An approach that exemplifies such a competence-building model is the training of *interpersonal cognitive problem-solving* (ICPS) skills. Children as young as 4 years of age differ in the cognitive abilities required to solve interpersonal problems with peers and adults. In addition, these abilities distinguish children who display behavioral difficulties from those who do not (Spivack and Shure, 1974). This has led a number of workers to posit that training in these skills will enable children to cope with a variety of interpersonal stresses that are thought to contribute to the development of behavior disorders.

Shure and Spivack's (1982) project to train inner-city black children of low SES is an example of such a program. The training program consisted of twelve weeks of twenty-minute lessons taught to small groups of children. The youngsters were first taught to listen to and observe others. They also learned that others had thoughts, feelings, and motives in problem situations. After being taught these prerequisite skills, the children were taught two interpersonal problem-solving skills: considering alternative solutions and realizing possible consequences of hypothetical situations. In addition to these structured lessons, teachers encouraged children to use their problem-solving skills when actual problems occurred outside the formal training sessions.

Participants in the project had one of four experiences during nursery school and the following year in kindergarten. Some children experienced the three-month-training program

both years (TT group), while others were trained in nursery school but not in kindergarten (TC group). Of those children who were in a control group in nursery school, and thus did not get training that year, some were given training during kindergarten (CT group), while others did not receive training either year (CC group). Shure and Spivack obtained several measures to evaluate the impact of their program. The Preschool Interpersonal Problem-Solving Test (PIPS) measured the ability to generate alternative solutions to two types of problems: (1) obtaining a toy from another child and (2) averting mother's anger after damaging an object. The What Happens Next Game (WHNG) evaluated the ability to name multiple consequences of two types of interpersonal acts: (1) grabbing a peer's toy and (2) taking something from an adult without first asking. To further assess the children, teachers completed the Hahnemann Preschool Behavior Scale, allowing ratings of either adjusted, inhibited, or impulsive.

How successful was the program in teaching interpersonal cognitive problem-solving skills? Trained children increased their ability to generate alternative solutions and to realize consequences significantly more than did corresponding control children. These gains occurred for adjusted children as well as for those who had initially been rated as inhibited or impulsive. Training produced results whether it occurred in preschool or a year later in kindergarten. Receiving training twice rather than just once improved the children's ability to generate alternatives, but the second training period did not add appreciably to the ability to recognize consequences.

Evaluation of the impact that training had on the children's adjustment focused on two questions: Did inhibited and impulsive children become better adjusted following training? Did training help prevent the development of adjustment problems? It does appear that the adjustment of impulsive and inhibited children who received training improved (see Figure 13–2). Furthermore, improvement was related to acquisition of interpersonal cognitive prob-

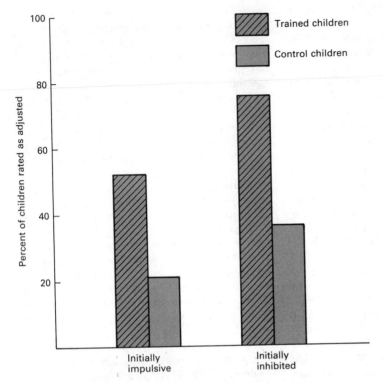

Figure 13–2 The percentage of children who were rated as adjusted following nursery school. *Adapted from Shure and Spivack, 1982.*

lem-solving skills. That is, the PIPS and WHNG scores of children whose behavior improved during either nursery school or kindergarten increased significantly more than the scores of those whose behavior did not improve.

It also appeared that training in ICPS skills helped prevent behavior problems from occurring. Eighty-six percent of the trained children who were initially rated as adjusted maintained that adjustment through nursery school and at six-month follow-up. This is in contrast to only 58 percent of the comparable untrained group. In addition, for those TC and CC children for whom information was available at the end of kindergarten, eight of nine treated children, but only four of ten control children, remained adjusted a full year later. Aberrant behavior was also less likely to persist among trained children. Among TC children initially judged as aberrant, only 10 percent remained so through the end of kindergarten, significantly less than the 71 percent of CC controls. These benefits

of ICPS training seem especially important considering that earlier findings (Spivack and Swift, 1977) suggest increased maladjustment as inner-city children progress through the early grades.

These results and others from Shure and Spivack's group are certainly encouraging, and they suggest the feasibility of a competence-based approach in general and of training in ICPS skills in particular. Since Shure and Spivack worked with socioeconomically disabled youngsters, however, the usefulness of the program is less clear for other populations. Among middle-class preschoolers the ability to generate alternative solutions has been associated with behaving more flexibly, persistently, and resourcefully in interpersonal problems situations (Arend, Gove, and Sroufe, 1979). However, less is known about other ICPS skills (for example, consequences) and the relationship of these skills to adjustment in this population. Evaluations of the effectiveness of ICPS training programs for older children have not yielded consistent results. Among children of this age group, cognitive ICPS change has generally been obtained, but as yet the link between improvement in cognitive skills and changes in behavior has not been well established.

A program initiated by Gesten and his colleagues, however, is encouraging (Gesten, Rains, Rapkin, Weissberg, Flores de Apocada, Cowen, and Bowen, 1982). Suburban second- and third-grade children received a classroom-based seventeen-session social problem-solving training program. At the end of the nine-week program, trained children performed significantly better than controls on alternative and consequential thinking and on a simulated behavioral peer problem task. Surprisingly, though, teacher ratings of adjustment at this point in time generally favored the controls. However, when the children were again evaluated one year later, this situation had changed. The new teachers, who did not know whether the children had been trained, rated trained students better than controls on seven of ten competence and pathology factors. However, the linkage between improved ICPS skills and adjustment was still less clear than indicated for preschool children.

Much remains to be learned about training children in interpersonal problem-solving skills. At the very least, the population that will most benefit must be determined. In addition, the question of skill maintenance must still be evaluated. Nonetheless, ICPS training and the competence approach from which it arises is at present a highly exciting area of research.

THE RIGHTS OF CHILDREN

During the last few decades concern for children has been couched more and more under the rubric of *rights*. A right is defined as an inherent guarantee (Shore, 1979). It is owned by the person and forms a philosophical foundation for legislation and specific programs and strategies. Psychologists and others who work with children are attempting to gain a consen-

sus on children's rights that might serve as a framework for policy regarding the care and treatment of the young. They also are working to implement these rights.

Children's rights can be viewed as emphasizing two domains. The first might be termed the "human rights" emphasis. Simply stated, advocates argue that each child has the right as a human being to certain conditions. The Joint Commission on the Mental Health of Children (1969) spelled out these fundamental rights: to be wanted, to be born healthy, to exist in a healthy environment, to have basic needs satisfied, to receive continuous loving care, to acquire necessary intellectual and emotional skills, and to receive care through appropriate agencies that seek to keep children as close as possible to their normal social environment (Shore, 1979). The second, and more controversial, emphasis has been on legal rights. The quest for change in children's legal rights developed in the context of growing advocacy for minority or special groups, as represented by the civil rights and women's liberation movements.

Child welfare advocates who stand for human rights and legal rights have sometimes been called "child savers" and "kiddie libbers," respectively (e.g., Mnookin, 1978). Underlying their advocacy is the recognition that children's needs are not being met and that the needs of youth do not always coincide with those of parents and of the state. As an example of the complexities involved in meeting children's needs, let us look at the quite common situation in which some kind of child placement is at issue due to the inability of the family to care for the child.

The Problem of Child Placement

The dilemma of if, when, and how to place children outside of their natural homes is a serious challenge faced by the child welfare systems. Knitzer (1981) has described what she believes to be the most repeatedly documented problems in these systems:

1. Too frequently children are unnecessarily removed from their homes. This usually oc-

curs because alternatives such as day care, respite services for parents, crisis intervention, or emergency housing are unavailable.

2. Once removed, children are too often placed in settings that are unnecessarily restrictive or too far from their homes.

3. Contact with natural families is often cut off when children are placed.

4. Public officials fail to monitor the quality of the care received or do not make sufficient effort to see that prompt decisions are made about reuniting families or, should this fail, terminating parental rights and having the child adopted. Thus, children remain in care for long periods and often must deal with multiple placements. Even the most well-adjusted child would have difficulty coping with these situations.

5. There is an absence of meaningful data about children who are at risk or who are already placed outside of their homes. As a result, it is difficult to target services to specific needs.

To illustrate this last point, 1971 was the last year for which data were available on the number of children adopted nationally. Furthermore, a survey of 140 child welfare agencies revealed that officials could not provide data on the ages of 49 percent of the children, length of care for 53 percent, number of moves for 87 percent, and legal status for 73 percent (Children's Defense Fund, 1979).

How does one overcome these problems and make decisions about a particular child's placement? The common standard for judging alternatives is the "best interests of the child." As obvious as this may sound, it is a difficult and complex standard to apply. The issue of custody in divorce cases and the decision whether to institutionalize a disturbed or handicapped child illustrate some of these complexities (Mnookin, 1978).

The high divorce rate in this country and the increasing frequency of fathers' requests to keep their children make the issue of child custody relatively common. For example, consider the case of a boy who has strong emotional ties to both his mother and his father, who are divor-

cing. Suppose, too, that neither parent would put the child in danger if he or she had custody. Nevertheless, the judge has to decide which parent should have the child. Let us assume that the court has substantial information about past home life and present alternatives. What could professional child workers tell the judge to aid the decision-making process? Present knowledge does not enable us to reliably predict the consequences of a particular decision for a particular child. It would seem unwise to ask the child to choose one parent and perhaps jeopardize his relationship with the other. Furthermore, the young child may not have the capacity or the maturity to determine his or her own best interests. Which set of values is the judge to employ in determining the child's best interest? Should a long-term or a short-term perspective be taken? The conditions that may make the child happy at 7 or 10 years of age may not lead to desirable outcomes at age 30. Should the judge be concerned with the child's happiness or with the child's spiritual training? Are stability and security more important than intellectual stimulation? The decision about the child's best interest is far from clear.

The complexity involved in determining "best interest" can also be seen in the question of institutionalization. When it becomes difficult to provide services in the community for adults, they can voluntarily commit themselves to an institution. Alternatively, they can be involuntarily committed if they represent a danger to themselves or others—not an easy decision in itself. But what about a seriously disturbed or handicapped child? Should parents be able to commit a child after consultation with a professional? Should the child be able to object? Should there be a hearing that allows a judge to resolve conflicting desires? If the judge decides that the child should remain in the home, what is the likelihood that the family, which initiated placement hearings, will be able to care for the child?

Dilemmas such as the ones posed above have repeatedly plagued those involved in the placement of children. Many child advocates argue that they know what is best for children. However, in their attempts to add the child's viewpoint to the process, few have systematically sought to assess what children's views really are.

What Children Think about Their Rights

What role can children play in determining their own best interest? This question is of particular importance to those interested in "liberating" children. It is important to know the extent to which a child can participate in his or her own legal defense or interests. Understanding children's views involves knowledge of cognitive development, situational variables, and family child-rearing patterns. Although available research is limited, it is nevertheless interesting to ask, "What is the child's view of his or her rights?"

Melton (1980) examined the child's ability to conceptualize rights. Low SES and high SES first-, third-, fifth-, and seventh-grade youngsters were interviewed and asked what they thought a right was. In the second part of the interview, twelve vignettes were presented. These represented situations in which a child might assert a right. Included were conflicts with school officials (for example, access to school records), other authorities (for example, custody hearings), parents (for example, privacy of a diary), and peers (older children ordering younger children away from a public park). The children's responses were scored for (1) level of reasoning ability displayed and (2) whether the child suggested that the youngster in the story should express a right.

The results of this study indicate that children may have the cognitive capacity to participate in decisions involving their rights earlier than is frequently expected. Most children had some idea of the nature of rights by third or fifth grade. Older children had developed views in which rights were perceived as based on fairness and competence rather than on what authority figures allow. High SES children displayed reasoning based on fairness and competence and expressed positive attitudes toward children's rights an average of two years earlier than lower SES children.

Beyond their cognitive capacities, what are children's own preferences for adult versus child

control? Margolin (1982) showed children in second through sixth grade a series of illustrations of cartoon figures. The figures were depicted in situations in which children are currently denied self-determination by either conventional parental control or legal statute. The situations included: what children can watch on television, when they should go to bed, what they should eat, what movies they should see, whether they should drive a car, where they should live, and whether they should vote. The participants in the study were asked to say whether they had the right to decide each of these things. The questions were phrased so as to encourage disagreement with adult authority. The majority of responses indicated that the children felt that restrictions on their "right" of self-determination were appropriate (see Table 13-2). The exception to this was that 66 percent of the children felt that they should be able to vote for the president. Boys more than girls tended to choose self-determination, but except for television viewing, the majority supported restrictions. Older children tended to favor self-determination in television, driving, movies, and residence.

These results suggest that children do not necessarily desire to free themselves from adult protection. Thus, it would be wise for proponents of children's rights to consider both the child's age and specific areas of behavior as they incorporate the child's view into a balance between protection and liberation.

Progress in Children's Rights

Child advocates, though faced with a difficult and complex task, have not been silent. They have been active through a number of avenues (Knitzer, 1981). The issue of child placement can again serve as an example. Lawyers and others have used class action and individual test case litigation to advance and help reform child welfare policies. Efforts have also been made to convince states to revise child welfare statutes. Particular emphasis was given to creating or strengthening independent review mechanisms that would enable children to move through the foster care system more rap-

Table 13-2   Percentage of
Children Favoring
Self-Determination

Situation	
Television	
Combined	45
Girls	38
Boys	52
Food	
Combined	30
Girls	21
Boys	40
Bedtime	
Combined	36
Girls	28
Boys	43
Driving	
Combined	32
Girls	22
Boys	41
Movies	
Combined	36
Girls	29
Boys	42
Residence	
Combined	30
Girls	22
Boys	37
Voting	
Combined	66
Girls	65
Boys	67

Adapted from Margolin, 1982.

idly. For example, New York substantially modified funding formulas to increase incentives and resources for preventive and reunification (of families) services. Another avenue for reform has been the establishment of demonstration projects designed to prevent initial child placement or to shorten the stay in care. The Oregon Permanency Planning Project is an example of this kind of effort (Pike, 1976). The project demonstrated that with planning, legal backup, and services, children for whom return to the home had not been seen as an option

could return to their families, while others could be successfully adopted by relatives or foster families.

Perhaps one of the most influential contributions to child advocacy was the publication of two provocative books. In *Beyond the Best Interests of the Child* (1973) and later in *Before the Best Interests of the Child* (1979), Joseph Goldstein, Anna Freud, and Albert J. Solnit created controversy and challenged the child welfare field to think about its practices and the impact of those practices on healthy psychological development. In the first book the authors examined both legal and psychological aspects of child care *following* the state's decision to intervene and take legal control of the child. The second book took a step backward in the process and tackled the perhaps more difficult issue of when the state should have the right to intervene in the life of the family.

In the late 1970s the federal government, through Congress, began to question its role in child placement. The outgrowth of this process was the enactment of P.L. 96–272, the Adoption Assistance and Child Welfare Act of 1980. This law provides for appreciably increased funding for services designed to prevent placement in the first place or ensure permanent placement. It makes funding contingent upon the state's ability to provide adequate due process and other protection for children. The state is also required to demonstrate the capacity to monitor and gather information on its overall child welfare system. Child advocates worked to see that the law was structured to respond to the major problems of the child welfare system, as outlined above. P.L. 96–272 is not a panacea, of course, but it is an important beginning. Continued efforts and vigilance will be needed to assure that it is implemented in a manner helpful to children at risk of being placed or already in placement.

Despite recent activity on behalf of children's rights, it is incorrect to assume that societal reforms have always led to clear benefit for children. Two examples illustrate this point. Binet reacted to a perceived injustice when, in 1907, he sought to replace subjective school placement procedures with the use of objective intelligence tests. These tests eventually facilitated the identification of categories of mental retardation and deprivation. Yet today many workers argue that reliance on IQ tests and the process of labeling have created new injustice. Recall, too, that early in this century reform-minded professionals and laypersons advocated the creation of separate, special classes for physically handicapped and mentally disabled children. In contrast, today's effort has become one of "mainstreaming" children back into regular classes (Takanishi, 1978). These examples illustrate how yesterday's causes often become today's dilemmas. They do not imply, of course, that society should ignore the issue of children's rights or go back to old ways. Rather, they call for even greater effort in the care of the young.

THE CHALLENGE OF THE FUTURE: WHO IS FOR CHILDREN?

Concern for the welfare of children is widespread at the present time. Clear indication of this was given by the publication in 1978 of an entire issue of the *Journal of Social Issues* devoted to the rights of children, and by a special issue in 1979 of the *American Psychologist* on psychology's contribution and responsibility to children. Even more dramatic was the United Nation's declaration making 1979 the International Year of the Child, a move to highlight the needs of youth in all corners of the world. All of this reflects the considerable discussion today about the changing world and how it affects children. We seem very much aware of food shortages, health care needs, changing family structure, transitions in sex roles, and the possible effects of progress in transportation and communication (e.g., Anthony and Chiland, 1980).

In spite of these positive signs, however, children in the United States and in most other countries are not receiving adequate care. Edelman (1981) recently made this clear by listing some of the pressing concerns of the Children's Defense Fund.

1. Over 17 percent of our children—10 million—are poor, making them the poorest of any group in America, including the elderly. In 1979 one in every six preschoolers lived in a family at or below the poverty line.
2. An estimated 570,000 children are born annually to teenagers. Seven out of ten mothers under fifteen years of age receive no prenatal care in the first three months of pregnancy; over one-fifth receive no such care or receive it very late.
3. Ten million children, or one in six, get virtually no health care.
4. Only about one-sixth of our poorest children receive the periodic screening to which they are entitled, and when they are screened, about 40 percent of the detected problems go untreated.
5. The national commitment to preschool intervention remains precarious, with Head Start and other programs continuously engaging in fights for funding.
6. American policy still does not reflect the fact that only one in seventeen families is the stereotypic traditional family. Most mothers work outside the home. Still, licensed day care can take care of only 10 percent of the needs. The debate for standards for day care drags on. By 1990 at least 1 million more day care placements and 1.6 million child care workers will be needed.
7. At least half a million children live in out-of-home placement, and many will grow up there. Tens of thousands are placed inappropriately and then forgotten.
8. Mental health care for children is shockingly inadequate. Few resources and staff are available for children. Those in foster care and correctional facilities receive little of the care they require. Funding patterns work against treatment of children in the least restrictive setting. Inappropriate hospitalization occurs for lack of alternatives, and institutions are not of adequate quality.

In addition to her litany of children's needs, Edelman painted a bleak picture for the 1980s. Economic and sociopolitical pressures exist that may work against programs for families. Since the general population is becoming older, support may be diverted into needed programs for adults. Moreover, children have been—and re-

main—an easy group to ignore: They do not vote, contribute to campaigns, or lobby. In Edelman's words, "Amidst protestations of 'Who can be against children?' too few people are *for* children when it really matters" (1981, p. 111).

Nevertheless, Edelman does have some rec-

Table 13-3   Common Myths Faced by Children's Advocates and the Reality

Myths	Reality
Only Other People's Children Have Problems	Violence, drug abuse, and pregnancy belong to the middle-class as well as the lower classes. Handicapping conditions strike all social classes and races, although the poor may suffer most. Suicide has increased more among white teenage males than any other group.
Families Are Self-sufficient and Should Take Care of Themselves	No family is self-sufficient in rearing its young. We no longer can deny that one in five children live in a one-parent family. Day care and other support services are required.
No One Should Take Responsibility for Children Except Their Parents	Children may be a primary responsibility of the family but why should it be the case that other socializers do not care for the young? Most of the time others are buck-passing.
Helping Children Whose Families Cannot Fully Provide for Them Condones and Rewards Failure and Erodes Family Values	Turning our backs on children because we believe their parents did not do what they "should" is unreasonable. It leads to a policy in which we condemn people for being lazy but do not provide jobs, or condemn for child abuse but do give support to alleviate stress.
Child Advocates Want the Government to Take Control over Families' and Children's Lives	This is a red herring. The government already is involved. No one wants intrusion, but we must assure that what government does helps instead of hinders.
Meeting Children's Needs and Protecting Their Rights Will Divide Families and Pit Parents and Children Against Each Other	The goal is not to pit the generations but to provide services. It includes needs and rights in many institutions besides the family: schools, health, juvenile systems, welfare systems.
Children's Issues Should Be Above the Political Process	The political process is the established route for change and so must be used.
Providing Needed Services Is Too Expensive	Providing services is less expensive than trying to remedy problems once they exist. The real issue is what we value and are thus willing to pay for. Can a nation that spent $21.3 billion on tobacco products in 1980 afford preventive services for its children? Of course it can.

From Edelman, 1981.

ommendations. First, she suggests that ways must be found to combat so-called myths or assumptions that hinder commitment to the young and their families. These myths, as shown in Table 13-3, stem from both philosophical and practical considerations. Many are deeply rooted in the American way of life, such as the idea that the child belongs exclusively to the family, which, in turn, must shoulder virtually all responsibility and control (e.g., Shore, 1979). Those who work with children can help uncover and destroy these myths. But they must also be fiscally hard-nosed about the cost-effectiveness of programs. Good evaluation of projects that work or do not work is sorely required. So too are efforts to implement gains already accomplished, such as P.L. 94-142 (p. 223) and the Adoption Assistance and Child Welfare Act (p. 330). Considerable effort must also be expended in the political arena to establish a network of legislators and others concerned about the young. In the final analysis, Edelman speaks of the importance of persistence, repeating a story about Sojourner Truth, who tenaciously fought against slavery and the maltreatment of women. When a heckler once allowed that he cared for Sojourner's speech no more than for a flea bite, stubborn Sojourner retorted, "Maybe not, but . . . I'll keep you scratching" (Lerner, 1972, p. 524, cited by Edelman, 1981). Perhaps this kind of tenacity, combined with know-how and hard work, can advance our knowledge and commitment to the young.

SUMMARY

Concerns for children of any society are partially set by existing social, political, and economic conditions. In the U.S., current concern has been shaped by the broad social thrust of the 1960s and by recently accumulated knowledge of children's development.

One of the areas in which improvement is sought is in prevention of behavior problems. When etiology is well established and primarily biological (e.g., genetic processes, nutritional deficits), mental health problems appear pre-

ventable in large measure. However, necessary biological preconditions have not been firmly established for most behavioral dysfunctions. Thus, a broad public health model, as described by Caplan, is commonly employed.

Caplan's model includes primary prevention (reduction of the rate of new cases), secondary prevention (reduction of the duration of existing cases), and tertiary prevention (reduction of residual effects of disorders). Emphasis has been placed on primary and secondary efforts, with specific programs varying enormously in focus and setting. The Rochester Primary Mental Health Project, Head Start, the Voluntary Intervention and Treatment Program, intervention with families adjusting to sudden infant death, and research into the causes of schizophrenia are a few examples of efforts toward prevention.

In principle the benefits of prevention seem indisputable. Nevertheless, resistance to and criticism of this mode are common. Professionals are trained for treatment and respond to already existing problems. Preventive efforts are fragmented at the national level. Serious question has been raised about the efficacy of prevention, particularly primary prevention. Finally, ethical dilemmas are of particular concern in programs that operate across large segments of the population.

One of the ways in which good mental health might be fostered is through the building of competence in children. Competence, which has been variously defined, includes many aspects of functioning (e.g., personality, social perceptions, motor skills, cognition). Programs that teach parents to interact optimally with their offspring could prove fruitful. So too might programs that train children directly, as in Spivack and Shure's attempt to increase interpersonal cognitive problem-solving skills in low SES youngsters. Results from this effort demonstrate that the young can be taught such skills and that training can increase adjustment.

When we turn to the issue of children's rights, we turn to another kind of concern for the young. The "human rights" emphasis advocates that all children have an inherent right to have basic biological and psychological needs met. The legal rights emphasis, which covers several complex domains (e.g., child placement, institutionalization), advocates for children through the legal system. The task that both "child savers" and "kiddie libbers" have taken upon themselves is to gain consensus on children's rights and to make that consensus the framework for social policy regarding the care and treatment of the young.

In spite of the fact that concern for children is widely expressed at the present time, the needs of the young are largely unmet. Edelman, for example, points to poverty, poor medical care, unmet family needs, inappropriate child placement, and shockingly inadequate mental health care. She argues that child workers must understand and destroy social myths that hinder the welfare of children, construct cost-efficient programs, and advocate in the political arena.

GLOSSARY

ABA′ (reversal) research design Single-subject experimental design in which the relevant behavior is measured during a baseline period (A), a period in which a manipulation is made (B), and a period in which the manipulation is removed (A′). A fourth period involving the reintroduction of the manipulation (B′) is added when treatment is the goal.

Accommodation In Piagetian theory, the process of adapting one's mental constructions or schemas of the world to fit with new experiences.

Adaptive behavior scales Psychological instruments that measure an individual's ability to perform in the everyday environment, for example, to wash one's hair, interact socially, and communicate. Used mostly for evaluation of retarded or severely disturbed persons, these scales depend heavily on parental or caretaker reports.

Amniocentesis A procedure used to examine the development of the fetus. A long needle injected into the abdomen of the pregnant woman extracts fetal cells and amniotic fluid, which are evaluated for biochemical and chromosomal defects.

Amphetamines Drugs which act as stimulants, producing high levels of energy. Side effects such as sleeplessness and nervousness can result from large doses.

Anaclitic depression A period of withdrawal and sadness in very young children in reaction to prolonged separation from their parents.

Antisocial behavior A pattern of behavior that violates widely held social norms and brings harm to others (e.g. stealing, lying). The terms psychopathic or sociopathic are also often used to describe such patterns of behavior by individuals who appear to exhibit no remorse or shame after harming others.

Aphasia A general term referring to language disturbances not caused by general intellectual deficiency. *Developmental aphasia* refers to receptive and expressive language disorders in childhood.

Assimilation In Piagetian theory, the process of taking in or interpreting new information according to existing mental constructions or schemas of the world.

Attachment A strong socioemotional bond between individuals. Usually discussed in terms of the child-parent or child-caretaker relationship, attachment is generally viewed as having strong influence on a child's development.

Autonomic nervous system A part of the nervous system that consists of ganglia along the spinal cord and nerves to peripheral organs (e.g. glands and blood vessels). It regulates functions usually considered involuntary, such as the operation of smooth muscles and glands. The system controls physiological changes associated with the expression of emotion.

Behavior modification An approach to the treatment of behavior disorders that is based primarily on learning principles. Also referred to as *behavior therapy*.

Biofeedback Procedures by which the individual is provided immediate information (feedback) about some aspect of physiological functioning (e.g. muscle tension, skin temperature). These procedures are believed to be helpful in treating certain physical disorders since it is assumed that the individual can come to control bodily functioning through such feedback.

Broncho-dilator Substances inhaled or taken in oral form which expand (dilate) the air passages and are therefore frequently included in the treatment of asthma.

Bulimia Episodes of uncontrolled excessive eating, often followed by self-induced vomiting or laxative abuse.

Central nervous system In humans, the brain and spinal cord. (*See* autonomic nervous system)

Cephalocaudal growth Growth that takes place from the head (cephalic) region to the tail (caudal) region. Early physical growth and motor development generally occur in the cephalocaudal direction.

Child guidance movement An early to mid-20th century effort in the U.S. to treat and prevent childhood mental disorders. Importance was given to influences of familial and wider social systems on the child.

Chromosome A threadlike structure in the cell nucleus that contains the genetic code. With the exception of the gametes, human cells possess 23 pairs, 22 pairs of autosomes and 1 pair of sex chromosomes. The gametes possess 23 single chromosomes.

Chromosome aberrations Abnormalities in the number and/or structure of the chromosome complement that often lead to fetal death or anomalies in development.

Classical conditioning A form of learning, also referred to as Pavlovian conditioning. An individual comes to respond to a stimulus (conditioned stimulus or CS) that did not previously elicit a response. Classical conditioning occurs when a CS is paired with another stimulus (the unconditioned stimulus, or UCS) that does elicit the desired response (unconditioned response, or UCR). When this response is elicited by the conditioned stimulus alone it is called a conditioned response (CR).

Classificatory variable In research methodology, attributes of subjects (e.g., age, sex, diagnosis) that are investigated in some way. Classificatory variables are sometimes erroneously taken for independent variables. (*See* mixed research design)

Clinical case study Descriptive method of research in which an individual case of disturbed behavior is described. Case studies typically include the behavioral manifestations themselves, history and background of the person, test results, treatments, and outcome. The case study can be informative but cannot be generalized to other persons or situations with confidence.

Clinical utility A criterion for judging the adequacy of a classification system, diagnosis, or assessment instrument. Judgments are based on how fully the observed phenomena are described and on how useful the descriptions are.

Compulsions Behaviors the child feels compelled to repeat over and over again, even though they appear to have no rational basis.

Concordant In genetic research, refers to individuals who are similar in particular attributes, for example, concordant for hair color or activity level.

Concurrent validity A measure of the degree to which a diagnostic category suggests additional features, that are not included in the definition of the diagnosis, but that are found in persons with the diagnosis.

Conditioned stimulus (CS) A neutral stimulus, which through repeated pairing with a stimulus (unconditioned stimulus) that already elicits a particular response, comes to elicit a similar response (conditioned response).

Content validity A measure of the degree to which an assessment instrument measures what it is intended to measure.

Contingency management A group of procedures that seek to modify or change behavior by altering the contingencies (causal relationships) between stimulus and response events.

Continuity theories of development Theories of development that postulate that growth occurs in a gradual, continuous fashion rather than in clearly defined stages or steps. Continuity theories emphasize the role of experience and learning in development.

Control group In an experiment, a group of subjects who are treated differently than subjects who receive the experimental manipulation and later compared with them. The purpose of control groups is to insure that the results of the experiment can be attributed to the manipulation rather than to other variables.

Correlational research A research strategy aimed at establishing whether two or more variables covary, or are associated. (*See* positive correlation and negative correlation.) The establishment of a correlation permits prediction of one variable from the other, but does not establish a causal relationship.

Crisis intervention A method of prevention of disorders that provides services to persons who have experienced developmental crises (e.g., adolescence upset) or accidental crises (e.g., loss of a loved one).

Critical period A relatively limited period of time during which an organism may be particularly sensitive to specific influences. Strictly viewed, the critical period hypothesis postulates that certain inputs at certain times set up irreversible patterns of behavior.

Crossing over A genetic mechanism in which sections of a chromosome pair are exchanged in meiosis.

Cross-sectional research A research strategy that observes and compares different groups of subjects at one point in time. It is a highly practical way to gather certain kinds of information.

Deficit vs. difference model Antagonistic models to explain atypical functioning of poor children, the deficit model suggests that these children are deficient by reason of inheritance and/or inferior subculture. The difference model argues that poor children are not deficient but learn different content and styles that disadvantage them on intelligence tests and in institutions that stress middle-class values.

Delinquency A legal term that refers to an illegal act by a person under 18. Such behavior may be illegal for an adult as well, such as theft, or may only be illegal when committed by a juvenile, for example, truancy.

Delusion An idea or belief that appears contrary to reality and is not widely accepted in the culture (e.g., delusions of grandeur or persecution).

Dependent variable In the experimental method of research, the measure of behavior that may be influenced by the manipulation (independent variable).

Development Change in structure and function that occurs over time in living organisms. Typically viewed as change from the simple to the complex, development is the result of transactions between biological and environmental variables.

Developmental level The level at which an individual is functioning with regard to physical, intellectual, or socioemotional characteristics. Individuals can be assigned to a developmental level based on age-norms or theoretical constructions.

Developmental quotient (DQ) A measure of performance on infant tests of intelligence, paralleling the intelligence quotient (IQ) derived from intelligence tests for older children.

Developmental vs. difference controversy Theoretical dispute about atypical functioning, especially about mental retardation. The developmental view argues that retarded persons function intellectually in the same ways as do the nonretarded, but that they develop more slowly and perhaps reach a ceiling. The difference view maintains that the intellective processes of retarded persons are qualitatively different than normal processes.

Diagnosis The decision that the pattern of behaviors or symptoms displayed by a person indicates a certain disorder or disease.

Diathesis A constitutional predisposition toward a a disease or disorder

Differential reinforcement of other behaviors (DRO) In behavior modification, refers to applying relatively more reinforcement to desirable behaviors that are incompatible with specific undesirable behaviors.

Differentiation Process whereby growth becomes progressively refined. For example, motor development that initially involves global action of the arm comes to include refined movement of the wrist and fingers.

Discordant In genetic research, refers to individuals who are dissimilar in particular attributes, for example, discordant in hair color or activity level.

Discrimination The process by which an individual comes to learn that a particular stimulus, but not others, signals that a certain response is likely to be followed by a particular consequence.

Disinhibition The process by which responses already in the child's repertoire, for example, pushing, increase after observing a model exhibit acts in the same class of behavior, such as hitting and yelling.

Displacement According to psychoanalytic theory, an unconscious defense mechanism whereby an emotional reaction toward some important object is instead expressed toward some other, less threatening object.

Diversion programs This approach to delinquency attempts to intervene by providing services (e.g. education, vocational training) that will *divert* delinquent youth away from the juvenile justice system.

Dizygotic twins Twins resulting from two independent unions of ova and sperm that occur at approximately the same time. Dizygotic twins are genetically no more alike than are nontwin siblings.

DNA Deoxyribonucleic acid. The chemical carrier of the genetic code that is found in the chromosomes. The spiral-shaped DNA molecule is composed of sugar, phosphates, and nucleotides. The nucleotides carry the hereditary information that directs protein synthesis.

Dyscalculia General term for the inability to perform arithmetic operations. Many skills are involved, such as spatial and language abilities.

Dyslexia General term referring to the inability to

read. *Developmental dyslexia* denotes problems in reading during childhood.

Echolalia   The repetition of the speech of others, either immediately or delayed in time. A pathological speech pattern commonly found in infantile autism and psychoses.

Ego   According to psychoanalytic theory, this is the structure of the mind that operates predominantly at the conscious level. It mediates between instinctual urges and reality and is responsible for decision making.

Electroencephalograph (EEG)   A recording of the electrical activity of the brain.

Empirical   The process of verification or proof by accumulating information or data through observation or experiment (in contrast to reliance on impression or theory).

Epidemiology   The study of the occurrence of a (behavior) disorder within a specific population. Occurrence may be expressed as prevalence or incidence. (*See* prevalence, incidence)

Eros (libido)   This is Freud's term for the id's impulse to seek pleasure and gratification. It is sometimes equated with sexual instinct.

Etiology   The cause or origin of a disease or behavior disorder.

Etiological validity   The degree to which a diagnostic label indicates that the same cause is present in different individuals with this disorder.

Executive function   A term that refers to the ability to select, monitor, evaluate, and revise strategies employed in memory.

Experimental research   A research strategy that can establish causal relationships between variables. In the experiment subjects are treated by the independent variable to determine possible effects on the dependent variable. Comparison groups are included to control for extraneous influences and the procedures are carefully controlled by the researchers.

External validity   In research methodology, refers to the degree to which findings of an investigation can be generalized to other populations and situations.

Extinction   A weakening of a learned response that is produced when reinforcement that followed the response no longer occurs.

Factor analysis   A statistical procedure which correlates each item with every other item, and then groups items that tend to correlate with each other into clusters of related items (factors).

Frustration-aggression hypothesis   The proposition that frustration always leads to aggression and that aggression is only caused by frustration.

Gametes   The sex cells that unite to form the zygote. In females the gametes are the ova (or eggs); in males the gametes are the spermatozoa (or sperm).

Gene   The smallest unit of the chromosome that transmits genetic information. With the exception of the gametes, genes occur in pairs, one on each of the paired chromosomes.

Generalization   The process by which a response is made to a new stimulus that is different but similar to the stimulus present during learning.

Generalized imitation   The tendency to imitate across persons, situations, and time.

Genotype   The complement of genes that a person inherits; the genetic endowment.

Hallucination   A sensory perception (e.g., hearing a noise, seeing an object) that occurs in the absence of any apparent environmental stimulation.

Hypothesis   In science, a proposition or ''educated guess'' put forth for evaluation by some scientific method.

Id   According to psychoanalytic theory this is developmentally the earliest of the structures of the mind—it is present at birth. The source of all psychic energy, the Id operates entirely at the unconscious level, seeking immediate gratification of all instinctual urges (the pleasure principle).

Impulsivity   The tendency to act quickly without reflection. Hyperactive children are viewed as impulsive.

Incidence   In studying the occurrence of a behavior disorder, incidence refers to the number of new cases in a given population in a given time period. (*See* prevalence)

Independent variable   In the experimental method of research, the variable manipulated by the researcher.

Instrumental learning   Also frequently termed operant conditioning, this is the process by which a response is acquired, maintained, or eliminated as a function of environmental consequences (e.g., reward and punishment).

Intelligence quotient (IQ), deviation   A standard score derived from statistical procedures that reflects the direction and degree to which an individual's performance on an intelligence test deviates from the average score of the individual's age group.

Intelligence quotient (IQ), ratio   The ratio of mental age (MA), derived from performance on tests of intelligence, to chronological age (CA), multiplied by 100. $IQ = MA/CA \times 100$.

Interactional model of development The view that development is the result of the interplay of organismic and environmental variables. (*See* transactional model of development)

Internalizing disorders The large category of disorders—many of which are traditionally referred to as neuroses—in which the problems exhibited seem directed more at the self than at others; for example fears, depression, and withdrawal.

Internal validity In research methodology, refers to the degree to which findings can be attributed to certain factors. Frequently concerns the degree to which a result of an *experiment* can be attributed to the experimental manipulation (the independent variable), rather than to extraneous factors.

Inter-rater reliability The extent to which different raters agree on a particular diagnosis or measurement.

Introversion-extroversion A dimension of social behavior or personality. Introversion refers to the degree to which an individual is inner-oriented, shy, and uneasy in social situations. Extroversion is the degree to which an individual is outgoing and at ease socially.

Laterality The use of one side of the body over the other, for example, in right-handedness. Laterality in brain functioning is assumed to be the basis of such behavioral functioning.

Learned helplessness Passivity and a sense of lack of control over one's environment that is learned through experiences where one's behavior was ineffective in controlling events.

Least restrictive environment A term that refers to the idea that handicapped individuals have a right to be educated with and to live with the nonhandicapped to the extent that is maximally feasible. (See Public Law 94–142.)

Libido The energy associated with Eros.

Longitudinal research A research strategy that observes the same subjects over a relatively long period of time, measuring behavior at certain points. It is particularly helpful in tracing developmental change.

Mainstreaming The placing of handicapped individuals into the least restrictive environments in which they are capable of functioning. More specifically, the placement of handicapped children in regular, rather than special, classes. (See Public Law 94–142)

Masked depression This term refers to cases where a child's depression is "masked" by other problems such as hyperactivity or delinquency. These "depressive equivalents" are thought to be manifestations of the underlying depression.

Maturation Changes that occur in individuals of a species relatively independent of the environment provided that basic conditions are satisfied. For example, most humans will walk, given normal physical capacity, nourishment, and opportunity for movement.

Maturational lag A slowness or falling behind in development; often implies a lag in brain or nervous system development.

Mediational processes Strategies by which stimuli are connected so that learning and thinking are facilitated. Examples are the use of imagery, words, clustering, and rehearsal.

Memory Complex process by which perceived information can be recalled in some way. According to a widely-held model, information is first taken in by a sensory register, is passed to short-term storage, and then to long-term storage.

Mental age (MA) The age-score corresponding to the chronological age (CA) of children whose test performance the examinee equals. For the average child, $MA = CA$.

Mental hygiene movement An effort organized in the United States early in the 20th century to bring effective, humane treatment to the mentally ill and to prevent mental disorders. Clifford Beers, who wrote *A Mind That Found Itself*, was a driving force in the movement, which was closely associated with the child guidance movement.

Meiosis In maturation of the gametes, the specialized cell division that results in the ova and sperm containing half of the number of chromosomes found in other cells.

Metamemory The understanding or awareness of the working of one's memory or the strategies used to facilitate memory.

Migraine headache A severe form of headache caused by instability of the vascular system that results in sustained dilation, an increase in size of the extracranial arteries.

Minimal brain dysfunction (MBD) The hypothesis or assumption that the central nervous system or brain is functioning in a pathological way to a degree that is not clearly detectable. MBD is hypothesized as the cause of hyperactivity and learning disabilities, as well as other behavior disorders.

Mitosis The common type of cell division that results in two identical daughter cells. During mitosis each chromosome pair is duplicated, with one pair going to each daughter cell.

Mixed research design A research design in which subjects are assigned into groups on the basis of some attribute (i.e., a classificatory variable such as age), and then an experimental manipulation is applied. In interpretation of results, care must be taken not to view the classificatory variable as an independent variable.

Monozygotic twins Twins resulting from one union of an ovum and sperm. The single zygote divides early into two, with the new zygotes having identical genes (and thus being of the same sex).

Morphology In language, the study of word formation.

Multiple baseline research design Single-subject experimental design that typically entails the consecutive manipulation of two (or more) behaviors. With the behaviors being manipulated one at a time, the behavior not being treated serves as a comparison to evaluate change in the other.

Mutation Spontaneous change in the genes that can be transmitted to the next generation. One of the genetic mechanisms that accounts for variation in species and individuals.

Nature vs. nurture controversy The continuing debate about the relative influence of innate and experiential factors on the shaping of the individual. Also known as the maturation vs. learning and heredity vs. environment controversy.

Negative correlation When two (or more) variables are negatively correlated they co-vary such that high scores on one variable are associated with low scores on the other, and vice versa.

Negative reinforcement The process whereby the withdrawal of a stimulus contingent on a particular response increases the probability of that response reoccurring.

Neurophysiological assessment The use of procedures that *directly* measure the physiological integrity of the nervous system. The EEG is the most well known of these measures.

Neuropsychological assessment The use of psychological tests and behavioral measures to *indirectly* evaluate the functioning of the nervous system. Performance on these measures is known or presumed to reflect specific aspects of the functioning of the brain.

Neurosis A traditional term employed to describe any of a group of nonpsychotic disorders that are characterized by unusual levels of anxiety and associated problems. Phobias, obsessions, and compulsions are examples of disorders in this category.

Neurotransmitter A chemical that carries the electrical impulse from one neuron across the synaptic cleft to another neuron. Examples are serotonin, dopamine, and norepinephrine.

Normal distribution (curve) The bell-shaped theoretical distribution or probability curve that describes the way in which many attributes (e.g., height, intelligence) are assumed to occur in the population. Extreme values of the attribute occur with less frequency than middle values of the attribute.

Norms Data based on information gathered from a segment of the population that represents the entire population. Norms serve as standards to evaluate individual development or functioning.

Nuclear family A family unit consisting of the father, mother, and children.

Observational learning The learning that occurs through viewing the behavior of others. Modeled behavior can be presented in live or symbolic form.

Observer bias The degree to which a person's observations are distorted by expectations of what behavior will occur.

Obsessions Recurring and intrusive irrational thoughts over which the individual feels no control.

Operant conditioning *See* instrumental learning.

Operational criteria (definition) A specified set of observable operations that are measurable and allow one to define some concept. For example, maternal deprivation might be defined by measuring the time the child is separated from its mother.

Overcorrection Behavior modification technique in which an individual engaging in an undesirable behavior (e.g., self-injury, enuresis) must then practice a behavior that is incompatible with the undesirable act.

Overlearning The procedure whereby learning trials are continued beyond the point at which the child has completed the stated criteria. This is intended to increase the likelihood that the new behavior will be maintained.

Paired-associate learning Learning phenomenon in which an individual is initially presented paired stimuli (e.g. words, pictures) and later, when shown one stimulus of a pair, must recall or reproduce the other.

Paradigm The set of assumptions and conceptions shared by a group of scientists that are used in collecting data and interpreting the phenomena of interest.

Paradoxical drug effect An effect of a drug that contradicts the expected effect. An example is the quieting of many hyperactive children by stimulant medications.

Partial correlation statistical procedure A statistical procedure that aids in the interpretation of a demonstrated correlation by removing the effects of one or more specific variables.

Participant modeling A treatment method in which observation of a model is followed by the observer joining the model in gradual approximations of the desired behavior.

Pearson product-moment correlation A widely used statistical procedure to determine whether a correlation exists between two variables. The procedure entails the calculation of the Pearson coefficient, r, which ranges in value from -1.00 to $+1.00$. A coefficient of -1.00 is a perfect negative correlation, while $+1.00$ is a perfect positive correlation. The value of 0 means that the variables do not co-vary in the sample tested.

Perceptual-motor training Approach to rectify general and specific learning disabilities that is based on the assumption that basic perceptual and motor functioning has gone awry or has developed abnormally. Training emphasizes exercises in sensory reception and motor responses, such as practicing right/left orientation, balancing, and learning simple forms and shapes.

Perinatal Referring to the period of development at or around the time of birth.

Perspective *See* paradigm.

Phenotype The observable attributes of an individual that result from genetic endowment, developmental processes, and the transactions of these.

Phobia Anxiety and avoidance of some object or situation that is judged to be an excessive, overly persistent, unadaptive, or inappropriate fear.

Phonology The study of speech sounds.

Pica The habitual eating of substances usually considered inedible such as dirt, paper, and hair.

Placebo A treatment—psychological or chemical—that alters a person's behavior because of an expectation that he or she has that change will occur. Placebos are often employed as control treatments to evaluate whether a treatment being tested is effective for reasons other than the person's belief in it.

Polygenetic inheritance Inheritance of a characteristic that is influenced by many genes rather than a single one.

Positive correlation When two (or more) variables are positively correlated they co-vary with each other such that high scores on one variable are associated with high scores on the other variable, and low scores on the one variable are associated with low scores on the other.

Positive reinforcement A stimulus is presented following a particular response—and contingent upon that response—thereby increasing the likelihood that the response will occur in the future.

Predictive validity The extent to which predictions about future behavior can be made by knowing an individual's diagnosis or performance on some test.

Preformation An antiquated doctrine that the human organism is preformed in the gametes and that development is an enlargement of the already existing parts.

Premorbid adjustment This term refers to the psychological, social, and academic/vocational adjustment of a person prior to onset of the symptoms of a disorder or its diagnosis.

Prenatal Referring to the period of development that occurs during pregnancy.

Preparedness Refers to the idea that organisms are genetically influenced to learn particular responses or associations more readily than others. For example, an organism might be biologically predisposed to be sensitive to a certain object and more likely to learn a fear response to it.

Prevalence In studying the occurrence of a behavior disorder, prevalence refers to the number of cases in the population at a given time. It may be expressed by number of cases or percent of the population. (*See* incidence)

Primary prevention The prevention of disorders in the population by methods that preclude their occurrence. Examples are parent education in child management and counseling of individuals who have suffered trauma.

Projection A defense mechanism whereby the ego protects against unacceptable thoughts or impulses by attributing them to another person or some object.

Projective tests Psychological tests which present ambiguous stimuli to the person. The subject's response is presumed to reflect unconsious thoughts and feelings that are unacceptable to the ego and therefore cannot be expressed directly. This unconscious material is projected onto the test material and thereby expressed indirectly.

Pronoun reversal Deviant speech pattern in which speakers refer to themselves as "you" or "she" or "he" and refer to others as "I" or "me". Often found in autistic children.

Proximodistal growth   Growth that takes place from the central axis of the body outward to the periphery. Early physical growth and motor development tend to occur in the proximodistal direction.

Psychoactive drugs   Chemical substances that influence psychological processes (e.g., behavior, thinking, emotions) by their influence on nervous system functioning. Examples are stimulants and tranquilizers.

Psychomotor retardation   A slowing of movement often associated with depression that may involve slowed speech, slowed body movements, and decreased energy level.

Psychopath   See antisocial behavior.

Psychosomatic disorders   Disorders involving actual physical symptoms that are presumed to be caused, at least in part, by psychological factors such as stress.

Public Law 94–142   The federal *Education for all Handicapped Children Act of 1975,* which sets guidelines for the rights of handicapped children to appropriate education. It assures appropriate public education and services in the least restrictive environment, a role for parents in decision making, and assistance to the states.

Public Law 96–272   The federal *Adoption Assistance and Child Welfare Act of 1980,* which is designed to provide better welfare services to children and to protect their rights in child adoption and placement.

Punishment   A response is followed by either an unpleasant stimulus or the removal of a pleasant stimulus, thereby decreasing the frequency of that response.

Random assignment   In research, the assignment of individuals to different groups in such a way that each individual has an equal chance of being assigned to any group. Such chance assignment helps make the groups comparable on factors that might influence the findings.

Recidivism   The return to a previous undesirable pattern. The juvenile delinquent who returns to commit a crime after completing a treatment program is illustrative of recidivism.

Reflexes   Automatic, unlearned responses to specific stimulation. Examples are the sucking, coughing, and Moro reflexes. Reflexes are considered relatively simple acts, some of which give way to voluntary, learned responses.

Reinforcement   A process whereby a stimulus presented contingent on the occurrence of a particular behavior results in an increase in the likelihood of that behavior. See positive reinforcement and negative reinforcement.

Relapse   The reoccurrence of a problem after it has been successfully treated.

Reliability   The degree to which an observation is consistently made. The term can be applied to a test or other measurement or to a system of classification.

Repression   According to psychoanalytic theory, the most basic defense mechanism. Thoughts or impulses unacceptable to the ego are forced back into the unconscious.

Response prevention   A behavioral treatment procedure in which the person is not allowed to, or discouraged from, engaging in a compulsive ritual or behavior.

Risk   Vulnerability to a disorder. Individuals at risk for a particular disorder are said to be vulnerable to develop that condition.

Rumination   The voluntary regurgitation of food by infants.

School phobia   An extreme reluctance to go to school which is frequently accompanied by somatic complaints. The term *school refusal* is preferred by some clinicians, since an actual fear of school may not be present.

Scientific method   An empirical approach to understanding the wide array of natural phenomena. The scientific approach involves systematic observation, measurement and testing of relationships, and explanations of phenomena.

Secondary prevention   The prevention of disorders in the population by shortening the duration of existing cases through early diagnosis and treatment.

Self-injurious behavior   Repetitious action that damages the self physically, such as head banging, scratching the self, and pulling one's own hair. Often observed in psychotic and mentally retarded children, but occurs in a small percentage of young, normal children.

Self-stimulatory behavior   Sensory-motor behavior that serves as stimulation for the child. Often refers to a pathological process, for example, as when an autistic child repetitiously flaps his or her hands.

Semantics   The study of the meanings in language (or more generally, in signs).

Separation anxiety   Excessive anxiety regarding separation from the mother or other major attachment figures.

Sequential research designs   Various research designs that combine the longitudinal and cross-sectional strategies in order to maximize the strengths of these methods.

Single-subject experimental designs Research designs that entail working with one individual in ways that permit inferences about causality. (*See* ABA and Multiple baseline designs)

Socioeconomic status (SES) Classification of people according to social class. Indices of SES include monetary level, amount of education, and occupational level. Many factors vary with SES, such as medical care and child-rearing practices.

Sociopath See antisocial behavior.

Somatogenesis The viewpoint that development or a particular disorder is due to biological—rather than psychological—causes.

Special education A term employed to describe the efforts of educators to deal with the problems of atypical children.

Stage theories of development Explanations of development that postulate that growth occurs in a recognizable order of noncontinuous stages or steps, which are qualitatively different from each other. Examples: Piaget's cognitive theory and Freud's psychosexual theory.

Statistical significance In research, refers to a low probability that the findings are merely chance occurrences. By tradition a finding is statistically significant when there is a 5 percent probability or less than it occurred by chance. ($p \leq .05$).

Stimulants A drug which increases alertness and activity. Amphetamines are one example of stimulants.

Stimulus overselectivity Selectively attending to certain aspects of a stimulus configuration while ignoring other aspects. Overselectivity is not attributed to specific sensory deficits, but etiology is not understood.

Superego The third of Freud's three structures of the mind. It is the conscience or self-critical part of the individual that reflects society's morals and standards as they have been learned from parents and others.

Sympathetic nervous system A part of the autonomic nervous system which, among other things, accelerates heart rate, contracts blood vessels, inhibits intestinal activity, and in general seems to prepare the organism for stress or activity.

Symptom substitution The notion, derived largely from the psychodynamic perspective, that if one treats just the observed problem behavior, a new problem or symptom will occur since the underlying illness or psychological conflict has not been treated.

Syndrome A group of behaviors or symptoms which tend to occur together in a particular disorder.

Syntax The aspect of grammar that deals with the way words are put together to form phrases, clauses, and sentences.

Systematic desensitization A behavioral treatment of anxiety. The client visualizes a hierarchy of scenes, each of which elicits more anxiety than the previous scene. These visualizations are paired with relaxation until they no longer produce anxiety.

Systematic direct observation Observation of specific behaviors of an individual or group of individuals in a particular setting, with the use of a specific observational code or instrument.

Temperament A variety of socioemotional behaviors viewed as relatively stable attributes of individuals, such as activity level, introversion-extroversion, and social responsiveness.

Teratogens Conditions or agents that tend to cause developmental malformations, defects, or death of the fetus.

Tertiary prevention The prevention of disorders in the population by reducing defective functioning that is residual to primary disorders. An example is support groups for persons who are returning to the community after hospitalization for mental disorders and may have to face negative stereotyping.

Test-retest reliability The degree to which the use of a test or diagnostic system yields the same result when applied to an individual at different times.

Thanatos According to psychoanalytic theory, it is the destructive, aggressive, death instinct. Thanatos and Eros are the two basic instincts of the id.

Time-out Behavior modification technique in which an individual displaying an undesirable behavior is removed from the immediate environment, usually by placement into an isolated room. Conceptually time-out is viewed as elimination of positive reinforcement or as punishment.

Token economy A behavioral treatment procedure developed from operant conditioning principles. A system of behaviors that earn or cost reward points, given in the form of some scrip, such as poker chips, is set up. These tokens can then be exchanged for prizes, activities, or privileges.

Transactional model of development The view that development is the result of the continuous interplay of organismic and environmental variables. It is conceptually similar to the interactional model of development but it emphasizes the ongoing, mutual influences of factors.

Tuberose sclerosis A disorder, transmitted by an

autosomal dominant gene, in which severe mental retardation and tumors of the skin and internal organs are exhibited.

Twin study   A type of research investigation frequently employed to examine the effects of hereditary and environmental variables. Pairs of genetically-identical monozygotic twins and genetically-different dizygotic twins are examined to determine whether the former are more alike than the latter.

Unconditioned stimulus   A stimulus which elicits a particular response prior to any conditioning trials. The loud noise that causes an infant to startle is an example of an unconditioned stimulus.

Validity   A term used in several different ways, all of which address issues of correctness, meaningfulness, and relevancy. (See internal validity, external validity, etiological validity, concurrent validity, and content validity and predictive validity.)

Vascular system   The circulatory system of blood vessels consisting of arteries, veins, and capillaries.

Zeitgeist   A German word for the general viewpoint and attitudes of a given society at a particular time. A literal translation is *zeit* (time) *geist* (spirit).

Zygote   The cell mass formed by the joining of an ovum and sperm; the fertilized egg.

REFERENCES

ABLON, S. L., & MACK, J. E. Sleep disorders. In J. D. Noshpitz (ed.), *Basic handbook of child psychiatry II.* New York: Basic Books, 1979.

ABRAHAM, K. Notes on the psychoanalytical investigation and treatment of manic-depressive insanity and allied conditions (1911). In K. Abraham, *Selected papers on psycho-analysis.* London: Hogarth Press, 1949.

ABRAHAM, S., & NORDSIECK, M. Relationship of excess weight in children and adults. *Public Health Reports,* 1960, *75,* 263–273.

ACHENBACH, T. M. The classification of children's psychiatric symptoms: A factor-analytic study. *Psychological Monographs,* 1966, *80* (7, Whole No. 615).

ACHENBACH, T. M. *Developmental psychopathology.* New York: The Ronald Press Co., 1974.

ACHENBACH, T. M. The Child Behavior Profile: I. Boys aged 6-11. *Journal of Consulting and Clinical Psychology,* 1978, *46,* 478–488. (a)

ACHENBACH, T. M. *Research in developmental psychology: Concepts, strategies, methods.* New York: Free Press, 1978. (b)

ACHENBACH, T. M. The Child Behavior Profile: An empirically based system for assessing children's behavioral problems and competencies. *International Journal of Mental Health,* 1979, *1,* 24–42.

ACHENBACH, T. M. DSM-III in light of empirical research on the classification of child psychopathology. *Journal of the American Academy of Child Psychiatry,* 1980, *19,* 395–412.

ACHENBACH, T. M., & EDELBROCK, C. S. The classification of child psychopathology: A review and analysis of empirical efforts. *Psychological Bulletin,* 1978, *85,* 1275–1301.

ACHENBACH, T. M., & EDELBROCK, C. S. Behavioral problems and competencies reported by parents of normal and disturbed children aged four through sixteen. *Monographs of the Society for Research in Child Development,* 1981, *46* (Whole No. 188).

ACHENBACH, T. M., & LEWIS, M. A proposed model for clinical research and its application to encopresis and enuresis. *Journal of the Academy of Child Psychiatry,* 1971, *10,* 535–554.

ACKERMAN, P. T., PETERS, J. E., & DYKMAN, R. A. Children with specific disabilities: Bender Gestalt Test findings and other signs. *Journal of Learning Disabilities,* 1971, *4,* 437–446.

ACKERSON, L. *Children's behavior problems: Vol. 2. Relative importance and interrelations among traits.* Chicago: University of Chicago Press, 1942.

ADAMS, P. *Obsessive children.* New York: Brunner/Mazel, 1973.

AGRAS, W. S., BARLOW, D. H., CHAPIN, H. N., ABEL, G. G., & LEITENBERG, H. Behavior modification of anorexia nervosa. *Archives of General Psychiatry,* 1974, *30,* 279–286.

AHRONS, C. R. The continuing co-parental relationship between divorced spouses. *American Journal of Orthopsychiatry,* 1981, *51,* 415–428.

AINSWORTH, M. D. S. Infant development and mother-infant interaction among Ganda and American families. In P. H. Leiderman, S. R. Tulkin, & A. Rosenfeld (eds.), *Culture and infancy: Variations in the human experience.* New York: Academic Press, 1977.

AINSWORTH, M. D. S., & BELL, S. M. Mother-infant interaction and the development of competence. In K. J. Connolly & J. S. Bruner (eds.), *The growth of competence.* London: Academic Press, 1974.

ALANEN, Y. Some thoughts of schizophrenia and ego development in the light of family investigations. *Archives of General Psychiatry,* 1960, *3,* 650–656.

ALBEE, G. W. The politics of nature and nurture. *American Journal of Community Psychology,* 1982, *10,* 4–36.

ALEXANDER, A. B. Systematic relaxation and flow rates in asthmatic children: Relationship to emotional precipitants and anxiety. *Journal of Psychosomatic Research,* 1972, *16,* 405–410.

ALEXANDER, A. B. Behavioral methods in the clinical management of asthma. In W. D. Gentry & R. B. Williams (eds.), *Behavioral approaches to medical practice.* Cambridge, Mass.: Ballinger, 1977.

ALEXANDER, A. B. The treatment of psychosomatic disorders. In B. B. Lahey & A. E. Kazdin (eds.), *Advances in clinical child psychology,* Vol. 3. New York: Plenum, 1980.

ALEXANDER, A. B., CROPP, G. J. A., & CHAI, H. Effects of relaxation training on pulmonary mechanics in children with asthma. *Journal of Applied Behavior Analysis,* 1979, *12,* 27–35.

ALEXANDER, A. B., & SOLANCH, L. S. Psychological aspects in the understanding and treatment of bronchial asthma. In J. M. Ferguson & C. B. Taylor (eds.), *The comprehensive handbook of behavioral medicine,* Vol. 2. New York: S. P. Medical & Scientific Books, 1981.

ALEXANDER, F. *Psychosomatic medicine.* New York: W. W. Norton and Co., 1950.

ALEXANDER, J. F. Defensive and supportive communications in normal and deviant families. *Journal of Consulting and Clinical Psychology,* 1973, *40,* 223–231.

ALEXANDER, J. F., HAAS, L. J., KLEIN, N. C., & WARBURTON, J. R. *Functional family therapy.* Paper presented at meeting of Western Psychological Association, Honolulu, Hawaii, May 1980.

ALEXANDER, J. F., & PARSONS, B. V. Short-term behavioral intervention with delinquent families: Impact on family process and recidivism. *Journal of Abnormal Psychology*, 1973, *81*, 219–225.

ALGOZZINE, B. The emotionally disturbed child: Disturbed or disturbing? *Journal of Abnormal Child Psychology*, 1977, *5*, 205–211.

ALLEN, K., HART, B., BUELL, J., HARRIS, F., & WOLF, M. Effects of social reinforcement on isolated behavior of a nursery school child. *Child Development*, 1964, *35*, 511–518.

AMERICAN PSYCHIATRIC ASSOCIATION. *Diagnostic and statistical manual of mental disorders*, 1st ed. Washington, D.C.: American Psychiatric Association, 1952.

AMERICAN PSYCHIATRIC ASSOCIATION. *Diagnostic and statistical manual of mental disorders*, 2nd ed. Washington, D.C.: American Psychiatric Association, 1968.

AMERICAN PSYCHIATRIC ASSOCIATION. *Diagnostic and statistical manual of mental disorders*, 3rd ed. Washington, D.C.: American Psychiatric Association, 1980.

ANASTASI, A. Heredity, environment, and the question "How?" *Psychological Review*, 1958, *65*, 197–208.

ANASTASI, A. *Psychological testing*. New York: Macmillan, 1968.

ANDERS, T. F. Neurophysiological studies of sleep in infants and children. *Journal of Child Psychology and Psychiatry*, 1982, *23*, 75–83.

ANDERS, T. F., & FREEMAN, E. D. Enuresis. In J. D. Noshpitz (ed.), *Basic handbook of child psychiatry II*. New York: Basic Books, 1979.

ANDERS, T. F., & WEINSTEIN, P. Sleep and its disorders in infants and children: A review. *The Journal of Pediatrics*, 1972, *50*, 311–324.

ANDERSON, L. D. The predictive value of infant tests in relation to intelligence at 5 years. *Child Development*, 1939, *10*, 202–212.

ANDERSON, R. P., HALCOMB, C. G., & DOYLE, R. B. The measurement of attentional deficits. *Exceptional Children*, 1973, *39*, 534–539.

ANDERSON, S., & MESSICK, S. Social competency in young children. *Developmental Psychology*, 1974, *10*, 282–293.

ANDRASIK, F., BLANCHARD, E. B., & EDLUND, S. R. A multiple baseline analysis of autogenic feedback in the treatment of chronic juvenile vascular headache. *Child & Family Behavior Therapy*, 1982.

ANDRASIK, F., & HOLROYD, K. A. A test of specific and nonspecific effects in the biofeedback treatment of tension headache. *Journal of Consulting and Clinical Psychology*, 1980, *48*, 575–586.

ANTHONY, E. J. Behavior disorders. In P. H. Mussen (ed.), *Carmichael's manual of child psychology*, Vol. II. New York: John Wiley, 1970.

ANTHONY, E. J. The psychiatric evaluation of the anxious child: Case record summarized from the clinic records. In E. J. Anthony & D. C. Gilpin (eds.), *Three further clinical faces of childhood*. New York: S P Medical & Scientific Books, 1981.

ANTHONY, E. J., & CHILAND, C. *The child in his family: Preventive child psychiatry in an age of transition*. New York: John Wiley, 1980.

ARAGONA, J., CASSADY, J., & DRABMAN, R. S. Treating overweight children through parental training and contingency contracting. *Journal of Applied Behavior Analysis*, 1975, *8*, 269–278.

AREND, R., GOVE, F. L., & SROUFE, A. L. Continuity of individual adaptation from infancy to kindergarten: A predictive study of ego-resiliency and curiosity in preschoolers. *Child Development*, 1979, *50*, 950–959.

ARIÈS, P. *Centuries of childhood*. Trans. R. Baldick. New York: Vintage Books (Knopf and Random House), 1962.

ARNOLD, J., LEVINE, A., & PATTERSON, G. R. Changes in sibling behavior following family intervention. *Journal of Consulting and Clinical Psychology*, 1975, *43*, 683–688.

ARTER, J. A., & JENKINS, J. R. Examining the benefits and prevalence of modality considerations in special education. *Journal of Special Education*, 1977, *11*, 281–298.

ARTER, J. A., & JENKINS, J. R. Differential diagnosis—prescriptive teaching: A critical appraisal. *Review of Educational Research*, 1979, *49*, 517–555.

ASHER, S. R. Children's peer relations. In M. E. Lamb (ed.), *Social and personality development*. New York: Holt, Rinehart and Winston, 1978.

ATKESON, B. M., & FOREHAND, R. Conduct disorders. In E. J. Mash & L. G. Terdal (eds.), *Behavioral assessment of childhood disorders*. New York: Guilford Press, 1981.

ATKINSON, R. C., & SHIFFRIN, R. M. Human memory: A proposed system and its control processes. In K. W. Spence & J. T. Spence (eds.), *The psychology of learning and motivation*. New York: Academic Press, 1968.

AYLLON, T., HAUGHTON, E., & OSMOND, H. O. Chronic anorexia: A behaviour problem. *Canadian Psychiatric Association Journal*, 1964, *9*, 145–154.

AYLLON, T., LAYMAN, D., & KANDEL, H. J. A behavioral-educational alternative to drug control of hyperactive children. *Journal of Applied Behavior Analysis*, 1975, *8*, 137–146.

AYLLON, T., & ROSENBAUM, M. S. The behavioral treatment of disruption and hyperactivity in school settings. In B. B. Lahey & A. E. Kazdin (eds.), *Advances in clinical child psychology*, Vol. 1. New York: Plenum, 1977.

AZRIN, N. H., & ARMSTRONG, P. M. The "mini-meal"—A method for teaching eating skills to the profoundly retarded. *Mental Retardation*, 1973, *11*, 9–13.

AZRIN, N. H., SCHAEFFER, R. M., & WESOLOWSKI, M. D. A rapid method of teaching profoundly retarded persons to dress by a reinforcement-guidance method. *Mental Retardation*, 1976, *14*, 29–33.

AZRIN, N. H., SNEED, T. J., & FOXX, R. M. Dry bed: Rapid elimination of childhood enuresis. *Behaviour Research and Therapy*, 1974, *12*, 147–156.

AZRIN, N. H., & THIENES, P. M. Rapid elimination of enuresis by intensive learning without a conditioning apparatus. *Behavior Therapy*, 1978, *9*, 342–354.

BAER, D. M., & SHERMAN, J. A. Reinforcement control of generalized imitation in young children. *Journal of Experimental Child Psychology*, 1964, *1*, 37–49.

BAKER, B. L. Symptom treatment and symptom substitution in enuresis. *Journal of Abnormal Psychology*, 1969, *74*, 42–49.

BAKER, H., & WILLS, U. School phobia: Classification and

treatment. *British Journal of Psychiatry*, 1978, *132*, 492–499.

BAKER, L., & CANTWELL, D. P. Specific developmental disorders of childhood and adolescence: Developmental language disorder. In H. I. Kaplan, A. M. Freedman, & B. J. Sadock (eds.), *Comprehensive textbook of psychiatry/ III*, Vol. 3. Baltimore, Md.: Williams & Wilkins, 1980.

BAKER, L., CANTWELL, D. P., RUTTER, M., & BARTAK, L. Language and autism. In E. Ritvo (ed.), *Autism: Diagnosis, current research and management*. New York: Spectrum Publ., 1976.

BAKWIN, H. Enuresis in twins. *American Journal of Diseases in Childhood*, 1971, *121*, 222–225.

BAKWIN, H., & BAKWIN, R. M. *Behavior disorders in children*, 4th ed. Philadelphia: Saunders, 1972.

BALLA, D., & ZIGLER, E. Personality development in retarded persons. In N. R. Ellis (ed.), *Handbook of mental deficiency*. Hillsdale, N.J.: Lawrence Erlbaum Associates, 1979.

BANDURA, A. Influence of models' reinforcement contingencies on the acquisition of imitative responses. *Journal of Personality and Social Psychology*, 1965, *1*, 589–595.

BANDURA, A. Self-efficacy: Towards a unifying theory of behavior change. *Psychological Review*, 1977, *84*, 191–215. (a)

BANDURA, A. *Social learning theory*. Englewood Cliffs, N.J.: Prentice-Hall, 1977. (b)

BANDURA, A., GRUSEC, J. E., & MENLOVE, F. L. Vicarious extinction of avoidance behavior. *Journal of Personality and Social Psychology*, 1967, *5*, 16–23.

BANDURA, A., & MENLOVE, F. L. Factors determining vicarious extinction of avoidance behavior through symbolic modeling. *Journal of Personality and Social Psychology*, 1968, *8*, 99–108.

BARATZ, S. S., & BARATZ, J. C. Early childhood intervention: The social science base of institutional racism. *Harvard Educational Review*, 1970, *40*, 29–50.

BARKLEY, R. A. Predicting the response of hyperkinetic children to stimulant drugs. *Journal of Abnormal Child Psychology*, 1976, *4*, 327–348.

BARKLEY, R. A. Recent developments in research on hyperactive children. *Journal of Pediatric Psychology*, 1978, *3*, 158–163.

BARKLEY, R. A. Hyperactivity. In E. J. Mash & L. G. Terdal (eds.), *Behavioral assessment of childhood disorders*. New York: Guilford Press, 1981. (a)

BARKLEY, R. A. *Hyperactive children*. New York: Guilford Press, 1981. (b)

BARKLEY, R. A., COPELAND, A., & SIVAGE, C. A self-control classroom for hyperactive children. *Journal of Autism and Developmental Disorders*, 1980, *10*, 75–89.

BARRIOS, B. A., HARTMANN, D. P., & SHIGETOMI, C. Fears and anxieties in children. In E. J. Mash & L. G. Terdal (eds.), *Behavioral assessment of childhood disorders*. New York: Guilford Press, 1981.

BARSCH, R. H. Achieving perceptual motor efficiency. Seattle, Wash.: Special Child Publications, 1967.

BARTON, E. S., GUESS, D., GARCIA, E., & BAER, D. M. Improvement of retardates' mealtime behaviors by

timeout procedures using multiple baseline techniques. *Journal of Applied Behavior Analysis*, 1970, *3*, 77–84.

BATESON, G., JACKSON, D. D., HALEY, J., & WEAKLAND, J. Toward a theory of schizophrenia. *Behavioral Science*, 1956, *1*, 251–264.

BATTLE, E., & LACEY, B. A. Context for hyperactivity in children over time. *Child Development*, 1972, *43*, 757–772.

BAUER, D. H. An exploratory study of developmental changes in children's fears. *Journal of Child Psychology and Psychiatry*, 1976, *17*, 69–74.

BAUMRIND, D. Some thoughts on ethics of research—after reading Milgram's "Behavioral study of obedience." *American Psychologist*, 1964, *19*, 421–423.

BAUMRIND, D. Reciprocal rights and responsibilities in parent-child relations. *Journal of Social Issues*, 1978, *34*, 179–196.

BAYLEY, N. On the growth of intelligence. *American Psychologist*, 1955, *10*, 805–818.

BAYLEY, N. *Bayley Scales of Infant Development: Birth to two years*. New York: Psychological Corporation, 1969.

BAYLEY, N. Development of mental abilities. In P. H. Mussen (ed.), *Carmichael's manual of child psychology*, Vol. 1. New York: John Wiley, 1970.

BECK, A. T. *Depression: Clinical, experimental, and theoretical aspects*. New York: Harper & Row, Pub., 1967.

BECK, A. T., WARD, C. H., MENDELSON, M., MOCK, J. E., & ERBAUGH, J. K. Reliability of psychiatric diagnosis: II. A study of consistency of clinical judgements and ratings. *American Journal of Psychiatry*, 1962, *119*, 351–357.

BECKER, W. C. Consequences of parental discipline. In M. L. Hoffman and W. L. Hoffman (eds.), *Review of child development research*, Vol. 1. New York: Russell Sage Foundation, 1964.

BECKER, W. C., PETERSON, D. R., HELLMER, L. A., SHOEMAKER, D. J., & QUAY, H. C. Factors in parental behavior and personality as related to problem behavior in children. *Journal of Consulting Psychology*, 1959, *23*, 107–118.

BELL, R. A. A reinterpretation of the direction of effects of studies of socialization. *Psychological Review*, 1968, *75*, 81–95.

BELLAK, L. *The Thematic Apperception Test and Children's Apperception Test*. New York: Grune & Stratton, 1971.

BELLMAN, M. Studies on encopresis. *Acta Pediatrica Scandinavica*, 1966, *179* (Supplement).

BELMONT, L., & BIRCH, H. G. Lateral dominance, lateral awareness, and reading disability. *Child Development*, 1965, *36*, 57–71.

BELMONT, L., & MAROLLA, F. A. Birth order, family size, and intelligence. *Science*, 1973, *182*, 1096–1101.

BELSKY, J. Child maltreatment. An ecological integration. *American Psychologist*, 1980, *35*, 320–335.

BELSKY, J. Early human experience: A family perspective. *Developmental Psychology*, 1981, *17*, 3–23.

BEMIS, K. M. Current approaches to the etiology and treatment of anorexia nervosa. *Psychological Bulletin*, 1978, *85*, 593–617.

BEMPORAD, J. R. Encopresis. In B. B. Wolman, J. Egan,

& A. O. Ross (eds.), *Handbook of treatments of mental disorders in childhood and adolescence.* Englewood Cliffs, N.J.: Prentice-Hall, 1978.

BEMPORAD, J. R. Adult recollections of a formerly autistic child. *Journal of Autism and Developmental Disorders,* 1979, *9,* 179-197.

BENDER, L. *Instructions for the use of the Visual Motor Gestalt Test.* New York: American Orthopsychiatric Association, 1946.

BENDER, L. One hundred cases of childhood schizophrenia treated with electric shock. *Trans. American Neurological Association,* 1947, *72,* 165-169.

BENDER, L. Childhood schizophrenia. In S. I. Harrison & J. F. McDermott (eds.), *Childhood psychopathology.* New York: International Universities Press, 1972.

BENDER, L. The family patterns of 100 schizophrenic children observed at Bellevue, 1935-1952. *Journal of Autism and Childhood Schizophrenia,* 1974, *4,* 279-292.

BENEDICT, R. Anthropology and the abnormal. *Journal of General Psychology,* 1934, *10,* 59-82. (a)

BENEDICT, R. *Patterns of culture.* Boston: Houghton-Mifflin, 1934. (b)

BENTON, A. Some conclusions about dyslexia. In A. L. Benton & D. Pearl (eds.), *Dyslexia.* New York: Oxford University Press, 1978.

BERECZ, J. M. Phobias of childhood: Etiology and treatment. *Psychological Bulletin,* 1968, *70,* 694-720.

BEREITER, C. An academic preschool for disadvantaged children: Conclusions from evaluation studies. In J. C. Stanley (ed.), *Preschool programs for the disadvantaged.* Baltimore, Md.: John Hopkins University Press, 1972.

BERG, I., NICHOLS, K., & PRITCHARD, C. School phobia— Its classification and relationship to dependency. *Journal of Child Psychology and Psychiatry and Allied Disciplines,* 1969, *10,* 123-141.

BERMAN, A. Research associating learning disabilities with juvenile delinquency. In J. Gottlieb & S. S. Strichart (eds.), *Developmental theory and research in learning disabilities.* Baltimore, Md.: University Park Press, 1981.

BERSCHEID, E., & WALSTER, E. Physical attractiveness. In L. Berkowitz (ed.), *Advances in experimental social psychology.* New York: Academic Press, 1974.

BETTLEHEIM, B. *The empty fortress.* New York: Free Press, 1967. (a)

BETTLEHEIM, B. Where self begins. *New York Times,* February 12, 1967. (b)

BIJOU, S. W., BIRNBRAUER, J. S., KIDDER, J. D., & TAGUE, C. Programmed instruction as an approach to teaching reading, writing, and arithmetic to retarded children. *Psychological Record,* 1966, *16,* 505-522.

BIJOU, S. W., PETERSON, R. F., HARRIS, F. R., ALLEN, K. E., & JOHNSTON, M. S. Methodology for experimental studies of young children in natural settings. *The Psychological Record,* 1969, *19,* 177-210.

BILLER, H. B. Paternal and sex-role factors in cognitive and academic functioning. In J. K. Cole & R. Dienstbier (eds.), *Nebraska symposium on motivation.* Lincoln, Nebr.: University of Nebraska Press, 1974.

BIRCH, H. G., & GUSSOW, J. D. *Disadvantaged children: Health, nutrition, and school failure.* New York: Grune & Stratton, 1970.

BIRNBRAUER, J. S. Mental retardation. In H. Leitenberg (ed.), *Handbook of behavior modification and behavior therapy.* Englewood Cliffs, N.J.: Prentice-Hall, 1976.

BIRNS, B. Individual differences in human neonates' responses to stimulation. *Child Development,* 1965, *36,* 249-256.

BIRNS, B. The emergence and socialization of sex differences in the earliest years. *Merrill-Palmer Quarterly,* 1976, *22,* 229-254.

BJORNTORP, P., CARLGREN, G., ISAKSSON, B., KROTKIEWSKI, M., LARSSON, B., & SJOSTROM, L. Effect of an energy-reduced dietary regimen in relation to adipose tissue cellularity in obese women. *Amercian Journal of Clinical Nutrition,* 1975, *23,* 445-452.

BLANCHARD, E. B., & YOUNG, L. D. Clinical applications of biofeedback. *Archives of General Psychiatry,* 1974, *30,* 573-589.

BLEEKER, E. R., & ENGLE, B. T. Learned control of cardiac rate and cardiac conduction in Wolff-Parkinson-White syndrome. *Seminars in Psychiatry,* 1973, *5,* 465-479.

BLISS, E. L., & BRANCH, C. H. H. *Anorexia nervosa: Its history, psychology, and biology.* New York: Paul Hoeber, 1960.

BLOOM, B. L. The logic and urgency of primary prevention. *Hospital and community psychiatry,* 1981, *32,* 839-843.

BLOOM, B. S. *Stability and change in human characteristics.* New York: John Wiley, 1964.

BLUMBERG, M. L. Psychopathology of the abusing parent. *American Journal of Psychotherapy,* 1974, *28,* 21-29.

BOLLES, R. C. Reinforcement, expectancy, and learning. *Psychological Review,* 1972, *79,* 394-409.

BORKOVEC, T. D. Autonomic reactivity to sensory stimulation in psychopathic, neurotic and normal delinquents. *Journal of Consulting and Clinical Psychology,* 1970, *35,* 217-222.

BORKOWSKI, J. G., & CAVANAUGH, J. C. Maintenance and generalization of skills and strategies by the retarded. In N. R. Ellis (ed.), *Handbook of mental deficiency.* Hillsdale, N.J.: Lawrence Erlbaum Associates, 1979.

BORNSTEIN, B. Analyses of a phobic child. *Psychoanalytic Study of the Child,* 1949, *Vol. III-IV,* 181-226.

BORNSTEIN, M., BELLACK, A., & HERSEN, M. Social skills training for unassertive children: A multiple baseline analysis. *Journal of Applied Behavior Analysis,* 1977, *10,* 183-195.

BORNSTEIN, P., & QUEVILLON, R. Effects of a self-instructional package on overactive preschool boys. *Journal of Applied Behavior Analysis,* 1976, *9,* 179-188.

BOWEN, M. Introduction: Family systems theory. In S. I. Harrison & J. F. McDermott, Jr. (eds.), *New directions in child psychopathology,* Vol. 1. New York: International Universities Press, 1980.

BOWERMAN, C. E., & KINCH, J. W. Changes in family and peer orientation between the fourth and tenth grades. In M. Gold & E. Douvan (eds.), *Adolescent development.* Boston: Allyn & Bacon, 1969.

BOWLBY, J. Grief and mourning in infancy and early childhood. *Psychoanalytic Study of the Child,* 1960, *15,* 9-52.

BOWLBY, J. *Attachment and loss,* Vol. 1. London: Hogarth; New York: Basic Books, 1969.

BOYCE, T. W., JENSEN, E. W., CASSEL, J. C., COLLIER, A. M., SMITH, A. H., & RAIMEY, C. T. Influence of life events and family routines on childhood respiratory tract illness. *Pediatrics,* 1977, *60,* 609–615.

BRADFIELD, R., PAULOS, J., & GROSSMAN, H. Energy expenditure and heart rate of obese high school girls. *American Journal of Clinical Nutrition,* 1971, *24,* 1482–1486.

BRAGINSKY, D. D., & BRAGINSKY, B. M *Hansels and Gretels: Studies of children in institutions for the mentally retarded.* New York: Holt, Rinehart and Winston, 1971.

BRAUKMANN, C. J., & FIXSEN, D. L. Behavior modification with delinquents. In M. Hersen, R. M. Eisler, & P. M. Miller (eds.), *Progress in behavior modification,* Vol. 1. New York: Academic Press, 1975.

BREGER, L. *From instinct to identity: The development of personality.* Englewood Cliffs, N.J.: Prentice-Hall, 1974.

BREGMAN, E. O. An attempt to modify the emotional attitudes of infants by the conditioned response technique. *Journal of Genetic Psychology,* 1934, *45,* 169–198.

BRIDGER, W. H.., & MANDEL, I. J. Abolition of the PRE by instructions in GSR conditioning. *Journal of Experimental Psychology,* 1965, *69,* 476–482.

BRIM, O. G. Family structure and sex role learning by children. *Sociometry,* 1958, *21,* 1–16.

BROADHURST, D. D., EDMUNDS, M., & MacDICKEN, R. A. Early childhood programs and the prevention and treatment of child abuse and neglect. National Center on Child Abuse and Neglect. DHEW Publication No. OHDS 79-30198. Washington, D.C.: U.S. Government Printing Office, 1979.

BRODKIN, A. M. Family therapy: The making of a mental health movement. *American Journal of Orthopsychiatry,* 1980, *50,* 4–17.

BRONFENBRENNER, U. Socialization and social class through time and space. In E. E. Maccoby, T. M. Newcomb, & E. L. Hartley (eds.), *Readings in social psychology.* New York: Holt, 1958.

BRONFENBRENNER, U. The roots of alienation. In U. Bronfenbrenner and M. A. Mahoney (eds.), *Influences on human development.* Hinsdale, Ill.: Dryden Press, 1972.

BRONFENBRENNER, U. *A report on longitudinal evaluations of preschool programs, Volume II: Is early intervention effective?* Washington, D.C.: Department of Health, Education, and Welfare, 1974.

BRONFENBRENNER, U. Who needs parent education? *Teachers College Record,* 1978, *79,* 766–787.

BRONHEIM, S. P. Pulmonary disorders: Asthma and cystic fibrosis. In P. R. Magrab (ed.), *Psychological management of pediatric problems,* Vol. 1. Baltimore, Md.: University Park Press, 1978.

BROPHY, J. E., & GOOD, T. L. Teachers' communication of differential expectations for children's classroom performance: Some behavioral data. *Journal of Educational Psychology,* 1970, *61,* 365–374.

BROWN, A. L. The role of strategic behavior in retardate memory. In N. R. Ellis (ed.), *International review of research in mental retardation.* New York: Academic Press, 1974.

BROWN, A. L., & BARCLAY, C. R. The effects of training specific mnemonics on the metamnemonic efficiency of retarded children. *Child Development,* 1976, *47,* 71–80.

BROWN, C. C. (ed.). *Infants at risk: Assessment and intervention.* Pediatric Round Table: 5. Johnson & Johnson Baby Products, 1981.

BROWN, R., & HERRNSTEIN, R. J. *Psychology.* Boston: Little, Brown, 1975.

BROWN, W. T., MEZZACAPPA, P. M., & JENKINS, E. C. Screening for fragile X syndrome by testicular size measurement. *Lancet,* November 7, 1981, 1088.

BROWNELL, K. D., & VENDITTI, E. M. The etiology and treatment of obesity. In W. E. Fann, I. Karacan, A. D. Pokorny, & R. L. Williams (eds.), *Phenomenology and the treatment of psychophysiologic disorders.* New York: Spectrum Publ., 1982.

BRUCH, H. The insignificant difference: Discordant incidence of anorexia nervosa in monozygotic twins. *American Journal of Psychiatry,* 1969, *126,* 85–90.

BRUCH, H. *Eating disorders: Obesity, anorexia nervosa, and the person within.* New York: Basic Books, 1973.

BRUCH, H. *The golden cage: The enigma of anorexia nervosa.* New York: Vintage Books, 1979.

BRUININKS, R. H., THURLOW, M. L., THURMAN, S. K., & FIORELLI, J. S. Deinstitutionalization and community services. In J. Wortis (ed.), *Mental retardation and developmental disabilities,* Vol. XI. New York: Brunner/Mazel, 1980.

BRUMBACK, R. A., JACKOWAY, M. K., & ⁷EINBERG, W. A. Relations of intelligence to childhoᴏ depression in children referred to an educational diagnosis center. *Perceptual and Motor Skills,* 1980, *50,* 11–17.

BRYAN, T. H., & BRYAN, J. H. *Understanding learning disabilities.* Port Washington, N. Y. Alfred Publishing Co., 1975.

BRYAN, T., & BRYAN, J. H. Learning disorders. In H. E. Rie & E. D. Rie (eds.), *Handbook of minimal brain dysfunctions.* New York: Wiley-Interscience, 1980.

BRYANT, K. Speech and language development. In M. J. Krajicek and A. I. Tearney (eds.), *Detection of developmental problems in children.* Baltimore, Md.: University Park Press, 1977.

BUCKLEY, P. D. The Bender Gestalt Test: A review of reported research with school-age subjects, 1966–1977. *Psychology in the Schools,* 1978, *15,* 327–338.

BULLEN, B. A., REED, R. B., & MAYER, J. Physical activity of obese and non-obese adolescent girls appraised by motion picture sampling. *American Journal of Clinical Nutrition,* 1964, *14,* 211–233.

BURCHARD, J. D., & HARIG, P. T. Behavior modification and juvenile delinquency. In H. Leitenberg (ed.), *Handbook of behavior modification and behavior therapy.* Englewood Cliffs, N.J.: Prentice-Hall, 1976.

BURSTEIN, S., & MEICHENBAUM, D. The work of worrying in children undergoing surgery. *Journal of Abnormal Child Psychology,* 1979, *7,* 127–132.

BUSCH-ROSSNAGEL, N. A., & VANCE, A. K. The impact of the schools on social and emotional development. In B.

B. Wolman (ed.), *Handbook of developmental psychology.* Englewood Cliffs, N.J.: Prentice-Hall, 1982.

BUSS, A., & PLOMIN, R. *A temperament theory of personality development.* New York: Wiley-Interscience, 1975.

BUSS, A. H., PLOMIN, R., & WILLERMAN, L. The inheritance of temperament. *Journal of Personality,* 1973, *41,* 513–524.

BUTTERFIELD, E. C., & BELMONT, J. M. Assessing and improving the executive cognitive functions of mentally retarded people. In I. Bialer & M. Sternlicht (eds.), *Psychological issues in mental retardation.* New York: Psychological Dimensions, 1977.

BUTTERFIELD, E. C., & DICKERSON, D. J. Cognitive theory and mental development. In N. R. Ellis (ed.), *International review of research in mental retardation.* New York: Academic Press, 1976.

BUXTON, M. N., ARKEL, Y., LAGOS, J., DESPOSITO, F., LOWENTHAL, H., & SIMRING, S. Stress and platelet aggregation in hemophiliac children and their family members. *Research Communications in Psychology, Psychiatry, and Behavior,* 1981, *6,* 21–48.

CALDWELL, B. M., BRADLEY, R. H., & ELARDO, R. Early stimulation. In J. Wortis (ed.), *Mental retardation and developmental disabilities.* New York: Brunner/Mazel, 1975.

CAMPAGNA, A. F., & HARTER, S. Moral judgment in sociopathic and normal children. *Journal of Personality and Social Psychology,* 1975, *31,* 199–205.

CAMPBELL, D. T., & STANLEY, J. C. *Experimental and quasi-experimental designs for research.* Chicago: Rand McNally, 1963.

CAMPBELL, M., ANDERSON, L. T., MEIER, M., COHEN, I. L., SMALL, A. M., SAMIT, C., & SACHAR, E. J. A comparison of haloperidol and behavior therapy and their interaction in autistic children. *Journal of the Academy of Child Psychiatry,* 1978, *17,* 640–655.

CAMPBELL, M., GELLER, B., & COHEN, I. L. Current status of drug research and treatment with autistic children. *Journal of Pediatric Psychology,* 1977, *2,* 153–161.

CAMPIONE, J. C., & BROWN, A. L. Memory and metamemory development in educable retarded children. In R. V. Kail, Jr., & J. W. Hagen (eds.), *Perspectives on the development of memory and cognition.* Hillsdale, N.J.: Lawrence Erlbaum Associates, 1977.

CANTWELL, D. P. (ed.). *The hyperactive child.* New York: Spectrum Publ., 1975.

CANTWELL, D. P. The diagnostic process and diagnostic classification in child psychiatry: DSM-III. *Journal of the American Academy of Child Psychiatry,* 1980, *19,* 345–355. (a)

CANTWELL, D. P. Specific developmental disorders of childhood and adolescence: Developmental arithmetic disorder. In H. I. Kaplan, A. M. Freedman, & B. J. Sadock (eds.), *Comprehensive textbook of psychiatry/III,* Vol. 3. Baltimore, Md.: Williams & Wilkins, 1980. (b)

CANTWELL, D. P. Foreword in R. A. Barkley, *Hyperactive children.* New York: Guilford Press, 1981.

CANTWELL, D. P., BAKER, L., & RUTTER, M. Family factors. In M. Rutter & E. Schopler (eds.), *Autism: A reappraisal of concepts and treatment.* New York: Plenum, 1978.

CANTWELL, D. P., RUSSELL, A. T., MATTISON, R., &

WILL, L. A comparison of DSM-II and DSM-III in the diagnosis of childhood psychiatric disorders: I. Agreement with expected diagnosis. *Archives of General Psychiatry,* 1979, *36,* 1208–1213.

CANTWELL, D. P., & SATTERFIELD, J. H. The prevalence of academic underachievement in hyperactive children. *Journal of Pediatric Psychology,* 1978, *3,* 168–171.

CAPLAN, G. *The principles of preventive psychiatry.* New York: Basic Books, 1964.

CAPLAN, M., & DOUGLAS, V. Incidence of parental loss in children with depressed mood. *Journal of Child Psychology and Psychiatry,* 1969, *10,* 225–232.

CAPUTE, A. J., ACCARDO, P. J., VINING, E. P. G., RUBENSTEIN, J. E., & HARRYMAN, S. *Primitive reflex profile.* Baltimore, Md.: University Park Press, 1978.

CARBERRY, A. T., & HANDAL, P. J. The use of the AML scale with a Headstart population: Normative and validation studies. *American Journal of Community Psychology,* 1980, *8,* 353–363.

CARLSON, G., & CANTWELL, D. P. A survey of depressive symptoms, syndrome and disorder in a child psychiatric population. *Journal of Child Psychology and Psychiatry,* 1980, *21,* 19–25.

CARLSON, G. A., & CANTWELL, D. P. Suicidal behavior and depression in children and adolescents. *Journal of the American Academy of Child Psychiatry,* 1982, *21,* 361–368.

CARR, E. G. The motivation of self-injurious behavior: A review of some hypotheses. *Psychological Bulletin,* 1977, *84,* 800–816.

CARR, E. G., NEWSOM, C. D., & BINKOFF, J. A. Stimulus control of self-destructive behavior in a psychotic child. *Journal of Abnormal Child Psychology,* 1976, *4,* 139–153.

CARRON, A. V., & BAILEY, D. A. Strength development in boys from 10 through 16 years. *Monographs of the Society for Research in Child Development,* 1974, *39* (4), No. 157, 1–37.

CATTELL, P. *The measurement of intelligence of infants and young children.* New York: Psychological Corporation, 1960.

CERRETO, M. C., & TUMA, J. M. Distribution of DSM-II diagnoses in a child psychiatric setting. *Journal of Abnormal Child Psychology,* 1977, *5,* 147–153.

CHAR, J., & LUBETSKY, S. Childhood psychoses in the preschool child. *Journal of Autism and Developmental Disorders,* 1979, *9,* 271–277.

CHARLES, L., & SCHAIN, R. A four-year follow-up study of the effects of methylphenidate on the behavior and academic achievement of hyperactive children. *Journal of Abnormal Child Psychology,* 1981, *9,* 495–505.

CHARLESWORTH, R., & HARTUP, W. Positive social reinforcement in the nursery school peer group. *Child Development,* 1967, *38,* 993–1002.

CHARNEY, E., GOODMAN, H. C., McBRIDE, M., LYON, B., & PRATT, R. Childhood antecedents of adult obesity: Do chubby infants become obese adults? *The New England Journal of Medicine,* 1976, *295,* 6–9.

CHESS, S. Autism in children with congenital rubella. *Journal of Autism and Childhood Schizophrenia,* 1971, *1,* 33–47.

CHESS, S. The influence of defect on development in children with congenital rubella. *Merrill-Palmer Quarterly,* 1974, *20,* 255–274.

CHESS, S., & THOMAS, A. Differences in outcome with early intervention in children with behavior disorders. In M. Roff, L. Robins, & M. Pollack (eds.), *Life history research in psychopathology*, Vol. 2. Minneapolis: University of Minnesota Press, 1972.

CHESS, S., & THOMAS, A. Temperamental individuality from childhood to adolescence. *Journal of the American Academy of Child Psychiatry*, 1977, *16*, 218–226.

CHILDREN'S DEFENSE FUND. *An examination of public responsibility to children in out-of-home care*. Washington, D.C.: CDF, 1979.

CHRISTOPHERSEN, E. R., BARNARD, J. D., FORD, D., & WOLF, M. M. The family training program: Improving parent-child interaction patterns. In E. J. Marsh, L. C. Handy, & L. A. Hamerlynck (eds.), *Behavior modification approaches to parenting*. New York: Brunner/Mazel, 1976.

CLARKE-STEWART, K. A. And daddy makes three: The father's impact on mother and young child. *Child Development*, 1978, *49*, 466–478.

CLEMENT, P. W. Elimination of sleepwalking in a seven-year-old boy. *Journal of Consulting and Clinical Psychology*, 1970, *34*, 22–26.

CLEMENTS, S. D. *Minimal brain dysfunction in children*. NINDS Monograph No. 3, Public Health Service Bulletin #1415. Washington, D.C.: U.S. Department of Health, Education and Welfare, 1966.

CLINGEMPEEL, W. G., & REPPUCCI, N. D. Joint custody after divorce: Major issues and goals for research. *Psychological Bulletin*, 1982, *91*, 102–127.

COATES, T. J., & THORESEN, C. E. Obesity among children and adolescents. The problem belongs to everyone. In B. Lahey & A. Kazdin (eds.), *Advances in clinical child psychology*. New York: Plenum, 1978.

CODDINGTON, R. D. The significance of life events as etiologic factors in the diseases of children: I - A survey of professional workers. *Journal of Psychosomatic Research*, 1972, *16*, 7–13.

COHEN, D. J., & SHAYWITZ, B. A. Preface to the special issue on neurobiological research in autism. *Journal of Autism and Developmental Disorders*, 1982, *12*, 103–107.

COHEN, H. J., & FILIPCZAK, J. *A new learning environment*. San Francisco: Jossey-Bass, 1971.

COHEN, S. *Social and personality development in childhood*. New York: Macmillan, 1976.

COLES, G. S. The learning-disabilities test battery: Empirical and social issues. *Harvard Educational Review*, 1978, *48*, 313–340.

COLLIER, B., & ETZWILER, D. Comparative study of diabetes knowledge among juvenile diabetics and their parents. *Diabetes*, 1971, *20*, 51–57.

COMBS, M., & SLABY, D. Social skills training in children. In A. Kazdin & B. Lahey (eds.), *Advances in clinical child psychology*. New York: Plenum, 1977.

CONGER, J., & KEANE, S. Social skills intervention in the treatment of isolated or withdrawn children. *Psychological Bulletin*, 1981, *90* (3), 478–495.

CONNERS, C. K. A teacher rating scale for use with drug studies with children. *American Journal of Psychiatry*, 1969, *126*, 884–888.

CONNERS, C. K. Symptom patterns in hyperkinetic, neurotic, and normal children. *Child Development*, 1970, *4*, 667–682.

CONNERS, C. K. Rating scales for use in drug studies with children. *Psychopharmacology Bulletin*, 1973, 24–29.

CONNERS, C. K. Discussion of Dr. Rapoport's chapter. In J. G. Schulterbrandt & A. Raskin (eds.), *Depression in childhood: Diagnosis, treatment, and conceptual models*. New York: Raven Press, 1977.

CONNERS, C. K. Psychotropic drug treatment of children. In J. G. Bernstein (ed.), *Clinical psychopharmacology*. Littleton, Mass.: PSG Publishing, 1978.

CONNERS, C. K. Artificial colors in the diet and disruptive behavior. In R. M. Knights & D. J. Bakker (eds.), *Treatment of hyperactive and learning disabled children*. Baltimore, Md.: University Park Press, 1980.

CONNERS, C. K., KRAMER, K., & GUERRA, F. Auditory synthesis and dichotic listening in children with learning disabilities. *Journal of Special Education*, 1969, *3*, 163–170.

CONNERS, C. K., & WERRY, J. S. Pharmacotherapy. In H. C. Quay & J. S. Werry (eds.), *Psychopathological disorders of childhood*, 2nd ed. New York: John Wiley, 1979.

COOLIDGE, J. C., HAHN, P. B., & PECK, A. L. School phobia: Neurotic crisis or way of life. *American Journal of Orthopsychiatry*, 1957, *27*, 296–306.

COOPER, A. M. A case of bronchial asthma treated by behavior therapy. *Behaviour Research and Therapy*, 1964, *1*, 351–356.

COOPER, M. *Pica*. Springfield, Ill.: Chas. C Thomas, 1957.

CORMAN, L., & GOTTLIEB, J. Mainstreaming mentally retarded children: A review of the research. In N. R. Ellis (ed.), *International review of research in mental retardation*, Vol. 9. New York: Academic Press, 1978.

COSTELLO, C. G. Childhood depression. In E. J. Mash & L. G. Terdal (eds.), *Behavioral assessment of childhood disorders*. New York: Guilford Press, 1981.

COWEN, E. L. The wooing of primary prevention. *American Journal of Community Psychology*, 1980, *8*, 258–284.

COWEN, E. L., GERSTEN, E. L., & WILSON, A. B. The primary mental health project (PMHP): Evaluation of current program effectiveness. *American Journal of Community Psychology*, 1979, *3*, 293–303.

COWEN, E., PEDERSON, A., BABIGIAN, H., IZZO, L., & TROST, N. Long term follow-up of early detected vulnerable children. *Journal of Consulting and Clinical Psychology*, 1973, *41*, 438–446.

COWEN, E. L., TROST, M. A., LORIAN, R. P., DORR, D., IZZO, L. D., & ISAACSON, R. V. *New ways in school mental health: Early detection and prevention of school maladaptation*. New York: Human Sciences Press, 1975.

CRANDALL, V. Achievement behavior in young children. In *The young child: Reviews of research*. Washington, D.C.: National Association for the Education of Young Children, 1967.

CREER, T. L. Asthma: Psychological aspects and management. In E. Middleton, C. Reed, & E. Ellis (eds.), *Allergy: Principles and practice*. St. Louis, Mo.: C. V. Mosby, 1978.

CREER, T. L. Asthma. *Journal of Consulting and Clinical Psychology*, 1982, *50*, 912–921.

CREER, T. L., WEINBERG, E., & MOLK, L. Managing a

hospital behavior problem: Malingering. *Journal of Behavior Therapy and Experimental Psychiatry,* 1974, *5,* 259-262.

CREER, T. L., & YOCHES, C. The modification of an inappropriate behavioral pattern in asthmatic children. *Journal of Chronic Diseases,* 1971, *24,* 507-516.

CRISP, A. H. Premorbid factors in adult disorders of weight, with particular reference to primary anorexia nervosa (weight phobia): A literature review. *Journal of Psychosomatic Research,* 1970, *14,* 1-22.

CROMWELL, R. L. A social learning approach to mental retardation. In N. R. Ellis (ed.), *Handbook of mental deficiency.* New York: McGraw-Hill, 1963.

CRONBACH, L. J. Five decades of public controversy over mental testing. *American Psychologist,* 1975, *30,* 1-14.

CRUIKSHANK, W. M. *Learning disabilities.* Syracuse, N. Y.: Syracuse University Press, 1977.

CUSHNA, B. The psychological definition of mental retardation: A historical review. In L. S. Szymanski & P. E. Tanguay (eds.), *Emotional disorders of mentally retarded persons.* Baltimore, Md.: University Park Press, 1980.

CYTRYN, L., & LOURIE, R. S. Mental retardation. In H. I. Kaplan, A. M. Freedman, & B. J. Sadock (eds.), *Comprehensive textbook of psychiatry/III,* Vol. 3. Baltimore, Md.: Williams & Wilkins, 1980.

CYTRYN, L., & McKNEW, D. Proposed classification of childhood depression. *American Journal of Psychiatry,* 1972, *129,* 149-155.

CYTRYN, L., & McKNEW, D. Factors influencing the changing clinical expression of the depressive process in children. *American Journal of Psychiatry,* 1974, *131,* 879-881.

CYTRYN, L., McKNEW, D. H., & BUNNEY, W. E. Diagnosis of depression in children: A reassessment. *American Journal of Psychiatry,* 1980, *137,* 22-25.

CZUDNER, G., & ROURKE, B. P. Simple reaction time in brain damaged and normal children under regular and irregular preparatory interval conditions. *Perceptual and Motor Skills,* 1970, *31,* 767-773.

DALBY, J. T. Environmental effects on prenatal development. *Journal of Pediatric Psychology,* 1978, *3,* 105-109.

DALLY, P. J. *Anorexia nervosa.* New York: Grune & Stratton, 1969.

D'ANDRADE, R. G. Sex differences and cultural institutions. In E. E. Maccoby (ed.), *The development of sex differences.* Stanford, Calif.: Stanford University Press, 1966.

DAVID, O. J., HOFFMAN, S. P., SVERD, J., CLARK, J., & VOELLER, K. Lead and hyperactivity. Behavioral response to chelation: a pilot study. *American Journal of Psychiatry,* 1976, *133,* 1155-1158.

DAVIDS, A. *Issues in abnormal child psychology.* Monterey, Calif.: Brooks/Cole, 1973.

DAVIDSON, M. D., KUGLER, M. M., & BAUER, C. H. Diagnosis and management in children with severe and protracted constipation and obstipation. *Journal of Pediatrics,* 1963, *62,* 261-275.

DAVIDSON, W. S., & SEIDMAN, E. Studies of behavior modification and juvenile delinquency: A review, meth-

odological critique, and social perspective. *Psychological Bulletin,* 1974, *81,* 998-1011.

DAVIS, M. S. Variation in patients' compliance with doctors' orders: Analysis of congruence between survey responses and results of empirical investigations. *Journal of Medical Education,* 1966, *41,* 1037-1048.

DAVISON, G. C., & NEALE, J. M. *Abnormal psychology.* New York: John Wiley, 1978, 1982.

DeFRIES, J. C., & PLOMIN, R. Behavioral genetics. In M. R. Rosenzweig & L. W. Porter (eds.), *Annual review of psychology.* Palo Alto, Calif: Annual Reviews Inc., 1978.

deJONGE, G. A. Epidemiology of enuresis: A survey of the literature. In I. Kolvin, R. C. MacKeith, & S. R. Meadow (eds.), *Bladder control and enuresis.* Philadelphia: Lippincott, 1973.

DELAMATER, A. M., LAHEY, B. B., & DRAKE, L. Toward an empirical subclassification of "Learning Disabilities": A psychophysiological comparison of "Hyperactive" and "Nonhyperactive" subgroups. *Journal of Abnormal Child Psychology,* 1981, *9,* 65-77.

DeLEON, G., & MANDELL, W. A comparison of conditioning and psychotherapy in the treatment of functional enuresis. *Journal of Clinical Psychology,* 1966, *22,* 326-330.

DELFINI, L. F., BERNAL, M. E., & ROSEN, P. M. Comparison of deviant and normal boys in home settings. In E. J. Mash, L. A. Hammerlynck, & L. C. Handy (eds.), *Behavior modification and families.* New York: Brunner/Mazel, 1976.

DELONG, G. R. A neurologic interpretation of infantile autism. In M. Rutter & E. Schopler (eds.), *Autism: A reappraisal of concepts and treatment.* New York: Plenum, 1978.

DELPRATO, D. J. Hereditary determinants of fears and phobias: A critical review. *Behavior Therapy,* 1980, *11,* 79-103.

DeLUISE, M., BLACKBURN, G. L., & FLIER, J. S. Reduced activity of the red-cell sodium-potassium pump in human obesity. *New England Journal of Medicine,* 1980, *303,* 1017-1022.

DE MAUSE, L. (ed.). *The history of childhood.* New York: Psychohistory Press, 1974.

DeMYER-GAPIN, S., & SCOTT, T. J. Effects of stimulus novelty on stimulation-seeking in anti-social and neurotic children. *Journal of Abnormal Psychology,* 1977, *86,* 96-98.

DENNIS, W., & DENNIS, M. G. The effects of cradling practices upon the onset of walking in Hopi children. *Journal of Genetic Psychology,* 1940, *56,* 77-86.

DENO, E. Special education as developmental capital. *Exceptional Children,* 1970, *37,* 229-237.

DePANFILIS, D. Clients who refer themselves to child protective services. *Children Today,* March-April 1982, *11,* 21-25.

deSILVA, P., RACHMAN, S., & SELIGMAN, M. E. P. Prepared phobias and obsessions: Therapeutic outcome. *Behaviour Research and Therapy,* 1977, *15,* 65-77.

DesLAURIERS, A. M. The cognitive-affective dilemma in early infantile autism: The case of Clarence. *Journal of Autism and Child Schizophrenia,* 1978, *8,* 219-229.

DEVINE, V. T. *The coercion process: A laboratory analogue.* Unpublished doctoral thesis, State University of New York at Stony Brook, 1971.

DIAMOND, S., & DALESSIO, D. J. *The Practicing Physicians's Approach to Headache,* 2nd ed. Baltimore, Md.: Williams and Wilkins, 1978.

DILLER, L. Psychological aspects of physically handicapped children. In B. B. Wolman (ed.), *Manual of child psychopathology.* New York: McGraw-Hill, 1972.

DION, K. Physical attractiveness and evaluations of children's transgressions. *Journal of Personality and Social Psychology,* 1972, *24,* 207-213.

DION, K., BERSCHEID, E., & WALSTER, E. What is beautiful is good. *Journal of Personality and Social Psychology,* 1972, *24,* 285-290.

DODGE, K. A., COIE, J. D., & BRAKKE, N. P. Behavior patterns of socially rejected and neglected preadolescents: The roles of social approach and aggression. *Journal of Abnormal Child Psychology,* 1982, *10,* 389-410.

DOLEYS, D. M. Behavioral treatments for nocturnal enuresis in children: A review of the recent literature. *Psychological Bulletin,* 1977, *84,* 30-54.

DOLEYS, D. M. Assessment and treatment of childhood encopresis. In A. J. Finch & P. C. Kendall (eds.), *Clinical treatment and research in child psychopathology.* New York: Spectrum Publ., 1979. (a)

DOLEYS, D. M. Assessment and treatment of childhood enuresis. In A. J. Finch & P. C. Kendall (eds.), *Clinical treatment and research in child psychopathology.* New York: Spectrum Publ., 1979. (b)

DOLEYS, D. M., CARTELLI, L. M., & DOSTER, J. Comparison of patterns of mother-child interaction. *Journal of Learning Disabilities,* 1976, *9,* 42-46.

DOLL, E. A. The essentials of an inclusive concept of mental deficiency. *American Journal of Mental Deficiency,* 1941, *46,* 214-219.

DOLL, E. A. *Vineland Social Maturity Scale.* 1965 Edition. Circle Pines, Mn.: American Guidance Service, 1965.

DOLLARD, J., DOOB, L. W., MILLER, N. E., MOWRER, O. H., & SEARS, R. R. *Frustration and aggression.* New Haven: Yale University Press, 1939.

DORFMAN, D. D. The Cyril Burt question: New findings. *Science,* 1978, *201,* 1177-1186.

DOUGLAS, J. Early hospital admissions and later disturbances of behaviour and learning. *Developmental Medicine and Child Neurology,* 1975, *17,* 456-480.

DOUGLAS, V. I. Higher mental processes in hyperactive children. In R. M. Knights & D. J. Bakker (eds.), *Treatment of hyperactive and learning disordered children.* Baltimore, Md.: University Park Press, 1980. (a)

DOUGLAS, V. I. Treatment and training approaches to hyperactivity: Establishing internal or external control. In C. K. Whalen & B. Henker (eds.), *Hyperactive children.* New York: Academic Press, 1980. (b)

DRABMAN, R. S., CORDUA, G. D., HAMMER, D., JARVIE, G. J., & HORTON, W. Developmental trends in eating rates of normal and overweight preschool children. *Child Development,* 1979, *50,* 211-216.

DRABMAN, R. S., HAMMER, D., & JARVIE, G. J. Eating styles of obese and nonobese black and white children in a naturalistic setting. *Addictive Behaviors,* 1977, *2,* 83-86.

DRABMAN, R., SPITALNIK, R., HAGAMEN, M. B., & VAN WITSEN, B. The "fine-two" plan: An integrated approach to treating severely disturbed children. *Hospital and Community Psychiatry,* 1973, *24,* 33-36.

DROTAR, D. Psychological perspectives in chronic childhood illness. *Journal of Pediatric Psychology,* 1981, *6,* 211-228.

DROTAR, D., BASKIEWICZ, A., IRVIN, N., KENNELL, J. H., & KLAUS, M. H. The adaptation of parents to the birth of an infant with a congenital malformation: A hypothetical model. *Pediatrics,* 1975, *56,* 710-717.

DUBEY, D. R. Organic factors in hyperkinesis: A critical evaluation. *American Journal of Orthopsychiatry,* 1976, *46,* 353-366.

DUBEY, D. R., KAUFMAN, K. F., & O'LEARY, S. G. *Behavioral and reflective parent-training for hyperactive children: A comparison.* Paper presented at the annual meeting of the American Psychological Association, San Francisco, August 1977.

DUBEY, D. R., KENT, R. N., O'LEARY, S. G., BRODERICK, J. E., & O'LEARY, K. D. Reactions of children and teachers to classroom observers: A series of controlled investigations. *Behavior Therapy,* 1977, *8,* 887-897.

DUNBAR, J. M., & AGRAS, W. S. Compliance with medical instruction. In J. M. Ferguson & C. B. Taylor (eds.), *The comprehensive handbook of behavioral medicine,* Vol. 3. New York: Spectrum Publ., 1980.

DUNN, L. M. Special education for the mildly retarded— is much of it justifiable? *Exceptional Children,* 1968, *35,* 5-22.

DURLAK, J. A., STEIN, M. A., & MANNARINO, A. P. Behavioral validity of a brief teacher rating scale (the AML) in identifying high-risk acting-out schoolchildren. *American Journal of Community Psychology,* 1980, *8,* 101-115.

DWECK, C. S. Learned helplessness: A developmental approach. Discussion of the chapters of Dr. McKinney and Watson. In J. G. Schulterbrandt & A. Raskin (eds.), *Depression in childhood: Diagnosis, treatment, and conceptual models.* New York: Raven Press, 1977.

DYKMAN, R. A., ACKERMAN, P. T., CLEMENTS, S. D., & PETERS, J. E. Specific learning disabilities: An attentional deficit syndrome. In H. R. Myklebust (ed.), *Progress in learning disabilities,* Vol. II. New York: Grune & Stratton, 1971.

EDELBROCK, C., & ACHENBACH, T. M. A typology of child behavior profile patterns: Distribution and correlates for disturbed children aged 6-16. *Journal of Abnormal Child Psychology,* 1980, *8,* 441-470.

EDELMAN, M. W. Who is for children? *American Psychologist,* 1981, *36,* 109-116.

EELLS, K. Some implications for school practice of the Chicago studies of cultural bias in intelligence tests. *Harvard Educational Review,* 1953, *23,* 284-297.

EGGERS, C. Course and prognosis of childhood schizophrenia. *Journal of Autism and Childhood Schizophrenia,* 1978, *8,* 21-36.

EICHORN, D. H. Biological correlates of behavior. In H.

W. Stevens (ed.), *Child psychology,* Vol. 1. Chicago: University of Chicago Press, 1963.

EID, E. E. Follow-up study of physical growth of children who had excessive weight gain in the first six months of life. *British Medical Journal,* 1970, *2,* 74–76.

EISENBERG, L. Hyperkinetic reactions. In J. D. Noshpitz (ed.), *Basic handbook of child psychiatry,* Vol. 2. New York: Basic Books, 1979.

EKSTEIN, R., FRIEDMAN, S., & CARUTH, E. The psychoanalytic treatment of childhood schizophrenia. In B. B. Wolman (ed.), *Manual of child psychopathology.* New York: McGraw-Hill, 1972.

ELLIS, P. L. Empathy: A factor in antisocial behavior. *Journal of Abnormal Child Psychology,* 1982, *10,* 123–134.

EME, R. F. Sex differences in childhood psychopathology: A review. *Psychological Bulletin,* 1979, *86,* 574–595.

EMERY, R. E. Interparental conflict and the children of discord and divorce. *Psychological Bulletin,* 1982, *92,* 310–330.

EMPEY, L. T. *American delinquency: Its meaning and construction.* Homewood, Ill.: Dorsey Press, 1978.

ENGLISH, H. B. Three cases of the "conditioned fear response." *Journal of Abnormal and Social Psychology,* 1929, *24,* 221–225.

EPSTEIN, L. H., COBURN, P. C., BECKER, D., DRASH, A., & SIMINERIO, L. Measurement and modification of the accuracy of determinations of glucose concentration. *Diabetes Care,* 1980, *3,* 535–536.

EPSTEIN, L. H., FIGUEROA, J., FARKAS, G. M., & BECK, S. The short-term effects of feedback on accuracy of urine glucose determinations in insulin dependent diabetic children. *Behavior Therapy,* 1981, *12,* 560–564.

EPSTEIN, L. H., WING, R. R., KOESKE, R., ANDRASIK, F., & OSSIP, D. J. Child and parent weight loss in family-based behavior modification programs. *Journal of Consulting and Clinical Psychology,* 1981, *49,* 674–685.

EPSTEIN, S. Explorations in personality today and tomorrow: A tribute to Henry A. Murray. *American Psychologist,* 1979, *34,* 649–653.

ERICKSON, M. T. *Child psychopathology: Assessment, etiology, and treatment.* Englewood Cliffs, N.J.: Prentice-Hall, 1978.

ERON, L. D. Parent-child interaction, television violence, and aggression in children. *American Psychologist,* 1982, *37,* 197–211.

ERON, L. D., HUESMANN, L. R., LEFKOWITZ, M. M., & WALDER, L. O. Does television violence cause aggression? *American Psychologist,* 1972, *27,* 253–263.

ETAUGH, C. Effects of nonmaternal care on children: Research evidence and popular views. *American Psychologist,* 1980, *35,* 309–319.

ETZWILER, D. What the juvenile diabetic knows about his disease. *Pediatrics,* 1962, *29,* 135–141.

ETZWILER, D., & ROBB, J. Evaluation of programmed education among juvenile diabetics and their families. *Diabetes,* 1972, *21,* 967–971.

EXNER, J. E., JR. *The Rorschach: A comprehensive system.* New York: Wiley-Interscience, 1974.

EYBERG, S. M., & JOHNSON, S. M. Multiple assessment of behavior modification with families: Effects of contin-

gency contracting and order of treated problems. *Journal of Consulting and Clinical Psychology,* 1974, *42,* 594–606.

FALSTEIN, E. I., FEINSTEIN, S., & JUDAS, I. Anorexia Nervosa in the male child. *American Journal of Orthopsychiatry,* 1956, *26,* 751–773.

FANTZ, R. L. The origin of form perception. *Scientific American,* 1961, *204,* 66–72.

FAUST, M. S. Developmental maturity as a determinant of prestige in adolescent girls. *Child Development,* 1960, *31,* 173–184.

FEDERAL BUREAU OF INVESTIGATION. *Crime in the United States: Uniform crime reports, 1978.* Washington, D.C.: U.S. Government Printing Office, 1979.

FEDERAL BUREAU OF INVESTIGATION. *Crime in the United States: Uniform crime reports, 1979.* Washington, D.C.: U.S. Government Printing Office, 1980.

FEINGOLD, B. F. *Why your child is hyperactive.* New York: Random House, 1975.

FELDMAN, F., CANTOR, D., SOLL, S., & BACHRACH, W. Psychiatric study of a consecutive series of 34 patients with ulcerative colitis. *British Medical Journal,* 1967, *3,* 14–17.

FELDMAN, G. M. The effect of biofeedback training on respiratory resistance of asthmatic children. *Psychosomatic Medicine,* 1976, *38,* 27–34.

FELNER, R. D., STOLBERG, A., & COWEN, E. L. Crisis events and school mental health referral patterns of young children. *Journal of Consulting and Clinical Psychology,* 1975, *43,* 305–310.

FERBER, H., KEELEY, S. M., & SHEMBERG, K. M. Training parents in behavior modification: Outcome of and problems encountered in a program after Patterson's work. *Behavior Therapy,* 1974, *5,* 415–419.

FERGUSON, H. B., & PAPPAS, B. A. Evaluation of psychophysiological, neurochemical, and animal models of hyperactivity. In R. L. Trites (ed.), *Hyperactivity in children.* Baltimore, Md.: University Park Press, 1979.

FERGUSON, L. R. The competence and freedom of children to make choices regarding participation in research: A statement. *Journal of Social Issues,* 1978, *34,* 114–121.

FERSTER, C. B. Positive reinforcement and behavioral deficits of autistic children. *Child Development,* 1961, *32,* 437–456.

FERSTER, C. B. The repertoire of the autistic child in relation to principles of reinforcement. In L. Gottschalk & A. H. Averback (eds.), *Methods of research of psychotherapy.* New York: Appleton-Century-Crofts, 1966.

FERSTER, C. B. Behavioral approaches to depression. In R. J. Friedman & M. M. Katz (eds.), *The psychology of depression: Contemporary theory and research.* Washington, D.C.: Winston, 1974.

FEUERSTEIN, M., WARD, M. M., & LEBARON, S. W. M. Neuropsychological and neurophysiological assessment of children with learning and behavior problems: A critical appraisal. In B. B. Lahey & A. E. Kazdin (eds.), *Advances in clinical child psychology,* Vol. 2. New York: Plenum, 1979.

FIELD, T. Early peer relations. In P. S. Strain (ed.), *The* utilization of classroom peers as behavior change agents. New York: Plenum, 1981.

FINCH, S. M. Psychological factors affecting physical conditions (Psychosomatic disorders). In H. I. Kaplan, A. M. Freedman, & B. J. Sadock (eds.), *Comprehensive textbook of psychiatry/III,* Vol. 3. Baltimore, Md.: Williams & Wilkins, 1980.

FINLEY, W. W. An "EEG study of sleep of enuretics at three age levels. *Clinical Electroencephalography,* 1971, *1,* 35–39.

FINLEY, W. W., BESSERMAN, R. L., BENNETT, L. F., CLAPP, R. K., & FINLEY, P. M. The effect of continuous, intermittent, and "placebo" reinforcement on the effectiveness of the conditioning treatment for enuresis nocturna. *Behaviour Research and Therapy,* 1973, *11,* 289–297.

FINLEY, W. W., & PERRY, R. R. Relationship of EEG findings to enuresis nocturna in children with psychiatric disorders. *Clinical Electroencephalography,* 1973, *4,* 62–69.

FINNEY, J. W., RUSSO, D. C., & CATALDO, M. F. Reduction of pica in young children with lead poisoning. *Journal of Pediatric Psychology,* 1982, *7,* 197–207.

FISH, B., & RITVO, E. R. Psychoses of childhood. In J. D. Noshpitz (ed.), *Basic handbook of child psychiatry,* Vol. 2. New York: Basic Books, 1979.

FISHER, E. B., JR., DELAMATER, A. M., BERTELSON, A. D., & KIRKLEY, B. G. Psychological factors in diabetes and its treatment. *Journal of Consulting and Clinical Psychology,* 1982, *50,* 993–1003.

FIXSEN, D. L., PHILLIPS, E. L., & WOLF, M. M. Achievement place: Experiments in self-government with pre-delinquents. *Journal of Applied Behavior Analysis,* 1973, *6,* 31–47.

FIXSEN, D. L., WOLF, M. M., & PHILLIPS, E. L. Achievement place: a teaching-family model of community-based group homes for youth in trouble. In L. Hammerlynck, L. Handy, and E. Mash (eds.), *Behavior change: Methodology, concepts and practice.* Champaign, Ill.: Research Press, 1973.

FLAVELL, J. H. *The developmental psychology of Jean Piaget.* New York: Van Nostrand, 1963.

FLAVELL, J. H. *Cognitive development.* Englewood Cliffs, N.J.: Prentice-Hall, 1977.

FLAVELL, J. H., BEACH, D. R., & CHINSKY, J. M. Spontaneous verbal rehearsal in a memory task as a function of age. *Child Development,* 1966, *37,* 283–299.

FLAVELL, J. H., & WELLMAN, H. M. Metamemory. In R. V. Kail, Jr., & J. W. Hagen (eds.), *Perspectives on the development of memory and cognition.* Hillsdale, N.J.: Lawrence Erlbaum Associates, 1977.

FLEISCHMAN, M. J. A replication of Patterson's "Intervention for boys with conduct problems." *Journal of Consulting and Clinical Psychology,* 1981, *49,* 342–351.

FODOR, E. M. Delinquency and susceptibility to social influence among adolescents as a function of level of moral development. *Journal of Social Psychology,* 1972, *86,* 257–260.

FODOR, E. M. Moral development and parent behavior antecedents in adolescent psychopaths. *Journal of Genetic Psychology,* 1973, *122,* 37–43.

FOLSTEIN, S., & RUTTER, M. A twin study of individuals with infantile autism. In M. Rutter & E. Schopler (eds.), *Autism: A reappraisal of concepts and treatment.* New York: Plenum, 1978.

FOREHAND, R. Child noncompliance to parental requests: Behavioral analysis and treatment. In M. Hersen, R. M. Eisler, & P. M. Miller (eds.), *Progress in behavior modification,* Vol 5. New York: Academic Press, 1977.

FOREHAND, R., KING, H. E., PEED, S., & YODER, P. Mother-child interactions: Comparisons of a noncompliant clinic group and a non-clinic group. *Behaviour Research and Therapy,* 1975, *13,* 79–84.

FOREHAND, R., & SCARBORO, M. E. An analysis of children's oppositional behavior. *Journal of Abnormal Child Psychology,* 1975, *3,* 27–31.

FOREHAND, R., WELLS, K. C., & GRIEST, D. L. An examination of the social validity of a parent training program. *Behavior Therapy,* 1980, *11,* 488–502.

FORGUS, R. H. The effects of early perceptual learning in the behavioral organization of adult rats. *Journal of Comparative Physiological Psychology,* 1954, *47,* 331–336.

FOSTER, G. G., & SALVIA, J. Teacher response to the label of learning disabled as a function of demand characteristics. *Exceptional Children,* 1977, *43,* 533–534.

FOXX, R. M., & MARTIN, E. D. Treatment of scavenging behavior by overcorrection. *Behaviour Research and Therapy,* 1975, *13,* 153–162.

FRAIBERG, S. On the sleep disturbances of early childhood. *The psychoanalytic study of the child,* Vol. 5. New York: International Universities Press, 1950.

FRANKEL, A. Juvenile diabetes—The look from within. In Z. Laron (ed.), *Modern problems in pediatrics (Vol. 12): Diabetes in juveniles: Medical and rehabilitation aspects.* New York: Karger, 1975.

FRANKEL, M. S. Social, legal, and political responses to ethical issues in the use of children as experimental subjects. *Journal of Social Issues,* 1978, *34,* 101–113.

FREEDMAN, D. G., & KELLER, B. Inheritance of behavior in infants. *Science,* 1963, *140,* 196–198.

FREEMAN, E. H., FEINGOLD, B. F., SCHLESINGER, K., & GORMAN, F. J. Psychological variables in allergic disorders: A review. *Psychosomatic Medicine,* 1964, *26,* 543–575.

FRENCH, T. M., & ALEXANDER, F. Psychogenic factors in bronchial asthma. *Psychosomatic Medicine Monograph,* 1941, *4,* 2–94.

FREUD, A. Adolescence. *The Psychoanalytic Study of the Child,* 1958, *13,* 255–278.

FREUD, A. *Normality and pathology in childhood.* New York: International Universities Press, 1965.

FREUD, S. *An outline of psycho-analysis.* Translated and newly edited by J. Strackey. New York: W. W. Norton and Co., 1949.

FREUD, S. Analysis of a phobia in a five-year-old boy (1909). *Standard Edition,* Vol. 10. Ed. and trans. James Strachey. London: The Hogarth Press, 1953.

FREUD, S. From the history of an infantile neurosis. In *Col-*

lected papers, Vol. 3. New York: Basic Books, 1959. (Originally published 1918.)

FREUD, S. Civilization and its discontents (1930). In *Standard edition of the complete psychological works of Sigmund Freud,* Vol. 21. London: Hogarth Press, 1961.

FRIEDMAN, R. M., SANDLER, J., HERNANDEZ, M., & WOLFE, D. A. Child abuse. In E. J. Mash & L. G. Terdal (eds.), *Behavioral assessment of childhood disorders.* New York: Guilford Press, 1981.

FRODI, A. M., LAMB, M. E., LEAVITT, L. A., DONOVAN, W. L., NEFF, C., & SHERRY, D. Fathers' and mothers' responses to the faces and cries of normal and premature infants. *Developmental Psychology,* 1978, *14,* 490–498.

FROSTIG, M. Visual perception, integrative functions, and academic learning. *Journal of Learning Disabilities,* 1972, *5,* 1–15.

FROSTIG, M., & HORNE, D. The Frostig Program for the Development of Visual Perception. Chicago: Follett Corp., 1964.

FROSTIG, M., LEFEVER, W., & WHITTLESEY, J. R. B. *Administration and scoring manual for the Marianne Frostig developmental test of visual perception.* Palo Alto, Calif.: Consulting Psychologists Press, 1966.

FURMAN, W. Promoting social development: Developmental implications for treatment. In B. B. Lahey & A. E. Kazdin (eds.), *Advances in clinical child psychology,* Vol. 3. New York: Plenum, 1980.

FURMAN, W., RAHE, D., & HARTUP, W. Rehabilitation of socially withdrawn preschool children through mixed-age and same-age socialization. *Child Development,* 1979, *50,* 915–922.

GAD, M. T., & JOHNSON, J. H. Correlates of adolescent life stress as related to race, SES, and levels of perceived social support. *Journal of Clinical Child Psychology,* 1980, *9,* 13–16.

GALTON, F., *Hereditary genius.* London: Macmillan, 1869.

GARCIA, J., McGOWAN, B. K., & GREEN, K. F. Biological constraints on conditioning. In A. H. Black & W. F. Prokasy (eds.), *Classical conditioning II: Current research and theory.* New York: Appleton-Century-Crofts, 1972.

GARDNER, R. A. Minimal brain dysfunction. In J. R. Bemporad (ed.), *Child development in normality and psychopathology.* New York: Brunner/Mazel, 1980.

GARMEZY, N. The experimental study of children vulnerable to psychopathology. In A. Davids (ed.), *Child personality and psychopathology,* Vol. 2. New York: Wiley-Interscience, 1975.

GARN, S., COLE, P. E., & BAILY, S. M. Effect of parental fatness levels on the fatness of biological and adoptive children. *Ecology of Food and Nutrition,* 1976, *6,* 1–34.

GARNER, A. M., & THOMPSON, C. W. Factors in the management of juvenile diabetes. *Pediatric Psychology,* 1974, *2,* 6–7.

GARNER, A. M., & THOMPSON, C. W. Juvenile diabetes. In P. R. Magrab (ed.), *Psychological management of pediatric problems: Vol. 1: Early life conditions and chronic disorders.* Baltimore, Md.: University Park Press, 1978.

GARVEY, W. P., & HEGREVES, J. P. Desensitization techniques in the treatment of school phobia. *American Journal of Orthopsychiatry,* 1966, *36,* 147–152.

GELDER, M. Behaviour therapy for neurotic disorders. *Behavior Modification,* 1979, *3,* 469–495.

GELLES, R. J. Violence toward children in the United States. In R. Bourne & E. H. Newberger (eds.), *Critical perspectives on child abuse.* Lexington, Mass.: Lexington Books-Heath, 1979.

GERARD, M. W. Enuresis: A study in etiology. *American Journal of Orthopsychiatry,* 1939, *9,* 48–58.

GERSTEN, J. C., LANGNER, T. S., EISENBERG, J. G., SIMCHA-FAGAN, O., & McCARTHY, E. D. Stability and change in types of behavioral disturbance of children and adolescents. *Journal of Abnormal Child Psychology,* 1976, *4,* 111–127.

GESELL, A., & AMATRUDA, C. S. *Developmental diagnosis,* 2nd ed. New York: Hoeber, 1947.

GESTEN, E. L., RAINS, M. H., RAPKIN, B. D., WEISSBERG, R. P., FLORES DE APOCADA, R., COWEN, E. L., & BOWEN, R. *Training children in social problem-solving competencies: A first and second look.* American Journal of Community Psychology, 1982, *10*(1), 95–115.

GIBBONS, D. C. *Delinquent behavior,* 2nd ed. Englewood Cliffs, N.J.: Prentice-Hall, 1976.

GIL, D. G. *Violence against children.* Cambridge, Mass.: Harvard University Press, 1970.

GIL, D. G. Unraveling child abuse. In R. Bourne & E. H. Newberger (eds.), *Critical perspectives on child abuse.* Lexington, Mass.: Lexington Books-Heath, 1979.

GINSBURG, H. *The myth of the deprived child: Poor children's intellect and education.* Englewood Cliffs, N.J.: Prentice-Hall, 1972.

GIOVANNONI, J. M., & BILLINGSLEY, A. Child neglect among the poor: A study of parental adequacy in families of three ethnic groups. In S. Chess and A. Thomas (eds.), *Annual progress in child psychiatry and child development.* New York: Brunner/Mazel, 1971.

GITTELLMAN-KLEIN, R. Definitional and methodological issues concerning depressive illness in children. In J. G. Schulterbrandt & A. Raskin (eds.), *Depression in childhood: Diagnosis, treatment, and conceptual models.* New York: Raven Press, 1977.

GITTELMAN, R. The role of psychological tests for differential diagnosis in child psychiatry. *Journal of the American Academy of Child Psychiatry,* 1980, *19,* 413–438.

GITTELMAN, R., ABIKOFF, H., POLLACK, E., KLEIN, D. F., KATZ, S., & MATTES, J. A controlled trial of behavior modification and methylphenidate in hyperactive children. In C. K. Whalen & B. Henker (eds.), *Hyperactive children.* New York: Academic Press, 1980.

GLADSTON, R. Observations on children who have been physically abused and their parents. *American Journal of Psychiatry,* 1965, *122,* 440–443.

GLICKLICH, L. B. A historical account of enuresis. *Pediatrics,* 1951, *8,* 859–876.

GLIDDEN, L. M. Training of learning and memory in retarded persons: Strategies, techniques, and teaching tools. In N. R. Ellis (ed.), *Handbook of mental deficiency.* Hillsdale, N.J.: Lawrence Erlbaum Associates, 1979.

GLOW, R. A., GLOW, P. H., & RUMP, E. E. The stability of child behavior disorders: A one-year test-retest study of Adelaide versions of the Conners teacher and parent rating scales. *Journal of Abnormal Child Psychology*, 1982, *10*, 33–60.

GLUECK, S., & GLUECK, E. T. *Unraveling juvenile delinquency.* New York: Commonwealth Fund, 1950.

GLUECK, S., & GLUECK, E. *Towards a typology of juvenile offenders: Implications for therapy and prevention.* New York: Grune & Stratton, 1970.

GODDARD, H. H. *The Kallikak family.* New York: Macmillan, 1912.

GOLDBERG, H. K., & SCHIFFMAN, G. B. *Dyslexia.* New York: Grune & Stratton, 1972.

GOLDBERG, J. O., & KONSTANTAREAS, M. M. Vigilance in hyperactive and normal children on a self-paced task. *Journal of Child Psychiatry and Psychology*, 1981, *22*, 55–63.

GOLDBERG, S. Prematurity: Effects on parent-infant interaction. *Journal of Pediatric Psychology*, 1978, *3*, 137–144.

GOLDFARB, W. Infant rearing and problem behavior. *American Journal of Orthopsychiatry*, 1943, *13*, 249–265.

GOLDFARB, W. Childhood psychosis. In P. H. Mussen (ed.), *Carmichael's manual of child psychology*, Vol. 2. New York: John Wiley, 1970.

GOLDFARB, W. Pervasive developmental disorders of childhood. In H. I. Kaplan, A. M. Freedman, & B. J. Sadock (eds.), *Comprehensive textbook of psychiatry/III*, Vol. 3. Baltimore, Md.: Williams & Wilkins, 1980.

GOLDFARB, W., GOLDFARB, N., & SCHOLL, H. The speech of mothers of schizophrenic children. *American Journal of Psychiatry*, 1966, *122*, 1220–1227.

GOLDFARB, W., SPITZER, R. L., & ENDICOTT, J. A study of psychopathology of parents of psychotic children by structured interview. *Journal of Autism and Childhood Schizophrenia*, 1976, *6*, 327–338.

GOLDSTEIN, J., FREUD, A., & SOLNIT, A. J. *Beyond the best interests of the child.* New York: Free Press, 1973.

GOLDSTEIN, J., FREUD, A., & SOLNIT, A. J. *Before the best interests of the child.* New York: Free Press, 1979.

GOLDSTON, S. E. An overview of primary prevention programming. In D. C. Klein & S. E. Goldston (eds.), *Primary prevention: An idea whose time has come.* DHEW Publication No. (ADM) 77–447. Washington, D.C.: U.S. Government Printing Office, 1977.

GORDON, D. A., & YOUNG, R. D. School phobia: A discussion of aetiology, treatment and evaluation. *Psychological Reports*, 1976, *39*, 783–804.

GOTTLIEB, M. I. The learning-disabled child: Controversial issues revisited. In M. I. Gottlieb, P. W. Zinkus, & L. J. Bradford (eds.), *Current issues in developmental pediatrics: The learning-disabled child.* New York: Grune & Stratton, 1979.

GOTTMAN, J., GONSO, J., & RASMUSSEN, B. Social interaction, social competence and friendship in children. *Child Development*, 1975, *46*, 709–718.

GOTTMAN, J., GONSO, J., & SCHULER, P. Teaching social skills to isolated children. *Journal of Abnormal Child Psychology*, 1976, *4*, 179–186.

GOULD, M. S., WUNSCH-HITZIG, R., & DOHRENWEND, B.

Estimating the prevalence of childhood psychopathology. *Journal of the American Academy of Child Psychiatry*, 1981, *20*, 462–476.

GOYEN, J. D., & LYLE, J. G. Effect of incentives and age on the visual recognition of retarded readers. *Journal of Experimental Child Psychology*, 1971, *11*, 266–273.

GOYETTE, C. H., CONNERS, C. K., & ULRICH, R. F. Normative data on revised Conners parent and teacher rating scales. *Journal of Abnormal Child Psychology*, 1978, *6*, 221–236.

GRACE, W. J., & GRAHAM, D. T. Relationship of specific attitudes and emotions to certain bodily diseases. *Psychosomatic Medicine*, 1952, *14*, 243–251.

GRAHAM, P. J. Epidemiological studies. In H. C. Quay & J. S., Werry (eds.), *Psychopathological disorders of childhood*, 2nd ed. New York: John Wiley, 1979.

GRAZIANO, A. M., DEGIOVANNI, I. S., & GARCIA, K. A. Behavioral treatment of children's fears: A review. *Psychological Bulletin*, 1979, *86*, 804–830.

GRAZIANO, A. M., MOONEY, K. C., HUBER, C., & IGNASIAK, D. Self-control instruction for children's fear-reduction. *Journal of Behavior Therapy and Experimental Psychiatry*, 1979, *10*, 221–227.

GREEN, A. H. Child abuse. In B. B. Wolman (ed.), *Handbook of treatment of mental disorders in childhood and adolescence.* Englewood Cliffs, N.J.: Prentice-Hall, 1978.

GREENLAND, C. Lethal family situations: An international comparison of deaths from child abuse. In E. J. Anthony & C. Chiland (eds.), *The child in his family: Preventive child psychiatry in an age of transitions.* New York: John Wiley, 1980.

GREENO, J. G. Psychology of learning, 1960–1980: One participant's observations. *American Psychologist*, 1980, *35*, 713–728.

GRIEST, D. L., & WELLS, K. C. Behavioral family therapy with conduct disorders in children. *Behavior Therapy*, 1983, *14*, 37–53.

GRINDER, R. E. *A history of genetic psychology.* New York: John Wiley, 1967.

GROSSMAN, H. J. (ed.), *Manual on terminology and classification in mental retardation.* Washington, D.C.: American Association on Mental Deficiency, 1977.

GROSSMAN, H. J. (ed.), *Classification in Mental Retardation.* Washington, D. C.: American Association on Mental Deficiency, 1983.

GROSSMANN, F., THANE, K., & GROSSMANN, K. E. Maternal tactual contact of the newborn after various postpartum conditions of mother-infant contact. *Developmental Psychology*, 1981, *17*, 158–169.

GROUP FOR THE ADVANCEMENT OF PSYCHIATRY. *Psychopathological disorders in childhood: Theoretical considerations and a proposed classification.* New York: Jason Aronson, 1966.

GUNN, P., BERRY, P., & ANDREWS, R. J. The temperament of Down's syndrome infants: A research note. *Journal of Child Psychology and Psychiatry*, 1981, *22*, 189–194.

HAFNER, A. J., QUAST, W., & SHEA, M. J. The adult adjustment of one thousand psychiatric patients: Initial findings from a twenty-five year follow-up. In R. O. Wirt, G. Winokur, & M. Roff (eds.), *Life history in psy-*

chopathology, Vol. 4. Minneapolis: University of Minnesota Press, 1975.

HAGAMEN, M. B. Childhood psychosis: Residential treatment and its alternatives. In B. B. Wolman (ed.), *Handbook of treatment of mental disorders in childhood and adolescence.* Englewood Cliffs, N.J.: Prentice-Hall, 1978.

HAGAMEN, M. B. Autism and childhood schizophrenia. In J. E. Bemporad (ed.), *Child development in normality and psychopathology.* New York: Brunner/Mazel, 1980. (a)

HAGAMEN, M. B. Family adaptation to the diagnosis of mental retardation in a child and strategies of intervention. In L. S. Szymanski & P. E. Tanguay (eds.), *Emotional disorders of mentally retarded persons.* Baltimore, Md.: University Park Press, 1980. (b)

HALLAHAN, D. P., & KAUFFMAN, J. M. *Exceptional children: Introduction to special education.* Englewood Cliffs, N.J.: Prentice-Hall, 1978.

HALMI, K. A. Anorexia nervosa: Demographic and clinical features in 94 cases. *Psychosomatic Medicine,* 1974, *36,* 18–25.

HALMI, K., & BRODLAND, G. Monozygotic twins concordant and discordant for anorexia nervosa. *Psychological Medicine,* 1973, *3,* 521–524.

HAMMILL, D. D., & LARSEN, S. C. The relationship of selected auditory perceptual skills and reading ability. *Journal of Learning Disabilities,* 1974, *7,* 429–435.

Handbook on women workers. Washington, D.C.: U.S. Department of Labor, 1975.

HANSEN, H., BELMONT, L., & STEIN, Z. Epidemiology. In J. Wortis (ed.), *Mental retardation and development disabilities,* Vol. XI. New York: Brunner/Mazel, 1980.

HARE, R. D. *Psychopathy: Theory and research.* New York: John Wiley, 1970.

HARLEY, J. P., & MATTHEWS, C. G. Food additives and hyperactivity in children: Experimental investigations. In R. M. Knights and D. J. Bakker (eds.), *Treatment of hyperactive and learning disordered children.* Baltimore, Md.: University Park Press, 1980.

HARLOW, H. F., & HARLOW, M. K. The affectional systems. In A. M. Schrier, H. F. Harlow, & F. Stolnitz (eds.), *Behavior of nonhuman primates,* Vol. 2. New York: Academic Press, 1965.

HARLOW, H. F., & HARLOW, M. K. The young monkeys. In P. Cramer (ed.), *Readings in developmental psychology today.* Del Mar Calif.: CRM Books, 1970.

HARRIS, S. L. DSM-III—Its implications for children. *Child Behavior Therapy,* 1979, *1,* 37–46.

HARRIS, S. L., & FERRARI, M. Developmental factors in child behavior therapy. *Behavior Therapy,* 1983, *14,* 54–72.

HARRIS, S. L., & MILCH, R. E. Training parents as behavior therapists for their autistic children. *Clinical Psychology Review,* 1981, *1,* 49–63.

HARRISON, N. S. *Understanding behavioral research.* Belmont, Calif.: Wadsworth, 1979.

HARRISON, S. I., & McDERMOTT, J. F. *Childhood psychopathology.* New York: International Universities Press, 1972.

HARTER, S., & ZIGLER, E. The assessment of effectance motivation in normal and retarded children. *Developmental Psychology,* 1974, *10,* 169–180.

HARTUP, W. W. Peer interaction and social organization. In P. H. Mussen (ed.), *Carmichael's manual of child psychology,* Vol. 2. New York: John Wiley, 1970.

HARTUP, W. W. Peer interaction and the behavioral development of the individual child. In E. Schopler & R. J. Reichler (eds.), *Psychopathology and child development.* New York: Plenum, 1976.

HARTUP, W. W. Peer relations and the growth of social competence. In M. W. Kent & J. E. Rolf (eds.), *The primary prevention of psychopathology,* Vol. 3. Hanover, N.H.: University Press of New England, 1979.

HARTUP, W. W. Peers, play, and pathology: A new look at the social behavior of children. In T. Field, S. Goldberg, D. Stern, & A. Sostek (eds.), *High-risk infants and children: Adult and peer interactions.* New York: Academic Press, 1980.

HASTINGS, J. E., & BARKLEY, R. A. A review of psychophysiological research with hyperkinetic children. *Journal of Abnormal Child Psychology,* 1978, *6,* 413–448.

HAWTON, K. Attempted suicide in children and adolescents. *Journal of Child Psychology and Psychiatry,* 1982, *23,* 497–503.

HAYWOOD, H. C. Psychometric motivation and the efficiency of learning and performance in the mentally retarded. In B. W. Richards (ed.), *Proceedings of the First Congress of the International Association for the Scientific Study of Mental Deficiency.* Reigate, Surrey, England: Michael Jackson, 1968.

HAYWOOD, H. C., MEYERS, C. E., & SWITZKY, H. N. Mental retardation. In M. R. Rosenzweig & L. W. Porter (eds.), *Annual review of psychology.* Palo Alto, Calif.: Annual Reviews Inc., 1982.

HAYWOOD, H. C., & WEAVER, S. J. Differential effects of motivational orientations and incentive conditions on motor performance in institutionalized retardates. *American Journal of Mental Deficiency,* 1967, *72,* 459–467.

HEBB, D. O. *The organization of behavior.* New York: John Wiley, 1949.

HELD, M. L., & SNOW, D. L. MMPI, internal-external control and problem checklists of obese adolescent females. *Journal of Clinical Psychology,* 1972, *28,* 523–525.

HENKER, B., & WHALEN, C. K. The changing faces of hyperactivity: Retrospect and prospect. In C. K. Whalen & B. Henker (eds.), *Hyperactive children.* New York: Academic Press, 1980.

HERMELIN, B., & O'CONNER, N. *Psychological experiments with autistic children.* London: Pergamon Press, 1970.

HERSEN, M., & BARLOW, D. H. *Single case experimental designs: Strategies for studying behavior change.* New York: Pergamon Press, 1976.

HERSOV, L. A. Persistent non-attendance at school. *Journal of Child Psychology and Psychiatry,* 1960, *1,* 130–136. (a)

HERSOV, L. A. Refusal to go to school. *Journal of Child Psychology and Psychiatry,* 1960, *1,* 137–145. (b)

HESS, R. D., & SHIPMAN, V. C. Maternal attitudes toward the school and the role of the pupil: Some social class comparisons. In A. H. Passow (ed.), *Developing programs for the educationally disadvantaged.* New York: Teachers College, Columbia University, 1968.

HESTON, L. L. Psychiatric disorders in foster home reared children of schizophrenic mothers. *British Journal of Psychiatry,* 1966, *112,* 819–825.

HETHERINGTON, E. M. Effects of father absence on personality development in adolescent daughters. *Developmental Psychology,* 1972, *7,* 313–326.

HETHERINGTON, E. M. Divorce: A child's perspective. *American Psychologist,* 1979, *34,* 851–858.

HETHERINGTON, E. M., & FRANKIE, C. Effects of parental dominance, warmth and conflict on imitation in children. *Journal of Personality and Social Psychology,* 1965, *2,* 188–194.

HETHERINGTON, E. M., & MARTIN, B. Family interaction. In H. C. Quay and J. S. Werry (eds.), *Psychopathological disorders of childhood,* 2nd ed. New York: John Wiley, 1979.

HETHERINGTON, E. M., STOUWIE, R., & RIDBERG, E. H. Patterns of family interaction and child rearing attitudes related to three dimensions of juvenile delinquency. *Journal of Abnormal Psychology,* 1971, *77,* 160–176.

HEWETT, J. M. Teaching speech to an autistic child through operant conditioning. *American Journal of Orthopsychiatry,* 1965, *35,* 927–936.

HILGARD, E. R., & BOWER, G. H. *Theories of learning.* New York: Appleton-Century-Crofts, 1966.

HINKLE, L. E., & WOLF, S. Importance of life stress in the course and management of diabetes mellitus. *Journal of the American Medical Association,* 1952, *148,* 513–520.

HOBBS, N. Mental health's third revolution. *American Journal of Orthopsychiatry,* 1964, *34,* 822–833.

HOBBS, N. *The futures of children.* San Francisco: Jossey-Bass, 1975.

HOBBS, N. *The troubled and troubling child.* San Francisco: Jossey-Bass, 1982.

HODAPP, R. M., & MUELLER, E. Early social development. In B. B. Wolman (ed.) *Handbook of developmental psychology.* Englewood Cliffs, N.J.: Prentice-Hall, 1982.

HOFFMAN, L. W. Effects of maternal employment on the child—A review. *Developmental Psychology,* 1974, *10,* 204–228.

HOFFMAN, L. W. Changes in family roles, socialization, and sex differences. *American Psychologist,* 1977, *32,* 644–657.

HOFFMAN, M. L. Development of moral thought, feeling, and behavior. *American Psychologist,* 1979, *34,* 958–966.

HOLLINGSWORTH, C. E., TANGUAY, P. E., GROSSMAN, L., & PABST, P. Long-term outcome of obsessive-compulsive disorder in childhood. *Journal of the American Academy of Child Psychiatry,* 1980, *19,* 134–144.

HOLMES, L. B. Genetic counseling for the older pregnant woman: New data and questions. *New England Journal of Medicine,* 1978, *298,* 1419–1421.

HONZIK, M. P., MacFARLAND, J. W., & ALLEN, L. The stability of mental test performance between 2 and 18 years. *Journal of Experimental Education,* 1948, *17,* 309–324.

HOPS, H. Children's social competence and skill: Current research practices and future directions. *Behavior Therapy,* 1983, *14,* 3–18.

HOPS, S., & GREENWOOD, C. R. Social skills deficits. In E. J. Mash & L. G. Terdal (eds.), *Behavioral assessment of childhood disorders.* New York: Guilford Press, 1981.

HOROWITZ, F. D. Improving our knowledge of children's thoughts. *American Psychologist,* 1979, *34,* 892–893.

HOY, E., WEISS, G., MINDE, K., & COHEN, N. The hyperactive child at adolescence: Cognitive, emotional and social functioning. *Journal of Abnormal Child Psychology,* 1978, *6,* 311–324.

HUDGINS, W., & PRENTICE, N. M. Moral judgment in delinquent and nondelinquent adolescents and their mothers. *Journal of Abnormal Psychology,* 1973, *82,* 145–152.

HUMPHREYS, L., FOREHAND, R., McMAHON, R., & ROBERTS, M. Parent behavioral training to modify child noncompliance: Effects on untreated siblings. *Journal of Behavior Therapy and Experimental Psychiatry,* 1978, *9,* 235–238.

HUNDLEBY, J. D., CARPENTER, R. A., ROSS, R. A. J., & MERCER, G. W. Adolescent drug use and other behaviors. *Journal of Child Psychology and Psychiatry,* 1982, *23,* 61–68.

HUNSAKER, J. H. A two-process approach to nocturnal enuresis: Preliminary results. *Behavior Therapy,* 1976, *6,* 560–561.

HUNT, J. McV. *Intelligence and experience.* New York: The Ronald Press Co., 1961.

HUNT, J. McV. Psychological development: Early experience. *Annual review of psychology,* 1979, *30,* 103–143.

HUTT, S. J., & HUTT, C. *Direct observation and measurement of behavior.* Springfield, Ill.: Chas. C Thomas, 1970.

ILLINGWORTH, R. S. Predictive value of developmental tests in the 1st year. *Journal of Child Psychology and Psychiatry,* 1961, *2,* 210–215.

INHELDER, B. *The diagnosis of reasoning in the mentally retarded.* Trans. W. B. Stephens. New York: Day, 1968 (French ed., 1943).

ISRAEL, A. C., & O'LEARY, K. D. Developing correspondence between children's words and deeds. *Child Development,* 1973, *44,* 575–581.

ISRAEL, A. C., PRAVDER, M. D., & KNIGHTS, S. A peer-administered program for changing the classroom behavior of disruptive children. *Behavioural Analysis and Modification,* 1980, *4,* 224–238.

ISRAEL, A. C., & SIMON, L. G. *Behavior problems of obese children in a weight reduction program.* Manuscript submitted for publication, 1983.

ISRAEL, A. C., & STOLMAKER, L. S. Behavioral treatment of obesity in children and adolescents. In M. Hersen, R. M. Eisler, & P. M. Miller (eds.), *Progress in Behavior Modification,* Vol. 10. New York: Academic Press, 1980.

ISRAEL, A. C., STOLMAKER, L., & GUILE, C. A. *The contribution of training parents in child management skills to the behavioral treatment of childhood obesity.* Manuscript submitted for publication, 1983.

ISRAEL, A. C., STOLMAKER, L. S., & PRINCE, B. The relationship between impulsivity and eating behavior in children. *Child and Family Behavior Therapy,* in press.

ISRAEL, A. C., STOLMAKER, L., SHARP, J. P., SILVERMAN, W., & SIMON, L. G. *Two methods of increasing parental in-*

volvement in the treatment of childhood obesity. Manuscript in preparation, 1983.

JABBOUR, J. T., DUENAS, D. A., GILMARTIN, R. C., & GOTTLIEB, M. I. *Pediatric neurology handbook.* Flushing N.Y.: Medical Examination Publishing Co., 1976.

JACKSON, C. M. Some aspects of form and growth. In W. J. Robbins, S. Brody, A. F. Hogan, C. M. Jackson, and C. W. Greed (eds.), *Growth.* New Haven: Yale University Press, 1929.

JACOB, R. G., O'LEARY, K. D., & ROSENBLAD, C. Formal and informal classroom settings: Effects on hyperactivity. *Journal of Abnormal Child Psychology,* 1978, *6,* 47–59.

JACOBS, P. A., BRUNTON, M., & MELVILLE, M. M. Agressive behavior, mental subnormality, and the XYY male. *Nature,* 1965, *208,* 1351–1352.

JANSKY, J. J. Specific developmental disorders of childhood and adolescence: Developmental reading disorder. In H. I. Kaplan, A. M. Freedman, & B. J. Sadock (eds.), *Comprehensive textbook of psychiatry/III,* Vol. 3. Baltimore, Md.: Williams and Wilkins, 1980.

JASON, L. A. A behavioral approach in enhancing disadvantaged children's academic abilities. *American Journal of Community Psychology,* 1977, *5,* 413–421.

JASTAK, J. F., & JASTAK, S. R. *The Wide Range Achievement Test,* rev. ed. Wilmington, Del.: Guidance Associates, 1965.

JEFFREY, D. B., & KRAUSS, M. R. The etiologies, assessments, and treatments of obesity. In S. N. Haynes & L. A. Gannon (eds.), *Psychosomatic disorders: A psychophysiological approach to etiology and treatment.* New York: Gardner, 1981.

JEFFREY, D. B., LEMNITZER, N. B., HESS, J. M., HICKEY, J. S., McLELLARN, R. W., & STROUD, J. *Children's responses to television food advertising: Experimental evidence of actual food consumption.* Paper presented at a meeting of the American Psychological Association, New York City, September 1979.

JEFFREY, R. W., WING, R. R., & STUNKARD, A. J. Behavioral treatment of obesity: The state of the art 1976. *Behavior Therapy,* 1978, *9,* 189–199.

JEHU, D., MORGAN, R. T. T., TURNER, A., & JONES, A. A controlled trial of the treatment of nocturnal enuresis in residential homes for children. *Behaviour Research and Therapy,* 1977, *15,* 1–16.

JENKINS, E. C., BROWN, W. T., DUNCAN, C. J., BROOKS, J., BEN-YISHAY, M., GIORDANO, F. M., & NITKOWSKY, H. M. Feasibility of fragile X chromosome prenatal diagnosis demonstrated. *Lancet,* December 5, 1981, 1292.

JENSEN, A. R. How much can we boost IQ and scholastic achievement? *Harvard Educational Review,* 1969, *39,* 1–123.

JENSEN, A. R. Sir Cyril Burt in perspective. *American Psychologist,* 1978, *33,* 499–503.

JENSEN, A. R., & ROHWER, W. D. The effect of verbal mediation on the learning and retention of paired-associates by retarded adults. *American Journal of Mental Deficiency,* 1963, *68,* 80–84.

JERSILD, A. T., & HOLMES, F. B. Children's fears. *Child Development Monograph,* No. 20, 1935.

JESPERSEN, J. O. *Language: Its nature, development, and origin.* London: Allen and Unwin, 1922.

JESSOR, R., & JESSOR, S. L. *Problem behavior and psychosocial development.* New York: Academic Press, 1977.

JOHNSON, M. L., BURKE, M. S., & MAYER, J. Relative importance of inactivity and overeating in the energy balance of obese high school girls. *American Journal of Clinical Nutrition,* 1956, *4,* 37–44.

JOHNSON, S. M., & BOLSTAD, O. D. Methodological issues in naturalistic observation: Some problems and solutions for field research. In L. A. Hamerlynck, L. C. Handy, & E. J. Mash (eds.), *Behavior change: Methodology, concepts, and practice.* Champaign, Ill.: Research Press, 1973.

JOHNSON, S. M., & CHRISTENSEN, A. Multiple criteria follow-up of behavior modification with families. *Journal of Abnormal Child Psychology,* 1975, *3,* 135–154.

JOHNSON, S. M., & LOBITZ, G. K. Parental manipulation of child behavior in home observations. *Journal of Applied Behavior Analysis,* 1974, *7,* 23–32. (a)

JOHNSON, S. M., & LOBITZ, G. K. The personal and marital status of parents as related to observed child deviance and parenting behaviors. *Journal of Abnormal Child Psychology,* 1974, *3,* 193–208. (b)

JOHNSON, S. M., WAHL, G., MARTIN, S., & JOHANSSON, S. How deviant is the normal child? A behavioral analysis of the preschool child and his family. In R. D. Rubin. J. P. Brady, & J. D. Henderson (eds.), *Advances in behavior therapy,* Vol. 4. New York: Academic Press, 1973.

JOHNSON, S. W. *Arithmetic and learning disabilities.* Boston: Allyn and Bacon, 1979.

JOINT COMMISSION ON THE MENTAL HEALTH OF CHILDREN. *Crises in child mental health: Challenge for the 70's.* New York: Harper & Row, Pub., 1969.

JONES, M. C. A laboratory study of fear: The case of Peter. *Pedagogical Seminary,* 1924, *31,* 308–315.

JONES, R. R., REID, J. B., & PATTERSON, G. R. Naturalistic observations in clinical assessment. In P. McReynolds (ed.), *Advances in psychological assessment,* Vol. 3. San Francisco: Jossey-Bass, 1975.

JOSSELYN, I., LITTNER, N., & SPURLOCK, J. Psychologic aspects of ulcerative colitis in children. *Journal of American Medical Women's Association,* 1966, *21,* 303–306.

JUDD, L. J. Obsessive-compulsive neurosis in children. *Archives of General Psychiatry,* 1965, *12,* 136–143.

JURKOVIC, G. J. The juvenile delinquent as a moral philosopher: A structural-developmental perspective. *Psychological Bulletin,* 1980, *88,* 709–727.

JURKOVIC, G. J., & PRENTICE, N. M. Dimensions of moral interaction and moral judgment in delinquent and nondelinquent families. *Journal of Consulting and Clinical Psychology,* 1974, *42,* 256–262.

JURKOVIC, G. J., & PRENTICE, N. M. Relation of moral and cognitive development to dimensions of juvenile delinquency. *Journal of Abnormal Psychology,* 1977, *86,* 414–420.

KAFFMAN, M., & ELIZUR, E. Infants who become enuretics: A longitudinal study of 161 Kibbutz children. *Mon-*

ographs of the Society for Research in Child Development, 1977, 42 (4, Serial No. 170).

KAGAN, J. Reflection-impulsivity and reading ability in primary grade children. *Child Development,* 1965, *36,* 609–628.

KAHN, E., & COHEN, L. H. Organic driveness: A brain syndrome and an experience—with case reports. *New England Journal of Medicine,* 1934, *210,* 748–756.

KALES, A., JACOBSON, A., PAULSON, M., KALES, J., & WALTER, R. Somnambulism: Psychophysiological correlates. I. All-night EEG studies. *Archives of General Psychiatry,* 1966, *14,* 586–594.

KALLMANN, F., & ROTH, B. Genetic aspects of preadolescent schizophrenia. *American Journal of Psychiatry,* 1956, *112,* 599–606.

KALNINS, I. V., CHURCHILL, M. P., & TERRY, G. E. Concurrent stresses in families with a leukemic child. *Journal of Pediatric Psychology,* 1980, *5,* 81–92.

KAMIN, L. G. *The science and politics of IQ.* New York: Halsted Press, 1974.

KANDEL, D. B. Epidemiological and psychosocial perspectives on adolescent drug use. *Journal of the American Academy of Child Psychiatry,* 1982, *21,* 328–347.

KANFER, F. H., KAROLY, P., & NEWMAN, A. Reduction of children's fear of the dark by competence-related and situational threat-related verbal cues. *Journal of Consulting and Clinical Psychology,* 1975, *43,* 251–258.

KANGAS, J., & BRADWAY, K. Intelligence at middle age: A 38-year follow-up. *Developmental Psychology,* 1971, *5,* 333–337.

KANNER, L. Autistic disturbances of affective contact. *Nervous Child,* 1943, *2,* 217–250.

KANNER, L. Problems of nosology and psychodynamics of early infantile autism. *American Journal of Orthopsychiatry,* 1949, *19,* 416–426.

KANNER, L. Do behavior symptoms always indicate psychopathology? *Journal of Child Psychology and Psychiatry,* 1960, *1,* 17–25.

KANNER, L. *Child psychiatry,* 4th ed. Springfield, Ill.: Chas. C. Thomas, 1972.

KANNER, L. *Childhood psychoses: Initial studies and new insights.* Washington, D.C.: V. H. Winston & Sons, 1973.

KANNER, L., & EISENBERG, L. Early infantile autism, 1943–1955. *American Journal of Orthopsychiatry,* 1956, *26,* 55–65.

KASHANI, J., & SIMONDS, J. F. The incidence of depression in children. *American Journal of Psychiatry,* 1979, *136,* 1203–1204.

KATZ, J. Hormonal abnormality found in patients with anorexia nervosa. *Journal of the American Medical Association,* 1975, *232,* 9–11.

KATZ-GARRIS, L. The right to education. In J. Wortis (ed.), *Mental retardation and developmental disabilities,* Vol. X. New York: Brunner/Mazel, 1978.

KAUFFMAN, A. S. Issues in psychological assessment: Interpreting the WISC-R intelligently. In B. B. Lahey & A. E. Kazdin (eds.), *Advances in clinical child psychology,* Vol. 3. New York: Plenum, 1980.

KAUFFMAN, J. M., & HALLAHAN, D. P. Learning disabil-

ity and hyperactivity (with comments on minimal brain dysfunction). In B. B. Lahey & A. E. Kazdin (eds.), *Advances in clinical child psychology,* Vol. 2. New York: Plenum, 1979.

KAUFMAN, I., & ROSENBLUM, L. A reaction to separation in infant monkeys: Anaclitic depression and conservation-withdrawal. *Psychosomatic Medicine,* 1967, *29,* 648–675.

KAUFMAN, M. R., & HEIMAN, M. (eds.). *Evolution of psychosomatic concepts: Anorexia nervosa, a paradigm.* New York: International Universities Press, 1964.

KAVALE, K. Meta-analysis of the relationship between visual perceptual skills and reading achievement. *Journal of Learning Disabilities,* 1982, *15,* 42–51.

KAVANAUGH, C. Emotional abuse and mental injury. *Journal of the American Academy of Child Psychiatry,* 1982, *21,* 171–177.

KAZDIN, A. E. Assessment techniques in childhood depression: A critical appraisal. *Journal of the American Academy of Child Psychiatry,* 1981, *20,* 358–375.

KAZDIN, A. E., & BOOTZIN, R. R. The token economy: An evaluative review. *Journal of Applied Behavior Analysis,* 1972, *5,* 343–372.

KAZDIN, A. E., & PETTI, T. A. Self-report and interview measures of childhood and adolescent depression. *Journal of Child Psychology and Psychiatry,* 1982, *23,* 437–457.

KELLAM, S. G., BROWN, C. H., & FLEMING, J. P. The prevention of teenage substance use: Longitudinal research and strategy. In T. J. Coates, A. C. Peterson, & C. Perry (eds.), *Adolescent health: Crossing the barriers.* New York: Academic Press, 1982.

KELLY, J. A., & DRABMAN, R. S. Generalizing response suppression of self-injurious behavior through an overcorrection punishment procedure: A case study. *Behavior Therapy,* 1977, *8,* 468–472.

KELLEY, T. L., MADDEN, R., GARDNER, E. F., & RUDMAN, H. C. *The Stanford Achievement Test.* New York: Harcourt Brace Jovanovich, 1964.

KELMAN, H. C. Human use of human subjects: The problem of deception in social psychological experiments. *Psychological Bulletin,* 1967, *67,* 1–11.

KELTY, M. Protection of persons who participate in applied research. In G. T. Hannah, W. P. Christian, & H. B. Clark (eds.), *Preservation of client rights.* New York: Free Press, 1981.

KEMPE, C. H., SILVERMAN, F. N., STEELE, B. F., DROEGEMUELLER, W., & SILVER, H. K. The battered-child syndrome. *Journal of American Medical Association,* 1962, *181,* 17–24.

KENDALL, P. C. Cognitive-behavioral interventions with children. In B. B. Lahey & A. E. Kazdin (eds.), *Advances in clinical child psychology,* Vol. 4. New York: Plenum, 1981.

KENDALL, P. C., & FINCH, A. J. Strategies for research in child psychopathology. In A. J. Finch and P. C. Kendall (eds.), *Clinical treatment and research in child psychopathology.* New York: Spectrum, 1979.

KENDALL, P. C., & HOLLON, S. D. *Cognitive-behavioral in-*

terventions: Theory, research, and procedures. New York: Academic Press, 1979.

KENNEDY, W. A. School phobia: Rapid treatment of 50 cases. *Journal of Abnormal Psychology,* 1965, *70,* 285–289.

KENNEDY, W. A., VAN DERIET, V., & WHITE, J. C., JR. A normative sample of intelligence and achievement of Negro elementary school children in the southeastern United States. *Monographs of the Society for Research in Child Development,* 1963, *28*(No. 6).

KENNELL, J. H., TRAUSE, M. A., & KLAUS, M. H. Evidence for a sensitive period in the human mother. In S. I. Harrison and J. F. McDermott (eds.), *New directions in childhood psychopathology.* New York: International Universities Press, 1980.

KENNY, T. J. Hyperactivity. In H. E. Rie & E. D. Rie (eds.), *Handbook of minimal brain dysfunctions.* New York: John Wiley, 1980.

KENT, R. N. A methodological critique of "Intervention for boys with conduct problems." *Journal of Consulting and Clinical Psychology,* 1976, *44,* 297–302.

KENT, R. N., O'LEARY, K. D., DIAMENT, C., & DIETZ, A. Expectation biases in observational evaluation of therapeutic change. *Journal of Consulting and Clinical Psychology,* 1974, *42,* 774–780.

KEOGH, B. K. Hyperactivity and learning disorders: Review and speculation. *Exceptional Child,* 1971, *38,* 101–109.

KEOGH, B. K., & BARKETT, C. J. An educational analysis of hyperactive children's achievement problems. In C. K. Whalen & B. Henker (eds.), *Hyperactive children.* New York: Academic Press, 1980.

KEOGH, B. K., & MARGOLIS, J. Learn to labor and to wait: Attentional problems of children with learning disorders. *Journal of Learning Disabilities,* 1976, *9,* 276–286.

KEPHART, N. C. *The slow learner in the classroom.* Columbus, Ohio: Chas. E. Merrill, 1960, 1971.

KESSEN, W. Research in the psychological development of infants: An overview. *Merrill-Palmer Quarterly,* 1963, *9,* 83–94.

KESSEN, W., HAITH, M. M., & SALAPATEK, P. H. Infancy. In P. H. Mussen (ed.), *Carmichael's manual of child psychology,* Vol. 1. New York: John Wiley, 1970.

KESSLER, J. N. History of minimal brain dysfunctions. In H. E. Rie and E. D. Rie (eds.), *Handbook of minimal brain dysfunctions.* New York: John Wiley, 1980.

KESSLER, J. W. *Psychopathology of childhood.* Englewood Cliffs, N.J.: Prentice-Hall, 1966.

KIMMEL, H. D., & KIMMEL, E. C. An instrumental conditioning method for the treatment of enuresis. *Journal of Behavior Therapy and Experimental Psychiatry,* 1970, *1,* 121–123.

KING, C. A., & YOUNG, R. D. Peer popularity and peer communication patterns: Hyperactive versus active but normal boys. *Journal of Abnormal Child Psychology,* 1981, *9,* 465–482.

KIRBY, F. D., & TOLER, H. C. Modification of pre-school isolate behavior: A case study. *Journal of Applied Behavior Analysis,* 1970, *3,* 309–314.

KIRK, S. A. *Behavioral diagnosis and remediation of learning disabilities.* Proceedings of the First Annual Meeting of the ACLD Conference on Exploration into the Problems of the Perceptually Handicapped Child. Chicago, Illinois, April 1963.

KIRK, S. A. *Educating exceptional children.* Boston: Houghton Mifflin, 1972.

KIRK, S. A., McCARTHY, J. J., & KIRK, W. D. *Illinois Test of Psycholinguistic Abilities.* Urbana, Ill.: University of Illinois Press, 1968.

KLEIN, N. C., ALEXANDER, J. F., & PARSONS, B. V. Impact of family systems intervention on recidivism and sibling delinquency: A model of primary prevention and program evaluation. *Journal of Consulting and Clinical Psychology,* 1977, *45,* 469–474.

KLOPFER, B., & KELLY, D. *The Rorschach technique.* Yonkers, N.Y.: World Book Company, 1942.

KNITZER, J. Child welfare: The role of federal policies. *Journal of Clinical Child Psychology,* 1981, *10,* 3–7.

KNOBLOCH, H., & PASAMANICK, B. *Gesell and Amatruda's developmental diagnosis.* New York: Harper & Row Pub., 1974.

KOEGEL, R. L., FIRESTONE, P. B., KRAMME, K. W., & DUNLAP, G. Increasing spontaneous play by suppressing self-stimulation in autistic children. *Journal of Applied Behavior Analysis,* 1974, *7,* 521–528.

KOHLBERG, L. Development of moral character and moral ideology. In M. Hoffman & L. Hoffman (eds.), *Review of child development research,* Vol. 1. New York: Russell Sage Foundation, 1964.

KOHLBERG, L. Moral stages and moralization: The cognitive-developmental approach. In T. Lickona (ed.), *Moral development and behavior: Theory, research and social issues.* New York: Holt, Rinehart and Winston, 1976.

KOHLBERG, L., LaCROSSE, J., & RICKS, D. The predictability of adult mental health from childhood behavior. In B. Wolman (ed.), *Manual of child psychopathology.* New York: McGraw-Hill, 1972.

KOHN, M. L. Social class and parent-child relationships: An interpretation. *American Journal of Sociology,* 1963, *68,* 471–480.

KOLATA, G. B. Behavioral teratology: Birth defects of the mind. *Science,* 1978, *202,* 732–734.

KOLKO, D. J., ANDERSON, L., & CAMPBELL, M. Sensory preference and overselective responding in autistic children. *Journal of Autism and Developmental Disorders,* 1980, *10,* 259–271.

KOLVIN, I. Psychoses in childhood—a comparative study. In M. Rutter (ed.), *Infantile autism: Concepts, characteristics, and treatment.* London: Churchill-Livingstone, 1971. (a)

KOLVIN, I. Studies in childhood psychoses. I. Diagnostic criteria and classification. *British Journal of Psychiatry,* 1971, *118,* 381–384. (b)

KOOCHER, G. P. Childhood, death, and cognitive development. *Developmental Psychology,* 1973, *9,* 369–375.

KOOCHER, G. P. Pediatric cancer: Psychosocial problems and the high costs of helping. *Journal of Clinical Child Psychology,* 1980, *9,* 2–5.

KOOCHER, G. P., & SALLAN, S. E. Pediatric oncology. In P. R. Magrab (ed.), *Psychological management of pediatric problems,* Vol. 1. Baltimore, Md.: University Park Press, 1978.

KOPPITZ, E. M. *The Bender Gestalt Test for young children.* New York: Grune & Stratton, 1964.

KOSKI, M. L. The coping processes in childhood diabetes. *Acta Paediatrica Scandinavica (Supplement),* 1969, *198,* 7–56.

KOSKI, M., & KUMENTO, A. The interrelationship between diabetic control and family life. In Z. Laron (ed.), *Pediatric and adolescent endocrinology (Vol. 3): Psychological aspects of balance of diabetes in juveniles.* New York: Karger, 1977.

KOTELCHUK, M. The infant's relationship to the father: Experimental evidence. In M. E. Lamb (ed.), *The role of the father in child development.* New York: John Wiley, 1976.

KOTSES, H., GLAUS, K. D., CRAWFORD, P. L., EDWARDS, J. E., & SCHERR, M. S. Operant reduction of frontalis EMG activity in the treatment of asthma in children. *Journal of Psychosomatic Research,* 1976, *20,* 453–459.

KOVACS, M., & BECK, A. T. An empirical-clinical approach toward a definition of childhood depression. In J. G. Schulterbrandt & A. Raskin (eds.), *Depression in children: Diagnosis, treatment, and conceptual models.* New York: Raven Press, 1977.

KOZLOFF, M. *Reaching the autistic child.* Champaign, Ill.: Research Press, 1973.

KUHN, T. S. *The structure of scientific revolutions.* Chicago: University of Chicago Press, 1962.

KURDEK, L. A. An integrative perspective of children's divorce adjustment. *American Psychologist,* 1981, *36,* 856–866.

LADD, G. Social skills and peer acceptance: Effects of a social learning method for training verbal social skills. *Child Development,* 1981, *52,* 171–178.

LaGRECA, A., & SANTOGROSSI, D. Social skills training with elementary school students: A behavioral group approach. *Journal of Consulting and Clinical Psychology,* 1980, *48,* 220–228.

LAHEY, B. B., DELAMATER, A., & KUPFER, D. Intervention strategies with hyperactive and learning-disabled children. In S. M. Turner, K. S. Calhoun, & H. E. Adams (eds.), *Handbook of clinical behavior therapy.* New York: Wiley-Interscience, 1981.

LAHEY, B., GREEN, K., & FOREHAND, R. On the independence of ratings of hyperactivity, conduct problems, and attentional deficits in children: A multiple regression analysis. *Journal of Consulting and Clinical Psychology,* 1980, *48,* 566–574.

LAHEY, B. B., VOSK, B. N., & HABIF, V. L. Behavioral assessment of learning disabled children: A rationale and strategy. *Behavioral Assessment,* 1981, *3,* 3–14.

LAMB, H. R., & ZUSMAN, J. A new look at primary prevention. *Hospital and Community Psychiatry,* 1981, *32,* 843–848.

LAMB, M. E. The role of the father: An overview. In M. E. Lamb (ed.), *The role of the father in child development.* New York: John Wiley, 1976.

LAMB, M. E. Social interaction in infancy and the development of personality. In M. E. Lamb (ed.), *Social and personality development.* New York: Holt, Rinehart and Winston, 1978.

LAMBERT, N. M., & SANDOVAL, J. The prevalence of learning disabilities in a sample of children considered hyperactive. *Journal of Abnormal Child Psychology,* 1980, *8,* 33–50.

LANDAUER, T. K., CARLSMITH, J. M., & LEPPER, M. Experimental analysis of the factors determining obedience of four-year-old children to adult females. *Child Development,* 1970, *41,* 601–611.

LANG, P. J., & MELAMED, B. G. Avoidance conditioning therapy of an infant with chronic ruminative vomiting. *Journal of Abnormal Psychology,* 1969, *74,* 139–142.

LANGHORNE, J., LONEY, J., PATERNITE, C., & BECHTHOLDT, H. Childhood hyperkinesis: A return to the source. *Journal of Consulting and Clinical Psychology,* 1976, *85,* 201–209.

LAPOUSE, R., & MONK, M. An epidemiologic study of behavior characteristics in children. *American Journal of Public Health,* 1958, *48,* 1134–1144.

LAPOUSE, R., & MONK, M. A. Fears and worries in a representative sample of children. *American Journal of Orthopsychiatry,* 1959, *29,* 803–818.

LAUER, R. M., CONNER, W. C., LEAVERTON, P. E., REITER, M. A., & CLARKE, W. R. Coronary heart disease risk factors in school children: The Muscatine study. *Journal of Pediatrics,* 1975, *86,* 697–706.

LAUFER, M. W., & DENHOFF, E. Hyperkinetic behavior syndrome in children. *Journal of Pediatrics,* 1957, *50,* 463–474.

LAUFER, M. W., DENHOFF, E., & SOLOMONS, G. Hyperkinetic impulse disorder in children's behavior problems. *Psychosomatic Medicine,* 1957, *19,* 39–49.

LAUFER, M. W., & SHETTY, T. Attentional deficit disorders. In H. I. Kaplan, A. M. Freedman, & B. J. Sadock (eds.), *Comprehensive textbook of psychiatry/III,* Vol. 3. Baltimore, Md.: Williams & Wilkins, 1980.

LAWLER, K. A., & ALLEN, M. T. Risk factors for hypertension in children: Their relationship to psychophysiological responses. *Journal of Psychosomatic Research,* 1981, *23,* 199–204.

LEACH, G. M. A comparison of the social behaviour of some normal and problem children. In N. Blurton Jones (ed.), *Ethological studies of child behaviour.* Cambridge: Cambridge University Press, 1972.

LEFF, R. Behavior modification and the psychoses of childhood: A review. *Psychological Bulletin,* 1968, *69,* 396–409.

LEFKOWITZ, M. Discussion of Dr. Gittelman-Klein's chapter. In J. G. Schulterbrandt & A. Raskin (eds.), *Depression in childhood: Diagnosis, treatment, and conceptual models.* New York: Raven Press, 1977.

LEFKOWITZ, M., & BURTON, N. Childhood depression: A critique of the concept. *Psychological Bulletin,* 1978, *85* (4), 716–726.

LEFKOWITZ, M., & TESINY, E. Assessment of childhood depression. *Journal of Consulting and Clinical Psychology,* 1980, *48,* 43–50.

LEITENBERG, H., AGRAS, W. S., & THOMSON, L. E. A sequential analysis of the effect of selective positive reinforcement in modifying anorexia nervosa. *Behaviour Research and Therapy,* 1968, *6,* 211–218.

LELAND, H. Mental retardation. In P. R. Magrab (ed.), *Psychological management of pediatric problems,* Vol. II. Baltimore, Md.: University Park Press, 1978.

LEMERT, E. M. *Instead of court: Diversion in juvenile justice.* Rockville, Md.: National Institute of Mental Health, 1971.

LEMERT, E. M. Diversion in juvenile justice: What hath been wrought. *Journal of Research in Crime and Delinquency,* 1981, *18,* 34–46.

LENNEBERG, E. H. *Biological foundations of language.* New York: John Wiley, 1967.

LEON, G. R., KENDALL, P. C., & GARBER, J. Depression in children: Parent, teacher, and child perspectives. *Journal of Abnormal Child Psychology,* 1980, *8,* 221–235.

LERNER, R. M., & SCHROEDER, C. Physique identification preference, and aversion in kindergarten children. *Developmental Psychology,* 1971, *5,* 538.

LEVENSTEIN, P. *VIP children reach school: Latest chapter.* Verbal Interaction Project. Progress Report, 1974.

LEVENTHAL, T., & SILLS, M. Self-image in school phobia. *American Journal of Orthopsychiatry,* 1964, *34,* 685–695.

LEVINE, M. D. Children with encopresis: A descriptive analysis. *Pediatrics,* 1975, *56,* 412–416.

LEVITT, E. E. The results of psychotherapy with children: An evaluation. *Journal of Consulting Psychology,* 1957, *21,* 189–196.

LEVITT, E. E. Psychotherapy with children: A further evaluation. *Behaviour Research and Therapy,* 1963, *1,* 45–51.

LEVY, F., DRUMBRELL, S., HOBBES, G., RYAN, M., WILTON, N., & WOODHILL, J. M. Hyperkinesis and diet: A double-blind crossover trial with a tartrazene challenge. *Medical Journal of Australia,* 1978, *1,* 61–64.

LEVY, F., & HOBBES, G. The diagnosis of attention deficit disorders (hyperkinesis) in children. *Journal of Child Psychiatry,* 1981, *20,* 376–384.

LEWINSOHN, P. A behavioral approach to depression. In R. J. Freidman & M. M. Katz (eds.), *The psychology of depression: Contemporary theory and research.* Washington D.C.: Winston, 1974.

LEWIS, S. A comparison of behavior therapy techniques in the reduction of fearful avoidance behavior. *Behavior Therapy,* 1974, *5,* 648–655.

LEWITTES, D. J., & ISRAEL, A. C. The effects of other-oriented consequences for ongoing delay of gratification in children. *Developmental Psychology,* 1978, *14,* 181–182.

LIEBERMAN, D. A. Behaviorism and the mind: A (limited) call for a return to introspection. *American Psychologist,* 1979, *34,* 319–333.

LIEBERT, R. M., & POULOS, R. W. Television as a moral teacher. In T. Lickona (ed.), *Moral development and behavior.* New York: Holt, Rinehart and Winston, 1976.

LIEBERT, R. M., & SCHWARTZBERG, N. S. Effects of mass media. *Annual Review of Psychology,* 1977, *28,* 141–173.

LIEBERT, R. M., & SPIEGLER, M. D. *Personality: Strategies and issues.* Homewood, Ill.: Dorsey Press, 1978.

LIEBERT, R. M., SPRAFKIN, J. N., & DAVISON, E. *The early window: Effects of television on children and youth.* New York: Pergamon Press, 1982.

LIEBERT, R. M., & WICKS-NELSON, R. *Developmental psychology.* Englewood Cliffs, N.J.: Prentice-Hall, 1981.

LILLY, M. S. (ed.), *Children with exceptional needs: A survey of special education.* New York: Holt, Rinehart and Winston, 1979. (a)

LILLY, M. S. Learning and behavior problems. A traditional categorical overview. In M. S. Lilly (ed.), *Children with exceptional needs.* New York: Holt, Rinehart and Winston, 1979. (b)

LILLY, M. S. Special education. Emerging issues. In M. S. Lilly (ed), *Children with exceptional needs.* New York: Holt, Rinehart and Winston, 1979. (c)

LILLY, M. S. Special education. Historical and traditional perspectives. In M. S. Lilly (eds.), *Children with exceptional needs.* New York: Holt, Rinehart and Winston, 1979. (d)

LINDQUIST, E. F., & HIERONYMUS, A. N. *Iowa Tests of Basic Skills Manuals.* New York: Houghton Mifflin, 1955–56.

LINKS, P. S., STOCKWELL, M., ABICHANDANI, F., & SIMEON, J. Minor physical anomalies in childhood autism. Part I. Their relationship to pre- and perinatal complications. *Journal of Autism and Developmental Disorders,* 1980, *10,* 273–285.

LINSCHEID, T. R. Disturbances of eating and feeding. In P. R. Magrab (ed.), *Psychological management of pediatric problems, Vol. 1: Early life conditions and chronic diseases.* Baltimore, Md.: University Park Press, 1978.

LIPSITT, L. P., ENGEN, T., & KAYE, H. Developmental changes in the olfactory threshold of the neonate. *Child Development,* 1963, *34,* 371–376.

LOBITZ, G. K., & JOHNSON, S. M. Normal versus deviant children: A multimethod comparison. *Journal of Abnormal Child Psychology,* 1975, *3,* 353–374. (a)

LOBITZ, G. K., & JOHNSON, S. M. Parental manipulation of the behavior of normal and deviant children. *Child Development,* 1975, *46,* 719–726. (b)

LOCKYER, L., & RUTTER, M. A five- to fifteen-year follow-up of infantile psychoses: III. Psychological characteristics. *British Journal of Psychiatry,* 1969, *115,* 765–882.

LONEY, J., LANGHORNE, J., & PATERNITE, G. An empirical basis for subgrouping the hyperkinetic/minimal brain dysfunction syndrome. *Journal of Abnormal Child Psychology,* 1978, *87,* 431–441.

LOPEZ, R. Hyperactivity in twins. *Canadian Psychiatric Association Journal,* 1965, *10,* 421–426.

LORAND, S. Anorexia nervosa: Report of a case. In M. R. Kaufman & M. Heiman (eds.), *Evolution of psychosomatic concepts: Anorexia nervosa, a paradigm.* New York: International Universities Press, 1964. (Reprinted from *Psychosomatic Medicine,* 1943, *5,* 282–292.)

LORENZ, K. *Evolution and modification of behavior.* Chicago: University of Chicago Press, 1965.

LORENZ, K. *On aggression.* New York: Bantam Books, 1967.

LORION, R. P., & COWEN, E. L. Referral to a school mental health project: A screening note. *American Journal of Community Psychology,* 1978, *6,* 247–251.

LORR, M., & JENKINS, R. L. Patterns of maladjustment in children. *Journal of Clinical Psychology,* 1953, *9,* 16–19.

LOTTER, V. Epidemiology of autistic conditions in young children. I. Prevalence. *Social Psychiatry,* 1966, *1,* 124–137.

LOTTER, V. Factors related to outcome in autistic children. *Journal of Autism and Childhood Schizophrenia,* 1974, *4,* 263–277. (a)

LOTTER, V. Social adjustment and placement of autistic children in Middlesex: A follow-up study. *Journal of Autism and Childhood Schizophrenia,* 1974, *4,* 11–32. (b)

LOTTER, V. Follow-up studies. In M. Rutter and E. Schopler (eds.), *Autism: A reappraisal of concepts and treatment.* New York: Plenum, 1978.

LOVAAS, O. I. *The autistic child: Language development through behavior modification.* New York: Irvington, 1977.

LOVAAS, O. I. Contrasting illness and behavioral models for the treatment of autistic children: A historical perspective. *Journal of Autism and Developmental Disorders,* 1979, *9,* 315–323.

LOVAAS, O. I., FREITAG, G., GOLD, V. J., & KASSORLA, I. C. Recording apparatus and procedure for observation of behavior of children in free play settings. *Journal of Experimental Child Psychology,* 1965, *2,* 108–120.

LOVAAS, O. I., KOEGEL, R., & SCHREIBMAN, L. Stimulus overselectivity in autism: A review of research. *Psychological Bulletin,* 1979, *86,* 1236–1254.

LOVAAS, O. I., KOEGEL, R. L., SIMMONS, J. Q., & LONG, J. S. Some generalization and follow-up measures on autistic children in behavior therapy. *Journal of Applied Behavior Analysis,* 1973, *6,* 131–165.

LOVAAS, O. I., & NEWSOM, C. D. Behavior modification with psychotic children. In H. Leitenberg (ed.), *Handbook of behavior modification and behavior therapy.* Englewood Cliffs, N.J.: Prentice-Hall, 1976.

LOVAAS, I. O., & SIMMONS, J. Q. Manipulation of self-destruction in three retarded children. *Journal of Applied Behavior Analysis,* 1969, *2,* 143–157.

LOVAAS, O. I., YOUNG, D. B., & NEWSOM, C. D. Childhood psychosis: Behavioral treatment. In B. B. Wolman (ed.), *Handbook of treatment of mental disorders in childhood and adolescence.* Englewood Cliffs, N.J.: Prentice-Hall, 1978.

LOVIBOND, S. H. *Conditioning and enuresis.* Oxford: Pergamon, 1964.

LOVIBOND, S. H., & COOTE, M. A. Enuresis. In C. G. Costello (ed.), *Symptoms of psychopathology.* New York: John Wiley, 1970.

LOWE, K., & LUTZKER, J. Increasing compliance to a medical regimen with a juvenile diabetic. *Behavior Therapy,* 1979, *10,* 57–67.

LOWMAN, J. Grief intervention and Sudden Infant Death Syndrome. *American Journal of Community Psychology,* 1979, *7,* 665–677.

LUBAR, J. F., & SHOUSE, M. N. Use of biofeedback in the treatment of seizure disorders and hyperactivity. In B. B. Lahey & A. E. Kazdin (eds.), Advances in clinical child psychology, Vol. 1. New York: Plenum, 1977.

LUNDBERG, O., & WALINDER, J. Anorexia nervosa and signs of brain damage. *International Journal of Neuropsychiatry,* 1967, *3,* 165–173.

LUPARELLO, T., LYONS, H. A., BLEECKER, E. R., & MCFADDEN, E. R., JR. Influences of suggestion on airways reactivity in asthmatic subjects. *Psychosomatic Medicine,* 1968, *30,* 819–825.

LUTZKER, J. R. Deviant family systems. In B. B. Lahey & A. E. Kazdin (eds.), *Advances in clinical child psychology,* Vol. 3. New York: Plenum, 1980.

LYLE, J. G., & GOYEN, J. D. Visual recognition, developmental lag, and strephosymbolia in reading retardation. *Journal of Abnormal Child Psychology,* 1968, *73,* 25–29.

LYNN, D. B. *The father: His role in child development.* Monterey, Calif.: Brooks/Cole, 1974.

MACCOBY, E. E., & JACKLIN, C. *The psychology of sex differences.* Stanford Calif.: Stanford University Press, 1974.

MACFARLAND, J. W., ALLEN, L., & HONZIK, M. P. *A developmental study of the behavior problems of normal children.* Berkeley: University of California Press, 1954.

MACFARLAND, J. W., ALLEN, L., & HONZIK, M. P. *A developmental study of the behavior problems of normal children between 21 months and 14 years.* Berkeley: University of California Press, 1954.

MACHOVER, K. *Personality projection in the drawing of the human figure.* Springfield, Ill.: Chas. C Thomas, 1949.

MACMILLAN, D. L. Motivational differences: Cultural-familial retardates vs. normal subjects on expectancy for failure. *American Journal of Mental Deficiency,* 1969, *74,* 254–258.

MACMILLAN, D. L., & KEOGH, B. K. Normal and retarded children's expectancy for failure. *Developmental Psychology,* 1971, *4,* 343–348.

MACRAE, J. M. Retests of children given mental tests as infants. *Journal of Genetic Psychology,* 1955, *87,* 111–119.

MADDOX, G. L., BACK, K. W., & LIEDERMAN, V. R. Overweight as social deviance and disability. *Journal of Health and Social Behavior,* 1968, *9,* 287–298.

MAHLER, M. S. *The psychoanalytic study of the child.* New York: International Universities Press, 1952.

MAHLER, M. S. Sadness and grief in infancy and childhood. *Psychoanalytic Study of the Child,* 1961, *16,* 332–351.

MAHONEY, M. J. Reflections on the cognitive-learning trend in psychotherapy. *American Psychologist,* 1977, *32,* 5–13.

MALINOWSKI, B. *Sex and repression in savage society.* New York: Harcourt Brace Jovanovich, 1927.

MALLICK, S. K., & McCANDLESS, B. R. A study of catharsis of aggression. *Journal of Personality and Social Psychology,* 1966, *4, 591–596.*

MALMQUIST, C. P. Childhood depression: A clinical and behavioral perspective. In J. G. Schulterbrandt & A. Raskin (eds.), *Depression in childhood: Diagnosis, treatment, and conceptual models.* New York: Raven Press, 1977.

MANSHEIM, P. Emotional and behavioral data in a case of the 48, XXYY syndrome. *Journal of Pediatric Psychology,* 1979, *4,* 363–370.

MARGOLIN, C. R. A survey of children's views on their

rights. *Journal of Clinical Child Psychology*, 1982, *11*, 96–100.

MARHOLIN, D., LUISELLI, J. K., & TOWNSEND, N. M. Overcorrection: An examination of its rationale and treatment effectiveness. In M. Hersen, R. M. Eisler, & P. M. Miller (eds.), *Progress in behavior modification*, Vol. 9. New York: Academic Press, 1980.

MARKS, I. M., & GELDER, M. G. Different onset ages in varieties of phobia. *American Journal of Psychiatry*, 1966, *123*, 218–221.

MARSTON, A. R., LONDON, P., & COOPER, L. M. Note on the eating behaviour of children varying in weight. *Journal of Child Psychology and Psychiatry and Allied Disciplines*, 1976, *17*, 221–224.

MARTIN, B. Parent-child relations. In F. D. Horowitz, E. M. Hetherington, S. Scarr-Salapatek, & G. M. Siegel (eds.), *Review of child development research*, Vol. 4. Chicago: University of Chicago Press, 1975.

MARTINSON, R. What works? — Questions and answers about prison reform. *The Public Interest*, 1974, *35*, 22–54.

MASH, E. J., & DALBY, J. T. Behavioral interventions for hyperactivity. In R. L. Trites (ed.), *Hyperactivity in children*. Baltimore, Md.: University Park Press, 1979.

MASON, E. Obesity in pet dogs. *Veterinarian Record*, 1970, *86*, 612–616.

MASOVER, L., & STAMPLER, J. Address to the Convention of the American Public Health Association, 1976. Cited in U.S. Senate Select Committee on Nutrition and Human Needs (eds.), *Dietary Goals for the United States*. Washington, D.C.: Government Printing Office, 1977, 75–77.

MASTERS, J. C. Developmental psychology. *Annual Review of Psychology*, 1981, *32*, 117–151.

MASTERS, J. C., & FURMAN, W. Popularity, individual friendship selection, and specific peer interaction among children. *Developmental Psychology*, 1981, *17*, 344–350.

MATARAZZO, J. E. *Wechsler's measurement and appraisal of adult intelligence*. Baltimore, Md.: Williams & Wilkins, 1972.

MATHÉ, A. A., & KNAPP, P. H. Emotional and adrenal reactions to stress in bronchial asthma. *Psychosomatic Medicine*, 1971, *33*, 323–338.

MATTIS, S. Dyslexia syndromes: A working hypothesis that works. In A. L. Benton & D. Pearl (eds.), *Dyslexia*. New York: Oxford University Press, 1978.

MATTIS, S., FRENCH, J. H., & RAPIN, I. Dyslexia in children and young adults: The independent neuropsychological syndromes. *Developmental Medicine and Child Neurology*, 1975, *17*, 150–163.

MATTISON, R., CANTWELL, D. P., RUSSELL, A. T., & WILL, L. A comparison of DSM-II and DSM-III in the diagnosis of childhood psychiatric disorders: II. Interrater agreement. *Archives of General Psychiatry*, 1979, *36*, 1217–1222.

MAYRON, L. M., OTT, J. N., NATIONS, R., & MAYRON, E. L. Light, radiation, and academic behavior: Initial studies on the effects of full-spectrum lighting and radiation shielding on behavior and academic performance of school children. *Academic Therapy*, 1974, *10*, 33–47.

McADOO, W. G., & DeMYER, M. K. Personality characteristics of parents. In M. Rutter & E. Schopler (eds.),

Autism: A reappraisal of concepts and treatment. New York: Plenum, 1978.

McASKIE, M. Carelessness or fraud in Sir Cyril Burt's kinship data? A critique of Jensen's analysis. *American Psychologist*, 1978, *33*, 496–498.

McCAAN, D. C., & PRENTICE, N. M. The facilitating effects of money and moral set on the moral judgment of adolescent delinquents. *Journal of Abnormal Psychology*, 1973, *82*, 81–84.

McCALL, R. B., APPLEBAUM, M. I., & HOGARTY, P. S. Developmental changes in mental performance. *Monographs of the Society for Research in Child Development*, 1973, *38* (Whole No. 150).

McCLEARN, G. E. The inheritance of behavior. In L. Postman (ed.), *Psychology in the making*. New York: Knopf, 1963.

McCLEARN, G. E. Genetic influences on behavior and development. In P. H. Mussen (ed.), *Carmichael's manual of child development*. New York: John Wiley, 1970.

McCORD, J., & McCORD, W. The effects of parental role model of criminality. *Journal of Social Issues*, 1958, *14*, 66–75.

McDERMOTT, J., & FINCH, S. Ulcerative colitis in children: Reassessment of a dilemma. *Journal of the American Academy of Child Psychiatry*, 1967, *6*, 512–525.

McGARVEY, B., GABRIELLI, W. F., JR., BENTLER, P. M., & MEDNICK, S. A. Rearing social class, education, and criminality: A multiple indication model. *Journal of Abnormal Psychology*, 1981, *90*, 354–364.

McLEAN, J., & CHING, A. Follow-up study of relationships between family situation and bronchial asthma in children. *Journal of the American Academy of Child Psychiatry*, 1973, *12*, 142–161.

McNEILL, D. The development of language. In P. H. Mussen (ed.), *Carmichael's manual of child psychology*, Vol. 1. New York: John Wiley, 1970.

McNEILL, D. How to resolve two paradoxes and escape a dilemma: Comments on Dr. Cazden's paper. In K. J. Connolly & J. S. Bruner (eds.), *The growth of competence*. London: Academic Press, 1974.

MEDNICK, S. A. A learning theory approach to research in schizophrenia. *Psychological Bulletin*, 1958, *55*, 316–327.

MEDNICK, S. A. Breakdown in individuals at high-risk for schizophrenia: Possible predispositional factors. *Mental Hygiene*, 1970, *54*, 50–63.

MEDNICK, S. A., & HUTCHINGS, B. Genetic and psychophysiological factors in asocial behaviour. *Journal of the American Academy of Child Psychiatry*, 1978, *17*, 209–223.

MEDNICK, S. A., & SCHULSINGER, F. Some premorbid characteristics related to breakdown in children with schizophrenic mothers. In D. Rosenthal and S. S. Kety (eds.), *The transmission of schizophrenia*. Elmsford, N.Y.: Pergamon Press, 1968.

MEDNICK, S. A., & WITKIN-LANOIL, G. H. Intervention in children at high-risk for schizophrenia. In G. W. Albee & J. M. Joffe (eds.), *Primary prevention of psychopathology. Vol. 1: The issues*. Hanover, N.H.: University Press of New England, 1977.

MEICHENBAUM, D. Examination of model characteristics

in reducing avoidance behavior. *Journal of Personality and Social Psychology,* 1971, *17,* 298–307.

MEICHENBAUM, D. *Cognitive-behavior modification.* New York: Plenum, 1977.

MEICHENBAUM, D. Teaching children self-control. In B. B. Lahey & A. E. Kazdin (eds.), *Advances in child clinical psychology,* Vol. 2. New York: Plenum, 1979.

MEICHENBAUM, D. H., & GOODMAN, J. Training impulsive children to talk to themselves: A means of developing self-control. *Journal of Abnormal Psychology,* 1971, *77,* 115–126.

MELAMED, B. G. Behavioral approaches to fear in dental settings. In M. Hersen, R. M. Eisler, & P. M. Miller (eds.), *Progress in behavior modification,* Vol. 7. New York: Academic Press, 1979.

MELAMED, B. G., & JOHNSON, S. B. Chronic illness: Asthma and juvenile diabetes. In E. J. Mash & L. G. Terdal (eds.), *Behavioral assessment of childhood disorders.* New York: Guilford Press, 1981.

MELAMED, B. G., & SIEGEL, L. J. Reduction of anxiety in children facing hospitalization and surgery by use of filmed modeling. *Journal of Consulting and Clinical Psychology,* 1975, *43,* 511–521.

MELAMED, B. G., YURCHESON, R., FLEECE, E. L., HUTCHERSON, S., & HAWES, R. Effects of film modeling on the reduction of anxiety-related behaviors in individuals varying in level of previous experience in the stress situation. *Journal of Consulting and Clinical Psychology,* 1978, *46,* 1357–1367.

MELTON, G. B. Children's concepts of their rights. *Journal of Clinical Child Psychology,* 1980, *9,* 186–190.

MERCATORIS, M., & CRAIGHEAD, W. E. The effects of nonparticipant observation on teacher and pupil classroom behavior. *Journal of Educational Psychology,* 1974, *66,* 512–519.

MERLUZZI, T. V., RUDY, T. E., & GLASS, C. R. *The information-processing paradigm: Implications for chemical science.* New York: Guilford Press, 1981.

MESIBOV, G. B., SCHROEDER, C. S., & WESSON, L. Parental concerns about their children. *Journal of Pediatric Psychology,* 1977, *2,* 13–17.

MESSER, S. B. Reflection-impulsivity: A review. *Psychological Bulletin,* 1976, *83,* 1026–1052.

MIKLICH, D. R., RENNE, C. M., CREER, T. L., ALEXANDER, A. B., CHAI, H., DAVIS, M. H., HOFFMAN, A., & DANKER-BROWN, P. The clinical utility of behavior therapy as an adjunctive treatment for asthma. *Journal of Allergy and Clinical Immunology,* 1977, *5,* 285–294.

MILGRAM, S. Behavioral study of obedience. *Journal of Abnormal and Social Psychology,* 1963, *67,* 371–378.

MILICH, R., & LONEY, J. The role of hyperactivity and aggressive symptomatology in predicting adolescent outcome among hyperactive children. *Journal of Pediatric Psychology,* 1979, *4,* 93–112.

MILICH, R., LONEY, J., & LANDAU, S. Independent dimensions of hyperactivity and aggression: A validation with playroom observation data. *Journal of Abnormal Psychology,* 1982, *91,* 183–198.

MILLER, F. J., BILLEWICZ, W. Z., & THOMSON, A. M.

Growth from birth to adult life of 442 Newcastle-Upon-Tyne children. *British Journal of Preventative and Social Medicine,* 1972, *26,* 224–230.

MILLER, L. C., BARRETT, C. L., & HAMPE, E. Phobias of childhood in a prescientific era. In A. Davids (ed.), *Child personality and psychopathology: Current topics,* Vol. 1. New York: John Wiley, 1974.

MILLER, L. C., BARRETT, C. L., HAMPE, E., & NOBLE, H. Comparison of reciprocal inhibition psychotherapy and waiting list control for phobic children. *Journal of Abnormal Psychology,* 1972, *79,* 269–279.

MILLER, N. E. Learning of visceral and glandular responses. *Science,* 1969, *163,* 434–445.

MILLER, W. A., & ERBE, R. W. Prenatal diagnosis of genetic disorders. *Southern Medical Journal,* 1978, *71,* 201–207.

MILLICAN, F. K., & LOURIE, R. S. The child with pica and his family. In E. J. Anthony and C. Koupernik (eds.), *The child in his family,* Vol. 1. New York: Wiley-Interscience, 1970.

MINDE, K., LEWIN, D., WEISS, G., LAVIGUEUR, H., DOUGLAS, V., & SYKES, E. The hyperactive child in elementary school: A 5-year controlled follow-up. *Exceptional Children,* 1971, *38,* 215–221.

MINUCHIN, S., BAKER, L., ROSMAN, B., LIEBMAN, R., MILMAN, L., & TODD, T. A conceptual model of psychosomatic illness in children. *Archives of General Psychiatry,* 1975, *32,* 1031–1038.

MINUCHIN, S., ROSMAN, B. L., & BAKER, L. *Psychosomatic Families: Anorexia nervosa in context.* Cambridge, Mass.: Harvard University Press, 1978.

MISCHEL, W. On the interface of cognition and personality: Beyond the person-situation debate. *American Psychologist,* 1979, *34,* 740–754.

MISHLER, E. G., & WAXLER, N. E. Family interactional processes and schizophrenia: A review of current theories. *Merrill-Palmer Quarterly,* 1965, *11,* 269–315.

MNOOKIN, R. Children's rights: Beyond kiddie libbers and child savers. *Journal of Clinical Child Psychology,* 1978, *7,* 163–167.

MOFFITT, T. E., GABRIELLI, W. F., MEDNICK, S. A., & SCHULSINGER, F. Socioeconomic status, IQ, and delinquency. *Journal of Abnormal Psychology,* 1981, *90,* 152–156.

MOORE, K. L. *Before we are born.* Philadelphia: Saunders, 1974.

MORRIS, R. J., & KRATOCHWILL, T. R. *Treating children's fears and phobias: A behavioral approach.* Elmsford, N.Y.: Pergamon Press, 1983.

MORRISON, G. C., & COLLIER, J. G.: Family treatment approaches to suicidal children and adolescents. *Journal of the American Academy of Child Psychiatry,* 1969, *8,* 140–153.

MOSS, H. A. Sex, age, and state as determinants of mother-infant interaction. *Merrill-Palmer Quarterly,* 1967, *13,* 19–36.

MOSTOFSKY, D. I., & BALASCHAK, B. A. Psychobiological control of seizures. *Psychological Bulletin,* 1977, *84,* 723–750.

MOWRER, O. H. A stimulus-response analysis of anxiety and its role as a reinforcing agent. *Psychological Review,* 1939, *46,* 553–565.

MOWRER, O. H., & MOWRER, W. M. Enuresis: A method for its study and treatment. *American Journal of Orthopsychiatry,* 1938, *8,* 436–459.

MUNSINGER, H. Children's resemblance to their biological and adoptive parents in two ethnic groups. *Behavior Genetics,* 1975, *5,* 239–254.

MURPHY, L. B., & MORIARTY, A. E. *Vulnerability, coping, and growth.* New Haven: Yale University Press, 1976.

MURRAY, H. A. *Thematic Apperception Test.* Cambridge, Mass.: Harvard University Press, 1943.

MUSSEN, P. H., & JONES, M. C. Self-conceptions, motivations, and interpersonal attitudes of early and late maturing boys. *Child Development,* 1957, *28,* 243–256.

MYERS, C. E., NIHIRA, K., & ZETLIN, A. The measurement of adaptive behavior. In N. R. Ellis (ed.), *Handbook of mental deficiency.* Hillsdale, N.J.: Lawrence Erlbaum Associates, 1979.

MYERS, D. I., & GOLDFARB, W. Studies of perplexity in mothers of schizophrenic children. *American Journal of Orthopsychiatry,* 1961, *31,* 551–564.

NANNIS, E. D., SUSMAN, E. J., STROPE, B. E., WOODRUFF, P. J., HERSH, S. P., LEVINE, A. S., & PIZZO, P. A. Correlates of control in pediatric cancer patients and their families. *Journal of Pediatric Psychology,* 1982, *7,* 75–84.

National Advisory Committee on Handicapped Children: First Annual Report. Washington, D.C.: U.S. Office of Education, 1968.

NEALE, J. M., & OLTMANNS, T. F. *Schizophrenia.* New York: John Wiley, 1980.

NEEDLEMAN, H. L., GUNNOE, G., LEVITON, A., REED, R., PERESIE, H., MAHER, C., & BARNETT, P. Deficits in psychological and classroom performance of children with elevated dentine lead levels. *New England Journal of Medicine,* 1979, *300,* 689–695.

NEISSER, U. *Cognitive psychology.* Englewood Cliffs, N.J.: Prentice-Hall, 1967.

NELSON, K. Structure and strategy in learning to talk. *Monographs of the Society for Research in Child Development,* 1973, *38* (no. 149).

NELSON, K. Concept, word, and sentence: Interrelations in acquisition and development. *Psychological Review,* 1974, *81,* 267–285.

NELSON, K. Individual difference in language development: Implications for development and language. *Developmental Psychology,* 1981, *17,* 170–187.

NEMIAH, J. C. Phobic disorder (Phobic neurosis). In H. I. Kaplan, A. M. Freedman, & B. J. Sadock (eds.), *Comprehensive textbook of psychiatry/III,* Vol. 2. Baltimore, Md.: Williams & Wilkins, 1980.

NEUHAUS, E. C. A personality study of asthmatic and cardiac children. *Psychosomatic Medicine,* 1958, *20,* 181–194.

NEWELL, K. M., & KENNEDY, J. A. Knowledge of results and children's motor learning. *Developmental Psychology,* 1978, *14,* 531–536.

NEWSOM, C., & RINCOVER, A. Autism. In E. J. Mash and L. G. Terdal (eds.), *Behavioral assessment of children's disorders.* New York: Guilford Press, 1981.

NIHIRA, K., FOSTER, R., SHELLHAUS, M., & LELAND, H. *AAMD adaptive behavior scale.* Washington D.C.: American Association on Mental Deficiency, 1974.

NISBETT, R. E. Hunger, obesity and the VMH. *Psychological Review,* 1972, *79,* 433–453.

NOCELLA, J., & KAPLAN, R. M. Training children to cope with dental treatment. *Journal of Pediatric Psychology,* 1982, *7,* 175–178.

NORDYKE, N. S., BAER, D. M., ETZEL, B. C., & LE BLANC, J. M. Implications of the stereotyping of modification of sex role. *Journal of Applied Behavior Analysis,* 1977, *10,* 553–557.

NYE, F. I. Child adjustment in broken and in unhappy unbroken homes. *Marriage and Family Living,* 1957, *19,* 356–360.

O'CONNOR, N., & TIZARD, J. *The social problems of mental deficiency.* New York: Pergamon Press, 1956.

O'CONNOR, R. D. Modification of social withdrawal through symbolic modeling. *Journal of Applied Behavior Analysis,* 1969, *2,* 15–22.

O'CONNOR, R. D. The relative efficacy of modeling, shaping, and combined procedures. *Journal of Abnormal Psychology,* 1972, *79,* 327–334.

ODEN, S., & ASHER, S. Coaching children in skills for friendship making. *Child Development,* 1977, *48,* 495–506.

OFFER, D., SABSHIN, M., & MARCUS, D. Clinical evaluation of normal adolescents. *American Journal of Psychiatry,* 1965, *121,* 864–872.

OGBU, J. U. Origins of human competence: A cultural-ecological perspective. *Child Development,* 1981, *52,* 413–429.

ÖHMAN, A., ERIXON, G., & LÖFBERG, I. Phobias and preparedness: Phobic versus neutral pictures as conditioned stimuli for human autonomic responses. *Journal of Abnormal Psychology,* 1975, *84,* 41–45.

O'KEEFE, A. (ed.). *What Head Start means to families.* Washington D.C.: U.S. Department of Health and Human Services, 1979.

O'LEARY, K. D. Behavior modification in the classroom: A rejoinder to Winnett and Winkler. *Journal of Applied Behavior Analysis,* 1972, *5,* 505–511.

O'LEARY, K. D. *The etiology of hyperactivity.* Paper presented at the Second Annual Italian Behavior Therapy Association Meeting, Venice, Italy, 1978.

O'LEARY, K. D. Pills or skills for hyperactive children. *Journal of Applied Behavior Analysis,* 1980, *13,* 191–204.

O'LEARY, K. D., & JOHNSON, S. B. Psychological assessment. In H. C. Quay & J. S. Werry (eds.), *Psychopathological disorders of childhood,* 2nd ed. New York: John Wiley, 1979.

O'LEARY, K. D., & O'LEARY, S. G. *Classroom management: The successful use of behavior modification,* 2nd ed. Elmsford, N.Y.: Pergamon Press, 1977.

O'LEARY, K. D., PELHAM, W. E., ROSENBAUM, M. A., & PRICE, G. H. Behavioral treatment of hyperkinetic children. *Clinical Pediatrics,* 1976, *15,* 510–515.

O'LEARY, K. D., ROSENBAUM, A., & HUGHES, P. C. Fluorescent lighting: A purported source of hyperactive behavior. *Journal of Abnormal Child Psychology,* 1978, *6,* 285–289.

O'LEARY, S. G., & DUBEY, D. R. Applications of self-control procedures by children: A review. *Journal of Applied Behavior Analysis,* 1979, *12,* 449–465.

O'LEARY, S. G., & O'LEARY, K. D. Behavioral treatment for hyperactive children. In R. M. Knights & D. J. Bakker (eds.), *Treatment of hyperactive and learning disordered children.* Baltimore, Md.: University Park Press, 1980.

O'LEARY, S. G., & PELHAM, W. E. Behavioral therapy and withdrawal of stimulant medication with hyperactive children. *Pediatrics,* 1978, *61,* 211–217.

O'LEARY, S. G., & STEEN, P. L. Subcategorizing hyperactivity: The Stony Brook Scale. *Journal of Consulting and Clinical Psychology,* 1982, *50,* 426–432.

OLLENDICK, T. H. Fear reduction techniques with children. In M. Hersen, R. M. Eisler, & P. M. Miller (eds.), *Progress in behavior modification,* Vol. 8. New York: Academic Press, 1979.

OLLENDICK, T. H., & CERNY, J. A. *Clinical behavior therapy with children.* New York: Plenum, 1981.

OLLENDICK, T. H., & MATSON, J. L. Overcorrection: An overview. *Behavior Therapy,* 1978, *9,* 830–842.

ORNITZ, E. M. Neurophysiologic studies. In M. Rutter & E. Schopler (eds.), *Autism: A reappraisal of concepts and treatment.* New York: Plenum, 1978.

ORNITZ, E. M., & RITVO, E. R. Perceptual inconstancy in early infantile autism. *Archives of General Psychiatry,* 1968, *18,* 76–98.

ORRIS, J. B. Visual monitoring performance in three subgroups of male delinquents. *Journal of Abnormal Psychology,* 1969, *74,* 227–229.

ORTON, S. T. *Reading, writing, and speech problems in children.* New York: W. W. Norton and Co., 1937.

PADILLA, E. R., ROHSENOW, D. J., & BERGMAN, A. B. Predicting accident frequency in children. *Pediatrics,* 1976, *58,* 223–226.

PALKES, H., & STEWART, M. Intellectual ability and performance of hyperactive children. *American Journal of Orthopsychiatry,* 1972, *42,* 35–39.

PALMER, F. H., & SEMLEAR, T. Early intervention: The Harlem study. In R. M. Liebert, R. W. Poulos, & G. D. Marmor (eds.), *Developmental psychology.* Englewood Cliffs, N.J.: Prentice-Hall, 1977.

PARKE, R. D., & COLLMER, C. W. Child abuse: An interdisciplinary analysis. In E. M. Hetherington (ed.), *Review of child development research.* Chicago: University of Chicago Press, 1975.

PARSONS, B. V., & ALEXANDER, J. F. Short-term family intervention: A therapy outcome study. *Journal of Consulting and Clinical Psychology,* 1973, *41,* 195–201.

PARTRIDGE, J. W., GARNER, A. M., THOMPSON, C. W., & CHERRY, T. Attitudes of adolescents toward their diabetes. *American Journal of Diseases of Children,* 1972, *124,* 226–229.

PASCHALIS, A. P., KIMMEL, H. D., & KIMMEL, E. Further study of diurnal instrumental conditioning in the treatment of enuresis nocturna. *Journal of Behavior Therapy and Experimental Psychiatry,* 1972, *3,* 253–256.

PATTERSON, G. R. Interventions for boys with conduct problems: Multiple settings, treatments, and criteria. *Journal of Consulting and Clinical Psychology,* 1974, *42,* 471–481.

PATTERSON, G. R. *Families.* Champaign, Ill.: Research Press, 1975.

PATTERSON, G. R. The aggressive child: Victim and architect of a coercive system. In L. A. Hamerlynck, L. C. Handy, & E. J. Mash (eds.), *Behavior modification and families.* New York: Brunner/Mazel, 1976.

PATTERSON, G. R. Naturalistic observation in clinical assessment. *Journal of Abnormal Child Psychology,* 1977, *5,* 309–322.

PATTERSON, G. R. Mothers: The unacknowledged victims. *Monographs of the Society for Research in Child Development,* 1980, *45,* (Serial No. 186).

PATTERSON, G. R., & GULLION, M. E. *Living with children: New methods for parents and teachers.* Champaign, Ill.: Research Press, 1968.

PATTERSON, G. R., LITTMAN, R. A., & BRICKER, W. Assertive behavior in children: A step toward a theory of aggression. *Monographs of the Society for Research in Child Development,* 1967, *32* (Serial No. 113).

PATTERSON, G. R., REID, J. B., JONES, R. R., & CONGER, R. E. *A social learning approach to family intervention,* Vol. 1. Eugene, Ore.: Castalia, 1975.

PEARCE, J. Depressive disorders in childhood. *Journal of Child Psychology and Psychiatry,* 1977, *18,* 79–83.

PEASE, D., WOLENS, L., & STOCKDALE, D. F. Relationships and prediction of infant tests. *Journal of Genetic Psychology,* 1973, *122,* 31–35.

PEED, S., ROBERTS, M., & FOREHAND, R. Evaluation of the effectiveness of standardized parent training program in altering the interaction of mothers and their noncompliant children. *Behavior Modification,* 1977, *1,* 323–350.

PESHKIN, M. M. Intractable asthma of childhood: Rehabilitation at the institutional level with a follow-up of 150 cases. *International Archives of Allergy,* 1959, *15,* 91–101.

PETERSON, D. R. Behavior problems of middle childhood. *Journal of Consulting Psychology,* 1961, *25,* 205–209.

PETERSON, L., & RIDLEY-JOHNSON, R. Pediatric hospital response to survey on prehospital preparation for children. *Journal of Pediatric Psychology,* 1980, *5,* 1–7.

PETERSON, L., & SHIGETOMI, C. One year follow-up of elective surgery child patients receiving preoperative preparation. *Journal of Pediatric Psychology,* 1982, *7,* 43–48.

PHILLIPS, E. L. Achievement Place: Token reinforcement procedures in a home-style rehabilitation setting for 'predelinquent' boys. *Journal of Applied Behavior Analysis,* 1968, *1,* 213–223.

PHILLIPS, E. L., PHILLIPS, E. A., FIXSEN, D. L., & WOLF, M. M. Achievement place: Modification of the behaviors of predelinquent boys within a token economy. *Journal of Applied Behavior Analysis,* 1971, *4,* 45–59.

PHILLIPS, E. L., PHILLIPS, E. A., FIXSEN, D. L., & WOLF, M. M. Behavior shaping for delinquents. *Psychology Today,* 1973, *1,* 74–79.

PHILLIPS, E. L., PHILLIPS, E. A., WOLF, M. M., & FIXSEN, D. L. Achievement Place: Development of the elected manager system. *Journal of Applied Behavior Analysis,* 1973, *6,* 541–561.

PHILLIPS, L., BROVERMAN, I. K., & ZIGLER, E. Social competence and psychiatric diagnosis. *Journal of Abnormal Psychology,* 1966, *71,* 209–214.

PIAGET, J. *The moral judgment of the child.* Trans. M. Gabain. New York: Free Press, 1965. (Originally published 1932.)

PIAGET, J. Intellectual evolution from adolescence to adulthood. *Human Development,* 1972, *15,* 1–12.

PIERCE, C. M. Enuresis and encopresis. In A. M. Friedman, H. T. Kaplan, & B. J. Sadock (eds.), *Comprehensive textbook of psychiatry/II,* Baltimore, Md.: Williams & Wilkins, 1975.

PIKE, V. Permanent planning for foster children: The Oregon project. *Children Today,* 1976, *5,* 21–25.

PINKERTON, P. Psychogenic megacolon in children: The implications of bowel negativism. *Archives of Diseases in Childhood,* 1958, *33,* 371–380.

PIOTROWSKI, Z. A. *Perceptanalysis.* New York: Macmillan, 1957.

PLOMIN, R., & DEFRIES, J. C. Genetics and intelligence: Recent data. *Intelligence,* 1980, *4,* 15–24.

PLOTKIN, W. B., & RICE, K. M. Biofeedback as a placebo: Anxiety reduction facilitated by training in either suppression or enhancement of alpha brainwaves. *Journal of Consulting and Clinical Psychology,* 1981, *49,* 590–596.

POLLACK, M., & WOERNER, M. G. Pre- and perinatal complications and "childhood schizophrenia": A comparison of five controlled studies. *Journal of Child Psychology and Psychiatry,* 1966, *7,* 235–242.

POPPEN, R., STARK, J., EISENSON, J., FORREST, T., & WERTHEIM, G. Visual sequencing performance of aphasic children. *Journal of Speech and Hearing Research,* 1969, *12,* 288–300.

PORTER, B., & O'LEARY, K. D. Marital discord and childhood behavior problems. *Journal of Abnormal Child Psychology,* 1980, *8,* 287–295.

POTTER, H. W. Mental retardation in historical perspective. In S. I. Harrison & J. F. McDermott (eds.), *Childhood psychopathology.* New York: International Universities Press, 1972.

POULOS, R. W., HARVEY, S. E., & LIEBERT, R. M. Saturday morning television: A profile of the 1974–75 children's season. *Psychological Reports,* 1976, *39,* 1047–1057.

PRINZ, R. J., CONNOR, P. A., & WILSON, C. C. Hyperactive and aggressive behaviors in childhood: Intertwined dimensions. *Journal of Abnormal Child Psychology,* 1981, *9,* 191–202.

PRINZ, R. J., ROBERTS, W. A., & HANTMAN, E. Dietary correlates of hyperactivity behavior in children. *Journal of Consulting and Clinical Psychology,* 1980, *48,* 760–769.

PRUGH, D. G., STAUB, E. M., SANDS, H. H., KIRSCHBAUM, R. M., & LENIHAN, E. A. A study of the emotional reactions of children and families to hospitalization and illness. *American Journal of Orthopsychiatry,* 1953, *23,* 70–106.

PURCELL, K. Childhood asthma, the role of family relationships, personality, and emotions. In A. Davids (ed.), *Child personality and psychopathology: Current topics,* Vol. 2. New York: John Wiley, 1975.

PURCELL, K., BRADY, K., CHAI, H., MUSER, J., MOLK, L., GORDON, N., & MEANS, J. The effect on asthma in children of experimental separation from the family. *Psychosomatic Medicine,* 1969, *31,* 144–164.

QUAY, H. C. Dimensions of personality in delinquent boys as inferred from the factor analysis of case history data. *Child Development,* 1964, *35,* 479–484.

QUAY, H. C. Psychopathic personality as pathological stimulation-seeking. *American Journal of Psychiatry,* 1965, *122,* 180–183.

QUAY, H. C. Patterns of aggression, withdrawal, and immaturity. In H. C. Quay & J. S. Werry (eds.), *Psychopathological disorders of childhood.* New York: John Wiley, 1972.

QUAY, H. C. Psychopathic behavior. In I. C. Uzgiris and F. Weizmann (eds.), *The structuring of experience.* New York: Plenum, 1977.

QUAY, H. C. Classification. In H. C. Quay & J. S. Werry (eds.), *Psychopathological disorders of childhood,* 2nd ed. New York: John Wiley, 1979.

QUAY, H. C., & LOVE, C. T. The effect of a juvenile diversion program on rearrests. *Criminal Justice and Behavior,* 1977, *4,* 377–396.

QUAY, H. C., & PETERSON, D. R. *Manual for the Behavior Problem Checklist.* Unpublished manuscript, University of Illinois, 1967; Revised edition, University of Miami, 1975.

QUAY, H. C., SPRAGUE, R. L., SHULMAN, H. S., & MILLER, A. L. Some correlates of personality disorder and conduct disorder in a child guidance clinic sample. *Psychology in the Schools,* 1966, *3,* 44–47.

RABKIN, J. G., & STRUENING, E. L. Life events, stress and illness. *Science,* 1976, *194,* 1013–1020.

RAINER, J. D. Genetics and psychiatry. In H. I. Kaplan, A. M. Freedman, & B. J. Sadock (eds.), *Comprehensive textbook of psychiatry/III,* Vol. 3. Baltimore, Md.: Williams & Wilkins, 1980.

RAINS, P. M., KITSUSE, J. I., DUSTER, T., & FREIDSON, E. The labeling approach to deviance. In N. Hobbs (ed.), *Issues in the classification of children,* Vol. 1. San Francisco: Jossey-Bass, 1975.

RANDO, T. A. An investigation of grief and adaptation in parents whose children have died from cancer. *Journal of Pediatric Psychology,* 1983, *8,* 3–20.

RANK, B. Adaptation of the psychoanalytic technique for the treatment of young children with atypical development. *American Journal of Orthopsychiatry,* 1949, *19,* 130–139.

RANK, B. Intensive study and treatment of preschool children who show marked personality deviations or "atypical development" and their parents. In G. Caplan (ed.), *Emotional problems of early childhood,* New York: Basic Books, 1955.

RAPAPORT, J. L. Pediatric psychopharmacology and childhood depression. In J. G. Schulterbrandt & A. Raskin (eds.), *Depression in childhood: Diagnosis, treatment, and conceptual models.* New York: Raven Press, 1977. (a)

RAPAPORT, J. L. Report of subcommittee on the treatment of depression in children. In J. G. Schulterbrandt & A. Raskin (eds.), *Depression in childhood: Diagnosis, treatment, and conceptual models.* New York: Raven Press, 1977. (b)

RAPAPORT, J. L., BUCHSBAUM, M. S., ZAHN, T. P., WEINGARTNER, H., LUDLOW, C., & MIKKELSEN, E. J.

Dextroamphetamine: Cognitive and behavioral effects in normal prepubertal boys. *Science,* 1978, *199,* 560-563.

RAPOPORT, J. L., QUINN, P. O., BURG, C., & BARTLEY, L. Can hyperactives be identified in infancy? In R. L. Trites (ed.), *Hyperactivity in children.* Baltimore, Md.: University Park Press, 1979.

RAPPAPORT, J. *Community psychology: Values, research, and action.* New York: Holt, Rinehart and Winston, 1977.

REED, E. W. Genetic anomalies in development. In F. D. Horowitz (ed.), *Review of child development research.* Chicago: University of Chicago Press, 1975.

REITAN, R. M. *Manual for administration of neuropsychological test batteries for adults and children.* Indianapolis: Reitan, 1969.

REITAN, R. M., & BOLL, T. J. Neuropsychological correlates of minimal brain dysfunction. *Annals of the New York Academy of Sciences,* 1973, *205,* 65-88.

REITAN, R. M., & DAVISON, L. W. (eds.), *Clinical neuropsychology: Current status and applications.* New York: Winston/Wiley, 1974.

REKERS, G. A., & LOVAAS, I. O. Behavioral treatment of deviant sex role behaviors in a male child. *Journal of Applied Behavior Analysis,* 1974, *7,* 173-190.

RENNE, C., & CREER, T. L. The effects of training on the use of inhalation therapy equipment by children with asthma. *Journal of Applied Behavior Analysis,* 1976, *1,* 1-11.

RICHMOND, J. B., EDDY, E., & GREEN, M. Rumination: A psychosomatic syndrome of infancy. *Pediatrics,* 1958, *22,* 49-55.

RIDBERG, E. H., PARKE, R. D., & HETHERINGTON, E. M. Modification of impulsive and reflective cognitive styles through observation of film mediated models. *Developmental Psychology,* 1971, *5,* 369-377.

RIE, H. E. Depression in childhood: A survey of some pertinent contributions. *Journal of American Academy of Child Psychiatry,* 1966, *5,* 653-685.

RIE, H. E. Historical perspectives of concepts of child psychopathology. In H. E. Rie (ed.), *Perspectives in child psychopathology.* New York: Aldine-Atherton, 1971.

RIEDER, R. O., BROMAN, S. H., & ROSENTHAL, D. The offspring of schizophrenics. *Archives of General Psychiatry,* 1977, *34,* 789-799.

RIMLAND, B. *Infantile autism.* New York: Appleton-Century-Crofts, 1964.

RIMLAND, B. The differentiation of childhood psychoses: An analysis of checklists for 2,218 psychotic children. *Journal of Autism and Childhood Schizophrenia,* 1971, *1,* 161-174.

RIMLAND, B. Infantile autism: Status and research. In A. Davids (ed.), *Child personality and psychopathology: Current topics,* Vol. 1. New York: Wiley-Interscience, 1974.

RINCOVER, A., & KOEGEL, R. L. Research on the education of autistic children: Recent advances and future directions. In B. B. Lahey & A. E. Kazdin (eds.), *Advances in clinical child psychology,* Vol. 1. New York: Plenum, 1977.

RISLEY, T. R., & WOLF, M. M. Establishing functional speech in echolalic children. *Behaviour Research and Therapy,* 1967, *5,* 73-88.

RIST, R. C. Student and teacher expectations: The self-fulfilling prophecy in ghetto education. *Harvard Educational Review,* 1970, *40,* 411-451.

RITVO, E. R., & FREEMAN, B. J. Current status of biochemical research in autism. *Journal of Pediatric Psychology,* 1977, *2,* 149-152.

RITVO, E. R., ORNITZ, E. M., GOTTLIEB, E., POUSSAINT, A. F., MARON, B. J., DITMAN, K. S., & BLINN, K. Arousal and nonarousal enuretic events. *American Journal of Psychiatry,* 1969, *126,* 77-84.

RITVO, E. R., RABIN, K., YUWILER, A., FREEMAN, B. J., & GELLER, E. Biochemical and hematological studies: A critical review. In M. Rutter & E. Schopler (eds.), *Autism: A reappraisal of concepts and treatment.* New York: Plenum, 1978.

RIVINUS, T. M. Personal communication. April 20, 1979.

RIVINUS, T. M., DRUMMOND, T., & COMBRINCK-GRAHAM, L. A group-behavior treatment program for overweight children: Results of a pilot study. *Pediatric and Adolescent Endocrinology,* 1976, *1,* 212-218.

ROBINS, L. N. *Deviant children grown up: A sociological and psychiatric study of sociopathic personality.* Baltimore, Md.: Williams and Wilkins, 1966.

ROBINS, L. N. Antisocial behavior disturbances of childhood: Prevalence, prognosis, and prospects. In E. J. Anthony (ed.), *The child in his family,* Vol. 3. New York: John Wiley, 1974.

ROBINS, L. N., MURPHY, G. E., WOODRUFF, R. A., JR., & KING, L. J. The adult psychiatric status of black school boys. *Archives of General Psychiatry,* 1971, *24,* 338-345.

ROBINSON, N. M., & ROBINSON, H. B. *The mentally retarded child.* New York: McGraw-Hill, 1976.

ROFF, J. D., KNIGHT, R., & WERTHEIM, E. Disturbed preschizophrenics: Childhood symptoms in relation to adult outcome. *Journal of Nervous and Mental Disease,* 1976, *162,* 274-281.

ROFF, M. Childhood social interactions and young adult bad conduct. *Journal of Abnormal and Social Psychology,* 1961, *63,* 333-337.

ROFF, M., SELLS, S., & GOLDEN, M. *Social adjustment and personality development in children.* Minneapolis: University of Minnesota Press, 1972.

ROLLINS, N., & BLACKWELL, A. The treatment of anorexia nervosa in children and adolescents: Stage I. *Journal of Child Psychology and Psychiatry,* 1968, *9,* 81-91.

ROSE, H. E., & MAYER, J. Activity, caloric intake, and the energy balance of infants. *Pediatrics,* 1968, *41,* 18-29.

ROSEN, A. C., REKERS, G. A., & BENTLER, P. M. Ethical issues in the treatment of children. *Journal of Social Issues,* 1978, *34,* 122-136.

ROSEN, B. M., BAHN, A. K., & KRAMER, M. Demographic and diagnostic characteristics of psychiatric clinic outpatients in the USA, 1961. *American Journal of Orthopsychiatry,* 1964, *34,* 455-468.

ROSENBERG, M. *Society and the adolescent self-image.* Princeton: Princeton University Press, 1965.

ROSENHAN, D. On being sane in insane places. *Science,* 1973, *179,* 250-258.

ROSENTHAL, D. *Genetic theory and abnormal behavior.* New York: McGraw-Hill, 1970.

ROSENTHAL, D. Heredity in criminality. *Criminal Justice and Behavior,* 1975, *2,* 3-21.

ROSENTHAL, T., & BANDURA, A. Psychological modeling: Theory and practice. In S. L. Garfield & A. E. Bergin (eds.), *Handbook of psychotherapy and behavioral change: An empirical analysis.* New York: John Wiley, 1978.

ROSENZWEIG, M. R., BENNETT, E. L., & DIAMOND, M. C. Brain changes in response to experience. *Scientific American,* 1972, *226,* 22-29.

ROSS, A. O. The clinical child psychologist. In B. J. Wolman (ed.), *Manual of child psychopathology.* New York: McGraw-Hill, 1972.

ROSS, A. O. *Psychological disorders of children: A behavioral approach to theory, research and therapy.* New York: McGraw-Hill, 1974.

ROSS, A. O. *Psychological aspects of learning disabilities and reading disorders.* New York: McGraw-Hill, 1976.

ROSS, A. O. *Child behavior therapy: Principles, procedures, and empirical basis.* New York: John Wiley, 1981.

ROSS, A. O., LACEY, H. M., & PARTON, D. A. The development of a behavior checklist for boys. *Child Development,* 1965, *36,* 1013-1027.

ROSS, A. O., & PELHAM, W. E. Child psychopathology. *Annual review of psychology,* 1981, *32, 243-278.*

ROSS, D. M., & ROSS, S. A. *Hyperactivity.* New York: John Wiley, 1976.

ROSSI, A. M. Some pre-World War II antecedents of community mental health theory and practice. *Mental Hygiene,* 1962, *46,* 78-98.

ROTHNER, A. D. Headaches in children: A review. *Headache,* 1979, *19,* 156-162.

ROURKE, B. Neuropsychological research in reading retardation: A review. In A. L. Benton & D. Pearl (eds.), *Dyslexia.* New York: Oxford University Press, 1978.

ROURKE, B. P., & STRANG, J. D. Neuropsychological significance of variations in patterns of academic performance: Motor, psychomotor, and tactile-perceptual abilities. *Journal of Pediatric Psychology,* 1978, *3,* 62-66.

ROUTH, D. K. Developmental and social aspects of hyperactivity. In C. K. Whalen and B. Henker (eds.), *Hyperactive children.* New York: Academic Press, 1980.

ROUTH, D. K., & ROBERTS, R. D. Minimal brain dysfunction in children: Failure to find evidence for a behavioral syndrome. *Psychological Reports,* 1972, *31,* 307-314.

ROUTH, D. K., SCHROEDER, C. S., & KOOCHER, G. P. Psychology and primary health care for children. *American Psychologist,* 1983, *38,* 95-98.

ROVET, J., & NETLEY, C. Processing deficits in Turner's Syndrome. *Developmental Psychology,* 1982, *18,* 77-94.

RUBIN, R. A., & BALOW, B. Measures of infant development and socioeconomic status as predictors of later intelligence and school achievement. *Developmental Psychology,* 1979, *15,* 225-227.

RUGH, R., & SHETTLES, L. B. *From conception to birth.* New York: Harper & Row, Pub., 1971.

RUSSELL, G. F. M. Anorexia nervosa: Its identity as an illness and its treatment. In J. H. Price (ed.), *Modern trends in psychological medicine: II.* New York: Appleton-Century-Crofts, 1970.

RUSSO, D. C., CARR, E. G., & LOVAAS, O. I. Self-injury in pediatric populations. In J. J. Ferguson & C. B. Taylor (eds.), *The comprehensive handbook of behavioral medicine,* Vol. 3. New York: Spectrum Publ., 1980.

RUTTER, M. Prognosis: Psychotic children in adolescence and early adult life. In J. K. Wing (ed.), *Early childhood autism.* London: Pergamon Press, 1966.

RUTTER, M. Parent-child separation: Psychological effects on the children. *Journal of Child Psychology and Psychiatry,* 1971, *12,* 233-260.

RUTTER, M. The development of infantile autism. *Psychological Medicine,* 1974, *4,* 147-163. (a)

RUTTER, M. Epidemiological and conceptual considerations in risk research. In E. J. Anthony & C. Koupernik (eds.), *The child in his family: Children at psychiatric risk.* New York: John Wiley, 1974. (b)

RUTTER, M. *Helping troubled children.* New York: Plenum, 1975.

RUTTER, M. Developmental issues and prognosis. In M. Rutter & E. Schopler (eds.), *Autism: A reappraisal of concepts and treatment.* New York: Plenum, 1978. (a)

RUTTER, M. Diagnosis and definition. In M. Rutter & E. Schopler (eds.), *Autism: A reappraisal of concepts and treatment.* New York: Plenum, 1978. (b)

RUTTER, M. Language disorder and infantile autism. In M. Rutter & E. Schopler (eds.), *Autism: A reappraisal of concepts and treatment.* New York: Plenum, 1978. (c)

RUTTER, M. Prevalence and types of dyslexia. In A. L. Benton & D. Pearl (eds.), *Dyslexia.* New York: Oxford University Press, 1978. (d)

RUTTER, M., GRAHAM, P., & YULE, W. *A neuropsychiatric study in childhood.* Clinics in Developmental Medicine, Nos. 35/36. London: Heinemann, 1970.

RUTTER, M., LEBOVICI, S., EISENBERG, L., SNEZNEVSKIJ, A. V., SADOUN, R., BROOKE, E., & LIN, T. Y. A triaxial classification of mental disorders in childhood: An international study. *Journal of Child Psychology and Psychiatry,* 1969, *10,* 41-61.

RUTTER, M., & SHAFFER, D. DSM-III: A step forward or back in terms of the classification of child psychiatric disorders? *Journal of the American Academy of Child Psychiatry,* 1980, *19,* 371-394.

RUTTER, M., TIZARD, J., & WHITMORE, K. (eds.), *Education, health, and behavior.* London: Longmans, 1970.

RUTTER, M., TIZARD, J., YULE, W., GRAHAM, P., & WHITMORE, K. Research report: Isle of Wight studies, 1964-74. *Psychological Medicine,* 1976, *6,* 313-332.

RUTTER, M., & YULE, W. The concept of specific reading retardation. *Journal of Child Psychology and Psychiatry,* 1975, *16,* 181-197.

RUTTER, M., YULE, W., & GRAHAM, P. Enuresis and behavioral deviance: Some epidemiological considerations. In I. Kolvin, R. C. MacKeith, & S. R. Meadow (eds.), *Bladder control and enuresis.* Philadelphia: Saunders, 1973.

SABATINO, D. A. When a definition is in trouble, there may

be trouble with the definition. *Journal of Pediatric Psychology,* 1979, *4,* 221–232.

SACHS, R., DeLEON, G., & BLACKMAN, S. Psychological changes associated with conditioning functional enuresis. *Journal of Clinical Psychology,* 1974, *30,* 271–276.

SAFER, D. J., & ALLEN, R. P. *Hyperactive children: Diagnosis and management.* Baltimore, Md.: University Park Press, 1976.

SAJWAJ, T., LIBET, J., & AGRAS, S. Lemon-juice therapy: The control of life-threatening rumination in a six-month-old infant. *Journal of Applied Behavior Analysis,* 1974, *7,* 557–563.

SALLADE, J. A comparison of the psychological adjustment of obese vs. nonobese children. *Journal of Psychosomatic Research,* 1973, *17,* 89–96.

SAMEROFF, A. J., & CHANDLER, M. J. Reproductive risk and the continuum of caretaking casualty. In F. D. Horowitz (ed.), *Review of child development research.* Vol. 4. Chicago: University of Chicago Press, 1975.

SANDLER-COHEN, R., BERMAN, A. L., & KING, R. A. Life stress and symptomatology: Determinants of suicidal behavior in children. *Journal of the American Academy of Child Psychiatry,* 1982, *21,* 178–186.

SANTOSTEFANO, S. *A biodevelopmental approach to clinical child psychology.* New York: Wiley-Interscience, 1978.

SATTERFIELD, J. H. Neurophysiologic studies with hyperactive children. In D. P. Cantwell (ed.), *The hyperactive child.* New York: Spectrum Publ., 1975.

SATTERFIELD, J. H., CANTWELL, D. P., SAUL, R. E., & YUSIN, A. Intelligence, academic achievement and EEG abnormalities in hyperactive children. *American Journal of Psychiatry,* 1974, *131,* 391–395.

SATZ, P., & FLETCHER, J. M. Minimal brain dysfunctions: An appraisal of research concepts and methods. In H. E. Rie and E. D. Rie (eds.), *Handbook of minimal brain dysfunctions.* New York: John Wiley, 1980.

SCARR, S. Genetic factors in activity motivation. *Child Development,* 1966, *37,* 663–673.

SCARR, S. Social introversion-extroversion as a heritable response. *Child Development,* 1969, *40,* 823–832.

SCARR, S., & WEINBERG, R. A. The I. Q. performance of black children adopted by white families. *American Psychologist,* 1976, *31,* 726–739.

SCHACHAR, R., RUTTER, M., & SMITH, A. The characteristics of situationally and pervasively hyperactive children: Implications for syndrome definition. *Journal of Child Psychology and Psychiatry,* 1981, *22,* 375–392.

SCHACHT, T., & NATHAN, P. E. But is it good for psychologists? Appraisal and status of DSM-III. *American Psychologist,* 1977, *32,* 1017–1025.

SCHAEFER, E. S. A circumplex model for maternal behavior. *Journal of Abnormal and Social Psychology,* 1959, *59,* 226–235.

SCHAFFER, H. R., & EMERSON, P. E. Patterns of response to physical contact in early human development. *Journal of Child Psychology and Psychiatry,* 1964, *5,* 1–13.

SCHAPIRO, J. An historical overview of education and the learning-disabled child. In M. I. Gottlieb, P. W. Zinkus, & L. J. Bradford (eds.), *Current issues in developmental pe-*

diatrics: The learning-disabled child.* New York: Grune & Stratton, 1979.

SCHOPLER, E. Changes of direction with psychotic children. In A. Davids (ed.), *Child personality and psychopathology: Current topics,* Vol. 1. New York: John Wiley, 1974.

SCHOPLER, E. Limits of methodological differences in family studies. In M. Rutter & E. Schopler (eds.), *Autism: A reappraisal of concepts and treatment.* New York: Plenum, 1978.

SCHOPLER, E., ANDREWS, C. E., & STRUPP, K. Do autistic children come from upper-middle-class parents? *Journal of Autism and Developmental Disorders,* 1979, *9,* 139–152.

SCHRAG, P., & DIVOKY, D. *The myth of the hyperactive child.* New York: Dell Pub. Co., 1975.

SCHREIBMAN, L., KOEGEL, R. L., CHARLOP, H., & EGEL, A. L. Autism. In A. S. Bellack, M. Hersen, & A. E. Kazdin (eds.), *International handbook of behavior modification and therapy.* New York: Plenum, 1982.

SCHROEDER, C. S. Psychologists in a private pediatric practice. *Journal of Pediatric Psychology,* 1979, *4,* 5–18.

SCHROEDER, S. R., MULICK, J. A., & ROJAHN, J. The definition, taxonomy, epidemiology, and ecology of self-injurious behavior. *Journal of Autism and Developmental Disorders,* 1980, *10,* 417–432.

SCHULSINGER, H. A ten-year follow-up of children with schizophrenic mothers. *Acta Psychiatrica Scandinavica,* 1976, *63,* 371–386.

SCHULTERBRANDT, J., & RASKIN, A. (eds.). *Depression in children: Diagnosis, treatment, and conceptual models.* New York: Raven Press, 1977.

SCHULTZ, E. W., SALVIA, J. A., & FEINN, J. Prevalence of behavioral symptoms in rural elementary school children. *Journal of Abnormal Child Psychology,* 1974, *1,* 17–24.

SEARS, R. R. *Your ancients revisited: A history of child development.* Chicago: University of Chicago Press, 1975.

SEARS, R. R., MACCOBY, E. E., & LEVIN, H. *Patterns of child rearing.* Evanston, Ill.: Row Peterson, 1957.

SEASHORE, H. G., WESMAN, A. G., & DOPPELT, J. E. The standardization of the Wechsler Intelligence Scale for Children. *Journal of Consulting Psychology,* 1950, *14,* 99–110.

SELIGMAN, M. E. P. Phobias and preparedness. *Behavior Therapy,* 1971, *2,* 307–320.

SELIGMAN, M. E. P. Depression and learned helplessness. In R. J. Friedman & M. M. Katz (eds.), *The psychology of depression: Contemporary theory and research.* Washington D.C.: Winston, 1974.

SELIGMAN, M. E. P., ABRAMSON, L. Y., SEMMEL, A., & VON BAEYER, C. Depressive attributional style. *Journal of Abnormal Psychology,* 1979, *88,* 242–247.

SELIGMAN, R., GLESER, G., RAUH, J., & HARRIS, L. The effect of earlier parental loss in adolescence. *Archives of General Psychiatry.* 1974, *31,* 475–479.

SELMAN, R. Toward a structural analysis of developing interpersonal relations concepts: Research with normal and disturbed preadolescent boys. In A. D. Pick (ed.), *Min-*

nesota symposia on child psychology, Vol. 10. Minneapolis: University of Minnesota Press, 1976.

Selvini, M. P. Anorexia nervosa. In S. Arieti (ed.), *World biennial of psychiatry and psychotherapy.* Vol. 1. New York: Basic Books, 1971.

Selye, H. *The stress of life.* New York: McGraw-Hill, 1956.

Serbin, L., & O'Leary, K. D. How nursery schools teach girls to shut up. *Psychology Today,* December 1975.

Shaffer, D. The association between enuresis and emotional disorder: A review of the literature. In I. Kolvin, R. C. MacKeith, & S. R. Meadow (eds.), *Bladder control and enuresis.* Philadelphia: Saunders, 1973.

Shaffer, D., & Fisher, P. The epidemiology of suicide in children and young adolescents. *Journal of the American Academy of Child Psychiatry,* 1981, *20,* 545–565.

Shaffer, D., & Greenhill, L. A. Critical note on the predictive validity of "The Hyperactive Syndrome." *Journal of Child Psychology and Psychiatry,* 1979, *20,* 61–72.

Shallenberger, P., & Zigler, E. Rigidity, negative reaction tendencies, and cosatiation effects in normal and feebleminded children. *Journal of Abnormal and Social Psychology,* 1961, *63,* 20–26.

Shantz, C. The development of social cognition. In E. M. Hetherington (ed.), *Review of child development research,* Vol. 5. Chicago: University of Chicago Press, 1975.

Shapiro, D., Schwartz, G. E., & Tursky, B. Control of diastolic blood pressure in man by feedback and reinforcement. *Psychophysiology,* 1972, *9,* 256–304.

Shapiro, T., Burkes, L., Petti, T. A., & Ranz, J. Consistency of "nonfocal" neurological signs. *Journal of the American Academy of Child Psychiatry,* 1978, *17,* 70–79.

Shepherd, M., Oppenheim, A. N., & Mitchell, S. Childhood behavior disorders and the child guidance clinic: An epidemiological study. *Journal of Psychology and Psychiatry,* 1966, *7,* 39–52.

Sherman, B., Halmi, K., & Zamudio, R. LH and FSH response to gonadotrophin releasing hormone in anorexia nervosa: Effect of nutritional rehabilitation. *Journal of Clinical Endocrinology and Metabolism,* 1975, *41,* 135–142.

Shetty, T. Neurophysiologic and biochemical aspects of hyperkinesis. In E. Denhoff and L. Stern (eds.), *Minimal brain dysfunction.* New York: Masson Publishing, 1979.

Shinn, M. Father absence and children's cognitive development. *Psychological Bulletin,* 1978, *85,* 295–324.

Shore, M. F. Legislation, advocacy, and the rights of children and youth. *American Psychologist,* 1979, *34,* 1017–1019.

Shuey, A. M. *The testing of Negro intelligence.* Lynchburg, Va.: Bell, 1966.

Shure, M. B., & Spivack, G. Interpersonal problem-solving in young children: A cognitive approach to prevention. *American Journal of Community Psychology,* 1982, *10,* 341–356.

Silberman, C. E. *Crisis in the classroom.* New York: Random House, 1970.

Siegel, P. S. Incentive motivation and the mentally retarded person. In N. R. Ellis (ed.), *Handbook of mental deficiency.* Hillsdale, N.J.: Lawrence Erlbaum Associates, 1979.

Silver, L. B. The relationship between learning disabilities, hyperactivity, distractibility, and behavioral problems. *Journal of Child Psychiatry,* 1981, *20,* 385–397.

Skinner, B. F. *Walden two.* London: Macmillan, 1948.

Skinner, B. F. *Science and human behavior.* New York: Macmillan, 1953.

Skinner, B. F. *The technology of teaching.* New York: Appleton-Century-Crofts, 1968.

Skrzypek, G. J. Effect of perceptual isolation and arousal on anxiety, complexity preference, and novelty preference in psychopathic and neurotic delinquents. *Journal of Abnormal Psychology,* 1969, *74,* 321–329.

Slaby, R. G. Verbal regulation of aggression and altruism. In W. Hartup & J. DeWit, (eds.), *Determinants and origins of aggressive behavior.* The Hague: Mouton, 1975.

Smith, D. W., & Wilson, A. A. *The child with Down's syndrome.* Philadelphia: Saunders, 1973.

Solnick, J. V., Braukmann, C. J., Bedlington, M. M., Kirigin, K. A., & Wolf, M. M. The relationship between parent-youth interaction and delinquency in group homes. *Journal of Abnormal Child Psychology,* 1981, *9,* 107–119.

Solyom, I., Beck, P., Solyom, C., & Hugel, R. Some etiological factors in phobic neurosis. *Canadian Psychiatry Association Journal,* 1974, *19,* 69–78.

Sours, J. A. The anorexia nervosa syndrome. *International Journal of Psycho-Analysis,* 1974, *55,* 567–576.

Sours, J. A. Enuresis. In B. B. Wolman, J. Egan, & A. O. Ross (eds.), *Handbook of treatment of mental disorders in childhood and adolescence.* Englewood Cliffs, N.J.: Prentice-Hall, 1978.

Soyka, L. F. Current status of medications for MBD. In E. Denhoff and L. Stern (eds.), *Minimal brain dysfunction.* New York: Masson Publishing, 1979.

Spache, G. D. *Spache Diagnostic Reading Scales.* Monterey, Calif.: California Test Bureau, 1963.

Spence, M. A. Genetic studies. In E. R. Ritvo (ed.), *Autism: Diagnosis, current research and management.* New York: Spectrum, Publ., 1976.

Sperling, M. Animal phobia in a 2-year-old child. *Psychoanalytic Study of the Child,* 1952, *7,* 115–125.

Sperling, M. Dynamic considerations and treatment of enuresis. *Journal of the American Academy of Child Psychiatry,* 1965, *4,* 19–31.

Spinetta, J. J. The dying child's awareness of death: A review. *Psychological Bulletin,* 1974, *81,* 256–260.

Spitz, H. H. Toward a relative psychology of mental retardation, with special emphasis on evolution. In N. R. Ellis (ed.), *International review of research in mental retardation.* New York: Academic Press, 1976.

Spitz, R. A. Anaclitic depression. In *The psychoanalytic study of the child,* Vol. 2. New York: International Universities Press, 1946.

Spitzer, R. L., & Cantwell, D. P. The DSM-III classification of the psychiatric disorders of infancy, childhood, and adolescence. *Journal of the American Academy of Child Psychiatry,* 1980, *19,* 356–370.

Spivack, G., & Shure, M. B. *Social adjustment of young children.* San Francisco: Jossey-Bass, 1974.

SPIVACK, G., & SWIFT, M. "High risk" classroom behaviors in kindergarten and first grade. *American Journal of Community Psychology*, 1977, *5*, 385–397.

SPOCK, B. *Baby and child care.* New York: Pocket Books, 1974.

SROUFE, L. A. Drug treatment of children with behavior problems. In F. D. Horowitz, E. M. Hetherington, S. Scarr-Salapatek, & G. M. Siegel (eds.), *Review of child development research.*, Vol. 4. Chicago: University of Chicago Press, 1975.

SROUFE, L. A. The coherence of individual development. *American Psychologist*, 1979, *34*, 834–841.

STANLEY, L. Treatment of ritualistic behavior in an eight-year-old girl by response prevention: A case report. *Journal of Child Psychology and Psychiatry*, 1980, *21*, 85–90.

STEELE, B. F., & POLLACK, D. A. A psychiatric study of parents who abuse infants and small children. In R. E. Helfer and H. Kempe (eds.), *The battered child.* Chicago: University of Chicago Press, 1968.

STEIN, A. H., & FRIEDRICH, L. K. Television content and young children's behavior. In J. P. Murray, E. A. Rubinstein, & G. A. Comstock (eds.), *Television and social behavior, Vol II: Television and social learning.* Washington, D.C.: U.S. Government Printing Office, 1972.

STEIN, A. H., & FRIEDRICH, L. K. Impact of television on children and youth. In E. M. Hetherington (ed.), *Review of child development research.* Chicago: University of Chicago Press, 1975.

STEIN, K. B., SARBIN, T. R., & KULIK, J. A. Further validation of antisocial personality types. *Journal of Consulting and Clinical Psychology*, 1971, *36*, 177–182.

STEIN, Z., & SUSSER, M. Social factors in the development of sphincter control. *Developmental Medicine and Child Neurology*, 1967, *9*, 692–706.

STEPHANIC, P. A., HEALD, F. P., & MAYER, J. Caloric intake in relation to energy output of obese and nonobese adolescent boys. *American Journal of Clinical Nutrition*, 1959, *7*, 55–62.

STEWART, M. A. Treatment of bedwetting. *Journal of the American Medical Association*, 1975, *232*, 281–283.

STEWART, M. A., CUMMINGS, C., SINGER, S., & DEBLOIS, C. S. The overlap between hyperactive and unsocialized aggressive children. *Journal of Child Psychiatry and Psychology*, 1981, *22*, 35–45.

ST. JAMES-ROBERTS, I. Neurological plasticity, recovery from brain insult, and child development. In H. W. Reese & L. P. Lipsitt (eds.), *Advances in child development and behavior*, Vol. 14. New York: Academic Press, 1979.

STONE, N. W., PENDLETON, V. M., VAILL, M. B., SLATIN, M., MITCHAM, C., & GEORGETTE, F. Primary prevention in mental health: A Head Start demonstration model. *American Journal of Orthopsychiatry*, 1982, *52*, 360–363.

STOTT, L. H., & BALL, R. S. Infant and preschool mental tests: Review and evaluation. *Monographs of the Society for Research in Child Development*, 1965, *30* (No. 3).

STRAIN, P. S. Effects of peer social initiations on withdrawn preschool children: Some training and generalization ef-

fects. *Journal of Abnormal Child Psychology*, 1977, *5*, 445–455.

STRAIN, P. S., & FOX, J. J. Peers as behavior change agents for withdrawn classmates. In B. B. Lahey & A. E. Kazdin (eds.), *Advances in clinical child psychology*, Vol. 4. New York: Plenum, 1981.

STRAUSS, A. A., & KEPHART, N. C. *Psychopathology and education of the brain-injured child.* Vol. II. New York: Grune & Stratton, 1955.

STRAUSS, A. A., & LEHTINEN, L. *Psychopathology and education of the brain-injured child.* New York: Grune & Stratton, 1947.

STREAN, H. S. *New approaches in child guidance.* Metuchen, N.J.: The Scarecrow Press, 1970.

STRICHART, S. S., & GOTTLIEB, J. Learning disabilities at the crossroads. In J. Gottlieb & S. S. Strichart (eds.), *Developmental theory and research in learning disabilities.* Baltimore, Md.: University Park Press, 1981.

STRODTBECK, F. L. The hidden curriculum in the middle-class home. In J. D. Krumboltz (ed.), *Learning and the educational process.* Chicago: Rand-McNally & Co., 1965.

STUNKARD, A. J. Eating patterns and obesity. *Psychiatric Quarterly*, 1959, *33*, 284–295.

STUNKARD, A. J., D'AQUILI, E., FOX, S., & FILION, R. D. Influence of social class on obesity and thinness in children. *Journal of the American Medical Association*, 1972, *221*, 579–584.

STUNKARD, A. J., & MAHONEY, M. J. Behavioral treatment of eating disorders. In H. Leitenberg (ed.), *Handbook of behavior modification and behavior therapy.* Englewood Cliffs, N.J.: Prentice-Hall, 1976.

STUNKARD, A. J., & PESTKA, J. The physical activity of obese girls. *American Journal of Diseases of Children*, 1962, *103*, 812–817.

STURGE, C. Reading retardation and anti-social behavior. *Journal of Child Psychology and Psychiatry*, 1982, *23*, 21–31.

SUOMI, S. J., & HARLOW, H. H. Social rehabilitation of isolate-reared monkeys. *Developmental Psychology*, 1972, *6*, 487–496.

SUSSMAN, M. B. The family today. *Children Today.* March-April 1978.

SUTTON-SMITH, B., & ROSENBERG, B. G. *The sibling.* New York: Holt, Rinehart and Winston, 1970.

SWANSON, J. M., & KINSBOURNE, M. Artificial color and hyperactive behavior. In R. M. Knights & D. J. Bakker (eds.), *Treatment of hyperactive and learning disordered children.* Baltimore, Md.: University Park Press, 1980.

SZUREK, S. Psychotic episodes and psychotic maldevelopment. *American Journal of Orthopsychiatry*, 1956, *26*, 519–543.

TAGER-FLUSBERG, H. On the nature of linguistic functioning in early infantile autism. *Journal of Autism and Developmental Disorders*, 1981, *11*, 45–56.

TAKANISHI, R. Childhood as a social issue: Historical roots of contemporary child advocacy movements. *Journal of Social Issues*, 1978, *34*, 8–28.

TAL, A., & MIKLICH, D. R. Emotionally induced decreases in pulmonary flow rates in asthmatic children. *Psychosomatic Medicine*, 1976, *38*, 190–200.

TANGUAY, P. Clinical and electrophysiological research. In E. Ritvo (ed.), *Autism: Diagnosis, current research and management.* New York: Spectrum Publ. 1976.

TANNER, J. M. The regulation of human growth. *Child Development,* 1963, *34,* 816–847.

TANNER, J. M. Physical growth. In P. H. Mussen (ed.), *Carmichael's manual of child development,* Vol. 1. New York: John Wiley, 1970.

TAPLIN, P. S., & REID, J. B. Effects of instructional set and experimenter influence on observer reliability. *Child Development,* 1973, *44,* 547–554.

TATE, B. G., & BAROFF, G. S. Aversive control of self-injurious behavior in a psychotic boy. *Behaviour Research and Therapy,* 1966, *4,* 281–287.

TEMPLER, D. I. Anorexic humans and rats. *American Psychologist,* 1971, *26,* 935.

TERDAL, L., JACKSON, R. H., & GARNER, A. M. Mother-child interactions: A comparison between normal and developmentally delayed groups. In E. J. Mash, L. A. Hamerlynck, & L. C. Handy (eds.), *Behavior modification and families.* New York: Brunner/Mazel, 1976.

TERMAN, L. M., & MERRILL, M. A. *Stanford-Binet Intelligence Scale. Manual for the third revision, Form L-M.* Boston: Houghton Mifflin, 1960.

THOMAS, A., & CHESS, S. Evolution of behavior disorders into adolescence. *American Journal of Psychiatry,* 1976, *133,* 539–542.

THOMAS, A., CHESS, S., & BIRCH, H. G. The origin of personality. *Scientific American,* 1970, *223,* 102–109.

THOMAS, A., CHESS, S., SILLEN, J., & MENDEZ, O. Cross cultural study of behavior in children with special vulnerabilities to stress. In D. F. Ricks, A. Thomas, & M. Roff (eds.), *Life history research in psychopathology,* Vol. 3. Minneapolis: University of Minnesota Press, 1974.

THOMAS, M. *Comparing theories of child development.* Belmont, Calif.: Wadsworth, 1979.

THOMPSON, C. W., GARNER, A. M., & PARTRIDGE, J. W. Sick? or diabetic? A research report. *Diabetes Bulletin,* 1969, *45,* 2–3.

THOMPSON, W. R. The inheritance and development of intelligence. *Research Publications of the Association for Research in Nervous and Mental Diseases,* 1954, *33,* 209–331.

THOMPSON, W. R., & GRUSEC, J. E. Studies of early experience. In P. H. Mussen (ed.), *Carmichael's manual of child psychology,* Vol. 1. New York: John Wiley, 1970.

THORNDIKE, E. L. *The elements of psychology.* New York: Seiler, 1905.

THORNDIKE, E. L. *The psychology of wants, interests, and attitudes.* New York: Appleton-Century-Crofts, 1935.

THURSTONE, L. L., & THURSTONE, T. G. Factorial studies of intelligence. *Psychometric Monographs,* 1941, No. 2.

TOOLAN, J. M. Depression and suicide in children: An overview. *American Journal of Psychotherapy,* 1981, *35,* 311–322.

TRESEMER, D., & PLECK, J. Sex-role boundaries and resistance to sex-role change. *Women's Studies,* 1974, *2,* 61–78.

TRICKETT, P. K., & SUSMAN, E. J. The impact of the child-rearing environment on the social and emotional development of the physically abused school-age child: Prelim-inary results. Paper presented at the Annual Convention of the American Psychological Association, Washington D.C., August 1982.

TRITES, R. L., DUGAS, E., LYNCH, G., & FERGUSON, H. B. Prevalence of hyperactivity. *Journal of Pediatric Psychology,* 1979, *4,* 179–188.

TRYPHONAS, H. Factors possibly implicated in hyperactivity. In R. L. Trites (ed.), *Hyperactivity in children.* Baltimore, Md.: University Park Press, 1979.

TUDDENHAM, R. D. The nature and measurement of intelligence. In L. Postman (ed.), *Psychology in the making.* New York: Knopf, 1963.

TYLER, L. E. *Tests and measurements.* Englewood Cliffs, N.J.: Prentice-Hall, 1963.

ULLMANN, C. A. Teachers, peers, and tests as predictors of adjustment. *Journal of Educational Psychology,* 1957, *48,* 257–267.

ULLMANN, L. P., & KRASNER, L. *A psychological approach to abnormal behavior,* 2nd ed. Englewood Cliffs, N.J.: Prentice-Hall, 1975.

URBAIN, E., & KENDALL, P. Review of social-cognitive problem-solving interventions with children. *Psychological Bulletin,* 1980, *88,* 109–143.

U.S. BUREAU OF THE CENSUS, *Statistical Abstract of the U.S.: 1979.* Washington, D.C.: U.S. Government Printing Office, 1979.

U.S. DEPARTMENT OF HEALTH AND HUMAN SERVICES. *Lasting effects after preschool.* Washington D.C.: Superintendent of Documents, U.S. Government Printing Office, 1979.

U.S. DEPARTMENT OF HEALTH AND HUMAN SERVICES. *Head Start. A child development program.* Washington D.C.: Superintendent of Documents, U.S. Government Printing Office, 1980.

U.S. DEPARTMENT OF JUSTICE. *Sourcebook of criminal justice statistics—1980.* Washington, D.C.: U.S. Government Printing Office, 1980.

UZGIRIS, I. C. Organization of sensorimotor intelligence. In M. Lewis (ed.), *Origins of intelligence.* New York: Plenum, 1976.

UZGIRIS, I. C., & HUNT, J. McV. *Assessment in infancy: Ordinal scales of psychological development.* Urbana, Ill.: University of Illinois Press, 1975.

VACHON, L., & RICH, E. S., JR. Visceral learning in asthma. *Psychosomatic Medicine,* 1976, *38,* 122–130.

VANCE, B. T. Social disability. *American Psychologist,* 1973, *28,* 498–511.

VANDERSALL, T. A. Ulcerative colitis. In B. B. Wolman, J. Egan, & A. O. Ross (eds.), *Handbook of treatment of mental disorders in childhood and adolescence.* Englewood Cliffs, N.J.: Prentice-Hall, 1978.

VARNI, J. W., LOVAAS, O. I., KOEGEL, R. L., & EVERETT, N. An analysis of observational learning in autistic and normal children. *Journal of Abnormal Child Psychology,* 1979, *7,* 31–43.

VELLUTINO, F. R. *Dyslexia: Theory and research.* Cambridge, Mass.: The MIT Press, 1979.

VERNICK, J., & KARON, M. Who's afraid of death on a leukemia ward? *American Journal of Diseases of Children,* 1965, *109,* 393–397.

VERNON, D., FOLEY, J., SIPOWICZ, R., & SCHULMAN, J. *The psychological responses of children to hospitalization and illness.* Springfield, Ill.: Chas. C Thomas, 1965.

VERNON, D., SCHULMAN, J., & FOLEY, J. Changes in children's behavior after hospitalization. *American Journal of Diseases in Children,* 1966, *111,* 581–593.

VITAL AND HEALTH STATISTICS. *Infant Mortality Rates: Socioeconomic Factors.* Series 22, No. 14. Rockwell, Md.: U.S. Department of Health, Education, and Welfare, 1972.

WAHLER, R. G. Deviant child behavior within the family: Developmental speculations and behavior change strategies. In H. Leitenberg (ed.), *Handbook of behavior modification and behavior therapy.* Englewood Cliffs, N.J.: Prentice-Hall, 1976.

WAHLER, R. G., BERLAND, R. M., COE, T. D., & LESKE, G. Social systems analysis: Implementating an alternative behavior model. In A. Rogers-Warren & S. F. Warren (eds.), *Ecological perspectives in behavior analysis.* Baltimore, Md.: University Park Press, 1977.

WAHLER, R. G., & GRAVES, M. G. Setting events in social networks: Ally or enemy in child behavior therapy? *Behavior Therapy,* 1983, *14,* 19–36.

WALKER, C. E. Toilet training, enuresis, and encopresis. In P. R. Magrab (ed.), *Psychological management of pediatric problems,* Vol. 1. Baltimore, Md.: University Park Press, 1978.

WALKER, H., GREENWOOD, C., HOPS, H., & TODD, N. Differential effects of reinforcing topographic components of social interaction. *Behavior Modification,* 1979, *3,* 291–321.

WALLANDER, J. L., & CONGER, J. C. Assessment of hyperactive children: Psychometric, methodological, and practical considerations. In M. Hersen, R. M. Eisler, & P. M. Miller (eds.), *Progress in behavior modification.* New York: Academic Press, 1981.

WALTERS, R. H., & BROWN, M. Studies of reinforcement of aggression: III. Transfer of responses to an interpersonal situation. *Child Development,* 1963, *34,* 563–571.

WALTON, D. The application of learning theory to the treatment of a case of bronchial asthma. In H. J. Eysenck (ed.), *Behavior therapy and the neuroses.* New York: Macmillan, 1960.

WARD, C. H., BECK, A. T., MENDELSON, M., MOCK, J. E., & ERBAUGH, J. K. The psychiatric nomenclature: Reasons for diagnostic disagreement. *Archives of General Psychiatry,* 1962, *7,* 198–205.

WARREN, M. Q. The case for differential treatment of delinquents. *Annals of the American Academy of Political and Social Science,* 1969, *381,* 47–59.

WARREN, M. Q., & PALMER, T. B. *The community treatment project after five years.* Sacramento, Calif.: California Youth Authority, 1966.

WATERMAN, J. M., SOBESKY, W. E., SILVERN, L., AOKI, B., & McCAULAY, M. Social perspective-taking and adjustment in emotionally disturbed, learning-disabled, and normal children. *Journal of Abnormal Child Psychology,* 1981, *9,* 133–148.

WATERS, E., WIPPMAN, J., & SROUFE, A. Social competence in preschool children as a function of the security of earlier attachment to the mother. *Child Development,* 1980, *51,* 208–216.

WATSON, J. B. Psychology as the behaviorist views it. *Psychological Review,* 1913, *20,* 158–177.

WATSON, J. B. *Behaviorism.* Chicago: University of Chicago Press, 1963.

WATSON, J. B., & RAYNER, R. Conditioned emotional reactions. *Journal of Experimental Psychology,* 1920, *3,* 1–14.

WEATHERLEY, D. Self-perceived rate of physical maturation and personality in late adolescence. *Child Development,* 1964, *35,* 1197–1210.

WEBER, L. *The English infant school and informal education.* Englewood Cliffs, N.J.: Prentice-Hall, 1971.

Webster's new collegiate dictionary. Springfield, Mass.: Merriam, 1973.

WECHSLER, D. *Measurement and appraisal of adult intelligence,* 4th ed. Baltimore, Md.: Williams & Wilkins, 1958.

WECHSLER, D. *Wechsler Preschool and Primary Scale of Intelligence.* New York: Psychological Corporation, 1967.

WECHSLER, D. I. *WISC-R manual. Wechsler Intelligence Scale for Children-Revised.* New York: Psychological Corporation, 1974.

WEIKART, D. P. Relationship of curriculum, teaching, and learning in preschool education. In J. C. Stanley (ed.), *Preschool programs for the disadvantaged.* Baltimore, Md.: Johns Hopkins University Press, 1972.

WEINER, P. S. Developmental language disorders. In H. E. Rie & E. D. Rie (eds.), *Handbook of minimal brain dysfunctions.* New York: Wiley-Interscience, 1980.

WEINGARTNER, H., RAPOPORT, J. L., BUCKSBAUM, M. S., BUNNEY, W. E., EBERT, M. H., MIKKELSON, E. J., & CAINE, E. D. Cognitive processes in normal and hyperactive children and their responses to amphetamine treatment. *Journal of Abnormal Psychology,* 1980, *89,* 25–37.

WEINRAUB, M., & FRANKEL, J. Sex differences in parent-infant interaction during free play, departure, and separation. *Child Development,* 1977, *48,* 1240–1249.

WEISS, B. Food additives and environmental chemicals as sources of childhood behavior disorders. *Journal of Child Psychiatry,* 1982, *21,* 144–152.

WEISS, G. Controlled studies of efficacy of long-term treatment with stimulants of hyperactive children. In E. Denhoff & L. Stern (eds.), *Minimal brain dysfunction.* New York: Masson Publishing, 1979.

WEISSBERG, R. P., COWEN, E. L., LOTYCZEWSKI, B. S., & GESTEN, E. L. The primary mental health project: Seven consecutive years of program outcome research. *Journal of Consulting and Clinical Psychology,* 1983, *51,* 100–107.

WEISZ, J. R., & YEATES, K. O. Cognitive development in retarded and nonretarded persons: Piagetian tests of the similar structure hypothesis. *Psychological Bulletin,* 1981, *90,* 153–178.

WEISZ, J. R., & ZIGLER, E. Cognitive development in retarded and nonretarded persons: Piagetian tests of the similar sequence hypothesis. *Psychological Bulletin,* 1979, *86,* 831–851.

WELLS, K. C., FOREHAND, R., & GRIEST, G. L. Generality of treatment effects from treated to untreated behaviors resulting from a parent training program. *Journal of Clinical Child Psychology,* 1980, *9,* 217–219.

WENDER, P. H. *Minimal brain dysfunction in children.* New York: Wiley-Interscience, 1971.

WERKMAN, S. Anxiety disorders. In H. I. Kaplan, A. E. M. Freedman, & B. J. Sadock (eds.), *Comprehensive textbook of psychiatry/III,* Vol. 3. Baltimore, Md.: Williams & Wilkins, 1980.

WERNER, E. E. *The children of Kauai.* Honolulu: University of Hawaii Press, 1971.

WERRY, J. S. Studies of the hyperactive child: IV. An empirical analysis of the minimal brain dysfunction syndrome. *Archives of General Psychiatry,* 1968, *19,* 9–16.

WERRY, J. S. The childhood psychoses. In H. C. Quay & J. S. Werry (eds.), *Psychopathological disorders of childhood,* 2nd ed. New York: John Wiley, 1979. (a)

WERRY, J. S. Organic factors. In H. C. Quay & J. S. Werry (eds.), *Psychopathological disorders of childhood,* 2nd ed. New York: John Wiley, 1979. (b)

WERRY, J. S. Psychosomatic disorders, psychogenic symptoms, and hospitalization. In H. C. Quay & J. S. Werry (eds.), *Psychopathological disorders of childhood,* 2nd ed. New York: John Wiley, 1979. (c)

WERRY, J. S., & COHRSSEN, J. Enuresis: An etiologic and therapeutic study. *Journal of Pediatrics,* 1965, *67,* 423–431.

WEST, K. L. MMPI correlates of ulcerative colitis. *Journal of Clinical Psychology,* 1970, *26,* 214–219.

WESTIN-LINDGREN, G. Achievement and mental ability of physically late and early maturing schoolchildren related to their social background. *Journal of Child Psychology and Psychiatry,* 1982, *23,* 407–420.

WHALEN, C. K., & HENKER, B. Psychostimulants and children: A review and analysis. *Psychological Bulletin,* 1976, *83,* 1113–1130.

WHITE, M. A thousand consecutive cases of enuresis: Results of treatment. *The Medical Officer,* 1968, *120,* 151–155.

WHITE, R. W. Motivation reconsidered: The concept of competence. *Psychological Review,* 1959, *66,* 297–333.

WHITE, W. C., & DAVIS, M. T. Vicarious extinction of phobic behavior in early childhood. *Journal of Abnormal Child Psychology,* 1974, *2,* 25–32.

WHITEHILL, M., DeMYER-GAPIN, S., & SCOTT, T. J. Stimulation-seeking in antisocial pre-adolescent children. *Journal of Abnormal Psychology,* 1976, *85,* 101–104.

WHITING, B. B., & WHITING, J. W. M. *Children of six cultures.* Cambridge: Harvard University Press, 1975.

WHITING, J. W. M., & CHILD, I. L. *Child training and personality: A cross-cultural study.* New Haven: Yale University Press, 1953.

WHITMAN, T. L., & SCIBAK, J. W. Behavior modification research with the severely and profoundly retarded. In N. R. Ellis (ed.), *Handbook of mental deficiency.* Hillsdale, N. J.: Lawrence Erlbaum Associates, 1979.

WILLERMAN, L. Activity level and hyperactivity in twins. *Child Development,* 1973, *44,* 288–293.

WILLIAMS, C. D. The elimination of tantrum behavior by extinction procedures: Case report. *Journal of Abnormal and Social Psychology,* 1959, *59,* 269.

WILLIAMS, H. E., & McNICOL, K. N. The spectrum of asthma in children. *Pediatric Clinics of North America,* 1975, *22,* 43–52.

WILLIAMS, R. H. (ed.). *Textbook of endocrinology,* 5th ed. Philadelphia: Saunders, 1974.

WINDLE, W. F. (ed.). *Neurological and psychological deficits of asphyxia neonatorum.* Springfield, Ill.: Chas. C Thomas, 1958.

WINETT, R. A., & WINKLER, R. C. Current behavior modification in the classroom: Be still, be quiet, be docile. *Journal of Applied Behavior Analysis,* 1972, *5,* 499–504.

WING, L. The syndrome of early childhood autism. *British Journal of Medicine,* September, 1970, 381–392.

WINSBERG, B. G., YEPES, L. E., & BIALER, I. Pharmacologic management of children with hyperactive/aggressive/inattentive behavior disorders. *Clinical Pediatrics,* 1976, *15,* 471–477.

WITKIN, H. A., MEDNICK, S. A., SCHULSINGER, F., BAKKESTRØM, E., CHRISTIANSEN, K. O., GOODENOUGH, D. R., HIRSCHHORN, K., LUNDSTEEN, C., OWEN, D. R., PHILIP, J., RUBIN, D. B., & STOCKING, M. Criminality in XYY and XXY men. *Science,* 1976, *193,* 547–555.

WOLFE, B. E. Behavioral treatment of childhood gender disorders. *Behavior Modification,* 1979, *4,* 550–575.

WOLMAN, B. B. Psychoanalytic theory of infantile development. In B. B. Wolman (ed.), *Handbook of child psychoanalysis: Research theory and practice.* New York: Van Nostrand Reinhold, 1972.

WOODWARD, W. M. Piaget's theory and the study of mental retardation. In N. R. Ellis (ed.), *Handbook of mental deficiency.* Hillsdale, N.J.: Lawrence Erlbaum Associates, 1979.

WORK, H. H. Mental retardation. In J. D. Noshpitz (ed.), *Basic handbook of child psychiatry,* Vol. 2. New York: Basic Books, 1979.

WORLD HEALTH ORGANIZATION. *Manual of the international statistical classification of diseases, injuries, and causes of death,* 9th revision. Geneva: World Health Organization, 1977.

WRIGHT, H. F. Observational child study. In P. H. Mussen (ed.), *Handbook of research methods in child development.* New York: John Wiley, 1960.

WRIGHT, L. Handling the encopretic child. *Professional Psychology,* 1973, *4,* 137–144.

WRIGHT, L. Outcome of a standardized program for treating psychogenic encopresis. *Professional Psychology,* 1975, *6,* 453–456.

WRIGHT, L. Conceptualizing and defining psychosomatic disorders. *American Psychologist,* 1977, *32,* 625–628.

WRIGHT, L., SCHAEFER, A. B., & SOLOMONS, G. *Encyclopedia of pediatric psychology.* Baltimore, Md.: University Park Press, 1979.

WRIGHT, L., & WALKER, C. E. Behavioral treatment of encopresis. *Journal of Pediatric Psychology,* 1976, *4,* 35–37.

YAMAMOTO, K. Children's ratings of the stressfulness of experiences. *Developmental Psychology,* 1979, *15,* 581–582.

YANDO, R. M., & KAGAN, J. The effects of teacher tempo on the child. *Child Development,* 1968, *39,* 27–34.

YARROW, L. J. Attachment and dependency. In J. L. Gewritz (ed.), *Attachment and dependency.* New York: V. H. Winston & Sons, 1972.

YARROW, L. J., & PEDERSEN, F. A. Attachment: Its origins

and course. In *The young child: Reviews of research.* Vol. II. Washington D.C.: National Association for the Education of Young Children, 1972.

YEN, S., McINTIRE, R. W., & BERKOWITZ, S. Extinction of inappropriate sleeping behavior: Multiple assessment. *Psychological Reports,* 1972, *30,* 375–378.

YOUNG, E. R., & PARISH, T. S. Impact of father absence during childhood on the psychological adjustment of college females. *Sex Roles,* 1977, *3,* 217–227.

YOUNG, G. C., & MORGAN, R. T. T. Overlearning in the conditioning treatment of enuresis. *Behaviour Research and Therapy,* 1972, *10,* 419–420.

YULE, W. The epidemiology of child psychopathology. In B. B. Lahey & A. E. Kazdin (eds.), *Advances in clinical child psychology,* Vol. 4. New York: Plenum, 1981.

YULE, W., & RUTTER, M. The epidemiology and social implications of specific reading retardation. In R. Knights and D. J. Bakker (eds.), *The neuropsychology of learning disorders: Theoretical approaches.* Baltimore, Md.: University Park Press, 1976.

YURCHENCO, H. *A mighty hard road: The Woody Guthrie story.* New York: McGraw-Hill, 1970.

ZALESKI, A., GARRARD, J. W., & SHOKIER, M. H. K. Nocturnal enuresis: The importance of a small bladder capacity. In I. Kolvin, R. C. MacKeith, & S. R. Meadow (eds.), *Bladder control and enuresis.* Philadelphia: Saunders, 1973.

ZAX, M., & COWEN, E. L. Early identification and prevention of emotional disturbance in a public school. In E. L. Cowen, E. A. Gardner, & M. Zax (eds.), *Emergent approaches to mental health problems.* N.Y.: Appleton-Century-Crofts, 1967.

ZEAMAN, D., & HOUSE, B. J. The role of attention in retardate discrimination learning. In N. R. Ellis (ed.), *Handbook of mental deficiency.* New York: McGraw-Hill, 1963.

ZEAMAN, D., & HOUSE, B. J. A review of attention theory. In N. R. Ellis (ed.), *Handbook of mental deficiency.* Hillsdale, N.J.: Lawrence Erlbaum Associates, 1979.

ZEGIOB, L. E., ARNOLD, S., & FOREHAND, R. An examination of observer effects in parent-child interactions. *Child Development,* 1975, *46,* 509–512.

ZIGLER, E. Developmental versus difference theories of mental retardation and the problem of motivation. *American Journal of Mental Deficiency,* 1969, *73,* 536–556.

ZIGLER, E. The effectiveness of Head Start: Another look. *Educational Psychologist,* 1978, *13,* 71–77.

ZIGLER, E., ABELSON, W. D., TRICKETT, P. K., & SEITZ, V. Is an intervention program necessary in order to improve economically disadvantaged children's IQ scores? *Child Development,* 1982, *53,* 340–348.

ZIGLER, E., & deLABRY, J. Concept-switching in middle-class, lower-class, and retarded children. *Journal of Abnormal and Social Psychology,* 1962, *65,* 267–273.

ZIGLER, E., & PHILLIPS, L. Social competence and outcome in psychiatric disorders. *Journal of Abnormal and Social Psychology,* 1961, *63,* 264–271.

ZIGLER, E., & TRICKETT, P. K. IQ, social competence, and evaluation of early childhood intervention programs. *American Psychologist,* 1978, *33,* 789–798.

ZINKUS, P. W. Behavioral and emotional sequelae of learning disorders. In M. I. Gottlieb, P. W. Zinkus, & L. J. Bradford (eds.), *Current issues in developmental pediatrics: The learning-disabled child.* New York: Grune & Stratton, 1979.

ZIV, A. Children's behavior problems as viewed by teachers, psychologists, and children. *Child Development,* 1970, *41,* 871–879.

ZUNG, W. W. A self-rating depression scale. *Archives of General Psychiatry,* 1965, *12,* 63–70.

NAME INDEX

Abel, G. G., 124
Abichandani, F., 175
Abikoff, H., 245
Ablon, S. L., 134, 135
Abraham, K., 55, 56
Abraham, S., 115
Accardo, P. J., 23
Achenbach, T. M., 7, 10, 36, 70, 82, 85n, 95-98, 103, 107, 108, 258
Ackerman, P. T., 101, 249
Adams, P., 151
Agras, S., 113
Agras, W. S., 124, 303, 304
Ahrons, C. R., 260
Ainsworth, M.D.S., 28, 29, 323
Alanen, Y., 180
Albee, G. W., 322
Alexander, A. B., 286, 287, 291-92, 302
Alexander, F., 290
Alexander, J. F., 260, 279, 280
Algozzine, B., 14, 99
Allen, K. E., 106
Allen, L., 36, 37, 140, 161, 201, 259
Allen, M. T., 285
Allen, R. P., 231, 232, 234
Amatruda, C. S., 109
Anastasi, A., 19, 201
Anders, T. F., 127, 134, 135, 136
Anderson, L., 172
Anderson, L. D., 199
Anderson, S., 324
Andrasik, F., 302
Andrews, C. E., 173
Andrews, R. J., 208-9
Anthony, E. J., 5, 7, 150-51
Aoki, B., 156
Applebaum, M. I., 201
Arend, R., 326
Aries, P., 9
Arkel, Y., 285

Armstrong, P. M., 226
Arnold, J., 267
Arnold, S., 107
Arter, J. A., 254
Asher, S. R., 34, 35
Atkinson, R. C., 217, 218
Ayllon, T., 124, 254, 255
Azrin, N. H., 130, 131, 226

Babigian, H., 154
Bachrach, W., 293
Back, K. W., 116
Baer, D. M., 10, 188, 226
Bahn, A. K., 92
Bailey, D. A., 24
Baily, S. M., 115
Baker, B. L., 130, 131
Baker, H., 148-49
Baker, L., 67, 125-26, 173-76, 249, 298
Bakwin, H., 128, 134
Bakwin, R. M., 134
Balaschak, B. A., 302
Ball, R. S., 201
Balla, D., 219, 220
Balow, B., 109, 199
Bandura, A., 10, 62-64, 146, 147, 267
Baratz, J. C., 323
Baratz, S. S., 323
Barclay, C. R., 218
Barkett, C. J., 234, 242
Barkley, R. A., 7, 232, 235-41, 244, 245
Barlow, D. H., 124
Barnard, J. D., 272
Baroff, G. S., 189
Barrett, C. L., 141, 148
Barrios, B. A., 139, 142
Barsch, R. H., 252
Bartak, L., 173
Bartel, 252
Barton, E. S., 226

Baskiewicz, A., 222
Battle, E., 7
Bauer, C. H., 133
Bauer, D. H., 142
Bayley, N., 109, 199
Beach, D. R., 216
Bechtholdt, H., 235
Beck, A. T., 92, 158, 163, 164
Beck, P., 142
Beck, S., 304
Becker, W. C., 32, 33, 260
Bedlington, M. M., 279
Beers, C., 10, 13
Bell, R. A., 32
Bell, S. M., 29, 323
Bellak, A., 104
Bellman, 132
Belmont, J. M., 217-18
Belmont, L., 33, 237, 238, 251
Belsky, J., 32, 33, 317
Bemis, K. M., 120, 122
Bemporad, J. R., 132, 171
Bender, L., 100, 177-78, 183, 186
Benedict, R., 3
Bennett, E. L., 39, 130
Bentler, P. M., 16, 276
Benton, A., 248
Berecz, J. M., 140, 143
Bergman, A. B., 285
Berkowitz, S., 135
Berland, R. M., 280
Berman, A. L., 159, 247
Bernal, M. E., 272
Berry, P., 208
Berscheid, E., 25
Bertelson, A. D., 295
Besserman, R. L., 130
Bettleheim, B., 174, 187
Bialer, I., 240
Bijou, S. W., 10, 106, 226

Biller, H. B., 34
Billewicz, W. Z., 115
Billingsley, A., 31
Binet, A., 12, 13, 198, 330-31
Binkoff, J. A., 190
Birch, H. G., 30, 31, 37, 251
Birnbrauer, J. S., 225-27
Birns, B., 7, 37
Bjorntorp, P., 118
Blackburn, G. L., 118
Blackman, S., 131
Blackwell, A., 122
Bleecker, E. R., 291
Bleuler, 167
Blinn, K., 128
Bliss, E. L., 120
Bloom, B. L., 311, 322
Blumberg, M. L., 316
Boll, T. J., 103
Bolstad, O. D., 106
Borkovec, T. D., 264
Borkowski, J. G., 216-18
Bornstein, P., 245
Bowen, M., 67, 68, 327
Bower, G. H., 25
Bowerman, C. E., 34
Boyce, T. W., 285
Bradley, R. H., 212, 240
Bradway, K., 200
Brady, K., 289-90
Braginsky, B. M., 225
Braginsky, D. D., 225
Brakke, N. P., 158
Branch, C.H.H., 120
Braukmann, C. J., 278, 279
Breger, L., 26
Breuer, J., 8
Bricker, W., 266, 271
Brim, O. G., 33
Broadhurst, D. D., 316
Broca, 230
Broman, S. H., 182
Bronfenbrenner, U., 31, 34
Bronheim, S. P., 285
Bronner, A., 12, 13
Brooke, E., 94
Brophy, J. E., 35
Brown, A. L., 217-18
Brown, C. C., 312
Brown, C. H., 277
Brown, R., 263
Brownell, K. D., 118
Bruch, H., 120, 122, 124
Bruininks, R. H., 225
Brunton, M., 265
Bryan, J. H., 230, 247-49, 251, 252
Bryan, T. H., 230, 247-49, 251, 252
Buckley, P. D., 101
Bullen, B. A., 117
Bunney, W. E., 160
Burchard, J. D., 278
Burke, M. S., 117
Burkes, L., 102
Burstein, S., 305
Burton, N., 162
Busch-Rossnagel, N. A., 35
Buss, A. H., 28
Butterfield, E. C., 217-18
Buxton, M. N., 285

Caldwell, B. M., 212
Campbell, D. T., 71, 72
Campbell, M., 172, 175, 186
Campione, J. C., 217-18
Cantor, D., 293
Cantwell, D. P., 92, 93, 98, 100, 158,
    159, 173-76, 230, 233, 234, 236, 241,
    249, 252
Caplan, G., 311, 319, 332
Caplan, M., 162
Capute, A., 23
Carlsmith, J. M., 272
Carlson, G. A., 158, 159
Carpenter, R. A., 277
Carpenter, K., 122
Carr, E. G., 189, 190
Carron, A. V., 24
Cartelli, L. M., 272
Caruth, E., 187
Cassel, J. C., 285
Cataldo, M. F., 115
Cattell, P., 109
Cavanaugh, J. C., 216-18
Cerny, J. A., 16
Cerreto, M. C., 92
Chai, H., 289-92
Chandler, M. J., 103
Chapin, H. N., 124
Char, J., 178-79
Charles, J., 242, 245
Charlesworth, R., 156
Charlop, H., 172
Charney, E., 115
Cherry, T., 295
Chess, T., 3, 7, 37-40, 175, 235, 259
Child, I. L., 112
Chinsky, J. M., 216
Christensen, A., 271
Christophersen, E. R., 272
Churchill, M. P., 294
Clapp, R. K., 130
Clarke-Stewart, K. A., 32
Clements, S. D., 134-35, 231, 249
Clingempeel, W. G., 261
Coddington, R. D., 284
Coe, T. D., 280
Cohen, D. J., 175
Cohen, H. J., 276, 278
Cohen, I. L., 186
Cohrssen, J., 130
Cole, P. E., 115, 158
Coles, G. S., 247, 248
Collier, A. M., 285
Collier, B., 295
Collier, J. G., 159
Collmer, C. W., 316, 317
Combrinck-Graham, L., 120
Combs, M., 156
Conger, J. C., 156
Conger, R. E., 269
Conners, C. K., 107, 163, 186, 237, 240,
    242, 244, 249
Connor, P. A., 235
Cooper, A. M., 291
Cooper, L. M., 116
Cooper, M., 113
Coote, M. A., 128
Copelane, A., 245
Copernicus, 45

Cordua, G. D., 116
Corman, L., 224
Costello, C. G., 164
Cowen, E. L., 154, 261, 312, 313, 322,
    327
Crandall, V., 35
Creer, T. L., 291, 292
Cronbach, L. J., 201
Cropp, G.J.A., 291-92
Cruikshank, W. M., 252
Cummings, C., 235
Cushna, B., 198
Cytryn, L., 21, 160, 196, 206, 210, 211,
    222
Czudner, G., 249

Dalby, J. T., 53, 244, 245
D'Andrade, R. G., 5
Danker-Brown, P., 291
Darwin, C., 9
David, O. J., 238
Davids, A., 149
Davidson, M. D., 133
Davidson, W. S., 278
Davis, M. H., 291
Davis, M. S., 303
Davis, M. T., 78-80
Davison, E., 267
Davison, G. C., 45, 82, 182, 320
Davison, L. W., 101
DeBlois, C. S., 235
DeFries, J. C., 49, 213
DeJonge, G. A., 127
DeLabry, J., 219-20
Delamater, A. M., 245, 248, 252, 254,
    295
DeLeon, G., 130, 131
Delfini, L. F., 272
DeLong, G. R., 175
Delprato, D. J., 145, 146
DeLuise, M., 118
DeMause, L., 9
DeMyer, M. K., 173, 174
DeMyer-Gapin, S., 264
Denhoff, E., 230
Dennis, M. G., 24
Dennis, W., 24
DePanfilis, D., 318, 319
Descartes, R., 283
DeSilva, P., 145
DesLauriers, A. M., 171
Desposito, F., 285
Devine, V. T., 271
Diament, C., 106
Diamond, M. C., 39
Dickerson, D. J., 217-18
Dietz, A., 106
Diller, L., 25
Dion, K., 25
Ditman, K. S., 128
Divoky, D., 242
Dodge, K. A., 158
Doleys, D. M., 129, 130, 132, 133, 272
Doll, E. A., 113, 202-3
Dollard, J., 266
Doob, L. W., 266
Doppelt, J. E., 201
Dorfman, D. D., 214

Doster, J., 272
Douglas, J., 305
Douglas, V. I., 162, 232
Down, L., 207
Drabman, R. S., 116, 225
Drake, L., 248
Droegemueller, W., 316
Drotar, D., 222
Drumbrell, S., 237
Drummond, T., 120
Dubey, D. R., 239, 244
Duenas, E., 46
Dugas, E., 232
Dunbar, J. M., 303, 304
Dunalp, G., 81
Dunn, L. M., 66-67, 224
Duster, T., 99
Dweck, C. S., 163
Dykman, R. A., 101, 249

Eddy, E., 112
Edelbrock, C. S., 36, 95-98, 103, 107,
    108, 258
Edelman, M. W., 331-34
Edmunds, M., 316
Eells, K., 201
Egel, A. L., 172
Eggers, C., 168, 179-80, 184
Eichorn, D. H., 24
Eid, E. E., 115
Eisenberg, J. G., 259
Eisenberg, L., 94, 170, 173, 236-38, 240
Eisenson, J., 249
Ekstein, R., 187
Elardo, R., 212
Elizur, E., 128
Ellis, P. L., 261
Eme, R. F., 7, 265
Emerson, P. E., 29, 37
Emery, R. E., 260, 261
Empey, L. T., 274, 275, 278
Endicott, J., 180, 181
Engen, T., 25
English, H. B., 144
Epstein, L. H., 304, 305
Erbaugh, J. K., 92
Erbe, R. W., 207
Erickson, M. T., 9, 58-59, 126
Erixon, G., 145
Eron, L. D., 268-69
Etaugh, C., 33
Etzel, B. C., 15
Etzwiler, D., 295, 296
Everett, N., 188
Exner, J. E., Jr., 104
Eyberg, S. M., 271

Falstein, E. I., 123
Fantz, R. L., 25
Farkas, G. M., 304
Faust, M. S., 24
Feingold, B. F., 51, 237, 289
Feinn, J., 7, 14
Feinstein, S., 123
Feldman, F., 292
Feldman, G. M., 289, 293
Felner, R. D., 261
Ferber, H., 271
Ferguson, H. B., 232, 236

Ferguson, L. R., 86
Fernald, G., 12, 13
Ferrari, M., 142
Ferster, C. B., 162, 174, 187
Feuerrstein, M., 100, 101, 103, 248
Field, T., 153, 155
Figueroa, J., 304
Filipczak, J., 276, 278
Finch, A. J., 80
Finch, S. M., 293
Finley, P. M., 130
Finley, W. W., 127, 128, 130
Finney, J. W., 115
Fiorelli, J. S., 232
Firestone, P. B., 81
Fish, B., 182
Fisher, E. G., Jr., 295
Fisher, P., 159
Fixsen, D. L., 278, 279
Flavell, J. H., 26, 216, 218
Fleece, E. L., 303
Fleischman, M. J., 271
Fleming, J. P., 277
Fletcher, J. M., 230, 231
Flier, J. S., 118
Flores de Apocada, R., 327
Fodor, E. M., 263
Foley, J., 305
Fölling, 21
Folstein, S., 175, 176
Ford, D., 272
Forehand, R., 107, 272-74, 280
Forgus, R. H., 39
Forrest, T., 249
Foster, G. G., 98
Foster, R., 203
Fox, J. J., 157
Foxx, R. M., 130
Fraiberg, S., 136
Frankel, A., 295
Frankel, J., 32
Frankel, M. S., 86, 87
Freedman, D. G., 28
Freeman, B. J., 175
Freeman, E. D., 127
Freeman, E. H., 289
Freidson, E., 99
Freitag, G., 185
French, J. H., 251
French, T. M., 289
Freud, A., 9, 11, 58, 123, 132, 330
Freud, S., 8-13, 16, 29, 39, 54-59, 123,
    128, 139, 143, 265
Friedman, R. M., 316, 317
Friedman, S., 187
Friedrich, L. K., 267, 268
Frodi, A. M., 32
Frostig, M., 109, 252, 253-54
Fuller, 225
Furman, W., 156-58

Gabrielli, W. F., 276
Gad, M. T., 285
Galton, F., 213
Garber, J., 161
Garcia, E., 226
Garcia, J., 145
Gardner, E. F., 109
Gardner, R. A., 231

Garmezy, N., 40
Garn, S., 115
Garner, A. M., 272, 295, 297
Garrard, J. W., 130
Garvey, W. P., 149
Gelder, M. G., 142, 152-53
Geller, B., 186
Geller, E., 175
Gelles, R. J., 316
Gerard, M. W., 127, 128
Gersten, E. L., 312
Gersten, J. C., 259
Gesell, A., 12-13, 109
Gesten, E. L., 313, 327
Gibbons, D. C., 276
Gil, D. G., 316, 317
Gilmartin, R. C., 46
Ginsburg, H., 323
Giovannoni, J. M., 31
Gittelman, R., 104, 245
Gladston, R., 316
Glass, C. R., 217
Gleser, G., 162
Glidden, L. M., 217-18
Glueck, E. T., 260, 275
Glueck, S., 260, 275
Goddard, H. H., 213
Gold, V. J., 185
Goldberg, H. K., 250
Goldberg, J. O., 92
Goldberg, S., 32
Golden, M., 154
Goldfarb, N., 181
Goldfarb, W., 39, 167, 180-83, 192
Goldstein, J., 230, 330
Goldston, S. E., 320
Good, T. L., 35
Goodman, H. C., 115
Goodman, J., 64
Gordon, D. A., 149
Gordon, N., 289-90
Gorman, F. J., 289
Gottlieb, E., 128
Gottlieb, J., 224, 252, 254
Gottlieb, M. I., 46, 246
Gottman, J., 156
Gove, F. L., 326
Goyen, J. D., 249
Goyette, C. H., 240
Graham, P., 103, 127, 258-59
Graves, M. G., 68, 280
Graziano, A. M., 142, 146
Green, A. H., 316, 317
Green, K. F., 145
Green, M., 112
Greenhill, L. A., 235
Greenland, C., 316, 317
Greenwood, C., 153, 156
Greer, 288
Griest, D. L., 68, 274, 280
Griest, G. L., 273
Grinder, R. E., 12, 21
Grossman, H. J., 196, 202, 204, 206
Grossman, L., 151
Grossmann, F., 32
Grossmann, K. E., 32
Grusec, J. E., 19, 39, 63
Guerra, F., 249
Guess, D., 226

Guile, C. A., 121
Gullion, M. E., 271
Gunn, P., 208
Gussow, J. D., 30, 31
Guthrie, W., 46

Haas, L. J., 279
Habif, V. L., 247, 252, 254
Hafner, A. J., 260
Hagamen, A. J., 171, 176, 180, 221, 222, 225
Haith, M. M., 23
Haley, J., 68
Hall, G. S., 12, 13
Hallahan, D. P., 67, 205, 206, 245-47, 254
Halmi, K. A., 123
Hammer, D., 116
Hammill, D. D., 254
Hampe, E., 141, 148
Hanf, 273
Hansen, H., 237, 238
Hantman, E., 237
Hare, R. D., 264
Harig, P. T., 278
Harley, J. P., 237
Harlow, H. F., 39
Harlow, M. K., 39
Harper, 126
Harris, F. R., 106
Harris, L., 162
Harris, S. L., 142, 191
Harrison, N. S., 70
Harrison, S. I., 196
Harryman, S., 23
Harter, S., 220
Hartmann, D. P., 139
Hartmann, H., 9, 58
Hartup, W. W., 34, 35, 153, 156-58
Harvey, S. E., 118
Hastings, J. E., 236
Haughton, E., 124
Hawes, R., 303
Hawton, K., 159
Haywood, H. C., 215, 217, 218, 220, 224
Heald, F. P., 117
Healy, W., 12, 13
Hebb, D. O., 39
Hegreves, J. P., 149
Heiman, M., 123
Hellmer, L. A., 260
Henker, B., 237, 239, 243, 245, 246
Hermelin, B., 173
Hernandez, M., 316
Herrnstein, R. J., 263
Hersov, L. A., 148
Hess, J. M., 119
Hess, R. D., 31
Heston, L. L., 182
Hetherington, E. M., 33, 34, 103, 163, 182, 238-39, 260, 261, 267, 276
Hickey, J. S., 119
Hieronymous, A. N., 109
Hilgard, E. R., 25
Hinkle, L. E., 297
Hippocrates, 45, 50
Hobbes, G., 237
Hobbs, N., 65-66, 99
Hodapp, R. M., 32

Hoffman, A., 291
Hoffman, L. W., 33
Hoffman, M. L., 261
Hoffman, H., 232
Hogarty, P. S., 201
Hollingsworth, C. E., 151, 152
Holmes, F. B., 140
Holmes, L. B., 207
Holroyd, K. A., 302
Honzik, M. P., 36, 37, 140, 161, 201, 259
Hops, H., 154
Hops, S., 153, 156
Horne, D., 253
Horton, W., 116
House, B. J., 216, 220
Hoy, E., 7, 242
Huesmann, L. R., 268-69
Hugel, R., 142
Hughes, P. C., 238
Hull, 10
Humphreys, L., 273
Hundleby, J. D., 277
Hunsaker, J. H., 130
Hunt, J. McV., 29, 32, 39, 197, 215, 217
Hunter, 44
Hutcherson, S., 303
Hutchings, B., 265
Hutt, C., 74
Hutt, S. J., 74

Illingworth, R. S., 199
Irvin, N., 222
Israel, A. C., 115-17, 119-21
Itard, J. M., 196, 223
Izzo, L. D., 154

Jabbour, J. T., 46
Jackson, C. M., 23
Jackson, R. H., 272
Jacob, R. G., 232
Jacobs, P. A., 265
Jacobson, A., 134
Jansky, J. J., 248, 250, 251
Jarvie, G. J., 116
Jason, L. A., 324
Jastak, J. F., 109
Jastak, S. R., 109
Jeffrey, D. B., 118, 119
Jeffrey, R. W., 118
Jehu, D., 130
Jenkins, J. R., 254
Jensen, A. R., 214, 216
Jensen, E. W., 285
Jersild, A. T., 140
Jespersen, J. O., 27
Jessor, R., 277
Jessor, S. L., 277
Johansson, S., 272
Johnson, J. H., 285
Johnson, M. L., 117
Johnson, S. B., 104, 297
Johnson, S. M., 106, 107, 260, 271, 272
Johnston, M. S., 106
Jones, A., 130
Jones, M. C., 24, 60, 139, 146
Jones, R. R., 267, 269
Josselyn, I., 293
Judas, I., 123

Judd, L. J., 151
Jurkovic, G. J., 97, 262, 263

Kaffman, M., 128
Kagan, J., 238, 248
Kahn, E., 100, 230
Kales, A., 134
Kales, J., 134
Kallmann, F., 182
Kalnins, I. V., 294
Kamin, L. G., 201, 214
Kandel, D. B., 277
Kandel, H. J., 254, 255
Kanfer, F. H., 147
Kangas, J., 200
Kanner, L., 5, 7, 9, 13, 112-13, 114, 127, 128, 135, 168-70, 183, 193
Karoly, P., 147
Karon, M., 308
Kashani, J., 158
Kassorla, I. C., 185
Katz, J., 122
Katz, S., 245
Katz-Garris, L., 223
Kauffman, A. S., 103
Kauffman, J. M., 67, 205, 206, 245-47, 254
Kaufman, K. F., 244
Kaufman, M. R., 123
Kavale, K., 252
Kavanaugh, C., 316
Kaye, H., 25
Kazdin, A. E., 163, 164
Keane, S., 156
Keeley, S. M., 271
Kellam, S. G., 277
Keller, B., 28
Kelley, T. L., 109
Kelly, D., 104
Kelman, H. C., 85
Kelty, M., 85
Kempe, C. H., 316
Kendall, P., 80, 156, 161
Kennedy, J. A., 24
Kennedy, W. A., 149, 150, 201
Kennell, J. H., 32, 222
Kenny, T. J., 235, 239
Kent, R. N., 106, 271
Keogh, B. K., 234, 242
Kephart, N. C., 230, 252
Kessen, W., 23, 40
Kessler, J. N., 230
Kessler, J. W., 57, 136, 149, 266
Kidder, J. D., 226
Kimmel, E. C., 130, 131
Kimmel, H. D., 130, 131
Kinch, J. W., 34
King, C. A., 234
King, H. E., 272
King, L. J., 259
King, R. A., 159
Kinsbourne, M., 237
Kirby, F. D., 156
Kirigin, K. A., 279
Kirk, S. A., 109, 245-46, 253, 254
Kirk, W. D., 109
Kirkley, B. G., 295
Kitsuse, J. I., 99
Klaus, M. H., 32, 222

Klein, D. F., 245
Klein, N. C., 279-80
Klein, M., 9, 58
Klopfer, B., 104
Knapp, P. H., 291
Knight, R., 98
Knitzer, J., 327, 329
Knobloch, H., 7, 12
Koegel, R., 81, 172, 188, 192
Kohlberg, L., 8, 262, 263
Kolata, G. B., 53
Kolko, D. J., 172
Kolvin, I., 167
Konstantareas, M. M., 82
Koocher, G. P., 112, 307, 308
Koppitz, E. M., 100, 101
Koski, M. L., 295, 297
Kotelchuk, M., 29
Kotses, H., 302
Kovacs, M., 158, 163, 164
Kozloff, M., 191, 192
Kraeplin, 45, 50, 92, 167
Kramer, K., 249
Kramer, M., 92
Kramme, K. W., 81
Kratochwill, T. R., 146
Krauss, M. R., 118
Kugler, M. M., 133
Kuhn, T., 44
Kupfer, D., 245, 252, 254
Kurdek, L. A., 260, 261

Lacey, B. A., 7
Lacey, H. M., 95
LaCrosse, J., 8
Lagos, J., 285
Lahey, B. B., 245, 247, 248, 252, 254
Lamb, H. R., 322
Lamb, M. E., 29, 32, 39
Lambert, N. M., 232
Landau, S., 235
Landauer, T. K., 272
Lang, P. J., 113
Langhorne, J., 235
Langner, T. S., 259
LaPouse, R., 7, 140, 142
Larsen, S. C., 254
Laufer, M. W., 230, 240
Laurendeau, 215
Lawler, K. A., 285
Layman, D., 254, 255
Leach, G. M., 74-75
LeBaron, S.W.M., 100, 101, 248
LeBlanc, J. M., 15
Lebovici, S., 94
Lefever, W., 109
Leff, R., 192
Lefkowitz, M. M., 162, 164, 268-69
Lehtinen, L., 230
Leitenberg, H., 124
Leland, H., 203, 225
Lemert, E. M., 276
Lemnitzer, N. B., 119
Lenneberg, E. H., 28
Leon, G. R., 161
Lepper, M., 272
Lerner, R. M., 116
Leske, G., 280
Leventhal, T., 150

Levin, H., 32
Levine, A. S., 267
Levitt, E. E., 7
Levy, F., 237
Lewinsohn, P., 162
Lewis, M., 98
Lewis, S., 146, 147
Lewittes, D. J., 116
Libet, J., 113
Liebert, R. M., 20n, 52, 56, 74, 118, 126, 267
Liebman, R., 298
Liederman, V. R., 116
Lilly, M. S., 66, 67, 99, 223, 247
Lin, T. Y., 94
Lindquist, E. F., 109
Links, P. S., 175
Linscheid, T. R., 112
Lipsitt, L. P., 25
Littman, R. A., 266, 271
Lobitz, G. K., 107, 260, 272
Locke, J., 20
Lockyer, L., 183
Loevinger, 26
Löfberg, I., 145
Lombroso, 264
London, P., 116
Loney, J., 7, 234, 235, 242
Long, J. S., 192
Lopez, R., 235-36
Lorand, S., 123
Lorenz, K., 39
Lorion, R. P., 312
Lotter, V., 7, 167, 175, 183, 184
Lotyczewski, B. S., 313
Lourie, R. S., 21, 113, 114, 196, 206, 210, 211, 222
Lovaas, I. O., 15-16, 172, 185, 188-90, 192
Love, C. T., 98, 276
Lovibond, S. H., 128-30
Lowe, K., 296, 304
Lowenthal, H., 285
Lowman, J., 319, 320
Lubar, J. F., 302
Lubetsky, S., 178-79
Lundberg, O., 123
Luparello, T., 291
Lutzker, J. R., 280, 296, 304
Lyle, J. G., 249
Lynch, G., 232
Lynn, D. B., 31, 34
Lyon, B., 115
Lyons, H. A., 291

McAdoo, W. G., 173, 174
Macalpine, 44
McAskie, M., 214
McBride, M., 115
McCaan, D. C., 263
McCall, R. B., 201
McCarthy, E. D., 259
McCarthy, J. J., 109
McCaulay, M., 156
McClearn, G. E., 49, 213
Maccoby, E. E., 32
McCord, J., 260
McCord, W., 260
McDermott, J., 196, 293

MacDicken, R. A., 316
McFadden, E. R., Jr., 291
MacFarland, J. W., 36, 37, 201
MacFarlane, J. W., 140, 161, 259
McGarvey, B., 276
McGowan, B. K., 145
Machover, K., 104
McIntire, R. W., 135
Mack, J. E., 134, 135
McKenzie, J., 289
McKnew, D., 160
McLellarn, R. W., 119
McMahon, R., 273
McNeill, D., 28, 324
McNicol, K. N., 288
MacRae, J. M., 199
Madden, R., 109
Maddox, G. L., 116
Mahler, M. S., 178, 180
Malinowski, B., 58
Malmquist, C. P., 160
Mandell, W., 130
Mansheim, P., 73
Marcus, D., 275
Margolin, C. R., 329
Marks, I. M., 142
Marolla, F. A., 33
Maron, B. J., 128
Marston, A. R., 116
Martin, B., 32, 33, 103, 163, 182, 260, 261, 267
Martin, S., 272
Mash, E. J., 244, 245
Mason, E., 115
Masover, L., 118-19
Masters, J. C., 156, 265
Matarazzo, J. E., 200
Mathé, A. A., 291
Mattes, J., 245
Matthews, C. G., 237
Mattis, S., 251, 252
Mattison, R., 92
Mayer, J., 117
Mayron, E. L., 238
Mayron, L. M., 238
Means, J., 289-90
Mednick, S. A., 265, 276, 320-22
Meichenbaum, D., 64, 244, 305
Melamed, B. G., 113, 297, 303, 306
Melton, G. B., 329
Melville, M. M., 265
Mendel, G., 46
Mendelson, M., 92
Mendez, O., 3
Menlove, F. L., 63
Mercer, G. W., 277
Merluzzi, T. V., 217
Merrill, M. A., 108
Mesibov, G. B., 126, 258
Messer, S. B., 233
Messick, S., 324
Meyer, A., 10
Meyers, C. E., 215, 217, 218, 224
Miklich, D. R., 290-91
Milch, R. E., 191
Milgram, S., 85
Milich, R., 7, 234, 235, 242
Miller, A. L., 97
Miller, F. J., 115

Miller, L. C., 140-42, 148
Miller, N. E., 266
Miller, W. A., 207
Millican, F. K., 113, 114
Milman, L., 298
Minde, K., 7, 234, 242
Minuchin, S., 67, 68, 125-26, 292, 298
Mitchell, S., 6, 7
Mnookin, R., 328
Mock, J. E., 92
Moffitt, T. E., 276
Molk, L., 289-90, 292
Monk, M., 7, 140, 142
Morgan, R.T.T., 130
Moriarty, A. E., 40
Morris, R. J., 146
Morrison, G. C., 159
Moss, H. A., 32
Mostofsky, D. I., 302
Mowrer, O. H., 10, 129, 143, 266
Mowrer, W. M., 129
Mueller, E., 32
Mulick, J. A., 189, 191
Munsinger, H., 213
Murphy, G. E., 259
Murphy, L. B., 40
Murray, H. A., 104
Muser, J., 289-90
Mussen, P. H., 24
Myers, C. E., 202, 203
Myers, D. I., 181

Nations, R., 238
Neale, J. M., 45, 82, 182, 320, 321
Needleman, H. L., 238
Nelson, K., 28
Netley, C., 209
Neuhaus, E. C., 288
Newell, K. M., 24
Newman, A., 147
Newsom, C. D., 61, 170, 172, 184, 188, 190
Nichols, K., 236
Nihira, K., 202, 203
Nisbett, R. E., 118
Noble, H., 148
Nordsieck, M., 115
Nordyke, N. S., 15
Nye, F. I., 261

O'Conner, N., 173
O'Connor, N., 206
Offer, D., 275
Ogbu, J. U., 324
Öhman, A., 145
O'Keefe, A., 315
O'Leary, K. D., 7, 35, 61-62, 104, 106,
   232, 238, 241-43, 261
O'Leary, S. G., 61-62, 235, 242, 244
Ollendick, T. H., 16, 146
Oltmanns, T. F., 321
Oppenheim, A. N., 6, 7
Ornitz, E. M., 128, 171, 172, 175, 176
Orris, J. B., 264
Orton, S. T., 250, 251
Osmond, H. O., 124
Ott, J. N., 238

Pabst, P., 151
Padilla, E. R., 285

Palazolli, 68
Palkes, H., 101, 234
Palmer, F. H., 278, 314
Pappas, B. A., 236
Parish, T. S., 34
Parke, R. D., 238, 316, 317
Parsons, B. V., 279, 280
Parton, D. A., 95
Partridge, J. W., 295
Pasamanick, B., 7, 12
Paschalis, A. P., 130
Paternite, C., 235
Paternite, G., 235
Patterson, G. R., 106, 266, 267, 269,
   270, 271, 272, 280
Paulson, M., 134
Pavlov, 10, 59
Pearce, J., 158
Pease, D., 109
Pedersen, F. A., 29
Pederson, A., 154
Peed, S., 272, 273
Pelham, W. E., 168, 170, 172, 176, 232,
   236, 241, 243, 244
Perry, R. R., 128
Peshkin, M. M., 287
Pestolozzi, J., 9
Peters, J. E., 101, 249
Peterson, D. R., 95, 97, 99, 260
Peterson, L., 305, 306
Peterson, R. F., 106
Petti, T. A., 102, 164
Pflaunder, 129
Phillips, E. A., 279
Phillips, E. L., 278, 279
Piaget, J., 26-28, 41, 214-15, 262
Pike, V., 330
Pinard, 215
Pinchon, 143
Pinel, 223
Piotrowski, Z. A., 104
Pleck, J., 5
Plomin, R., 28, 49, 213, 235
Plotkin, W. B., 302
Pollack, D. A., 316
Pollack, E., 245
Pollack, M., 182
Poppen, R., 249
Porter, B., 261
Potter, H. W., 196
Poulos, R. W., 118, 267
Poussaint, A. F., 128
Pratt, R., 115
Prentice, N. M., 97, 263
Price, G. H., 243
Prince, B., 116
Prinz, R. J., 235, 237
Ptolemy, 45
Purcell, K., 285, 289-90, 289

Quast, W., 260
Quay, H. C., 7, 95-97, 99, 139, 162,
   258, 260, 264, 275, 276
Quevillon, R., 245

Rabin, K., 175
Rachman, S., 145
Rahe, D., 157, 158
Raimey, C. T., 285

Rainer, J. D., 207
Rains, M. H., 327
Rains, P. M., 99
Rando, T. A., 307
Rank, B., 180
Ranz, J., 102
Rapaport, J. L., 163
Rapin, I., 251
Rapkin, B. D., 327
Rapoport, J. L., 242
Rappaport, J., 313, 323
Raskin, A., 160, 163
Rauh, J., 162
Rayner, R., 59-60, 139, 143, 145
Reed, E. W., 48, 209
Reed, R. B., 117
Reid, J. B., 106, 267, 269
Reitan, R. M., 101, 103
Rekers, G. A., 15-16
Renne, C. M., 291, 292
Reppucci, N. D., 261
Rice, K. M., 302
Rich, E. S., Jr., 289, 292
Richmond, J. B., 112
Ricks, D., 8
Ridberg, E. H., 238, 276
Ridley-Johnson, R., 306
Rie, H. E., 5, 9, 11, 44, 196
Rieder, R. O., 182
Rimland, B., 175, 185
Rincover, A., 170, 172, 184, 192
Rist, R. C., 35, 36
Ritvo, E. R., 128, 171, 172, 175, 182
Rivinus, T. M., 120
Robb, J., 296
Roberts, M., 272, 273
Roberts, R. D., 235
Roberts, W. A., 237
Robins, L. N., 7, 8, 259
Robinson, H. B., 197, 199, 200, 201,
   206, 208, 209, 212, 214, 217, 251
Robinson, N. M., 197, 199, 200, 201,
   206, 208, 209, 212, 214, 217, 251
Roff, J. D., 98
Roff, M., 154
Rohsenow, D. J., 285
Rohwer, W. D., 216
Rojahn, J., 189, 191
Rollins, N., 122
Rose, H. E., 117
Rosen, A. C., 16
Rosen, B. M., 92
Rosen, P. M., 272
Rosenbaum, A., 238
Rosenbaum, M. A., 243
Rosenberg, B. G., 33
Rosenberg, M., 35
Rosenblad, C., 232
Rosenthal, D., 182, 209, 265
Rosenthal, T., 146
Rosenzweig, M. R., 39
Rosman, B. L., 67, 125-26, 298
Ross, A. O., 11, 95, 148, 168, 170, 172,
   175, 176, 232, 241, 251, 254
Ross, D. M., 236, 241, 244
Ross, R.A.J., 277
Ross, S. A., 236, 241, 244
Roth, B., 182
Rourke, B. P., 249, 251, 252

Rousseau, J. J., 19
Routh, D. K., 112, 231, 233, 235
Rovet, J., 209
Rubenstein, J. E., 23
Rubin, R. A., 109, 199
Rudman, H. C., 109
Rudy, T. E., 217
Rugh, R., 39, 53
Russell, A. T., 92
Russell, G.F.M., 123
Russo, D. C., 115, 189, 190
Rutter, M., 92–93, 94, 103, 127, 140,
    163, 167, 168, 170, 171, 173–76, 183,
    232, 235, 238, 251–52, 257, 259,
    260, 261
Ryan, M., 237

Sabatino, D. A., 246, 248
Sabshin, M., 275
Sachs, R., 131
Sadoun, R., 94
Safer, D. J., 231, 232, 234
St. James-Roberts, I., 54
Sajwaj, T., 113
Salapatek, P. H., 23
Sallade, J., 116
Sallan, S. E., 308
Salvia, J. A., 7, 14, 98
Sameroff, A. J., 103
Sandler, J., 316
Sandler-Cohen, R., 159
Sandoval, J., 232
Santostefanao, S., 12
Satz, P., 230, 231
Saul, R. E., 100
Scarboro, M. E., 272
Scarr, S., 28, 213
Schachar, R., 232, 235, 238
Schaefer, A. B., 114, 128
Schaefer, E. S., 33
Schaeffer, R. M., 226
Schaffer, H. R., 29, 37, 127
Schain, R., 242, 245
Schapiro, J., 246
Scharf, 263
Schiffman, G. B., 250
Schlesinger, K., 289
Scholl, H., 181
Schopler, E., 173
Schrag, P., 242
Schreibman, L., 172
Schroeder, C., 112, 116, 126, 258
Schroeder, S. R., 189, 191
Schulman, J., 305
Schulsinger, F., 276, 320–21
Schulterbrandt, J., 160, 163
Schultz, E. W., 7, 14
Schwartzberg, N. S., 118
Scibak, J. W., 226, 226
Scott, T. J., 264
Sears, R. R., 12, 32, 83, 266
Seashore, H. G., 201
Seidman, E., 278
Seligman, M.E.P., 145, 163
Seligman, R., 162
Sells, S., 154
Selman, R., 156
Selvini, M. P., 68, 124

Semlear, T., 314
Sequin, 223
Serbin, L., 7
Shaffer, D., 92–93, 159, 235
Shallenberger, P., 219
Shantz, C., 156
Shapiro, T., 102
Sharp, J. P., 119, 120
Shaywitz, B. A., 175
Shea, M. J., 260
Shellhaus, M., 203
Shemberg, K. M., 271
Shepherd, M., 6, 7
Sherman, J. A., 188
Shettles, L. B., 39, 53
Shetty, T., 237, 240, 241
Shiffrin, R. M., 217, 218
Shigetomi, C., 139, 305
Shinn, M., 34
Shipman, V. C., 31
Shoemaker, D. J., 260
Shokier, M.H.K., 130
Shore, M. F., 327
Shouse, M. N., 302
Shuey, A. M., 201
Shulman, H. S., 97
Shure, M. B., 325, 326, 333
Siegel, L. J., 306
Siegel, P. S., 219
Silberman, C. E., 35
Sillen, J., 3
Sills, M., 150
Silver, H. K., 316
Silver, L. B., 234
Silverman, F. N., 316
Silverman, W., 119, 120
Silvern, L., 156
Simcha-Fagan, O., 259
Simeon, J., 175
Simmons, J. Q., 190, 192
Simon, L. G., 116, 117, 119, 120
Simon, T., 12, 13
Simonds, J. F., 158
Simring, S., 285
Singer, S., 235
Sipowicz, R., 305
Sivage, C., 245
Skinner, B. F., 10, 60, 63
Skrzypek, G. J., 97, 264
Slaby, D., 156
Smith, A., 232, 235, 238
Smith, A. H., 285
Smith, D. W., 209
Sneed, T. J., 130
Sneznevskij, A. V., 94
Sobesky, W. E., 156
Solanch, L. S., 287, 292
Soll, S., 293
Solnick, J. V., 279
Solnit, A. J., 330
Solomons, G., 114, 128, 230, 244
Solyom, C., 142
Solyom, I., 142
Sours, J. A., 128
Soyka, L. F., 242
Spache, G. D., 109
Spence, M. A., 10, 175
Spiegler, M. D., 74
Spinetta, J. J., 307

Spitalnik, R., 225
Spitz, H. H., 216, 217–18
Spitzer, R. L., 93, 180, 181
Spivack, G., 325, 326, 333
Spock, B., 151–52
Sprafkin, J. N., 267
Sprague, R. L., 97
Sroufe, A. L., 326
Sroufe, L. A., 41, 241
Stampler, J., 118–19
Stanley, J. C., 71, 72
Stanley, L., 152–53
Stark, J., 249
Steele, B. F., 316
Steen, P. L., 235
Stein, A. H., 267, 268
Stein, K. B., 277
Stein, Z., 132, 237, 238
Stephanic, P. A., 117
Stewart, M. A., 101, 129, 234, 235
Stockdale, D. F., 109
Stockwell, M., 175
Stolberg, A., 261
Stolmaker, L. S., 115, 116, 119, 120, 121
Stone, N. W., 314
Stott, L. H., 201
Stouwie, R., 276
Strain, P. S., 157
Strang, J. D., 252
Strauss, A. A., 230
Strean, H. S., 12
Strichart, S. S., 252, 254
Strodtbeck, F. L., 324
Stroud, J., 119
Strupp, K., 173
Stunkard, A. J., 116, 118
Sturge, C., 247
Susman, E. J., 317, 322
Susser, M., 132
Sussman, M. B., 34
Sutton-Smith, B., 33
Swanson, J. M., 237
Swift, M., 326
Switzky, H. N., 215, 217, 218, 224
Szurek, S., 180

Tager-Flusberg, H., 173
Tague, C., 226
Tal, A., 290–91
Tanguay, P. E., 151
Tanner, J. M., 23, 37
Taplin, P. S., 106
Tate, B. G., 189
Templer, D. I., 123
Terdal, L., 272
Terman, L. M., 83, 108, 198
Terry, G. E., 294
Tesiny, E., 164
Thane, K., 32
Thienes, P. M., 131
Thomas, A., 3, 7, 37, 38, 40, 235, 259
Thomas, M., 20
Thompson, C. W., 295, 297
Thompson, W. R., 19, 39, 49
Thomson, A. M., 115
Thomson, L. E., 124
Thorndike, E. L., 10, 145
Thurlow, M. L., 225
Thurman, S. K., 225

Thurstone, L., 197
Thurstone, T. G., 197
Tizard, J., 103, 140, 206, 259
Todd, T., 298
Toler, H. C., 156
Tolman, 10
Toolan, J. M., 159
Trause, M. A., 32
Tresemer, D., 5
Trickett, P. K., 317
Trites, R. L., 232
Trost, N., 154
Tryphonas, H., 237
Tuddenham, R. D., 12, 197
Tuma, J. M., 92
Turner, A., 130
Tyler, L. E., 200

Ullmann, C. A., 154
Ulrich, R. F., 240
Urbain, E., 156
Uzgiris, I. C., 215

Vachon, L., 289, 292
Vance, A. K., 35
Vance, B. T., 324
Van DeRiet, V., 201
Vandersall, T. A., 293
Van Witsen, B., 225
Varni, J. W., 188
Vellutino, F. R., 251, 254
Venditti, E. M., 118
Vernick, J., 308
Vernon, D., 305
Vining, E.P.G., 23
Vosk, B. N., 247, 252,
    254

Wahl, G., 272
Wahler, R. G., 68, 272, 280
Walder, L. O., 268-69
Walinder, J., 123
Walker, C. E., 126, 133
Walster, E., 25
Walter, R., 134
Walters, R. H., 266
Walton, D., 291
Warburton, J. R., 279
Ward, C. H., 92
Ward, M. M., 100, 101, 248
Warren, M. Q., 276, 278
Waterman, J. M., 156

Watson, J. B., 10, 11, 13, 59-60, 63,
    139, 143, 145
Watzlawick, 68
Weakland, J., 68
Weatherley, D., 24
Weaver, S. J., 220
Weber, L., 35
Wechsler, D., 108, 200
Weinberg, R. A., 213
Weinberg, E., 292
Weiner, P. S., 249
Weingartner, H., 242
Weinraub, M., 32
Weinstein, P., 134, 135
Weiss, B., 237
Weiss, G., 7, 24, 242
Weissberg, R. P., 313, 327
Weisz, J. R., 215
Wellman, H. M., 218
Wells, K. C., 68, 273, 274, 280
Werkman, S., 151
Werner, E. E., 230, 236
Werry, J. S., 53, 100, 103, 130, 132,
    133, 162, 167, 174, 180, 182, 186,
    187, 239, 293
Wertheim, E., 98
Wertheim, G., 249
Wesman, A. G., 203
Wesolowski, M. D., 226
Wesson, L., 126, 258
Westin-Lindgren, G., 24
Whalen, C. K., 237, 239, 243, 245, 246
White, J. C., Jr., 201
White, M., 130
White, R. W., 220, 323
White, W. C., 78-80
Whitehill, M., 264
Whiting, B. B., 153
Whiting, J.W.M., 112, 153
Whitman, T. L., 226, 226
Whitmore, K., 103, 140, 259
Whittlesey, J.R.B., 109
Wicks-Nelson, R., 20n, 52, 56, 126
Will, L., 92
Willerman, L., 28, 235
Williams, C. D., 61
Williams, H. E., 288
Williams, R. H., 123
Wills, U., 148-49
Wilson, A. A., 209
Wilson, A. B., 312, 313
Wilson, C. C., 235

Wilton, N., 237
Windle, W. F., 205
Winett, R. A., 35
Wing, L., 180
Wing, R. R., 118
Winkler, R. C., 35
Winsberg, B. G., 240
Witkin, H. A., 265
Witkin-Lanoil, G. H., 320, 321-22
Witmer, 11
Woerner, M. G., 182
Wolens, L., 109
Wolf, M. M., 272, 278, 279
Wolf, S., 297
Wolfe, B. E., 15
Wolfe, D. A., 316
Wolman, B. B., 56
Woodhill, J. M., 237
Woodruff, R. A., Jr., 259
Woodward, W. M., 214
Work, H. H., 206, 211
Wright, H. F., 104
Wright, L., 114, 128, 132, 133, 135, 283,
    293, 295

Yamamoto, K., 284
Yando, R. M., 238
Yarrow, L. J., 29
Yeates, K. O., 215
Yen, S., 135
Yepes, L. E., 240
Yoches, C., 292
Yoder, P., 272
Young, D. B., 172, 188, 190
Young, E. R., 34
Young, G. C., 130
Young, R. D., 149, 234
Yule, W., 103, 127, 151, 251, 259
Yurchenco, H., 46
Yurcheson, R., 303
Yusin, A., 100
Yuwiler, A., 175

Zaleski, A., 130
Zax, M., 312
Zeaman, D., 216, 220
Zegiob, L. E., 107
Zetlin, A., 202
Zigler, E., 215, 219-20, 314
Zinkus, P. W., 246
Ziv, A., 153
Zung, W. W., 164

SUBJECT INDEX

ABA' design, 81, 82
Abuse, child, 40, 315–19
Accommodation, 26
Achievement Place, 278–79
Acquisition, communication and language, 27–28
Adaptability, criteria for, 40
Adaptive behavior, 201–3
  defined, 197
  peer relations and, 153–54
Adipose cellularity theory, 118
Adoption Assistance and Child Welfare Act of 1980 (P.L. 96–272), 330
Adoption studies, 50
Advocacy, child, 327–31
Affective disturbance, 171
Age
  chronological and mental, 198, 199
  as factor in behavior disorders, 96–97, 142, 206
  of onset, 167
  social, 203
Agression, 265–72
Alcohol, 52
  abuse, 276–77
Amenorrhea, 122, 123
Amniocentesis, 53n
Amphetamines, 50, 240, 242
Anal-sadistic phase, 266
Anal stage, 55–56, 266
Anorexia nervosa, 120–26
Antipsychotics, 186
Antisocial Personality Disorder, 263–64

Anxiety
  castration, 56
  psychodynamic concept of, 57
  separation, 149
Anxiety-Withdrawal syndrome. See Internalizing disorders
Aphasia, 249
Arithmetic disorder, 252
Articulation disorder, 249–50
Aspirin, 52
Assessment, 99–109
  intellectual-educational, 108–9
  of learning disabilities, 252–55
  neurophysiological, 100
  neuropsychological, 100–103
  observational, 104–7
  performing, 109
  personality-behavior, 103–7
  of physical functioning, 99–103
Assimilation, 26
Asthma, 283–92
  etiology, 285–87, 289–91
  prevalence and prognosis, 285
  psychological aspects of, 287–92
Attachment, 28–29, 41
Attention
  in discrimination learning, 215–16
  selective, 172
Attention deficit disorder, 93, 232, 234
Attractiveness, physical, 24–25
Autism. See Infantile autism
Avoidant Disorder, 153

Barbiturates, 52
Baseline data, 81

Battered child, 316
Bayley Scales of Infant Development, 109, 199
Bedwetting. See Enuresis
Before the Best Interests of the Child (Goldstein, Freud, Solnit), 330
Behavioral/social learning perspective, 10, 59–63 (See also Etiology; Treatments)
Behavior disorders, defined, 2–6
Behavior Problem Checklist, 95
Beliefs, self-efficacy, 64
Bender Visual-Motor Gestalt Test, 100–101
Benzedrine, 240, 242
Berkeley Child Guidance Study, 36
Beyond the Best Interests of the Child (Goldstein, Freud, Solnit), 330
Bias, observer, 106–7
Binet Scales, 197–98
Biofeedback, 292, 301
Biological/physiological perspective, 45–54 (See also Etiology; Treatments)
  biochemical influences, 50–52
  genetic influence, 46–50
  structural and physiological damage, 52–54
Brain damage, 53–54
Bulimia, 121–22

Cancer, pediatric, 298–300
Caregivers, 307–8
CARS, 312

CASE II project (Contingencies Applicable for Special Education), 278
Case study, clinical, 72–74
Categorization, 66 (See also Classification)
Cattell Intelligence Tests for Infants and Young Children, 109
Causality (Causation), 77–78
Checklists, 107–8, 185 (See also specific checklists)
Chemical ingestion, 53
Chigaco Circle Study, 269
Child abuse, 40, 315–19
Child and Family Mental Health Project, The, 314
Child Behavior Checklist, 107, 116
Child guidance movement, 10–12
Childhood disorders
  commonness of, 6–8
  history of, 8–13
Child Psychiatry (Kanner), 13
Children's Apperception Test (CAT), 104
Children's Defense Fund, 331
Chromosomes, 20–21
  aberrations, 48–50, 207–9, 210
Chronic illness, psychological consequences of, 294–300
Classification, 90–99
  clinically derived, 91–94
  dangers of, 98–99
  of depression, 160
  empirical approaches to, 94–95, 97
  of fears and phobias, 140–41
  similarity of derived syndromes and, 95–98
Client, working with, 13–16
Clinical description. See specific disorders
Clinics, psychological, 11
Coaching-instructional techniques, 156
Coding, behavior, 106
Coercion theory, 269–72
Cognition, 26, 214–19
Cognitive-behavioral perspective, 63–64 (See also Etiology; Treatments)
Colitis, ulcerative, 292–94
Communication, 26–28, 156
  in autism, 172–73
  treatment of delinquency and, 279–80
Competence, 323–27
  criteria for, 40–41
  social, 155–56
Compliance behavior, 272, 273–74
Conception, 22–23
Concrete operations, 26

Conditioning, 59–62
  classical, 59–60
  instrumental (operant), 60–62
Conduct disorders, 93, 256–81
  aggression, 265–72
  causes and correlates of, 260–65
  definitions of, 257–60
  juvenile delinquency, 274–80
  oppositional-noncompliant behavior, 272–74
  parents and, 258–59
Conners Parent Rating Scale, 240
Conners Teacher Rating Scale, 240, 242
Consanguinity study, 49
Consent, informed and proxy, 86–87
Control, experimental, 78
Control process, 217–18
Coordination, eye-hand, 253
Correlational research methodology, 75–78
Crib death, 319–20
Criminality, biological factors in, 264–65
Crisis intervention, 319–20
Critical period hypothesis, 39
Crossing over, 20–21
Cylert, 242

Data, baseline, 81
Death and dying, 30, 52–53, 307–8, 319–20
Defects, birth, 40, 52–53
Defense mechanisms, 57
Deinstitutionalization, 224–25
Delinquency, juvenile, 274–80
Dementia praecox, 167
Denial, 57
Dental treatment, fear reduction in, 303
Deoxyribonucleic acid (DNA), 20
Depression, 50, 158–64
Deprivation, social, 219
Description, clinical. See specific disorders
Desensitization, systematic, 146, 281
Determination, multiple, 39
Determinism, 54
Development, 18–42
  defined, 19–20
  disordered behavior and, 2
  Freudian view of, 8–9
  genetic, 20–21
  intellectual, 25–28
  interactional, 20
  issues in, 36–41
  levels, of, 36–37
  moral, 260–63
  peer relations and, 153
  physical, 21–25
  social, 28–29

Development (*cont.*)
  social context of, 29–36
  transactional model, 20
Developmental disorders, pervasive, 93
Developmental lines, concept of, 58
Developmental period, defined, 197
Developmental perspectives. See Development; Etiology; Treatments
Developmental quotient (DQ), 109, 199
Developmental scales, 109
Developmental vs. difference controversy, 215
Deviance, 2
Dexedrine, 242
Dextroamphetamine, 242
Diabetes mellitus, 52, 294–300
Diagnostic and Statistical Manual of Mental Disorders (DSM), 91–93, 94
Diagnostic Checklist for Behavior Disturbed Children, 185
Diagnostic-prescriptive teaching technique, 254
Diathesis-stress concept, 45–46
Diet
  deficiencies, maternal, 52
  in etiology of hyperactivity, 236–37
  Feingold, 236
Differences, individual, 37–38
"Difficult" children, 37–38
Dimensional rating scales, 107–8
Directionality, problem of, 77–78
Discrimination, 59
  definition, 61
  expressive/receptive, 188–89
  figure-ground, 253
  learning, 215–16
Disinhibition, 63
Displacement, 57
Disturbing Behavior Checklist, 99
Diversion program, 277–78
Divorce, 260, 261
DNA, 30
Down's Syndrome, 50, 207–9
Draw-a-Person test, 104
Drugs
  abuse, 276–77
  attitudes toward, 249
  for psychoses, 186
DSM-III, 167
  diagnostic criteria of, 121, 170, 177, 234, 257–58
  validity of, 92–93
Dying. See Death and dying
Dyscalculia, 252
Dyslexia, 250–52

Dysphasia, 249
Dysphoria, 158

Eating disorders, 93, 111–26
  anorexia nervosa, 120–26
  obesity, 115–20
  pica, 113–15
  rumination, 112–13
Echolalia, 173
Ecological/environmental factors.
  See Etiology; Treatments
Education
  through Head Start, 313–14
  of mentally retarded, 222–27
  special, 64–66, 226
  teachers, 14
Education for all Handicapped
  Children Act of 1975
  (P.L. 94–142), 15, 223–24
Ego, 54–55
Electra complex, 56
Electroconvulsive shock, 186
Electroencephalograph (EEG), 100,
  101, 128
Elimination disorders, 126–33
  encopresis, 132–33
  enuresis, 126–32
Embryo, period of the, 22
Employment, maternal, 33
Empty Fortress, The (Bettleheim),
  174
Encopresis, 132–33
Enuresis, 126–32
Environment, 20, 21, 41, 59 (*See also*
  Etiology; Treatments)
  least restrictive, 223–24, 226
Epidemiologic studies, 6–7
Epidemiology, of mental retardation,
  205–6
Eros instinct, 54
Ethical issues
  in prevention, 322–23
  in research, 85–87
  in treatment, 15–16, 115–16
Etiology
  of anorexia nervosa, 122–26
  of asthma, 285–87, 289–91
  of conduct disorders, 260–65
  of depression, 162–63
  of encopresis, 132–33
  of enuresis, 127–29
  of fears and phobias, 142–46
  of hyperactivity, 235–39
  of infantile autism, 173–76
  of late onset psychoses, 180–82
  of learning disabilities, 248–49
  of mental retardation, 206–14
    chromosome aberrations,
     207–9, 210
    family and sociological factors,
     211–12

Etiology (*cont.*)
    Mendelian inheritance, 209–10
    prenatal, perinatal, postnatal
     variables, 210
  of obesity, 118–19
  of pica, 114–15
  of rumination (mercyism), 112–13
  of school phobia, 149–50
  of sleep disorders, 134–36
  of ulcerative colitis, 293
Executive function, 218
Experience, early, 39–40
Experimental research methodology,
  78–82
Externalizing syndrome. *See*
  Conduct disorders
Extinction, 61, 189–90

Factor analysis, 95
Failure, expectancies for, 220–21
Family, Families, 31–36
  of anorexics, 122
  broken, effects of, 260, 261
  conduct disorders and, 260, 261
  death of child and, 307
  interactions
    coercive, 269–72
    modification of, 279–80
  juvenile diabetes and, 297–98
  of leukemic children, 294
  mental retardation and, 210–14,
    221–22
  middle class, 3–4
  poverty and stability of, 30–31
  psychoanalytic theory of, 31
  single-parent, 33–34
  stress, 40
  structure of, 33–34
Family systems perspective, 67–68
  (*See also* Etiology; Treatments)
Fat cell theory, 118
Fathers. *See* Family, Families;
  Parents
FBI Crime Index Offenses, 274
Fears and phobias, 60, 139–50
  clinical description and
    classification, 140–41
  developmental characteristics,
    140–42
  etiological paradigms, 142–46
  school phobia, 148–50
  treatment of, 146–48
Feedback 24
Fetus, period of the, 22–23
Fixation, 55
Formal operations, 26
Frostig Developmental Test of
  Visual Perception, 109

Galactosemia, 211
Gametes, 20

Gender
  disorder, 15–16
  prevalence of behavior disorders
    and, 6
  sociocultural norms and, 5
General intellectual functioning,
  defined, 196–97
Generalization, 59, 61, 191
Genes, 20–21, 46
Genetic influences, 46–50 (*See also*
  Etiology: Treatments)
Genital stage, 56–57
Gesell Development Schedules, 109
Goodenough-Harris Drawing Test,
  201

Hallucinogens, 186
Halstead Neuropsychological Test
  Battery for Children, 100
Hartup disease, 211
Headache, 301–2
Head Start, 313–15, 323
Heart rate, 101
Hereditary influence. *See*
  Etiology; Genetic influences;
  Treatments
Heroin, 52
Herpes Simplex, 2, 52
Home Start, 314
Home support programs, 225
Homosexuality, 56
Hormones, 52
Hospitalization, 304–7
Human Figure Drawing Test, 104
Huntington's chorea, 46, 48
Hyperactivity, 51, 232–45
  definition, 232–35
  etiology, 235–39
  identification of, 239–40
  minimal brain dysfunction and,
    230–32
  nature of, 232–35
  treatment of, 240–45
Hyperkinetic syndrome. *See*
  Hyperactivity
Hypothalamus, 123
Hypothesis testing, 70
Hypotheses (*See also* Models;
  Perspectives)
  coercion, 269–72
  concerning self-injurious behavior,
    189–90
  critical period, 39
  frustration-aggression, 266
  perceptual deficit, 251

ICD-9, 167
Id, 54–55
Identity, loss, of, 178–79
Illinois Test of Psycholinguistic
  Abilities, 109

Imipramine hydrochloride (Tofranil), 129, 242
Imprinting, 39
Impulsivity, 233, 234
Inattention, 234
Incidence, 6-7
Individualized education program (IEP), 223
Infantile autism, 167, 168-76
  core defect in, 171-73
  DSM-III and ICD-9 criteria for, 170
  etiology, 173-76
  parents and, 173-75
Influenza A, 52
Information processing, 215-19
Inhibition, 63
Institutionalization, 225, 277, 278
"Insulin reactions," 295
Integration, sensory, 251
Intelligence
  nature and measurement of, 197-201
  nature-nurture controversy about, 213-14
  tests, 108-9
Intelligence quotient (IQ), 198, 199-201
Interactions, 40, 156
Interdisciplinary approach, 13-14
Internalizing disorders, 138-65
  depression, 158-64
  fears and phobias, 139-50
    developmental characteristics, 140-42
    etiological paradigms, 142-46
    school phobia, 148-50
    treatment, 146-48
  obsessive-compulsive disorders, 151-53
  overanxiety, 150-51
  related to peer status and social competence, 155-56
  withdrawal, 153-58
International Classification of Disease, Ninth Revision (ICD-9), 93-94, 167
Interpersonal cognitive problem-solving (ICPS), 325-27
Intervention
  crisis, 319-20
  early, 313-15
  psychological, in asthma, 291-92
Interviews, 103
Introversion-extroversion, 28
Invulnerability, 40-41
Iowa Test of Basic Skills, 109
IQ, 199-201
Irritants, psychological, 289-91

Judgments, value, 15-16

Klinefelter's syndrome, 209

Labeling, dangers of, 98-99
Language, 26-28, 188-89, 249
Later onset psychoses, 176-83
  clinical features, 177-80
  etiology, 180-82
Law of Effect, 10
Laxative abuse, 122
Lead, 51, 114, 237-38
Learned behavior, 266-69
Learned helplessness, 163
Learning, 59, 214-19 (*See also* Perspectives)
  behavioral/social, 59-63
  definitional problems, 25
  discrimination, 215-16
  imitative, 62-63
  mental retardation and, 215-19
  observational, 62-63, 143-44
  paired-associate, 216
  processes, 25-26
  selective, 172
Learning disabilities, 245-55
  causes of, 248-49
  definition and clinical description, 246-48
  etiology, 248-49
  minimal brain dysfunction and, 230-32
  specific types of, 249-52
  treatment and assessment, 252-55
Least restrictive environment, 223-24, 226
Lesch-Nyhan Syndrome, 46-47
Leukemia, acute lymphoplastic, 298-300
Libido, 54
Lighting, fluorescent, 237-38
Lithium, 186
Long-term store, 217
Lying, "protective" or "benign," 308

Mainstreaming, 65-66, 224
Maple syrup urine disease, 211
Marital discord, 260, 261
Matching Familiar Figures Tests (MFFT), 233
Maturation, 12-13, 24
  categories of, 24
Maturational-learning controversy. *See* Nature-nurture controversy
Measurement, 71
Mediation, in paired-associate learning, 216
Medical regimens, compliance with, 303-4
Megavitamins, 186
Meiosis, 20
Melanesians, 2-3

Memory, 217-19
  family adjustment to, 221-22
Mental age (MA), 198, 199
Mental hygiene movement, 10-12
Mental retardation, 93, 195-228
  adaptive behavior and, 201-3
  cognition and learning, 214-19
  definition, 196-97
  epidemiology, 205-6
  etiology, 206-14
  family adjustment to, 221-22
  intelligence measurement and, 197-201
  levels of, 203-5
  personality and motivational variables, 219-21
  treatment and educational issues, 222-27
Metabolic disorders, 209-10, 211
Metamemory, 218
Methodologies. *See* Research
Methylphenidate, 242
Mind, structures of, 54-55
Mind That Found Itself, A (Beers), 10, 13
Minimal brain dysfunction (MBD), 53, 100, 230-32
Minority groups, 224
Misconduct, 233-34
Modeling, 62-63
  participant, 146-47
  peer, 157-58
Models, 20, 54-57, 146, 226, 323 (*See also* Perspectives)
Morphine, 52
Mosaicism, 207
Mother-child relationship, 29
Mothers. *See* Family, Families; Parents
Motivation, mastery, 220
Multiple baseline design, 82
Multiple Response Recording, 185-86
Mutation, 21

Nature-nurture controversy, 19-20, 213-14
  about intelligence, 197-201
Neglect, child, 40
Nervous system, 100, 236, 264
Neurosis, use of term, 139
Neurotransmitters, 50, 51, 175
New York Longitudinal Study, 37
Niemann Pick disease, 211
Nightmares, 134, 135
Night terrors, 134, 135
Noncompliance behavior, 272-74
Norms, 2-5

Obesity, 115-20
Observation, 71, 74-75
  systematic direct, 74-75

Obsessive-compulsive disorder, 151–53
Oedipus complex, 56
Oppositional-noncompliant
    behavior, 272–74
Oral stage, 55
Oregon Permanency Planning
    Project, 330
Overactivity, 232
Overanxiety, 150–51
Overcontrolled syndrome. *See*
    Internalizing disorders
Overcorrection, 190–91
Overdetermination, 39
Overgeneralization, 98
Overlearning, 130
Overselectivity, stimulus, 172
Overweight. *See* Obesity
Ovum, period of the, 22

P.L. 94–142 (Education for All
    Handicapped Children Act of
    1975), 15, 223–24
P.L. 96–272 (Adoption Assistance
    and Child Welfare Act of 1980),
    330
Paradigms. *See* Perspectives
Parent-child relationship, 31, 32–33
    etiology of conduct disorders and,
    260
Parents
    asthma symptoms and, 289–90
    attachment to, 29
    attitudes of, 107
    autism and, 173–75
    conduct disorders and, 258–59
    dimensions of behavior, 32–33
    effect on aggressive behavior of,
    267, 268
    interaction with, 14
    involvement of, in Head Start,
    314, 315
    later onset psychoses and, 180–82
    noncompliant behavior and, 272,
    273
    skills program for, 271–72
    training of, 324–25
    as therapists, 191–92
Partialing, 77–78
Pavor Nocturnus, 134
Peak expiratory flow rate (PERF),
    290, 291, 292
Pearson r, 76n
Pedigree analysis, 49
Peer Nomination Inventory for
    Depression (PNID), 164
Peer relations, 153–56, 325
    influence of, 34–35
    internalizing disorders related to,
    155–56
    modeling for withdrawn and,
    157–58

Pemoline, 242
Penis envy, 56
Perceptual-motor approaches, to
    learning disabilities, 252–54
Perspectives, 43–68 (*See also*
    Etiology; Treatments)
    behavioral/social learning, 10,
    59–63
    biological/physiological, 45–54
    biochemical influences, 50–52
    genetic influences, 46–50
    structural and physiological
    damage, 52–54
    cognitive-behavioral, 63–64
    defined, 44–45
    family systems, 67–68
    psychodynamic, 54–59
    psychoeducational, 64–67
    treatment mode and, 15–16
Pervasive Developmental Disorders, 167
Phallic stage, 56
Phenothiazines, 50
Phenylketonuria (PKU), 21
Phobias, *See* Fears and phobias
Physical conditions, psychological
    factors affecting, 282–309
    asthma, 283–92
    cancer, 298–300
    diabetes mellitus, 294–98
    dying, dealing with, 307–8
    modification of, 300–302
    treatment of, 303–7
    ulcerative colitis, 292–94
Physical functioning, assessement of,
    99–103
Pica, 113–15
Pittsburgh Adjustment Survey
    Scales, 95
Placebo effect, 72
Placement, problem of, 327–29
Play, 58
Pleasure principle, 55
PMHP, 312–13
Poverty and the poor, 40
    child abuse and, 317
    family stability and, 30–31
Preformation, 21–22
Prematurity, 40
Prenatal influences, 40, 52–53
Pre-operational period, 26
Preparedness, evolutionary, concept
    of, 145
Preschool Interpersonal Problem-
    Solving Test (PIPS), 325
Prevalence, 6–7
    of asthma, 285
    of conduct disorders, 258–59
    of depression, 158–60
    of obsessive-compulsive disorder,
    151–52
    of overanxiety, 151

Prevalence (*cont.*)
    of school phobia, 148–49
    of socially-withdrawn behavior,
    153
Prevention, 311–23
    of child abuse, 315–19
    crisis intervention, 319–20
    Head Start, 313–15
    issues in, 322–23
    Rochester Primary Mental Health
    Project (PMHP), 312–13
    of schizophrenia, 320–22
Principles of Preventive Psychiatry
    (Caplan), 311
Problems, stability of, 7–8
Problem solving, 216–17, 325–27
Projection, 57
Project on the Classification of
    Exceptional Children, 99
Project Re-ED, 65–66
Pronoun reversals, 173
Psychiatrists, 14
Psychoanalytic theory, classical,
    54–59
Psychodynamic perspective, 54–59
    (*See also* Etiology: Treatments)
Psychoeducational perspective,
    64–67 (*See also* Etiology;
    Treatments)
Psychologists, 13–14
Psychology, 14
    cognitive, 217
    ego, 58
Psychology as a Behaviorist Views It
    (Watson), 10, 13, 59
Psychoses, 166–94
    definitional problems, 167–68
    infantile autism, 168–76
    later onset, 176–83
    outcome of, 182–84
    treatment of, 184–92
        behavior modification, 187–92
        physical methods of, 186
        traditional therapies, 187
Psychosexual stages, 55–57
Psychosomatic disorders. *See*
    Physical conditions,
    psychological factors affecting
Punishment, 61, 190–91, 271

Radiation, 52
Random assignment, 78
Raven's Progressive Matrices, 201
Reaching the Autistic Child (Kozloff),
    191
Reaction formation, 57
Reactive Attachment Disorder of
    Infancy, 160
Reactivity, 107
Reading disorder, 250–52
Reasoning, moral, 262–63

Receptive discrimination, 188–89
Reciprocity, concept of, 271
Reflexes, neonatal, 23
Reification, 98–99
Reinforcement, 188
  effectiveness of, 219
  of other behaviors (DRO), 191
  positive and negative, 61, 269–71
  social, 279
Reitan-Indiana Neuropsychological
  Test Battery for Children, 101,
  103
Relaxation therapy, 291–92, 301
Reliability, 71
  of behavior coding, 106
  of empirically derived
    classification systems, 97
  interrater, 91
  of IQ tests, 200
  test-retest, 91
Repression, 57
Research, 69–89
  ethical issues in, 85–87
  longitudinal and cross-sectional,
    83–85
  methods of, 72–83
    correlational, 75–78
    experimental, 78–82
    mixed designs, 82–83
    simple descriptive, 72–75
  science, nature of, 70–72
Response prevention, 152–53
Reversal design, 82
Rh incompatibility, 52
Rights of children, 327–31
Rip Van Winkle Study (Eron,
  Huesmann, Lefkowitz and
  Walder), 268–69
Risk, 40–31
Ritalin, 242, 245
Rochester Primary Mental Health
  Project (PMHP), 312–13
Role theory, 32, 33–34
Rorschach test, 104
Rubella, 52, 53, 175
Rumination, 112–13

Scales, 107–9 (See also
  specific scales)
Schilder's disease, 211
Schizoid disorder, 153
Schizophrenia, 50–51, 167, 177–83
  (See also Later onset psychoses)
  prevention of, 320–22
School, 35–36
School phobia, 148–50
Science, nature of, 70–72
Sclerosis, tuberose, 175
Screening, 312
Self-control, 116
Self-determination, child, 329, 330

Self-efficacy beliefs, 64
Self-injurious behavior (SIB),
  189–91
Sensorimotor disturbances in
  austic children, 171
Sensorimotor period, 26
Sensory averaged evoked response
  (SER), 101
Sensory integration, 251
Sensory register, 217
Separation-loss theory of
  depression, 162–63
Sequential designs, 84–85
Serotonin, 175
Set point theory, 118
Sex. See Gender
Sex linkage, 46
Shape constancy, 254
Shaping, definition, 61
Shock, electroconvulsive, 186
Short-term store, 217
Siblings, 33
Significance, statistical, 76–77, 77n
Skin conductance, 101
Sleep disorders, 133–36, 133–36
Sleep Terror Disorder, 134
Sleepwalking, 134
Social exchange theory, 191–92
Social interaction, modalities of, 59
Socialization, differential, 7
Social learning theory. See Behavior/
  social learning perspective;
  Etiology; Treatments
Social quotient (SQ), 203
Social services, from Head Start,
  314
Social workers, 10, 14, 24
Sociocultural factors, in mental
  retardation, 210–14
Socioeconomic status (SES), 29–31,
  201, 212, 275–76
Soft neurological signs, 100
Somatogenesis, 45
Somnambulism, 134
Space, position in, 254
Spache Diagnostic Reading Scales,
  109
Spatial relationships, 254
Special education, 64–66, 226
  teachers, 14
"Special education for the mildly-
  retarded—is much of it
  justifiable?" (Dunn), 66
Specific Developmental Disorders,
  247
Stability
  of conduct disorders, 259–60
  problems, 7–8
Stages, psychosexual, 55–57
Standard deviations, 205
Stanford Achievement Test, 109

Stanford-Binet Test, 108, 198
Statistical significance, 76–77, 77n
Status asthmaticus, 283
Stereotyped movement disorders, 93
Stimulants, 186
Stimulus overselectivity, 172
Stress, life and illness, 284–85
Subaverage, defined, 197
Substitutions, 250
Success, expectancies for, 220–21
Sudden Infant Death Syndrome
  (SIDS), 319–20
Suicide, child and adolescent, 159
Superego, 54–55
Syndromes, 95–98, 258 (See also
  specific syndromes)
Syphilis, 52, 175
Systems theory, 67–68

Tay-Sachs disease, 46, 47
Teachers, special education, 14
Television, effects of, 118–19,
  266, 267–69
Teratogens, 52–53
Tests (See also specific tests and
  scales)
  ability and achievement, 109
  intelligence, 66, 108–9, 197–201
  psychological, 103–4
  standardized, 185, 201
Thalidomide, 52
Thanatos instinct, 54
Thematic Apperception Test (TAT),
  104
Theoretical orientations. See
  Perspectives
Thinking, primary process, 55
Three Essays on the Theory of Sexuality
  (Freud), 9, 13
Tobacco, 52
Tofranil, 129, 242
Token economy programs, 61–62
Training
  autogenic, 301
  dry-bed, 130–31
  generalization of, 191
  language, 188–89
  of parents, 324–25
    as therapists, 191–92
  retention control, 130
  strategy
Transference, 187
Translocation, 207
Treatments
  for aggressive children, 269–72
  of anorexia nervosa, 124–26
  of asthma, 289–92
  dental, fear reduction in, 303
  of depression, 163–64
  drug, attitudes toward, 249
  of encopresis, 133

Treatments (*cont.*)
  of enuresis, 129–32
  ethical issues in, 15–16, 115–16
  factors determining mode of, 14–16
  of hyperactivity, 240–45
  of learning disabilities, 252–55
  of mental retardation, 222–27
  of noncompliant behavior, 273
  of obesity, 119–20
  of obsessive-compulsive disorders,
    152–53
  of phobias, 146–48
  of pica, 114–15
  psychological facilitation of
    medical, 302–7
  of psychologically affected
    physical conditions, 303–7
  of psychoses, 186–92
  of rumination (mercyism), 112–13
  of school phobia, 150
  of sleep disorders, 134–36
  of ulcerative colitis, 293–94
  of withdrawn child, 156–58
Tricyclic antidepressants, 186
Trisomy 21, 207–8
Troubled and Troubling Child, The
  (Hobbs), 65
Tuberose sclerosis, 175
Turner's syndrome, 209

Twin studies, 49–50, 176
Two-factor theory, 143

Ulcerative colitis, 292–94
Unconscious, 54
Underarousal, 263–64
Undercontrolled syndrome. *See*
  Conduct disorders
Urine alarm, 129–30
Urine glucose levels, teting of,
  304–5
Utility, clinical, 91

Validity
  of DSM-III, 92–93
  of empirically derived
    classification systems, 97
  etiological, 91
  of intelligence tests, 200
  of observational systems, 106–7
  types of, 71–72, 91
Variables
  classificatory, 82
  dependent, 79
  implicated in mental retardation,
    210
  independent, 78
  motivational and personality,
    219–21

Variables (*cont.*)
  problem of, 77–78
  psychogenic, 173–75, 180–82
Verbal deficit, 251
Vineland social maturity scale,
  202–3
Voluntary Intervention and
  Treatment Program (VITP),
  318–19

Wechsler scales, 100–103, 108,
  198–99
Weight
  effect of television on, 118–19
  birth, 30
Werry-Weiss-Peters Activity Rating
  Scale, 239–40
What Happens Next Game
  (WHNG), 325
"Who's Afraid of Death on a
  Leukemia Ward?" (Vernick
  and Karon), 308
Why Your Child is Hyperactive
  (Feingold), 236–37
Wide Range Achievement Test, 109
Wilson's disease, 211
Withdrawal, social, 153–58

Zygote, 22